Women Without Superstition

Women Without Superstition

"No Gods – No Masters"

THE COLLECTED WRITINGS OF WOMEN FREETHINKERS OF THE NINETEENTH AND TWENTIETH CENTURIES

Edited by Annie Laurie Gaylor

Freedom From Religion Foundation
Madison, Wisconsin

Published by the Freedom From Religion Foundation, Inc.
PO Box 750, Madison WI 53701 (608) 256-8900
© 1997 by Annie Laurie Gaylor
All rights reserved. First edition 1997
Printed in the United States of America
Library of Congress Catalog Card Number: 96-90833
ISBN 1-877733-09-1

BOOK DESIGN BY JANE TENENBAUM

Permission to excerpt from Margaret Sanger's *Autobiography* granted by
Alexander C. Sanger.

Permission to reprint "What Makes An Atheist Tick?" by Sylvia Fraser,
September 11, 1965, granted by the *Toronto Star*.

Permission to reprint "The Debit Account" by Margaret Knight granted by
Barbara Smoker, president, National Secular Society.

Permission to reprint "A Search of the Scriptures" by Ruth Hurmence Green
from *The Book of Ruth* granted by the Freedom From Religion Foundation,
Inc.

Permission to reprint "Profile of an Atheist" by Craig Phelon, granted by the
San Antonio Express-News.

Permission to reprint "Truth or the Consequences" by Kay Nolte Smith,
granted by Prof. Phillip J. Smith.

Permission to reprint the speech "From Housewife to Heretic" granted by
Sonia Johnson.

Permission to reprint "U.S. Patriots: Without God on their Side" by Barbara
Ehrenreich, January-February 1981, granted by *Mother Jones* © 1981,
Foundation for National Progress.

Permission to reprint "Subject to Debate" by Katha Pollitt, December 26,
1994, granted by *The Nation*, © The Nation Company, L.P.

Permission to reprint "On Islamic Fundamentalism" by Taslima Nasrin
granted by Tom Ferrick, Humanist Chaplaincy at Harvard University, and
the Humanist Association of Massachusetts.

Permission also granted by individual authors Meg Bowman, Anne Nicol
Gaylor, Sherry Matulis, Queen Silver, Barbara Smoker, and Barbara G.
Walker to use or excerpt their copyrighted selections.

In Loving Memory of
BLANCHE FEARN
1911–1995
"A Woman Without Superstition"

Dedicated to My Mother
ANNE
who has contributed thirty years of her life
to uplifting women
and ensuring freedom from religion;

and

to

My Daughter
SABRINA
a fourth-generation freethinker,
whose middle name "Delata"
is Delaware for "Thought"

This book was made possible by the generosity
of a grant from the
JAMES HERVEY JOHNSON FOUNDATION
San Diego

CONTENTS

Alphabetical Contents

PREFACE

I regard the Bible as I do the other so-called sacred books of the world. They were all produced in savage times, and, of course, contain many things that shock our sense of justice. In the days of darkness women were regarded and treated as slaves. They were allowed no voice in public affairs. Neither man nor woman were civilized, and the gods were like their worshipers. It gives me pleasure to know that women are beginning to think and are becoming dissatisfied with the religion of barbarians.

Eva A. Ingersoll
The Woman's Bible Part II, Appendix, 1898

THE TITLE *Women Without Superstition* comes from the accolade given by the nineteenth century's most famous freethinker to his wife. Robert Green Ingersoll dedicated his first book to Eva, "a woman without superstition." Can there be greater praise?

The subtitle of this anthology, "No Gods—No Masters," was the motto Margaret Sanger chose for her 1914 publication, *The Woman Rebel*. Ever since encountering Sanger's motto I have felt it expresses in a nutshell the feminist viewpoint toward patriarchal religion. "No Gods—No Masters" gallantly rejects the master/slave hierarchy of male power over women and supernatural power over all humankind that is ordained in the Hebrew and Christian testaments.

The pansy on the dust jacket was chosen because pansies at one time became a symbol of freethought, a custom that ought to be revived. With their little intelligent "faces," they have always been one of my favorite flowers. The word comes from the French *pensée*, meaning "thought" or "fancy," from the verb *penser*, "to think." The purple, yellow and white colors on the dust jacket represent feminism since these three colors were adopted by the American women's suffrage movement.

This collection makes available for the first time the work and writings of women freethinkers which otherwise must be scavenged from the dustbin of history. The "heretical" thoughts and often eloquent writings of women without superstition should not be forgotten in the musty corridors of a few libraries. One should not have to spend hours of often discouraging labor at the computer terminal, or tramp through university libraries, or experience eyestrain in front of microfilmed documents just to be able to read some of the views of women freethinkers! Ideas and accomplishments, not just names, should be remembered. In many cases, even their names have been forgotten.

Women Without Superstition is intended in part to acquaint feminists with the freethinking heritage of the women's rights movement, and the freethought ideals that so often motivated and underpinned the convictions of many feminist foremothers. The women's movement has not acknowledged the debt it owes to the unorthodox, freethinking women in its ranks. Their nonreligious views often have been suppressed, as if shameful, when in fact repudiation of patriarchal religion is an essential step in freeing women.

Similarly, the work of women freethinkers to liberate minds and governments from religious dogma has all too often been ignored or relegated to footnotes by historians of freethought. This is regrettable considering that women freethinkers of the nineteenth century were often praised, recognized, published, even feted by contemporaries. Freethinkers today, male and female, seem hungry to know more about this largely forgotten aspect of the freethought movement. The barrier has been the difficulty in finding information about their lives and writings. This collection reclaims the rightful place of women freethinkers.

Reading only their ideas without a context does not do justice to these women. Most are or were activists and doers, movers and shakers, with lives as fascinating as their writings. Finding biographical information often was as daunting as locating their freethought writings, therefore more background is offered than in the usual anthology.

This anthology would need to be twice as long to include every woman who has, by her unorthodoxy, contributed to freethought or feminism. Quakers and Unitarian-Universalist women, as well as the modern feminist theologians, popularizers of goddess worship and women's studies scholars have all made contributions in battling patriarchal religions. These contributions, for the most part, have been recognized, whereas the contributions of women freethinkers have been marginalized.

Writers featured are English-speaking; most are historic figures from the United States. I have not focused on poets or literary figures. Some women's writings do not appear here due to difficulty in locating them. Some requests for submissions or permission to reprint were ignored. Other writers were omitted because I simply have run out of space! The last section includes additional biographical summaries.

Chapters are arranged chronologically by date of the author's birth. To avoid footnotes and make source identification simple, most quotes in the biographies are documented briefly in the text by author, book title and page number. (Since it is cited so frequently and had multiple, changing authors, *The History of Woman Suffrage* citations include only title, volume and date.) If the same source is used in succession, only following page numbers are indicated. Full publishing information is available in the bibliography, which is arranged by chapter/author. Titles with quote marks indicate it is not the original title. Original spelling, grammar and (most) punctuation have been preserved; "[sic]" is used sparingly, but typographical errors in original sources have been corrected.

Authors are referred to by first name in the biographical sketches. I am sure they would not consider this blasphemous! So many of the featured women changed names after marrying or remarrying that a first-name basis is not only friendly but sensible.

Readers spoiled by today's consciousness may share my own initial dismay at the ubiquitous generic-male language ("mankind . . . he") found in the writings of many of these strong feminists, even when writing about women's rights! Too bad language reform was a janie-come-lately to the feminist cause!

As this is a fat book full of details about fifty exceptional women offering a barrage of powerful ideas, I recommend selecting one or two women a night to read so their thoughts can be properly digested. Please don't miss the special Elizabeth Cady Stanton Freethought Reader (Chapter Ten) for a tantalizing taste of the depth of her freethought views.

There are striking commonalities in the writings of women freethinkers. Many were freethinkers who, to borrow my husband's metaphor, sprang up in comparative isolation like wildflowers, whose reasoning, experiences, study of religion or reading of the bible compelled them to reach the same conclusions about the harm of religion to women, intellect or society, and to speak out. I call it the "Ruth Green phenomenon." Ruth became an atheist and wrote *The Born Again Skeptic's Guide to the Bible* after reading the bible, virtually without contact with other freethinkers or freethought writings. On the other hand, much of this writing did not come out of a vacuum. Many of the authors of the late nineteenth century knew each other, or were exposed to each others' writings, a phenomenon that fed upon itself until feminist freethinking was truly in flower.

❦

The writers featured are *freethinkers*, not necessarily atheists, although that label accurately describes many of them. Freethought means the use of reason in forming opinions about religion, rather than basing belief on faith, authority or tradition. Some of the women defy categorizing or were Deists in the classical Enlightenment sense, or their views may have changed over a lifetime. The prerequisite for inclusion is that their selected writings analyze religion using *reason*, not faith.

I define *religion* as a belief in a supernatural being who must be worshipped and obeyed as the creator and ruler of the universe, whose dicta are found in so-called sacred writings. Some contributors, however, use the loosest definition of the word—applying it to any system of philosophy or ethics, not necessarily the supernatural. Several writers, such as Elizabeth Cady Stanton, turn the word on its head by adopting Thomas Paine's irreverent concept of a "religion of humanity." The word "religion" takes on a sinister cast when one examines its root, *religare*, meaning "to bind," which in turn means "to hold, to make prisoner, to restrain." The women featured in this collection have worked to break the ties that bind womankind and restrain intellect. Most emphatically, the contributors to this anthology eschew *superstition*—a belief inconsistent with the known laws of science and reason. Among the pioneers of social change striving to move humankind forward, they have directed their energies to *this* world, not toward an unseen, unprovable and unknowable one.

Matilda Joslyn Gage has pointed out that one of the monks who authored the infamous Witches Hammer handbook for killing women twisted etymology to argue that the word "woman" (*femina*) literally means "faithless" (contending *fe* = faith, *mina* or *minus* = less). Sprenger's absurd claim nevertheless can be turned by today's women into a compliment worthy of Col. Robert Ingersoll himself. In the following pages, I hope you will enjoy meeting or becoming better acquainted with these faithless women and their writings.—*Annie Laurie Gaylor, November 1996*

*Monument to Anne Hutchinson
at Massachusetts State House
(Cyrus Dallin, Sculptor)*

INTRODUCTION

The world has seemingly awaited the advent of heroic souls who once again should dare all things for the truth. The woman who possesses love for her sex, for the world, for truth, justice and right, will not hesitate to place herself upon record as opposed to falsehood, no matter under what guise of age or holiness it appears.

Matilda Joslyn Gage
Woman, Church & State, *1893*

THE WOMEN WHO HAVE PLACED themselves on record as opposed to falsehood have included some of the most remarkable "heroic souls" in the Western world:

A Scottish heiress becomes the confidante of General Lafayette and the toast of 1819 New York City, embarks on a tour in which she engages in unparalleled public criticism of the clergy, opens a Hall of Science, becomes editor of the *Free Enquirer,* and starts a model abolition colony. A cantakerous patriot who despises missionaries and throws religious tracts off steamer boats by the boxful, is pushed down a steep flight of stairs by a religionist, and convicted of being a "common scold" after feuding with a church congregation. A Polish daughter of an Orthodox rabbi becomes not just an unabashed atheist lecturer, but the first woman canvasser for women's rights. One of the most respected literary and "career women" in mid-nineteenth century America re-examines religion, fights for freedom in Italy, and dies in a shipwreck off New York City with her husband and baby. A young English girl who is to become a great Victorian novelist is warned by her beloved father that if she stops going to church, she must leave home.

A mother of seven commands the nascent American women's movement from her fireside, and devotes the end of her life to freeing women from religion. A dutiful Quaker daughter, offered a dollar by her mother to read the bible, is transformed into a lifelong rebel against its teachings. A suffragist who opens her morning paper to read that the nation's most prominent rector has started a series of lectures against women's rights, books a hall that very day for lectures to rebut his claims, and wins national attention for women's rights. A prim suffragist causes a scandal when she tells a minister that his mother ought to spank him for giving an antiwoman lecture. The leader of her state suffrage movement is declared "an undesirable member" after she writes publicly about the problems the bible has caused women.

The earnest political beliefs of "godless" anarchists make them targets of assassins, governments and public opinion. A teenaged Michigan girl, sent to a convent, emerges a fiery feminist and enemy of cant, becomes a poet and reformer, and survives an assassination attempt. A freethinker interested in marriage reform slits her wrists rather than serve a second sentence under the cruel Comstock Act.

A gentle, red-haired nurse and mother, who is arrested and jailed many times and whose public speeches are cancelled by the Catholic Church, almost single-handedly introduces the world to birth control. A young black actress becomes world-famous for playing a "simpleminded" slave in one of the most successful movies of all time, and is committed her entire life to ending the "slavery of religion." A former medical missionary to India realizes during an epiphany that there is no god, writes a leaflet about her convictions, and drops off copies door to door in her Canadian neighborhood.

An academic British psychologist scandalizes Great Britain by going on the BBC radio to suggest that parents can raise more moral children without religion. A victim of 1950's rape, repression and illegal abortion survives to become a spokeswoman for abortion rights and a voice for freethought. A Missouri grandmother and "halfhearted Methodist" finds reading the bible more traumatic than breast cancer, becoming an outspoken "atheist in a foxhole." A devout Mormon mother's tentative support for the Equal Rights Amendment leads to her dramatic excommunication in front of the world, and her complete change of heart about religion. A writer as a girl reads about the killing of women as witches and becomes an atheist, wondering: "How can anyone belong to a church that treated its members this way?" A nonreligious woman physician in a Moslem world goes into hiding after being condemned to die by holy men because of her poetry and fiction.

Many women freethinkers have "dared all things for the truth." Everyone featured in this collection has a life story worth remembering, as well as thoughts worth reading. Largely untold have been not only their stories but the history of women fighting to be free of religious strictures.

The status of women and the history of the women's rights movement cannot be understood except in the context of women's fight to be free from religion. As Barbara Ehrenreich has observed: "If there was one cause which had a logical and consistent affinity with free thought, it was feminism."

Let Your Women Keep Silence

Women have played such a crucial role in the move away from religious belief and dogma because organized religion has been the principle enemy of women's rights. Out of sheer self defense, women have been among the most impassioned critics of the church, and among the most ardent supporters of the constitutional principle of separation of church and state.

Among the most influential and damaging bible verses about women:

> Unto the woman he said, I will greatly multiply thy sorrow and thy conception; in sorrow thou shalt bring forth children; and thy desire shall be to thy husband, and he shall rule over thee. (Genesis 3:16)

> Thou shalt not suffer a witch to live. (Exodus 22:18)

> But I would have you know, that the head of every man is Christ; and the head of every woman is the man; and the head of Christ is God. . . . For the man is not of the woman; but the woman of the man. Neither was the man created for the woman; but the woman for the man. (1 Corinthians 11:3, 8–9)

> Let your women keep silence in the churches; for it is not permitted unto them to speak; but they are commanded to be under obedience, as also saith the law. And if they will learn anything, let them ask their husbands at home; for it is a shame for women to speak in the church. (1 Corinthians 14:34–35)

> Let the woman learn in silence in all subjection. But I suffer not a woman to teach nor to usurp authority over the man, but to be in silence. For Adam was first formed, then Eve. And Adam was not deceived, but the woman being deceived was in the transgression. (1 Timothy 2:11–14)

When the woman's movement started in the Western world, the exhortations of 1 Timothy and 1 Corinthians were the rule of the land. Women were classed with children and, in the parlance of the day, "idiots." Not only were they disenfranchised, they had no identity beyond daughter or wife. They had no custody rights. Their husbands could spend their pay checks and inherit their property. Married women could not sign contracts, sue or be sued. The term for it is "civil death," but its origin was strictly biblical.

American Jezebels

Early nineteenth-century female proponents of the abolition of slavery, of temperance and of women's rights were, by definition, all heretics. Regardless of their private views on religion, by their actions they were defying the injunctions to "keep silent" and "be in subjection."

The first female heretic on the North American shore was Anne Hutchinson. Arriving in the Puritan theocracy of Boston in 1634, Hutchinson became a serious threat to that church-state when she began holding discussion groups for women in her home, daring to critique the sermons and theology of male ministers. Authorities became alarmed when men, too, began listening to her, and her follower Sir Henry Vane even (temporarily) defeated John Winthrop as governor. Hutchinson's supporters were persecuted, Hutchinson was banished by the Massachusetts General Court for sedition and heresy in 1637, then she was excommunicated, "cast out" and delivered to "Satan" as a "Heathen" and a "Leper." Governor John Winthrop denounced her as an "American Jezebel." Hutchinson was only the first of many women to be persecuted by the Puritans—Hutchinson's Quaker supporter Mary Dyer was hanged in the Boston Commons in 1660 as a heretic, and the Salem witch trials followed. Hutchinson's followers settled briefly on the island of Aquidneck, Rhode Island, and, under her influence, adopted a civil, secular government which made the first declaration of religious freedom in America: "It is ordered that none shall be accounted a delinquent for doctrine." Reveling in freedom of conscience, she never entered another church and no church was built at her short-lived colony.

"She was the first woman in America to demand the right of individual judgment upon religious questions," wrote Elizabeth Cady Stanton about the woman she called our "rebellious foremother."

It would be nearly two hundred years before another woman spoke publicly to "promiscuous assemblies" of men and women in North America. Freethinker Frances Wright, during her unprecedented lecture series on "free inquiry" and freethought in 1828–1829, was attacked by mobs, and labeled the "Red Harlot of Infidelity," a "blasphemer" and, in what was intended as the ultimate insult, a "female Tom Paine."

The next women to speak publicly on a major platform were effectively silenced not by clergy enemies, although they tried, but by a clergy friend. The silencing of Sarah Grimké ranks as one of the most treacherous "black collar" betrayals of a woman. She and her sister Angelina, daughters of slaveholders who converted to Quakerism, began speaking out before female audiences against slavery in 1837. Men began attending their popular lectures, resulting in the Pastoral Letter by the Congregational Church of Massachusetts censuring them. [See Appendix] Sarah, in response to the Church's attempts to censor women abolitionists, realized the parallels between the position of slaves and that of all women. She began speaking out about women's rights. Her *Letters on the Equality of the Sexes*, the first American book addressing the woman question, examined "the perverted interpretation of Holy Writ."

Sarah's trusted friend, Presbyterian minister Theodore Weld, who was engaged to her sister Angelina, frankly believed the "woman question" he professed to support must not jeopardize the abolition movement. Weld wrote Sarah a letter couched as friendly advice, claiming, falsely, that other abolitionists were too polite to tell her that her poor speaking abilities were harming the cause. Sarah Grimké never spoke publicly again. The sisters' notorious speaking tour had lasted less than a year. They spent much of the rest of their lives dominated by Weld.

While these two sisters were silenced by a minister, others rose to take their places. Abolitionist Abby Kelley earned the hatred of the clergy, eventually leaving the Society of Friends and continuing her abolition and later suffrage work "without benefit of clergy." Nearly three hundred men walked out of the American Anti-Slavery Society meeting in 1840 in New York to protest Abby's presence on the business committee. The male segregationists formed the American and Foreign Anti-Slavery Society forbidding women to vote or hold office. At a Connecticut Anti-Slavery Society meeting, the Rev. Henry G. Ludlow ordered Abby to be silenced when she attempted to speak. When the body voted to permit her to speak, the minister grew hysterical, launching a tirade against "the sorcery of a woman's tongue," "the rule of women" and a "petticoat government." Rev. Ludlow's bullying was effective; for the rest of the two-day convention, Abby and any other women trying to speak were ordered to "Put down your hand" or informed "Your vote will not be counted." Later that year Congregationalist minister Gordon Hayes in Washington, Connecticut, launched a scurrilous attack during his sermon, declaring it "a sin and a shame for women to teach men." Warming to his subject, Rev. Hayes turned to Revelation, and called Abby a "Jezebel." This label is still used by Christian fundamentalists against women transgressing their biblically-anointed place, most notably directed at feminist First Lady Hillary Rodham Clinton.

On her wedding trip with her husband, abolition agent Henry Stanton, Elizabeth Cady Stanton attended the 1840 World's Anti-Slavery Convention in London. On this fateful trip, the men voted on the basis of scriptural edicts to exclude women from participation, relegating them to a curtained-off area. Stanton's experience was her feminist awakening. When Stanton with four Quaker women organized the 1848 Seneca Falls convention, the first public meeting calling for suffrage and rights for women, the meeting won the wrath of clergy around the nation.

The Mob Conventions

The level of outrage that attended women speaking in public was illustrated by what happened when the Philadelphia Female Anti-Slavery Society raised money to build Pennsylvania Hall as a place for abolitionists and reformers to meet. Four days after it was opened in May 1838, with women speaking in public freely, and blacks and whites mingling, a mob burned it to the ground.

The treatment of Abby Kelley and female abolitionists replayed itself wherever women, in defiance of the New Testament, gathered to speak. The May 12, 1853 "Brick Church Meeting" in New York, voted 34–32 against women being recognized as temperance delegates. "Throughout this protracted, disgraceful assault on American womanhood, the clergy baptized each new insult and set of injustice in the name of the Christian religion, and uniformly asked God's blessing on proceedings that would have put to shame an assembly of Hottentots," recalled Elizabeth Cady Stanton in *The History of Woman Suffrage*. Speakers, mostly clergy, condemned any public role for women, Stanton wrote, "quoting Scripture and the Divine Will to sanction their injustice."

A roster of ministers attended and attacked the resolutions of the first several national women's rights conventions, sermonizing against them afterward. The annual woman's rights convention meeting at the Broadway Tabernacle in September 1853, went down in history as the "mob convention." The mobs, mainly clergy or religionists acting on biblical precepts, sabotaged the convention with hisses, groans, stamping, and rude, ridiculing remarks, forcing it to shut down.

The religion-incited mobs continued wherever women spoke in public. "In the early days of woman-suffrage agitation, I saw that the greatest obstacle we had to overcome was the bible. It was hurled at us on every side," recalled Stanton toward the end of her life

The bible and other "holy books" continue to be hurled at women working for their freedom. Christian holy men have invoked the bible to oppose reproductive freedom, from the Y.M.C.A.-backed nineteenth-century postal censor and religious fanatic Anthony Comstock, and the powerful Archbishop Patrick Hayes of New York, who shut down Margaret Sanger's public meeting on birth control in 1921, to the clergy ringleaders of today's terrorism against abortion clinic personnel and patients. The Catholic, fundamentalist and Mormon churches also organized their congregations against the Equal Rights Amendment, defeating the ratification process. The religious war against women's rights continues unabated today around the world. Whether the issue is violence, birth control, abortion, education, or dress reform, the message against freedom for women is the same from the fundamentalist branches of Christianity, Islam, Judaism or Hinduism.

Women Secularists

Every freedom won for women, large or small, from women wearing bloomers to riding bicycles to not wearing bonnets in church, to being permitted to attend universities and enter professions, to vote and to own property, was opposed by the churches.

Therefore it is no surprise that the first to speak out for women's rights were the secularists, freethinkers and unorthodox. As nineteenth-century freethought activist Susan H. Wixon observed: "Freethought has always been the best friend woman had—the noblest, truest ally and champion." It was a freethinking Deist, Mary Wollstonecraft, who wrote the first significant call for woman's rights, *A Vindication of the Rights of Woman*, in 1792. It was ardent rationalist and anti-cleric Frances Wright who first took up the public cry on behalf of reason and women, becoming the premiere woman to lecture publicly in the United States and to call for women's equality.

It was a freethinking judge, Thomas Hertell, who was the first to introduce legislation to protect the property rights of women, to the scorn of fellow New York state legislators. It was an atheist, Ernestine L. Rose, who became the first to lobby for passage of Hertell's Married Woman's Property Act, and the first canvasser for woman's rights on our continent. Like Wollstonecraft and Wright, Rose was subject to vituperation, even libeled by clergy as being "a thousand times lower than a prostitute." It was Quaker heretic Lucretia Mott, whose motto of "Truth for authority, not authority for truth," helped to awaken the young Elizabeth Cady Stanton, who sparked the modern woman's movement. Stanton, editor of *The Woman's Bible* and author of innumerable speeches and articles condemning the role of religion in women's lives, was the first to call for woman suffrage, and devoted the end of her life to lifting women out of superstition. Her "coadjutant," Susan B. Anthony, was an agnostic. Their feminist partner, Matilda Joslyn Gage, was a freethinker who formed the first national feminist organization to work for the separation of church and state in 1890 and wrote *Woman, Church and State* in 1893. Freethinking women filled state and national suffrage ranks, as demonstrated by the writings and achievements of such activists as Lillie Devereux Blake, Marilla M. Ricker, Ellen Battelle Dietrick, Josephine K. Henry, Susan H. Wixon, and Helen H. Gardener.

Many freethinking women were catalysts, pushing the exploration of broader questions, such as marriage, sexual rights and wrongs, divorce reform, challenging the position of woman as the Proverbial drudge and "helpmeet." Freethinking women pioneered what Lois Waisbrooker called woman's "natural, inherent right to herself." Poet and radical freethinker Voltairine de Cleyre wrote in 1890: "The question of souls is old—we demand our bodies, now. We are tired of promises, God is deaf, and his church is our worst enemy." De Cleyre offered a comical look at the "virtuous" drudge of Proverbs in her address, "Woman Versus Orthodoxy," and wrote searingly of the issue of battered women a century ago. British iconoclast Annie Besant, anarchist atheist Emma Goldman and targets of censor Anthony Comstock, such as Elmina Slenker, were among the freethinkers who helped pave the way for woman rebel Margaret Sanger to ignite the birth control movement worldwide. Freethinker Charlotte Perkins Gilman, one of the most famous women writers of the turn of the century, addressed the "family values" question: "One religion after another has accepted and perpetuated man's original mistake in making a private servant of the mother of the race."

Try to imagine feminism without these women and their contributions!

Similarly, freethinking women filled early abolitionist ranks, such as Lydia Maria Child, Lucy N. Colman and many early feminist activists, including Harriet Martineau and Susan B. Anthony. Indeed, the fact that abolitionists were overwhelmingly unorthodox is proved by the fact that, in the pre-Civil War era, the term "abolition" and the insult "infidel" were often used synonymously, as Hypatia Bradlaugh Bonner pointed out.

Freethinking women have been well-represented in artistic and literary circles, from George Eliot to "Ouida" in the last century, to Meridel Le Sueur, Zona Gale, Ayn Rand, Barbara G. Walker, Margaret Atwood, Katha Pollitt, Barbara Ehrenreich and Taslima Nasrin in the twentieth century, to name but a few.

Women freethinkers were also, naturally, significant in the freethought movement. Wollstonecraft championed the Enlightenment, writing: "the being cannot be termed rational or virtuous, who obeys any authority, but that of reason." Frances Wright began lecturing in response to revival meetings, urging believers to use their reason and "to turn their churches into halls of science, and exchange their teachers of faith for expounders of nature." Ernestine L. Rose was a famous and unabashed atheist long before "the Great Agnostic" Robert G. Ingersoll became known. Her classic 1861 lecture, "A Defence of Atheism," pointed out, perhaps for the first time, that "all children are Atheists, and were religion not inculcated into their minds they would remain so. . . ."

Emma Martin wrote freethought pamphlets in Great Britain in the 1840s, daringly handing out anti-missionary writings at mission conventions. American Ella E. Gibson wrote the first book offering a feminist analysis of women in the bible in the 1870s. Others who started or carried on organized freethought work include Annie Besant and Hypatia Bradlaugh Bonner, Marilla M. Ricker, truth-seeking Susan H. Wixon, Etta Semple, a Kansas freethought editor who was the target of an assassin, child freethinker Queen Silver, BBC's "unholy menace" Margaret Knight, Marian Sherman, M.D., of Canada, "born-again skeptic" author Ruth Green, and a host of current activists.

Women have been among the most ardent supporters of secularism. At the time Frances Wright was speaking out against the religious revival in the United States, Anne Royall was fearlessly dedicating herself to fighting the God-in-the-Constitution party organizing in the 1820s. Matilda Joslyn Gage warned of an alliance between Catholics and Protestants seeking to put God in the Constitution one hundred years ago; her warning, unfortunately, is as timely today. Elizabeth Cady Stanton led the campaign to ensure that Sabbatarians would not close the World's Fair of 1893 on Sundays. It was a woman, Vashti McCollum, who brought the first lawsuit successfully challenging religious instruction in public schools in the United States. Today, women such as Barbara Smoker in Great Britain and Anne Nicol Gaylor in the United States direct national secular groups. Taslima Nasrin, who has a *fatwa* hanging over her head from Moslem fundamentalists, is a modern-day freedom fighter in the international battle of "woman versus orthodoxy."

"Salvation" Through Women?

Freethought has no gender, but its female proponents, cognizant of religion's control of women, naturally have written about the special harm done to women by religion. While an apologetic sector of the women's movement always has argued that the bible has been "misinterpreted" to subjugate women, most freethinking women have taken the opposite position. Feminism and other human rights cannot be argued by authority, much less by divine authority. "Do you tell me that the Bible is against our rights? Then I say that our claims do not rest upon a book written no one knows when, or by whom. . . . Books and opinions, no matter from whom they came, if they are in opposition to human rights, are nothing but dead letters. . . ." said Ernestine L. Rose during a debate on the matter at a women's rights convention in 1856.

Many of these writers addressed the harm of what suffragist Helen Battelle Dietrick termed the "idée fixe" of Christianity: Eve's sin/original sin. As Matilda Joslyn Gage wrote, "the real foundation of the Church is the doctrine of woman's inferiority by reason of her original sin." Helen H. Gardener, in her elegant book, *Men, Women and Gods*, noted in 1885: "This religion and the Bible require of woman everything, and give her nothing. They ask her support and her love, and repay her with contempt and oppression." Suffragist Josephine K. Henry later echoed: "Is not the Church to-day a masculine hierarchy, with a female constituency, which holds woman in Bible lands in silence and subjection? . . . It demands everything from her and gives her nothing in return."

Dietrick was among the many writers who spoke in terms of salvation of the world through the emancipation of women. As women compose the bulk of adherents, it is women "who must deliver the world from the curse of theology-engendered hatred," Dietrick urged. Voltairine de Cleyre, in invoking past freethought heroines, spoke of the need for a feminist/freethought "resurrection." Susan B. Anthony wrote: "I am a full and firm believer in the revelation that it is through *woman the race is to be redeemed.*"

Many women freethinkers have sought to "save" women—from religion. Elizabeth Cady Stanton stated: "My heart's desire is to lift women out of all these dangerous, degrading superstitions, and to this end will I labor my remaining days on earth," a vow reiterated by women who followed her. Margaret Sanger "wanted each woman to be a rebellious Vashti, not an Esther." Twentieth-century feminist Sonia Johnson once remarked, "One of my favorite fantasies is that next Sunday not one single woman, in any country of the world, will go to church."

In response to the inevitable assertion that the bible and Christianity elevated woman's status, perhaps no writer was so eloquent as Elizabeth Cady Stanton:

"So far from woman owing what liberty she does enjoy, to the Bible and the church, they have been the greatest block in the way of her development. The vantage ground woman holds to-day is due to all the forces of civilization, to science, discovery, invention, rationalism, the religion of humanity chanted in the golden rule round the globe centuries before the Christian religion was known. It is not to Bibles, prayer books, catechisms, liturgies, the canon law and church creeds and organizations, that woman owes one step in her progress, for all these alike have been hostile, and still are, to her freedom and development."

What British atheist Hypatia Bradlaugh Bonner pointed out in 1919 remains true: "The rise which has taken place recently in the status of women in certain countries is due almost wholly, if not entirely, to the decline in religious belief. . . . The more women know, the less they will 'believe.' "

Contributions to Freethought

Women Without Superstition features stimulating and thought-provoking writings by women pursuing every avenue of religious assumption and freethought conviction. The authors dissect the nature of belief, prayer, vicarious atonement, biblical claims, the preachments of Jesus, and onto-logical arguments. (Don't miss intriguing discussions on ants and reli-gion, pages 232 and 340.) Besides including essays and excerpts from books and periodicals, *Women Without Superstition* includes glimpses of other facets of the lives of women freethinkers, from autobiographical sketches to newspaper interviews and profiles. The centerpiece of this collection is the Elizabeth Cady Stanton Freethought Reader (Chapter Ten) contain-ing excerpts from more than forty of her writings about religion. Stanton on the question of religion is pure pleasure—yet most of these writings have never appeared in book form. The depth of her freethought works has never been plumbed.

Also showcased is Ernestine L. Rose's 1861 classic "A Defence of Athe-ism," which, dismayingly, has never before been reprinted in an anthology or in book form. Voltairine de Cleyre is a "lost" but powerful freethinker, much of whose writings remain timely and deserve resuscitation. Emma Goldman memorably dissected the Sermon on the Mount in her essay, "The Failure of Christianity." Charlotte Perkins Gilman, in her scorch-ingly logical analysis of "death-based religions," had a brilliant mind woe-fully underutilized by the freethought movement. Ruth Hurmence Green's "What I Found When I Searched the Scriptures" is a modern-day classic. So is Barbara Ehrenreich's analysis of the state of religion and state/church separation in latter-day twentieth century America.

Analyzing the bible and the character of its deity has been of special interest to women writers. Biblical exploits led early bible critic Ella E. Gibson to exclaim that "any family which permits such a volume to lie on their parlor-table ought to be ostracized by all respectable society" and latter-day biblical analyst Ruth Hurmence Green to vow "never to be seen in public with an unconcealed bible." Green added that she stopped believing in a god because "I could not admire in a deity what I condemned in human beings." Catherine Fahringer, after reviewing bible stories, realized: "I'm nicer than God!"

Women freethinkers have been particularly concerned with the nature of knowledge about religious claims. Charlotte Perkins Gilman, in the vein of Frances Wright, whimsically pointed out that "Men could think and think, talk and argue, advance, deny, assert, and controvert, and write innumerable books [about religion], without being hampered at any time by any fact." As Anne Nicol Gaylor noted: "It is possible to speculate endlessly about the nonexistent."

Ethics is another topic of interest to many of the women freethinkers. "Good works instead of long prayers," advised Anne Royall. "The lash of a hereafter is no guide for us here," observed thoughtful Ernestine L. Rose. Margaret Knight told BBC audiences in her 1955 broadcast: "Ethical teaching is weakened if it is tied up with dogmas that will not bear examination."

Perhaps most striking, however, is the theme of the importance of *this* world, improving life here on earth, a continual refrain in the writings of women.

"We are on the earth, and they tell of us heaven; we are human beings, and they tell us of angels and devils; we are matter, and they tell us of spirit; we have five senses whereby to admit truths, and a reasoning faculty by which to build our belief upon them; and they tell us of dreams dreamed thousands of years ago, which all our experience flatly contradicts," lectured Frances Wright in 1828.

British freethinker Emma Martin wrote in the 1840s: "Religion, with an upward glancing eye, asks what there is *above*. Philosophy looks around her and seeks to make a happy home of earth." People "lose themselves, while looking for God," warned Martin.

"Our life is short," counseled Ernestine L. Rose, "and we cannot spare an hour from the human race, even for all the gods in creation."

"I believe that this world needs all our best efforts and earnest endeavors twenty-four hours a day," wrote Helen H. Gardener.

Busy suffragists Elizabeth Cady Stanton and Susan B. Anthony agreed that they had no time to "commune with the angels." Stanton wrote at seventy:

"I can say that the happiest period of my life has been since I emerged from the shadows and superstitions of the old theologies, relieved from all gloomy apprehensions of the future, satisfied that as my labors and capacities were limited to this sphere of action, I was responsible for nothing beyond my horizon, as I could neither understand nor change the condition of the unknown world. Giving ourselves, then, no trouble about the future, let us make the most of the present, and fill up our lives with earnest work here."

"I do not believe in God, because I believe in man," wrote Emma Goldman.

Analyzes author Barbara G. Walker: "Faith in God necessarily implies a lack of faith in humanity."

Charlotte Perkins Gilman protested that humans are "directing our best efforts toward the sky. . . . Improvement in the human race is not accomplished by extracting any number of souls and placing them in heaven, or elsewhere. It must be established on earth." She added: "Surely fathers, not to speak of mothers, should be more concerned about what will happen to their living children in the world we are making, than about what may happen to themselves after they are dead!"

What do "faithless" women have faith in? Themselves, their rights, the potential of humankind, and the natural world.

"Let us use our energy and our initiative to solve our problems without relying on prayers and wishful thinking," said Ruth Hurmence Green. "When we have faith in ourselves, we will find we do not need to have faith in gods."

—Annie Laurie Gaylor

Women Without
Superstition

Women Without Superstition

1

Mary Wollstonecraft

REVOLUTIONARY FOR WOMANKIND

April 27, 1759 – September 10, 1797

> · . . . *the being cannot be termed rational or virtuous, who obeys any authority, but that of reason.*
>
> **A Vindication of the Rights of Woman,** *1792*

THE FIRST INFLUENTIAL BOOK calling for equality of the sexes was written by a freethinking Deist, Mary Wollstonecraft. The word "reason" appears more than one hundred and fifty times in the index to a modern release of Mary Wollstonecraft's two related works, *A Vindication of the Rights of Men* (1790) and *A Vindication of the Rights of Woman* (1792).

Scourged as "a hyena in petticoats" for her modern views, Mary was a child of the Enlightenment, with an unceasing faith in reason. Her Deism invoked a god that was Nature, perfection and the source of reason. Biographer Eleanor Flexner and others have suggested the evidence shows that Mary later lost even this faith, adopting an agnostic point of view.

Mary expressed strong opinions against conventional religion, the ministry, astrology, the monarchy, many customs of the wealthy, and slavery. She championed women's rights, children's rights and animal rights. She counseled the benefits of breast-feeding, early education, dress reform, rational parenting and called for a national system of free, coeducational primary day schools.

A Vindication of the Rights of Woman rebutted the accepted views of the day toward women by such authors as Rousseau, protested the circumscribed sphere of womankind, and society's assumptions that women feel rather than think. "Teach them to think" and treat women as the "rational creatures" that they were. Women "must only bow to the authority of reason, instead of being the *modest* slaves of opinion." (Wollstonecraft, *A Vindication of the Rights of Men with A Vindication of the Rights of Woman:* 124)

Mary was the second of seven children born in London to Elizabeth Dickson and weaver Edward John Wollstonecraft, who drank, spent an inheritance and left his daughters to fend for themselves. She became a companion to a widow, did needlework, worked as a governess, and opened her own school.

Mary had become acquainted with Richard Price, who was a dissenting minister, a friend to Joseph Priestley and correspondent with such men as Jefferson, Hume and Franklin. Her first book, *Thoughts on the Education of Daughters*, was published in London in 1786. She moved back to London to write, meeting influential writers, artists, and scientists through her publisher Joseph Johnson. In 1788, her novel *Mary, A Fiction* and a children's book *Original Stories from Real Life* were published, along with her translation of *On the Importance of Religious Opinions* by Jacques Necker. Her children's book was reissued in 1791 with illustrations by William Blake, and a third edition came out in 1796. She began writing for the *Analytical Review* and also compiled *The Female Reader*, an anthology published under the pseudonym "Mr. Creswick, Teacher of Elocution."

Edmund Burke, a member of Parliament, wrote his *Reflections on the Revolution in France*, attacking the American and French Revolutions, after reading Mary's review of a sermon by Richard Price. Mary wrote the first rebuttal of Burke's polemic five weeks later, *A Vindication of the Rights of Men*, published anonymously. Thomas Paine's own *Rights of Men* appeared afterward. Mary's answer rejected all arguments from authority or precedent.

Her seminal *A Vindication of the Rights of Woman* was published in 1792. Although a sensation in her day, it would not be republished for a century. Nevertheless, nineteenth-century women's rights advocates read and treasured it.

Mary devoted part of the last chapter of the book to exposing faith healers and fortune-tellers, classified as "Some Instances of the Folly Which the Ignorance of Women Generates." "In this metropolis a number of lurking leeches infamously gain a subsistence by practising on the credulity of women," she cautioned. (p. 276)

In Paris when Louis XVI was taken prisoner, having watched the scene from a window, she fled to escape arrest in May 1793, and wrote a history of the French revolution. She met Gilbert Imlay, and they lived as husband and wife, Imlay's American citizenship protecting her from arrest. By the time her daughter Fanny was born in April 1794, Imlay had left her. To stave off her despairing threats to commit suicide, Imlay sent her with the baby to Scandinavia on business. Her letters on Norway and Sweden were later published. Returning to London to find Imlay living with an actress, she jumped into the Thames, but was rescued.

In 1796, she and William Godwin fell in love. He wrote of her book, *Letters Written During a Short Residence in Sweden, Norway, and Denmark*: "If ever there was a book calculated to make a man in love with its author, this appears to me to be the book." The couple married on March 29, 1797, after discovering that Mary was pregnant. Future admirers such as Voltairine de Cleyre were particularly impressed by the couple's independent domestic arrangements: they continued to live in close but separate lodgings, sending notes back and forth. While pregnant, Mary worked on "Letters on the Management of Children," which contained her deeply held views on the need to respect children and their rights.

Following a rather uneventful pregnancy, the thirty-eight-year-old author delivered a daughter, Mary, on August 30. Three hours after delivery, the midwife summoned Godwin in panic: Mary had not delivered the placenta. When a hospital physician either used his hand or a spoonlike utensil to pull out the placenta, Mary hemorrhaged, fainting from the agony of the crude procedure. Several days later, it was clear she had a serious infection, perhaps "puerperal fever, " commonplace before the importance of medical hygiene was recognized. Or the doctor may have punctured her uterus. After ten days of intense suffering, she died.

Bereaved Godwin wrote *Memoirs of the Author of a Vindication of the Rights of Woman* four months after her death, published along with her unfinished novel and letters. When her private life went public, Mary Wollstonecraft became a symbol of ignominy to conservatives and proper society. One biographer discovered that in the index of the first issue of the *Anti-Jacobin Review*, readers looking up "Prostitution" were advised, "See Mary Wollstonecraft."

At twenty-two, Mary's first daughter Fanny committed suicide, writing in a note: "I have long determined that the best thing I could do was to put an end to the existence of a being whose birth was unfortunate . . . . Perhaps to hear of my death will give you pain, but you will soon have the blessing of forgetting that such a creature ever existed." The teenaged Mary ran off with poet Percy Shelley, and, at age nineteen, wrote the remarkable *Frankenstein*. After Shelley's tragic drowning in Italy, she courted respectability for their one surviving son. Aside from her friendship with Frances Wright, she avoided becoming embroiled in the cause of woman.

Margaret Fuller, who in many ways walked in Wollstonecraft's footsteps, wrote in *Woman in the Nineteenth Century*: "Mary Wolstonecraft [sic], like Madame Dudevant (commonly known as George Sand) in our day, was a woman whose existence better proved the need of some new interpretation of Woman's Rights than anything she wrote. Such beings as these, rich in genius, of most tender sympathies, capable of high virtue and a chastened harmony, ought not to find themselves, by birth, in a place so narrow, that, in breaking bonds, they become outlaws."

"Rational Creatures"

These excerpts are taken from a 1995 reprint of A Vindication of the Rights of Men and A Vindication of the Rights of Woman (1790, 1792) by Mary Wollstonecraft. She wrote nothing lengthy on religion, but the following quotes, arranged by subject matter, are typical of her views on reason versus orthodoxy. Page numbers are included for easy reference.

"Rational Creatures"

[Women's] first duty is to themselves as rational creatures, and the next, in point of importance, as citizens. . . . (*Rights of Woman*, Ch. IX: 235)

"Virtue & Reason"

. . . every being may become virtuous by the exercise of its own reason. . . .
In fact, it is a farce to call any being virtuous whose virtues do not result from the exercise of its own reason. (*Rights of Woman*, Ch. II: 89–90)
. . . the being cannot be termed rational or virtuous, who obeys any authority, but that of reason. (*Rights of Woman*, Ch. XIII: 291)

"Blind Obedience"

Strengthen the female mind by enlarging it, and there will be an end to blind obedience. . . . (*Rights of Woman*, Ch. II: 93)

"Submit to Reason"

A slavish bondage to parents cramps every faculty of the mind; . . . Children cannot be taught too early to submit to reason, . . . (*Rights of Woman*, Ch. XI: 247–248)

"Eve"

Probably the prevailing opinion, that woman was created for man, may have taken its rise from Moses's poetical story; yet, as very few, it is presumed, who have bestowed any serious thought on the subject, ever supposed that Eve was, literally speaking, one of Adam's ribs, the deduction must be allowed to fall to the ground; or, only be so far admitted as it proves that man, from the remotest antiquity, found it convenient to exert his strength to subjugate his companion, and his invention to shew that she ought to have her neck bent under the yoke, because the whole creation was only created for his convenience or pleasure. (*Rights of Woman*, Ch. II: 95)

"Slavery To Ministers"

Slavery to monarchs and ministers, which the world will be long freeing itself from, and whose deadly grasp stops the progress of the human mind, is not yet abolished. (*Rights of Woman*, Ch. III: 117)

. . . The clergy, I speak of the body, not forgetting the respect and affection which I have for individuals, perform the duty of their profession as a kind of fee-simple, to entitle them to the emoluments accruing from it; and their ignorant flock think that merely going to church is meritorious. (*Rights of Men*, 36–37)

What, but the rapacity of the only men who exercised their reason, the priests, secured such vast property to the church, when a man gave his perishable substance to save himself from the dark torments of purgatory; and found it more convenient to indulge his depraved appetites, and pay an exorbitant price for absolution, than listen to the suggestions of reason, and work out his own salvation: in a word, was not the separation of religion from morality the work of the priests . . . ? (*Rights of Men*, 40)

"Divine Right of Husbands"

I love man as my fellow; but his scepter, real, or usurped, extends not to me, unless the reason of an individual demands my homage; and even then the submission is to reason, and not to man. (*Rights of Woman*, Ch. II: 107)

But should it be proved that woman is naturally weaker than man, whence does it follow that it is natural for her to labour to become still weaker than nature intended her to be? Arguments of this cast are an insult to common sense, and savour of passion. The *divine right* of husbands, like the divine right of kings, may, it is to be hoped, in this enlightened age, be contested without danger, . . . (Ch. III: 112)

Matthew 7:16

. . . What but a pestilential vapour can hover over society when its chief director is only instructed in the invention of crimes, or the stupid routine of childish ceremonies? Will men never be wise? - will they never cease to expect corn from tares, and figs from thistles? (*Rights of Woman*, Ch. I: 83)

"Demi-Gods"

Men neglect the duties incumbent on man, yet are treated like demi-gods; religion is also separated from morality by a ceremonial veil, yet men wonder that the world is almost, literally speaking, a den of sharpers or oppressors. (*Rights of Woman*, Ch. IX: 230)

"Hell Stalks Abroad"

. . . Man preys on man; and you mourn for the idle tapestry that decorated a gothic pillar, and the dronish bell that summoned the fat priest to prayer. You mourn for the empty pageant of a name, when slavery flaps her wing, . . . Why is our fancy to be appalled by terrific perspectives of a hell beyond the grave?—Hell stalks abroad;—the lash resounds on the slave's naked sides; and the sick wretch, who can no longer earn the sour bread of unremitting labour, steals to a ditch to bid the world a long good night. . . . (*Rights of Men*: 62)

2

Anne Newport Royall

LOBBYIST FOR THE SEPARATION OF CHURCH & STATE

June 11, 1769 – October 1, 1854

Good works instead of long prayers.

Anne Royall's motto

ECCENTRIC AUTHOR, PASSIONATE DEFENDER OF THE ENLIGHTENMENT, and ardent foe of the "Christian party in politics," outspoken Anne Royall was arrested, at the behest of religionists, and convicted of being a "common scold" by a Washington, D.C., jury in 1829. A South Carolina editor averred that Anne was actually "an uncommon scold." Probably the first lobbyist in the United States Congress to oppose a union of church and state, Anne exposed government corruption, fought to retain Sunday mail delivery, and championed public schools free from religious bias or control. She knew and interviewed every president from John Adams to Franklin Pierce. Hating the proliferation of religious tracts and societies, Anne dumped tracts off steamboats, tore them into pieces and flung them out of hotel rooms, and drove out missionaries from the halls of Congress, wielding an old green cotton umbrella. Her mottos: "Free thought, free speech and a free press" and "Good works instead of long prayers."

One of her several biographers, George Stuyvesant Jackson, wrote of her:

"She was nationally known, liked, feared, ignored, detested; but she would be heard whatever the reactions, for in her personality were curiously if not harmoniously blended the philosophy of Voltaire with the evangelism of Carry Nation; the persistence of Joan of Arc with the pen of H.L. Mencken. . . . With it all, however, she was very nearly the pattern of the true liberal in any day: above party, above corruption, above the fashions of the time in defense of what she considered the best for a free country with justice for its citizens."

Writing at the turn of the nineteenth century, biographer Sarah Harvey Porter speculated that the reason her books were ignored by posterity "lies in the woman's bitterly hostile attitude to the prevailing theology of her day."

Anne Newport was born in Baltimore, moved with her family to wilderness in Pennsylvania, then to Sweet Spring, Virginia. Major William Royall, a wealthy Revolutionary soldier, hired her impoverished mother as a servant in 1785. In 1797, Royall shocked family and neighbors by marrying twenty-eight-year-old Anne, who was more than twenty years his junior. A Freemason, he knew Washington, Jefferson, and Lafayette, and was an admirer of Voltaire and Paine. Anne, with the run of Royall's library, embraced the Age of Reason:

"When our reason is cultivated and our minds enlightened by education, we are enabled to strip off that disguise which knavery, bigotry and superstition wears." (Anne to Matt, February 7, 1818, Royall, *Letters from Alabama: 176*)

Her views were Deistic, repudiating dogma and hell: ". . . I spurn the narrow mind which is attached to a sect or party, to the exclusion of the rest of mankind." (Anne to Matt, December 21, 1817, *Letters:* 105)

After her husband died in 1813, Anne, a wealthy, childless widow of forty-four, spent the next decade in Alabama. Royall's relatives, who had been written out of his will, contested it and managed to break it in 1823, leaving Anne without any means except what she could earn by pen. She set off on a series of nomadic adventures to Tennessee and Virginia, New York, and New England, writing her first travel book, *Sketches of History, Life and Manners in the United States* (1826), followed by the three-volume *Black Books* (1828–1829) [see selections], *Mrs. Royall's Pennsylvania* (1829), *The Southern Tour* (1830–1831) and *Letters from Alabama* (1830). These letters had been written in 1817–1822 to a respectable young attorney named Matthew Dunbar.

On May 3, 1821, she wrote Matt, ungrammatically: "What think you, Matt, of the christian religion? Between you and I, and the bed post, I begin to think it is all a plot of the priests. I have ever marked those professors, whenever humanity demanded their attention, the veriest savages under the sun." (*Letters:* 218–219)

Anne financed trips by selling books and taking subscriptions for new ones, sometimes begging or using credit. Described as a small, frail scarecrow, she was intrepid, sloshing by foot through the mud of Cumberland Pass, taking boats at night, roughing it on the frontier. Many feared to cross her, for her books castigated individuals who snubbed her and praised businesses and people who treated her well. Her books and escapades brought fame, but any fortune she amassed was soon spent or given away.

Anne reviled missionaries and piety, fought evangelicals in Congress, and destroyed the tracts of the Sunday School Union wherever she found them, such as in the Library of Congress. When, on July 4, 1827, Rev. Ezra Stiles Ely of Philadelphia announced plans for "a Christian party in politics" and the election of

Christians only to government, Anne went into action. To suggest a church and state party was outright treason, she believed. She spent one August afternoon at West Point in the blistering sun destroying religious literature. Her complaints about religious ritual there resulted in a Congressional investigation led by the grandfather of Theodore Roosevelt, Rep. James J. Roosevelt.

Although she was not a feminist, Anne felt a loyalty to her own sex, providing sympathy and charity for "fallen women." Like Frances Wright, Anne was appalled at the influence of ministers over American women, and condemned the "contamination" of American Indians by missionaries. In a letter written to a disapproving Cincinnati minister on September 3, 1830, Anne wrote her oft-repeated maxim that she would rather see *one* good action, than hear ten thousand good words. Claiming to have been raised among the Indians as a "heathen," she wrote that she never read the bible, fearing it would influence her to behave as bible believers did.

She worked hard but unsuccessfully to stop the Sabbatarians from halting Sunday mail distribution. She taunted religionists, whom she called "blue-skins" and "black coats," making personal calls on Dr. Ely and prominent preacher Lyman Beecher.

On December 17, 1827, despite warnings not to enter the anti-Masonic state of Vermont, Anne called on an anti-Mason shopkeeper in Burlington, who pushed her down a ten-foot flight of icy stairs. She landed in a snowbank, but dislocated her ankle, and broke several bones, which confined her to an unfriendly boarding house for months.

While outrageously free-spoken, this quality made her entertaining, accounting in part for the success of her books. But the religious hysteria against her mounted after she settled in Washington, D.C., and began feuding with a nearby evangelical church, the Engine House Congregation, whose members stoned her house and harassed her by singing hymns outside her door. The church got her arrested under a colonial law punishing "common scolds." The first Circuit Court case in May 1829 was thrown out, but in the second appearance she was convicted. Persecutors brought a ducking stock into the courtroom, but she was let off with a fine of ten dollars and costs, and fifty dollars as a peace bond. Depending on which history is believed, President Andrew Jackson went to pay her fines but was beaten to it either by defense witness, Secretary of War Jon Eaton, or two sympathetic reporters. Her notoriety caused her to be mobbed by students at the University of Virginia, and some towns refused her admittance.

At sixty-two, Anne launched a D.C. weekly newspaper out of her home, the *Paul Pry* (1831–1836) succeeded by the *Huntress* (1836–1854), which folded three months before her death at age eighty-five. Not a scandal sheet, *Paul Pry*'s purpose was "to educate the people to respect, maintain, and defend free government." She took ads, wrote editorials, reported news, and toured every govern-ment department, describing every federal employee, from the Secretary of State to the Post Office's janitor. She exposed malfeasance in public office, promoted justice for Indians, editorialized on all the issues of the day, promoted labor rights, the abolition of flogging in the Navy, gradual abolition of slavery by states, build-ing canals and roads, and public funding for scientific research. She fought the power of the Bank of the United States, reveling when President Jackson vetoed a bill in 1832 renewing its charter.

A newspaper in Alabama was named for her during her lifetime, as well as a canal boat operating in Hollidaysburg, Pennsylvania. Today, a paddle-boat at free-thought Lake Hypatia, Alabama, bears her name.

It took John Quincy Adams twenty-five years to win Anne her husband's war pension. On July 29, 1848, Congress amended a statute and at age seventy-nine, Anne was offered $480 a year or the flat sum of $1,200, choosing cash. William Royall's vindictive heirs interceded; she received exactly ten dollars of her pen-sion. She died almost penniless.

Phineas T. Barnum visited her in 1836, and described her in his autobiogra-phy as "a monomaniac upon political subjects, [but] she was nevertheless a good-hearted, generous woman." In his *Memoirs*, John Quincy Adams ambiguously recalled Anne Royall as "a virago errant in enchanted armor."

Missionaries

*These remarks are excerpted from the chapter "Missionaries," **Black Book, Volume III** (1829). Imagine what Anne Royall might have written about today's television evangelists!*

... FROM MAINE TO GEORGIA—from the Atlantic to Missouri, they swarm like locusts; and, under the name of *foreign* missions, *home* missions, *Bible* missions, *tract* societies, societies for educating *pious* young men, to spread the gospel, *pincushion* societies, *cent* societies, *mite* societies, *widows'* societies, *children's* societies, *rag-tag* societies, and Sunday school societies, they have laid the whole country under contribution! Figures cannot calculate the amount collected by those public and private robbers: it is more than would liberate every slave in the United States; it would pay the British debt! They say, "We do not force people to give." I see no difference between forcing a man out of his money, at the mouth of a pistol, and forcing it from him by *trick* and cunning; the crime is the same. . . .

The late proceedings of those daring invaders to establish a national religion have opened the eyes of all lovers of liberty and religion. . . . I have been told they have thrown off the mask and are preaching to the people to elect none but godly men to represent them in the General and State Legislatures; as to godly men, I believe they are very scarce, but what they mean by godly people, is people of their own stamp; to bring this about, they are establishing presses over the whole country, and this they are able to do as they have the greatest revenue in the country. Having tasted the sweets of money, which has the same effect on them that drinking has upon a drunkard, the more he drinks the dryer he is, so the more they get, the more they want; and taking the advantage of this run-mad delusion of spreading the gospel to obtain it, they think to get these godly men into the General Government; get two-thirds of the states to alter the Constitution; come out with their national religion, and then let the people get their throats ready. May the arm of the first member of Congress, who proposes a national religion, drop powerless from his shoulder; his tongue cleave to the roof of his mouth and all the people say amen.

Let no one view this as an idle chimera; look at the vast sums of money they have obtained, let any sober man say why are all those presses and booksellers set up, have these any thing to do with converting the heathen? no, nor is it done with that view, it is done to blind mankind; make him a bigot, to fashion him into a tool; and thus, by slow but sure means, effect their purposes. See what they have done in a few years [the foreign mission board was instituted in 1810], they have contaminated the whole country, their name is legion; see the skill, the industry and the energy displayed by those band of pirates, to amass money, their God is mamon [*sic*] and they worship no other. One of two things seems inevitable, either the country must put down these men, or they will put down the country; on this point there can be but one opinion, they are determined and will not stop short of despotism.

In all countries, and in all ages, from the Druids down to brother Beecher, priests have aimed at universal power; this may be accounted for thus: all men wish others to think as they do on all subjects, but more particularly on religion; this is natural, and such is the nature of man, that he devises means to compel others to think as he does; but no means are so effectual as power, and no means are more successful in acquiring power than money. . . .

. . . like a pestilence [they] cover the land; not to scatter blessings amongst the distressed, root out ignorance, (as somebody wisely said of them,) or diffuse the lights of knowledge, to ennoble the age, or amend mankind; not to break the chains of slavery, or teach man his religious or political duties, or cultivate the arts and sciences, no; quite the reverse. Their object and their interest is to plunge mankind into ignorance, to make him a bigot, a fanatic, a hypocrite, a heathen, to hate every sect but his own, (the orthodox,) to shut his eyes against the truth, harden his heart against the distress of his fellow man, and purchase heaven by money. . . .

They preach up the Juggernaut, (the true Juggernauts are amongst ourselves,) and draw such pictures of heathens going to Hell by thousands, that they frighten ignorant women and children into compliance. They will take no denial, "you will go to Hell if you do not give money to spread the gospel;" some will take out their watch and give the people so many minutes to consider upon the matter, and in case of refusal, everlasting torment in Hell is denounced against them. "Oh, sir, I have but one dollar to buy me clothes, indeed sir I cannot spare it." "Oh give it, to send the gospel to the heathen, and trust to the Lord." Why don't they trust to the Lord? No! They trust to the cash. . . .

If those millions squandered on designing missionaries had been deposited in funds for the support of yourselves, when old age, misfortune, or sickness (from which none are exempt,) overtakes you, or for the distressed of your race, what a heaven of happiness you would have created on earth: ye would now be an ornament to your sex, and ages to come would call you blessed. But it is in vain to try—a priest-ridden female is lost to reason. Why? because she has surrendered her reason to the priests—missionaries I mean—the orthodox; they are the grand deceivers. . . .

Fanaticism and bigotry require any food but common sense, and reason, which would break the charm of those spellbound fanatics. . . .

I find that the whole weight of relieving human misery and distress falls on the shoulders of those *Heretics and Infidels*; and though great part of this distress has been occasioned by those ravening wolves' hopeful converts, if the amount of a piece of bread would save the life of a fellow man, he might perish in the street for them, who ever saw them relieve the poor. These *Heretics* are the men that feed the hungry, cloth the naked, take in the stranger, visit the sick and the prisoner. . . .

These *bible* people remind me of another calamity similar to this missionary scheme, when our people, or any christian power would go to Africa for the pious purpose of kidnapping negroes, the mother would cry out to her children "run, run, the *christians* are coming," so when ever you hear "bibles," run for your life, if you do not want your pockets picked, or to be insulted and slandered as I was . . . and if you hear "*hopeful* convertions" [sic] or the "gospel," don't stop to look behind you.

. . . Do these Presbyterians, or orthodox . . . think we have forgotten what use they made of power, when they had it? Do they think we have forgotten how they drenched England in blood, created a civil war, (what they are in a fair way to do here) and, when they could no longer retain the power of killing there, came over to this country, and began it afresh—dipping their hands in the blood of harmless, unresisting people? Do they think we have forgotten how they whipped, branded, banished, and imprisoned the innocent Quakers? Five of those who were banished, happening to return privately, to settle some private business, were taken and hung by those monsters, at *one* time. Do they think we have forgotten how they put innocent men, women, and children to death, in cool blood, under the pretence of witchcraft? "Even refused to bury the victims of their inhuman barbarity; but left them hanging on the gibbets, exposed to wild beasts, and birds of prey." The innocence of youth, the infirmities of old age, virgin modesty, fortune, honor, virtue, and the most dignified employments of the state, were no security; they hung a lawyer, because he refused to plead against those innocent sufferers; they hung seventeen in *one* day. Children of ten years of age were put to death; young girls were stripped naked, (by God's people, the ministers,) and the marks of witchcraft searched for, on their bodies, with the most indecent curiosity. Those spots of the scurvy, which age impresses upon the bodies of old men, were taken for evident signs of the infernal power. When witnesses failed, those blood-spilling monsters put the innocent creatures to tortures, to extort confessions dictated by their executioners, themselves; and they have the impudence to dictate to us now, to go to blood-spilling again; nothing else, under heaven. What else is it? They are in full possession of every liberty, but that of hanging heretics. . . . What did Calvin, their leader, do? Did he not burn an innocent man, by piece-meal—kept him three days in torture, by the flames—was this monster a Christian? True, all sects have been persecutors; but these persecutions were the acts of their tyrannical kings, pontiffs, and rulers. Not so those bloody Calvinists: they, when they have the power, devour their equals, their fellow men, with that wanton, savage ferocity, with which wild beasts destroy each other; and worse; for the wild beast only kills to satisfy his hunger; but those monsters of hypocrisy kill for the pure pleasure of seeing blood flow. It is bred in them; it is in their grain, and will never be extinguished; it is in the nature of their tenets, and a distinguishing trait of this sect. . . . Instead of inculcating those virtues which ennoble human nature, enlarge the powers of thinking, or advance their future happiness by a liberal course of improvement, they are taught that sordid avarice, and haughtiness, is religion; they tell the student that hating his neighbor, is religion; that all sects but his own are heretics, and must be exterminated to make way for God's people. . . .

Frances Wright

3

Frances Wright

THE FREE ENQUIRER

September 6, 1795 – December 13, 1852

I am not going to question your opinions. I am not going to meddle with your belief. I am not going to dictate to you mine. All that I say is, examine, inquire. Look into the nature of things. Search out the grounds of your opinions, the for and the against. Know why you believe, understand what you believe, and possess a reason for the faith that is in you.

"Divisions of Knowledge," *1828*

FRANCES WRIGHT WAS THE FIRST WOMAN TO SPEAK PUBLICLY to men and women from the podium in the United States, the first to publicly advocate women's equality, and certainly the first to question the utility of religion and denounce the power of the clergy. She was a pioneering antislavery activist, social reformer, early advocate of free public schools, and editor of the *Free Enquirer.*

She sat at the feet of freethought philosopher Jeremy Bentham, won praise from Thomas Jefferson and became the confidante of General Lafayette. The nineteenth-century woman's rights movement lionized her as a path-blazer of unparalleled brilliance. Her likeness was placed in the frontispiece of the first volume of *The History of Woman Suffrage.*

But to the United States press and clergy of her day, she was "The Red Harlot of Infidelity," "a bold blasphemer, and a voluptuous preacher of licentiousness . . . impervious to the voice of virtue, and case-hardened against shame!" Catherine E. Beecher, writing in the 1830s, declared her "disgusting." Freethought historian J.M. Robertson granted her only three paragraphs in *A History of Freethought in the Nineteenth Century*, dismissing her as "a reformer rather than a thinker." In fact, her words broke as many barriers as her actions did.

Her eye-opening definition of religion: "a belief in, and homage rendered to, existences unseen and causes unknown." She entreated others to follow her own rule, and speak only about what they *knew*, urging them "to turn their churches into halls of science, and exchange their teachers of faith for expounders of nature." (Wright, *Life, Letters and Lectures*: 73, 91, 67)

Her credo: "I am neither Jew nor Gentile, Mahomedan nor Theist; I am but a member of the human family, and would accept of truth by whomsoever offered—that truth which we can all find, if we will but seek—in things, not in words; in nature, not in human imagination; in our own hearts, not in temples made with hands." (p. 101)

"Time is it to arrest our speculations respecting unseen worlds and inconceivable mysteries, and to address our inquiries to the improvement of our human condition, and our efforts to the practical illustration of those beautiful principles of liberty and equality enshrined in the political institutions, and, first and chief, in the national declaration of independence." (p. 103)

❧

Orphaned as a baby in Dundee, Scotland, Frances was raised in London by her mother's aristocratic relatives. She grew to be an arresting five feet, ten inches. When she became famous, she influenced fashion with her simplicity, especially the arrangement of her curly hair in a liberating style of ringlets. The young heiress had a strong social conscience, falling in love with the idea of America as a teenager. Spending her late teens with her Scottish aunt and uncle, who was a moral philosopher at the University of Glasgow, she wrote two plays, "Altorf" and "A Few Days in Athens," published later to acclaim.

In 1818, Frances and loyal sister Camilla, a year younger, traveled to America for two years. After "Altorf" was successfully staged in New York in 1819, Frances shocked society by having the temerity to place her byline on the published play.

She returned to England in 1820 and wrote *Views of Society & Manners in America*, "By an Englishwoman," which, praising the United States and attacking Tories, caused a sensation. The book brought her to the attention of Jeremy Bentham and General Lafayette, the hero of the American Revolution. A widower in his sixties, Lafayette invited her to visit him in France. An amorous friendship began. Frances, who carried conspiratorial messages across the Channel for Lafayette, frequently stayed with his family.

At twenty-nine, Frances returned with Camilla to America, traveling separately but in Lafayette's grand wake when he was invited back to America for a hero's welcome in the fall of 1824. She and Camilla stayed at Monticello for two weeks when Jefferson hosted Lafayette. The sisters officially became U.S. citizens in 1825. They traveled widely on their own, Frances riding hundreds of miles on horseback. On the frontier, she became one of the first women to adopt "turkish pants." A visit to Robert Owen's commune in New Harmony, Indiana, inspired a plan: to educate slaves for freedom at a model communal plantation. President James Monroe and Chief Justice John Marshall were consulted by Lafayette on her behalf, and Andrew Jackson advised purchasing land in Tennessee. The settlement "Nashoba" (Chickasaw for the Wolf River) was located near a trading post called Memphis.

Underfunded and understaffed from the start, Nashoba broke ground on March 3, 1826. Frances determined that the only religion there would be "kind feeling and kind action." Joining in the manual labor of clearing swamp, subsisting on cornmeal and river water, Frances nearly died of malaria. Recuperating at New Harmony, she met Robert Dale Owen, who became a trusted friend. After a sojourn in Europe, Frances returned to Nashoba in 1828 with Frances Trollope, the mother of the novelist, who was horrified at the primitive conditions. Poor, malaria-ravished Camilla, left to manage the unraveling experiment, had married a co-worker and was pregnant. The press began vilifying Nashoba as "Fanny Wright's Free Love Colony."

❧

At age thirty-four, Frances became the first woman in America to be the main speaker on a public occasion, delivering a July 4th address at New Harmony. She launched a career as freethought lecturer with three consecutive Sunday lectures at the Cincinnati Courthouse beginning August 10, 1828, now seeking to "destroy the slavery of the mind." Her impetus was a revival there:

. "The victims of this odious experiment on human credulity and nervous weakness were invariably women. . . . the despair of Calvin's hell itself seemed to have fallen upon every heart, and discord to have taken possession of every mansion." (*Life, Letters and Lectures:* viii)

In a short autobiography published with her lectures, Frances explained: "It was in this year, 1828, that the standard of 'the Christian Party in Politics' was openly unfurled. . . . This was an evident attempt, through the influence of the clergy over the female mind—until this hour lamentably neglected in the United States—to effect a union of Church and State. . . ." (p. 34).

Frances set out on a history-making quest to disabuse these duped women of their religious fantasies by an earnest series of lectures calling for the education of women and rejecting religion. She toured the west as far as St. Louis, traveling to Baltimore in December 1828, which pronounced itself wonderstruck. She lectured in Philadelphia at the old State House, then in New York City. Labeled the "Priestess of Beelzebub," and condemned by the press as "a female monster," she was physically attacked, a protester once setting a smoke-barrel on fire. After another lecture her carriage was overturned. Once the gaslight was cut off, leaving an audience of 2,000 in the dark. Frances, who continued to lecture by candlelight, was carried down the street in triumph.

Mrs. Trollope, who witnessed Frances' debut lectures in Cincinnati, wrote of it in her book about America, *Domestic Manners of the Americans:*

"That a lady of fortune, of family, and education, whose youth had been passed in the most refined circles of private life, should present herself to the people in this capacity would naturally excite surprise anywhere . . . but in America, where women are guarded by a seven-fold shield of habitual insignificance, it has caused an effect that can scarcely be described. 'Miss Wright of Nashoba is going to lecture at the Court House' sounded from street to street and from house to house. I shared the surprise but not the wonder; I knew her extraordinary gift of eloquence, her almost unequalled command of words, and the wonderful power of her rich and thrilling voice; and I doubted not if it were her will to do it, she had the power of commanding attention and enchanting the ear of any audience before whom it was her pleasure to appear. . . . But . . . all my expectations fell far short of the splendour, the brilliance, the overwhelming eloquence of this extraordinary orator . . . It is impossible to imagine anything more striking than her appearance. Her tall and majestic figure, the deep and almost solemn expression of her eyes, the simple contour of her finely formed head, unadorned excepting by its own natural ringlets. Her garment of plain white muslin which hung about her in folds that recalled the drapery of a Grecian statue, all contributed to produce an effect unlike anything I had ever seen before, or expect to see."

Young Walt Whitman caught a lecture, recalling how "we all loved her: fell down before her," how she was "sweeter, nobler, grander—multiplied by twenty—than all who traduced her," considering her one of the most maligned, least understood characters in history.

❦

Her first lecture on the nature of knowledge warned of the "hired preachers and licensed teachers of old doctrines and old ways" who exploit ignorant women: "Above, her agitated fancy hears the voice of a god in thunders; below, she sees the yawning pit; and, before, behind, around, a thousand phantoms, conjured from the prolific brain of insatiate priestcraft, confound, alarm, and overwhelm her reason!" (*Life, Letters and Lectures:* 17, 20)

Lecture II, on free inquiry, continued a feminist theme: "However novel it may appear, I shall venture the assertion, that, until women assume the place in society which good sense and good feeling alike assign to them, human improvement must advance but feebly. . . . whenever we establish our own pretensions upon the sacrificed rights of others, we do in fact impeach our own liberties, and lower ourselves in the scale of being!" (p. 24)

Lecture III urged overthrowing superstition: "Instead of establishing facts, we have to overthrow errors; instead of ascertaining what *is*, we have to chase from our imaginations what is *not*." She called churches the most formidable enemy of human progress. (pp. 39, 44)

In a lecture on "Morals," Frances observed that, "so far from entrenching human conduct within the gentle barriers of peace and love, religion has ever been, and now is, the deepest source of contentions, wars, persecutions for conscience sake, angry words, angry feelings, backbitings, slanders, suspicions, false judgments, evil interpretations, unwise, unjust, injurious, inconsistent actions. . . . we have seen that no religion stands on the basis of *things known*; none bounds its horizon within the field of human observation; and, therefore, as it can never present us with indisputable facts, so must it ever be at once a source of error and of contention." (p. 70)

"A necessary consequent of religious belief is the attaching ideas of merit to that belief, and of demerit to its absence. Now here is a departure from the first principle of true ethics. Here we find ideas of moral wrong and moral right associated with something else than beneficial action. The consequence is, we lose sight of the real basis of morals, and substitute a false one. Our religious belief usurps the place of our sensations, our imaginations of our judgment. . . . We no longer look to actions, trace their consequences, and *then* deduce the rule; we first make the rule, and then, right or wrong, force the action to square with it." (pp. 73–74)

In her lecture on opinions, Frances observed that persecution for opinion had "raised the gloomy walls and dug the foul caverns of the Inquisition. It was this invented the rack, and the wheel, and the faggot, and the death-pang, and the dungeon, where the Moor, and the Jew, and the philosopher, and the suspected heretic expired, unpitied, unremembered, before thanksgiving, heaven-invoking bigotry." (pp. 87, 85)

Frances noted that in "employing *teachers of opinions*, instead of *teachers of facts*," who expounded "inexplicable creeds" and "unintelligible mysteries," rivers of blood had been shed, all for "establishing and protecting the dogma of a trinity in unity, predestination to salvation or damnation, the divine presence or absence in a wafer of bread or the liquor in a wine cup, the saving efficacy of the sign of the cross, or the sprinkling of cold water on the forehead of an infant." (p. 90)

❧

Practicing what she preached, Frances purchased an old church for $7,000 in the Bowery and renamed it "Hall of Science." The world's first Hall of Science opened its doors in April 1829, for lectures and meetings, at one time offering a health clinic, with a storefront bookstore selling Paine, Shelley, Godwin, and Richard Carlile's birth control tract, "Every Woman's Book." She and Owen launched the

Free Enquirer, its motto "to promote the cause of human improvement." Phiquepal D'Arusmont and some of his pupils from the abandoned New Harmony commune joined her and helped print the newspaper in the basement. In an ironic foreshadowing of her own future, Frances wrote of the legal discrimination, injustices and cruelties faced by a woman upon marriage, who swore away her person, property, "and, as it but too often is, her peace, her honor, and her life."

Camilla joined Frances in New York, but her baby did not survive the summer of 1829. When Frances launched the Working Men's Party, with a radical platform of a ten-hour workday, the *New York Advertiser* decried her as "Lost to society, to earth and to heaven, godless and hopeless." She lectured successfully in Boston despite clergy-led boycotts. Once a minister tried to block her from entering the lecture hall. The Mayor of New York disparaged her as a "female Tom Paine." The candidates of the Working Men's Party, smeared as "Fanny Wrightists," lost, but the party continued.

Frances escorted Nashoba's slaves to Haiti, then she, Camilla, and D'Arusmont sailed for Europe. Her health broken, Camilla died in 1831. Frances, at thirty-five, and the Frenchman, fifty-two, became lovers, setting in motion the tragedy of Frances' remaining life. Finding herself alone and pregnant, Frances married D'Arusmont, and cut herself off from friends, keeping secret the birth of her daughter, Frances Sylva. Frances set off on solo lectures, including a four-year visit to the United States to resume lecturing, again attacked by the press and thugs. She edited the *Manual of American Principles* in 1836–1837.

In 1844, with a new inheritance, she purchased a house in Cincinnati, drawing up a trust to make her daughter an heiress, granting her husband a comfortable lifetime annuity. He sued to take over her American properties. She divorced him, and lost custody of her daughter.

Frances fell on the ice and broke her hip, suffering greatly until her premature death on December 13, 1852. Sylva, who became a Christian and referred to the *Free Enquirer* as "infidel trash," raised a marble monument to the memory of the mother she never understood at Spring Grove Cemetery, Cincinnati.

A tribute to Frances Wright was made at the twentieth anniversary convention of women's suffrage in New York on October 19, 1870, by Paula Davis:

"To this heroic woman, who left ease, elegance, a high social circle of rich culture, and with true self-abnegation gave her life, in the country of her adoption, to the teaching of her highest idea of truth, it is fitting that we pay a tribute to just, though late, respect. . . . She bore the calumny, reproach and persecution to which she was subjected for the truth, as calmly as Socrates. Looking down the serene heights of her philosophy she pitied and endured the scoffs and jeers of the multitude, and fearlessly continued to utter her rebukes against oppression, ignorance and bigotry." (*History of Woman Suffrage* II: 430)

Lectures

Excerpted are two of Frances Wright's 1828–1829 lectures later compiled in
Life, Letters and Lectures.

Divisions of Knowledge

. . . I must intreat you to inquire what the knowledge is, that you learn from your spiritual teachers. "The knowledge by faith," they will answer for you. "And faith," they will add, "is the knowledge of things unseen." Can there be any such knowledge? I put it to your reason. Knowledge we have shown to be ascertained facts. Things unseen! Can human understanding know any thing about them? More I will ask: could it be of any utility were even such knowledge possible? And do ye hire teachers to teach you non-existent knowledge, impossible knowledge, and knowledge which, even under the supposition of its possibility, could serve no conceivable purpose? We are on the earth, and they tell us of heaven; we are human beings, and they tell us of angels and devils; we are matter, and they tell us of spirit; we have five senses whereby to admit truths, and a reasoning faculty by which to build our belief upon them; and they tell us of dreams dreamed thousands of years ago, which all our experience flatly contradicts.

Again I must intreat your patience—your gentle hearing. I am not going to question your opinions. I am not going to meddle with your belief. I am not going to dictate to you mine. All that I say is, examine, inquire. Look into the nature of things. Search out the grounds of your opinions, the *for* and the *against*. Know why you believe, understand *what* you believe, and possess a reason for the faith that is in you.

But your spiritual teachers caution you against inquiry—tell you not to read certain books; not to listen to certain people; to beware of profane learning; to submit your reason, and to receive their doctrines for truths. Such advice renders them suspicious counsellors. By their own creed, you hold your reason from their God. Go! ask them why he gave it.

Be not afraid! If that being which they tell us of exist, we shall find him in his works. If that revelation be his which they tell us to revere, we shall find all nature and its occurrences, all matter and its phenomena, bearing testimony to its truth. Be not afraid! In admitting a creator, refuse not to examine his creation; and take not the assertions of creatures like your-selves, in place of the evidence of your senses and the conviction of your understanding.

But you will say, the clergy are moral teachers no less than religious. They form and amend our practice as well as dictate our belief.

My friends! we have ascertained the contrary. We have seen that from Maine to Missouri—from hence each way to our antipodes—the hired preachers of all sects, creeds, and religions, never do, and never can, teach any thing but what is in conformity with the opinions of those who pay them. We have substantiated the fact, that they never did, and never can, touch the master-vice, whatever it be, and wherever found. We know that they ever have, and ever must, persecute truth, by whomsoever discov-ered—by Galileo, or by Leslie and Lawrence; we know that they have stifled enquiry, wherever started, in every age and every nation on the globe; and that hardly a fact in science or a truth in philosophy, but has been purchased with the blood, or the liberty, or the domestic peace of a martyr. We have traced this conduct of your teachers to its cause. Remove the cause, and the effect shall cease. Give premiums for the discovery and revelation of knowledge, not for its repression! Take for your teachers experimental philosophers, not spiritual dreamers! Turn your churches into halls of science, and devote your leisure day to the study of your own bodies, the analysis of your own minds, and the examination of the fair material world which extends around you! Examine the expenses of your present religious system. Calculate all that is spent in multiplying churches and salarying their ministers; in clothing and feeding travelling preachers, who fill your streets and highways with trembling fanatics, and your very forests with frantic men and hysterical women. Estimate all the fruits of honest industry which are engulfed in the treasuries of Bible societies, tract associations, and christian missions; in sending forth teachers to cen-tral Africa and unexplored India, who know not the geography of their own country; and, hardly masters of their native tongue go to preach of things unseen to nations unknown; compassing the earth to add error to ignorance, and the frenzy of religious fanaticism to the ferocity of savage existence. See the multitude and activity of your emissaries! Weigh the expenses of your outlay and outfit, and then examine if this cost and this activity could not be more usefully employed. By a late estimate, we learn the yearly expenses of the existing religious system, to exceed in these

United States twenty millions of dollars. Twenty millions! For teaching what? Things unseen, and causes unknown! Why, here is more than enough to purchase the extract of all just knowledge—that is, of things *seen* and causes *known*, gathered by patient philosophy through all past time up to the present hour. Things unseen sell dear. Is it not worth our while to compare the value with the cost, and to strike the balance between them?

If we consider that there is no arriving at just practice but through just opinions, and no arriving at just opinions but through just knowledge, we must perceive the full importance of the proposed inquiry. Twenty millions would more than suffice to make us wise; and, alas! do they not more than suffice to make us foolish? I entreat you, but for one moment, to conceive the mental and moral revolution there would be in this nation, were these twenty millions, or but one half—but one third of that sum, employed in the equal distribution of accurate knowledge. Had you, in each of your churches, a teacher of elementary science, so that all the citizens, young and old, might cultivate that laudable curiosity without which the human animal is lower than the brute, we should not then see men staggering under intoxication, nor lounging in imbecile idleness; nor should we hear women retailing scandal from door to door, nor children echoing ribaldry in the streets, and vying with the monkey in mischief.

"But" you will say, "the clergy preach against these things." And when did mere preaching do any good? Put something in the place of these things. Fill the vacuum of the mind. Awaken its powers, and it will respect itself. Give it worthy objects on which to spend its strength, and it will riot no more in wantonness. Do the clergy this? Do they not rather demand a prostration of the intellect—a humbling and debasing of the spirit? Is not their knowledge that of things unseen, speaking neither to the senses, nor to the faculties? Are not their doctrines, by their own confession, incomprehensible? Is not their morality based upon human depravity? Preach they not the innate corruption of our race? Away with this libel of our nature! Away with this crippling, debasing, cowardly theory! Long, long enough hath this foul slander obscured our prospects, paralyzed our efforts, crushed the generous spirit within us! Away with it! such a school never made a race of freemen. And, see! in spite of the doctrine, to what heights of virtue and intelligence hath not man attained! Think of his discoveries in science—spite of chains, and dungeons, and gibbets, and anathemas! Think of his devotion to principle! Even when in error, great in his devotion! Think of the energy stronger than power, the benevolence supreme over selfishness, the courage conquering in death, with which he fought, and endured, and persevered through ages until he won his haven of liberty in America! Yes! he has won it. The noble creature has proved his birthright. May he learn to use and to enjoy it. . . .

With such guides, and engaged in such investigations and undertakings, as I have ventured to recommend, you will all meet on common ground. You will no longer see in each other Calvinists, Baptists, Catholics, Lutherans, Methodists, and I know not what; you will see only human beings. The halls of science are open to all; her truths are disputed by none. She says not to one, *"eat no meat on Fridays;"* to another *"plunge into the river;"* to a third, *"groan in the spirit;"* to a fourth, *"wait for the spirit;"* to a fifth, *"eat bread in the Lord;"* to a sixth, *"eat the Lord in bread;"* to a seventh, *"dance in divine praise;"* to a eighth, *"dance not at all;"* to a ninth, *"perceive in things visible the shadows of things unseen;"* to a tenth, *"there is for you salvation;"* and to nine hundred and ninety-nine thousandths of the human race, *"ye were born for eternal fire."* Science says nothing of all this. She says, only, "observe, compare, reason, reflect, understand:" and the advantage is, that we can do all this without quarrelling.

Religion

It has been my object in this, as in my previous discourses, to develope with you the nature of knowledge, to substantiate in what it consists, and where and how it may be found. I have farther, on the present occasion, attempted to prove that you are now engaged in the pursuit of what is not knowledge. That you are now paying your quota of the twenty millions per annum towards the support of a system of error, which from the earliest date of human tradition, has filled the earth with crime, and deluged its bosom with blood, and which, at this hour, fills your country with discord, and impedes its progress in virtue, by lengthening the term of its ignorance. . . .

I will pray ye to observe how much of our positive misery originates in our idle speculations in matters of faith, and in our blind, our fearful forgetfulness of facts—our cold, heartless, and, I will say, *insane* indifference to visible causes of tangible evil, and visible sources of tangible happiness? Look to the walks of life I beseech ye—look into the public prints—look into your sectarian churches—look into the bosoms of families—look into your own bosoms, and those of your fellow-beings, and see how many of our disputes and dissensions, public and private—how many of our unjust actions—how many of our harsh judgments—how many of our uncharitable feelings—spring out of our ignorant ambition to rend the vail which wraps from our human senses the knowledge of things unseen, and from our human faculties the conception of causes unknown? And oh, my fellow beings! do not these very words *unseen* and *unknown*, warn the enthusiast against the profanity of such inquiries, and proclaim to the philosopher their futility? Do they not teach us that religion is no subject for instruction, and no subject for discussion? Will they not convince us, that as beyond the horizon of our observation, we can *know* nothing, so within that horizon is the only safe ground for us to meet in public?

I know how far from this simple conviction we now are. Perhaps at this very moment, the question, *what does she believe*, is uppermost in the thoughts of two-thirds of my hearers. Should such be their thoughts, I will reply to them.

With respect to myself, my efforts have been strenuously directed to ascertain what *I know*, to understand what *can be known*, and to increase my *knowledge* as far as possible. In the next place, I have endeavoured to communicate my *knowledge* to my fellow-creatures; and strictly laid down to myself the rule, never to speak to them of that of which I have *not* knowledge. If beyond the horizon of things seen—without the range of our earthly planet, and apart from the nature of our human race, any speculations should force themselves on my fancy, I keep them to myself, even as I do the dreams of my nightly sleep, well satisfied that my neighbour will have his speculations and his dreams also, and that his, whatever they may be, will not coincide precisely with mine.

Satisfied by experience, no less than observation, of the advantage to be derived from this rule of practice, viz. to communicate with others only respecting my knowledge, and to keep to myself my belief, I venture to recommend the same to my fellow creatures; and, in conformity with this rule, would urge them, as soon as possible, to turn their churches into halls of science, and exchange their teachers of faith for expounders of nature. Every day we see sects splitting, creeds new modelling, and men forsaking old opinions only to quarrel about their opposites. I see three Gods in one, says the trinitarian, and excommunicates the socinian, who sees a godhead in unity. I see a heaven but no hell, says the universalist, and disowns fellowship with such as may distinguish less. "I see a heaven and a hell also, beyond the stars," said lately the orthodox friend, and expelled his shorter-sighted brethren from the sanctuary. I seek them both in the heart of man, said the more spiritual follower of Penn, and straightway builded him up another temple, in which to quarrel with his neighbour, who perhaps only employs other words to express the same ideas. For myself, pretending to no insight into these mysteries, possessing no means of intercourse with the inhabitants of other worlds, confessing my absolute incapacity to see either as far back as a first cause, or as far forward as a last one, I am content to state to you, my fellow creatures, that all my studies, reading, reflection, and observation, have obtained for me no knowledge beyond the sphere of our planet, our earthly interests, and our earthly duties; and that I more than doubt, whether, should you expend all your time and all your treasure in the search, you will be able to acquire any better information respecting unseen worlds, and future events, than myself. Whenever you shall come to the same conclusion, you will probably think the many spacious edifices which rear their heads in your city, are somewhat misapplied, and the time of the individuals who minister therein, somewhat misemployed: you will then doubtless perceive that they who wish to muse; or pray, had better do it after the manner designated by the good Jesus, namely, by entering their closet and shutting the door; and farther perceive, that the true Bible is the book of nature, the wisest teacher he who most plainly expounds it, the best priest our own conscience, and the most orthodox church a hall of science. I look round doubtless upon men of many faiths, upon calvinists, unitarians, methodists, baptists, catholics, and I know not what beside, and yet, my friends, let us call ourselves by what names we will, are we not creatures occupying the same earth, and sharing the same nature? and can we not consider these as members of one family, apart from all our speculations respecting worlds, and existences, and states of being, for which, in ages past, men cut each other's throats, and for which they now murder each other's peace? . . .

I purpose to develop with you that just rule of life, which no system of religion ever taught, or can ever teach; which exists apart from all faith, all creeds, and all written laws, and which can alone be found by following, with an open eye, a ready ear, and a willing heart, the steps of knowledge; by exercising the senses, faculties, and feelings, which appertain to our nature; and, instead of submitting our reason to the authority of fallible books and fallible teachers, by bringing always the words of all books and all teachers to the test of our reason.

Harriet Martineau

4

Harriet Martineau

FREE ROVING PHILOSOPHER

June 12, 1802 – June 27, 1876

. . . I would not exchange my freedom from old superstition, if I were to be burned at the stake next month, for all the peace and quiet of orthodoxy, if I must take the orthodoxy with the peace and quiet.

Letter to Mr. Atkinson, *February 1848 (Harriet Martineau's Autobiography)*

ACCLAIMED BRITISH AUTHOR HARRIET MARTINEAU pronounced herself "a free rover on the broad, bright breezy common of the universe." (*Autobiography* I: 85–89)

Harriet is called "the first sociologist," mapping out sociological methodology before the word was coined, according to twentieth-century sociologist Alice S. Rossi. Harriet was a significant role model in the woman's movement: a respected female author winning acclaim for her own thought, who supported herself by her nonfiction, writing fifty books and more than sixteen hundred articles, signed by her own name. She boasted of being "probably the happiest single woman in England." (I: 102)

Since she had been raised in a Unitarian family, Unitarians claimed her as one of theirs, provoking her to write at the end of her life: ". . . I hope and believe my old co-religionists understand and admit that I disclaim their theology *in toto*, and that by no twisting of language or darkening of its meanings can I be made out to have any thing whatever in common with them about religious matters. . . . they must take my word for it that there is nothing in common between their theology and my philosophy." (I: 120–121)

Her earliest inner rebellion was at chapel: "The duties preached were those of inferiors to superiors, . . . I used to thirst to hear some notice of the oppression which servants and children had . . . to endure. . . ." (I: 16)

Sixth of eight children of a silk manufacturer in Norwich, England, Harriet seemed lost in the shuffle of an unsympathetic household. Sensitive Harriet cried every day from the age of eight to fourteen. Growing deaf by age twelve, delicate, fearful, and "plain," Harriet blossomed into a woman uniformly praised for her disposition, warm heart, hospitality, and confident strength of character.

She was devoutly, if confusedly, religious. Her Unitarian family must have suffered a "wonderful slovenliness of thought, as well as ignorance, that we could have taken Unitarianism to be Christianity," she later commented, regarding as "pernicious" the sect's practice "of taking any liberties they please with the revelation they profess to receive." (I: 28, 29)

She turned to writing when family fortunes altered. Her first book was *Devotions for Young People* (1823). Her next was a religious novel, *Christmas Day*. When the British and Foreign Unitarian Association offered prizes for the three best tracts on converting Roman Catholics, Jews, and Mohammedans to Unitarianism in 1830, Harriet won them all. She turned to monthly tracts on political and economic issues about the poor laws, taxation and paupers. She was soon famous and sought after for her opinions.

"My business in life has been to think and learn, and to speak out with absolute freedom what I have thought and learned. The freedom is itself a positive and never-failing enjoyment to me, after the bondage of my early life." (I: 101–102)

At age thirty-two in 1834, Harriet took a two-year visit to America, writing the two-volume *Society in America*, a definitive work on the status of American women, whom she found unhealthily obsessed with religion, as Frances Wright had. Her work was as acclaimed as de Tocqueville's. Her warm reception turned nasty after Harriet endorsed William Lloyd Garrison and the Abolitionists. She spent the final three months of her tour mobbed, condemned, and fearing for her life.

During a period of invalidism, Harriet published a series of essays, including the story "The Hour and the Man," a tribute to Toussaint L'Ouverture. She turned down the first of three offers of a government pension. In 1846, Harriet claimed a "scientific" mesmeric cure, making her "transition from religious inconsistency and irrationality to free-thinking strength and liberty" during this period. (I: 466)

In 1846, Harriet visited Egypt, Palestine, and Arabia with friends, writing *Eastern Life, Past and Present* (1848), examining the genealogy of Egyptian, Hebrew, Christian and Mohammedan faiths. Critics pounced on the "mocking spirit of infidelity." Three years later, her freethought was made clear when *On the Laws of Man's Nature and Development*, letters between herself and H. G. Atkinson, was published.

In the controversial book, she had written: "There is no theory of a God, of an author of Nature, of an origin of the Universe, which is not utterly repugnant to my faculties; which is not (to my feelings) so irrelevant as to make me blush; so misleading as to make me mourn. I can now hardly believe that it was I who once read Milton with scarcely any recoil from the theology. . . ."

Harriet pondered: "I certainly had no idea how little faith Christians have in their own faith till I saw how ill their courage and temper can stand any attack on it." (*Autobiography*, II: 44)

She wanted to write a book for "the Secularist order of parents . . . who could obtain few story-books for their children which were not stuffed with what was in their eyes pernicious superstition." Not confident of her ability to write fiction, Harriet wrote *Household Education* (1848), and was pleased to learn that "there are a good many Christian parents who can accept suggestion and aid from one who will not pronounce their Shibboleth. . . " (I: 550–551)

She translated and condensed the six volumes of French atheist and philosopher Auguste Comte into two, to his approval, a project completed in 1853. Told she had fatal heart disease in 1855, Harriet wrote her autobiography, but survived until 1876. When Harriet's diagnosis became known, she received correspondence from believers: "One sends me a New Testament (as if I had never seen one before) with the usual hopes of grace &c., though aware that the bible is no authority with me; and, having been assured that I am 'happy,' this correspondent has the modesty to intimate that I ought not to be happy, . . .

"The lesson taught us by these kindly commentators on my present experience is that dogmatic faith compels the best minds and hearts to narrowness and insolence." (II: 109–110)

Another correspondent took the liberty of regretting that Harriet's espousal of causes was undermined by her freethinking. Harriet exclaimed: "what signifies the pursuit of any one reform, like those specified,—Anti-slavery and the Woman question,—when the freedom which is the very soul of the controversy, the very principle of the movement,—is mourned over in any other of its manifestations? The only effectual advocates of such reforms as those are people who follow truth wherever it leads. . . . My own feeling of concern arises from seeing how much moral injury and suffering is created by the superstitions of the Christian mythology. . . ." (II: 110)

The final passage of her autobiography records her pleased conviction that theology would soon be extinct.

William Lloyd Garrison wrote on July 4, 1876, that "the service she rendered to the antislavery cause was inestimable." Florence Nightingale, on Sept. 29, 1876, wrote that Harriet Martineau "was born to be a destroyer of slavery, in whatever form, in whatever place, all over the world, wherever she saw or thought she saw it."

"Release From Superstition"

*These excerpts tracing her evolution from Unitarian believer to freethinker and "free rover" are taken from **Harriet Martineau's Autobiography, Volumes I and II**, written in 1855, and published posthumously in 1877.*

... I CERTAINLY NEVER BELIEVED, more or less, in the "essential doctrines" of Christianity, which represent God as the predestinator of men to sin and perdition, and Christ as their rescuer from that doom. I never was more or less beguiled by the trickery of language by which the perdition of man is made out to be justice, and his redemption to be mercy. I never suffered more or less from fear of hell. The Unitarianism of my parents saved me from that. But nothing could save me from the perplexity of finding so much of indisputable statement of those doctrines in the New Testament, nor from a covert sense that it was taking a monstrous liberty with the Gospel to pick and choose what made me happy, and reject what I did not like or could not receive. When I now find myself wondering at Unitarians who do so,—who accept heaven and reject hell,—who get rid somehow of the reign of Christ and the apostles on earth, and derive somehow a sanction of their fancy of a heaven in the stars, peopled with old acquaintances, and furnished for favourite pursuits, I try to recal [sic] the long series of years during which I did the same thing, with far more, certainly, of complacency than misgiving. I try to remember how late on in life I have said that I confidently reckoned on entering the train of Socrates in the next world, and getting some of his secrets out of Pythagoras, besides making friendship with all the Christian worthies I especially inclined to. When I now see the comrades of my early days comfortably appropriating all the Christian promises, without troubling themselves with the clearly-specified condition,—of faith in Christ as a Redeemer,— I remind myself that this is just what I did for more than the first half of my life. The marvel remains how they now, and I then, could possibly wonder at the stationary or declining fortunes of their sect,—so evidently as Unitarianism is a mere clinging, from association and habit, to the old privilege of faith in a divine revelation, under an actual forfeiture of all its essential conditions. (*Vol.* I: 30–31)

❦

For above thirty years I have seen more and more clearly how awful, and how irremediable except by the spread of a true philosophy, are the evils which arise from that monstrous remnant of old superstition,—the supposition of a self-determining power, independent of laws, in the human will; and I can truly say that if I have had the blessing of any available strength under sorrow, perplexity, sickness and toil, during a life which has been any thing but easy, it is owing to my repose upon eternal and irreversible laws, working in every department of the universe, without any interference from any random will, human or divine.

. . . The fatalistic element of the Essene doctrine strongly pervades the doctrine and morality of Christ and the apostles; and its curious union with the doctrine of a special providence is possible only under the theocratic supposition which is the basis of the whole faith— . . . the practice of prayer, as prevailing throughout Christendom, is wholly unauthorized by the New Testament. Christian prayer, as prevailing at this day, answers precisely to the description of that phariasic prayer which Christ reprobated. His own method of praying, the prayer he gave to his disciples, and their practice, were all wholly unlike any thing now understood by Christian prayer, in protestant as well as catholic countries. I changed my method accordingly, . . . the evidence grew wonderfully strong that management; and that even so much self-reference as was involved in "working out one's own salvation with fear and trembling" was demoralizing. Thus I arrived,— after long years,—at the same point of ease or resignation about my spiritual as my temporal affairs, and felt that (to use a broad expression uttered by somebody) it was better to take the chance of being damned than be always quaking one's self in the fear of it. (Not that I had any literal notion of being damned,—any more than any other born and bred Unitarian.). . . I need hardly say that I soon drew back in shame from offering to a Divine being a homage which would be offensive to an earthly one. . . .

It is clear however that a Christianity which never was received as a scheme of salvation,—which never was regarded as essential to salvation,— which might be treated, in respect to its records, at the will and pleasure of each believer,—which is next declared to be independent of its external evidences, because those evidences are found to be untenable,—and which is finally subjected in its doctrines, as in its letter, to the interpretation of each individual,—must cease to be a faith, and become a matter of speculation, of spiritual convenience, and of intellectual and moral taste. . . . But at length I recognised the monstrous superstition in its true character of a great fact in the history of the race, and found myself, with the last link of my chain snapped,—a free rover on the broad, bright breezy common of the universe. (I: 85–89)

❦

I had long perceived the worse than uselessness of enforcing principles of justice and mercy by an appeal to the example of God. I had long seen that the orthodox fruitlessly attempt to get rid of the difficulty by presenting the two-fold aspect of God,—the Father being the model of justice, and the Son of love and mercy,—the inevitable result being that he who is especially called God is regarded as an unmitigated tyrant and spontaneous torturer, while the sweeter and nobler attributes are engrossed by the man Jesus,—whose fate only deepens the opprobrium of the Divine cruelty: while the heretics whose souls recoil from such a doctrine, and who strive to explain away the recorded dogmas of tyranny and torture, in fact give up the Christian revelation by rejecting its essential postulates. . . . I had long given up, in moral disgust, the conception of life after death as a matter of compensation for the ills of humanity, or a police and penal source of "the divine government." I had perceived that the doctrines of the immortality of the soul and the resurrection of the body were incompatible; and that, while the latter was clearly impossible, we were wholly without evidence of the former. (I: 468–469)

❦

When I experience the still new joy of feeling myself to be a portion of the universe, resting on the security of its everlasting laws, certain that its Cause was wholly out of the sphere of human attributes, and that the special destination of my race is infinitely nobler than the highest proposed under a scheme of 'divine moral government,' how could it matter to me that the adherents of a decaying mythology,—(the Christian following the heathen, as the heathen followed the barbaric-fetish) were fiercely clinging to their Man-God, their scheme of salvation, their reward and punishment, their arrogance, their selfishness, their essential pay-system, as ordered by their mythology? As the astronomer rejoices in new knowledge which compels him to give up the dignity of our globe as the centre, the pride, and even the final cause of the universe, so do those who have escaped from the Christian mythology enjoy their release from the superstition which fails to make happy, fails to make good, fails to make wise, and has become as great an obstacle in the way of progress as the prior mythologies which it took the place of nearly two thousand years ago. . . . To the emancipated, it is a small matter that those who remain imprisoned are shocked at the daring which goes forth into the sunshine and under the stars to study and enjoy, without leave asked, or fear of penalty. (II: 45–46)

❦

. . . I have now had three months' experience of the fact of constant expectation of death; and the result is, as much regret as a rational person can admit at the absurd waste of time, thought and energy that I have been guilty of in the course of my life in dwelling on the subject of death. . . . And now that I am awaiting it at any hour, the whole thing seems so easy, simple and natural. . . . I attribute this very much, however, to the nature of my views of death. The case must be much otherwise with Christians,—even independently of the selfish and perturbing emotions connected with an expectation of rewards and punishments in the next world. They can never be quite secure from the danger that their air-built castle shall dissolve at the last moment, and that they may vividly perceive on what imperfect evidence and delusive grounds their expectation of immortality or resurrection reposes. . . . An unselfish and magnanimous person cannot be solaced, in parting with mortal companions and human sufferers, by personal rewards, glory, bliss, or anything of the sort. I used to think and feel all this before I became emancipated from the superstition; and I could only submit, and suppose it all right because it was ordained. But now, the release is an inexpressible comfort; and the simplifying of the whole matter has a most tranquillizing effect. I see that the dying . . . naturally and regularly, unless disturbed, desire and sink into death as into sleep. . . . We know, by all testimony, that persons who are brought face to face with death by an accident which seems to leave no chance of escape, have no religious ideas or emotions whatever. . . . Under the eternal laws of the universe, I came into being, and, under them, I have lived a life so full that its fulness is equivalent to length. . . . since I attained a truer point of view: and the relief from old burdens, the uprising of new satisfactions, and the opening of new clearness,—the fresh air of Nature, in short, after imprisonment in the ghost-peopled cavern of superstition,—has been as favourable to my moral nature as to intellectual progress and general enjoyment. . . . (II: 104–107)

꘡

. . . the time cannot be far off when, throughout the civilised world, theology must go out before the light of philosophy. . . . Precisely in proportion to Man's ignorance of his own nature, as well as of other things, is the tendency of his imagination to inform the outward world with his own consciousness. The fetish worshipper attributes a consciousness like his own to every thing about him; the imputation becomes more select and rare through every rising grade of theology, till the Christian makes his reflex of himself invisible and intangible, or, as he says, "spiritual.". . . About this matter, of the extinction of theology by a true science of human nature, I cannot but say that my expectation amounts to absolute assurance; and that I believe that the worst of the conflict is over. I am confident that a bright day is coming for future generations. Our race has been as Adam created at nightfall. The solid earth has been but dark, or dimly visible, while the eye was inevitably drawn to the mysterious heavens above. There, the successive mythologies have arisen in the east, each a constellation of truths, each glorious and fervently worshipped in its course; but the last and noblest, the Christian, is now not only sinking to the horizon, but paling in the dawn of a brighter time. The dawn is unmistakable; and the sun will not be long in coming up. The last of the mythologies is about to vanish before the flood of a brighter light. . . . (II: 122–124)

5

Lydia Maria Child

ABOLITIONIST, AUTHOR, ANTI-THEOLOGIAN

February 11, 1802 – October 20, 1880

It is impossible to exaggerate the evil work theology has done in the world.
The Progress of Religious Ideas Through Successive Ages, 1855

CONSIDERED ONE OF THE "FIRST WOMEN OF LETTERS" in the United States, Lydia Maria Francis Child was a famous abolitionist, author, novelist and journalist. Today Americans continue singing the song whose words she wrote, beginning: "Over the river and through the wood to grandfather's house we go."

Maria (as she preferred to be known) joined the Unitarians in 1820, although she was unchurched most of her life. *The Progress of Religious Ideas Through Successive Ages*, a three-volume work published in 1855, repudiated revelation and creeds.

Her Calvinist father, a Massachusetts baker, went from poverty to prosperity with his "Medford Crackers." Maria, as a child, slept with a bible under her pillow. Her views broadened after her older brother Convers became a professor at Harvard Divinity School and held a Unitarian parish. Maria's popular first book, *Hobomok* (1824), a daring love story about a noble Indian and a white woman, resulted in her induction into the Boston Athenæum. She ran a school in Watertown for three years, started the first U.S. journal for children, a bimonthly, and wrote a novel, *The Rebels, or Boston Before the Revolution* (1825).

Her marriage to Harvard graduate David Lee Child in 1828 produced no children. While her perpetually debt-ridden husband edited a whig journal, Maria, burdened with housework and boarders, supported the family through her popular writings, including *The Frugal Housewife* (1820), published in seven editions by 1832, followed by *The Mother's Book* and *The Little Girl's Own Book*. In *The First Settlers of New England*, Maria blamed Calvinist-based racism for the treatment of Indians, as she later condemned the use of scripture to support slavery.

Maria wrote one of the earliest, most significant antislavery books, *An Appeal in Favor of That Class of Americans Called Africans*, denouncing racism, miscegenation laws, segregation in churches and public facilities, and the sexual degradation of slave women. *An Appeal* recruited many of the future leaders of the antislavery movement to the abolition cause. But the welcome mat was withdrawn by Boston society. She continued producing abolitionist writings as well as conventional books such as *The Family Nurse* (1837). Her interest in the nascent woman question was addressed in the two-volume *The History of the Condition of Women, in Various Ages and Nations* (1835).

Maria moved to New York City to edit the weekly *National Anti-Slavery Standard* in 1840. Although its literary quality was praised, its editor was subjected to constant criticism for being too moderate and resigned in 1843. Maria supported herself by regular columns for the *Boston Courier*, published as *Letters from New-York* (1843–1845), reprinted eleven times through 1879. Books written in the 1840s included *Fact and Fiction* (1846), stories examining the plight of "fallen women."

She had distanced herself from the abolition cause, but got back into the fray in 1860. After John Brown's raid in 1859, she offered to nurse him in prison, and was denounced by the wife of the Virginia senator who authored the Fugitive Slave Act. About 300,000 copies of the exchange between Maria and Mrs. Mason were printed in pamphlet form. One of Maria's most famous lines, in response to Mason's argument that Southern women were nice to slave women during childbirth, was: ". . . here at the North, after we have helped the mothers, *we do not sell the babies.*" Maria wrote three other prominent antislavery pamphlets, including *The Patriarchal Institution.* The following year she edited the writings of former slave Harriet Jacobs, *Incidents in the Life of a Slave Girl*, and in 1865 paid for and published *The Freedman's Book*, excerpts by many prominent African-Americans written for the benefit of freed slaves.

After her death at age seventy-eight from heart disease, John Greenleaf Whittier recited a memorial poem in her honor at her funeral, which was presided over by Wendell Phillips.

❦

Maria was significant both to the woman's and the freethought movement, while distancing herself from both. She wrote *The Progress of Religious Ideas* because, when young, she had longed to find an objective representation of the world religions. "I wished to show that *theology* is not *religion*; with the hope that I might help to break down partition walls; to ameliorate what the eloquent Bushnell calls 'baptized hatreds of the human race.'"

When a child, she was offended that "the records of all other religions were unscrupulously analyzed, or contemptuously described as 'childish fables,' or 'filthy

superstitions.' . . . and I was still more displeased with the scoffing tone of sceptical writers, who regarded all religions as founded on imposture. Either way, the
one-sidedness of the representation troubled my strong sense of justice." (Child,
Progress of Religious Ideas I: vii)

Anticipating outcry, Maria was propitiatory toward Christians, presenting her
book "with extreme timidity." Holding unclassifiable views somewhat akin to
those of Anne Hutchinson, Maria believed in something she referred to as "Providence," advising everyone to show "sincere reverence for that inward voice" of
conscience. (III: 461)

She hated theology, dogma and doctrines, toward the end of her life defining
religion simply as working for the welfare of the human race. Although praising
the example and precepts of Jesus in a manner similar to Thomas Jefferson, she
predicted Christianity's demise. Jesus' divinity was irrelevant; only moral principle counted. Church Fathers "petrified all thought into formulas, and when
hungry souls asked for bread, gave them a stone. . . . In the process, errors of faith
came to be regarded as more sinful, than the greatest moral delinquencies." (III:
450).

"As a general thing, Christians have manifested very little kindness, or candour,
in their estimate of other religions; but the darkest blot on their history is their
treatment of the Jews," wrote Maria. "The Jews of Rome and Alexandria, whom
the Christian Fathers considered as deservedly accursed by men, and outcasts
from God's mercy, were better, and far more enlightened, than those savage tribes
of the desert, who went about slaughtering women and children, in the name of
Jehovah, and who were nevertheless reverenced as the only people God had chosen for his own, on the face of the whole earth." (III: 439, 441)

Humanity, she predicted, will outgrow any "Written Revelation." Attempting to "resuscitate decaying forms" brings only "elaborate and far-fetched explanations and allegories." (III: 419)

Following Maria Child's death, *The Truth Seeker* remembered her in many of
its profiles and retrospectives, on the strength of her stirring statements against
theology and doctrine in her "Concluding Chapter" of *The Progress of Religious
Ideas*. [See selection]

The Progress of Religious Ideas

This is excerpted from the concluding chapter of Volume III of **The Progress of Religious Ideas Through Successive Ages** *(1855).*

THE EXISTENCE OF VERY PIOUS FEELINGS, in conjunction with intolerance, cruelty, and selfish policy, has never ceased to surprise and perplex those who have viewed it calmly from a distance. Constantine, after he had manifested such zeal for bishops, and shown the greatest reliance on the efficacy of prayer, caused the death of his own son, and his sister's husband, and her son, from the fear that they might become formidable as rivals in the empire. Constantius, who was zealous for Christianity, pursued the same course with regard to his uncle and cousins. Theodosius, the most pious of them all, was relentless in his persecution of sects that differed in the slightest degree from the established church; and he ordered thousands of innocent people, including women and children, to be slaughtered, to gratify his resentment. From that time down to the present day, such instances abound; and it is common to explain them by the supposition of deliberate hypocrisy in religious professions. But I am convinced that piety toward God may be perfectly sincere in those who manifest great selfishness and violence toward their fellow creatures; because the two results proceed from different elements in man's nature, which must be harmoniously proportioned and combined to form a consistent religious character; but which, nevertheless, are often disproportioned, and even completely separated. Conscientiousness and reverence for the supernatural are distinct things; and either one or the other may predominate in character. I have known exceedingly conscientious and humane people, who would be uneasy for days, if they had struck a dog, or given a cent too little in change, or uttered an equivocation, who, nevertheless, could not be much impressed by the most solemn ceremonies of the church, or excited by the most fervent preaching. On the other hand, I have known extremely devotional people, who wept over the Bible, and could not live happily without frequent worship, who nevertheless abused animals, and dealt hardly with the poor, without being troubled by any degree of the remorse they would have felt, if they had fallen asleep for the night without uttering a prayer. John Newton was a memorable example to the point. He wrote in strains of the most affecting piety, spent much of his time in reading of Christ, and praying to him, and thankfully recorded "sweet seasons of communion with God," while he was carrying on the slave-trade on the coast of Africa. . . .

It is impossible to exaggerate the evil work theology has done in the world. What destruction of the beautiful monuments of past ages, what waste of life, what disturbance of domestic and social happiness, what perverted feelings, what blighted hearts, have always marked its baneful progress! How the flowery meadow of childhood has been blasted by its lurid fires! Alas, what a world that was for infancy to open its wondering eyes upon, when exorcisms to cast out Devils were murmured over its innocent brow! When Pagan priests poured sacrificial wine into its tender stomach, and Christian deacons forced open its reluctant mouth, to pour in more wine, that the Devil might be expelled, which they supposed had taken possession of the poor little suffering lamb! What a spiritual atmosphere that was for childhood to breathe, when zealous mothers dragged their little ones, with hot haste, to the place of martyrdom, and taught them it was sinful to be attracted by birds and butterflies on the way! When monks scourged and nearly starved a little boy, to test whether his father had become sufficiently holy to witness their cruelty without any remains of human emotion!

Even if nothing worse than wasted mental effort could be laid to the charge of theology, that alone ought to be sufficient to banish it from the earth, as one of the worst enemies of mankind. What a vast amount of labour and learning has been expended, as uselessly as emptying shallow puddles into sieves! How much intellect has been employed mousing after texts, to sustain preconceived doctrines! Little or no progress toward truth is usually made, because passages of ancient books are taken up hundreds of years after they were written, and are used in a sense altogether foreign from the original intention, in order to sustain some opinion, or tradition of the then present time. And the human mind is not left free to pursue even *this* distorting process; but colleges of supervisors are appointed to instruct the young in what light everything *ought* to be viewed. One college covers the eyes of all its students with red spectacles, so that every object seems on fire. Another insists that blue spectacles are the only proper medium; consequently its pupils maintain that all creation is ghastly pale. Whereupon red spectacles rush to battle with blue spectacles, to prove that the whole landscape is flame-coloured. If one who uses his natural eyesight comes between them, and says, ever so gently: "Nay, my friends, you are both mistaken. The meadows are of an emerald green, and the sunshine is golden," he is rudely shoved aside, as an heretic, or an infidel. One party calls out to him: "Did you ever look at the landscape through red spectacles?" Another shouts: "Did you ever examine it by the only right method, which is through blue spectacles?" And if he cannot answer in the affirmative, they both vociferate: "Then you had better keep silence; for you are altogether incapable of forming a correct opinion on the subject."

Alas, what millions of men have been thus employed, in all countries, ever since the world began! What a blooming paradise would the whole earth be, if the same amount of intellect, labour, and zeal, had been expended on science, agriculture, and the arts! Polemical controversy must necessarily be useless, even if it were nothing worse; because it is always striving to settle infinite questions by the exercise of finite faculties. . . .

Ernestine L. Rose
(The Schlesinger Library, Radcliffe College)

6

Ernestine L. Rose

ATHEIST & AMERICA'S FIRST WOMAN'S RIGHTS CANVASSER

January 13, 1810 – August 4, 1892

I was a rebel at the age of five.

NINETEENTH-CENTURY AMERICA'S MOST OUTSPOKEN ATHEIST was also America's first lobbyist for woman's rights. Ernestine L. Rose adopted without embarrassment or apology the label "atheist" well before Robert G. Ingersoll discovered freethought or launched his career as "the Great Agnostic." She had the distinction of being barred as an atheist from the nation's capitol as a speaker by the Chaplain, Mr. Milburn, in 1854.

Born Ernestine Louise Siismondi Potowski in the Jewish ghetto in Piotrkow, Poland, she was the affectionate only child of an orthodox rabbi, living in a wall within a wall, constricted by Judaism, and anti-Semitism. Questioning the religious fasting that threatened her beloved father's health, she once said, "If God is pleased in making you sick and unhappy, I hate God." (*History of Woman Suffrage* I: 95–98)

One Saturday, Ernestine reportedly was rebuked by her shocked father, when he noticed her combing her hair. He ordered her to drop her comb at once, because she was sinning against God. Ernestine, bewildered by the special care taken to dress her up and decorate the house for the Sabbath, decided to take matters into her own hands and "ask Him myself." She left the room for a few moments and returned triumphant: "I asked God if it was a sin and He didn't say anything." Case closed.

Defying conventions by studying the Torah in Hebrew, Ernestine rejected the bible and Judaism by age fourteen. Her mother died when she was sixteen, leaving her an inheritance of property, which her father offered as dowry, engaging her without her permission to an older man. When she tried to break the engagement, the man reminded her that she would then forfeit her dowry. She took the unprecedented step of arguing her case before the High Tribunal of the

Regional Polish Court in Kalish, winning a legal document entitling her to her property. Returning home, she found a new stepmother, age sixteen, awaiting her.

At seventeen years of age, in 1827, Ernestine Potowski set out alone for Berlin despite laws restricting foreign Jews from lengthy stays or from conducting business there. Ernestine later told her American friends that she sought and obtained audience with the Prussian king, urging him to abolish the restrictions. He was impressed enough with the teenager to instead grant her the right to stay in Germany on any terms. To support herself, she invented an early "odor-eater," made of perfumed paper chemically treated to emit pleasant odors to mask kitchen smells. This lifelong business helped to support her lecture tours.

At nineteen, she left Germany by way of Holland, where legend has it she was shipwrecked, and again gained an audience with the reigning king of the land, to successfully plead the case of a Dutch mother unjustly imprisoned. By age twenty-two, she had immigrated to England, where Robert Owen, the famed reformer, invited her to address a meeting of workers, and dubbed her "my daughter."

She supported herself by tutoring German and Hebrew, and by her perfume trade. She met and married William Ella Rose, a jeweler and silversmith, in the mid-1830s. They left for America in 1836, establishing a silversmith shop in New York City. The couple was child-free.

Ernestine came to the attention of the freethought press after she challenged a preacher to a debate during a public meeting on December 14, 1837. Some audience members threatened, "Drag her out!"

Ernestine became America's first woman's rights activist after drawing up a petition in support of a Married Woman's Property Act, a bill proposed in 1836 by freethinker Judge Thomas Hertell, a member of the New York legislature. Going door to door, she was met by wife after wife echoing the same refrain: "We don't want any more rights—we have rights enough." It became a suffrage legend that Ernestine garnered only five signatures in five months. However, twelve years later in 1848, the Married Women's Property Act of New York was passed, a landmark for American women.

Dubbed the "Frances Wright of the Fifties" and "Queen of the Platform," Ernestine became the second foreign woman to lecture publicly, like Wright, promoting woman's rights, abolition and freethought. In an address before the American Anti-slavery Society in 1853 she stated: "Emancipation from every kind of bondage is my principle. I go for the recognition of human rights, without distinction of sect, party, sex, or color."

She later wrote Susan B. Anthony on January 9, 1877, about her lecture tours: "All that I can tell you is, that I used my humble powers to the uttermost, and raised my voice in behalf of Human Rights in general, and the elevation and

Rights of Woman in particular, nearly all my life. . . . Yet in spite of hardships, for it was not as easy to travel at that time as now; and the expense, as I never made a charge or took up a collection, I look back to that time, when a stranger and alone, I went from place to place, in high-ways and by-ways, did the work and paid my bills with great pleasure and satisfaction; for the cause gained ground, and in spite of heresies I had always good audiences, attentive listeners, and was well received wherever I went . . ." (*HWS* I: 99)

She lectured in at least twenty-three states, often making return visits and addressing legislative bodies. She attended the first National Woman's Rights Convention in Worcester, Massachusetts, in 1850, and nearly all the National and State Conventions afterward, until 1869. She and other New York feminists launched a woman's suffrage petition campaign in that state as early as 1851. She once risked tar and feathering by visiting South Carolina and speaking out against slavery in 1847. In Charleston, clergy from the pulpit tried to keep parishioners away from her talks, calling her "the female devil, so bold as to contest the right of the South to hold their own slaves." (D'Hericourt, *The Revolution*, Sept. 16, 1869)

With Susan B. Anthony, she took on a four-week lecture tour of the slave-border cities in 1854. In Washington, D.C., Anthony tried to secure the use of the Capitol on a Sunday morning for Ernestine's talk, and was turned down by the chaplain in charge. Anthony recorded in her diary on March 24, 1854 a revealing conversation which shed light on Ernestine's isolation as a public atheist: "[No] one knows how I have suffered from not being understood," Ernestine confessed. Anthony concluded: "Mrs. Rose is not appreciated, nor cannot be by this age," analyzing that almost every other reformer "shrinks from being identified with one in whose view their ultraism is sheer conservatism." (Dubois, *Elizabeth Cady Stanton-Susan B. Anthony*: 75–76)

"Agitate! Agitate! ought to be the motto of every reformer," Ernestine urged. "Agitation is the opposite of stagnation—the one is life, the other death."

She spoke at the First National Infidel Convention meeting in New York City on May 4, 1845, with four hundred participants from fourteen states, including Robert Owen, Josiah P. Mendum, publisher of the *Boston Investigator*, a freethought weekly, and its editor, Horace Seaver. The *New York Herald* reported: "Seated by our side was the venerable Robert Owen, and the highly accomplished, talented and intellectually beautiful Mrs. Rose." Ernestine told this gathering:

"Ignorance is the evil—knowledge will be the remedy. Knowledge not of what sort of beings we shall be hereafter, or what is beyond the skies, but a knowledge pertaining to *terra firma*, and we may have all the power, goodness and love that we have been taught belongs to God himself."

The *New York Herald* quoted her remarks by mimicking her Polish accent, but reported that her speech was met by "thunders of applause."

She helped to organize Thomas Paine memorials, a custom started in 1824 by Benjamin Offen. On January 29, 1850, the one hundred and thirteenth birthday of Thomas Paine, the Rose couple helped organize a celebration at the Chinese Museum, attended by eight hundred people who danced the night away.

In May, 1850, a heckling mob incited by *New York Herald* editor James Gordon Bennett, halted the three-day American Antislavery Society convention featuring Ernestine as speaker.

The *New York Herald* (October 23, 1850) headlined its coverage of the First National Woman's Rights Convention in Worcester, Massachusetts (where Ernestine spoke) in this manner: "Woman's Rights convention - Awful Combination of Socialism, Abolitionism, and Infidelity." At the Third National Woman's Convention meeting in Syracuse on September 8–10, 1852, Rose opposed a resolution by Rev. Antoinette Brown to reconcile Christianity with women's rights, pointing out this was mere opinion and not authority, that Brown was entitled to such interpretation, but it should not be Convention doctrine:

"For my part, I see no need to appeal to any written authority, particularly when it is so obscure and indefinite as to admit of different interpretations. When the inhabitants of Boston converted their harbor into a teapot rather than submit to unjust taxes, they did not go to the Bible for their authority; for if they had, they would have been told from the same authority to 'give unto Caesar what belonged to Caesar.' Had the people, when they rose in the might of their right to throw off the British yoke, appealed to the bible for authority, it would have answered them, 'Submit to the powers that be, for they are from God.' No! on Human Rights and Freedom, on a subject that is as self-evident as that two and two make four, there is no need of any written authority."

A two-day debate was ended by Lucretia Mott, who reminisced about the bible question and the antislavery experience. Saying that "self-evident truths needed no argument or outward authority," Mott called to table the resolution, which carried unanimously. (*HWS* I: 536–537, 540)

The harassment of woman's rights advocates by ministers and mobs continued, most notably at a four-day bible convention called by William Lloyd Garrison and other abolitionists, freethinkers and women's rights advocates "for the purpose of freely and fully canvassing the authority and influence of the Jewish and Christian Scriptures." More than two thousand attended the event at Melodeon Hall in Hartford, Connecticut, in June 1853, the majority hostile, including seven hundred divinity students. When Ernestine, the only woman speaker, was lecturing, someone turned off the gas meter, and the lights went out. As the *New York Herald* reported, "Groaning, hissing, stamping, barking, crowing, and every token of disapprobation were most liberally lavished upon her, but she bore it bravely." Garrison described the rabble as "like a troop of demons let loose from the pit." When the lights came back on, Ernestine made even her detractors laugh and applaud by saying, "When the lights were extinguished it reminded me of one of the true things we find in the Bible, that some there are 'who love darkness better than light.' "

A Woman's Rights Convention meeting at the Broadway Tabernacle in New York City on September 6–7, 1853, became known as "The Mob Convention" in feminist annals, with the clergy and the *Daily Herald* inciting hecklers. Rose was heckled so mercilessly that she could not continue speaking. What subject was so controversial it had to be censored? Her practical lecture on the inability of women in New York State to make out wills! Ernestine adjourned the convention on September 8. (*HWS* I: 573)

Ernestine took the brunt of press criticism directed at an Albany Convention meeting February 14–15, 1854, when the *Albany Register* editorialized on March 7, 1854:

"People are beginning to inquire how far public sentiment should sanction or tolerate these unsexed women, who make a scoff of religion, who repudiate the Bible and blaspheme God; who would step out from the true sphere of the mother, the wife, and the daughter, and taking upon themselves the duties and the business of men, stalk into the public gaze, and by engaging in the politics, the rough controversies, and trafficking of the world, upheave existing institutions, and overturn all the social relations of life.

"It is a melancholy reflection, that among our American women who have been educated to better things, there should be found any who are willing to follow the lead of such foreign propagandists as the ringleted, glove-handed exotic, Ernestine L. Rose. We can understand how such men as the Rev. Mr. May, or the sleek-headed Dr. Channing may be deluded by her to becoming her disciples . . .

"In no country in the world, save possibly one, would her infidel propagandism and preachings in regard to the social relations of life be tolerated! She would be prohibited by the powers of government from her efforts to obliterate from the world the religion of the Cross—to banish the Bible as a text-book of faith, and to overturn social institutions that have existed through all political and governmental revolutions from the remotest time. . . . But in this country, such is the freedom of our institutions, and we rejoice that it should be so, that she, and such as she, can give their genius for intrigue full sway. They can exhibit their flowing ringlets and beautiful hands, their winning smiles and charming stage attitudes to admiring audiences, who, while they are willing to be amused, are in the main safe from their corrupting theories and demoralizing propagandism." (*HWS* I: 608–609)

In a letter to *The Albany Daily State Register,* she of the "flowing ringlets and beautiful hands" responded most graciously, correcting one error about her past, and noting: "Every one who ever advanced a new idea, no matter how great and noble, has been subjected to criticism, and therefore we too must expect it. . . . I chose to make this country my home in preference to any other, because if you carried out the theories you profess, it would indeed be the noblest country on earth." (*HWS* I: 610)

She fared better in the write-up of *The Albany Transcript,* which proclaimed her "the queen of the company," rising "to a high standard of oratorical power. . . . full of eloquence and pathos, and she has as great a power to chain an audience as any of our best male speakers." (*HWS* I: 606)

An attempt was made, before the fifth national convention in Philadelphia on October 18, 1854, to prevent Ernestine from presiding at the convention, a maneuver squelched by Susan B. Anthony. Following a debate with a Philadelphia minister, William Lloyd Garrison startled the convention by proposing a resolution pointing out "that the most determined opposition it encounters is from the clergy generally, whose teachings of the Bible are intensely inimical to the equality of woman with man." It passed unanimously, along with a second resolution embodying his earlier expressed belief that "The human mind is greater than any book. The mind sits in judgment on every book. If there be truth in the book, we take it; if error, we discard it. . . . In this country, the Bible has been used to support slavery and capital punishment; while in the old countries, it has been quoted to sustain all manner of tyranny and persecution. We must look at all things rationally." The resolution likewise passed, as did a final resolution praising Ernestine for "the courtesy, impartiality, and dignity with which she has presided over its proceedings." (*HWS* I: 384–385)

When Ernestine was invited to speak in Bangor, Maine, in December 1855, the *Bangor Mercury* published attacks against her by three clergymen. Rev. G.D. Little argued, "it would be shameful to listen to this woman, a thousand times below a prostitute." Her two lectures were well-received, with the town's other newspapers generally agreeing "a census of the dead and wounded discloses none but members of the assailing party."

At the Seventh National Convention, held in New York on November 25 and 26, 1856, Ernestine Rose responded to a male opponent, more polite than the usual heckler, who invoked religion to oppose women's rights:

". . . As we believe our cause to be based on truth, we know it can bear the test of reason, and, like gold doubly refined, will come out purer and brighter from the fiery ordeal. The young man , . . based his principal argument against us, 'Because,' said he, 'you can bring no authority from revelation or from nature.' . . . It is true we do not go to revelations written in books; but ours is older than all books, . . . That revelation is no less than the living, breathing, thinking, feeling, acting revelation manifested in the nature of woman. In her manifold powers, capacities, needs, hopes, and aspirations, lies her title-deed, and whether that revelation was written by nature or nature's God, matters not, for here it is. No one can disprove it. No one can bring an older, broader, higher, and more sacred basis for human rights. Do you tell me that the Bible is against our rights? Then I say that our claims do not rest upon a book written no one knows when, or by whom. Do you tell me what Paul or Peter says on the subject? Then again I reply that our claims do not rest on the opinions of any one, not even on those of Paul and Peter, for they are older than they. Books and opinions, no matter from whom they came, if they are in opposition to human rights, are nothing but dead letters. . . .

". . . Sisters, . . . I entreat you, if you have an hour to spare, a dollar to give, or a word to utter—spare it, give it, and utter it, for the elevation of woman! And when your minister asks you for money for missionary purposes, tell him there are higher, and holier, and nobler missions to be performed at home. When he asks for colleges to educate ministers, tell him you must educate woman, that she may do away with the necessity of ministers, so that they may be able to go to some useful employment. If he asks you to give to the churches (which means to himself) then ask him what he has done for the salvation of woman. When he speaks to you of leading a virtuous life, ask him whether he understands the causes that have prevented so many of your sisters from being virtuous, and have driven them to degradation, sin, and wretchedness. When he speaks to you of a hereafter, tell him to help to educate woman, to enable her to live a life of intelligence, independence, virtue, and happiness here, as the best preparatory step for any other life. And if he has not told you from the pulpit of all these things; if he does not know them; it is high time you inform him, and teach him his duty here in this life." (*HWS* I: 661–663)

In June 1857, she attended a "fearless discussion" for "friends of freethought" at the Rutland Free Convention, Vermont, on such questions as the Sabbath, the bible, marriage, slavery, and many "et ceteras." During the discussion on marriage, the happily married Ernestine proposed a resolution: "That the only true and natural marriage is an exclusive conjugal love based on perfect equality between one man and one woman; the only true home is the isolated home based on this exclusive love." *The New York Times*, as a result, charged that "Mrs. Ernestine Rose" goes for "free love on principle." Although she refuted this in a letter, the groundless charge was to stick like a burr.

At the tenth woman's suffrage convention at the Cooper Institute, New York, on May 10–11, 1860, when Elizabeth Cady Stanton urged the convention to take up divorce reform, Ernestine made an eloquent plea for women's right to divorce. (*HWS* I: 729–732)

She became embroiled in a debate on the pages of the *Boston Investigator* when its editor, Horace Seaver, published an anti-Jewish diatribe on October 28, 1863. She replied, "Then let us as Infidels . . . not add to the prejudice already existing towards the Jews, or any other sect." The controversy raged on for ten weeks of published arguments back and forth. Although the debate became increasingly bitter, their friendship survived.

She also became embroiled in the famous suffragist rift over the "Negro's Hour," siding with Stanton and Anthony in protesting the inclusion of the word "male" into the Constitution through the adoption of the Fourteenth Amendment, and the exclusion of the word "sex" from the Fifteenth. Ernestine was the first to propose a new group, the American Equal Rights Association (AERO), which advocated "educated suffrage" instead of "manhood suffrage." The women, feeling already betrayed by the Republican party and Congress, became bitter when the male abolitionists abandoned the woman suffrage plank at this time, arguing male Negroes were more entitled than women of all races. Then Ernestine proposed that AERO become the National Woman Suffrage Association:

"Why is it, my friends, that Congress has enacted laws to give the negro of the South the right to vote? Why do they not at the same time protect the negro woman? If Congress really means to protect the negro race, they should have acknowledged woman just as much as man; not only in the South, but here in the North, the only way to protect her is by the ballot." (*HWS* II: 396)

Within five days, it was a done deed, with Stanton president, and Rose and Anthony on the Executive Committee—no male leadership invited. In June 1869, less than a month after she obtained her United States citizenship, Rose—suffering greatly from neuralgia and rheumatism—sailed with her husband for Europe, after being feted by many of her friends. She received gifts of money from the *Boston Investigator* as well as a touching tribute from the conservative *Hebrew Leader*, whose editor, Rabbi Jonas Bondi, perhaps remembering her plea for tolerance on the pages of the *Boston Investigator*, wrote in the May 21, 1869 issue:

"Among all the advocates of human freedom and moral and social progress, who have labored in this country for the last twenty-five or thirty years, none has exhibited more constancy, devotion, sacrifice, earnestness and ability, than Ernestine L. Rose, and but for the fact that such genuine reformers are never suitably appreciated in their day and generation, she would now be the most popular, as she has long been the best female lecturer in the United States."

Rose's main link to the United States was *The Boston Investigator*, for which she wrote occasional letters after settling in England. Friends included Moncure D. Conway and George Jacob Holyoake. She made occasional public appearances on behalf of women and freethought. At a two-day General Conference of

Liberal Thinkers held in June 1878, at Conway's South Place Chapel, attended by an old friend, Col. Thomas Wentworth Higginson, she spoke briefly:

"My friend, Col. Higginson, had no pocket for the old definition of religion. My pocket is so full of humanity alone that I have no pocket for anything else. I go for man . . . All the emotion we can possibly possess, all the feeling of which human nature is capable, all belongs to man. If there be one God or ten thousand gods, they do not need it, but man does and woman does, and to me it is stealing from man what belongs to man to give to a god, and to render to him things that cannot benefit him. . . . Our life is short and we cannot spare an hour from the human race, even for all the gods in creation."

On January 25, 1882, her husband died at sixty-nine of a heart attack. Charles Bradlaugh, the noted British atheist, delivered the funeral oration and Conway also spoke. Hypatia Bradlaugh Bonner, Bradlaugh's daughter, became a close friend toward the end of Ernestine's life.

Rose was buried at Highgate Cemetery with her husband. Freethinker George Jacob Holyoake spoke at her graveside:

"More than comely in features, which had dignity of contour, Mrs. Rose had a voice which at once arrested attention by its strength and melody. She spoke with easy accuracy, and with eloquence and reason. . . . In her youth her dark hair and gleaming eyes showed she had the fire of Judith in her. . . . Like her great co-worker in the anti-slavery movement, Lucretia Mott, Mrs. Rose took truth for authority, not authority for truth. . . . The slave she helped to free from the bondage of ownership, and the minds she had set free from the bondage of authority were the glad and proud remembrance of her last days." (*Boston Investigator*, August 6, 1892)

Susan B. Anthony, asked to prepare a "Roll of Honor" of nineteenth-century suffrage workers, wrote on December 30, 1899, that Mary Wollstonecraft, Frances Wright, and Ernestine L. Rose were the earliest champions of women's rights. Freethinker Lillie Devereux Blake wrote that the women of New York ought never to forget the debt of gratitude they owed Ernestine for their rights.

Stanton, Anthony and Matilda Joslyn Gage wrote in tribute of her while she was still alive:

"All through these eventful years Mrs. Rose has fought a double battle; not only for the political rights of her sex as women, but for their religious rights as individual souls; to do their own thinking and believing. How much of the freedom they now enjoy, the women of America owe to this noble Polish woman, can not be estimated, for moral influences are too subtle for measurement.

"Those who sat with her on the platform in bygone days, well remember her matchless powers as a speaker; and how safe we all felt while she had the floor, that neither in manner, sentiment, argument, nor repartee, would she in any way compromise the dignity of the occasion.

"She had a rich musical voice, with just enough of foreign accent and idiom to add to the charm of her oratory. As a speaker she was pointed, logical, and impassioned. She not only dealt in abstract principles clearly, but in their application touched the deepest emotions of the human soul." (*HWS* I: 100)

A Defence of Atheism

This lecture was delivered in Mercantile Hall, Boston, on April 10, 1861, and was later published in pamphlet form by the J. P. Mendum, (Boston) Investigator office. This is its first appearance in book form.

MY FRIENDS:—IN UNDERTAKING THE INQUIRY of the existence of a God, I am fully conscious of the difficulties I have to encounter. I am well aware that the very question produces in most minds a feeling of awe, as if stepping on forbidden ground, too holy and sacred for mortals to approach. The very question strikes them with horror, and it is owing to this prejudice so deeply implanted by education, and also strengthened by public sentiment, that so few are willing to give it a fair and impartial investigation,—knowing but too well that it casts a stigma and reproach upon any person bold enough to undertake the task, unless his previously known opinions are a guarantee that his conclusions would be in accordance and harmony with the popular demand. But believing as I do, that Truth only is beneficial, and Error, from whatever source, and under whatever name, is pernicious to man, I consider no place too holy, no subject too sacred, for man's earnest investigation; for by so doing only can we arrive at Truth, learn to discriminate it from Error, and be able to accept the one and reject the other.

Nor is this the only impediment in the way of this inquiry. The question arises, Where shall we begin? We have been told, that "by searching none can find out God," which has so far proved true; for, as yet, no one has ever been able to find him. The most strenuous believer has to acknowledge that it is only a belief, but he *knows* nothing on the subject. Where, then, shall we search for his existence? Enter the material world; ask the Sciences whether they can disclose the mystery? Geology speaks of the structure of the Earth, the formation of the different strata, of coal, of granite, of the whole mineral kingdom.—It reveals the remains and traces of animals long extinct, but gives us no clue whereby we may prove the existence of a God.

Natural history gives us a knowledge of the animal kingdom in general; the different organisms, structures, and powers of the various species. Physiology teaches the nature of man, the laws that govern his being, the functions of the vital organs, and the conditions upon which alone health and life depend. . . . But in the whole animal economy—though the brain is considered to be a "microcosm," in which may be traced a resemblance or relationship with everything in Nature—not a spot can be found to indicate the existence of a God.

Mathematics lays the foundation of all the exact sciences. It teaches the art of combining numbers, of calculating and measuring distances, how to solve problems, to weigh mountains, to fathom the depths of the ocean; but gives no directions how to ascertain the existence of a God.

Enter Nature's great laboratory—Chemistry.—She will speak to you of the various elements, their combinations and uses, of the gases constantly evolving and combining in different proportions, producing all the varied objects, the interesting and important phenomena we behold. She proves the indestructibility of matter, and its inherent property—motion; but in all her operations, no demonstrable fact can be obtained to indicate the existence of a God.

Astronomy tells us of the wonders of the Solar System—the eternally revolving planets, the rapidity and certainty of their motions, the distance from planet to planet, from star to star. It predicts with astonishing and marvellous precision the phenomena of eclipses, the visibility upon our Earth of comets, and proves the immutable law of gravitation, but is entirely silent on the existence of a God.

In fine, descend into the bowels of the Earth, and you will learn what it contains; into the depths of the ocean, and you will find the inhabitants of the great deep; but neither in the Earth above, nor the waters below, can you obtain any knowledge of his existence. Ascend into the heavens, and enter the "milky way," go from planet to planet to the remotest star, and ask the eternally revolving systems, Where is God? and Echo answers, Where?

The Universe of Matter gives us no record of his existence. Where next shall we search? Enter the Universe of Mind, read the millions of volumes written on the subject, and in all the speculations, the assertions, the assumptions, the theories, and the creeds, you can only find Man stamped in an indelible impress his own mind on every page. In describing his God, he delineated his own character: the picture he drew represents in living and ineffaceable colors the epoch of his existence—the period he lived in.

It was a great mistake to say that God made man in his image. Man, in all ages, made his God in his own image; and we find that just in accordance with his civilization, his knowledge, his experience, his taste, his refinement, his sense of right, of justice, of freedom, and humanity,—so has he made his God. But whether coarse or refined; cruel and vindictive, or kind and generous; an implacable tyrant, or a gentle and loving father; it still was the emanation of his own mind—the picture of himself.

But, you ask, how came it that man thought or wrote about God at all? The answer is very simple. Ignorance is the mother of Superstition. In proportion to man's ignorance is he superstitious—does he believe in the mysterious. The very name has a charm for him. Being unacquainted with the nature and laws of things around him, with the true causes of the effects he witnessed, he ascribed them to false ones—to supernatural agencies. The savage, ignorant of the mechanism of a watch, attributes the ticking to a spirit. The so-called civilized man, equally ignorant of the mechanism of the Universe, and the laws which govern it, ascribes it to the same erroneous cause. Before electricity was discovered, a thunderstorm was said to come from the wrath of an offended Deity. To this fiction of man's uncultivated mind, has been attributed all of good and of evil, of wisdom and of folly. Man has talked about him, written about him, disputed about him, fought about him,—sacrificed himself, and extirpated his fellow man. Rivers of blood and oceans of tears have been shed to please him, yet no one has ever been able to demonstrate his existence.

But the Bible, we are told, reveals this great mystery. Where Nature is dumb, and Man ignorant, Revelation speaks in the authoritative voice of prophecy. Then let us see whether that Revelation can stand the test of reason and of truth.—God, we are told, is omnipotent, omniscient, omnipresent,—all wise, all just, and all good; that he is perfect. So far, so well; for less than perfection were unworthy of a God. The first act recorded of him is, that he created the world out of nothing; but unfortunately the revelation of Science—Chemistry—which is based not on written words, but demonstrable facts, says that Nothing has no existence, and therefore out of Nothing, Nothing could be made. Revelation tells us that the world was created in six days. Here Geology steps in and says, that it requires thousands of ages to form the various strata of the earth. The Bible tells us that the earth was flat and stationary, and the sun moves around the earth. Copernicus and Galileo *flatly* deny this *flat* assertion, and demonstrate by Astronomy that the earth is spherical, and revolves around the sun. Revelation tells us that on the fourth day God created the sun, moon, and stars. This, Astronomy calls a moon story, and says that the first three days, before the great torchlight was manufactured and suspended in the great lantern above, must have been rather dark.

The division of the waters above from the waters below, and the creation of the minor objects, I pass by, and come at once to the sixth day.

Having finished, in five days, this stupendous production, with its mighty mountains, its vast seas, its fields and woods; supplied the waters with fishes—from the whale that Jonah swallowed to the little Dutch herring; peopled the woods with inhabitants—from the tiger, the lion, the bear, the elephant with his trunk, the dromedary with his hump, the deer with his antlers, the nightingale with her melodies, down to the serpent which tempted mother Eve; covered the fields with vegetation, decorated the gardens with flowers, hung the trees with fruits; and surveying this glorious world as it lay spread out like a map before him, the question naturally suggested itself. What is it all for, unless there were beings capable of admiring, of appreciating, and of enjoying the delights this beautiful world could afford? And suiting the action to the impulse, he said, "Let us make man." "So God created man in his own image; in the image of God created he him, male and female created he them."

I presume by the term "image" we are not to understand a near resemblance of face or form, but in the image or likeness of his knowledge, his power, his wisdom, and perfection. Having thus made man, he placed him (them) in the garden of Eden—the loveliest and most enchanting spot at the very head of creation, and bade them (with the single restriction not to eat of the tree of knowledge), to live, to love, and to be happy.

What a delightful picture, could we only rest here! But did these beings, fresh from the hand of omnipotent wisdom, in whose image they were made, answer the great object of their creation? Alas! no. No sooner were they installed in their Paradisean home, than they violated the first, the only injunction given them, and fell from their high estate; and not only they, but by a singular justice of that very merciful Creator, their innocent posterity to all coming generations, fell with them! Does that bespeak wisdom and perfection in the Creator, or in the creature? But what was the cause of this tremendous fall, which frustrated the whole design of the creation? The Serpent tempted mother Eve, and she, like a good wife, tempted her husband. But did God not know when he created the Serpent, that it would tempt the woman, and that *she* was made out of such frail materials, (the rib of Adam,) as not to be able to resist the temptation? If he did not know, then his knowledge was at fault; if he did, but could not prevent that calamity, then his power was at fault; if he knew and could, but would not, then his goodness was at fault. Choose which you please, and it remains alike fatal to the rest.

Revelation tells us that God made man perfect, and found him imperfect; then he pronounced all things good, and found them most desperately bad. "And God saw that the wickedness of man was great in the earth, and that every imagination of the thought of his heart was evil continually. And it repented the Lord that he had made man on the earth, and it grieved him at his heart." "And the Lord said, I will destroy man whom I have created, from the face of the earth; both man and beasts, and the creeping things, and the fowls of the air, for it repenteth me that I have made them." So he destroyed everything, except Noah with his family, and a few household pets. Why he saved *them* is hard to say, unless it was to reserve materials as stock in hand to commence a new world with; but really, judging of the character of those he saved, by their descendants, it strikes me it would have been much better, and given him far less trouble, to have let them slip also, and with his improved experience made a new world out of fresh and superior materials.

As it was, this wholesale destruction even, was a failure. The world was not one jot better after the flood than before. His chosen children were just as bad as ever, and he had to send his prophets, again and again, to threaten, to frighten, to coax, to cajole, and to flatter them into good behaviour. But all to no effect. They grew worse and worse; and having made a covenant with Noah after he had sacrificed of "every clean beast and of every clean fowl,"—"The Lord smelt the sweet savour; and the Lord said in his heart, I will not again curse the ground any more for man's sake; for the imagination of man's heart is evil from his youth; neither will I again smite any more everything living, as I have done." And so he was forced to resort to the last sad alternative of sending "his only begotten son," his second self, to save them. But alas! "his own received him not," and so he was obliged to adopt the Gentiles, and die to save the world. Did he succeed, even then? Is the world saved? Saved! From what? From ignorance? It is all around us. From poverty, vice, crime, sin, misery, and shame? It abounds everywhere. Look into your poor-houses, your prisons, your lunatic asylums; contemplate the whip, the instruments of torture, and of death; ask the murderer, or his victim; listen to the ravings of the maniac, the shrieks of distress, the groans of despair; mark the cruel deeds of the tyrant, the crimes of slavery, and the suffering of the oppressed; count the millions of lives lost by fire, by water, and by the sword; measure the blood spilled, the tears shed, the sighs of agony drawn from the expiring victims on the altar of fanaticism;—and tell me from what the world was *saved?* And why was it not saved? Why does God still permit these horrors to afflict the race? Does omniscience not know it? Could omnipotence not do it? Would infinite wisdom, power, and goodness allow his children thus to live, to suffer, and to die? No! Humanity revolts against such a supposition.

Ah! not now, not here, says the believer. Hereafter will he save them. Save them hereafter! From what? From the apple eaten by our mother Eve? What a mockery! If a rich parent were to let his children live in ignorance, poverty, and wretchedness, all their lives, and hold out to them the promise of a fortune at some time hereafter, he would justly be considered a criminal, or a madman. The parent is responsible to his offspring— the Creator to the creature.

The testimony of Revelation has failed. Its account of the creation of the material world is disproved by science. Its account of the creation of man in the image of perfection, is disproved by its own internal evidence. To test the Bible God by justice and benevolence, he could not be good; to test him by reason and knowledge, he could not be wise; to test him by the light of the truth, the rule of consistency, we must come to the inevitable conclusion that, like the Universe of matter and of mind, this pretended Revelation has also failed to demonstrate the existence of a God.

Methinks I hear the believer say, you are unreasonable; you demand an impossibility; we are finite, and therefore cannot understand, much less define and demonstrate the infinite. Just so! But if I am unreasonable in asking you to demonstrate the existence of the being you wish me to believe in, are you not infinitely more unreasonable to expect me to believe—blame, persecute, and punish me for not believing—in what you have to acknowledge you cannot understand?

But, says the Christian, the world exists, and therefore there must have been a God to create it. That does not follow. The mere fact of its existence does not prove a Creator. Then how came the Universe into existence? We do not know but the ignorance of man is certainly no proof of the existence of a God. Yet upon that very ignorance has it been predicated, and is maintained. From the little knowledge we have, we are justified in the assertion that the Universe never was created, from the simple fact that not one atom of it can ever be annihilated. To suppose a Universe created, is to suppose a time when it did not exist, and that is a self-evident absurdity. Besides, where was the Creator before it was created? Nay, where is he now? Outside of that Universe, which means the all in all, above, below, and around? That is another absurdity. Is he contained within? Then he can be only a part, for the whole includes all the parts. If only a part, then he could not be its Creator, for a part cannot create the whole. But the world could not have made itself. True; nor could God have made himself; and if you must have a God to make the world, you will be under the same necessity to have another to make him, and others still to make them, and so on until reason and common sense are at a stand-still.

The same argument applies to a First Cause. We can no more admit of a first than a last cause. What is a first cause? The one immediately preceding the last effect, which was an effect to a cause in its turn—an effect to causes, themselves effects. All we know is an eternal chain of cause and effect, without beginning as without end.

But is there no evidence of intelligence, of design, and consequently of a designer? I see no evidence of either. What is intelligence? It is not a thing, a substance, an existence in itself, but simply a property of matter, manifesting itself through organizations. We have no knowledge of, nor can we conceive of, intelligence apart from organized matter; and we find that from the smallest and simplest insect, through all the links and gradations in Nature's great chain, up to Man—just in accordance with the organism, the amount, and quality of brain, so are the capacities to receive impressions, the power to retain them, and the abilities to manifest and impart them to others; namely, to have its peculiar nature cultivated and developed, so as to bear mental fruits, just as the cultivated earth bears vegetation—physical fruits. Not being able to recognize an independent intelligence, I can perceive no design or designer except in the works of man.

But, says Paley, does the watch not prove a watchmaker—a design, and therefore a designer? How much more then does the Universe? Yes; the watch shows design, and the watchmaker did not leave us in the dark on the subject, but clearly and distinctly stamped his design on the face of the watch. Is it as clearly stamped on the Universe? Where is the design, in the oak to grow to its majestic height? or in the thunderbolt that rent it asunder? In the formation of the wing of the bird, to enable it to fly, in accordance with the promptings of its nature? or in the sportsman to shoot it down while flying? In the butterfly to dance in the sunshine? or its being crushed in the tiny fingers of a child? Design in man's capacity for the acquisition of knowledge, or in his groping in ignorance? In the necessity to obey the laws of health, or in the violation of them, which produces disease? In the desire to be happy, or in the causes that prevent it, and make him live in toil, misery, and suffering?

The watchmaker not only stamped his design on the face of the watch, but he teaches how to wind it up when run down; how to repair the machinery when out of order; and how to put a new spring in when the old one is broken, and leave the watch as good as ever. Does the great Watchmaker, as he is called, show the same intelligence and power in keeping, or teaching others to keep, this contemplated mechanism—Man—always in good order? and when the life-spring is broken replace it with another, and leave him just the same? If an Infinite Intelligence designed man to possess knowledge, he could not be ignorant; to be healthy, he could not be diseased; to be virtuous, he could not be vicious; to be wise, he could not act so foolish as to trouble himself about the Gods, and neglect his own best interests.

But, says the believer, here is a wonderful adaptation of means to ends; the eye to see, the ear to hear, &c. Yes, this is very wonderful; but not one jot more so, than if the eye were made to hear, and the ear to see. The supporters of Design use sometimes very strange arguments. A friend of mine, a very intelligent man, with quite a scientific taste, endeavored once to convince me of a Providential design, from the fact that a fish, which had always lived in the Mammoth Cave of Kentucky, was entirely blind. Here, said he, is strong evidence; in that dark cave, where nothing was to be seen, the fish needed no eyes, and therefore it has none. He forgot the demonstrable fact that the element of light is indispensable in the formation of the organ of sight, without which it could not be formed, and no Providence, or Gods, could enable the fish to see. That fish story reminds me of the Methodist preacher who proved the wisdom and benevolence of Providence in always placing the rivers near large cities, and death at the end of life; for Oh! my dear hearers, said he, what would have become of us had he placed it at the beginning?

Everything is wonderful, and wonderful just in proportion as we are ignorant; but that proves no "design" or "designer." But did things come by chance? It exists only in the perverted mind of the believer, who, while insisting that God was the cause of everything, leaves *Him* without any cause. The Atheist believes as little in the one as in the other. He knows that no effect could exist without an adequate cause; that everything in the Universe is governed by laws.

The Universe is one vast chemical laboratory, in constant operation, by her internal forces. The laws or principles of attraction, cohesion, and repulsion, produce in never-ending succession the phenomena of composition, decomposition, and recomposition. The *how*, we are too ignorant to understand, too modest to presume, and too honest to profess. Had man been a patient and impartial inquirer, and not with childish presumption attributed everything he could not understand, to supernatural causes, given names to hide his ignorance, but observed the operations of Nature, he would undoubtedly have known more, been wiser, and happier.

As it is, Superstition has ever been the great impediment to the acquisition of knowledge. Every progressive step of man clashed against the two-edged sword of Religion, to whose narrow restrictions he had but too often to succumb, or march onward at the expense of interest, reputation, and even life itself.

But, we are told, that Religion is natural; the belief in a God universal. Were it natural, then it would indeed be universal; but it is not. We have ample evidence to the contrary. According to Dr. Livingstone, there are whole tribes or nations, civilized, moral, and virtuous; yes, so honest that they expose their goods for sale without guard or value set upon them, trusting to the honor of the purchaser to pay its proper price.

Yet these people have not the remotest idea of a God, and he found it impossible to impart it to them. And in all ages of the world, some of the most civilized, the wisest, and the best, were entire unbelievers; only they dared not openly avow it, except at the risk of their lives. Proscription, the torture and the stake, were found most efficient means to seal the lips of heretics; and though the march of progress has broken the infernal machines, and extinguished the fires of the Inquisition, the proscription, and more refined but not less cruel and bitter persecutions of an intolerant and bigoted public opinion, in Protestant countries, as well as in Catholic, on account of belief, are quite enough to prevent men from honestly avowing their true sentiments upon the subject. Hence there are few possessed of the moral courage of a Humboldt.

If the belief in a god were natural, there would be no need to teach it. Children would possess it as well as adults, the layman as the priest, the heathen as much as the missionary. We don't have to teach the general elements of human nature;—the five senses, seeing, hearing, smelling, tasting, and feeling. They are universal; so would religion be were *it* natural, but it is not. On the contrary, it is an interesting and demonstrable fact, that all children are Atheists, and were religion not inculcated into their minds they would remain so. Even as it is, they are great sceptics, until made sensible of the potent weapon by which religion has ever been propagated, namely, fear—fear of the lash of public opinion here, and of jealous, vindictive God hereafter. No; there is no religion in human nature, nor human nature in religion. It is purely artificial, the result of education, while Atheism is natural, and, were the human mind not perverted and bewildered by the mysteries and follies of superstition, would be universal.

But the people have been made to believe that were it not for religion, the world would be destroyed:—man would become a monster, chaos and confusion would reign supreme. These erroneous notions conceived in ignorance, propagated by superstition, and kept alive by an interested and corrupt priesthood who fatten the credulity of the public, are very difficult to be eradicated.

But sweep all the belief in the supernatural from the face of the earth, and the world would remain just the same. The seasons would follow each other in their regular succession; the stars would shine in the firmament; the sun would shed his benign and vivifying influence of light and heat upon us; the clouds would discharge their burden in gentle and refreshing showers; and cultivated fields would bring forth vegetation; summer would ripen the golden grain, ready for harvest; the trees would bear fruits; the birds would sing in accordance with their happy instinct, and all Nature would smile as joyously around us as ever. Nor would man degenerate. Oh! no. His nature, too would remain the same. He would have to be obedient to the physical, mental, and moral laws of his being, or to suffer the natural penalty for their violation; observe the mandates of society, or receive the punishment. His affections would be just as warm, the love of self-preservation as strong, the desire for happiness and the fear of pain as great. He would love freedom, justice, and truth, and hate oppression, fraud, and falsehood, as much as ever.

Sweep all belief in the supernatural from the globe, and you would chase away the whole fraternity of spectres, ghosts, and hobgoblins, which have so befogged and bewildered the human mind, that hardly a clear ray of the light of Reason can penetrate it. You would cleanse and purify the heart of the noxious, poisonous weeds of superstition, with its bitter, deadly fruits—hypocrisy, bigotry, and intolerance, and fill it with charity and forbearance towards erring humanity. You would give man courage to sustain him in trials and misfortune, sweeten his temper, give him a new zest for the duties, the virtues, and the pleasures of life.

Morality does not depend on the belief in any religion. History gives ample evidence that the more belief the less virtue and goodness. Nor need we go back to ancient times to see the crimes and atrocities perpetrated under its sanction. We have enough in our own times. Look at the present crisis—at the South with 4,000,000 of human beings in slavery, bought and sold like brute chattels under the sanction of religion and of God, which the Reverends Van Dykes and the Raphalls of the North fully endorse, and the South complains that the reforms in the North are owing to Infidelity. Morality depends on an accurate knowledge of the nature of man, of the laws that govern his being, the principles of right, of justice, and humanity, and the conditions requisite to make him healthy, rational, virtuous, and happy.

The belief in a God has failed to produce this desirable end. On the contrary, while it could not make man better, it has made him worse; for in preferring blind faith in things unseen and unknown to virtue and morality, in directing his attention from the known to the unknown, from the real to the imaginary, from the certain here to a fancied hereafter, from the fear of himself, of the natural result of vice and crime, to some whimsical despot, it perverted his judgment, degraded him in his own estimation, corrupted his feelings, destroyed his sense of right, of justice, and of truth, and made him a moral coward and a hypocrite. The lash of a hereafter is no guide for us here. Distant fear cannot control present passion. It is much easier to confess your sins in the dark, than to acknowledge them in the light; to make it up with a God you don't see, than with a man whom you do. Besides, religion has always left a back door open for sinners to creep out of at the eleventh hour. But teach man to do right, to love justice, to revere truth, to be virtuous, not because a God would reward or punish him hereafter, but because it is right; and as every act brings its own reward or its own punishment, it would best promote his interest by promoting the welfare of society. Let him feel the great truth that our highest happiness consists in making all around us happy; and it would be an infinitely truer and safer guide for man to a life of usefulness, virtue, and morality, than all the beliefs in all the Gods ever imagined.

The more refined and transcendental religionists have often said to me, if you do away with religion, you would destroy the most beautiful element of human nature—the feeling of devotion and reverence, ideality, and sublimity. This, too, is an error. These sentiments would be cultivated just the same, only we would transfer the devotion from the unknown to the known; from the Gods, who, if they existed, could not need it, to man who does. Instead of reverencing an imaginary existence, man would learn to revere justice and truth. Ideality and sublimity would refine his feelings, and enable him to admire and enjoy the ever-changing beauties of Nature; the various and almost unlimited powers and capacities of the human mind; the exquisite and indescribable charms of a well cultivated, highly refined, virtuous, noble man.

But not only have the priests tried to make the very term Atheism odious, as if it would destroy all of good and beautiful in Nature, but some of the reformers, not having the moral courage to avow their own sentiments, wishing to be popular, fearing least their reforms would be considered Infidel, (as all reforms assuredly are,) shield themselves from the stigma, by joining in the tirade against Atheism, and associate it with everything that is vile, with the crime of slavery, the corruptions of the Church, and all the vices imaginable. This is false, and they know it. Atheism protests against this injustice. No one has a right to give the term a false, a forced interpretation, to suit his own purposes, (this applies also to some of the Infidels who stretch and force the term Atheist out of its legitimate significance). As well might we use the terms Episcopalian, Unitarian, Universalist, to signify vice and corruption, as the term Atheist, which means simply a disbelief in a God, because finding no demonstration of his existence, man's reason will not allow him to believe, nor his conviction to play the hypocrite, and profess what he does not believe.

Give it its true significance, and he will abide the consequence; but don't fasten upon it the vices belonging to yourselves. Hypocrisy is the prolific mother of a large family!

In conclusion, the Atheist says to the honest conscientious believer, Though I cannot believe in your God whom you have failed to demonstrate, I believe in man; if I have no faith in your religion, I have faith, unbounded, unshaken faith in the principles of right, of justice, and humanity. Whatever good you are willing to do for the sake of your God, I am full as willing to do for the sake of man. But the monstrous crimes the believer perpetrated in persecuting and exterminating his fellowman on account of difference of belief, the Atheist, knowing that belief is not voluntary, but depends on evidence, and therefore there can be no merit in the belief of any religions, nor demerit in a disbelief in all of them, could never be guilty of. Whatever good you would do out of fear of punishment, or hope of reward hereafter, the Atheist would do simply because *it is* good; and *being so*, he would receive the far surer and more certain reward, springing from well-doing, which would constitute his pleasure, and promote his happiness.

Margaret Fuller
(Courtesy of Constance Threinen)

7

Margaret Fuller

HIGH-PRIESTESS OF TRANSCENDENTALISM

May 23, 1810 – July 19, 1850

Give me truth; cheat me by no illusion.

Memoirs I: 303

BORN SARAH MARGARET FULLER IN CAMBRIDGEPORT, Massachusetts, she became one of the foremost nineteenth-century women writers and critics, winning an esteemed place in the early woman's movement upon the publication of *Woman in the Nineteenth Century* (1845). A role model of the independent woman, she died at forty at the peak of her powers, in a tragic shipwreck off Fire Island.

The first of nine children, she wrote poignantly of her suffering under the tutelage of her exacting father Timothy Fuller, a Unitarian and Harvard-educated lawyer and politician. Desiring a son and finding her precociously bright, he overstimulated her mind with classical lessons by age six. "The consequence was a premature development of the brain, that made me a 'youthful prodigy' by day, and by night a victim of spectral illusions, nightmare, and somnambulism. . . ." she wrote in an autobiographical fragment, later appearing in the posthumous *Memoirs.* "But I do wish that I had read no books at all till later,—that I had lived with toys, and played in the open air. Children should not cull the fruits of reflection and observation early, but expand in the sun, and let thoughts come to them. . . . With me, much of life was devoured in the bud." She attributed the acute migraines she suffered to her early training. (Chevigny, *The Woman and the Myth: Margaret Fuller's Life and Writings:* 37, 45)

One of her earliest memories was the death of her younger sister, and the terrible funeral procession. "I did not then, nor do I now, find any beauty in these ceremonies. What had they to do with the sweet playful child?" (p. 36)

She attended a school in Gorton in her early teens, mingling with Harvard students. Her intellectual prowess made her appear freakish; male friends and authors referred to her energy and mind as "masculine."

When her father died in 1835, Margaret assumed financial headship of her family. She taught first at Bronson Alcott's controversial Temple School, which was decried by ministers and mobs, then at a spin-off school in Providence. Her first translation, *Eckermann's Conversations with Goethe*, was published in 1939. She assumed editorship of the Transcendentalist *Dial* for two years beginning in 1840. Transcendentalism, led by Ralph Waldo Emerson, who had quit the ministry and rejected sectarian religion, was a refuge for Margaret in its espousal of individual self-development and its emphasis on literature, intellect and idealism. Emerson at this time was profoundly opposed to activism, preaching a detachment she emulated. However, as she wrote of Goethe, Margaret ultimately refused to subordinate the intellectual to the spiritual.

Margaret is credited with holding the original consciousness-raising group, offering "Conversation classes" for women, for a fee, in Cambridge and Boston from 1839–1844. Her goal: to provide higher education to women, help them "systemize thought" in the face of society's discouragement, and determine "What are we born to do?" It has been pointed out that these classes were the first such gatherings of women in North America since Anne Hutchinson's more heretical discussions. Margaret, then an admirer of Madame de Staël, consciously emulated her salons. Sidestepping the controversies of the day, she refused to discuss abolition at all. The first topic: Greek mythology. Abolitionist Harriet Martineau, who attended a lecture, pilloried Margaret's "Conversations," considering Margaret a product of a pedantic age and a repressive nation:

". . . The difference between us was that while she was living and moving in an ideal world, talking in private and discoursing in public about the most fanciful and shallow conceits which the transcendentalists of Boston took for philosophy, she looked down upon persons who acted instead of talking finely, and devoted their fortunes, their peace, their repose, and their very lives to the preservation of the principles of the republic. While Margaret Fuller and her adult pupils sat 'gorgeously dressed,' talking about Mars and Venus, Plato and Göthe, and fancying themselves the elect of the earth in intellect and refinement, the liberties of the republic were running out as fast as they could go. . . ."

Martineau felt that Margaret only found herself and "her heart" during her European stay. (Martineau, *Autobiography* I: 381–382)

But American feminist Elizabeth Cady Stanton took another view of "Conversations." According to Stanton, they "were in reality a vindication of woman's right to think. . . . Miss Fuller was the precursor of the Woman's Rights agitation of the last thirty-three years," she wrote in 1881. (*History of Woman Suffrage* I: 801–802)

Margaret wrote her first book, *Summer on the Lakes* (1844), after traveling to the frontier of the Midwest, making trenchant observations on the harm of missionaries to American Indians. [See selection]

At age thirty-four, she became the first woman staff member of *The New York Tribune*, after Horace Greeley, at his wife's urging, offered her a position as literary critic, thereby opening the doors of journalism to women. She wrote about reform for women prisoners and the plight of prostitutes, and opposed capital punishment. In 1845, she wrote *Woman in the Nineteenth Century*, adapted from an article published in the *Dial*, championing the cause of women. While digressive, the book did not equivocate in addressing societal assumptions: "It is the fault of MARRIAGE and of the present relation between the sexes, that the woman *belongs* to the man, instead of forming a whole with him." Margaret praised women abolitionists, such as the Grimkés and Abby Foster. Her writing reflected a kind of merged paganism, Unitarianism, and Transcendentalism, but Margaret defined religion as "the thirst for truth and good, not the love of sect and dogma," and observed: "Women are, indeed, the easy victims both of priestcraft and self-delusion; but this would not be, if the intellect was developed in proportion to the other powers." (*Woman and the Myth*: 275, 261)

🌿

What were her views on religion? At age nineteen, she had written friends a letter, later reprinted in the first volume of *Memoirs*: "I have hesitated much whether to tell you what you ask about my religion. You are mistaken! I have not formed an opinion. I have determined not to form settled opinions at present. Loving or feeble natures need a positive religion, a visible refuge, a protection, as much in the passionate season of youth as in those stages nearer to the grave. But mine is not such." (p. 166)

When William Henry Channing put together *Memoirs*, he edited out heresies, such as this passage from a credo written in 1842, in which she did not accept the special divinity of Christ: "You see how wide the gulf that separates me from the Christian Church. . . . Do you not place Christ then in a higher place than Socrates, for instance, or Michael Angelo? Yes! Because if his life was not truer, it was deeper, and he is a representative of the ages. But then I consider the Greek Apollo as one also! . . .

". . . I do not reject the church either. Let men who can with sincerity live in it. I would not—for I believe far more widely than any body of men I know. And as nowhere I worship less than in the places set apart for that purpose, I will not seem to do so. The blue sky seen above the opposite roof preaches better than any brother, because, at present, a freer, simpler medium of religion." (pp. 170–171)

On December 30, 1847, Margaret wrote about witnessing a nun taking the veil: "Poor thing! . . tares and wormwood must be her portion. She was then taken behind a grating, her hair cut, and her clothes exchanged for the nun's vestments; the black-robed sisters who worked upon her looking like crows or ravens at their ominous feasts . . . where it [monastic seclusion] is enforced or repented of, no hell could be worse. . . ." (p. 441)

In one of her final letters, to friends Marcus and Rebecca Spring (December 12, 1849), she wrote: ". . . If so, you are a Christian; you know I never pretended to be except in dabs and sparkles here and there." (p. 490)

Margaret's freethinking motto was "Give me truth; cheat me by no illusion," from a poem published in *Memoirs*. New Englanders considered her downright "pagan." Even Emerson found her "exotic." Indeed, when she read Christian teachings, she wrote that they made her cry out "for her dear old Greek gods." (p. 147)

The editors of the posthumous *Memoirs*, according to biographer Bell Gale Chevigny, bowdlerized her writings: ". . . pantheism and repudiation of dogma had two adverse affects: it made some of her writing diffuse to the point of unintelligibility and some spiritually unacceptable to her editors." (p. 169) Margaret Fuller's disparagements or reservations about Jesus were censored by Channing, a Christian Socialist minister, in *Memoirs*. Chevigny, in analyzing extant originals with *Memoirs*, found that Channing had added pious salutations such as "O Father" if her writing seemed irreverent. Margaret, in final analysis, appeared to be a Deist in the mold of Mary Wollstonecraft.

❧

She traveled to England, Scotland and France with companions in 1846, becoming a foreign correspondent for Greeley, befriending Italian republican revolutionary Guiseppe Mazzini and French author George Sand. With Europe in revolutionary foment, Margaret became radicalized. The following year she stayed in Rome, meeting a handsome younger Italian nobleman, Giovanni Angelo Ossoli. History still debates when or if they married, but Margaret, known for her truthfulness, belatedly announced they had married secretly.

Her son Angelo was born on September 5, 1848. Margaret directed a hospital in Rome during the siege of Rome by the French in 1849. The republican cause lost, the family sailed for America on May 17, 1850, and drowned on July 19, just fifty yards short of their destination. It took twelve hours from the time the ship was wrecked until Margaret and her family drowned, while salvagers, not rescuers, gathered on the shore.

Wrote Stanton: "Margaret Fuller possessed more influence upon the thought of America, than any woman previous to her time." (*History of Woman Suffrage* I: 802)

Summer on the Lakes

This is excerpted from Chapter VI of Margaret Fuller's first book **Summer on the Lakes** *(1844), written after she toured northern Illinois, Wisconsin and Mackinaw Island.*

... OUR PEOPLE AND OUR GOVERNMENT have sinned alike against the first–born of the soil, and if they are the fated agents of a new era, they have done nothing—have invoked no god to keep them sinless while they do the hest of fate.

Worst of all is it when they invoke the holy power to mask their iniquity; when the felon trader, who all the week has been besotting and degrading the Indian with rum mixed with red pepper and damaged tobacco, kneels with him on Sunday before a common altar to tell the rosary which recalls the thought of Him crucified for love of suffering men, and to listen to sermons in praise of "purity"!!

"My savage friends," cries the old, fat priest, "you must, above all things, aim at *purity*."

Oh! my heart swelled when I saw them in a Christian church. Better their own dog-feasts and bloody rites than such mockery of that other faith.

"The dog," said an Indian, "was once a spirit; he has fallen for his sin, and was given by the Great Spirit in this shape to man as his most intelligent companion. Therefore we sacrifice it in highest honor to our friends in this world—to our protecting geniuses in another."

There was religion in that thought. The white man sacrifices his own brother and to Mammon, yet he turns in loathing from the dog-feast.

"You say," said the Indian of the South to the missionary, "that Christianity is pleasing to God. How can that be? Those men at Savannah are Christians."

Yes, slavedrivers and Indian traders are called Christians, and the Indian is to be deemed less like the Son of Mary than they! Wonderful is the deceit of man's heart!

... The few who have not approached them with sordid rapacity, but from love to them as men having souls to be redeemed, have most frequently been persons intellectually too narrow, too straitly bound in sects or opinions to throw themselves into the character or position of the Indians, or impart to them anything they can make available. The Christ shown them by these missionaries is to them but a new and more powerful Manitou; the signs of the new religion but the fetishes that have aided the conquerors.

Here I will copy some remarks made by a discerning observer, on the methods used by the missionaries, and their natural results:

"Mr. _____ and myself had a very interesting conversation upon the subject of the Indians, their character, capabilities, &tc. After ten years' experience among them, he was forced to acknowledge that the results of the missionary efforts had produced nothing calculated to encourage . . ."

Thus the missionary vainly attempts by once or twice holding up the cross to turn deer and tigers into lambs; vainly attempts to convince the red man that a heavenly mandate takes from him his broad lands. He bows his head, but does not at heart acquiesce. He cannot. It is not true; and if it were, the descent of blood through the same channels for centuries has formed habits of thought not so easily to be disturbed. . . .

I have no hope of liberalizing the missionary, of humanizing the sharks of trade, of infusing the conscientious drop into the flinty bosom of policy, of saving the Indian from immediate degradation and speedy death. . . .

Yet let every man look to himself how far this blood shall be required at his hands. Let the missionary, instead of preaching to the Indian, preach to the trader who ruins him of the dreadful account which will be demanded of the followers of Cain, in a sphere where the accents of purity and love come on the ear more decisively than in ours. Let every legislator take the subject to heart, and if he cannot undo the effects of past sin, try for that clear view and right sense that may save us from sinning still more deeply. And let every man and every woman in their private dealings with the subjugated race, avoid all share in embittering by insult or unfeeling prejudice the captivity of Israel.

8

Emma Martin

EARLY BRITISH FREETHOUGHT PAMPHLETEER

1812 – 1851

*There is yet another consideration which is fatal to the Christian religion,
and that is its persecuting spirit. It calls in the aid of Ecclesiastical and civil
laws, and the iron hand of custom to condemn, and if possible to punish those
who may express different opinions to its own. . . . Perish the cause which has
no more rational argument in its favour than that which the stake or prison
can supply!*

"A Few Reasons for Renouncing Christianity"

DESERVING THE ACCOLADE "HEROINE OF FREETHOUGHT" is a pioneering British freethinker Emma Martin, who was one of the first female lecturers and pamphle-
teers in freethought, also seeking to serve the cause of women over her short
lifetime.

Born in Bristol, England, Emma received strict religious training. That and a
youthful "melancholy turn of mind" inclined her toward religion.

"It never occurred to my mind, nor did any controversy ever suggest the
thought, that possibly the bible itself might not be what it appeared," she wrote
in the autobiographical pamphlet, "A Few Reasons for Renouncing Christianity
and Professing and Disseminating Infidel Opinions." After weighing the Socinian
and Catholic controversies, she selected a sect called Particular Baptists, becoming an enthusiastic, then disillusioned member at age nineteen.

Married young, Emma unhappily became aware of "the degraded condition
of woman," the need for improved education and better employment. She eventually separated from her husband. Once awakened to the wrongs of her sex as a
class, it was not long before she began to investigate the claims of religion, declaring herself a freethinker and infidel.

"Who could have palmed such an immense imposture upon mankind?" she asked. "Just think of my astonishment when I found its doctrines, its crucifixion, its sacraments, its holy-days, &c., had been in the world thousands of years before the Christian era."

In her ardor to reach the religious masses, Emma prepared a brief address to Christian Congregations on the folly of supporting missionary societies. She personally distributed her spirited letter on the subject, announcing her lectures, charging the missionary societies with wasting donations and injuring the recipients of their propaganda.

In "The Missionary Jubilee Panic, and the Hypocrites Prayer, Addressed to the Supporters of Christian Missions" (1844) Emma wrote:

"How strange it is that you regard the *real* evils of the *present* life, as of less fearful moment, than the contingencies of some future one!"

"I hate the sickly sentimentality of vaunted Christians, whose *tears* are as much under the control of fashion as their dress.

"The people perish for want and you cry 'more churches,' they ask for bread and you give them *stones.*

"They pine in ignorance, and you call for BIBLES, . . .

"The people need things for the *present* life, and you ask for more money to purchase for them *eternal* life. . . .

"Let the immense premises devoted to the puerile and false publications of the Tract Society be converted into houses of industry, where fallen and wretched outcasts may be restored to prosperity, health and virtue.

"Use your Bible Presses for the *diffusion of useful knowledge.*"

In "A Few Reasons for Renouncing Christianity," Emma asked:

"Is it not fatal to its pretensions of divine authorship, that we have the astounding fact, that for the greater part of the human family Christ died in vain, for they are not, nor will be saved? Imagine a being claiming to be a God, and setting about any undertaking in which he signally fails."

She wrote: "Religion, with an upward glancing eye, asks what there is *above*. Philosophy looks around her and seeks to make a happy home of earth. Religion asks what God would have her do:—Philosophy, what nature's laws advise. Religion has never given us laws in which cruelty and vice may not be seen, but Philosophy's pure moral code may be thus briefly stated:—

"Happiness is the great object of human existence. . . ."

In "The Bible No Revelation or the Inadequacy of Language to Convey a Message from God to Man," she wrote: "I would rather give my daughters a set of physiological and obstetric books for their perusal, than allow them to read the Levitical law, or the stories of the two Tamars, of Bathsheba, Lot, and others, . . ."

According to freethought historian John M. Robertson, Emma became an

Owenite and once formed a "short-lived free union." In addition to writing her own remarkable freethought pamphlets, she translated the maxims of Guicciardini.

Freethinker George Jacob Holyoake wrote of her:

"Beautiful in·expression, quick in wit, strong in will, eloquent in speech, coherent in conviction, and of a stainless character, she was incomparable among public women. She was one of the few among the early advocates of English Socialism who saw that the combat against religion could not be confined to an attack on forms of faith—to a mere comparison of creeds—and she attached only a secondary importance to the abuses of Christianity, when she saw that the whole was an abuse of history, reason, and morality." (Underwood, *Heroines of Freethought:* 234)

When a clerical friend insulted her by mailing a religious tract called "The Sinner's Friend," she wrote him a dignified reply:

"I have, sir, children, whose happiness is dearer to me than my own, for they have, I hope, a longer term of existence before them than I can look for; the possession, therefore, of principles which, if they are false, would be so detrimental to their interests, must have been to me a matter of deep solicitude, not only because they must necessarily share in any odium which attaches to the name of their mother, but also because their education must be erroneous, and eternal happiness be risked by unbelief. Allow me, then, to ask you whether I, who became an Infidel after twelve years of study and practice of Christian principles; after seriously investigating the internal and external evidences of Christianity; after searching, as I have done, into the origin and principles of all religions; after making public profession of my disbelief, having so important a thing at stake as the welfare and happiness of my children—think you, sir, that 'The Sinner's Friend' can overthrow the reasoning of years. . . ?" (pp. 235–236)

Emma, a single mother responsible for the support of her children and an active freethought lecturer, found time to qualify as a physician for women, attending lectures on women's health and anatomy, and studying and interning in hospitals.

But her own health failed. She died of tuberculosis before her fortieth birthday at her home in Finchley Common. A rationalist funeral service was conducted by Holyoake, who compared her to Frances Wright and Harriet Martineau, calling her an indefatigable and efficient "worker for human improvement." Holyoake added: "Indeed, she was the most womanly woman of all the public advocates of Woman's Rights." (pp. 238–239)

Prayer

The Food of Priestcraft and Bane of Common Sense.

This was published in London as a pamphlet in the 1840s.

PRAYER IS THE PETITION MADE BY MAN to the supposed author of his existence, in belief of his will and power to grant the request.

We are commanded by the popular religion to "pray without ceasing."

As this is a very difficult task, it is of course not required of us without some reasons assigned for it; the object of this little essay is to examine those reasons in order to ascertain whether they are sufficient to justify the practice.

We are told that "if we ask we shall receive," and this presents an inducement so strong, that if it were *true*, there is no doubt but that the majority of mankind would indeed "pray without ceasing." But it is *not* true. How many are the fervent petitions, presented in faith by God's worshippers, which are never granted! "Ye ask, and have not, because ye ask amiss," says the new testament. But this could not be the case with *all* unanswered prayers.

The full heart, bursting with affliction, looked to the God in which it had been made to believe, for help. If such God existed, he could not think such confidence in his power or love "amiss," yet how many a "bruised reed" has been "broken" by the refusal of its most urgent prayer, made in its greatest need!

"Ye desire to have that ye may consume it upon your lusts," is the reproof administered to the disappointed petitioners. But the parent who has prayed for the preservation of life or virtue of his child, knows that such rebuke is in his case unmerited.

He prayed for health and virtue for one whom he believed *God* had entrusted to his care, for one whom *nature* bid him love and cherish, "his lusts" had nothing to do with such a petition! Why was it then refused?

The poor weak erring mortal who every now and then had fallen into some indiscretion—sin if you prefer it—prays to the God whom he believes capable of giving strength to the weak, that we would save him from the temptations which surround him. He prays in the humility which would rest on a stronger than himself. According to Christianity, this would not be amiss, nor was it to feed "his lusts," but on the contrary that he might be able to deny them. Why then were not *his* petitions granted?

The church has prayed for the success of Christ's kingdom. Its devout members have longed for the salvation of their fellow men,—they have proved their sincerity too by giving their money as well as their prayers for the promotion of that object. It was surely not one which was furnished by "their lusts," nor could they "ask amiss" when they prayed as they thought Christ had taught them—"Thy kingdom come." Yet, who can say that the scintlings of Christianity now visible in the world is any answer to eighteen hundred years of prayers from fervent generations?

When too is it remembered that a rapid movement towards scepticism had taken place within the last few years, contemporaneous with yet deeper devotion and more urgent prayers from the faithful, it appears to be demonstrable that Baal is not the only god who when men petition him, "must be asleep, or on a journey," &c., since their requests are not granted.

The church has prayed much more successfully for the "good estate of the catholic church," yet there may be some doubt whether in the latter petition more than in the former was not to be found the "asking that they might consume it upon their lusts." The purple and fine linen and sumptuous fare of the dignitaries of the church have been bestowed. The power of Christianity to amass worldly riches is, so far, unquestionable,—but its power to subdue passion and prejudice, to make the world imitators of the meek and humble one, is now more dubious then ever.

You have prayed;—prayed in vain—will not the wise abandon so profitless a pursuit? . . .

Can prayer change God?

Unless prayer could change the determination of God it would seem useless to offer it, yet there are many reasons why this is impossible.

1. God is said to be immutable, "that in him there is no variableness or shadow of turning," yet he must be continually changing if he suffered himself to be guided by the prayers of changeful man, who, to-day longs for the rose, and tomorrow weeps over the wound of the thorn.

Succeeding generations, from a change of tastes and habits, make opposite requests, and "grant us peace in out time, Oh! Lord," succeeds to "prosper thou our righteous cause, Oh Lord," and "subdue the King's enemies under his feet."

Is this immutable one a vane, to be veered about by the breath of prayer from whatsoever quarter it may blow?

2. It is impossible that *any* God *could* grant the various and contradictory prayers which even saints may present. The favourable answer to one prayer often involves the disappointment of an antagonistic request. "If it be possible let this cup pass from me," said Christ, but many had prayed for salvation for Israel, and if their salvation was to be won by his tasting death for every man, (strange that every man is obliged to taste death for himself also), it was not in the power of God himself to answer both prayers favourably.

3. If God is the moral ruler of the universe, as great events often depend on those which appear trifling, and as every one is necessary to connect the great chain of cause and effect, if he has determined *anything* of all that has, or shall happen, he has determined *all*, and it must be as useless to ask him to alter any part of the arrangement, as to ask him to undo the whole.

Christians seem to be pretty well aware of this, for the usual addenda to all their prayers is "nevertheless not my will but thine be done," and "if it please thee," or, "unless, in thy infinite wisdom thou hast otherwise determined"; which is very much like saying, You may give it me if you please, but I know that you will not give me any more for asking, so let it alone if you prefer to do so. Supple Christianity!

If prayer does not directly benefit man by the obtainment of his desires, in our further search into the reasons for the practice, we may ask,—

Is prayer meritorious?

The majority of the professors of the protestant religion will undoubtedly answer in the negative, but their conduct will contradict their words. They will *say* "we are unprofitable servants, we have done that which it was our duty to do," but they will *feel*, (if they are believers), all the more comfortable for the performance. The Catholic will be more honest, he will literally understand the scripture which says "the kingdom of Heaven suffereth violence, and the violent take it by storm," and so he will pour a torrent of words in hopes of swamping Heaven's determinations.

If one can be amused at the religious follies of fellow-beings, to whom these things are of such serious import, ample material is furnished for it in the Roman Catholic Book of Common Prayer, where we find directions for the obtainment of heaven's blessings in proportion to the *number of times* we repeat certain talismanic words. . . .

If there be any merit in devotion it becomes an important question,

HOW should men pray?

Some suppose it necessary to prostate themselves in order to get their requests attended to. Others think it necessary to perform certain ablutions first. Some make offerings of incense, fruits, and blood, aye, even the blood of their fellow-men, and think that such gifts will procure from their God a favourable attention to their prayers. Nor is it only among Hindoos, Mahometans or savages that differences of opinion exist. Christians affirm that the nominal head of their church taught them *how* to pray, and what to pray for; and they prove the *clearness* of the instructions, or their punctilious obedience of them, by the diversity of their practice. The churches of England and Rome so devoutly appreciate that "beautiful formula" the Lord's Prayer, that they repeat it several times over in each service, as though they were apprehensive of God's inattention, but hoped out of several repetitions he may chance to hear one. They seem to think prayer God's music, and they play often what they fancy are his favorite tunes.

Among Christian churches some stand while they address their prayers to God; others think it necessary to kneel. Some turn to the east and curtsey at certain magic words, while others make the sign of the cross and use *holy* water as the necessary accompaniments. Whence all these differences? If a God requires prayer of men, he would require it of *all*; and since it is very evident that all men cannot pray acceptably, since some accompany their prayers with ridiculous and others with cruel practices, and that they do this from ignorance, it follows, that there is no creative intelligence who requires of any man prayer, since he has not taught *all* men *how* to pray acceptably.

Perhaps the reader will have a sudden influx of Christian charity, and suppose that God overlooks all these *minor* differences, as he may be inclined to call forms and ceremonies when he is engaged in an infidel controversy.

If this be so and all *modes* be equally harmless, let the *gentle* reader use, for conscience sake, one of those by which the Hindoo worshipper honors the Goddess Kalee, as mentioned in the Missionary Quarterly Papers.

Prayer is useful in its effects upon the mind of the petitioner.

This is the most rational defence of prayer, let us glance at its pretensions.

I will take it for granted that the constant and sincere solicitation of God to make us virtuous, meek, charitable, &c., &c., is calculated to generate in us the disposition for which we pray. But what of this? If men were taught the pure charity which thinketh no evil:—the calm content that knows no impatience:—the sober temperance which knows no excess:—in fine, the pure morals which can do no wrong, then, they would be in a state to ask for good things only, but then they would not need the so called soothing, sin-checking influence of prayer, for they would be already all that you consider prayer may make them.

Men pray out of themselves, as they speak at other times out of themselves. "Out of the abundance of the heart the mouth speaketh." Thus, David cannot be supposed to have done any thing towards calming and purifying his heart when his prayer was, "let his children be orphans and his wife a widow." Nor is it wonderful when his religion allowed him to think that such prayers would be heard and answered by God, that on his death-bed, revenge and murder still breathed forth in his last instructions to his son and successor.

[David's praying to God to help him to commit murder has been imitated, at an humble distance, in modern times, by one, John Bridmore, aged sixty-five, who, according to *Bell's New Weekly Messenger,* was charged at the Lambeth Police Court, with having violated two sisters tender of age. One of them was too ill to attend, and the other stated, that the prisoner went down on his knees and made his evening prayer immediately before his commission of the offence. Did his prayer *purify* his heart? Or is it not possible, that even in the presence of his intended victims, he was praying for the success of his designs?]

Does prayer invigorate the mind?

On the contrary prayer is the palsy of effort. The person much inclined to ask God's assistance, learns to repose on the hope of its obtainment, instead of actively seeking the good desired by his own labour. They wait to see the "leadings of providence." They pause "lest they should seem to be troubled about many things," and neglect "the one thing needful."

They think it necessary to "seek first the kingdom of God, and his righteousness," and they expect that all other things shall be added to them.

If then prayer does not produce the blessings sought by it, and if its effect on the mind of the individual is not of an improving character, then,

What are its uses?

The priest knows them well, and applies them, to the continuance of his nefarious power. Does any member of the flock occasionally have "hard thoughts of God," doubts respecting the divinity of his religion, or suspicions of the righteousness of some "dispensation of providence," the priest declares him sinful and convinces him of the necessity for urgent prayer, that the "devil thus resisted may flee from him." Does a sermon appear to be, what it really is, a dry, profitless discourse, it is the fault of the hearer, he must *pray* that God will bless the word spoken, and render it profitable. The man who believes it a duty to pray for faith, "Lord I believe help thou my unbelief," has lost, for the time, the power to use his understanding on any matters of religion. He is the tame slave of the priest, his spiritual guide, who, over his creed, his morals, and his estate, exercises an almost unlimited sway.

Christians! shake off the supineness which your priests have created in you; dare to think for yourselves, nor suppose your God can be pleased with the sacrifice of your reason. The bended knee is not the attitude for study. Read the Bible with the eye of criticism not of faith. Suspend your devotions, and reflect on the reception of your past petitions. *Ask no more till they are granted.*

Elizabeth Cady Stanton
(From the collection of the Seneca Falls Historical Society)

9

Elizabeth Cady Stanton

"A FEARLESS, SERENE AGNOSTIC"

November 12, 1815 – October 26, 1902

I have endeavoured to dissipate these religious superstitions from the minds of women, and base their faith on science and reason, where I found for myself at last that peace and comfort I could never find in the Bible and the church. . . . The less they believe, the better for their own happiness and development. . . .

For fifty years the women of this nation have tried to dam up this deadly stream that poisons all their lives, but thus far they have lacked the insight or courage to follow it back to its source and there strike the blow at the fountain of all tyranny, religious superstition, priestly power, and the canon law.

"The Degraded Status of Woman in the Bible," *1896*

THE FIRST TO CALL FOR WOMAN SUFFRAGE in the United States, Elizabeth Cady Stanton devoted her life to freeing women not only from legal constraints, but from superstition.

Elizabeth authored the very text of the Nineteenth Amendment guaranteeing women's right to vote. More recognized and famous in her day than Susan B. Anthony, she has been neglected, comparatively, by later generations, while Anthony, her more conservative "coadjutor," is a household name, her likeness appearing on the dollar piece, her birthday still observed. Elizabeth's outspoken criticism of religion resulted in suppression of her contributions to the revolution of women, just as Thomas Paine's anti-theological *Age of Reason* resulted in diminution of Paine's role in the American Revolution.

Elizabeth was born in Johnstown, New York, into the prosperous home of Margaret Lindsay Cady and Daniel Cady, an eminent lawyer, judge and member of Congress. Eager to please her exacting father in the face of his bitter loss of all five sons, she excelled in Latin, Greek, mathematics, and horseback-riding. Overhearing pathetic pleas for legal help from disenfranchised women clients in her father's law office, Elizabeth resolved early to rid the statutes of "these odious laws."

With college barred to her, at fifteen she boarded at Emma Willard's seminary for girls in Troy. There she fell victim to a visiting evangelist, the Rev. Charles G. Finney, "who, as a terrifier or human souls, proved himself the equal of Savonarola. . . . Returning home, I often at night roused my father from his slumbers to pray for me, lest I should be cast into the bottomless pit before morning." (Stanton, *Eighty Years & More:* 41, 43)

Her family rescued her through a trip to Niagara and some sensible reading. "That disabused my mind of hell and the devil and of a cruel, avenging God, and I have never believed in them since." (Interview, *Chicago Record,* June 29, 1897)

When she was nearly twenty-four, she met and fell in love with Henry Stanton, a young abolitionist and antislavery agent. On their honeymoon in 1840, their wedding tour took them to the World's Anti-Slavery Convention in London. There she first met Quaker feminist Lucretia Mott, suffering with her and the other women the humiliation of having women's status as delegates debated and denied by male abolitionists. Women were curtained off from the meeting and not permitted to speak. It did not escape her notice that "The clerical portion of the convention was most violent in its opposition," who, "Bible in hand, argued woman's subjection, divinely decreed when Eve was created." (*Eighty Years:* 80–81) The Seneca Falls convention germinated in London. So, it seems, did *The Woman's Bible.*

Her youth was largely devoted to her role as housekeeper, mother (eventually of seven), wife, cook, and nurse. At thirty-two, a harried housewife and isolated mother living in Seneca Falls, New York, she instigated and planned, with Lucretia Mott, Mary Ann McClintock, Jane Hunt, and Martha C. Wright, the historic first woman's rights convention on July 19–20, 1848. Elizabeth's call for woman's suffrage as part of the "Declaration of Rights and Sentiments" was considered almost too shocking to utter. The suffrage plank, although much-disputed, not only won endorsement there but would galvanize women for the next seventy-two years.

She entered into a lifelong feminist partnership with Susan B. Anthony in 1851, confining herself because of domestic duties mainly to speech- and letter-writing, with major exceptions, until entering her fifties. Her interests were never confined, however, to suffrage. From the start of her woman's rights activism, Elizabeth was committed to a radical platform to uplift women, constantly criticizing religion's treatment of women.

Elizabeth defied the biblical edict of Deuteronomy 22:5 (condemning women who wear men's clothes as "abominations") firsthand when she began wearing the Turkish trousers introduced to her era by her cousin and best friend Elizabeth Smith Miller. While thrilled with the liberation the short skirt gave her, Elizabeth, who had felt "like a captive set free," was so tormented in public that she gave them up, except in the privacy of her own home.

Elizabeth did not give up on much else. Initially all alone in calling for a suffrage plank at the Seneca Falls convention, she held firm as many signers repudiated the document after the press and clergy ridiculed the gathering. For calling for divorce for women married to habitual drunkards, she lost a temperance post in a male power play. This would be the pattern of her crusades, until finally even Anthony differed in public from her over her criticism of the bible. "Such experiences," she wrote in her autobiography, "have given me confidence in my judgment." (*Eighty Years:* 467) This self-confidence was a course she recommended to others in "Solitude of Self," a speech delivered to the House Committee on the Judiciary on January 18, 1892.

In reminiscing over her lifetime of unpopular causes, Elizabeth once commented: "Women are afraid. It is unpopular to question the bible. They are creatures of tradition. They fear to question their position in the testament, as they feared to advocate suffrage fifty years ago. Now they are quarreling as to which were among the first to advocate it.

"You see they are not used to abuse as I am. In Albany, fifty years ago, when I went before the legislature to plead for a married woman's right to her own property, the women whom I met in society crossed the street rather than speak to me." (Interview, *Chicago Record*, June 29, 1897)

In various stages of gestation and nursing from the ages of twenty-six until forty-three, she was proud of her robust health and the relative ease of her deliveries in a century when childbirth was so risky. In a letter to Elizabeth Smith Miller, Elizabeth seemed to take special pleasure in thwarting the biblical command of Genesis 3:16 to bring forth children in sorrow:

Dear Liz:

The fact of my having a daughter you already know; but the particulars I must give you. Well, on Tuesday night I walked nearly three miles, shopped and made five calls. Then I came home, slept well all the night and on Wednesday morning at six awoke with a little pain which I well understood. Thereupon I jumped up, bathed and dressed myself, hurried the breakfast eating none myself of course, and got the house and all things in order, working bravely between the pains. I neither sat down nor laid down until half past nine when I gave up all my vocations and avocations, secular and domestic, and devoted myself wholly to the one matter then brought more especially before my mind. At ten o'clock the whole work was completed, the nurse and Amelia alone officiating. I had no doctor and Henry was in Syracuse. When the baby was twenty-four hours old, I got up, bathed, taking a sponge and sitz bath, put on the wet bandage, dressed, ate my breakfast, walked on the piazza, and, the day being beautiful, I took a ride of three miles on the plank road; then I came home, rested an hour or so, read the newspapers and wrote a long letter to mama. The short dress I wore until the last. It is grand for such occasions and I love it more than ever. And finally let me say that everything with me and the baby is as it should be. My joy in being the mother of a precious little girl is more than I can tell you. The baby is very large and plump, and her head is covered with black curly hair. Oh! how I do rejoice in her...." (Stanton to Miller, Seneca Falls, October 22, 1852, Library of Congress)

She wrote an impish letter of joy to Susan B. Anthony on the arrival of her "little heretic," her second and last daughter, Harriot. It is typical of Elizabeth's irrepressible irreverence:

Dear Friend:

Well, another female child is born into the world! Last Sunday afternoon, Harriot Eaton Stanton—oh! the little heretic thus to desecrate that holy holi-day—opened her soft blue eyes on this mundane sphere. Maggie's joy over her little sister is unbounded. I am very happy that the terrible ordeal is past and that the result is another daughter. But I feel disappointed and sad at the same time at this grievous interruption of my plans. I might have been born an orator before spring, you acting as midwife. . . . Yours in love, E.C. Stanton (Stanton to Anthony, January 24, 1856, Library of Congress)

During midlife and old age—what she correctly predicted would be her prime—Elizabeth came into her feminist own. She edited a feminist weekly news-paper, *The Revolution*, for two and a half years (1868–1870), and traveled under frontier conditions as a suffrage organizer and on the Lyceum circuit, lecturing for as many as five consecutive months a year for more than a decade. She was often invited into the homes of frontier women, where, to her discomfort, she would be asked to say "grace." At first she refused, then began using the opportu-nity to preach equality:

"I often saw weary little women coming to the table after most exhausting labors, and large, bumptious husbands spreading out their hands and thanking the Lord for the meals that the dear women had prepared, as if the whole came down like manna from heaven. So I preached a sermon in the blessing I gave. You will notice that it has three heresies in it: 'Heavenly Father and Mother, make us thankful for all the blessings of this life, and make us ever mindful of the patient hands that oft in weariness spread our tables and prepare our daily food. For humanity's sake, Amen.' " (Lutz, *Created Equal*: 201)

She wrote or coedited six books (*The History of Woman Suffrage* Volumes I–

III, *The Woman's Bible*, Volumes I and II, and her autobiography, *Eighty Years &*
More) and impatiently anticipated the great reforms and issues of twentieth century feminism. She was the first woman candidate for the U.S. House of Representatives (receiving twenty-four out of more than 22,000 votes cast in a less than
enthusiastic campaign in 1866). Although she considered the politics of organizations distasteful, she was a founder and first president of the National Woman
Suffrage Association in 1869, and upon its merger with the American Woman
Suffrage Association in 1890, she became the National American Woman Suffrage Association's controversial first president.

Elizabeth was feted in grand style upon her eightieth birthday in 1895 with
an audience of six thousand admirers at the Metropolitan Opera House, attended
by a wide array of feminists and freethinkers. Freethinker Lillie Devereux Blake
presented her with a silver loving cup from the New York City Woman Suffrage
League.

One onlooker gave a charming description of Elizabeth, reflecting her epic
standing in the feminist community:

"You know she is a very stout - fine looking old lady, with a fair, white skin,
black eyes, beautiful white hair and with a *slightly pug nose*, that gives her a very
alert expression as well as pleasing—. . . she looked motherly and ladylike & she
talks in the same way, easy, quiet, just as she looks, never at loss for words &
always something interesting to say, or at least - making her subject - interesting
or she won't say anything." (Miss Pike to Miss Putnam, New York, November
21, 1895, Library of Congress)

Elizabeth critiqued religion even at this public fete at the Metropolitan Opera House:

"As learned bishops and editors of religious newspapers are warning us against
further demands for new liberties, and clergymen are still preaching sermons on
the 'rib origin,' and refuse to receive women as delegates to their synods, it is
evident that our demands for equal recognition should now be made of the Church
for the same rights we have asked of the State for the last fifty years, for the same
rights, privileges and immunities that men enjoy. We must demand that the canon
law, the Mosaic code, the Scriptures, prayer books and liturgies be purged of all
invidious distinctions of sex, of all false teaching. . . ." (*The Open Court*, Chicago:
Open Court Publishing Co., no date, Library of Congress)

Only two weeks later, at the height of her respectability, Elizabeth challenged
convention once more when the first volume of *The Woman's Bible* was published,
becoming a best-seller with seven printings in six months. Her children reported
that Volume I went through three American and two English editions, selling
20,000 copies, and that the first U.S. edition of Volume II was 10,000 copies.

It was an unusual Stanton speech, address or article written for publication which did not at least make a passing reference to the harm of religion, whether her subject was slavery, marriage and divorce laws, or even her contemplation of "The Pleasures of Age," a formal talk she gave on the occasion of her seventieth birthday.

She managed to turn an assignment for *The Wheelman*, "Should Women Ride the Bicycle?," into a chance to entice women out of church. She recommended bicycling on Sunday mornings instead of listening to church sermons. "I believe that if women prefer a run in the open air on Sunday to a prosy sermon in a close church, they should ride by all means . . . this worship is far preferable to playing the role of 'miserable sinners' in the church service, and listening to that sanctimonious human wail, 'Good Lord deliver us.' " (Diary, May 20, 1896, *Elizabeth Cady Stanton Revealed* II: 318)

In her earliest extant letter to Susan B. Anthony, Elizabeth warned her new friend about Amelia Bloomer's unwillingness to condemn the Church's "equivocal position" on slavery. "She trusts to numbers to build up a cause rather than to principles, to the truth and the right. Fatal error!" Elizabeth condemned the abolitionists who insisted on compromising the movement in order to placate priests and rabbis, while failing to rebuke the Church for its role in maintaining slavery and woman's subjection, and turning "the cold shoulder on woman's cooperation. . . . The Church is a terrible engine of oppression, especially as concerns woman." (Stanton to Anthony, April 2, 1852. *ECS Revealed* II: 39–40)

In her official letter to the National Woman's Rights Convention in 1856, Elizabeth impatiently reflected on the paralyzing piety of woman: "She looks to heaven; whilst the more philosophical slave sets out for Canada." (*History of Woman Suffrage* I: 860)

As early as her 1860 "Antislavery" address, she invited those enslaved by the bondage of original sin to be "born into the kingdom of reason and free thought." In an address at the 1867 American Equal Rights Association, she said "the polling-booth shall be a beautiful temple . . . [the ballot] the mightiest engine yet . . . for the uprooting of ignorance, tyranny, superstition, the overturning of thrones, altars, kings, popes, despotisms, monarchies and empires." (*HWS* II: 187)

Her belief was "grounded on science, common sense, and love of humanity," not "fears of the torments of hell and promises of the joys of heaven." (Diary, September 25, 1882, *ECS Revealed* II: 195)

Toward the conclusion of her life, she quipped: "I am most truly a protestant, for I protest indifferently against all systems and all sects." (Diary, January 31, 1889, *ECS Revealed* II: 255)

Her practical nature increasingly outweighed any early allegiance to an idealized Christianity. "One word of thanks from a suffering woman outweighs with me the howls of all Christendom." (Stanton to Anthony, June 14, 1860, *ECS Revealed* II: 82)

Early political addresses were sprinkled generously with references to God, but as she found her own voice, increasing in confidence and battle-scarred by denunciations against her sacrilege in the popular press, invocations lessened. When such references occurred, "Nature" and "God" became interchangeable.

Religious hypocrisy was brought home to her through the Tilton-Beecher scandal, exposed by her former ally, Victoria Woodhull, in the *Woodhull and Claflin's Weekly*. Woodhull reported the common knowledge that liberal preacher Henry Ward Beecher was having an affair with his best friend's wife, Elizabeth Tilton. Beecher survived intact a church investigation and civil suit brought by Theodore Tilton by slandering famous feminists and blaming Elizabeth Tilton for seducing him, to the disgust of Stanton and her other friends. The century's most celebrated black-collar scandal could not pass her notice. To the consternation of Anthony and others, Elizabeth spoke out publicly and passionately against Beecher's treachery, religious hypocrisy and the double standard.

As she matured, she turned increasingly to freethought literature and the freethought press, lecturing before the Free Religious Association and Liberal Leagues. She was on terms of warm friendship with the leading freethinkers of the nineteenth century, from Ernestine Rose and Robert G. Ingersoll in the United States, to Charles Bradlaugh of England.

Elizabeth "enjoyed a warm and admiring friendship" with Ingersoll, according to his daughter Eva Ingersoll Wakefield. One of the few letters preserved out of their spirited and affectionate correspondence is of special interest, since Elizabeth increasingly agreed with Ingersoll that it was of more importance to get superstition out of woman's head than to put a ballot in her hand:

New York, March 8th, 1894

My dear Mrs. Stanton:

I am in favor of giving every right to women that I claim for myself, and I shall vote to do that if I ever have the chance.

True, I have done but little for what you call "the cause of woman,"—I have had other fish to fry.—I thought it of more importance to get superstition out of her head than to put a ballot in her hand.—

Besides, woman suffrage has had great leaders—you and Miss Anthony and many others have done great work and great good, and have said all that was worth saying. There was no need of me. In fact, I would have excited prejudice on account of my religious opinions.

Rest assured, I am on your side, and will vote your way and will give you aid and comfort,—and let you do the speaking.

Yours always,

R.G. Ingersoll

All send love

(*Letters of Ingersoll:* 706. The original letter, in the Library of Congress collection, ends "all send love," a line Eva deleted for publication.)

As Elizabeth became an outspoken freethinker, she ceased idealizing feminine self-sacrifice, which had been an early, orthodox theme in her temperance and suffrage writings. She made women's self-respect and esteem her special campaign, a centerpiece of her popular "Our Girls" speech:

"I think if every young girl should be so taught during her childhood and girlhood, that she would grow up with some definite purpose in life,—with something to accomplish which would tend to make her own life and the lives of other women better, the world would be very much improved. I believe in a definite purpose for girls. The thing which most retards, and militates against woman's self-development, is self-sacrifice. Put it down in capital letters, that self-development is a higher duty than self-sacrifice. Women have always believed that they were born to be sacrificed, and I have made it my duty and my life-work to teach them the contrary. If I have succeeded in that, I have attained sufficient success." (Interview by Haryot Holt Cahoon, "One Woman's Success," June 1898, Library of Congress)

The separation of church and state was of vital concern to Elizabeth, who warned suffragists not to capitalize on Frances Willard's suffrage help through the Women's Christian Temperance Union. At her opening speech at the National American Woman Suffrage Association convention of 1890, Elizabeth stated:

"As women are taking an active part in pressing on the consideration of Congress many narrow sectarian measures, such as more rigid Sunday laws, the stopping of travel, the distribution of the mail on that day, and the introduction of the name of God into the Constitution; and as this action on the part of some women is used as an argument for the disfranchisement of all, I hope this convention will declare that the Woman Suffrage Association is opposed to all union of Church and State, and pledges itself as far as possible to maintain the secular nature of our Government." (*HWS* IV: 166)

The freethought views of her later years are summed up in this paragraph from "The Pleasures of Age," published by *The Boston Investigator*, February 2, 1901:

"I can say that the happiest period of my life has been since I emerged from the shadows and superstitions of the old theologies, relieved from all gloomy apprehensions of the future, satisfied that as my labors and capacities were limited to this sphere of action, I was responsible for nothing beyond my horizon, as I could neither understand nor change the condition of the unknown world. Giving ourselves, then, no trouble about the future, let us make the most of the present, and fill up our lives with earnest work here."

In her autobiography, she added, "The happiest people I have known have been those who gave themselves no concern about their own souls, but did their uttermost to mitigate the miseries of others." (*Eighty Years:* 385)

It is fitting that the last article Elizabeth wrote before her death was "An Answer to Bishop Stevens," urging people to "embrace truth as it is revealed to-day by human reason." (*New York American & Journal*, October 27, 1902)

Elizabeth made good on her promise never to shadow "one young soul with any of the superstitions of the Christian religion." In a glowing reminiscence upon her mother's seventieth birthday, Margaret Stanton Lawrence recalled their secular home:

"We children, two girls and five boys (take notice I put the girls first, because we belong to the superior sex?) have only pleasant memories of a happy home, of a sunny, cheerful, indulgent mother, whose great effort was to save us from all the fears that shadow the lives of most children. God, was to us sunshine, flowers, affection, all that is grand and beautiful in nature. The devil had no place at our fireside, nor the Inferno in our dreams of the future." (Margaret Stanton Lawrence, "Sketch," *The New Era*, Chicago, Illinois, November 1885, Library of Congress)

Elizabeth had asked that Helen Gardener speak at her grave. At the memorial at the "Friends Meeting House" in Washington, D.C., Gardener stated:

"First of all, she wished it known that she died, as she had lived, a fearless, serene agnostic. Her philosophy kept her sane and sweet. No fear for her soul, no dread of any future life, prevented her from using all of her splendid energies to better conditions in this world. She worked for the welfare of the race, here and now, and believed that any possible world could and would take care of itself." (Gardener, Memorial, *Free Thought Magazine*, Chicago, Illinois, Memorial Number, January 1903)

[See "The Christian Church and Women," "The Degraded Status of Women in the Bible," and Chapter 10, "Elizabeth Cady Stanton: A Freethought Reader."]

Elizabeth Cady Stanton & Child

The Christian Church and Women

From the Index, Boston, c. 1888. This is a version of "Woman's Position in the Christian Church," a sermon originally delivered in Moncure D. Conway's Pulpit, South Place Chapel, London, September, 1882. A longer version appeared in The Boston Investigator, May 18, 1901. A slightly shorter version was included in the pamphlet "Bible and Church Degrade Woman."

... IT IS OFTEN ASSERTED that woman owes all the advantages of the position she occupies to-day to Christianity, but the facts of history show that the Christian Church has done nothing specifically for woman's elevation. In the general march of civilization, she has necessarily reaped the advantage of man's higher development, but we must not claim for Christianity all that has been achieved by science, discovery and invention.

If we admit that the truth it has taught, as an offset to its many errors, has been one of the factors in civilization, we shall concede all that can be fairly claimed. The prolonged slavery of woman is the darkest page in human history, and she has touched the depths of misery since in Bethlehem the Magi gathered round the child in the manger, who was hailed as the Savior of mankind. ...

I speak of the Christian Church, Catholic and Protestant, of the priesthood, the bulls of its popes, the decrees of its councils, the articles and resolutions of its general assemblies, presbyteries, synods, conferences, which, all summed up, compose the canon law, which has held Christendom during what are called the Dark Ages until now under its paralyzing influence, moulding civil law and social customs and plunging woman into absolute slavery.

The worst features of the canon law reveal themselves to-day in woman's condition as clearly as they did fifteen hundred years ago. The clergy in their pulpits teach the same doctrines in regard to her from the same texts, and echo the same old platitudes and false ideas promulgated for centuries by ecclesiastical councils. According to Church teaching, woman was an after-thought in the creation, the author of sin, being at once in collusion with Satan. Her sex was made a crime, marriage a condition of slavery, owing obedience; maternity a curse; and the true position of all womankind one of inferiority and subjection to all men; and the same ideas are echoed in our pulpits to-day.

England and America are the two nations in which the Christian religion is dominant; yet, by their ethics taught in the pulpit, the ideal woman is comparatively more degraded than in pagan nations. I say comparatively, for, because of the various steps in progress in education, science, invention and art, woman is now more fully the equal of man in these countries than in any other nation or period of the world. And yet the old ideas taught by the Church in the Dark Ages of her inferiority and depravity are still maintained, and, just in proportion as women are the equals of the men by their side, the more keenly they feel every invidious distinction based on sex. To those not conversant with the history of the Christian Church and the growth of the canon law, it may seem a startling assertion; but it is, nevertheless, true that the Church has done more to degrade woman than all other adverse influences put together. And it has done this by playing on the religious emotions (the strongest feelings of her nature) to her own complete subjugation. The same religious conscience that carried the widows to the funeral pyre of their husbands now holds some women in the Turkish seraglios, others in polygamy under the Mormon theocracy, and others in the Christian Churches, in which, while rich women help to build and support them, they may not speak or vote or enjoy any of the honors conferred on men, and all alike are taught that their degradation is of divine ordination, and thus their natural feelings of self-respect are held in abeyance to what they are taught to believe is God's will. Out of the doctrine of original sin grew the crimes and miseries of asceticism, celibacy, and witchcraft, woman becoming the helpless victim of all the delusions generated in the brain of man.

Having decided that she was the author of sin and the medium through whom the devil would effect the downfall of the Church, godly men logically inferred that the greater the distance between themselves and all womankind, the nearer they were to God and heaven. With this idea, they fought against all woman's influence, both good and evil. At one period, they crucified all natural affections for mother, sister, wife and daughter, and continued a series of persecutions that blackened the centuries with the most horrible crimes. This more than any other one influence was the cause of that general halt in civilization, that retrogressive movement of the Dark Ages, for which no historian has satisfactorily accounted. At no period of the world was the equilibrium of the masculine and feminine elements of humanity so disturbed. The result was moral chaos,—just what would occur in the material world, if it were possible to destroy the equilibrium of the positive and negative electricity or of the centripetal and centrifugal force.

For the supposed crimes of heresy and witchcraft, hundreds of women endured such persecutions and tortures that the most stolid historians are said to have wept in recording them; and no one can read them to-day but with a bleeding heart. And, as the Christian Church grew stronger, woman's fate grew more helpless. Even the Reformation and Protestantism brought no relief, the clergy being all along their most bitter persecutors, the inventors of the most infernal tortures. Hundreds and hundreds of fair young girls, innocent as the angels in heaven, hundreds and hundreds of old women, weary and trembling with the burdens of life, were hunted down by emissaries of the Church, dragged into the courts with the ablest judges and lawyers of England, Scotland and America on the bench, and tried for crimes that never existed but in the wild, fanatical imaginations of religious devotees. Women were accused of consorting with devils and perpetuating their diabolical propensities. Hundreds of these children of hypothetical origin were drowned, burned, and tortured in the presence of their mothers, to add to their death agonies. These things were not done by savages or pagans: they were done by the Christian Church. Neither were they confined to the Dark Ages, but permitted by law in England far into the eighteenth century. The clergy everywhere sustained witchcraft as Bible doctrine, until the spirit of rationalism laughed the whole thing to scorn, and science gave mankind a more cheerful view of life.

So large a place has the nature and position of woman occupied in the councils of the Church that the Rev. Charles Kingsley facetiously remarked that the Christian Church was swamped by hysteria from the third to the sixteenth century. Speaking of witchcraft, Lecky says the Reformation was the signal for a fresh outburst of the superstition in England, and there, as elsewhere, its decline was represented by the clergy as the direct consequence and the exact measure of the progress of religious scepticism. In Scotland, where the reformed ministers exercised greater influence than in any other country, and where the witch trials fell almost entirely into their hands, the persecution was proportionally atrocious. Probably the ablest defender of the belief was Glanvil, a clergyman of the English Establishment; and one of the most influential was Baxter, the greatest of the Puritans. It spread with Puritanism into the New World, and the executions in Massachusetts form one of the darkest pages in American history. The greatest religious leader of the last century, John Wesley, was among the latest of its supporters. He said giving up witchcraft was giving up the Bible. Scepticism on the subject of witches first arose among those who were least governed by the Church, advanced with the decline of the influence of clergy, and was commonly branded by them as a phase of infidelity.

One remarkable fact stands out in the history of witchcraft; and that is, its victims were chiefly women. Scarce one wizard to a hundred witches was ever burned or tortured.

Although the ignorance and crimes of the race have ever fallen most heavily on woman, yet in the general progress of civilization she has had some share. As man became more enlightened, she of necessity enjoyed the results; but to no form of popular religion has woman ever been indebted for one pulsation of liberty. Obedience and subjection have been the lessons taught her by all alike.

Lecky, in his *History of Rationalism* and his *European Morals*, gives facts sufficient to convince any woman of common sense that the greatest obstacle in the way of the freedom and elevation of her sex has been, and is, the teaching of the Church in regard to her rights and duties. Women have ever been the chief victims in the persecutions of the Church amid all its awful tragedies, and on them have fallen the heaviest penalties of the canon law. But the canon law did not confine itself to social relations; it laid its hand with withering touch on the civil law, and blighted many personal and property rights accorded woman under the Roman Code.

Speaking of the Roman Code before the introduction of Christianity, (Gaius) Maine says: "The jurisconsults had evidently at this time assumed the equality of the sexes as a principle to the code of equity. The situation of the Roman woman, whether married or single, became one of great personal and property independence; but Christianity tended somewhat from the very first to narrow this remarkable liberty. The prevailing state of religious sentiment may explain why modern jurisprudence has adopted these rules concerning the position of woman, which belong peculiarly to an imperfect civilization. No society which preserves any tincture of Christian institutions is likely to restore to married women the personal liberty conferred on them by middle Roman law. Canon law has deeply injured civilization."

Rev. Charles Kingsley says, "Whoever wishes to gain insight into that great institution, Canon Law, can do so most effectively by studying Canon Law in regard to woman. There will never be a good world for woman until the last remnant of Canon Law is civilized off the face of the earth. Meanwhile, all the most pure and high-minded women in England and Europe have been brought up under the shadow of the Canon Law, and have accepted it, with the usual divine self-sacrifice, as their destiny by law of God and nature, and consider their own womanhood outraged, when it, their tyrant, is meddled with." Women accept their position under the shadow of the canon law for the best of reasons,—they know nothing about it. And, if they should undertake to explore it, they would waste their lives in the effort. While spending a year in England, I heard that a learned clergyman in the Established Church, living near by, had a remarkable library of old and valuable books, and among others innumerable huge volumes of the canon laws. So, thinking I might readily find those affecting women, I made arrangements to spend a day in his library. The volumes as large as our largest family Bibles stood there in long rows, leather bound and clasped, without an index, and all in Latin. Seeing the formidable array, I said, Could you be kind enough to give me the volumes that contain canons specially affecting women? He said, Alas! I could not, without looking through all of them; and that, as you readily see, would involve more time than you and I have to spare. But, he added, as the customs of society, the position of woman in the Church, and the old common law of England have all been moulded by the canon law, you can judge the general spirit of these volumes by what you see and hear of woman's condition in every-day life.

This is one of the peculiarities of woman's position: she knows nothing of the laws, either canon or civil, under which she lives; and such churchmen as the Rev. Morgan Dix are determined we never shall. Nero was thought the chief of tyrants because he made laws, and hung them up so high the people could not read them. What shall we say of the great State of New York, that makes laws for women, and binds them in calf, and then forbids its daughters to enter the law schools where they might learn them, or to plead for the most unfortunate of their sex in our courts of justice?

As the result of the canon law, what is woman's position in the State and the Church to-day? We have woman disfranchised, with no voice in the government under which she lives, denied until recently the right to enter colleges or professions, laboring at half-price in the world of work, a code of morals that makes man's glory woman's shame; a civil code that makes her in marriage a nonentity, her person, her children, her earnings the property of her husband. In adjusting this institution of marriage, woman has never yet in the history of the world had one word to say. The relation has been absolutely established and perpetuated without her consent. We have thus far had the man marriage. He has made all the laws concerning it to suit his own convenience and love of power. He has tried every possible form of it, and is as yet satisfied with none of his experiments. If an inhabitant of some other planet could suddenly light in one of our law libraries, and read over our civil and criminal codes, he would be at a loss to know what kind of beings women are, so anomalous is the position we hold, with some rights partially recognized in one place and wholly obliterated in another. In the criminal code, we find no feminine pronouns. All criminals are designated as "he," "his," "him." We might suppose our fathers thought women were too pure and angelic ever to commit crimes, if we did not find in the law reports, cases in which women had been imprisoned and hung as "he," "his," "him." And yet, while the masculine pronoun can be made to do duty for punishments, when it comes to privileges we are excluded, because the laws and constitutions do not contain the feminine pronouns "she," "hers," "her." We are a kind of half human, half animal being, like those wonderful questioning sphinxes we see in the Old World.

And we present very much the same appearance in the Church. Go into any little country town, and the chief excitement among the women is found in fairs, donation parties, festivals, Church building, and decorating. The women are the chief, untiring pertinacious beggars for the church. They compose the vast majority of the congregations. Rich women give large sums to clear church debts, to educate young men for the ministry, and to endow theological seminaries. Poorer women decorate the temples for Christmas and Easter, make surplices and gowns, embroider table covers for the altar, and slippers for the rector; and all alike think they are serving God in sustaining the Church and the priesthood. In return, the whole tone of church teaching in regard to woman is, to the last degree, contemptuous and degrading. Perchance the very man educated by some sewing society of women will ascend the pulpit, and take his text in I Corinthians xiv., 34, 35: "Let your women keep silence in the churches:

for it is not permitted unto them to speak; but they are commanded to be under obedience, as also saith the law. And if they will learn anything, let them ask their husbands at home, for it is a shame for women to speak in the Church." Ephesians v. 23: "Wives, submit yourselves unto your own husbands, as unto the Lord. For the husband is the head of the wife, even as Christ is the head of the church." I Timothy II., 11, 12, 13: "Let the woman learn in silence with all subjection. But I suffer not a woman to teach, nor to usurp authority over the man. . . . For Adam was first formed, then Eve." I Corinthians XI., 8, 9: "For the man is not of the woman, but the woman of the man. Neither was the man created for the woman, but the woman for the man."

Now, my friends, what effect do you think such Epistles as these, written by Paul to the Ephesians, the Corinthians, and the Thessalonians, had on the men and women of those times; and what is the effect of sermons from such texts to-day, but to degrade woman and demoralize man? These teachings in regard to woman so faithfully reflect the provisions of the canon law that it is fair to infer that their inspiration came from the same source, written by men, translated by men, revised by men. If the Bible is to be placed in the hands of our children, read in our schools, taught in our theological seminaries, proclaimed as God's law in our temples of worship, let us by all means call a council of women in New York, and give it one more revision from the woman's stand-point.

Disraeli said that the early English editions contain six thousand errors in the translation from the Hebrew, which were constantly introduced and passages interpolated for sectarian purposes or to sustain new creeds. The *Church Union* says of the present translation that there are more than seven thousand variations from the received Hebrew text, and more than one hundred and fifty thousand from the received Greek text, making by these two authorities one hundred and sixty-three thousand errors. It is fair to suppose that at least one-half of these errors are with reference to woman's position. It would not be assuming too much, in view of all the facts of history, for woman hereafter to take the liberty of defining her own position, without the slightest reference to the Church, its canon law, or Biblical interpretations. But, to return to the temple of worship, the sermon finished, to which women reverently listen in silence, the choir performs its part in this travesty on womanhood.

In all the great cathedrals in England and in some here in New York, boys from ten to fifteen chant the hymns of praise that woman's lips may not profane, while they, oblivious to these insults to their sex, swell the listening crowd, and worship the very God they are told who made them slaves, and cursed them with sufferings that time can never mitigate.

When last in England, I visited the birthplace of Dean Stanley. The old homestead was occupied by a curate and his two daughters. They escorted us all over the place,—in the school where poor children were taught, in the old church where the dean had long preached. "Do you see that table cover in the altar?" said one of the daughters. "Sister and I worked that." "Did you spread it on the table?" said I. "Oh, no," she said: "no woman is allowed to enter this enclosure." "Why?" said I. "Oh! it is too sacred." "But," said I, "men go there; and it is said that women are purer, more delicate, refined, and naturally religious than they are." "Yes, but women are not allowed." "Shall *I* explain the reason to you?" I replied. "Yes," she said, with a look of surprise. "Well," said I, "it is because the Church believes that woman brought sin into the world, that she was the cause of man's fall from holiness, that she was cursed of God, and has ever since been in collusion with the devil. Hence, the Church has considered her unfit to sing in the choir or enter the Holy of holies." She looked very thoughtful, and said, "I never supposed these old customs had such significance." "Yes," I replied, "every old custom, every fashion, every point of etiquette, is based on some principle, and women ignorantly submit to many degrading customs, because they do not understand their origin." . . .

All these indignities have their root in the doctrine of original sin, gradually developed in the canon law,—a doctrine never taught in the primitive Christian Church. In spite of the life, character, and teachings of Jesus, ever proclaiming the essential equality and oneness of the whole human family, the priesthood, claiming apostolic descent, so interpret Christianity as to make it the basis of all religious and political disqualifications for women, sustaining the rights of *man* alone.

The offices woman held during the apostolic age she has been gradually deprived of through ecclesiastical enactments. Although, during the first four hundred years of the Christian Church, women were the chosen companions of Jesus and his followers, doing their utmost to spread the new faith, as preachers, elders, deacons, officiating in all the sacraments, yet these facts are carefully excluded from all the English translations of the Scriptures; while woman's depravity, inferiority, and subordination are dwelt upon wherever the text will admit of it. Under all the changes in advancing civilization for the last fifteen hundred years, this one idea of woman has been steadily promulgated; and to-day, in the full blaze of the sunlight of the nineteenth century, it is echoed in the pulpit by every sect and in the halls of legislation by every party.

*

In one of the essential doctrines of Christianity,—namely, self-sacrifice,—women have been carefully trained, until, as John Stuart Mill says, that has come to be their pet virtue. This is nowhere better illustrated than in their religion. There is no depth of personal degradation they have not touched in the religious worship and sacrifice of ancient civilizations, and no humiliation of the spirit that mortals can suffer, when ostracised by those in no way superior to themselves, that educated women in our day have not endured. Seeing this, I have endeavored at many of our suffrage conventions to pass some resolutions embodying the idea that woman's first duty was self-development; and at last, after a prolonged struggle and much imposition, even by women themselves, the following resolutions were passed at our thirtieth anniversary, held in Rochester, July 1878:—

Resolved, That, as the first duty of every individual is self-development, the lessons of self-sacrifice and obedience taught woman by the Christian Church have been fatal, not only to her own vital interests, but through her to those of the race.

Resolved, That the great Principle of the Protestant Reformation, the right of individual conscience and judgment, heretofore exercised by man alone, should now be claimed by woman; that, in the interpretation of Scripture, she should be guided by her own reason, and not the authority of the Church.

Resolved, That it is through the perversion of the religious element in woman, playing upon her hopes and fears of the future, holding this life with all its high duties in abeyance to that which is to come, that she and the children she has trained have been so completely subjugated by priestcraft and superstition.

The following Sunday, the Rev. A. H. Strong, D.D., President of the Baptist Theological Seminary of that city, preached a sermon especially directed against these resolutions, which met strong clerical criticism and opposition by all the fraternity in the State who chanced to see reports of

— 121 —

the proceedings.

One amusing episode in that convention is worthy of note. Frederick Douglass, who has always done noble service in our cause, was present. But his intellectual vision being a little obscured that warm afternoon, he opposed the resolutions, speaking with a great deal of feeling and sentiment of the beautiful Christian doctrine of self-sacrifice. When he finished, Mrs. Lucy Colman, always keen in pricking bubbles, arose and said: "Well, Mr. Douglass, all you say may be true; but allow me to ask you why you did not remain a slave in Maryland, and sacrifice yourself like a Christian to your master, instead of running off to Canada to secure your liberty like a man? We shall judge your faith, Frederick, by your deeds." The time has come when women, too, would rather run to Canada to taste some of the sweets of liberty than to sacrifice themselves forever in the thorny paths marked out for them by man.

❦

Whatever oppressions man has suffered, they have invariably fallen more heavily on woman. Whatever new liberties advancing civilization has brought to man, ever the smallest measure has been accorded to woman, as a result of church teaching. The effect of this is seen in every department of life.

There is nothing so cheap as womanhood in the commerce of the world. You can scarcely take up a paper that does not herald some outrage on woman, from the dignified matron on her way to church to the girl of fourteen gathering wild flowers on her way to school. I hold men in high places responsible for the actions of the lower orders. The sentiments and opinions expressed by clergymen and legislators mould the morals of the highway. So long as the Church and the State, in their creeds and codes, make woman an outcast, she will be the sport of the multitude. Whatever can be done to dignify her in the eyes of man will be a shield and helmet for her protection. If the same respect the masses are educated to feel for cathedrals, altars, symbols, and sacraments was extended to the mothers of the race, as it should be, all these distracting problems, in which their interests are involved, would be speedily settled. You cannot go so low down in the scale of being as to find men who would enter our churches to desecrate the altars or toss about the emblem of the sacrament, because they have been educated with a holy reverence for these things. But where are any lessons of reverence for woman taught to the multitude?

And yet is she not, as the mother of the race, more exalted than sacraments, symbols, altars, and vast cathedral domes? Are not the eternal principles of justice engraven on her heart more sacred than canons, creeds, and codes written on parchment by Jesuits, bishops, cardinals, and popes? Yet where shall we look for lessons of honor and respect to her?

Do our sons in the law schools rise from their studies of the invidious statutes and opinions of jurists in regard to women with a higher respect for their mothers? By no means. Every line of the old common law of England on which the American system of jurisprudence is based, touching the interests of woman, is, in a measure, responsible for the wrongs she suffers to-day.

Do our sons in their theological seminaries rise from their studies of the Bible, and the popular commentaries on the passages of Scripture concerning woman's creation and position in the scale of being, with an added respect for their mothers? By no means. They come oft-times fresh from the perusal of what they suppose to be God's will and law, fresh from communion with the unseen, perhaps with the dew of inspiration on their lips, to preach anew the subjection of one half the race to the other.

A very striking fact, showing the outrages women patiently endure through the perversion of their religious sentiments by crafty priests, is seen in the treatment of the Hindu widow, the civil law in her case, as in so many others, being practically annulled by theological dogmas.

"The most liberal of the Hindu schools of jurisprudence," says Maine, "that prevailing in Bengal proper, gives a childless widow the enjoyment of her husband's property under certain restrictive conditions during her life," and in this it agrees with many bodies of unwritten local custom. If there are male children, they succeed at once; but, if there are none, the widow comes in for her life before the collateral relatives. At the present moment, marriages among the upper classes of Hindus being very commonly infertile, a considerable portion of the soil of the wealthiest Indian provinces is in the hands of childless widows as tenants for life. But it was exactly in Bengal proper that the English, on entering India, found the suttee, or widow-burning, not merely an occasional, but a constant and almost universal practice with the wealthier classes; and, as a rule, it was only the childless widow, and never the widow with minor children, who burnt herself on her husband's funeral pyre. There is no question that there was the closest connection between the law and the religious custom; and the widow was made to sacrifice herself, in order that her tenancy for life might be gotten rid of. The anxiety of her family that the rite should be performed, which seemed so striking to the first English observers of the practice, was in fact explained by the coarsest motives; but the Brahmins who exhorted her to the sacrifice were undoubtedly influenced by a purely professional dislike to her enjoyment of property. The ancient rule of the civil law, which made her a tenant for life, could not be gotten rid of; but it was combated by the modern institution, which made it her duty to devote herself to a frightful death. The reasoning on this subject, current even in comparatively ancient times, is thus given in the *Mitakshava*: "The wealth of a regenerate man is designed for religious uses; and a woman's succession to such property is unfit, because she is not competent to the performance of religious rites." Thus the liberal provisions of the civil law were disposed of by burning the widow, and she was made willing for the sacrifice by a cultivated sense of religious duty.

What is true in this case is true of women in all ages. They have been trained by their religion to sacrifice themselves, body and soul, for the men of their families and to build up the churches. We do not burn the bodies of women to-day; but we humiliate them in a thousand ways, and chiefly by our theologies. So long as the pulpits teach woman's inferiority and subjection, she can never command that honor and respect of the ignorant classes needed for her safety and protection. There is nothing more pathetic in all history than the hopeless resignation of woman to the outrages she has been taught to believe are ordained of God.

The Degraded Status of Woman in the Bible

From the pamphlet "Bible and Church Degrade Woman," by E. C. Stanton, H. L. Green, publisher, Office of Free Thought Magazine, Chicago, Illinois, 1896.

THE PENTATEUCH MAKES WOMAN a mere afterthought in creation; the author of sin; cursed in her maternity; a subject in marriage; and claims divine authority for this fourfold bondage, this wholesale desecration of the mothers of the race. While some admit that this invidious language of the

Old Testament is disparaging to woman, they claim that the New Testament honors her. But the letters of the apostles to the churches, giving directions for the discipline of women, are equally invidious, as the following texts prove:

"Wives, obey your husbands. If you would know anything, ask your husbands at home. Let your women keep silence in the churches, with their heads covered. Let not your women usurp authority over the man, for as Christ is the head of the church so is the man the head of the woman. Man was prior in creation, the woman was of the man, therefore shall she be in subjection to him."

No symbols or metaphors can twist honor or dignity out of such sentiments. Here, in plain English, woman's position is as degraded as in the Old Testament.

As the Bible is in every woman's hands, and she is trained to believe it "the word of God," it is impossible to describe her feelings of doubt and distrust, as she awakens to her status in the scale of being; the helpless, hopeless position assigned her by the Creator, according to the Scriptures.

Men can never understand the fear of everlasting punishment that fills the souls of women and children. The orthodox religion, as drawn from the Bible and expounded by the church, is enough to drive the most imaginative and sensitive natures to despair and death. Having conversed with many young women in sanatoriums, insane asylums, and in the ordinary walks of life, suffering with religious melancholia; having witnessed the agony of young mothers in childbirth, believing they were cursed of God in their maternity; and with painful memories of my own fears and bewilderment in girlhood, I have endeavored to dissipate these religious superstitions from the minds of woman, and base their faith on science and reason, where I found for myself at last that peace and comfort I could never find in the Bible and the church. I saw the first step to this was to convince them that the Bible was neither written nor inspired by the Creator of the Universe, the Infinite Intelligence, the soul and center of Life, Love and Light; but that the Bible emanated, in common with all church literature, from the brain of man. Seeing that just in proportion as women are devout believers in the dogmas of the church their lives are shadowed with fears of the unknown, the less they believe, the better for their own happiness and development. It was the religious devotee that threw her child under the car of Juggernaut, that gave her body a living sacrifice on the funeral pyre of her husband, to please God and save souls; for the same reason the devotees of our day build churches and parsonages, educate young men for the ministry, endow theological seminaries, make surplices and embroider slippers for the priesthood.

It may not be amiss for man to accept the Bible, as it honors and exalts him. It is a title deed for him to inherit the earth. According to the Pentateuch he communes with the gods, in performing miracles he is equal in power and glory with his Creator, can command the sun and moon to stand still to lengthen the day and lighten the night, if need be, to finish his battles. He can stand in the most holy places in the temples, where woman may never enter; he can eat the consecrated bread and meat, denied her; in fact, there is a suspicion of unworthiness and uncleanness seductively infused into the books of Moses against the whole female sex, in animal as well as human life. *The first born male* kid is the only fit burnt offering to the Lord; if preceded by a female it is unfit.

As the Bible gives us two opposite accounts of the creation of woman and her true position, so the church gives two opposite interpretations of the will of God concerning her true sphere of action. When ecclesiastics wish to rouse woman's enthusiasm to lift a church debt or raise a pastor's salary, then they try to show that she owes all she is and all the liberty she enjoys to the Bible and Christian religion; they dwell on the great honor God conferred on the sex in choosing a woman to be the mother of his own begotten son.

But when woman asks for equal rights and privileges in the church, to fill the office of pastor, elder deacon or trustee, to be admitted as a delegate to the synods, general assemblies, or conferences, then the bishops quote texts to show that all these positions are forbidden by the Bible. And so completely have these clerical tergiversations perverted the religious element in woman's nature, and blinded her to her individual interests, that she does not see that her religious bondage is the source of her degradation.

The honor and worship accorded the ideal mother, of the ideal man, has done naught to elevate the real mother, of the real man. So far from woman owing what liberty she does enjoy, to the Bible and the church, they have been the greatest block in the way of her development. The vantage ground woman holds to-day is due to all the forces of civilization, to science, discovery, invention, rationalism, the religion of humanity chanted in the golden rule round the globe centuries before the Christian religion was known. It is not to Bibles, prayer books, catechisms, liturgies, the canon law and church creeds and organizations, that woman owes one step in her progress, for all these alike have been hostile, and still are, to her freedom and development. . . .

⁂

When the canon law with its icy fingers touched the old Roman civil law it robbed woman of many privileges she before enjoyed. The old English common law, too, reflects many of its hideous features and has infused its deadly poison into the statute laws of every state in this new republic. For fifty years the women of this nation have tried to dam up this deadly stream that poisons all their lives, but thus far they have lacked the insight or courage to follow it back to its source and there strike the blow at the fountain of all tyranny, religious superstition, priestly power and the canon law. . . .

Elizabeth Cady Stanton

10

Elizabeth Cady Stanton: A Freethought Reader

Unless otherwise identified, these excerpts are from handwritten manuscripts, writings and published articles or speeches in the Elizabeth Cady Stanton Papers, Library of Congress collection, now conveniently available as part of the comprehensive microfilm history project, Papers of Elizabeth Cady Stanton and Susan B. Anthony, edited by Patricia G. Holland and Ann D. Gordon. **The History of Woman Suffrage** *is abbreviated HWS, and Stanton's published collection of diaries and letters,* **Elizabeth Cady Stanton Revealed,** *is abbreviated ECS Revealed. Original spelling, grammar and punctuation from Stanton's holographs are unchanged. When Stanton's excerpts are taken from a published source, publisher's spelling has been followed.*

"I Had the Same Right To Think"

It was at the fateful World Anti-Slavery Convention in England in 1840 that Stanton had her "conversion" to freethought, in listening to Lucretia Mott, an unorthodox Quaker shunned as an infidel by many other Quakers and Friends:

I FOUND IN THIS NEW FRIEND a woman emancipated from all faith in manmade creeds, from all fear of his denunciations. Nothing was too sacred for her to question, as to its rightfulness in principle and practice. "Truth for authority, not authority for truth," was not only the motto of her life, but it was the fixed mental habit in which she most rigidly held herself. It seemed to me like meeting a being from some larger planet, to find a woman who dared to question the opinions of Popes, Kings, Synods, Parliaments, with the same freedom that she would criticise an editorial in the *London Times*, recognizing no higher authority than the judgment of a pure-minded, educated woman. When I first heard from the lips of Lucretia Mott that I had the same right to think for myself that Luther, Calvin, and John Knox had, and the same right to be guided by my own convictions, and would no doubt live a higher, happier life than if guided by theirs, I felt at once a new-born sense of dignity and freedom; it was like suddenly coming into the rays of the noon-day sun, after wandering with a rushlight in the caves of the earth. . . .

. . . I expressed to her my great satisfaction in her acquaintance, and thanked her for the many religious doubts and fears she had banished from my mind. She said, "There is a broad distinction between religion and theology. The one is a natural, human experience common to all well-organized minds. The other is a system of speculations about the unseen and the unknowable, which the human mind has no power to grasp or explain, and these speculations vary with every sect, age, and type of civilization. No one knows any more of what lies beyond our sphere of action than thou and I, and we know nothing." (*HWS* I: 422)

"The Greatest Humbug" – 1848

Stanton's first remarks against clergy and scoldings of devout women appeared in her address at the Seneca Falls Convention, naming the "immaculate priesthood" first among transgressors of the unprincipled male professions, launching a recurring theme against "one of the greatest humbugs of the day," the so-called Education Society in which women in sewing circles paid for the education of young men for the ministry, who later would take to the pulpit to condemn these same women:

Now, IS NOT THE IDEA PREPOSTEROUS, for such a being to educate a great, strong, lazy man, by working day and night with her needle, stitch, stitch, and the poor widow always throws in her mite, being taught to believe that all she gives for the decoration of the churches and their black-coated gentry, is given unto the Lord. (*"Address Delivered At Seneca Falls Convention and Rochester"*)

"Let Us Withdraw Our Mite" – 1852

Keenly interested in the root of women's oppression, Stanton used an early dalliance in the temperance movement as a chance to call for suffrage, divorce law reform and to criticize religion. As President of the New York State Temperance Convention, in an address on April 20, 1852, she essentially advised women to stop supporting the ministry, and "the unknown God." The closing of churches, she hinted, would be no loss:

. . . INASMUCH AS CHARITY BEGINS AT HOME, let us withdraw our mite from all associations for sending the Gospel to the heathen across the ocean, for the education of young men for the ministry, for the building up of a theological aristocracy and gorgeous temples to the unknown God, and devote ourselves to the poor and suffering about us. Let us feed and clothe the hungry and naked, gather children into schools, and provide reading-rooms and decent homes for young men and women thrown alone upon the world. Good schools and homes where the young could ever be surrounded by an atmosphere of purity and virtue, would do much more to prevent immorality and crime in our cities than all the churches in the land could ever possibly do toward the regeneration of the multitude sunk in poverty, ignorance, and vice. *(HWS* I: 482–483)

"Woman, The Greatest Dupe" – 1852

In a sweeping letter to the Syracuse temperance convention in September 1852, Stanton concluded with an eloquent, impatient plea to women to cast off religious chains. Stanton was still professing belief in an idealized Christianity at this stage; she later recognized religion was the root cause of woman's subjugation:

PRIESTCRAFT DID NOT END WITH THE BEGINNING of the reign of Protestantism. Woman has always been the greatest dupe, because the sentiments act blindly, and they alone have been educated in her. Her veneration, not guided by an enlightened intellect, leads her as readily to the worship of saints, pictures, holy days, and inspired men and books, as of the living God and the everlasting principles of Justice, Mercy, and Truth.

. . . Woman in her present ignorance is made to rest in the most distorted views of God and the Bible and the laws of her being; and like the poor slave "Uncle Tom," her religion, instead of making her noble and free, and impelling her to flee from all gross surroundings, by the false lessons of her spiritual teachers, by the wrong application of great principles of right and justice, has made her bondage but more certain and lasting, her degradation more helpless and complete. *(HWS* I: 850-851)

Antislavery Address – 1860

An eloquent Stanton issued this stunning denunciation of the harm of religious thought:

. . . SHALL HE FETTER HIS MIND WITH VAIN SPECULATIONS of an eternal hell, a royal heaven, an aristocracy of saints, an evil fiend of torment, a God who laughs at his calamities? You may look through all the systems of nature, you will find no inflictions on the human family so terrible so protracted as those which man has conjured up for himself. What are all the accidents at sea compared with the infernal tortures of the Spanish inquisition? What is a shipwreck to a conversion to the gloomy doctrines of a Calvin? What is death by lightning to a life long fear of hell? Who that has ever believed in the dogmas of the popular theology, that has for years gone mourning, groaning, grieving, fasting, praying in that slough of despond can fail to rejoice in the emancipation of any soul from such darkness, bondage. Who that sees a mind oppressed with the traditions of the ages, in its first agonizings for life, love, law would dare to obstruct its vision?—who would check its earnest longings with the cry behold a mystery. Who would bind its hopes, or decry its rights—to explore the universe for facts, thoughts. . . . The weary traveller long tossed about at sea is filled with joy to find himself on land once more. How good it is to stand upright, firm, to feel no motion swelling, heaving up and down.

"And sweeter far than foothold firm on solid land
"Is to the soul a faith that it can understand"
. . . Here where we have neither Pope, or King, no royal family, crown, or scepter, no nobility, rank, or class, nothing outward to cultivate or command our veneration, Law; the immutable principles of right, are all and everything to us. *(Stanton manuscript, "Antislavery," Speech to the Anniver-*

sary of the American Anti-Slavery Society, 1860, punctuation uncorrected. In-
terestingly, the two published versions of this speech during this era retained her
orthodoxies but edited out of the above handwritten passage her strongest con-
demnations of religion.)

Folly – 1860

Although not a primary object in her youth, separation of church and state became a
passionate interest. As early as 1860, she was developing a philosophy of civil law,
sagely advising:

A VERY WISE FATHER ONCE REMARKED, that in the government of his children, he forbid as few things as possible; a wise legislature would do the
same. It is folly to make laws on subjects beyond human prerogative, knowing that in the very nature of things they must be set aside. To make laws
that man cannot and will not obey, serves to bring all law into contempt. It
is very important in a republic, that the people should respect the laws, for
if we throw them to the winds, what becomes of civil government? *(Stanton manuscript, Address of May 15, 1860?)*

That Ancient Polling Booth – 1869

Her columns for The Revolution (1868–1870), in which she could write unedited to
her heart's content, were often playfully iconoclastic, as in this passage published on
March 29, 1869:

. . . I DISAGREE WITH PETER AND PAUL as to the effect on civilization of the
action of woman at that ancient polling booth, the apple tree, where our
first parents and his Satanic majesty held council together. That act was
the unlocking to the human family of all the realms of knowledge and
thought; but for that, Moses and Aaron, Samson and Solomon, Colum-
bus, Newton, Fulton and Cyrus Field, would have been to this hour list-
lessly sunning themselves on the grassy slopes of Paradise, ignorant of the
laws of their being and everything beyond their own horizon. Yes, when
Eve took her destiny in her own hand and set minds spinning down through

all the spheres of time, she declared humanity omnipotent, and to-day thinking people are wrapt in wonder and admiration at the inventions and discoveries of science, the grandeur of man's conceptions, and the magnitude of his works. . . .

When women are educated, with large brains and large waists, there will not be so many fools.

"The Man Marriage" – 1869

Stanton's conviction that women should feel free to interpret the bible to their point of view, as men did already, was expressed three decades before The Woman's Bible became a reality, in The Revolution on April 8, 1869. Stanton was convinced that a woman's reading of the bible could help suffragists elevate the status of women.

THERE IS NO ONE HERESY that has wrought such evil on the earth as that of making the mother of the race subservient to any power this side of the throne of God, and when puny man, with narrow views, so interprets the Bible as to make woman his lawful slave, he not only degrades her but the law of God also. . . .

Women have been listening, thinking, studying philosophy, Hebrew, Greek, first principles, and when they translate the Bible for themselves we shall have a new evangel of womanhood, wifehood and motherhood.

"The Catholic World" – 1869

Stanton has been called "antiCatholic" both in her day and the present for writing this piece, "The 'Catholic World' On Woman's Suffrage," published as a front-page editorial in The Revolution, appearing April 29, 1869. Point-by-point, she answered an attack of the woman's rights movement in a magazine called The Catholic World. Her warning that if the Catholic idea "finds lodgment in the minds of this people, we ring the death-knell of American liberties" remains as timely today as when it was printed. The essay makes an eloquent argument for the remarkable achievements of women in the face of patriarchy. "When lions paint pictures, they will not always represent men as conquerors, themselves as crouching slaves," she archly remarked.

Among women's achievements: "the fact that no slave breathes in this land to-day is largely due to the influence of such women as Lucretia Mott, Lydia Maria Child, Abby Foster, and Frances D. Gage." The essay is typical Stanton, alternating between eloquent opinion, factual summations, and darts of sardonic humor. "We are taught to pray 'Thy will be done on earth as it is in heaven.' If the thing cannot be done, why waste breath asking it?" Stanton sensibly demanded. One can see why Catholic patriarchs might be discomfited by her trenchant observation, in rebutting the Catholic World's prophecy that woman's suffrage will "break up and destroy the Christian family," that: "The office of 'paternity' should not be ignored by those who minister at the altar, as the rejection of the marriage institution tends to undermine the basis of society. It is in vain for men to preach the sacredness of relations they degrade in their lives, or wholly abjure for themselves."

A WRITER IN THE MAY NO. OF THIS MAGAZINE gives an essay of eleven pages on Woman's Sphere, in which he shows to his entire satisfaction: That suffrage is not a natural right. . . . That bad as things are, everything would be worse if woman had a voice in the laws, for she has degraded whatever she has touched, made home a pandemonium, enfeebled literature, and corrupted politics whenever she has had influence in national affairs. That the Protestant religion and the theory of our government is to blame for much of all this, and our fashionable boarding schools and *The Revolution* for the rest. The writer further shows that the only remedy for all this is Catholicism, substituting authority for individualism, educating our daughters in convents, and "wedding widows and spinsters to the Holy Spirit, that they may be mothers of minds and hearts." . . .

If we should take as much trouble to search our title to the right of Suffrage as to the acre of land we buy, we should find the original owner in both cases a mere squatter or savage, pirate or thief. Whoever will patiently unravel the history of the human family, will come to the conclusion that ecclesiastical, and civil organizations, on the above principle, that the few have the right to govern the many, have thus far been mere engines of oppression, robbing nine-tenths of the people of bread and education to keep one-tenth in luxury, idleness and bloated vice.

It is not possible for a foreigner and a Catholic, to take in the grandeur of the American idea of individual rights, as more sacred than any civil or ecclesiastical organizations. . . .

The fact that the few have seized the keys of heaven, pretending to be in the councils of the Most High—the riches of earth, the land, rivers, forests, mines of wealth, the industry of the people, and made laws to protect themselves in this wholesale monopoly, does not constitute them a *civil society* or apostolic order, with the right to dole out privileges or franchises, salvation or absolution to the rest of man or womankind. The human mind is ever oscillating between the extremes of authority and individualism; and if the former—the Catholic idea—finds lodgment in the minds of this people, we ring the death-knell of American liberties.

A religion is pure only as it dignifies man, lifts him above fear and superstition, and leaves him free to think.

A government is just only when the whole people share equally in its protection and advantages. . . .

The right to vote is the right of self-assertion. It is to throw round one's-self new outposts of individual sacredness, where each man can hold the drawbridge to his own civil, political and religious citadel, over which no King or Pope dare pass.

. . . To rebel against all authority, however hoary with time, when unjust and oppressive, is the only way to liberty and life. . . .

I am glad the life, liberty and happiness of my sex are not in the care and keeping of this pious Catholic, for we should be as summarily disposed of, for some imaginary heresy, as are all the able arguments on human rights of the last century, by this scratch of his bold pen. The women of this nation, good sir, will accept neither your premises nor your conclusions.

. . . A witty Frenchman describes the first conservative going about at the dawn of creation with upturned eyes and hands exclaiming, "My God! my God! conserve the chaos!!" Not more absurd than the men of our day who, in view of the moral chaos that surrounds them—the misery, weakness, imbecility, depravity and vice, that gather round their firesides—cry out against all changes in our social relations.

That Universal Creed – 1869

"Man to command, and woman to obey," has long been the darling theory of the stronger sex—. . . .

Christianity and chivalry, it is often remarked, have placed woman on a throne. . . . In science, literature, and art, *man* is the central word around which the word woman revolves as a mere nebulous satellite. In Holy Writ, also man is all in all. Genealogies begin with the father and end with the son. Eve never had any descendants! Moses, though careful to give both the names and histories of the sons of Adam, forgot to mention even the names of the daughters. It is man that fell and man that is to be redeemed, but who ever heard of the fall of woman! Earth, heaven, and hell are the three spheres assigned to man; but neither philosophers, divines, nor prophets have been able to determine even one for woman. . . .

Some have cursed her birth, and destroyed her as soon as known; others have tolerated her as "a desirable calamity"—as an evil, necessary to the continuation of the species, and fit only to be the slave and drudge of man; others have enshrined her as a being "too bright and good for human nature's daily food," and others, to guard her feminine purity, have forced upon her the sequestered life of a nunnery. All such disparaging views have a common origin in that universal creed: "man to command and woman to obey."

. . . If man is to command, it is evident that his right to do so must come either from nature or revelation. If it come from one, it must also come from the other, for there can be no real antagonism between nature and true revelation: for the same reason, if it do not come from one, it cannot come from the other. . . . The question, therefore, with perfect fairness and consistency, may be considered with reference to nature alone. First, I will consider briefly the Biblical side of the question. . . . Conservatism, shrinking from the light of reason, has marshalled its texts, and raised the shout of "infidelity," in the vain hope of checking reform. Thus has the Bible, too often been made the baluster of prejudice. It is worthy of note that no great reforms, whether political, scientific, social, or ecclesiastic, have ever been inaugurated that have not been compelled to pass the ordeal of Scriptural condemnation. The anathemas that were thundered forth from the Vatican against the great German reformer contained no word more terrible than "heretic." When Galileo announced his belief in the Copernican system, the vengeance of the priesthood vented itself in the cry of "heresy," and in the tortures of the Inquisition. That venerable old man of seventy years was compelled, with his hand upon the Gospels, to say that he "abjured, detested, and abhorred the heresy of the earth's motion around the sun." But as the old man tottered out from the presence of his persecutors, he muttered to himself: "It does move, nevertheless." So the world believes to-day. In the world's great *sentina* of false theories and notions, you search in vain for one that has not been labelled with a text. Well might the poet of poets put in the mouth of Bassanio:

> What damned error, but some sober brow
> Will bless it, and approve it with a text.

Slavery was defended until its latest hour as an institution of divine origin; and the cry of "infidelity" was made a gag to silence its opponents. Intemperance, too, has been ticketed with a "Thus saith the Lord." So the freedom of woman has been restricted to limits, said to have been fixed by the fiat of God; and, incredible as it is, men are not wanting whose chivalrous souls, without recoil, will permit them to say that their lordship over woman was divinely ordained. Despotism and oppression, from the remotest ages, have ever claimed the sanction of divine oracles. Millions of human beings have been put to death by the most horrid engines of torture that a diabolical ingenuity could invent; yet all this was said to be done to the glory of God.

"The Greatest Bugaboo"

YOU ASK FOR MY DEFINITION of "Free Love." I hasten to say that it means nothing; it is simply the cry of "wolf, wolf," to frighten the timid.

Each sage has some word of momentous import, with which to hound the lovers of truth and progress. Dr. Foster in his essays, tells us of the terrible power of the epithet "romantic" at one time. To say that a man, woman, or book was "romantic" would consign either to speedy oblivion. Then came "blue-stocking," which had such an appalling effect on all literary women that they wrote under the assumed names of the "stronger sex." Even in our own days Jessie Benton Fremont apologized repeatedly for the impropriety of writing a book.

Then came "infidel," that slayed its thousands. Science, philosophy, and reform alike writhed under its torturing blows. Combe, Spurgeon, Comte, Buckle, Spencer, Garrison, Phillips, and Abby Foster were all made bugbears to the trembling masses by the skillful use of that vague, undefined word "infidel." Then came "strong-minded," that sent the daughters of Eve scampering in all directions. "O, heaven defend us," cry they; "let us be silly, simpering, the feeblest of all created things, anything but strong-minded." Long use, however, has at least dulled somewhat the edge of this long expletive, and some new scare must be invented, to keep rebellious womanhood in check, and now comes "free love," most freely used by knaves and libertines, to condemn the virtuous and confound the brave.

The term cannot be defined; it means nothing; it belongs to the same family with "strong-minded," "infidel," "blue stocking," and "romantic," and is equally short lived; so let it too run its course, while we, fearing no bugbears, march on to the ballot box; for with the Butlers, Sargants, Chandlers and Ferrys all falling into line, victory must soon be ours.

Yours. *(Undated published letter from Mrs. E. Cady Stanton)*

"A Class of Men, Who, Like Minerva, Sprang from the Brains of Their Fathers"

For the Boston Investigator:

. . . Now, THE TIME HAS COME for woman herself to demand of the Church what she is demanding of the State—an equal voice in its laws and an equal share in its honors. Women, themselves, could secure this if they would withdraw from every church whose bishop in any way expresses such degrading opinions of the mothers of the race.

What is the origin of all such ideas?

It is that marriage is considered a defilement by the Church, and in one sect denied its priesthood. A woman, in order to be permitted to clean the floor of the 'holy of Holies' in some cathedrals, must be single!

Woman, according to the Bible, by eating the forbidden fruit precipitated the fall of the race, hence was cursed of God in her maternity, and all the race born in sin and iniquity, is the origin of the doctrine of infant damnation, considered one of the essential creeds of the Church, which hundreds of intelligent, highly educated men have just discussed for days in a great ecclesiastical convocation in our metropolis.

The degradation and defilement of woman is so clearly taught in the

Bible and sacred literature that the priests in some sects are forbidden all relations with her, while in others she is defiled by marriage, but, singularly enough, they are not.

There is a class of gentlemen leaders in the Church and State, in sacred and in profane literature, in history and in fiction, in art and in polite society, who evidently have a contempt for woman, who are always dictating as to her sphere of action, her manners, dress and home duties, her morals and mental capacity, who evidently neither respect nor appreciate the sex.

These gentlemen could never have known the tender care of a mother, the devoted love of a wife, the warm affection of a sister, nor the sweet reverence of a daughter, or they must have had some feeling of gratitude, kind regard and high appreciation for womankind.

But, perchance, like Minerva, they all sprang from the brains of their fathers, fully armed and equipped for the battle of life!

Tarrytown Suffrage Address – 1870

At Plymouth Hall, Tarrytown, New York, Stanton made one of her favorite points to a suffrage convention:

WE HAVE SETTLED THE POSSIBILITY in this country of having a state without a king, a church without a Pope, and now we are to prove it possible to have a family without a divinely ordained head. . . . By the same process of development, that man's blind faith in the authority of kings & Popes has been gradually superceded by new faith, & reliance in himself, has woman's blind faith in collective mankind, been substituted by new faith in herself. It is as disastrous to true government in the state, & home, to teach all womankind to submit to the authority of man, as divinely ordained, as it is to teach all mankind to bow down to the author[ity] of kings & Popes, as divinely ordained. *(Stanton Manuscript, untitled, 1870 Tarrytown Address)*

"No Time To Commune With Angels" – 1873

In a characteristic note on the subject, she wrote to a friend of her indifference to speculative views:

I AM SORRY I HAVE DISAPPOINTED Isabella Beecher Hooker by not devoting more time and thought to the next life. But the fact is I have always been so busy with mundane affairs that I have not had a moment to commune with the angels. If you have any heavenly experiences, do communicate them to I.B.H. and make your letter compensate in a measure for my indifference. To suppose this short life to be all of this world's experiences never did seem wholly satisfactory, but at the same time I see no proof of all these vague ideas floating in Mrs. Hooker's head. *(Stanton to Antoinette Brown Blackwell, June 10, 1873, ECS Revealed II: 142)*

"Gloomy Forebodings" – 1877

Stanton was deeply concerned about the tax-exempt status of churches:

For years many a thinking people have had gloomy forebodings as to the result of the immense power of the church in our political affairs. . . . And the first step in the disestablishment of the church & of all churches is the taxation of church property. The government has no right to tax infidels for everything that takes the name of religion. For every dollar of church property untaxed, all other properties must be taxed one dollar more, and thus the poor man's home bears the burden of maintaining costly edifices from which he & his family are as effectively excluded—as though a policeman stood to bar their entrance, and in smaller towns all sects are building, building, building, not a little town in the western prairies but has its three & four churches & this immense accumulation of wealth is all exempt from taxation. In the new world as well as the old these rich ecclesiastical corporations are a heavy load on the shoulders of the people, for what wealth escapes, the laboring masses are compelled to meet. If all the church property in this country were taxed, in the same ratio poor widows are to day, we could soon roll off the national debt. . . .

The clergy of all sects are universally opposed to free thought & free speech, & if they had the power even in our republic to day would crush any man who dared to question the popular religion. *(Stanton, Unidentified Lecture Fragment about Taxation of Church Property, 1877?)*

"Jehovah's Role In Suffrage Movement" – 1878

Stanton wrote Susan B. Anthony this humorous account of the suffragists who prayed for victory:

THE DAY FOLLOWING THE CLOSE OF THE CONVENTION, Isabella Beecher Hooker held a regular Moody and Sankey prayer meeting in the ladies' reception room right next to the Senate Chamber. Those present prayed, sang "Hold the Fort," "Guide us, oh thou great Jehovah" and "The Battle Hymn of the Republic," and made speeches from the tops of the tables. In the mean time the senators were assembling for the first time after the holidays and the corridors were crowded. Senator Sargent told us it was a regular mob. Mrs. Sargent and I did not attend the prayer meeting, for, as Jehovah has never taken a very active part in the suffrage movement, I thought I would stay at home and get ready to implore the committee, having more faith in their power to render us the desired aid. *(Stanton to Anthony, January 14, 1878, Elizabeth Cady Stanton Revealed, II: 154)*

Letter to Col. Ingersoll – 1880

When a Col. Miller sent Robert G. Ingersoll some of his own preserves, noting that he had mastered the skill when his wife and daughter went abroad, Col. Ingersoll noted in his thanks that he had often held "that women should be relegated to the ministry and men elevated to the kitchen."

When Mr. Miller shared this correspondence with Stanton, she wrote Ingersoll (Tenafly, March 20, 1880):

DEAR FRIEND:

Colonel Miller has sent me your letter on preserves, woman and the ministry. It is true that profession in the future will be as much improved by woman's thought as the home will be simplified and systematised by the scientific skill and arrangement of man's best thought. Every wife, mother and housekeeper feels at present that there is some screw loose in the household situation. We need more of man's mind there to organise and methodise, more of his inventive genius directed towards the every-day conveniences of life, to lessen labor and throw some new light on the problems arising from the stubborn elements of fire and water, so that the feminine soul need not be so sorely vexed with ranges, water-pipes, ovens that will not bake, drafts and leakages, things which she will never understand, for the mass of my sex hate facts, rules and machinery. For my part, I had rather write a sermon or a brief every day than make a coal fire in a range and keep it going twenty-four hours. Henry James says, "Woman is an inspirational being opposed to routine, authority, outward law;" hence the need of man ever by her side to catch her inspiration and give them form and force, and his need of her lest his routine authority and outward law degenerate into cold abstractions for want of the glow which her inspirations could give him.

Yours sincerely.

"When Shall We Learn?" – 1880

WITH THE ADVENT OF THE CHRISTIAN RELIGION, came more terrible tortures and persecutions than ever before. And woman has all along been the great sufferer. I note that a large majority of those who were tortured for sorcery were women. And those who will not accept the popular superstitions *to-day* suffer bitter persecutions, more and more refined, of course, as civilization advances. Instead of the tortures of the Inquisition, they endure ostracism. When shall we learn the lesson of individual freedom? *(Stanton to Henry Stanton, August 2, 1880, ECS Revealed: II: 171)*

Stanton's "Sermons" – 1883

Stanton gave several popular "sermons," usually to women-only crowds at churches, including "Is the Bible Opposed To Woman Suffrage?" and a similar talk, "Women in the Bible," apparently to meet demand when she was stranded on Sundays during various lecture tours. She consciously and pragmatically tailored her message to the orthodox, confessing in her diary that she "often spoke in the churches, when I would sow as much good seed as possible, though I was careful never to try and set out full-grown plants, especially if they were of a prickly nature, which was more often than not the species taken from my nursery." (January 31, 1889, ECS Revealed, II: 255)

The body of her "sermons" was an informational pep talk on bible heroines, reflecting her expedient eagerness to put a new spin on the bible, thereby motivating the conventionally religious woman of her time.

. . . WHATEVER THE THEORY OF THEIR TRUE POSITION representative women have in all ages walked outside the prescribed limits & done what they had the capacity to accomplish, and the women of the Bible form no exception. They preached prayed prophesied, expounded principles of government & Rulers, lead armies, saved nations & cities by their diplomacy & conquered their enemies by intrigue as well as courage. They communed with Spirits—told fortunes, solved the mysteries of the seen & unseen & in great emergencies trusting to their own nature strength & judgement rose superior to the customs, conventionalisms of their day & generation, & in no case is there a word of disapproval from prophet or Apostle.

Even in the midst of this pep talk, Stanton took care to point out the degraded status of biblical women:

THE MORAL CHARACTER OF A WOMAN'S ACTION is seldom considered so that she seconds man in all his plans and projects but when she claims any rights, honors or privileges for herself, for her individual happiness, or the benefit of her sex, then she is denounced for the slightest deviation from strict propriety or custom.

Stanton used bible verses to argue that "man and woman were a simultaneous creation, that Eve was not an unfortunate afterthought, and that the curse was not a direct fiat from heaven, but the result of violated law, to be got rid of by observing the rules of life." (Diary, May 21, 1883, ECS Revealed)

IN GENESIS 1ST 27, 28TH, WE HAVE THE ACCOUNT, "God created man in his own image," male & female created he *them* & gave *them* domination over the fish of the sea, the fowl of the air & every creeping thing that riseth upon the earth, but there is nothing said of mans authority over woman in this first Magna Charta of human rights. . . . The scene in the garden of

Eden which is supposed to conflict with this first account of the creation is metaphorical & allegorical, found alike in the scriptures of all nations. Though it is not to be understood literally yet there is a great truth bound up in that ancient poem, recognizing as it does woman's power as mother of the race. Just as in her degradation the race has been dragged down to vice misery & death, so in her elevation shall we be lifted up & become as Gods, knowing good & evil. . . .

But what a monstrous idea that woman should be cursed in her maternity. . . . Woman may trace her degradation in no small measure to the perversion of the religious element in humanity, destroying her own self respect & the respect of man for her by teaching the doctrine of Gods special displeasure visited on her for all time!

Surely Stanton would have felt in danger of another "woman's rights convulsion" to see woman's continued loyalty to the Church into the twenty-first century. Stanton's folksy, approving remarks about certain biblical heroines never mitigated her eloquent denunciations of the harm of the bible to women, in bible commentary that remains unparalleled in feminist writings:

To GO NO FURTHER BACK than the experience of our own times every reform that has marked the progress of the 19th century has been compelled to meet and conquer the objection. "The Bible is opposed to it.". . .

With this experience in all reforms it is not surprising that the demand for the enfranchisement of woman should be resisted by the same class for the same reasons. "The Bible is opposed to it" although the record says nothing in regard to a republican form of government, universal suffrage, or the political rights of women. . . .

The woman question as it comes up to day was never thought of by Moses Jesus or Paul, hence they said nothing that can be properly quoted on either side. "Obedience" to the powers that be was the one lesson of the past alike in the state, the church, & the home. But "resistance to the powers that be" is the higher lesson of the new civilization, through which we have caught a glimpse of freedom, we are now beginning to realize.

In contemplating the steady march of the race towards individualism, how puerile it seems to limit human freedom & the developement with isolated texts of scripture that have no significance whatever beyond the period & latitude where they were first uttered. And how dishonest to so interpret special directions and injunctions, as to conflict with accepted universal principles. . . .

When women read, translate & interpret the Bible, they will find the views now taken of woman's position unwarrantable and unfair. One might as well explore the solar system with a microscope as study history with a dictionary, or the Bible with a concordance.

As well decide the spheres of Jupiter & Venus without a knowledge of the planetary world as the true relation of man & woman for all time, by the customs of the Hebrews, Greeks & Romans, or the opinions of their philosophers centuries ago. . . .

Stanton announced during her sermon that she was prepared to purge the entire bible, if that were needed to free women:

FREDERICK DOUGLASS IN THE HEIGHT OF THE ANTISLAVERY STRUGGLE once said, 'Prove to me that the Bible sanctions slavery, and in the name of God and humanity, I would if possible make a bonfire of every Bible in the universe.'

And so say I. Prove to me that the Bible sanctions and teaches the universal subjection of woman to man as a principle formal order and I should be compelled to repudiate its authority and to do all in my power to weaken its hold on popular thought.

Making good on this vow is precisely what Stanton proceeded to do, increasingly devoting her energies to criticism of religion. (Stanton handwritten manuscript, "Is The Bible Opposed To Woman Suffrage?" Stanton's punctuation, short-hand uncorrected. Sermon preached twice in Strech, England in 1883, including at the Methodist church in Bristol, England, May 20, 1883)

"Unfulfilled Promises"

A resolution was once introduced at a Washington convention, directed at "women who call Christ Lord," reading, in part: "That we rejoice in the growing recognition among Christians that the teachings of Christ inculcate the equality of the rights of women and men . . ." Stanton protested:

PROMISES MADE TWO THOUSAND YEARS AGO, not yet fulfilled, cannot be said to be very inspiring to female disciples, in view of their present position.

. . . As the art of printing was not known in the time of the Jews we cannot in the nature of things have any absolutely reliable reports of what he [Jesus] did say regarding woman. Hence it would not be prudent to base our Resolutions in our conventions on his sayings or doings. *(Stanton manuscript, "An Interpolation?" no date)*

"His Satanic Majesty"

IF ONE TAKES THE ACCOUNT of the temptation as literal it places woman under great obligation to his Satanic majesty that he did not give that first apple to man for from his past record I fear he would never have shared his illumination with woman. *(Undated "Woman in the Bible" manuscript)*

"Roll Off The Terrible Superstitions" – 1885

Remarks at the 1885 National Woman Suffrage Association Convention:

YOU MAY GO OVER THE WORLD and you will find that every form of religion which has breathed upon this earth has degraded woman. There is not one which has not made her subject to man. Men may rejoice in them because they make man the head of the woman. I have been traveling the old world during the last few years and have found new food for thought. What power is it that makes the Hindoo woman burn herself on the funeral pyre of her husband? Her religion. What holds the Turkish woman in the harem? Her religion. By what power do the Mormons perpetuate their system of polygamy? By their religion. Man, of himself, could not do this; but when he declares, "Thus saith the Lord," of course he can do it. So long as ministers stand up and tell us that as Christ is the head of the church, so is man the head of the woman, how are we to break the chains which have held women down through the ages? You Christian women can look at the Hindoo, the Turkish, the Mormon women, and wonder how they can be held in such bondage. Observe to-day the work women are doing for the churches. *The church rests on the shoulders of women.* Have we ever yet heard a man preach a sermon from Genesis I: 27–28, which declares the full equality of the feminine and masculine element in the

Godhead? They invariably shy at that first chapter. They always get up in their pulpits and read the second chapter.

Now I ask you if our religion teaches the dignity of woman? It teaches us that abominable idea of the sixth century—Augustine's idea—that motherhood is a curse; that woman is the author of sin, and is most corrupt. Can we ever cultivate any proper sense of self-respect as long as women take such sentiments from the mouths of the priesthood? . . . The canon laws are infamous—so infamous that a council of the Christian church was swamped by them. In republican America, and in the light of the nineteenth century, we must demand that our religion shall teach a higher idea in regard to woman. People seem to think we have reached the very end of theology; but let me say that the future is to be as much purer than the past as our immediate past has been better than the dark ages. We want to help roll off from the soul of woman the terrible superstitions that have so long repressed and crushed her. *(HWS IV: 60–61)*

Has Christianity Benefited Woman? – 1885

THE ASSERTION THAT WOMAN OWES all the advantages of her present position to the Christian church, has been repeated so often, that it is accepted as an established truth by those who would be unwilling to admit that all the injustice and degradation she has suffered might be logically traced to the same source. A consideration of woman's position before Christianity, under Christianity, and at the present time, shows that she is not indebted to any form of religion for one step of progress, or one new liberty; on the contrary, it has been through the perversion of her religious sentiments that she has been so long held in a condition of slavery. All religions thus far have taught the headship and superiority of man, the inferiority and subordination of woman. Whatever new dignity, honor, and self-respect the changing theologies may have brought to man, they have all alike brought to woman but another form of humiliation. History shows that the condition of woman has changed with different forms of civilization, and that she has enjoyed in some periods greater honor and dignity and more personal and property rights than have been accorded her in the Christian era. History shows, too, that the moral degradation of woman is due more to the theological superstitions than to all other influences together. . . .

In the fifth century the church fully developed the doctrine of original sin, making woman its weak and guilty anchor. To St. Augustine, whose early life was licentious and degraded, we are indebted for this idea, which was infused into the canon law, and was the basis of all the persecutions woman endured for centuries, in the drift of Christian opinion from the extremes of polygamy to celibacy, from the virtues of chivalry to the cruelties of witchcraft, when the church taught its devotees to shun woman as a temptation and defilement. It was this persecution, this crushing out of the feminine element in humanity, more than all other influences combined, that plunged the world into the dark ages, shadowing the slowly rolling centuries till now with woman's agonies and death, paralyzing literature, science, commerce, education, changing the features of art, the sentiments of poetry, the ethics of philosophy, from the tender, the loving, the beautiful, the grand, to the stern, the dark, the terrible. Even the paintings representing Jesus were gradually changed from the gentle, watchful shepherd to the stern, unrelenting judge. Harrowing representations of the temptation, the crucifixion, the judgment-day, the Inferno, were intensified and elaborated by Dante and Milton. Painter and poet vied with each other in their gloomy portrayals, while crafty bishops coined these crude terrors into canons, and timid, dishonest judges allowed them to throw their dark shadows over the civil law. . . . This idea is the chief block in the way of woman's advancement at this hour. *(North American Review, May 1885)*

The Pleasures Of Age – 1885

In her autobiography, Stanton quipped that it took her a full week to think of some "pleasures of age," an address given at a gathering for her seventieth birthday.

IN THE FULLER DEVELOPMENT of the feminine element in humanity, we shall have the impress of woman's thought and sentiment in government and religion, exalting justice, and equality in the one, love and tenderness in the other, anger and vindictive punishment having no place in either. Harriet Martineau said that the happiest day of her life was the day that she gave up the charge of her soul. I can say that the happiest period of my life has been since I emerged from the shadows and superstitions of the old theologies, relieved from all gloomy apprehension of the future, satisfied that as my labors and capacities were limited to this sphere of action, I was responsible for nothing beyond my horizon, as I could neither understand nor change the conditions of the unknown world. Giving ourselves, then, no trouble about the future, let us make the most of the present, and fill up our lives and earnest work here. The time has passed for the saints to withdraw from the world, to atone for their sins in fasting and prayer. One good woman laboring at her profession of healing the sick, bearing messages of good cheer to many a bedside, always active on the watchtower of faith and hope, with bright face and busy hands, is of more value to her day and generation than a regiment of saints who spend their day weeping and praying over the sins of the people. There is just the same difference in dignity and importance between women engaged in some earnest life purpose, and those who do nothing, that there is between men who labor in the trades and professions, and those who spend their time in yachts, horse-races and general amusements. To my youthful coadjutors in the woman suffrage work, into whose hands we are now passing the lamp of this great reform, that has lighted us through so many dark days of persecution, I would say, rest assured that your labors in this movement will prove a double blessing—to yourselves in the higher development it will bring you, and to the world in the nobler type of womanhood henceforth to share an equal place with man. *(Stanton's Seventieth Birthday, November 12, 1885, reprinted in Boston Investigator)*

"Religion For Women And Children" – 1886

This eloquently addressed one of Stanton's special concerns, that Liberals and free-thinking men paternalistically, even opportunistically, shielded female relatives and the laboring classes from enlightened thought. Christianity's role as "a powerful police institution" is roundly condemned.

An out-and-out English agnostic remarked to a friend, who wondered that he still said grace at table and regularly attended divine worship: "We must keep up the church as the most powerful police institution we have; it would be an awful calamity to take their religion from the laboring classes, and especially from women and children. All these are more easily governed through their fears, as their capacity to reason is very limited."

In regard to the first proposition, all history shows that there have been more outrages committed by the Church, through its ecclesiastics, in the name of religion, on the sacred rights of humanity and the best interests of society, than by all other organizations together.

It has, indeed, been, in all ages, "a powerful police institution," to rob the poor, to suppress free thought, to make martyrs of noble men and women; but when has it ever risked its own safety to fight the battles of the people against the oppressions of the state? When, by wise counsels as a united body, has it ever averted the settlement of one vexed question by war? In the prolonged anti-slavery struggle for forty years, it spoke with no certain sound, until the clashing arms and roaring cannon proclaimed liberty throughout the nation. But when the indignant masses awake from the lethargy of ages the world over, as they have already in France, and see how they have been deceived, defrauded, and priest-ridden, they will repudiate the Church and the creeds that have so long held them in bondage. As, with more general education, with the light and knowledge of science, the people cannot be much longer swayed by worn-out superstitions, is it not better for their spiritual teachers to begin now to teach them what is true, as far as they themselves know, and to stop teaching them mere speculations and superstitions, the wild vagaries of unbalanced minds, the accumulated errors of the ages? They tell us, by way of excuse for their unfaithfulness, that the people are not ready for a more rational theology, that the undeveloped mind is not prepared for the whole truth about anything. But a measure of the truth, as far as it goes, must be better than error; and, if they are always deluded with falsehoods, how will they ever be prepared to accept what is reasonable? We must remember that truth is the natural food for the human soul, the atmosphere in which all its finest qualities most readily develop. Hence, those who hold the vantage-ground of thought should give freely of their richest treasures to those who would be delivered from the errors of the past. We pride ourselves on the munificent charities of this Christian civilization, on our unbounded almsgiving to the poor and needy; but behind those outstretched hands, those appealing eyes and pleading lips, are hungering souls oppressed with fear of an angry God, an all-powerful devil, a judgment day, and everlasting punishment. . . .

While the people would be unspeakably happy to be lifted out of all their harassing superstitions and harrowing fears of the eternal future, it is the height of cruelty and injustice for the educated classes, who live on their labor, grinding them to powder by a cunning system of legislation, dooming them in this life to ignorance, poverty, and rags, to fasten on their sorrowing souls the belief that their miseries here are but the fore-shadowing of infinitely worst [sic] suffering hereafter. If we think it is not safe to tell them the simple truth, that we know nothing of what lies beyond our mortal horizon, we might at least picture for them some beautiful visions of peace and joy. . . .

And, as to the women and children,—ah! how little strong men dream of all they suffer in a sincere belief of the gloomy doctrines of our Christian theology! Men, with their steady nerves, strong muscles, equable temperaments, trained to reason and self-reliance, in contact with the stern facts of life, cannot comprehend the multiplied and ever-present fears and apprehensions of coming danger that poison the lives of most women and children, growing out of their more nervous organization, more fertile imaginations, and that natural timidity that accompanies a sense of help-lessness in danger. Alas for the children! Their lives are beset with fears. They are afraid of their parents at home, of their teachers in school, of the police in the street, and of the omnipresent God and devil, at all times and in all places. It is folly to hope much from the lessons of love, taught in sweet-sounding phrases, so long as they are reminded every hour in the day that they are doing something to make God angry and the devil smile. While fathers and husbands rejoice in their emancipation from the bond-age of the Christian theology, and discuss with each other the rationalism of the great German thinkers, of the French scientists, and the English historians, laughing among themselves at all the gods and the devils of the theologies that have made humanity tremble, now crumbled to dust, how can they calmly contemplate, from day to day, the fact that all these with-ering, crippling superstitions are being fastened on the minds of their own trusting wives and daughters, and their innocent young children, whom they are bound to protect, not only from physical harm, but spiritual slavery!

How carefully they would guard their children from measles, whoop-ing-cough, and scarlet fever—diseases that will never give them one-half the suffering that will come to them with a faith in the doctrines of origi-nal sin, an angry God, a cunning devil ever whispering in their ears, coax-ing them to lie and steal and swear, a day of judgment, the last trump, and everlasting punishment in a lake of fire!

And alas, too, for the pale-stricken mothers of the race who believe all this, and still more that, through their folly, through that one fatal interview in the Garden of Eden, all this misery entered the world, and hence the pangs of maternity were to be their punishment,—the curse pronounced in the beginning on all Eve's daughters. And multitudes of women believe this to-day, in stead of referring their sufferings to their artificial habits of life,—to tight waists, heavy skirts, high heels, improper diet, and want of exercise. Passages of Scripture perpetuating all these cruelties and absurdities are still read in our pulpits, with a holy unction that makes them seem plausible to unthinking minds. How can educated men of common sense and kind feeling live side by side with women and children year after year, and never share with them the freedom and blessedness of a more rational religion? A system of theology that the agnostics, the scientists, the philosophers, the historians, and the most enlightened and progressive clergymen themselves repudiate cannot be the most nourishing spiritual pabulum for women and children, to say nothing of the laboring women.

I can truly say, after an experience of seventy years, that all the cares and anxieties, the trials and disappointments, of my whole life, are light in the balance with my sufferings in childhood and youth from the horrible dogmas I sincerely believed and the gloomy environments connected with everything associated with the name of religion. . . . The memory of my own suffering has saved me from the cruelty of ever shadowing one young soul with any of the superstitions of our Christian religion. *(The Index, March 11, 1886)*

"A Gospel Of Humiliation" – c. 1888

. . . If we should select all the passages of Scripture in regard to women & print them on a single page, with all the canon laws, & the opinions of Bishops & clergymen published within the forty years of woman's struggle for justice we should exclaim, This is indeed 'a gospel of humiliation' for women. . . .

. . . no form of religion that subordinates one half the race to the other, can be said to benefit that half denied individual responsibility & independence and none of the tortures of the inquisition are as cruel & wicked as has been the perversion of the religious element in woman's nature in making her believe that these laws & devices of men emanated from the Creator of the universe. And as if all these teachings were not sufficiently humiliating, they insistently proclaim that our nature & highest happiness calls for this kind of authorized subjection. . . .

They not only tell us that we enjoy the position of inferior & subject, but to reconcile us to the situation they tell us of the dignity & glory of "subordination," that Christ came to exalt those virtues so essentially womanly, ministering to others, humility, self sacrifice, subordination. The chicanery & tergiversations of these crafty teachers in trying to reconcile woman to being robbed of all her natural rights to life liberty & happiness is exasperating beyond measure to those who are awake to the real situation. . . .

There has been no such organized cruelty & contempt for womanhood in the history of the world as during the last 1800 years. The persecutions of sex that grew out of celibacy, asceticism & witchcraft were more terrible than woman ever endured under any other form of religion. It is not to christianity as taught in the scriptures or exemplified in the church, that woman is indebted for the modicum of justice she enjoys to day. Civilization with its arts, inventions, discoveries, its trade of commerce, its science & rationalism has given us the advantages of our present position in spite of the dogmas of the church & ecclesiastical domination. The religions of the past may do for man as they are the outgrowth of his wants & highest ideals, & all alike make him sovreign [sic] of the universe, & the mother of the race his subject. The religion of the future that shall recognize the equality & dignity of woman will be realized in a higher development in the near future. I have no quarrel with any of the creeds or catechisms or the thirty-nine articles of the Christian faith except as they touch directly or indirectly the creation & destiny of woman & there I will accept none of them, for they all alike degrade the sex & make woman a slave & subject when she should be an equal factor in the state the church & the home. In how many churches do you ever see a woman a trustee, a deacon an elder or a pastor, and if a woman were nominated for one of these offices, the majority of her own sex would vote against her so demoralized are women by church teachings in regard to their own rights, duties & interests.

It is the spirit of the canon law, reaching through the centuries, that holds the devotees of the church outside the general movement for woman's enfranchisement to-day. The most important subject for the consideration of the church, the state, & the family is the status of woman; around this centers all human progress. Yet women themselves think the sacraments, the altars, the spires of their temples of worship, a new organ & choir, of more importance than themselves. The Protestant world has divided into numberless sects, in the singing of psalms with metre & without, on the sprinkling of babies, on the doctrine of free will as against foreordination, salvation by faith, or by works, the plenary inspiration of the scriptures, but none have divided on the great fact of woman's creation, nature, destiny, & true position in the scale of being. She is still regarded as an after-thought, a mere helpmeet, a weaker vessel, the author of sin, cursed of God, to be forever as a just punishment under the domination of man. And the most lamentable feature in all this is that woman herself thinks that it is of more consequence that she should be dipped, joined the church, & take the communion, than that she should be recognized as man's equal on earth & in his ideal God as the Heavenly Mother. . . . Without fear of contradiction, I can safely say that every step in progress that woman has made she has been assailed by ecclesiastics that her most vigilant unwearied opponents have always been the clergy & the religious press has always been the most bitter & unfair in its criticisms . . . *(Untitled manuscript on Family, State & Church, c. 1888)*

On The Sprinkling of Babies

WE FIND THE WHOLE WORLD STIRRED UP today with the discussion as to whether the Pope is infallible when any man or woman with two grains of common sense knows he is not. . . . it is of very little importance whether the Pope is infallible, the conception of the Virgin Mary immaculate, whether children should be sprinkled when babies or dipped when twenty-one, whether the devil has a personality or hell a locality. *("The True Republic," speech c. 1880s)*

Sermon From Text, Genesis 1:27

"What we call God is the infinite ideal of humanity," she wrote, advocating "the Religion of Humanity." Stanton thoughtfully offered a psychological analysis of patriarchal religion to a Free Religious audience. She argued that the way to equalize the "great moral forces" which are out of equilibrium is "through the recognition & elevation of women," degraded by the world religions. "When Theodore Parker, in his morning prayer on a beautiful Sunday, addressed the All-loving as 'Our Father and our Mother,' he struck a chord which will one day vibrate through the heart of universal humanity. It was a thought worth infinitely more than all the creeds of Christendom," Stanton wrote. The reason for the endurance of the Catholic Church, "older than any civilized government on the globe," is its token emphasis on the Virgin Mary, she contended. Although predicated on her favorite bible verse, this Stanton speech was primarily devoted to a feminist dissection of the trinity:

ALL THE EVILS THAT HAVE RESULTED from dignifying one sex & degrading the other may be traced to this central error,—a belief in a trinity of *masculine* Gods from which the *feminine* element is wholly eliminated.

. . . The subjection of woman has existed as an invariable element in Christian civilization. It could not be otherwise with the Godhead represented as a trinity of males. . . . The race has not yet reached its maturity when governed by reason. It is still governed by its emotions, often by its reverse passions, as hate, fear, greed, rather than by love, attraction, devotion. It will glorify woman when it comes to its reason. Positivists, who have everything on reason, whose religion is *masculoid*, point to the church of humanity which makes woman & especially the mother the central figure, the actual Divinity. It remains for us to take the next step & reunite both in the trinity of Father, Mother & Child. . . .

There is no power by which the human soul can be held in such bondage as through the religious emotions; no realm of thought where it is so difficult to displace error with truth as the religious realm. And so long as we base our religions on the fundamental error of a *"male* God" it is in vain to struggle for woman's equal status in the church; and until her equality is recognized, all talk of establishing a religion of humanity is idle since one half of humanity is in social, religious, political subjection to the other. I have often thought that we should take the first step for woman's freedom, & for that of humanity—when we shall have outgrown the popular idea of a male God in the skies or elsewhere: Then we might see & worship God *in* humanity; Then we might love home & deify each other. . . .

When woman discards its creeds, dogmas, & authorities she too will be free, & a free enlightened woman is a divine being, the savior of mankind. . . .

Stanton also took a hopeful view of the power of freethought:

I BELIEVE WE HAVE REACHED A POINT where the world of thought is ready to accept anything which can be proved to be true, whether it is endorsed by the church or not. That is a great step in advance. People no longer ask is this in the Bible, or according to Bible teachings, but is it true? Is it according to the nature of things? Nor does God's word in a book, nor does the church, affirm or deny this, but does god's human reason say it? is it according to logic & mathematics? Then, can it be proved practically? does it tend to make us happy? will it work? will it pay? These are the questions we ask to day; they are signs & tokens of an extended emancipation that has come so gradually that we hardly realize it.

. . . Thanks to the law of Progress, woman is awaking to the degradation she has endured in the name of religion, & is interpreting the laws of life for herself. *(Stanton undated manuscript, "Sermon From Text, Genesis 1:27")*

"An Expurgated Bible" – 1889

A newspaper, probably the Woman's Tribune in Lincoln, Nebraska, published this commentary lauding a court decision in which bible-reading was barred from public schools as both a religious and sectarian exercise:

INASMUCH AS THE BIBLE DEGRADES WOMAN and in innumerable passages teaches her absolute subjection to man in all relations in the State, the Church, the home and the whole world of work, it is to her interest that the Bible, in its present form, should be taken from the schools and from the rising generation of boys, as it teaches lessons of disrespect for the mothers of the race.

Or else an expurgated edition of the book should be got out, putting in one volume the grand declarations, moral lessons, poetry, science and philosophy, and in another all the christian mythologies for those who would value it as ancient literature.

The first would then be fit to place in the hands of the rising generation. E.C.S.

Worship of God In Man – 1892

Stanton composed several variations on this theme, including a similar essay, "The Ultimate Religion." Known for her bible critiques, Stanton here offered her view of the "Religion of Humanity," of course defining religion in its broadest, natural meaning: "to bind again, to unite those who have been separated":

As I READ THE SIGNS OF THE TIMES, I think the next form of religion will be the "Religion of Humanity," in which men and women will worship what they see of the divine in each other; the virtues, the beatitudes, the possibilities ascribed to Deity reflected in mortal beings. . . .The new religion will teach the dignity of human nature, and its infinite possibilities for development. Its believers will not remain forever in the valley of humiliation, confessing themselves in the Church service, on each returning Sabbath day, to be "miserable sinners" imploring the "good Lord to deliver them" from the consequences of violated law; but the new religion will inspire its worshippers with self-respect, with noble aspirations to attain diviner heights from day to day than they yet have reached. It will teach individual honesty and honor in word and deed, in all the relations of life. It will teach the solidarity of the race, that all must rise or fall as one. Its creed will be Justice, Liberty, Equality for all the children of the earth. It will teach our practical duties to man in this life, rather than our sentimental duties to God in fitting ourselves for the next life. . . .

It is folly to talk of a just government and a pure religion, in a nation where the State and the Church alike sustain an aristocracy of wealth and ease, while those who do the hard work of the world have no share in the blessings and riches, that their continued labors have made possible for others to enjoy. Is it just that the many should ever suffer, that the few may shine? To reconcile men to things as they are, we have sermons from the texts, "Blessed are the poor in spirit, for theirs is the kingdom of Heaven," "The poor ye have always with you," "Servants obey your masters," "Render unto Caesar the things that are Caesar's." As if poverty, servility, and authority were decrees of Heaven!

Such decrees will not do for our day and generation; the school-master is abroad, Webster's spelling book is a classic. The laboring classes have tasted the tree of knowledge and like the gods they begin to know good and evil. With new liberties and education they demand corresponding improvements in their environments; as they reach new vantage ground from time to time and survey broader fields of usefulness, they learn their rights and duties, their relations to one another, and their true place in the march of civilisation. "Equal rights to all" is the lesson for this hour. *(The Open Court, September 1892?)*

Shall The World's Fair Be Closed On Sunday? – 1893

Stanton felt so passionately about one state-church issue that she undertook a personal crusade to circulate a pamphlet objecting to the Sunday closing of the World's Fair in Chicago, apparently paying for and distributing it herself. It was reprinted in various newspapers, as well as The Woman's Tribune. Congress had voted to withhold appropriations to the Fair if it opened on Sundays, after being petitioned by 100,000 Americans, mostly—to Stanton's disgust—"concerned women." She ably mustered quotes and opinions from the New Testament and church leaders such as Calvin and Luther, as well as from contemporaries, to disprove the claims of the Sabbatarians. Neither Jesus nor Paul advocated keeping the Sabbath, Calvin deferred a sermon to attend a Sunday play, and Martin Luther favored dancing on Sunday rather than observing a Jewish code. The Sunday closing laws, she averred, were antithetical to family happiness and morality. She launched her broadside at a time the vote was being reconsidered. Her efforts paid off. Although many exhibits were closed, the Fair opened on Sundays.

. . . IT IS IN VERY BAD TASTE as well as grossly unjust, for Christians, comprising as they do, so very small a portion of the human family, to force their religious observances on representatives of all the nations on the earth.

. . . It has been our boast that we have no State religion, that here all sects occupy a common ground, that all faiths are equally respected. Then why should the Sunday of the Christian be more binding than that of the

Jew, the Quaker, the Seventh-day Baptist, or of that increasingly large class of educated, liberal-minded people who do not believe in any penal Sundays, or imposed religious test, but who do believe in a change of employment one day in seven, when those who do the hard work of the world shall have free access to all the libraries, the galleries of art, the museums, the concerts and the public parks, there to enjoy whatever innocent amusements they may desire.

... In Great Britain where only the churches and drinking saloons are open, Sunday is indeed the most gloomy period in the week. In London everybody looks disconsolate, while in Paris they all seem happy, families going everywhere together, to libraries, picture galleries, concerts and pleasant excursions. .... This act of Congress is a fatal blow at one of the vital principles of our Government and should be resisted by all who know the danger of recognizing any union in State and Church.

Stanton rebuked Christian ladies of leisure for embracing the view that "Sunday is more precious than humanity." Her pamphlet ended with a cogent review of constitutional provisions and Supreme Court rulings, such as Supreme Court Justice Samuel F. Miller's court finding that "The law knows no heresy, is committed to the support of no dogma, the establishment of no sect." (Stanton, "Shall The World's Fair Be Closed On Sunday?," The National Bulletin of the Woman's Tribune, February 1893)

"Christmas on the Mayflower" – 1893

In this talk before the Foremothers Dinner on December 22, 1893, in New York, Stanton lauded Anne Hutchinson, the Massachusetts Bay Colony heretic, as "the first rebellious foremother."

SHE AFFIRMED THE RIGHT of individual conscience & judgment, in all matters of faith, placing reason above church discipline, creeds & scriptures. She demanded the same liberty of thought for women, as man claimed for himself, & an equal position in the church.

I really do not wonder, when the men of the present day read about the independence of the foremothers, and what one woman like Anne Hutchinson could do to set a whole colony on the ears, that they are afraid to emancipate 30,000,000 of her descendants at one blow. How nervous our clergy would be, if they knew that every Monday morning the women of their congregations would assemble and pick their sermons all to pieces, separating the wheat from the chaff and throwing the latter to the winds! *(Manuscript, "Christmas on the Mayflower")*

"Women Do Not Wish To Vote" – 1894

WOMEN ARE TOO PROUD TO ADMIT that they want what they think they cannot get. They fear the ridicule of the men of their households, of the press, the disapproval of their clergymen who quote the Bible against larger liberties for their sex. . . . This one lesson of subjection and self sacrifice has been taught by creeds, codes, customs and constitutions all through the centuries and no wonder that woman has learned it so well. The most powerful influence on the human mind is through religious emotions, and all the leading religions on the earth teach the subjection of one sex and the domination of the other, thus enfeebling the love of liberty on the one side and stimulating the love of tyranny on the other. *(This front-page article appeared in The National Bulletin, a suffrage organ, Vol. 2, No. 3, April 1894)*

The Woman's Bible – 1895, 1898

Elizabeth Cady Stanton's best-known contribution to freethought is her two-volume **The Woman's Bible** *(1895, 1898). Although she tried valiantly to interest a committee of women scholars to critique the bible, and assembled about thirty women, only seven of them contributed to Volume I, and eight participated in the writing of Volume II. Stanton did most of the writing, fortunately, as her contributions are most memorable.*

In trying to rouse the interest of her cousin Elizabeth Miller Smith in the project, Stanton explained its purpose:

"1st I endeavor to show that it should not have authority as the 'Word of God.'

"2nd That all living creatures human and animal, of the female sex, are degraded under the Mosaic dispensation.

"3rd That the Pentateuch is full of contradictions. The first chapter of Genesis gives one account of the creation; the second and third quite another.

"4th, That the spirit is unfriendly to women all through . . . I say in plain English that the Lord did not talk to Moses, that Moses never saw his face and that Moses did not write the Pentateuch . . . The vast majority of women worship the Bible as a kind of fetich. I am trying to lift them out of that superstition." (Stanton to Mrs. Miller, New York, July 21st, 1887, Library of Congress)

Part I of The Woman's Bible was a bestseller which received press coverage that would be unheard of in today's conservative media. It received pages of press comments on its advance sheets. Favorable were such comments as:

"It is to be doubted if either Bishop Doane or Bishop Coxe, would dare venture into dialectics with Mrs. Stanton."—Buffalo Courier

"Robert G. Ingersoll is the only person on earth capable of a work equal to Mrs. Stanton's sensation, 'The Woman's Bible.' "—Chicago Times Herald

Just as helpful in promoting the book were the predictably blistering notices:

"And now the new woman is going to have a new Bible. The work of the devil."—State Journal, Ohio

Most notices were milder, such as the Los Angeles Times' sarcastic but noncommittal remark: "The new women are about to revise the Bible so as to make it conform to the advanced ideas of the omniscient sisterhood."

"Like other 'mistakes,' this too, in due time, will be regarded as 'a step in progress,' " Stanton wrote firmly at the end of her autobiography:

"It requires no courage now to demand the right of suffrage, temperance legislation, liberal divorce laws, or for women to fill church offices—these battles have been fought and won and the principle governing these demands conceded. But it still requires courage to question the divine inspiration of the Hebrew Writings as to the position of woman. Why should the myths, fables, and allegories of the Hebrews be held more sacred than those of the Assyrians and Egyptians, from whose literature most of them were derived? Seeing that the religious superstitions of women perpetuate their bondage more than all other adverse influences, I feel impelled to reiterate my demands for justice, liberty, and equality in the Church as well as in the State." **(Eighty Years:** *467–68, the last page of her autobiography)*

Stanton hailed the changes since the bible had been written, when "rationalism took the place of religion, and reason triumphed over superstition." **(The Woman's Bible I:** *80)*

In an interview prior to the publication of Volume II, Stanton spoke enthusiastically about her hopes for **The Woman's Bible:**

"The conviction grew in my mind that as long as women allowed themselves to be overcome by the preachers there was little hope for their political enfranchisement. If women could only see and realize the true position they hold in the bible I believe the main obstacle to suffrage would be removed. . . .

"I consider the bible the most degrading book that has ever been written about women. . . ." (Chicago Record, June 29, 1897)

Introduction To The Woman's Bible

*This introduced Part I of **The Woman's Bible**, published in 1895.*

FROM THE INAUGURATION OF THE MOVEMENT for woman's emancipation the Bible has been used to hold her in the "divinely ordained sphere," prescribed in the Old and New Testaments.

The canon and civil law; church and state; priests and legislators; all political parties and religious denominations have alike taught that woman was made after man, of man, and for man, an inferior being, subject to man. Creeds, codes, Scriptures and statutes, are all based on this idea. The fashions, forms, ceremonies and customs of society, church ordinances and discipline all grow out of this idea.

Of the old English common law, responsible for woman's civil and political status, Lord Brougham said, "it is a disgrace to the civilization and Christianity of the Nineteenth Century." Of the canon law, which is responsible for woman's status in the church, Charles Kingsley said, "this will never be a good world for women until the last remnant of the canon law is swept from the face of the earth."

The Bible teaches that woman brought sin and death into the world, that she precipitated the fall of the race, that she was arraigned before the judgment seat of Heaven, tried, condemned and sentenced. Marriage for her was to be a condition of bondage, maternity a period of suffering and anguish, and in silence and subjection, she was to play the role of a dependent on man's bounty for all her material wants, and for all the information she might desire on the vital questions of the hour, she was commanded to ask her husband at home. Here is the Bible position of woman briefly summed up.

Those who have the divine insight to translate, transpose and transfigure this mournful object of pity into an exalted, dignified personage, worthy our worship as the mother of the race, are to be congratulated as having a share of the occult mystic power of the eastern Mahatmas.

The plain English to the ordinary mind admits of no such liberal interpretation. The unvarnished texts speak for themselves. The canon law, church ordinances and Scriptures, are homogeneous, and all reflect the same spirit and sentiments.

These familiar texts are quoted by clergymen in their pulpits, by statesmen in the halls of legislation, by lawyers in the courts, and are echoed by the press of all civilized nations, and accepted by woman herself as "The Word of God." So perverted is the religious element in her nature, that with faith and works she is the chief support of the church and clergy; the very powers that make her emancipation impossible. When, in the early part of the Nineteenth Century, women began to protest against their civil and political degradation, they were referred to the Bible for an answer. When they protested against their unequal position in the church, they were referred to the Bible for an answer.

This led to a general and critical study of the Scriptures. Some, having made a fetish of these books and believing them to be the veritable "Word of God," with liberal translations, interpretations, allegories and symbols, glossed over the most objectionable features of the various books and clung to them as divinely inspired. Others, seeing the family resemblance between the Mosaic code, the canon law, and the old English common law, came to the conclusion that all alike emanated from the same source; wholly human in their origin and inspired by the natural love of domination in the historians. Others, bewildered with their doubts and fears, came to no conclusion. While their clergymen told them on the one hand, that they owed all the blessings and freedom they enjoyed to the Bible, on the other, they said it clearly marked out their circumscribed sphere of action: that the demands for political and civil rights were irreligious, dangerous to the stability of the home, the state and the church. Clerical appeals were circulated from time to time conjuring members of their churches to take no part in the anti-slavery or woman suffrage movements, as they were infidel in their tendencies, undermining the very foundations of society. No wonder the majority of women stood still, and with bowed heads, accepted the situation.

Listening to the varied opinions of women, I have long thought it would be interesting and profitable to get them clearly stated in book form. To this end six years ago I proposed to a committee of women to issue a Woman's Bible, that we might have women's commentaries on women's position in the Old and New Testaments. It was agreed on by several leading women in England and America and the work was begun, but from various causes it has been delayed, until now the idea is received with renewed enthusiasm, and a large committee has been formed, and we hope to complete the work within a year.

Those who have undertaken the labor are desirous to have some Hebrew and Greek scholars, versed in Biblical criticism, to gild our pages with their learning. Several distinguished women have been urged to do so, but they are afraid that their high reputation and scholarly attainments might be compromised by taking part in an enterprise that for a time may prove very unpopular. Hence we may not be able to get help from that class.

Others fear that they might compromise their evangelical faith by affiliating with those of more liberal views, who do not regard the Bible as the "Word of God," but like any other book, to be judged by its merits. If the Bible teaches the equality of Woman, why does the church refuse to ordain women to preach the gospel, to fill the offices of deacons and elders, and to administer the Sacraments, or to admit them as delegates to the Synods, General Assemblies and Conferences of the different denominations? They have never yet invited a woman to join one of their Revising Committees, nor tried to mitigate the sentence pronounced on her by changing one count in the indictment served on her in Paradise.

The large number of letters received, highly appreciative of the undertaking, is very encouraging to those who have inaugurated the movement, and indicate a growing self-respect and self-assertion in the women of this generation. But we have the usual array of objectors to meet and answer. One correspondent conjures us to suspend the work, as it is "ridiculous" for "women to attempt the revision of the Scriptures." I wonder if any man wrote to the late revising committee of Divines to stop their work on the ground that it was ridiculous for men to revise the Bible. Why is it more ridiculous for women to protest against her present status in the Old and New Testament, in the ordinances and discipline of the church, than in the statutes and constitution of the state? Why is it more ridiculous to arraign ecclesiastics for their false teaching and acts of injustice to women, than members of Congress and the House of Commons? Why is it more audacious to review Moses than Blackstone, the Jewish code of laws, than the English system of jurisprudence? Women have compelled their legislators in every state in this Union to so modify their statutes for women that the old common law is now almost a dead letter. Why not compel Bishops and Revising Committees to modify their creeds and dogmas? Forty years ago it seemed as ridiculous to timid, time-serving and retrograde folk for women to demand an expurgated edition of the laws, as it now does to demand an expurgated edition of the Liturgies and the Scriptures. Come, come, my conservative friend, wipe the dew off your spectacles, and see that the world is moving. Whatever your views may be as to the importance of the proposed work, your political and social degradation are but an outgrowth of your status in the Bible. When you express your aversion, based on a blind feeling of reverence in which reason has no control, to the revision of the Scriptures, you do but echo Cowper, who, when asked to read Paine's "Rights of Man," exclaimed, "No man shall convince me that I am improperly governed while I feel the contrary."

Others say it is not politic to rouse religious opposition. This much-lauded policy is but another word for cowardice. How can woman's position be changed from that of a subordinate to an equal, without opposition, without the broadest discussion of all the questions involved in her present degradation? For so far-reaching and momentous a reform as her complete independence, an entire revolution in all existing institutions is inevitable.

Let us remember that all reforms are interdependent, and that whatever is done to establish one principle on a solid basis, strengthens all. Reformers who are always compromising, have not yet grasped the idea that truth is the only safe ground to stand upon. The object of an individual life is not to carry one fragmentary measure in human progress, but to utter the highest truth clearly seen in all directions, and thus to round out and perfect a well balanced character. Was not the sum of influence exerted by John Stuart Mill on political, religious and social questions far greater than that of any statesman or reformer who has sedulously limited his sympathies and activities to carrying one specific measure? We have many women abundantly endowed with capabilities to understand and revise what men have thus far written. But they are all suffering from inherited ideas of their inferiority; they do not perceive it, yet such is the true explanation of their solicitude, lest they should seem to be too self-asserting.

Again there are some who write us that our work is a useless expenditure of force over a book that has lost its hold on the human mind. Most intelligent women, they say, regard it simply as the history of a rude people in a barbarous age, and have no more reverence for the Scriptures than any other work. So long as tens of thousands of Bibles are printed every year, and circulated over the whole habitable globe, and the masses in all English-speaking nations revere it as the word of God, it is vain to belittle its influence. The sentimental feelings we all have for those things we were educated to believe sacred, do not readily yield to pure reason. I distinctly remember the shudder that passed over me on seeing a mother take our family Bible to make a high seat for her child at table. It seemed such a desecration. I was tempted to protest against its use for such a purpose, and this, too, long after my reason had repudiated its divine authority.

To women still believing in the plenary inspiration of the Scriptures, we say give us by all means your exegesis in the light of the higher criticism learned men are now making, and illumine the Woman's Bible, with your inspiration.

Bible historians claim special inspiration for the Old and New Testaments containing most contradictory records of the same events, of miracles opposed to all known laws, of customs that degrade the female sex of all human and animal life, stated in most questionable language that could not be read in a promiscuous assembly, and call all this "The Word of God."

The only points in which I differ from all ecclesiastical teaching is that I do not believe that any man ever saw or talked with God, I do not believe that God inspired the Mosaic code, or told the historians what they say he did about woman, for all the religions on the face of the earth degrade her, and so long as woman accepts the position that they assign her, her emancipation is impossible. Whatever the Bible may be made to do in Hebrew or Greek, in plain English it does not exalt and dignify woman. My standpoint for criticism is the revised edition of 1888. I will so far honor the revising committee of nine men who have given us the best exegesis they can according to their ability, although Disraeli said the last one before he died, contained 150,000 blunders in the Hebrew, and 7,000 in the Greek.

But the verbal criticism in regard to woman's position amounts to little. The spirit is the same in all periods and languages, hostile to her as an equal.

There are some general principles in the holy books of all religions that teach love, charity, liberty, justice and equality for all the human family, there are many grand and beautiful passages, the golden rule has been echoed and re-echoed around the world. There are lofty examples of good and true men and women, all worthy our acceptance and example whose lustre cannot be dimmed by the false sentiments and vicious characters bound up in the same volume. The Bible cannot be accepted or rejected as a whole, its teachings are varied and its lessons differ widely from each other. In criticising the peccadilloes of Sarah, Rebecca and Rachel, we would not shadow the virtues of Deborah, Huldah and Vashti. In criticising the Mosaic code we would not question the wisdom of the golden rule and the fifth Commandment. Again the church claims special consecration for its cathedrals and priesthood, parts of these aristocratic churches are too holy for women to enter, boys were early introduced into the choirs for this reason, woman singing in an obscure corner closely veiled. A few of the more democratic denominations accord women some privileges, but invidious discriminations of sex are found in all religious organizations, and the most bitter outspoken enemies of woman are found among clergymen and bishops of the Protestant religion.*

The canon law, the Scriptures, the creeds and codes and church discipline of the leading religions bear the impress of fallible man, and not of our ideal great first cause, "the Spirit of all Good," that set the universe of matter and mind in motion, and by immutable law holds the land, the sea, the planets, revolving round the great centre of light and heat, each in its own elliptic, with millions of stars in harmony all singing together, the glory of creation forever and ever.

ELIZABETH CADY STANTON.

* See the address of Bishop Doane, June 7th, 1895, in the closing exercises of St. Agnes School, Albany.

Conclusion – The Woman's Bible

*This concluded the Appendix of **The Woman's Bible,** Part II, 1898.*

. . . I HAVE BEEN DEEPLY IMPRESSED with the difficulty of substituting reason for superstition in minds once perverted by a false faith. Women have been taught by their religious guardians that the Bible, unlike all other books, was written under the special inspiration of the Great Ruling Intelligence of the Universe. Not conversant with works on science and higher criticism, which point out its fabulous pretensions, they cling to it with an unreasoning tenacity, like a savage to his fetich. Though it is full of contradictions, absurdities and impossibilities, and bears the strongest evidence in every line of its human origin, and in moral sentiment is below many of the best books of our own day, they blindly worship it as the Word of God.

When you point out what in plain English it tells us God did say to his people in regard to woman, and there is no escape from its degrading teaching as to her position, then they shelter themselves under false translations, interpretations and symbolic meanings. It does not occur to them that men learned in the languages have revised the book many times, but made no change in woman's position. Though familiar with "the designs of God," trained in Biblical research and higher criticism, interpreters of signs and symbols and Egyptian hieroglyphics, learned astronomers and astrologers, yet they cannot twist out of the Old or New Testaments a message of justice, liberty or equality from God to the women of the nineteenth century!

The real difficulty in woman's case is that the whole foundation of the Christian religion rests on her temptation and man's fall, hence the necessity of a Redeemer and a plan of salvation. As the chief cause of this dire calamity, woman's degradation and subordination were made a necessity. If, however, we accept the Darwinian theory, that the race has been a gradual growth from the lower to a higher form of life, and that the story of the fall is a myth, we can exonerate the snake, emancipate the woman, and reconstruct a more rational religion for the nineteenth century, and thus escape all the perplexities of the Jewish mythology as of no more importance than those of the Greek, Persian and Egyptian. (II: 214)

Woman's Bigotry – c. 1896

This fragment completes the story of Stanton's crusade against a blue-law curtailment of the World's Fair:

IT IS SAID THAT UNDER THE LEADERSHIP of the "W.C.T.U.," [Women's Christian Temperance Union] association 100,000 petitions were presented in Congress, asking that no appropriation be made to the Exposition unless the managers pledged themselves to close the gates on Sunday, the only day the masses could visit the grounds. Thus sacrificing large classes of citizens to the prejudices of a few for the sacredness of one day of the week above all others. If the Christians could close the gates on Sunday, why not the Jews do the same on Saturday?

Now they want God & the Christian religion recognized in the constitution. They have denied Robert Ingersoll's right to lecture in a certain Hall in Chicago, or the platform of any of their organizations.

The Women generally are in favor of the most rigid Sunday laws.

Three different conventions of women have passed resolutions against 'The Woman's Bible.' As if a revising committee of thirty women had not as good a right to express their opinion of what is taught in the Scriptures, as a committee of Bishops.

There is no persecution so bitter as that in the name of religion. I published a leaflet in favor of opening the World's Fair on Sunday. Five hundred copies by chance fell into the hands of one of my devout friends, as sweet a little woman as ever known in other respects. She threw them all into the fire. Dear—said I, you have committed a state prison offense however, I shall not incarcerate you, but if you had lived in the time of Calvin you would as readily [have] burned me & thought you did God service.

Much as I desire the suffrage, I would rather never vote, than to see the policy of our government, at the mercy of the religious bigotry of such women. My heart's desire is to lift women out of all these dangerous, degrading superstitions, & to this end will I labor my remaining days on earth.

Seeing the danger of a union in state & church in the old world, our fathers determined to lay the foundations of our republic, in the equal rights of all citizens, without regard to sect or creed, Quaker, Baptist, Jew,

Catholic, Protestant, Infidel, Agnostic, all enjoy the same freedom. Any encroachments on this principle should be firmly resisted. *(Holograph rough draft. c. 1896. A published version not quite as passionate but similar to this appears in the essay "The Effect of Woman Suffrage on Questions of Morals and Religion," from the pamphlet "Bible and Church Degrade Woman," 1896)*

"The Effect of Woman Suffrage on Questions of Morals and Religion" – 1896

Cognizant that some freethinking men feared "the effect of woman's religious bigotry on the secular nature of our government" should women win the vote, Stanton addressed those fears head on.

THERE IS NO DOUBT that in their present religious bondage, the political influence of women would be against the secular nature of our government, so carefully guarded by the fathers. They would, if possible, restore the Puritan Sabbath and sumptuary laws, and have the name of God and the Christian religion recognized in the National Constitution, thus granting privileges to one sect over another, involving no end of religious persecutions.

Admit all the danger herein set forth, shall we deny the right of self-government to women, because through ignorance they may at first abuse their power? No, no. . . .

Woman's education has been left too much to the church, which has made her a devotee, training her sentiments and emotions at the expense of her reason and common sense. . . .

We must turn the tide of her enthusiasm from the church to the state, arouse her patriotism; awaken her interest in great public questions, on which depend the stability of the republic and the elevation of the race, instead of wasting so much time and thought on the salvation of her own soul. In her education hereafter substitute reason for blind faith, science for theological superstitions; then will our most liberal men, our scientists, scholars and statesmen, find in the women of their households a reserve force for building a higher, purer civilization. *("The Effect of Woman Suffrage on Questions of Morals and Religion," in "Bible and Church Degrade Woman" pamphlet, 1896)*

"The Bible Hurled" – 1897

IN THE EARLY DAYS OF WOMAN-SUFFRAGE AGITATION, I saw that the greatest obstacle we had to overcome was the bible. It was hurled at us on every side. The ballot for woman was contrary to God's holy ordinance. Woman was born to be submissive, subjective; she must be subservient to her husband in all things and at all times. These were the admonitions of pulpit and press. *(An Interview with the Chicago Record, June 29, 1897)*

"Memory of My Own Sufferings" – 1898

I CAN TRULY SAY, after an experience of seventy years, that all the cares and anxieties, the trials and disappointments of my whole life, are light, when balanced with my sufferings in childhood and youth from the theological dogmas which I sincerely believed, and the gloom connected with everything associated with the name of religion, the church, the parsonage, the graveyard, and the solemn, tolling bell. . . . I early believed myself a veritable child of the Evil One, and suffered endless fears lest he should come some night and claim me as his own. To me he was a personal, ever-present reality, crouching in a dark corner of the nursery. Ah! how many times I have stolen out of bed, and sat shivering on the stairs, where the hall lamp and the sound of voices from the parlor would, in a measure, mitigate my terror. Thanks to a vigorous constitution and overflowing animal spirits, I was able to endure for years the strain of these depressing influences, until my reasoning powers and common sense triumphed at last over my imagination. The memory of my own suffering has prevented me from ever shadowing one young soul with any of the superstitions of the Christian religion. (**Eighty Years:** 24–26.)

"That Everlasting No! No! No!" – 1898

Religion had played a suffocating role in her childhood. Stanton recalled asking her stern Scotch Presbyterian nurse:

". . . WHY IS IT EVERYTHING WE LIKE TO DO IS A SIN, and that everything we dislike is commanded by God or someone on earth. I am so tired of that everlasting no! no! no! At school, at home, everywhere it is *no*! Even at church all the commandments begin 'Thou shalt not.' I suppose God will say 'no' to all we like in the next world, just as you do here." *(**Eighty Years**, 10–11. Clearly enjoying the impact of this anecdote, Stanton played fast and loose with it, attributing her rebellion at "Thou shalt not" to one of her sons in an interview in the Philadelphia Sunday Press, "Home Life A Century Ago" December 8, 1901)*

"Clerical Assumptions"

This fragmentary, undated handwritten manuscript offers a scorching critique of clergy prerogative and self-protective actions to retain what Stanton called its "monopoly" over birth, marriage and death, as well as repressive Sunday blue laws. Stanton was particularly indignant over Pittsburgh brethren who wanted to stop Monday newspapers being set on Sundays:

IF THE SUNDAY PAPERS contained a single column as questionable [as the] morals & decency in innumerable chapters in the Bible they would have been suppressed long ago as obscene literature. . . . The clergy would not object to see the whole American people after listening to pulpit platitudes for hours to sit the remainder of the day & far into the night Bibles in hand, reading about . . . . what Abraham Isaac & Jacob Solomon & Daniel did . . . *(Stanton undated, incomplete manuscript)*

Death of Ingersoll – 1899

NO DEATH OUTSIDE MY OWN FAMILY could fill me with such sadness. . . . he sacrificed wealth, position, social recognition, and calmly endured ridicule and bitter persecution to strengthen and perpetuate the conflict between science and theology. . . . The future will rank him among the great heroes of the nineteenth century. *(Boston Investigator, August 5, 1899)*

My Creed

In this, one of her last manuscripts, Stanton turns religious dogma on its head. God is nature:

. . . THE SUN MOON & STARS the constellations the days & nights, the seasons . . . The centripetal & centrifugal forces, positive & negative magnetism, the laws of gravitation cohesion attraction are all immutable & unchangeable one & all moving in harmony together.

This attorney's daughter considered the law "beneficent" but rejected the idea of Special Providence:

THE PAIN WE SUFFER in violating Law warns us against danger. Our sorrows in life are not caused by the direct fiat of a malevolent Being but by our own ignorance or indifference to the laws of our being. . . .

I see inexorable law everywhere, cause & effect, our sufferings & prayers do not mitigate one iota the effect of violated law either in the moral or material world[.] If we defy the law of gravitation, a broken neck or leg will be the penalty[.]

Prayer was useless, except for any "effect on ourselves":

IF WE ARE GOVERNED BY UNCHANGEABLE LAW where is the use of prayer?

We must understand that we hold our destiny in our own hands, whether for weal or woe are wholly responsible. Man has proved himself equal to the gravest responsibilities this life involves, he too possesses the elements of sovereignty wisdom goodness & power[.] To govern himself

& live in harmony with the laws of the universe is his first duty. The greatest ruler on earth is he that governs himself, . . . The Episcopal prayers chanted round the globe each returning Sabbath day "Oh Lord have mercy upon us miserable sinners" is most demoralizing. . . . *("My Creed," no date, transcription of nearly illegible script provided in Papers of Elizabeth Cady Stanton and Susan B. Anthony, Holland & Gordon, editors)*

An Honored Place for the Bible In English Literature – 1902

In two letters written close to her death, Stanton reiterated the views of a lifetime about the bible. In one of her last letters, she suggests the "honored place" for the bible is to delete all the "mythologies and abominations, all that degrades the mothers of the race" so that what is left "we might safely place in the schools and in the hands of our children," while the expurgations "might be preserved for those who would value it as a specimen of ancient literature."

I FOUND NOTHING GRAND in the history of the Jews nor in the morals inculcated in the Pentateuch. Surely the writers had a very low idea of the nature of their god. They made him not only anthropomorphic, but of the very lowest type, jealous and revengeful, loving violence rather than mercy. I know of no other books that so fully teach the subjection and degradation of woman. *(Stanton, "The Bible & Woman," Boston Investigator, April 19, 1902)*

❦

IT IS ONE OF THE MYSTERIES THAT WOMAN, who has suffered so intensely from the rule of the church, still worships her destroyer and "licks the hand that's raised to shed her blood." *("An Honored Place for the Bible In English Literature," New York American and (?), Sunday, October 5, 1902)*

Lucy N. Colman

11

Lucy N. Colman

THE ABOLITIONIST INFIDEL

July 26, 1818 – January 18, 1906

If your Bible is an argument for the degradation of woman, and the abuse by whipping of little children, I advise you to put it away, and use your common sense instead.

The Truth Seeker, *March 5, 1887*

AN ARDENT ABOLITIONIST, Lucy Newhall Colman left the New England church because of its complicity with slavery, later renouncing the Unitarian and Universalist creeds as well, becoming a reader and contributor to *The Truth Seeker* for a quarter-century.

Born in Sturbridge, Massachusetts, to the Danforth family, her mother a direct descendant of John and Priscilla Alden, she was married at eighteen to John M. Davis of Dighton, Massachusetts, and widowed at twenty-four when Davis died of consumption. She remarried at twenty-six and became a mother at twenty-eight:

"I always like to write the word 'Mother' with a capital M. To me it is the most wonderful word in all the language; it means joy that can never be equaled. I can never forget the ecstasy that came over me when I first looked in the face of my child, and knew that it was mine, but with the joy came the remembrance of the slave mother's agony as she looked upon her child and knew its fate," she wrote in "Reminiscence," her column for *The Truth Seeker.*

Her second husband, an engineer, was negligently killed in an accident on the New York Central Railroad, leaving her to support her seven-year-old daughter, Gertrude. The Railroad paid for a grand funeral, running extra trains and giving free fare to those in attendance, estimated at two thousand mourners. But when Lucy asked for financial assistance, it was refused. So was employment with the railroad company. She applied for various positions, such as clerk at the "ladies' window" in a post office, and was turned away each time because of her sex.

"This was a time of 'woman's wrongs,' " she wrote. "I had given up the church, more because of its complicity with slavery than from a full understanding of the foolishness of its creeds." (*Truth Seeker*, February 19, 1887)

She became a school teacher in Rochester, earning $350 a year for work that a man was paid $800 for performing. When offered a post at the "colored school" in Rochester, she took the position, then advised the parents to send their children to schools in their own districts, until the school was empty and surrounding schools integrated, all in the course of a year.

When Susan B. Anthony invited Lucy to read a paper at a New York convention of teachers, Lucy caused a sensation by urging the abolition of corporal punishment in Rochester schools.

"If your Bible is an argument for the degradation of woman, and the abuse by whipping of little children, I advise you to put it away, and use your common sense instead." The session raged into the night against the Infidel-Abolitionist.

Soon she gave up teaching for abolition work, planning her first meeting with abolitionist Amy Post, then traveling widely as an abolitionist lecturer in Michigan, Ohio, Indiana, Illinois, New York and Pennsylvania, and making some forays into Wisconsin and Iowa. She dabbled in spiritualism for a time, introduced to it at the Western Anti-Slavery Society in Michigan.

Lucy as an abolitionist was "mobbed" many times, even in the North. More than once she was pelted with eggs. Lucy invariably found the church to be the "bulwark of slavery" and ministers the ringleaders of mobs attacking her speeches. "God was often informed of my presence, and told of my hostility to him and his earthly church. . . . Neither threats nor prayers had any effect upon my stay." (*The Truth Seeker*, April 23, 1887)

She became an agent of the Western Society of the American Antislavery Society, forced to earn her own keep, which meant confining herself to one meal a day and going without a fire in her room.

Like most women abolitionists, she soon became involved in advocacy for women's rights. She was a "who's who in the ranks" of feminism and freethought in 1878, on the platform with Elizabeth Cady Stanton, Matilda Joslyn Gage, Parker Pillsbury, Frederick Douglass, and Ella E. Gibson.

Her daughter Gertrude entered the New England Woman's Medical College in 1862, and died within two weeks. Frederick Douglass conducted the funeral. Lucy then served as matron in the National Colored Orphan Asylum in Washington, D.C., and later taught at a "colored school" in Georgetown, holding many philanthropic positions.

In later years she was a firm freethinker, working with *The Truth Seeker* publication against Anthony Comstock's censorship. She penned *Reminiscences* about her adventurous life and died in her Syracuse home at eighty-eight.

Reminiscences

This originally appeared in The Truth Seeker, January 29, 1887. "Liberalism," which Colman refers to, was identified at that time with the freethought movement.

I DO NOT REMEMBER AT WHAT AGE I learned the astounding lesson that in this so-called Republican country there were several millions of human beings who were bought and sold like the beasts of the field; but it must have been almost in my babyhood, for I well remember being taught the cradle song by my mother, who died when I was five years of age. Let me give a few verses of this song, which Christian mothers taught their children:

> I thank the goodness and the grace
> That on my birth hath smiled,
> And made me in these Christian days
> A happy English child.
>
> I was not born, as thousands are,
> Where God was never known,
> And taught to pray a useless prayer
> To blocks of wood and stone.
>
> I was not born a little slave
> To labor in the sun,
> And wish I were but in my grave,
> And all my labor done.

I think my pious mother must have been sorely puzzled to answer satisfactorily to herself the questions which I was almost constantly asking her: "Why did God let children be slaves? and if God made little children, why did he make them black? if that were the reasons they were slaves? and was God good?" and many others of the same nature. This being a slave seemed to me, even at that time, the worst of all calamities, save one, that could befall anybody, and that other was the going to hell to be burnt forever in actual fire.

My poor little brain was so excited, in trying to find answers to these many questions, that I wonder that I did not entirely lose my senses and become idiotic. Perhaps the death of my mother, and the changes that naturally followed in the family, served to take my mind from this particular problem in theology.

About this time, from 1824 to 1830, there swept over New England what was called a "revival of religion." As I looked back upon it, it seems like some scourge or plague, so great was the sorrow that followed in its wake. Protracted meetings were everywhere the order of the day; sensational ministers were sought for, and employed to preach, with all the effect possible, the coming of the day of judgment and the sure doom of the impenitent.

Here was another problem to be solved—of what use was preaching or praying for those who were elected from the foundation of the world to be saved? And how worse than useless to try by any means to avert the doom of those who were fore-ordained to destruction! My queries, no matter to whom addressed, always received the same answer: "Child, Satan desires to have you, and so he is putting such questions into your head. Answer him, as did the savior, 'Get thee behind me;' and remember it is very wicked to reason upon the ways of God. You have the holy Bible; read that and accept it; it is God's word." At last, in despair, I began to read the Bible, consecutively, chapter by chapter; but, alas! I found it wholly inexplicable; and when I went to my good Christian aunt (who was in the place of mother to me) and begged her to tell me what such things meant, and why God used such filthy words, and what was the good of such laws, and why women were required to do things that were wrong in the nature of things, the only answer she could give me was, "I don't know; put away the Bible till you are older; read now the Psalms and the New Testament."

Such was the mental food given to children to digest sixty and seventy years ago. Is it better to-day? Liberalism has so permeated thought that like homeopathy in medicine (all pathies being so much afflicted by it that no respectable doctor salivates with calomel, or denies to a patient burning up with fever cold water), so the Protestant religion in all its different creeds is a mild mixture compared to what it was at the time of which I am writing. Perhaps for the reason that its hideousness is so nicely covered there is more need that Liberals be on the alert. Christianity demands entire subjection to its edicts; no matter that it keeps in the background the damnation of infants in another world, if it shall continue, as to-day, to teach, not only in Sunday-schools, but in public schools, supported by the entire public, the doctrines of the Bible. Until the majority of the people are allowed mental liberty, we are not safe. To-day, in this year 287 since Bruno gave his life in defense of liberty of thought, a citizen of New York is under arrest in the state of New Jersey for ridiculing the idea of the God of the universe being born of a woman and subject to all the ailments of babyhood. It is to be hoped that the jury will fail to convict, but the intelligence of a New Jersey juryman is, at the least, questionable. Freethinkers everywhere should use their utmost efforts to cause the removal from our statute-books of laws that make free speaking a crime. Within three years three persons have suffered imprisonment in England for caricaturing the God of the Established Church of that realm. Christians of this country and of England do not hesitate to go into foreign countries, decry their gods, and demolish the representatives of such gods, and if the nations object the sword soon settles the matter.

At the time when Mr. Garrison first published his demand for the immediate and unconditional emancipation of the slave, all *respectable* people considered themselves Christians. The different sects denied the name to each other, but each sect assumed the name for themselves. The Presbyterian, who was at that time Christian *par excellence*, refused to fellowship [with] the Unitarian, because the Unitarian denied that Jesus of Nazareth was the real God—he made him out a strange being, hardly intelligible to himself perhaps, but surely not God. Presbyterians and Unitarians alike denied the Christian name to Universalists, though the Universalist took excellent care of the son of God, making him not exactly equal to the Father God, but of great importance in the godhead to the human family, in that he had "willingly suffered death for every individual, and in so doing had paid to his Father (the principal God) the debt which Adam and Eve had entailed upon all their descendants forever and forever." This debt once paid, the Universalist persistently taught, had "destroyed death and hell, and even him that had the power of death—the devil." And so they were denied the Christian name, for of what use was a creed without a burning hell and a devil to so tempt human beings that few only could escape the eternal flames?

There lived at this time a lady in western Massachusetts somewhat famed as a writer, who left the Presbyterian church and joined the Unitarian. This lady was a great favorite with an aunt of hers, who considered this new heresy a sin fatal to salvation, but she was so warmly attached to this very sinful niece that she could not deny herself the pleasure of frequently visiting her. One day, when taking leave of the niece after a pleasant day's visit, the aunt embraced her friend very warmly, and, with the tears falling profusely, said to her: "Oh, do come and see me very often while we live, as you know when we die we shall be separated forever." Such was the assurance with which a certain class of Christians were endowed that they could with great certainty fix the eternal state of themselves and others.

Syracuse, January 17, 287.

Marian Evans ("George Eliot")

12

Marian Evans

"GEORGE ELIOT"

November 22, 1819 – December 22, 1880

The clergy are, practically, the most irresponsible of all talkers.
"Evangelical Teaching: Dr. Cumming," 1855

NÉE MARY ANN EVANS, the ranking Victorian British novelist became known by her penname "George Eliot."

"Mary Ann" lived her first twenty-one years at a farmstead in Derbyshire, where her father was estate manager. As the last child of her father's second marriage, she was a special favorite with him. Musically talented, she received, for a woman in her day, a good education, learning French, German and Italian, continuing out of school to read widely and take instruction. Influenced by a favorite governess, shy Mary Ann was a religious evangelical as an adolescent, even toying with Calvinism at one time. A religious poem was her first published work.

She was first exposed to freethought and skeptical reading through family friend Charles Bray, a manufacturer at Rosehill. Bray's brother-in-law, Charles Hennell, had recently written *An Inquiry into the Origins of Christianity*, rejecting miracles and the supernatural. Her eyes opened to religion, however painfully, conscientious Mary Ann gave up religion and stopped attending church. Her father refused to live with her, sending her to live with a sister, until Mary Ann consoled him by promising to reexamine her feelings. According to biographers, she learned a lesson that was a theme in her fiction: that human relationships are more important than sect or dogma.

Far from changing her views, Mary Ann proceeded to the monumental task of translating Strauss' *Das Leben Jesu*, her translation appearing anonymously in 1846. Drawn to the pantheism of Spinoza and Wordsworth, she also admired

George Sand.

After her father died in 1849, a liberated Mary Ann spent several months with friends in Geneva, then went to live with the Brays when she returned to England. She began a translation of Spinoza's *Tractatus-Theologico-Politicus* which was never finished. When George Chapman took over *The Westminister Review* from John Stuart Mill, Chapman offered her a position. Although unpaid, it allowed her to meet a wide array of writers and thinkers. Besides her heavy burden of editorial work, she translated Feuerbach's *The Essence of Christianity* (1854), the only book ever published under her own name. That year the shy, respectable writer scandalized British society by sending notices to friends announcing she had entered a free "union" with George Henry Lewes, editor of *The Leader*, who was unable to divorce his first, mentally-ill wife. The pair lived harmoniously together for the next twenty-four years, until his death, but suffered social ostracism, and financial hardship, as they were responsible not just for themselves but for Lewes' wife and children.

Mary Ann became salaried at the rate of £50 a year for editing the "Belles Lettres" section of *The Westminister*, and began writing essays and reviews. One of her most famous essays, published in 1855, was an analysis of Dr. Cumming, a popular evangelical preacher in Great Britain. [See selection] Under Lewes' supportive encouragement, "Marian," as she now called herself, began her impressive career. Her first story, "Amas Barton," later published in *Scenes of Clerical Life*, appeared in *Blackwood's Magazine* in 1857. Following successful *Scenes of Clerical Life* came *Adam Bede* (1859), *The Mill on the Floss* (1860), and *Silas Marner* (1861). She went to Italy to research Savonarola, writing *Romola* (1863), then traveled to Spain, writing the Positivist poem *The Spanish Gypsy* (1868). *Middlemarch* (1871) gave her financial independence. Her last two novels were lesser works.

Freethought themes in her writings, which invariably feature strong heroines, include her humanist vision of the importance of the welfare of humanity in *this* world. Her poem, "O May I Join the Choir Invisible" expressed her views: "O may I join the choir invisible/Of those immortal dead who live again/In minds made better by their presence . . ."

As the couple settled into a comfortable lifestyle, purchasing a house in the country, Lewes died of a heart attack in 1878. Marian became reclusive in her grief, working to publish his writings and establishing a scholarship in physiology in his memory.

At sixty-one in 1880, she married John Walter Cross, an admiring banker about twenty years younger than she. She died of pneumonia before her marriage was a year old. *Essays and Leaves from a Note-Book* was published in 1884. A volume of her letters and other writings was published in 1885.

Marian Evans

Evangelical Teaching: Dr. Cumming

This is excerpted from the title essay, which first appeared in Westminster Review, October 1855.

GIVEN, A MAN WITH MODERATE INTELLECT, a moral standard not higher than the average, some rhetorical affluence and great glibness of speech, what is the career in which, without the aid of birth or money, he may most easily attain power and reputation in English society? Where is that Goshen of mediocrity in which a smattering of science and learning will pass for profound instruction, where platitudes will be accepted as wisdom, bigoted narrowness as holy zeal, unctuous egoism as God-given piety? Let such a man become an evangelical preacher; he will then find it possible to reconcile small ability with great ambition, superficial knowledge with the prestige of erudition, a middling morale with a high reputation for sanctity. Let him shun practical extremes and be ultra only in what is purely theoretic: let him be stringent on predestination, but latitudinarian on fasting; unflinching in insisting on the Eternity of punishment, but diffident of curtailing the substantial comforts of Time; ardent and imaginative on the pre-millennial advent of Christ, but cold and cautious towards every other infringement of the *status quo*. Let him fish for souls not with the bait of inconvenient singularity, but with the dragnet of comfortable conformity. Let him be hard and literal in his interpretation only when he wants to hurl texts at the heads of unbelievers and adversaries, but when the letter of the Scriptures presses too closely on the genteel Christianity of the nineteenth century, let him use his spiritualizing alembic and disperse it into impalpable ether. Let him preach less of Christ than of Antichrist; let him be less definite in showing what sin is than in showing who is the Man of Sin, less expansive on the blessedness of faith than on the accursedness of infidelity. . . . In this way he will draw men to him by the strong cords of their passions, made reason-proof by being baptized with the name of piety. In this way he may gain a metropolitan pulpit; the avenues to his church will be as crowded as the passages to the opera; he has but to print his prophetic sermons and bind them in lilac and gold, and they will adorn the drawing-room table of all evangelical ladies, who will regard as a sort of pious 'light reading' the demonstration that the prophecy of the locusts whose sting is in their tail, is fulfilled in the fact of the Turkish commander's having taken a horse's tail for his standard, and that the French are the very frogs predicted in the Revelations.

Pleasant to the clerical flesh under such circumstances is the arrival of Sunday! Somewhat at a disadvantage during the week, in the presence of working-day interests and lay splendours, on Sunday the preacher becomes the cynosure of a thousand eyes, and predominates at once over the Amphitryon with whom he dines, and the most captious member of his church or vestry. He has an immense advantage over all other public speakers. The platform orator is subject to the criticism of hisses and groans. Counsel for the plaintiff expects the retort of counsel for the defendant. The honourable gentleman on one side of the House is liable to have his facts and figures shown up by his honourable friend on the opposite side. Even the scientific or literary lecturer, if he is dull or incompetent, may see the best part of his audience quietly slip out one by one. But the preacher is completely master of the situation: no one may hiss, no one may depart. Like the writer of imaginary conversations, he may put what imbecilities he pleases into the mouths of his antagonists, and swell with triumph when he has refuted them. He may riot in gratuitous assertions, confident that no man will contradict him; he may exercise perfect free-will in logic, and invent illustrative experience; he may give an evangelical edition of history with the inconvenient facts omitted:—all this he may do with impunity, certain that those of his hearers who are not sympathizing are not listening. For the Press has no band of critics who go the round of the churches and chapels, and are on the watch for a slip or defect in the preacher, to make a 'feature' in their article: the clergy are, practically, the most irresponsible of all talkers.

Susan B. Anthony
(The Schlesinger Library, Radcliffe College)

13

Susan B. Anthony

"A CREED OF PERFECT EQUALITY"

February 15, 1820 – March 13, 1906

Cautious, careful people, always casting about to preserve their reputation and social standing, never can bring about a reform. Those who are really in earnest must be willing to be anything or nothing in the world's estimation, and publicly and privately, in season and out, avow their sympathy with despised and persecuted ideas and their advocates, and bear the consequences.

The Life and Work of Susan B. Anthony, *Volume I, page 197*

AFTER ATTENDING AN INSULTING SERMON on "Woman and Scepticism" delivered in 1885 by Rev. Doctor Patton, President of Howard University, Susan B. Anthony made headlines by remarking as she shook his hand: "Doctor, your mother, if you have one, should lay you across her knee and give you a good spanking for that sermon." (Harper, *Life and Work of Susan B. Anthony* II: 596)

Susan had no tolerance for any sect, belief or group that did not embrace her creed: "the perfect equality of women."

"To-day Miss Anthony is an agnostic," Stanton noted in her autobiography. "As to the nature of the Godhead and of the life beyond her horizon she does not profess to know anything. Every energy of her soul is centered upon the needs of this world. To her, work is worship. She has not stood aside, shivering in the cold shadows of uncertainty, but has moved on with the whirling world, has done the good given her to do, and thus, in darkest hours, has been sustained by an unfaltering faith in the final perfection of all things." (Stanton, *Eighty Years & More*: 161)

Susan Brownell Anthony, second of eight children born to a Quaker father and Baptist mother, taught school from ages fifteen to thirty before devoting her life to reform. She worked first for abolition and temperance, drawn to feminism after meeting Elizabeth Cady Stanton in 1850.

Recalled Stanton: ". . . whenever I saw that stately Quaker girl coming across my lawn, I knew that some happy convocation of the sons of Adam was to be set by the ears, by one of our appeals or resolutions. . . . We never met without issuing a pronunciamento on some question. In thought and sympathy we were one, and in the division of labor we exactly complemented each other. In writing we did better work than either could alone." (pp. 165–166)

Muzzled at a temperance rally, in 1852 Susan organized the Woman's New York State Temperance Society, with Stanton at the helm, meeting new indignity when the World's Temperance Convention the next year refused to recognize women delegates. She shocked the 1853 New York State Teachers' Association—whose majority female membership, earning half-pay, was expected to remain in silence—by daring to speak at the gathering. Stanton wrote: "If all the witches that had been drowned, burned, and hung in the Old World and the New had suddenly appeared on the platform, threatening vengeance for their wrongs, the officers of that convention could not have been thrown into greater consternation." (*History of Woman Suffrage* I: 513)

For several years Susan traveled the mob circuit as a New York agent for William Lloyd Garrison's radical American Anti-Slavery Society. She called for overthrow of the government and its "blood-stained" Constitution of the fathers. Counseling a skeptical Stanton to put aside the woman question during the Civil War, she organized the Women's Loyal National League, which collected more than a hundred thousand signatures calling for constitutional emancipation of slaves. Congress drafted constitutional amendments to put "male" into the Constitution for the first time, and enfranchise only black men. Betrayed Anthony and Stanton accepted the offer of financing from a wealthy Democrat with a less than sterling reputation to publish the weekly *The Revolution*, to protest exclusion of women from the suffrage amendment. Its motto: "Men, Their Rights and Nothing More; Women, Their Rights and Nothing Less." Their benefactor proved fickle, and in May 1870, Susan sold the newspaper, assuming a $10,000 debt which it took her seven years of lecturing to discharge.

In May 1869, Susan, with Stanton, Ernestine Rose, Matilda Joslyn Gage and a host of other women, formed the National Woman Suffrage Association, splitting from suffragists who counseled it was the " [Male] Negro's Hour." The NWSA became the radical arm, while dissidents formed the American Woman Suffrage Association. Susan devoted the next thirty years to national and state suffrage campaigns. She was arrested and convicted for casting a ballot in the 1872 presidential election, never paying the $100 fine.

Plain-spoken and unmarried, Susan was an early magnet for public abuse, although after fifty years of tireless activism she affectionately became known as "Aunt Susan" (even "Saint Susan") by suffrage workers and the press.

Although she put suffrage above other concerns, it was far from her only interest. In 1860, she was widely condemned by abolitionists for sheltering a fugitive battered wife and daughter from a Massachusetts politician. She had a longstanding interest in women's labor, equal pay for equal work, prostitution, divorce and the economics of female dependence and subservience, freely speaking about "sex slavery." She was a passionate champion of coeducation and public schools.

Susan's most famous speech was about "bread and the ballot." She wrote: "Idle wishes, vain repinings, loud-sounding declamations never can bring freedom to any human soul. . . . Whoever consents to live by 'the sweat of the brow' of another human being inevitably humiliates and degrades herself. . . . No genuine equality, no real freedom, no true manhood or womanhood can exist on any foundation save that of pecuniary independence." (Harper, *Life and Work* I: 169)

Pre-Virginia Woolf, she wrote in her diary in 1853 that "Woman must have a *purse* of her own." In a letter to *The Revolution* published on July 20, 1871, she wrote in italics that *"independent bread alone can redeem woman from her curse of subjection to man."* (Sherr, *Failure Is Impossible—Susan B. Anthony In Her Own Words*: 49, 259)

Susan was the force behind the compilation of the massive *History of Woman Suffrage*, coediting the first four volumes, raising the money to publish and distribute this invaluable record. She engineered the controversial merging of the two suffrage organizations into the National American Woman Suffrage Association in 1890. However narrow she kept the suffrage platform as the NAWSA president for eight years, Susan expressed disappointment with the lack of concern with justice by suffragists:

"I wonder if when I am under the sod—or cremated and floating up in the air—I shall have to stir you and others up. How can you not be all on fire? . . . I really believe I shall explode if some of you young women don't wake up—and raise your voice in protest against the impending crime of this nation upon the new islands it has clutched from other folks—Do come into the living present & work to save us from any more *barbaric male governments*," she wrote old friend Clara Bewick Colby on December 17, 1898. (*Failure Is Impossible*: 185–186)

By her late seventies she had given seventy-five to one hundred speeches every year for forty-five years, and addressed Congress and the New York legislature for thirty years. At her eighty-sixth birthday celebration on February 15, 1906, Susan spoke in public for the last time, acknowledging the other foremothers of feminism: "with such women consecrating their lives, failure is impossible!" (Harper, *Life and Work* III: 1409)

She died on March 13, 1906.

❦

A shrewd political campaigner, Susan disagreed for strategy reasons with Stanton's desire to expose religion or other problems on the suffrage platform, seeing division as a handicap. An exasperated Stanton once told Clara Colby: "Miss Anthony has one idea and she has no patience with anyone who has two. I cannot sit on the door just like Poe's raven, and sing suffrage evermore. I am deeply interested in all the live questions of the day." (Lutz, *Created Equal*: 296)

After long debate at the 1885 woman suffrage convention on anti-biblical resolutions supported by Stanton, Susan opined: "I was on the old Garrisonian platform and found long ago that this matter of settling any question of human rights by people's interpretation of the Bible is never satisfactory. I hope we shall not go back to that war. No two can ever interpret alike, and discussion upon it is time wasted." Susan prevailed, and the resolution was tabled, but much publicized, prompting the derisive sermon that provoked Susan to say that a minister deserved to be spanked. (*History of Woman Suffrage*, IV: 59)

In a similar speech supporting Stanton for president of the newly merged National American Woman Suffrage Association, Susan said:

"I want our platform to be kept broad enough for the infidel, the atheist, the Mohammedan, or the Christian. I remember thirty years ago George William Curtis said to me: 'If you want your platform to succeed you must not allow Mrs. Ernestine L. Rose to stand upon it; she's a pronounced atheist.' I said: 'We shall never turn her out.' Now we have come to another phase of the fight, and if it is necessary, will fight forty years more to make our platform broad enough for the Christian to stand upon, whether she be a Catholic and counts her beads, or a Protestant of the straitest orthodox creed, as for the rights of the 'infidels' forty years ago. . . . These are the broad principles I want you to stand upon, that our platform may be kept as broad as the universe, that upon it may stand the representatives of all creeds and no creeds—Pagan, Jew, Gentile, Christian, Protestant or Catholic." (Lutz, *Created Equal*: 280; *History of Woman Suffrage* has a slightly different version, IV: 169)

In 1896, Susan wrote Stanton: "You say 'women must be emancipated from their superstitions before enfranchisement will be of any benefit,' and I say just the reverse, that women must be enfranchised before they can be emancipated from their superstitions. Women would be no more superstitious today than men, if they had been men's political and business equals and gone outside the four walls of home and the other four of the church into the great world, and come in contact with and discussed men and measures on the plane of this mundane sphere, instead of living in the air with Jesus and the angels. So you will have to keep pegging away, saying, 'Get rid of religious bigotry and then get political rights;'

while I shall keep pegging away, saying, 'Get political rights first and religious bigotry will melt like dew before the morning sun'; and each will continue still to believe in and defend the other." (*Life and Work* II: 857)

Susan was a stalwart friend to atheist Ernestine L. Rose, going with her on a month-long lecture tour of slave border cities. Susan noted in her diary on March 24, 1854, that when she asked the Speaker of the House for use of the Capitol for an address by Rose on Sunday morning, "He referred me to Mr. Milburn the Chaplain. Called on him. He could not allow her to speak there because she was not a member of some religious society. I remarked to him that ours was a country professing Religious as well as Civil Liberty and not to allow any and every faith to be declared in the Capitol of the nation, made the profession to religious freedom a perfect mockery." (Dubois, *Elizabeth Cady Stanton-Susan B. Anthony: Correspondence, Writings, Speeches:* 71)

At the Third National Woman's Convention in Syracuse, when feminists were harassed by ministers, in this instance, the vulgar Rev. Junius Hatch, a Congregationalist minister, Susan silenced him by commenting that he probably belonged to the "pin-cushion ministry, educated by women's sewing societies," an accusation that turned out to be true! (*HWS* I: 539)

A representative of the Women's Christian Temperance Union invited Susan to speak at a state gathering in 1890, stipulating nothing should be said that could be viewed as critical of Christianity. Susan wrote: "They never seem to think we have any feelings to be hurt when we have to sit under their reiteration of orthodox cant and dogma. The boot is all on one foot with the dear religious bigots—but if they will all pull together with us for suffrage we'll continue to bear and forbear, as we have done for the past forty years." (*Life and Work* II: 678)

Although Susan made occasional ceremonial references to God or fell back on her Quaker past, particularly in her younger days or when trying to impress authority, more frequently she made cynical comments. She relished turning religious language on its head: "Work is my gospel" (New York *Press*, February 6, 1905). In an interview by Nellie Bly appearing in the New York *World*, February 2, 1896, Susan stated: "I pray every single second of my life; not on my knees but with my work. My prayer is to lift women to equality with men. Work and worship are one with me. I know there is no God of the universe made happy by my getting down on my knees and calling him 'great.' " (*Failure Is Impossible:* 244, 249)

When addressing a women's temperance crusade in Rochester in 1874, she observed: "You never can talk down or sing down or pray down an institution which is voted into existence. . . . Frederick Douglass used to tell how, when he was a Maryland slave and a good Methodist, he would go into the farthest corner of the tobacco field and pray God to bring him liberty; but God never answered his prayers until he prayed with his heels. And so, dear friends, He never will answer yours for the suppression of the liquor traffic until you are able to pray with your ballots." (*Life and Work* I: 457)

She chastised suffrage workers for appealing to religion or prayer instead of to justice, rebuking a cohort in 1897: "It seems to me that by your using constantly the words 'God' and 'Jesus' as if they were material beings, when to you they are no longer such, you impress upon your audience, grounded as the vast majority yet are in the old beliefs, that you still hold to the idea of their personality. The world, especially women, love to cling to a personal, material help— God a strong man, Jesus a loving man." (*Life and Work* II: 922)

Like Stanton, Susan raised her eyebrows at Annie Besant's theosophy conversion. After hearing Besant's theories, she wrote Anna Howard Shaw in a letter on September 8, 1897: "I think it is the least attractive speculation of any of them, and it does not matter whether it is Calvinism, Unitarianism, Spiritualism, Christian Science, or Theosophy, they are all mere speculations. So I think you and I had better hang on to this mundane sphere and keep tugging away to make the conditions better for the next generation of women." (*Failure Is Impossible:* 264)

Susan was as impatient with religious claims as she was with attempts to put religion or irreligion on the suffrage platform, writing Stanton that "we'll chat over men, women and conditions—not theories, theosophies and theologies, they are all Greek to me." (*Life and Work* II: 919)

She was "stunned" to hear William Henry Channing admit belief in miracles in his old age. Susan deduced that "It is—it must be—simply the waning intellect returning to childish teachings." (*Life and Work* II: 563)

"I am a full and firm believer in the revelation that it is through *woman the race is to be redeemed.* And it is because of this faith that I ask for her immediate and unconditional emancipation from all political, industrial, social and religious subjection," Susan said during a speech toward the end of her life. (*Failure Is Impossible:* 259–296)

While she irritably rejected any connection with Stanton's *Woman's Bible* committee, when Susan's "cabinet" formulated a resolution repudiating connection with the first volume of the book at the January 23–28, 1896 NAWSA conference, Susan spoke out against it, but would not resign when it passed, as Stanton urged. [See selection] While scolding her friend over the *Woman's Bible*, Susan wrote Stanton: "But while I do not consider it my duty to tear to tatters the lingering skeletons of the old superstitions and bigotries, yet I rejoice to see them crumbling on every side." (Harper, *Life and Work:* 857)

"Miss Anthony on the Religious Press"

*This is excerpted from The Woman's Tribune, June 17, 1893, edited and pub-
lished weekly by Clara Bewick Colby. The speech was introduced in this manner:
"Miss Anthony was called on innumerable times to speak before the various sec-
tions of the Congress of Women [at the Columbia World Exposition] and always
she spoke with vigor, spontaneity and marvelous power. Those who have worked
with her for years were astonished at her versatility and untiring freshness. She
also spoke the next week at one of the meetings of the Women's Auxiliary Press
Congress and was on the regular programme of the closing day of the general
congress, when the subject of the religious press was under discussion. Her remarks created a great sensation delivered as they were before a number of divines
who imagine they are leading the thought of the day. Miss Anthony never writes
her speeches so we are glad that this was taken in full by a short-hand reporter."*

I AM ASKED TO SPEAK UPON "The Moral Leadership of the Religious Press."
For one who has for fifty years been ridiculed by both press and pulpit,
denounced as infidel by both, it is, to say the least, very funny. Nevertheless I am glad to stand here to-day as an object lesson of the survival of the
fittest, from ridicule and contempt. I was born into this earth right into
the midst of the ferment of the division of the Society of Friends, as it was
called, on the great question which has divided all the religious peoples of
Christendom, and my grandfather and grandmother and my father, all
Quakers, took the radical side, the Unitarian, which has been denounced
as infidel.

I passed through the experience of three great reforms, not only with
the secular press but with the religious press. The first one was that of
temperance, in which my father was the very earliest man in all Western
Massachusetts who put liquor out of his store before he was even yet a
married man. From that day in 1816 up to the day of his death, though a
manufacturer and a merchant nearly all of his life, he never sold a drop of
liquor and scarcely ever tasted a drop. Very naturally my first reform work
was in the cause of temperance, and I had my first little experience with
the religious press on that question. It was no light affair, I can assure you.

I went as a delegate of the New York State Woman's Temperance Association to Syracuse, at the time of the holding of the great annual con-

vention of the New York State Temperance Society, the men's society, and my credentials with the credentials of other women were presented. When the committee reported it was adversely, that it was very well for women to belong to the temperance society, but wholly out of the way for them to be accepted as delegates or to speak or to take any part in the meetings, and I want to say to you that the majority of the men of that convention were ministers. They were not of one denomination or another, but they were of all denominations. I want to say for the comfort of everybody that the most terrible Billingsgate, the most fearful denunciation, and the most opprobrious epithets that I ever had laid on my head were spoken that day by those ministers; and when there was time to report the proceedings the whole religious press of the country, the liberal, the Unitarian, as well as the orthodox, came down on my head for obtruding myself there, claiming that St. Paul had said: "Let your women keep silence in the churches," and no one but an infidel would attempt to speak there. I submit that was not leadership in the right direction.

Then next came the anti-slavery movement. And nobody can say for a moment that either the religious pulpit or the religious press was a leader in the great work of breaking the chains of the millions of slaves in this country; but, on the other hand, church after church was rent in twain; the press—take the old New York *Observer* or the old New York *Advocate*—used to make my hair stand straight for fear I might go to the bottomless pit because I was an abolitionist.

Then the next great question has been this woman question. When we started out on that the whole religious world was turned upside down with fright. We women were disobeying St. Paul; we women were getting out of sphere and would be no good anywhere, here or here after; and the way that I was scarified! I don't know, somehow or other the press both secular and religious, always took special pride in scarifying Miss Anthony. I used to tell them it was because I hadn't a husband or a son who would shoot the men down who abused me. Well, now they take special pains to praise. [Applause.] It is a wonderful revolution of the press.

I want to say that the religious press is exactly like the pulpit, and the religious press and pulpit are exactly in the position of the politician and of the political newspaper. The religious press has to be exactly what the people of the country want it to be, if it is not, there is no support for the newspaper. The religious press, instead of being a leader in the great moral reform, is usually a little behind [applause], and . . . I am glad that the spirit of freedom is abroad to-day. . . .

"Vote for Religious Liberty"

*The appendix of **The Woman's Bible** Part II (1898) contains this account of
"**The Woman's Bible** Repudiated," followed by a plea from Susan B. Anthony
to "vote for religious liberty."*

AT THE TWENTY-EIGHTH ANNUAL CONVENTION of the National-American Woman Suffrage Association, held in Washington, D. C., in January, 1896, the following, was reported by the Committee on Resolutions:

"That this Association is non-sectarian, being composed of persons of all shades of religious opinion, and that it has no official connection with the so-called 'Woman's Bible,' or any theological publication."

Charlotte Perkins Stetson moved to amend by striking out everything after the word "opinion."

Anna R. Simmons moved, as an amendment to the amendment, to omit the words "the so-called Woman's Bible, or."

This was followed by a long and animated discussion, in which the following persons participated:

Frances A. Williamson; Helen Morris Lewis, Annie L. Diggs, Carrie Chapman Catt, Rachel Foster Avery, Henry B. Blackwell, Laura M. Johns, Elizabeth U. Yates, Katie R. Addison, Alice Stone Blackwell and Rev. Anna Howard Shaw, speaking for the resolution; and Charlotte Perkins Stetson, Mary Bentley Thomas, J. B. Merwin, Clara B. Colby, Harriette A. Keyser, Lavina A. Hatch, Lillie Devereux Blake, Caroline Hallowell Miller, Victoria Conkling Whitney, Althea B. Stryker, and Cornelia H. Cary speaking against it.

The President, Susan B. Anthony, left the chair and spoke with much earnestness against the adoption of the resolution as follows:

"The one distinct feature of our Association has been the right of individual opinion for every member. We have been beset at every step with the cry that somebody was injuring the cause by the expression of some sentiments that differed with those held by the majority of mankind. The religious persecution of the ages has been done under what was claimed to be the command of God. I distrust those people who know so well what God wants them to do to their fellows, because it always coincides with their own desires. All the way along the history of our movement there has been this same contest on account of religious theories. Forty years ago one of our noblest men said to me: 'You would better never hold another convention than let Ernestine L. Rose stand on your platform,' because that talented and eloquent Polish woman, who ever stood for justice and freedom, did not believe in the plenary inspiration of the Bible. Did we banish Mrs. Rose? No, indeed! Every new generation of converts threshes over the same old straw. Twenty-five years ago a prominent woman, who stood on our platform for the first time, wanted us to pass a resolution that we were not free lovers; and I was not more shocked than I am to-day at this attempt. The question is whether you will sit in judgment on one who has questioned the Divine inspiration of certain passages in the Bible derogatory to women. If she had written approvingly of these passages, you would not have brought in this resolution because you thought the cause might be injured among the liberals in religion. In other words, if she had written your views, you would not have considered a resolution necessary. To pass this one is to set back the hands on the dial of reform. It is the reviving of the old time censorship, which I hoped we had outgrown.

"What you should do is to say to outsiders that a Christian has neither more nor less rights in our Association than an atheist. When our platform becomes too narrow for people of all creeds and of no creeds, I myself shall not stand upon it. Many things have been said and done by our orthodox friends that I have felt to be extremely harmful to our cause; but I should no more consent to a resolution denouncing them than I shall consent to this. Who is to draw the line? Who can tell now whether Mrs. Stanton's commentaries may not prove a great help to woman's emancipation from old superstitions that have barred her way? Lucretia Mott at first thought Mrs. Stanton had injured the cause of all woman's other rights by insisting upon the demand for suffrage, but she had sense enough not to bring in a resolution against it. In 1860, when Mrs. Stanton made a speech before the New York Legislature in favor of a bill making drunkenness a cause for divorce, there was a general cry among the friends that she had killed the woman's cause. I shall be pained beyond expression if the delegates here are so narrow and illiberal as to adopt this resolution.

You would better not begin resolving against individual action or you will find no limit. This year it is Mrs. Stanton; next year it may be me or one of yourselves who will be the victim.

"Are you going to cater to the whims and prejudices of people who have no intelligent knowledge of what they condemn? If we do not inspire in woman a broad and catholic spirit, they will fail, when enfranchised, to constitute that power for better government which we have always claimed for them. You would better educate ten women into the practice of liberal principles than to organize ten thousand on a platform of intolerance and bigotry. I pray you, vote for religious liberty, without censorship or inquisition. This resolution, adopted, will be a vote of censure upon a woman who is without a peer in intellectual and statesmanlike ability; one who has stood for half a century the acknowledged leader of progressive thought and demand in regard to all matters pertaining to the absolute freedom of women."

The Resolution was then adopted by a vote of 53 to 41.

Ella E. Gibson

14

Ella E. Gibson

THE "UNGODLY" WOMAN

May 8, 1821 – March 5, 1901

Christianity is an insult to the wisdom of the nineteenth century. To place before its progress and development a leader, ruler, king, savior, god, whose knowledge was less than a modern five-year-old school girl, is an outrage upon humanity.

The Godly Women of the Bible, *1870s*

ELLA E. GIBSON HAD THE DISTINCTION of being an ordained minister and an army chaplain before losing faith and penning what appears to be the earliest feminist analysis of the bible, *The Godly Women of the Bible, by an Ungodly Woman of the Nineteenth Century*, circa 1878.

Born in Winchendon, Massachusetts, she taught public school for twelve years in Massachusetts and New Hampshire, also writing for the press and giving public lectures. She organized Soldiers' Ladies Aid Societies in Wisconsin during the start of the Civil War, then joined the Eighth Wisconsin Volunteers ("Live Eagle Regiment"), and was elected chaplain of the First Wisconsin Regiment, Heavy Artillery. Her appointment apparently was approved by President Lincoln on November 10, 1864, but the Secretary of War refused to muster her because she was a woman. However, by an act of Congress, on March 3, 1869, pay for her services as chaplain was approved. She did not receive a pension until 1876. D.M. Bennett of *The Truth Seeker* revealed that much of her government stipend generously found its way into the freethought cause.

Ella had contracted malaria in the line of duty which severely disabled her, often confining her to bed. However, according to freethought biographer Samuel P. Putnam, this did not stop her from writing for nearly every Liberal paper in the United States, nor from editing "The Moralist" for a time in the early 1890s.

The Godly Women of the Bible by an Ungodly Woman of the Nineteenth Century

— 203 —

was first published by the Truth Seeker Company and apparently was in print continuously for the next three decades, including a posthumous reprint. Today the book is so rare that it is listed with only one university.

It was dedicated "to the believer in the infallible inspiration of the bible, and especially to woman," with the wish expressed that it might open the eyes of "any blind devotee." Ella wrote the book in ill health in intervals over three years. In the preface she confided her goal to write two other books, "Bible Laws and Usages of Woman" and the "Character of Jesus Christ as Portrayed in the Gospels," which apparently were never completed.

"The *first* is required to prove woman's oppression in this age of refinement and progression due to the unjust laws and infamous customs of the Bible; the *second* to show that Christianity is an insult to the wisdom of the nineteenth century. To place before its progress and development a leader, ruler, king, savior, god, whose knowledge was less than a modern five-year-old school girl, is an outrage upon humanity."

Ella took a more modern and less discreet approach than did the later *Woman's Bible* edited by Elizabeth Cady Stanton. "As the Bible opens with defaming woman (Eve), so it ends, as it begins, by fastening upon her the most odious epithet applied to her sex," concludes *Godly Women*. Where the *Woman's Bible* glosses rather hurriedly over Revelation, *Godly Women* quotes the worst verses of Chapter 17, which describe a harlot symbolizing the apostate church holding a golden cup in her hand "full of abominations and filthiness of her fornication." Ella also denounced the implications of Revelation 14:4 for describing the heaven-bound 144,000 men as "not defiled with women."

Wrote Ella: "All such statements are odious in the eyes of woman and an abomination in the sight of man—all men who are worthy of the name." She blamed the bible for its false teachings on the nature of female sexuality, which, in stories about Sarah, Lot's daughters, Rebecca, Leah, Rachel, Judah's daughter-in-law, Hannah, and Ruth, depicted sexually aggressive women, leading to "bitter disappointment" in contemporary men surprised to find wives "less amorous than affectionate."

She urged of the bible:

"Away with its false teachings, fables, pagan mythology, and abuse of woman, and assist her to free herself from these shackles and to overcome these vile aspersions descending down from the dark ages and settling like a pall over her existence and the existence of the race!"

Ella died at nearly eighty in Barre, Massachusetts.

The Godly Women of the Bible
By an Ungodly Woman of the Nineteenth Century

This is excerpted from the Preface and Conclusion of Ella E. Gibson's book, first published in the 1870s by the Truth Seeker.

No APOLOGY IS DEEMED NECESSARY for the production of "Godly Women." Women, held up to-day as pattern characters, should not be above or below the closest scrutiny and the severest criticism. If they cannot bear the investigation, let them fall. The ungodliness of the nineteenth century requires good manners and pure morals; and if these ancient godly women cannot stand the test, let Christendom withdraw them from the contest, consign them to the barbarous ages where they belong, and no longer urge them forward as holy examples for modern civilization to copy. If forced upon us as models of perfection, we progressive women shall resent the insult; therefore this volume. . . .

What an imposition to force revelation upon the world as superior to philosophy and the arts and sciences—yea, as their heralder and promoter! "No morality without the Bible" is an unmitigated falsehood, and its promulgators must either plead ignorance or knavery. Why should they longer be permitted to do either? Why not enlighten them, and then call them to an account for their libels and acts, the same as any other traducers and offenders? This seems just and proper; but whenever the doctrines of theology are doubted, the character of Bible heroes or heroines discussed, or their own criticised, the apologists of "a religion of faith, not works," hide themselves behind the sanctity and authority of the Bible, and seek to annihilate the philosopher under the false accusation of blasphemy and heresy, impugning his motives, defaming his morals, and questioning his sincerity. No one deserves thus to be misjudged, misrepresented, scorned, and ostracized, therefore many intelligent unbelievers in revelation conceal their views, seemingly assenting to doctrines they disbelieve, and hold their peace for fear they have not power to answer their tormentors. It is hoped that to such these reviews of "The Godly Women of the Bible" will prove an aid and encouragement, supplying them with a text-book, like "The Holy Bible Abridged," wherein they can readily find passages and proofs with which to controvert their accusers and convert their antagonists. . . .

❦

Woman's position under Judaism and Christianity, as portrayed in the Bible, is unworthy of herself and man to-day. Then why seek to maintain and perpetuate it by retaining such a book as authority? The abominable laws respecting her in the Old Testament and in the New, especially those of Paul in 1 Corinthians and elsewhere, are a disgrace to civilization and English literature; and any family which permits such a volume to lie on their parlor-table ought to be ostracized from all respectable society, unless there under protest. The time will come when King James's Bible (present version) will not be spoken of without a blush of shame tingling the cheek of modesty, or referred to except as a textbook obsolete, superannuated, blasphemous, false, pernicious, corrupt, immodest, obscene, and too immoral to be tolerated, even as a past nuisance, ancient, foreign, and worthless.

Woman, this is your work, to rise in rebellion against the book which promulgates such false and vile opinions in regard to yourselves, which is the origination of such erroneous views relative to your needs, motives, and desires, which, in every relation of life, misrepresents your position, aims, and interests; which clouds your hopes, stifles your ambition, circumscribes your opportunities, chains you down to slavish servitude in obedience to its mandates; gives to man, as man and husband, superior rights and privileges, exonerates him from all blame when most to blame, and installs him, right or wrong, Lord God over one-half of the human universe, and that half his mother, wife, and daughter, making him the fiat to which woman must universally defer, and limiting her education, privileges, possibilities, aspirations, and intuitions to his blind selfishness, controlled by passion, filthy lucre, ignorance, and power.

These pages have not been penned for pastime, but for a purpose, to call woman to her duties, to show her her responsibilities, to expose her dangers, to reveal her errors, to open her eyes to their origination, viz., the volume called the word of God, wherein she is maligned, outraged, victimized, enslaved, chattelized, polygamized, scourged, crushed, brutalized, and even denied the right of immortality, her very name suppressed, or merged within her husband's as unworthy of a place in history, her love trampled under foot, her affections scorned, motives questioned, sincerity doubted, her virginity despoiled, wifehood betrayed, and her very motherhood prostituted.

Yes, we charge all this and a thousand times more upon the Bible and the Bible God or Bible makers; woman being therein reviled and held up as a contemptible thing, fit only to be used by man as a menial, a toy, or a slave, as one of a numerous set of wives or concubines, to be discarded or kept at will or pleasure—even the Bible-God interfering to fill up seraglios, steal wives, prostitute damsels, and violate matrons and mothers.

Let us pause and estimate the value of such a book, its animus and its results on humanity—such women, or their history, as have been considered in this review, called godly or holy in this nineteenth century, and set up by Christianity as patterns for maidens, wives, and mothers to follow!

As we have delved into this rottenness, we have shamed our own face and the face of others in the quotations made from the sacred word, yet often omitting language too vulgar for *The Truth Seeker*, and have been compelled to ask pardon of the reader for a seeming breach of decency when an omission of some obscene passage would have failed to elucidate our subject or prove a statement. Our apology for this work is the Bible itself, itself so vile in its shamelessness that only itself could expose itself, for like the "Holy Bible Abridged" no language of ours could equal its obscenity or do it justice in portraying its filthiness; therefore, pardon is expected by the author, who took upon herself the unpleasant task and painful duty of probing the offensive ulcer, from whose festering foulness has emanated disease more contagious and fatal to the mental, moral, and physical well-being of the race than from all other sources combined.

This may be considered a wild statement, nevertheless true, though perhaps unprovable. No estimate can be made of the wrong done to woman by the existence and authority of the Bible, and if done to woman then to man and the race; therefore we implore our brother man to assist woman in discarding this filthy book, its pernicious doctrines, and unjust laws against, if not the better half of humanity, at least that half or portion with which he must coöperate in order to perpetuate the race and reproduce himself. If we ever again take our pen to expose the shortcomings of man, we trust this will not be the sin of omission that we must attack, viz., want of interest and lack of support in aiding woman to destroy the authority of a book which has been her greatest foe and most fruitful cause of oppression from man.

Woman, man is in your advance respecting this book, for having preceded you in its attempted destruction, and often has he encountered your fierce indignation when he would have sacrificed this hydra-headed ty-rant, your idol which has made you its too willing victim. Assist him in this work of annihilation, oppose him no longer. Realize that morals are not advanced or preserved through Bible teaching, progress secured, or science unfolded. The next great battle of the world is to be fought on the heights of reason between the truths of science and the errors of supersti-tion. On which side, O woman, will you be found in this mighty contest? Aiding and abetting your enemy, the Bible, or arrayed against it rendering assistance to your savior, reason, science, and truth? Oh, choose the latter, and unite with your brother man in exterminating from the earth the great-est scourge of the race, a false and pernicious theology, the doctrines of which are found within and sustained by the Hebrew and Christian scrip-tures, known as King James's Bible.

Matilda Joslyn Gage
(The Schlesinger Library, Radcliffe College)

15

Matilda Joslyn Gage

AUTHOR — WOMAN, CHURCH & STATE

March 25, 1826 – March 18, 1898

. . . in order to help preserve the very life of the Republic, it is imperative that women should unite upon a platform of opposition to the teaching and aim of that ever most unscrupulous enemy of freedom—the Church.

Woman's National Liberal Union Resolutions, *1890*

MATILDA JOSLYN GAGE, AN EARLY ACTIVIST in the American woman suffrage movement, was dedicated to freeing women from the teachings of the Christian church. She surfaced on the feminist scene in 1852, at twenty-six the youngest speaker at the National Woman's Rights Convention in Syracuse, New York. A founding member and onetime President of the National Woman Suffrage Association, a contributor to its newspaper *The Revolution*, Matilda was the forgotten third of the "triumvirate" composed of herself, Elizabeth Cady Stanton and Susan B. Anthony. An organized researcher, Matilda coedited with these women the first three volumes of *The History of Woman Suffrage*, each nearly one thousand pages.

Indignant over "the wrongs inflicted upon one-half of humanity by the other half in the name of religion; finding appeal and argument alike met by the assertion that God designed the subjection of woman, and yet that her position had been higher under Christianity than ever before," she refuted such arguments at the annual convention of the National Woman Suffrage Association in Washington, D.C. in 1878. (Gage, *Woman, Church, and State:* 5)

Popular response led to a forty-page essay, "Woman, Church, and State" appearing in the first volume of *The History of Woman Suffrage*. After twenty years of research, she completed the sketch with a book of the same name in 1893. Her research opened the eyes of contemporaries to woman-hating abuses stemming from such religious doctrines as celibacy, including the witch-hunts. Matilda, according to women's studies scholar Sally Roesch Wagner, was the first American to advance the notion of the "Matriarchate," a pre-Christian era during which female-based religions celebrated womanhood, ideas that were wiped out by the degrading dogmas of patriarchal Christianity.

A freethought activist, Matilda organized the Woman's National Liberal Union in 1890. Its unflinching, eloquent repudiation of the Religious Right of that era is eerily timely a century later. [See Resolutions and "Dangers of the Hour"]

❧

Matilda was encouraged to think freely growing up in Cicero, New York, an only child of Helen Leslie Joslyn and Dr. Hezekiah Joslyn, an advocate of abolition, woman's rights, freethought and temperance, whose house was a station on the underground railroad.

Elizabeth Cady Stanton wrote some of Matilda's history:

"Dr. Joslyn paid great attention to his daughter's education. From her earliest years it was a law of the household that her childish questions should not be put off with an idle reply, but must be reasonably answered; and when she was older, he himself instructed her in mathematics, Greek, and physiology. But that for which she feels most indebted to him, as she often says—the grandest training given her—was to think for herself. She was taught to accept no opinion because of its authority, but to question the truth of all things. Thus was laid the foundation of Mrs. Gage's reform tendencies and of her non-acceptance of masculine authority in matters of religion and politics. Nor was she, in a certain way, less indebted to her mother, a Scotch lady, belonging to the noble, old, and influential family of Leslie, a woman of refined and elevated tastes, universally respected and beloved. From this side Mrs. Gage inherited her antiquarian tastes and habits of delving into old histories, from which she has unearthed so many facts bearing upon woman's degradation." (*History of Woman Suffrage* I: 466)

Matilda attended the Clinton Liberal Institute at age fifteen. She gave her first talk at seventeen before a village literary society on the topic of astronomy. At eighteen in 1845, she married Henry H. Gage, a merchant. He eventually opened a successful dry goods business in Fayetteville, New York, where they settled. The frail Matilda gave birth to Helen, Thomas, Julie and Maud, and to a son who died in infancy.

Stanton recalled:

"Although Mrs. Gage was surrounded with a family of small children for years, yet she was always a student, an omnivorous reader and liberal thinker, and her pen was ever at work answering the attacks on the woman movement in the county and State journals. In the village of Manlius, where she lived some time after her marriage, she was the sole representative of this unpopular reform. When walking the street she would often hear some boy, shielded by a dry-goods box or a fence, cry out 'woman's rights.' " (*HWS* I: 465)

Matilda attracted favorable press for her stylish and ladylike appearance, but her views remained unorthodox. She served as vice-president and secretary of the New York State Woman Association in 1869, regularly attending state and national suffrage conventions. In the presidential election of 1872, Matilda tried to cast a ballot. Although failing in this mission, she defended Susan B. Anthony when she was tried in court for voting in the same election. Matilda spoke in sixteen townships in the spring of 1873 on Anthony's behalf, her theme: "The United States on trial, not Susan B. Anthony."

Matilda also organized a suffrage campaign involving nine women, all taxpayers, in a corporation tax election in which only taxpayers were eligible to vote. Matilda was denied her right to vote (in the barroom where it was held) on the grounds that she was married, while another was denied the vote on the grounds that she was single! When a legislative act went into effect in 1893 declaring no person ineligible to serve as a school officer, Matilda successfully registered to vote that fall. When her vote was challenged, two courts upheld her disenfranchisement.

As president of the National Woman Suffrage Association in 1875, Matilda spoke before committees in the U.S. House and Senate. She suggested that a "Declaration of Rights" for women, which she coauthored, be presented at the centennial celebration of the Declaration of Independence in Philadelphia in 1876. The Acting Vice President, Thomas W. Ferry, accepted the Declaration from Anthony and Matilda with a courtly bow.

She edited the *National Citizen and Ballot Box* from 1878–81, a four-page monthly for the National Woman Suffrage Association. In 1884 Matilda ran as an elector-at-large on the presidential ticket of Belva Lockwood, the first woman admitted before the U.S. Supreme Court.

Matilda and her husband were charter members of the Syracuse Liberal League. Matilda addressed the New York State Freethinkers Association at the 1878 and 1882 annual conventions.

With broad interests in civil liberties, she was declared an honorary member of the Council of Matrons of the Iroquois. At the July 19, 1878 convention of the National Woman Suffrage Association held in Rochester, New York, Matilda introduced a series of resolutions condemning the effort to force citizenship on Indians, and attacking prejudice against naturalizing Chinese immigrants. Apparently on behalf of Stanton, Matilda added three strongly-worded resolutions condemning the effect of religion on woman, urging that she be "guided by her own reason." Much to the delight of freethinkers, after prolonged debate, these three resolutions passed, inspiring more prolonged debate among the clergy.

Through the aegis of *National Citizen*, Matilda answered a clergy attack led by the president of the Baptist Theological Seminary in Rochester: "From Augustine down, theologians have tried to compel people to accept their special interpretation of the Scripture, and the tortures of the inquisition, the rack, the thumb-screw, the stake, the persecutions of witchcraft, the whipping of naked women through the streets of Boston, banishment, trials of heresy, the halter about Garrison's neck, Lovejoy's death, the branding of Captain Walker, shouts of infidel and atheist, have all been for this purpose." (*HWS* I: 126)

When Matilda introduced more resolutions at the next annual convention decrying a "false interpretation of Scripture," these likewise passed.

In an article appearing in a freethought periodical in 1888, Matilda called Frances Willard of the Women's Christian Temperance Union "the most dangerous person upon the American continent today."

❦

When Susan B. Anthony engineered a merger between the National Woman Suffrage Association and the more conservative American Woman Suffrage Association, working with Willard, who wanted the ballot to push her God-in-the-Constitution agenda, Matilda started her own group. In 1890, when Matilda convened the Woman's National Liberal Union, no woman had ever headed a national freethought group, nor would one until 1913 (when Libby C. Macdonald directed the Rationalist Association of North America). Women representing thirty-three states participated, included Susan H. Wixon and Voltairine de Cleyre. (De Cleyre followed suit by forming the Ladies Liberal League in Philadelphia in 1894.) Ida Craddock, a corresponding secretary of the American Secular Union, endorsed the gathering, for "the hour is eminently ripe for such a movement" (*Truth Seeker*, February 1, 1890). Craddock initially suggested affiliating the group with the Union but following the gathering, she wrote an article hailing its platform for being "far more radical" than that of the Union.

Perhaps Craddock's praise put some noses out of joint, for, although the call for the convention received favorable advance publicity in freethought periodicals, the fallout after Matilda was elected its president was venomous. Obviously threatened that a new Liberal group had been founded by a woman, Union official R. B. Westbrook condemned "The Gage Gathering" in an article (*The Truth Seeker*, March 8, 1890, later reprinted in *Freethought* and *The Boston Investigator*). In a jeremiad, he wrote that "her very bad grammar, her monotonous voice, her egotism and lack of manners, could all have been excused, had she not been guilty of such unsufferable self-assertion. . . . Let every person treat 'Mrs. Gage's Gathering' as a nullity. Let us put a Woman Suffrage plank in our 'Nine Demands' of Secularism, and then we shall not need any other 'gathering.' "

Even Robert Ingersoll's positive response to the resolutions, printed in the

June 7, 1890 *Truth Seeker*, could not save the Woman's League. [See Appendix] Unwilling to pour energies into a project where she would have to fight free-thinkers and other feminists as well as theocrats, Matilda never called a second convention. She devoted the next few years to completing *Woman, Church and State.*

Anthony Comstock commended an insulting decision by Matilda's local school board in Fayetteville, New York, to refuse the book, writing in 1894: "it is not a proper book for children to read," but did not prosecute her.

Matilda served on the *Woman's Bible* committee. According to Sally Roesch Wagner, Matilda dabbled in theosophy, but her beliefs in parapsychology were, however misguidedly, predicated on a rejection of the supernatural and a conviction that *natural laws* discovered under the matriarchate had been suppressed.

❦

Matilda spent her last years in Chicago with her daughter Maud, who was married to L. Frank Baum (who later wrote *The Wizard of Oz)*. On her deathbed, dying of a brain embolism, she composed a talk commemorating the fiftieth anniversary of the Seneca Falls convention.

Recalled Katherine Devereux Blake, the daughter of suffragist Lillie Blake:

"Mrs. Gage was a tireless student, a fine research worker, thorough in all she undertook; she had a deep sense of justice and at times an appalling frankness of speech—which I loved! One was never in doubt as to where Mrs. Gage stood, and she was invariably fair to others. She prepared many important suffrage documents, not always getting credit for them. In a letter written to my mother she says that she was the originator of the motto, so freely used by the suffragists over their own signatures: 'There is a word sweeter than Mother, Home, or Heaven; that word is Liberty.' She was absolutely honest in all her dealings, and I would take her word at any time as against anybody else's. I always loved and admired her greatly. I think that in some ways she was the greatest of those four women [Stanton, Anthony and Isabella Beecher Hooker]. Someone should write an adequate life of this great leader." (Blake, *Champion of Women:* 115) Sadly, to date no biography of Matilda Joslyn Gage has been published.

Carved on her tombstone at Fayetteville, New York, is her motto: "There is a word sweeter than Mother, Home, or Heaven; that word is Liberty." Another equally fitting epigraph might have been chosen from the preface of *Woman, Church, and State*:

". . . do not allow the Church or the State to govern your thought or dictate your judgment."

The Dangers of the Hour

Speech by Matilda Joslyn Gage at The Woman's National Liberal Convention, February 24, 1890.

For one hundred and fourteen years we have seen our country gradually advancing in recognition of broader freedom, fewer restrictions upon personal liberty, and the peoples of all nations looking towards us as the great exemplar of political and religious freedom. But of late a rapidly increasing tendency has been shown towards the destruction of our civil liberties. . . . The government is undergoing changes which are signs of danger. The red signal is out, if you are color blind and cannot see it the more the pity for you. An unreasoning confidence is the chronic state of the people. To them it does not seem possible there is danger to their free inheritance. They forget that liberty must ever be guarded. They forget the hereditary enslavement, the bondage of the human will to the church, and thousands bound do not heed this enslavement—to them it seems liberty. . . .

The danger menacing our country does not lie with the foreigners, nor the Anarchists, nor in municipal mismanagement. Free institutions are jeopardized because the country is false to its principles in the case of one-half of its citizens. But back of this falsity away down to the depths of causes deep in the hidden darkness of men's minds, must we look for the source of this perennial wrong. To a person of thought this is easily found in early religious training. Men have not yet learned to regard woman as a being of equal creation with themselves; do not yet believe that she stands on a par with them in natural rights even to the air she breathes. In order to secure victory for woman we must unfetter the minds of men from religious bondage. We have petitioned legislatures and congress, we have appeared before committees with the best arguments founded on justice, we have educated men politically, and yet the victory is not ours because the teachings of the church have stood in the way. Now our warfare must be upon another plan, now we must free men from that bondage of the will which is the most direful form of slavery, now we must show the falsity of that reed upon which men lean. In the old anti-slavery times men did not hesitate to call the American Church the bulwark of American slavery. In like manner to-day we shall proclaim the Church—American, English, Greek, Protestant, Catholic—to be the bulwark of woman's slavery. Man trained by the church from infancy that woman is secondary and inferior to him, made for him, to be obedient to him, the same idea permeating the Jewish and all Christian churches, all social, industrial and educational life, all civil and religious institutions, it is no subject of astonishment, if one gives a moment's thought, that woman's political enfranchisement is so long delayed. . . .

It has not been without bitter resistance by the clergy that woman's property and educational rights have advanced. Woman's anti-slavery work—her temperance work, her demand for personal rights, for political equality, for religious freedom and every step of kindred character has met with opposition from the church as a body and from the clergy as exponents of its views.

The St. Louis Globe-Democrat in an editorial of May 5, 1888, said: "There is no more striking anomaly in the history of civilization than the fact that the churches have profited in the greatest degree by the devotion of women, and yet have been among the slowest of organized institutions to concede to the sex the rights and advantages which it has managed to obtain. Most of the work done for the improvement of woman's condition as a member of society has been accomplished, not without a certain measure of Church sympathy, but without distinct and aggressive Church support. We refer particularly to the removal of insidious legal restrictions, and the development of sentiments of justice and fairness with regard to woman's political interests, and her relation to the philosophy of general progress."

Many insidious steps by both Catholic and Protestant prove the church now, as of old, the enemy of freedom. In 1884, a Plenary Council, preceded by an encyclical from the Pope laying out its line of work, was held in Baltimore. The two points against which the effort of the church is now chiefly directed, are marriage and public schools. In its control of these two questions it has ever found its chief sources of power. The Pope's encyclical declared that "civil marriage must be resented by the whole Catholic world." The establishment of parochial schools, in every parish was also commanded within two years unless excused therefrom by the bishop.

. . . It must be remembered that the Baltimore council was a body composed wholly of celibates governed by the chief celibate, the Pope of Rome, and that it decided upon a question of which it possessed no practical knowledge. It must also be recollected that no woman's voice was heard in this council in regard to a relation in which as wife, she takes an equal, and as mother a superior part. The judgment of these celibate men was alone to decide upon the form, obligation, validity and permanence of marriage, the church threatening penalties for their non-observance. In the decrees upon marriage of this council and the preceding encyclical two points are especially to be borne in mind. First, that woman is the chief victim—not alone the question decided without her voice but its indissolubility pressing most heavily upon her. For it must be remembered that while the church asserts marriage to be an indissoluble sacrament, her past history shows it to have been in the power of man, of the husband, to secure that release from its bonds that has ever been denied to the wife.

The second point not to be forgotten, is that the power possessed by the church during the middle ages was largely due to the control it had secured over domestic relations, and that no more severe blow has ever been inflicted upon it than the institution of civil marriage. This fact is well known to the church and its persistent effort to again secure control of this relation is for the purpose of once more acquiring the power it has lost in those countries where civil marriage exists. Wherever established by the state it has met with determined opposition by the church. Historians agree as to the power the church acquired by its hold upon marriage. Lecky says that when religious marriages were alone recognized they were a potent instrument in securing the power of the priesthood who were able to compel men to submit to the conditions they imposed in the formation of the most important contract in life.

Draper also declares the secret of much of the influence of the church in the middle ages lay in the control she has so skilfully gained over domestic life. The authority of the church over marriage has always been especially prejudicial to woman; it is from teachings of the church, that in the family power over the wife is given to the husband. It is the church and not the state, to which the teaching of woman's inferiority is due: it is the church which primarily commanded the obedience of woman to man. It is the church which stamps with religious authority the political and domestic degradation of woman. It is the church which has placed itself in opposition to all efforts looking towards her enfranchisement and it has done this under professed divine authority, and wherever we find laws of the state bearing with greater hardship upon woman than upon man, we shall ever find them due to the teachings of the church.

But while I have first referred to the encyclical of the Pope and the action of the plenary council, upon this question of marriage, Catholics are scarcely more greedy for power over this relation than are Protestants. The church has ever been a barrier to advancing civilization; when it was the strongest at the time spoken of, when it possessed the greatest control over marriage, civilization was at the lowest.

The Protestant pulpit is only less dangerous than the Catholic to the liberties of the people in that its organized strength is less. The old medieval control of the family under and through marriage is now as fully the aim of the Protestant church as of the Catholic. The General Episcopal convention has not convened of late years without canvassing the question of marriage and divorce. In 1886 a most stringent Canon upon this relation was proposed and although it failed of adoption, a similar effort was made at the recent triennial convention in New York the fall of 1889.

The Rev. George Z. Gray, dean of the Episcopal Theological School in Cambridge, Mass., is author of a book in which he asserts, referring to scripture as authority, that marriage is not a contract between equals, but an appropriation of the woman by the man, the wife becoming merged in him and owing him obedience, the right of divorce lying alone with the husband, the wife not an independent being possessing independent rights, but a veritable slave of the husband. Not alone the Episcopalians, but Congregationalists, Presbyterians and other sects oppose marriage as a civil contract declaring it a rite to be solemnized by the church alone, . . .

These are dangerous signs of the times as to the effort of the church to obtain increased power over the laity. It is also an attack of the church upon the state. The courts of this country have decided that marriage is a civil contract. As such a clergyman is no more fitted to take part in it than he would be to take acknowledgement of a deed, or take part in the legalization of any other contract. In fact a marriage performed by a clergyman of any denomination should be regarded as invalid in the light of civil law.

It is an infringement of individual rights, that either state or church should possess absolute control over this important relation,—one that enters the inmost life of the individual persons contracting it. The parties themselves as chiefly interested, should hold power over its forms. When consummated it might be placed upon record for their own safety as is done in case of other contracts.

. . . The other important subject against which the powers of the Catholic church has ever been arrayed, and whose touch we are beginning to feel in this country, is that of secular schools. As an ecclesiastical body the church is opposed to general education and to systems of public instruction in any part of the world. In Belgium, in 1879, when the state established communal schools under its own control the opposition of the clerical party was strenuous and bitter. The sacrament was refused to those whose children or grandchildren attended public schools; masters of state schools were excommunicated and communion refused to the children in attendance. The sacrament of extreme unction was also refused to parents whose children were in the state communal schools.

A curious division of penalty upon parents whose children were in these schools is notable as showing the opinion of the church as to where her chief power in ignorance lies—with women. The parents of girls attending state schools were excommunicated, but not those of boys.

The stronghold of the church has ever been the ignorance and degradation of women. Its control over woman in the two questions of marriage and education have given it keys of power more potent than those of Peter. With her uneducated, without civil or political rights, the church is sure of its authority; but once arouse woman to a disbelief in church teachings regarding her having brought sin into the world; once open to her all avenues of education, so that her teaching of the young in her charge will be a broader, more scientific character than in the past and the doom of the church is sealed. . . .

The Call for the Liberal Woman's Convention

Woman's National Liberal Union Convention For Organization, held February 24–25, 1890, Washington D.C., convened by Matilda Joslyn Gage.

FOR SEVERAL REASONS the woman suffrage reform advances slowly. Men trained from infancy by the Church, to a belief in woman's inferiority, are loath to concede her capable of self-government. Four new States have recently been admitted to the Union, neither one possessing a republican form of government as required by the Federal Constitution; neither one recognizing the right of self-government as inhering in its women citizens. Of Wyoming, now seeking Statehood, with a constitution providing for woman suffrage, the press declares that an applicant for admission, coming with this condition, may not find its entrance into Statehood thereby facilitated, but because of it, it "may be discovered by wary Congressmen to have insufficient population."

Such lessons as these should not be lost upon woman.

Existing woman suffrage societies have also ceased to be progressive. The new-comers, and many of the old ones, fear to take an advance step, and from motives of business or social policy, cater to their worst enemy, the Church. We therefore deem a broader platform necessary in order to reach the many-sided thought of the country; to more clearly show the cause of delay in the recognition of woman's demands; and to promote fearlessness in denunciation of that cause.

Again: A crisis in the nation's life is at hand. The encroachments of "The Christian Party in Politics," composed of both Catholics and Protestants—its aim a union of Church and State—were never as great as at the present time. The decrees of the Plenary Council, held in Baltimore, 1884, the speeches and resolutions of the recent Catholic Congress in the same city, the effort towards Parochial schools, &c., shows the drift of Catholic thought in this direction; but to no greater extent than is the like purpose of Protestant effort made known by the work of the National Reform Association, the American Sabbath Union, the Woman's Christian Temperance Union, the discussions, canons, and resolutions of State and National Ministerial Bodies, together with the various bills before Congress for religious education in schools, Sunday Rest, &c.

Therefore not alone to aid her own enfranchisement—valueless without religious liberty—but in order to help preserve the very life of the Republic, it is imperative that women should unite upon a platform of opposition to the teaching and aim of that ever most unscrupulous enemy of freedom—the Church.

Signed By Representatives From Twenty-Seven States.

Objects.

First. To assert Woman's natural rights to self-government, to show cause of delay in the recognition of her demands and to promote fearlessness in the denunciation of such cause.

Second. To preserve the secular nature of our Government and the principles of civil and religious liberty now incorporated in the Federal Constitution, and to arouse public thought to the imminent danger of a union of Church and State through a proposed amendment to the Constitution the object of which is to recognize the Christian religion as the foundation of our Government and the true basis of our laws.

Third. To show that the real foundation of the Church is the doctrine of woman's inferiority by reason of her original sin—a doctrine which we denounce as false in science and its foundation a theological myth.

RESOLUTIONS.

Resolved, That it is essential to the life of the Republic that the purely civil character of the Government be maintained and that Church and State be forever kept separate; that the legal foundation of our Government is not any creed of Christendom, nor any authority of the Church, nor a divine revelation, but it is simply the consent of the governed; that the State has not grown out of the Church, but should outgrow the need of any Church and be henceforth and forever independent of the Church.

Resolved, That the efforts now made by the Christian party to bring religion into politics in order to place a religious amendment in the Constitution of the United States, must be resisted, because the success of such efforts would make the Church the arbiter of the legislative functions of the Government and place dangerous irresponsible power in the hands of the priesthood.

Resolved, That according to the principle of the Government of the United States of America, the Church and State are and must be forever kept separate. The State should govern its civil affairs, give its protection to every form of religious belief and secure freedom from molestation to every sect in the exercise of its religious sentiments, and therefore any amendment to the Constitution proposed by the so-called Christian party in politics is destructive of existing civil liberty and should be energetically opposed.

Resolved, That the real endeavor of the Christian party in politics is to establish a papacy in place of the present secular form of government of the United States; that a papacy does not alone mean a Pope's one-man power in the Church, nor a claim of papal infallibility; nor an immoral pretense of power to bind or loose sins, nor the celebration of mass, nor use of holy water, nor the making of marriage a sacrament, nor the doctrine of extreme unction, nor consecrated ground for burial, nor the claim of any number of sacraments, nor the establishment of parochial schools to teach children what they cannot understand, nor a celibate priesthood, nor any form of theological doctrine regarding Heaven, Hell, or Purgatory; but that a papacy is any Church asserting divine authority for its teachings and therefore claiming the right to exercise civil power;—whether that Church call itself Roman, Greek, Anglican, or Protestant.

Resolved, That the centralization of power, whether in the Church or in the State, is dangerous to civil liberty and to individual rights, and therefore all attempts towards such centralization, either in Church or State, must be constantly and firmly opposed.

Resolved, That as our nation is composed of people holding various and conflicting religious views, Roman Catholics disagreeing with Protestant forms, both disagreeing with Jewish rites, and the Agnostic holding to no defined position, therefore it is wrong and unjust to impose religious instruction of any kind upon the pupils of our common schools, and in simple justice to all people we denounce and oppose every kind of religious instruction in our public schools.

Resolved, That the great principle of the Protestant Reformation, namely, the right of individual conscience and judgment heretofore claimed and exercised by man alone, should also be claimed and exercised by woman, who in her interpretation of the Scriptures should be guided by her own reason and not by the authority of any Church or creed.

Resolved, That as the first duty of every individual is self-development, the lessons of self-sacrifice and obedience taught woman by the Christian Church, have been fatal not only to her own vital interests but through her to the vital interest of the race.

Resolved, That every Church is the enemy of liberty and progress and the chief means of enslaving woman's conscience and reason, and therefore as the first and most necessary step towards her emancipation we should free her from the bondage of the Church.

Resolved, That the Christian Church of whatever name, is based on the theory that woman was created secondary and inferior to man and brought sin into the world, thus necessitating the sacrifice of a Saviour. That Christianity is false and its foundation a myth which every discovery in science shows to be as baseless as its former belief that the earth was flat.

Resolved, That morality is not theology, but has a basis independent of "Thou shalt," and "Thou shalt not"; that right is right and wrong is wrong, not because any being in the universe so declares, but in the nature of things, the origin of right being in truth and not in authority.

Resolved, That we seek the truth, come whence it may and lead where it will; with the Greek Plato we deem nothing so beautiful as truth; with Hindu Mahrajah we believe no religion can excel truth; and with the American Lucretia Mott we accept "truth for authority and not authority for truth."

Woman, Church and State

These selected quotations are extracted from the final chapter, "Past, Present, Future," of **Woman, Church and State**, *1893.*

THE MOST IMPORTANT STRUGGLE in the history of the church is that of woman for liberty of thought and the right to give that thought to the world.

Freedom for woman underlies all the great questions of the age. She must no longer be the scapegoat of humanity upon whose devoted head the sins of all people are made to rest.

Woman's increasing freedom within the last hundred years is not due to the church, but to the printing-press, to education, to free-thought and other forms of advancing civilization. The fashions of the christian world have changed but not its innermost belief.

[The church] . . . bids people live under faith outside of evidence, and in thus doing is guilty of immeasurable evils to mankind. A bark without compass, it steers upon a sea of night no star illumining the darkness; . . .

The most stupendous system of organized robbery known has been that of the church towards woman, a robbery that has not only taken her self-respect but all rights of person; the fruits of her own industry; her opportunities of education; the exercise of her own judgment, her own conscience, her own will.

Both church and state claiming to be of divine origin have assumed divine right of man over woman; while church and state have thought for man, man has assumed the right to think for woman.

During the Christian ages, the church has not alone shown cruelty and contempt for woman, but has exhibited an impious and insolent disregard of her most common rights of humanity. It has robbed her of responsibility, putting man in place of God. . . . It has denied her independent thought, declaring her a secondary creation for man's use to whom alone it has made her responsible. It has anathematized her sex, teaching her to feel shame for the very fact of her being. It has not been content with proclaiming her curse upon her creative attributes, but has thrust the sorrows and expiations of man's "curse" upon her, and in doing these things the church has wrought her own ruin. A religious revolution of the most radical kind, has even now assumed such proportions as to nearly destroy the basic creeds of various sects, and undermine the whole fabric of christendom. . . . With thought no longer bound by fear of everlasting punishment, mankind will cease to believe unproved assertions, simply because made by a class of men under assumed authority from God.

In knocking at the door of political rights, woman is severing the last link between church and state; the church must lose that power it has wielded with changing force since the days of Constantine, ever to the injury of freedom and the world.

The superstitions of the church, the miseries of woman, her woes, tortures, burnings, rackings and all the brutalities she has endured in the church, the state, and the family, under the sanction of christianity, would be incredible had we not the most undeniable evidence of their existence.

Possessing no proof of its [God's] existence, the church has ever fostered unintelligent belief. To doubt her "unverified" assertion has even been declared an unpardonable sin.

The careful student of history will discover that christianity has been of very little value in advancing civilization, but has done a great deal toward retarding it.

The church and civilization are antipodal; one means authority, the other freedom; one means conservatism, the other progress; one means the rights of God as interpreted by the priesthood, the other the rights of humanity as interpreted by humanity. Civilization advances by free-thought, free speech, free men.

Slavery and prostitution, persecutions for heresy, the inquisition with its six hundred modes of torture, the destruction of learning, the oppression of science, the systematized betrayal of confiding innocence, the recognized and unrecognized polygamy of man, the denial to woman of a right to herself, her thought, her wages, her children, to a share in the government which rules her, to an equal part of religious institutions, all these and a myriad more, are parts of what is known as christian civilization.

Nor has the church ever been the leader in great reforms. During the anti-slavery conflict, the American Church was known as "the bulwark of American slavery.". . . Penitentiaries and prisons, asylums and reformatories, all institutions of a repressive character which the church prides herself as having built up, are no less evil than the convents, monasteries and religious orders belonging to it. They have all risen through perversion of nature. Crimes and criminals are built up and born because of the great wrong first done to mothers; they are the offspring of church and state.

Woman will gain nothing by a compromising attitude toward the church, by attempt to excuse its great wrong toward her sex, or by palliation of its motives. On the contrary, a stern reference to facts, keeping the face of the world turned toward its past teachings, its present attitude, is her duty.

The world has seemingly awaited the advent of heroic souls who once again should dare all things for the truth. The woman who possesses love for her sex, for the world, for truth, justice and right, will not hesitate to place herself upon record as opposed to falsehood, no matter under what guise of age or holiness it appears. A generation has passed since the great struggle began, but not until within ten years has woman dared attack upon the veriest stronghold of her oppression, the Church.

Looking forward, I see evidence of a conflict more severe than any yet fought by reformation or science; a conflict that will shake the foundations of religious belief, tear into fragments and scatter to the winds the old dogmas upon which all forms of christianity are based. It will not be the conflict of man with man upon rites and systems; it will not be the conflict of science upon church theories regarding creation and eternity; it will not be the light of biology illuminating the hypothesis of the resurrection of the body; but it will be the rebellion of one half of the church against those theological dogmas upon which the very existence of the church is based. In no other country has the conflict between natural and revealed rights been as pronounced as in the United States; and in this country where the conflict first began, we shall see its full and final development. During the ages, no rebellion has been of like importance with that of Woman against the tyranny of Church and State; none has had its far reaching effects. We note its beginning; its progress will overthrow every existing form of these institutions; its end will be a regenerated world.

Women Without Superstition

16

Lois Waisbrooker

A "FEMALE ABRAHAM LINCOLN"

1826 – October 3, 1909

Until you let go of God and take hold of yourselves, of the innate powers of your own beings, there is no hope for you. . . . stop praying and go to work.

"The Curse of Godism," *c. 1896*

LOIS WAISBROOKER, HAILED AS A PROPHETESS OF BETTER DAYS, spent more than forty years of her life advocating women's rights—first suffrage, then ahead-of-her-time views on sex servitude and marriage relations.

Freethinker Ezra Heywood wrote, upon meeting Lois for the first time in 1875, that she "seemed to be a Roman Sibyl, Scott's Meg Merrilies, enacted by Charlotte Cushman, Margaret Fuller, and Sojourner Truth rolled into one. . . . She rose, went up the aisle, mounted the platform, and the tall, angular, weird, quaint kind of a she Abraham Lincoln was introduced to the audiences as 'Lois Waisbrooker.' " (Sears, *The Sex Radicals:* 232)

Born Adeline Eliza Nichols, she called herself "Lois." Her uneducated parents worked hard, her mother dying at age thirty-six. Lois had little education, working as a domestic drudge and never knowing what it was to be rested, she recalled in *Suffrage for Women*, a pamphlet published in 1868. After her marriage, Lois had several children, describing herself as a "childless widow" because her husband was not around and her children often were cared for by others due to her poverty and illness. She started a new life as a teacher of African-American children in country schools. In listening to a minister one Sunday, she realized:

". . . I must sit Sabbath after Sabbath under the ministrations of an ignorant man, or stay at home; and if the latter, should gain the reputation of being irreligious, and thus lose my influence with the people. I was a teacher of children, he of men and women; but while listening to the platitudes that fell from his lips, the conviction would force itself upon me that I was better qualified to teach that people than he was, with the question, 'Why should the fact that I am a woman be a reason that I should not?'—and the result of that summer's experience, of that questioning, is before the world." (Waisbrooker, *The Sex Revolution*, cited by McAllister: 37)

❦

After the Civil War, Lois became a lecturer on women's rights and "free love" issues. In 1869 she began writing tracts and novels, notably her views on suffrage in which she maintained "that we as a nation are motherless; or, rather, that our mother is but a servant; a petted one to be sure, but nonetheless a servant, [who] is forbidden to act, is unrepresented, is not one of the firm. . . ." (McAllister: 7).

She billed herself then as an "untrammeled Spiritualist speaker," becoming known in Boston's spiritualist community at the time Victoria Woodhull was famous. Whatever these "spiritualist" views, they were not Christian. Published in *The Truth Seeker* and elsewhere, writings in her last two decades firmly rejected "Godism" and Christianity. During the 1890s, Lois moved to Clinton, Iowa, then to Antioch, California, and finally to Topeka, Kansas, where she published a journal, *Foundation Principles*, dedicated to "Humanitarian Spiritualism."

As a regular contributor to Moses Harman's *Lucifer, The Light-Bearer*, Lois wrote candidly about women's sex servitude, rape, wartime rape, prostitution, and syphilis. One of her favorite quotes was Walt Whitman's statement, "sex contains all." As defined by the church, sex enslaved women, she believed, and was the source of untold misery.

In 1892, when she was sixty-six, Harman asked her to be guest editor of *Lucifer* while he was jailed under the Comstock Act after printing exposés about women's sexual servitude. To expose the hypocrisy of the Comstock Act, Lois reprinted an extract written for farmers about care of horse penises from a Department of Agriculture report. That issue of *Lucifer*, naturally, was banned by the Post Office. In 1894, she herself was charged with publishing obscenity in *Foundation Principles*.

"Noticed at Last" exalted the tongue-in-cheek headline of an article reporting her arrest: "Well! The sun will still shine, and people will still think. Thoughts will in time become deeds, and the prison walls that enclose martyrs for truth will disappear," she concluded. (McAllister: 42)

Feminist freethinker Matilda Joslyn Gage wrote a letter to *Lucifer* in support of Lois:

"Church power must be made to yield. The church, as I told a priest who called upon me this morning, is the great source of immorality, in its teaching that *woman was made for man*, to be obedient to him, and under 'the curse of God.' . . . Does the 'church' or the 'state' expect to gag the universe?

"I intend to live a good while yet to help put the vile tyrant down. Give us *free* thought, *free* speech, a *free* pen, a *free* people." (McAllister: 44)

Lois' two-year battle, *United States v. Waisbrooker*, ended with charges dropped on June 30, 1896. She moved to an anarchist colony in Home, Washington, in 1901, there publishing a feminist-anarchist monthly, *Clothed With the Sun*. In the hysterical clamp-down on radicals following the assassination of President McKinley, she was harassed and charged with obscenity for her article "The Awful Fate of Fallen Women." A jury in federal court found her guilty in July 1902, and she was fined one hundred dollars for writing "There is no sin in a mutual, loving relation."

In later recollections about her trial, she wrote *Lucifer* ("Very Strange," May 25, 1905): "Now, howl, ye slaves of church and state! Surely, there is nothing so cruel, so infernal, as is the idea that we must sacrifice health and even life to the supposed commands of some supposed God and to statutes founded upon such supposed commands."

She wrote a pamphlet in 1903 for the benefit of "ministers and teachers in need of enlightenment," called "Women's Source of Power." Another 1903 publication, *My Century Plant*, attacked the root of church power and counseled "how to free the earth from sex disease."

Her several propagandistic novels incorporated messages critical of religion, advocating the liberation of women from sex servitude, including *Helen Harlow's Vow* (in a ninth edition in 1890, published by Murray Hill Publishing Co.), and *A Sex Revolution* (1893). The latter feminist book deals with a main character who is guided by an "infidel" aunt in questioning church teachings. Her message: take personal action against existing hells on earth, rather than waiting for salvation or fearing other worlds.

She wrote a thirty-two page pamphlet, "The Curse of Godism," published by her own *Foundation Principles*. She delivered a speech, "The Folly of Worship," to the Liberal Convention in Ottawa, Kansas, on September 7, 1891, extracted in *Lucifer* on October 2, 1891. [See selection]

Lois Waisbrooker died in Antioch, California, at her son's home, shortly after penning "The Curse of Christian Morality," which was published after her death by Moses Harman. [See selection]

The Folly of Worship

This extract of a speech by Lois Waisbrooker before the September 1891 Liberal Convention in Ottawa, Kansas, appeared in the October 2, 1891 ("E.M. 291") issue of Lucifer, The Light-Bearer.

UNTIL YOU LET GO OF GOD and take hold of YOURSELVES, of the powers of your own being, there is no hope for you.

We are speaking of the God to whom people pray. We do not say that there is not a something beyond our comprehension; a life, a law, a power self-acting and eternal. But know this: Said power has no kinship with the God of the Christians, nor with the God of any other people whose worshipful ignorance causes them to build temples and pay tithes to win his favor.

Only think of it, men and women of the nineteenth century—think of a God who can be bought by your service, your prayers, your tears, your bowed head and bended knees—a God who can be induced to favor you—to pour out of his spirit upon you because of all this! No wonder that men in high places are for sale! God has his price, they have theirs. He will punish you in hell unless you meet his demands; the men who control the wealth of the world will starve you unless you meet their demands. Like God, like people. Then think of the folly of it!

If this ideal being—this monster creation of ignorance—really existed, the difference between such a being and man would be a thousand times greater than between man and the smallest insect. Let us imagine man receiving homage of ants, giving laws to ants, getting angry at wicked, disobedient ants "every day," and further—let us imagine ants in different parts of the earth building temples to man, ordaining a priesthood to stand between them and man, explaining man's will to the common ants, dealing out promises of future reward to obedient ones, and threats of future punishment to disobedient ones—imagine them sending missionaries to other ants to teach them how to win man's favor—imagine all this and see in the picture, the folly of worship, the curse of Godism.

Then think for a moment how you would despise a man who, were it possible to do so, would accept such homage from, and make such demands upon ants; and yet people are taught to believe that an infinite God demands your worship, is pleased with the temples that you build and consecrate to him. Use your reason, dear friends, and you will see that any being who would demand this of you, so far from being worthy of your homage would be beneath your contempt.

The Curse of Christian Morality

Lois Waisbrooker's last article, written when she was eighty-four, was published after her death by Moses Harman in the American Journal of Eugenics, January–February 1910, the last issue Harman edited before his death.

LECKY, THE HISTORIAN, IS REPORTED AS SAYING, "There should be no mercy shown to the woman who lapses from virtue, for the Christian standard must be maintained."

And what is that standard? It is that under no circumstances may a woman hold the sex relation unless she first pledges herself to some man during life. This done, she must be subject to her husband as "unto the Lord." Her feelings need not be considered; she belongs to the man and must yield to his wishes. If the woman who has no husband to obey dares to take her natural right, she is made an outcast and the brothel receives her.

Yes, I mean it. Woman has a natural, an inherent right to herself, a right which church and state refuse to allow her to exercise; but the time is coming when she will take that right and refuse to be crushed. I have known one such woman, one generation ahead of her time. She was teaching school in Iowa, but her home was in Ohio. She was a Spiritualist of Quaker descent; her mother nature was large. She wanted a child. She believed it to be her right, and she took the step. She wrote to her parents, told them she would go home if they said so, but if not, she had money enough to take care of herself where she was. They said Come home; and they tried to find out who the father was, but she would not tell them. She said, "The fault was mine, if it was a fault, and he shall not be annoyed." To the day of her death, when her son was a man of forty and a respected citizen, this woman never ceased to respect herself.

Such a woman is greater than Jesus on the cross, or Daniel in the lions' den, for the cross disappears and the lions flee before the majesty of her womanhood.

Sex is the fountain of all life, therefore of all power; and what has been the result of human law daring to say in what channel this life may flow if at all? Woman may be thus suppressed, but not man. Men visit the brothels for which the Christian standard is responsible, and the result is they are poisoned by the most loathsome of diseases—this until those who have investigated declare that not one family in ten is free from the hereditary taint. [Ed.—Waisbrooker is referring to syphilis.] A heavy price to pay for maintaining the Christian standard of virtue. Do I not well say that Christian morality is a curse?. . .

There is a cause for this persistent effort to maintain the Christian standard—*love of power.* Sex, as previously said, is the fountain of life, therefore of all power. It follows logically that if the church can control sex she controls everything. What matters it to her that nine-tenths of the people are poisoned by the outcasts she dooms to brothels so that she retains her power? The vital life expended in such relations, even in brothels, becomes a part of her heritage. Yes, the standard must be maintained, no matter what the effect.

O, mothers of the race! . . . Wake up! assert your right to yourselves, and live it. Harken! do you not hear the declarations of the Universal Life whispering through Mother Nature's attractions: "You belong to yourselves!" When you so listen to that voice as to take your freedom, the blood of your children will no longer be poisoned by sex disease, for that curse of Christian morality will no longer exist.

Then the power of the church will be gone, and people will have learned to conserve their creative life to their own upbuilding.

A noted physician who has left this life, but who was something of a philosopher, said: "The sexes seek each other for life." Well, what is it that thrills when lovers clasp hands or press lips? It is certainly something; and what can it be but the magnetism flowing from their creative life and blending to create more life for each?

But the Christian standard of virtue recognizes no such attraction as necessary. The wife who must be "subject to the husband as unto the Lord," gets no consideration for her attractions or repulsions. She is not supposed to feel anything of the kind. She is simply a sex slave. . . .

Whitman says that sex contains all. That statement cannot be gainsaid. There is not anywhere, visible or invisible, any one thing that is not the result of the action of the eternal two. The union always creates, but the character of that which is created is decided by the ruling party in the union.

The Christian standard of virtue, that which makes woman a subject, creates in such union slavery, tyranny, and the war spirit, because of the inevitable protest that nature makes. . . .

It is true that in spite of the effort to maintain the standard, the enslaved sex is growing away from it. But few women will now promise to obey, and men who are not saints are helping to give them a chance to break intolerable ties. There is now in the most progressed part of this country the possibility of divorce. True, the woman is not left free, she must live "pure" until she is again bound.

The thought sent out into the mental atmosphere by our Iowa school teacher so many years ago, is beginning to bear fruit, however. Within the last few years I have known two thinking women who have claimed the right to themselves, realizing as they do, that the relation has other uses than for offspring. Two of these are above the average of womanhood, are widely known and highly respected. They make no parade of their positions, but never hesitate to assert their claim if the subject comes up.

The Christian Bible says the son of the bond (bound) woman shall not be heir with the son of the free woman. Society now is the child of the bond woman but the free woman is coming, and the curse of Christian morality will cease to exist, for the standard can no longer be maintained.

Women Without Superstition

17

Elmina D. Slenker

PLAIN TRUTHS IN PLAIN WORDS

December 23, 1827 – 1908

When a mere girl, my mother offered me a dollar if I would read the Bible through; . . . despairing of reconciling many of its absurd statements with even my childish philosophy, . . . I became a sceptic, doubter, and unbeliever, long ere the "Good Book" was ended.

Studying the Bible, *1870*

THE FATHER OF ELIZABETH DRAKE, who was born in La Grange, New York, was expelled as a Shaker preacher when he became a "Liberal" and began holding heretical meetings. "Elmina" attributed her skeptical views to her mother's encouragement of offering her a dollar to read the bible.

Elmina, the oldest of six girls, eventually wrote for nearly all the Liberal journals. She met many reformers, including Ernestine Rose, Abby Kelley, and Parker Pillsbury. After advertising for an egalitarian husband in the *Water-Cure Journal*, she married Isaac Slenker, Quaker-style. The couple moved to Snowville, Virginia, in the early 1880s, where her husband operated woolen mills.

Elmina preached alcoholic and sexual temperance, gradually adopting "Dianaism," a philosophy which taught sexual sublimation and advocated practices which helped avoid unwanted pregnancies in a manner too plain-spoken for the guardians of the Comstock Act. In April 1887 when she was sixty, Elmina was arrested for mailing private, sealed letters giving advice on sex and marriage. Bail was set at two thousand dollars. Elmina was shown into a cold cell and given a blanket to spread on the floor, she later reported in *The Truth Seeker* (May 14, 1887).

A week later, she wrote the *Truth Seeker*: "I am here for the same reason my father was expelled as an unworthy member of the Quaker church—for speaking plain truths in plain words. We did not gild our pills with the gloss of delusive sophistry, but gave them in their simple nakedness, and the great world could not swallow them."

Her case was national news, reported by the *New York Times* disapprovingly when she refused to swear on a bible, and testified at a preliminary hearing that she did not believe in god, ghosts, heaven, hell, the bible or Christianity. She was vilified as "homely" by respectable press, which was cruel about her appearance (she had a harelip) and frowned on her short haircut.

Elmina spent six months in jail awaiting trial, unable to raise bail money. She was indicted on July 12 and held for trial in the United States District Court for the Western District of Virginia at Abington.

A freethinking attorney, Edward W. Chamberlain, represented her during her October 1887 trial, during which a jury found her guilty. However, Chamberlain contested the indictment as false because Elmina had not "knowingly" mailed obscene material, as required by the Comstock Act. Judge Paul set Elmina free on November 4, 1887. The case was a *cause célèbre* for freethought periodicals, covered in detail in *The Truth Seeker:* "What shall be said of the dirty agents employed for years in ensnaring an aged woman. . . ." (May 14, 1887) The National Defense Association, whose secretary was E. B. Foote, conducted the defense of Mrs. Slenker with expenses raised by *Truth Seeker* readers.

Elmina also wrote regularly for Moses Harman's *Lucifer: The Light-Bearer,* including an essay advocating the use of "contraceptics" appearing on July 23, 1886. She edited the *Little Freethinker* out of Snowville, Virginia and Chicago in 1892–1898. Her novels included *John's Way* (1878), *The Clergyman's Victims, Mary Jones, the Infidel School-Teacher* (1885) and *The Darwins* (1879).

❧

Her 153-page book, *Studying the Bible* (1870), is a brief, pithy response to various bible verses, made up of columns originally published in Josiah P. Mendum's freethought newspaper, the *Boston Investigator.*

Wrote Mendum in a preface dated January 1, 1870: "Many commentaries on the Bible, at different times, written by Infidels, have appeared, and done good service in the cause of truth against error. And we have now the pleasure of presenting, in the following pages, another and a novel commentary of the kind written by a woman. The author is Mrs. Elmina Drake Slenker, of Elizabethtown, East Tennessee, and the chapters here appended were published originally in the *Boston Investigator.* They excited much attention at the time, and at our suggestion they have been somewhat revised, and we now issue them in book form, for the benefit of the author, and as a useful contribution to the catalogue of Infidel works. The reader will find this commentary to be one of the keenest, liveliest, wittiest, and most sensible he ever met with,—the production of an intellect not much indebted, perhaps, to classical schools for its culture, but one which by strong natural ability is of no ordinary character. Though making no pretensions to literary acquirements, and writing as she could obtain occasional leisure from her household avocations, yet Mrs. Slenker has produced a valuable book for reference and preservation. We commend it with confidence to the Infidel public as a work with which they will all be satisfied, and we ask for it a generous patronage, as its circulation will not only help our cause, but essentially aid and encourage a worthy and deserving lady to continue her able efforts to promote reason and remove error and superstition."

Elmina applied common sense to standard bible texts, particularly analyzing the words and deeds of the New Testament Jesus. She wrote of the Sermon on the Mount that it was "nothing but a mass of absurdities and impossibilities,— sounding all very well as a romance, but for plain, practical, every-day life, it is simply nonsense." (*Studying the Bible*, p. 70)

She died in Snowville, Virginia, in her early eighties.

Studying the Bible

From the Introduction and Chapter 48 of **Studying the Bible** *(1870).*

WHEN A MERE GIRL, my mother offered me a dollar if I would read the Bible through; so with the tempting bait luring me on, I commenced the task, and, as I read, child-like asked questions, many of which proved, as is generally the case, too profound for the theological lore of my maternal relative, and at last despairing of reconciling many of its absurd statements with even my childish philosophy, I commenced jotting down extracts, accompanying each with a few of the ideas which they awakened, and the result was that I became a sceptic, doubter, and unbeliever, long ere the "Good Book" was ended: and indeed for that matter, the END was never reached, nor has it been to this day. Yet I read enough to know that it is a volume of fabulous contradictions, falsehoods, and nonsense, "from the fabled cosmogony in Genesis to the fabled destruction of the world in the Book of Revelations,"—a book which no one, with any pretensions to a knowledge of Nature and her laws, of man in his best and highest development, could believe to be a revelation from a Being as much superior to the *best* man as that best man would be to the "vilest sinner on God's footstool," or the wickedest wretch in the lowest and hottest apartment of his subterranean regions.

It is a book which would, in this enlightened (?) age, have been long ago laid upon the shelf, had its teachings not been engrafted upon the intellect of almost every child in civilized communities, almost as soon as it was able to talk or to understand. Almost every school-book, newspaper, almanac, every public lecture, every primer, every story told to the little child, is full of this one subject, and thus this Bible-religion becomes a belief grown up with the growth, welded to, and incorporated with, the young and expanding intellect, until it forms a part of the very organism itself. It will therefore take whole years of patient, persevering toil, years of study and persistent *un*-doing to clear away all the weeds, filth and rubbish that has so long encumbered the intellect of the race, and to plant therein the seeds of truth, wisdom, purity and freedom of thought! The *old* must be destroyed and rooted out, ere we can sow the *new*; so I will endeavor to do *my* part by sending forth to the world of truth-seekers a few of these jottings down of Scripture texts and the thoughts they called forth, hoping they may help to rid the world of such a mighty incubus as this old book has for so many centuries proved itself to be, bending down all science, knowledge and philosophy to the crude ideas and undeveloped intellect of a dead and buried past.

"Let Truth and Falsehood grapple. Who ever knew Truth put to the worse in a free and open encounter?"—Milton.

❦

"The effectual fervent prayer of a righteous man availeth much."—James v. 16.

If a prayer is *effectual* it must avail much, but who can prove that a single prayer ever was effectual?—that any single event in Nature was ever altered or changed by prayer? Fervent, earnest aspirations, may sometimes have a soothing, purifying effect on the heart of both supplicant and listener, and in this manner may do some good; but one can feel a heavy burden of grief or care lifted just as soon and just as surely, by philosophy and reason, by submitting quietly to the inevitable—resolving

"To patiently endure
any ill he cannot cure,"

as by praying to some imaginary nothing, and then winding up with the well known sentence, "Not my will, O Lord! but thine be done!" which is, after all, but resigning one's self to *the inevitable.*

The Infidel, or Atheist, whose mind has been educated and enlightened, can bear sorrow, disappointment, and affliction, just as calmly and resignedly as a Christian, and with far less whining, for he knows 'tis no use crying over "spilt milk." He knows that things which are born of circumstances over which he has no control, cannot be *prayed out of existence,* or diverted out of their legitimate channel, and he therefore resigns himself to them, and searches for other sources of happiness, looking ever on the sunny side, and when one cup of joy is dashed from his lips, he learns to fill for himself another from the first pure and legitimate fountain he can discover. . . .

Lillie Devereux Blake
(The Schlesinger Library, Radcliffe College)

18

Lillie Devereux Blake

THE RECTOR'S FOE

August 12, 1833 – December 30, 1913

Every denial of education, every refusal of advantages to women, may be traced to this dogma [of original sin], which first began to spread its baleful influence with the rise of the power of the priesthood and the corruption of the early Church.

Woman's Place To-Day, *1883*

LILLIE DEVEREUX BLAKE WORKED DILIGENTLY to secure rights for women during thirty years of activism, also supporting herself and her family with journalistic and fictional writings.

A Deist at most, Lillie made her freethought mark by a series of daring lectures refuting the anti-woman "Lenten lectures" of the Rev. Morgan Dix, rector of the Trinity Church in New York City, appearing in book form as *Woman's Place To-day* (1881). [See selection] She was on the revising committee of Elizabeth Cady Stanton's *The Woman's Bible*, tersely pointing out that literal translations showed that Potiphar was a *eunuch*, which throws "a new light on the story of Joseph and the woman who was Potiphar's wife only in name."

Elizabeth Johnson Devereux was born into wealth in Raleigh, North Carolina. (Freethought history buffs will be interested to note the Lillie was born one day after freethinker-to-be Robert G. Ingersoll.) Her father died suddenly when she was four. Her Episcopalian mother moved Lillie and her younger sister north. Inheritance was ticklish since it was left to the male line, but Lillie came into money as a young adult.

Lillie read widely all of her life, her feminism surfacing early. She wrote a melodramatic teenaged "treatise" in 1849: "I LIVE TO REDRESS THE WRONGS OF MY SEX," with a list of ten "rules to accomplish my aim" out of the Scarlett O'Hara school of flirtation. Newspaper accounts described her as a famous beauty through her plumper old age. (Blake, *Champion of Women*: 24)

In 1855 she married a handsome attorney of twenty-two. The young couple settled in St. Louis, freely spending Lillie's fortune. Her first daughter Elizabeth was born in 1857, the year Lillie turned seriously to "scribbling," tasting her first success with a short story in *Harper's Weekly*. They moved to New York City, where Katherine was born in 1858, the year Lillie completed her first novel, *Southwold*, published to favorable reviews in February 1859. Her life changed forever that May when her husband shot himself, the coroner's jury undecided between accident or suicide. She remarried in 1864.

Lillie discovered her fortune was spent, and struggled for money the rest of her life, supporting her family with her pen. In 1861 she supported herself as a war correspondent. By 1882, five hundred of her stories, articles, speeches and lectures, plus five novels, had been published, earning her about $3,600 for a lifetime of writing.

By thirty-five, she had turned her writing and energies almost exclusively to woman's rights, becoming a featured speaker at national suffrage conventions, her witty speeches attracting favorable press. In 1874, *Fettered for Life, or Her Lord and Master* was published, selling 1,300 copies on the day of publication.

In 1873 she made her first protest against Columbia University's exclusion of women, on behalf of her daughters, who were forced instead to attend Normal College. Dr. Morgan Dix, rector of Trinity Chapel, was the chairman of the committee which summarily dismissed Lillie's plea to admit women. In 1879, Lillie became president of the New York State Suffrage Association, building a powerful organization for eleven years which successfully campaigned for the defeat of an antisuffrage governor, won for rural women the right to vote at elections of school trustees, and got women admitted as census-takers.

When an antisuffrage lecture series by her nemesis, the Rev. Morgan Dix, was reprinted in the New York *Sun* on March 9, 1883, outraged Lillie secured a hall that day, hired a publicist and informed newspapers that her first rebuttal would be given on Sunday, March 11 at Frobisher's Hall. The nationally-noted lectures covered "Woman in Paganism and Christianity," "The Home," "The Causes of Divorce" (mainly, wrote Lillie, "that monstrous doctrine of the headship of man"), and "Woman's True Mission" (the world). Lillie said:

"Influenced by these surroundings, leading an almost cloistered life, this man has no more sympathy with the rhythm and pulse of the great heartbeat of to-day than a stained-glass window. He is a theological Rip Van Winkle, who has slept, not twenty but two hundred years. . . .

". . . he quaintly asserts that man should be the head of the family, because 'Adam was first formed, then Eve.' What does that prove? Either nothing, or that man is inferior to the fishes. For another sentence of equal truth, and proving that man should be subordinate to the finny tribe, might readily be framed thus: 'For the fishes were first formed, then Adam.' "

Her 1888 lecture, "Is It a Crime to Be A Woman?" was reviewed around the country. She indignantly recounted how a woman was sentenced to six months on Blackwell's Island for dressing as a man in order to make a waiter's salary.

Her special reform was the effort to place women matrons in New York City station houses to halt daily humiliations of women prisoners and homeless women. Lillie wrote and testified of the horror stories resulting from this inequity. One woman found insensible in the street was put into a cell overnight. In the morning, police discovered that she was not drunk but brutally battered; she died without recovering consciousness. Another woman picked up for drunkenness was found dead in her cell the next morning, her dead newborn beside her. Lillie won this twenty-year fight in 1892 after many setbacks. She lived to see some of the matrons promoted to detective work.

At Thanksgiving 1892, she organized the first of more than ten Pilgrim Mothers' Dinners, in response to a traditional New England male ritual. At her opening remarks, she quipped: "The Pilgrim mothers not only had to endure all that the Pilgrim fathers suffered, but had to endure the Pilgrim fathers as well." (*Champion of Women:* 180)

Lillie was on the main program at the International Congress of Women held in connection with the World's Columbian Exposition in 1893.

In 1895, Lillie was appointed to head a "Committee on Legislative Advice" by the National American Woman Suffrage Association, in accord with her strong belief that woman's rights not be sacrificed to woman suffrage. In 1899, she fought her removal by Susan B. Anthony as illegal. When Anthony retired, Lillie was encouraged by Elizabeth Cady Stanton to run as the natural successor of Anthony for president of the NAWSA against Carrie Chapman Catt. Stanton signed a circular listing Lillie's contributions, which included obtaining pensions for war nurses, making women eligible for civil service positions, and reforms in New York State, such as making both parents joint guardians of their children, enabling a woman to make a will without a husband's consent, and providing seats for saleswomen. Lillie withdrew before the vote "for the sake of harmony." Her daughter Katherine Blake blamed Anthony's suffrage single-mindedness for the demise of feminism shortly after the vote was won, believing her mother's vision, had she succeeded Anthony in the NAWSA, would have fulfilled the early promise of the woman's rights movement. Lillie's short-lived legislative group successfully protested the loss of citizenship for American women who married foreign men.

Lillie was placed in a sanitarium in 1910 and died at eighty after breaking her hip in 1913.

Woman in Paganism and Christianity

This is excerpted from the first of four lectures in reply to the Lenten Lectures on "Woman" by the Rev. Morgan Dix, D.D., Rector of Trinity Church, New York, collected as the book Woman's Place To-Day, in 1883.

WITHIN THE LAST FEW WEEKS a prominent clergyman has risen in our midst to tell us all about women—their history, their duties, and their place in the world. He is a man, and other men have applauded his conduct and endorsed his views. For three Friday evenings now this divine has had his say and no one has replied to him. But, considering the extraordinary nature of his utterances, it is certainly quite time that some woman should endeavor to present the views of women on subjects they may reasonably be supposed to understand.

Now, we have no fault to find with this reverend gentleman individually. He is a man of great learning, of wide culture, and of much excellence of character, a man whose broad benevolence has made him a benefactor to many, and he is no doubt perfectly honest in his views, as well as earnest in their presentation. But when this gentleman uses the position in which he stands, strongly intrenched with all the wealth of the wealthiest church in the country to sustain him, with his social standing, his congregation, his clerical brethren all giving him strength,—when he uses these great advantages to try to arrest the struggles of womanhood for freedom, to bind still tighter the chains she has half cast off, to stifle all her aspirations for a better life, then surely the time has come for some woman, speaking for her sex as well as her powers will permit, to reply to this clerical dictator.

For this divine, shunning the broad light of the nineteenth century, retires within the cloistered walls of Trinity Chapel, and from thence, refusing to see the sun at noonday, cries out, Let us live here with the past; this gentle twilight is better than the rude glare of day. Here, ladies, your silks and satins will be sheltered from all storms; let us then stop and dream in this cosy warmth and gentle shade.

Apparently the reverend doctor knows no world outside of the soft cushions of his velvet-lined pews. "Peace, prayer, retirement!" this, he says, should content all women. "Maternity is the glory of womanhood, and in this is she redeemed."

If from the easy chair of his study he dimly discerns the forms of women madly struggling in the great river of life, striving vainly for bread, for honest living, he says to them, Peace, retirement, these are women's happiness. If he sees a wretched mother shuddering on the brink of the river, and clasping to her breast a miserable baby that is her shame and her disgrace, to her he says, "Maternity is your highest function!" If he hears penetrating even through his curtained windows the voices of women who cry and plead for better opportunities for their sex, he bids them be silent; meekness, forbearance, patience are the virtues which most adorn womanhood.

Ah, he is himself too late, this respectable relic of the middle ages! The chariot of progress is moving on. At its front sits awakened womanhood with the glory of hope in her starry eyes, and not even the Rector of Trinity Church is strong enough to block the wheels of that triumphant car!

Now let us analyze a little in detail what this reverend gentleman has said. He declares first that all that woman has to-day she owes to the Church. Let us look a little into this statement, and see if a man of his cultivation ought to make it in the face of the facts of history. It has been a favorite objection against woman's emancipation to say that it was a "reform against nature," that women have always been subordinate, and therefore always will be. There is some excuse for such an assertion from a man who has read nothing and knows nothing, but from the learned doctor it is absolutely astonishing.

We might expect the Rev. John Jasper, of Richmond, Va., who declared that the earth stood still and the sun went round it, to make some such ignorant assertions, but from the Rev. Morgan Dix they are amazing!

Women in this country to-day are only asking for the liberties they enjoyed in Egypt 4,000 years ago. If we turn to that wonderful nation, whose stupendous monuments and gorgeous palaces still remain to tell what was the magnificence of their civilization, we shall find that woman occupied a position in the political, social, and business world that was equal to man's. In that wisest of all nations there were no cruel laws against women because of their sex. Their twin gods were Isis and Osiris, sister and brother, wife and husband, the woman's name always mentioned first. The queen also had equal power with the king, sometimes even greater, as Cleopatra was more influential than her husband Ptolemy, even after the Greek conquest.

The records on their monuments and the traditions of Egyptian history show men and women laboring together, dealing together in the market place, and sitting together at the council board. Property was transmitted in the female line, which was held to be the more surely legitimate. There was no thought in that land of denying to women the highest education. Wise women practised as physicians, pious women preached as priestesses, and learned women taught as the public instructors of both men and women, down to the time when the accomplished and beautiful Hypatia was torn to pieces by a Christian mob. . . .

Let us then see what this man-made Church has done for women: In the early days of Christianity women and men labored together to teach the new religion. Women were preachers and deaconesses, St. Paul himself frequently speaking of their work in his epistles. Indeed, their public ministrations in the Church continued until A.D. 365, when the Council of Laodicea, in its eleventh canon, forbade the ordination of women to the ministry; and women still continued to be deaconesses until the Council of Orleans in the year 511 took from them even this privilege.

But as the years passed on, the priesthood grew in arrogance and the desire for power. The gentle teachings of the early Christians were forgotten, the usurpations of Rome increased, and the supremacy of the priesthood was established by the absorption of wealth, and, as knowledge is power, by grasping all learning.

Education was discouraged for men and denied to women, and this monstrous body, the Church of the middle ages, was built up to be a giant of enormous potency.

In those days books were almost wholly in the hands of priests. Charles Martel, Richard Coeur de Lion, and the greatest warriors of the day could neither read nor write. Ignorance was the universal rule, and women were, of course, uneducated and consequently degraded.

But the most grievous wrong of that day, the cause of the gradual degradation of woman, was to be found in the establishment of the celibacy of the clergy. This doctrine that a priest must not marry was the fruitful source of infinite woe to women—a doctrine which, by the way, this reverend gentleman himself preached and practiced for a large portion of his life. No wonder he stands to-day as the apostle of woman's subordination, he who for so many years advocated that priestly isolation and denial of home life which for centuries wrought such misery to our sex.

This hideous doctrine of a celibate priesthood was maintained only by a constant struggle against the better and truer instincts of the heart. In order to sustain it women were declared to be by nature inferior, to be unfit to associate with men, to be unworthy and degrading in their influence over all who approached them. With this cruel set of maxims was the human heart preached down for a thousand years, and even to-day we suffer from those teachings which were rendered necessary to prevent men from entering the natural and happy relation of marriage.

In order to excuse this theory of woman's inferiority on account of her sex, which was utterly in conflict with pagan views, there was set up the absurd dogma that all women must be punished because of "Eve's sin;" a dogma borrowed from the ancient Jewish writings, and which is reiterated even by Dr. Dix to-day. How absurd this theory is. . . .

How far-reaching has been the wrong this theory has inflicted upon women it is difficult for us to understand; but it is at the root and foundation of every idea of woman's inferiority which afflicts us to-day. Every denial of education, every refusal of advantages to women, may be traced to this dogma, which first began to spread its baleful influence with the rise of the power of the priesthood and the corruption of the early Church.

St. Augustine, whose early life was most dissolute, was one of the first who taught this doctrine of Original Sin, and thenceforth this doctrine was reiterated and elaborated by the "fathers of the Church" as a powerful means of maintaining the celibacy of the clergy, the repetition of this idea tending constantly to the degradation of the sex.

St. Chrysostom, whose prayer Dr. Dix reads at every morning service, maintained this doctrine and described woman as "a necessary evil, a natural temptation, a desirable calamity, a domestic peril, a deadly fascination, and a painted ill."

All association with this weak and degraded half of humanity was discouraged among men; marriage was looked upon as a species of humiliation, and the Emperor Honorius banished the learned Jovinus because he asserted the possibility that a man might be saved who lived with his wife! These were the teachings of that Church to which Dr. Dix declares that women owe everything!

It was but an easy step, after marriage was declared degrading for men, to reduce women to utter subservience, to declare that all women should respect and obey all men: first the priest, then the husband, the father, the son, or indeed any man; and thus was built up that idea of man's superiority which has so firm a hold on society to-day.

Of course such views lead to utter immorality, and the so-called celibate priesthood were really most vicious in their lives. Where women were taught their inferiority they easily fell into slavery to all men, and in every community was established that class which is to-day the disgrace of our sex and of humanity.

At the end of fifteen hundred years of nominal Christianity this was woman's position. The old respect was gone. She had lost her property rights, her education, her political power. All women were in subjection to all men: they were denied the priesthood and the command of armies, in marriage they were held subordinate, and the chastity so esteemed by the pagan northern nations had given place to indiscriminate immorality.

With Protestantism, however, came the dawn of a new era, the first ray of light of the coming noonday. The right of freedom of thought, the right of private judgment, the right to criticise the Church and the priesthood, these new ideas were the harbingers of human liberty. . . .

From that day to this the struggle has gone on, the champions of liberty claiming personal freedom which has been gradually extended to the laborer, to the slave, and last of all to woman, who is still held in bondage by the teachings of the past and the arbitrary dictates of a masculine priesthood which even to-day re-echoes the spirit of the dark ages. . . .

Side by side with the doctrine of inferiority and submission taught to women went naturally the denial to them of all education; and when we reflect how persistently women were forbidden all instruction, it is no wonder that for centuries they have seemed utterly and abjectly inferior to men. . . .

Of course, as representing the Church which for centuries denied to women any education whatsoever, the Rector of Trinity is naturally foremost in trying to prevent the higher education of women. And it is well understood that Dr. Dix alone to-day prevents the opening of Columbia College to women.

If I may be pardoned a personal allusion I will briefly narrate the story of my own application to this university in 1873, on behalf of several young ladies who were anxious to avail themselves of the benefits of the institution. These applicants were all girls of unusual promise. One of them was a valedictorian of the Normal College here, one was a graduate of Michigan University, and they were all qualified and earnest students. As two of my ancestors has been presidents of the college I felt an especial claim on it; and on turning to the charter of the university I found that this claim on behalf of young women was apparently well founded.

. . . I made formal application to the Faculty, and at once found that the applicants had a friend in the president of the college, Mr. Barnard, then as now an earnest advocate of co-education. But the request of the young ladies to be admitted to examination was referred to a committee of which Dr. Morgan Dix was the chairman, and was peremptorily refused.

The position which he held ten years ago this reverend stumbling-block holds to-day. A decade with all its stirring life, with all its living facts, has not advanced him one tittle or opened his eyes to the needs of the day. . . .

And now comes Dr. Dix to define women's place and duties, and what does the worthy man consider should be their greatest pleasure? To adorn their minds with knowledge? To earn an honest livelihood? To make the path of life easier for others of their sex? Oh, no, none of these. They must go to church and listen to the singing of the Magnificat! They must not even sing themselves, but listen to the singing of this chant, intoned by a chorus of male voices. This, he says, is the touchstone to true woman-hood, and he finds in the words of the anthem *"Ecce Ancilla Domini,"* the utterance of that "sweet submission" which is woman's highest attribute.

Ah, my friends, there is a grander hymn even than the Magnificat, as there is "a word that is dearer than mother, home, or heaven, and that word is liberty." [—Matilda Joslyn Gage] A song should be sung by a grand and noble womanhood, not by a set of wretched, half-masculine crea-tures, such as Dr. Dix describes, miserable imitations of men striving vainly to contend with them, but educated and admirable women, who are doing women's work in caring for women, in laboring to make the world purer and better, who are devoted to their homes faithfully, and then to that larger home which is the world in which we live and in which we have every one of us work to do; women who will not lead lives of mere idleness and retirement, finding their occupation in the embroidering of altar cloths, and their pleasure in "listening" to the Magnificat; but women who shall lead lives of usefulness, for children, for friends, and for the state, and who in the grand chorus with their brothers shall sing that hymn to which the heart of every American is attuned . . . the hymn of liberty.

Ouida

19

Ouida

BESTSELLING VICTORIAN NOVELIST

January 1, 1839 – January 25, 1908

Christianity is a formula: it is nothing more.
"The Failure of Christianity," *1895*

NÉE MARIA LOUISA RAMÉ IN THE VILLAGE of Bury St. Edmunds, England, she built up a mysterious aura around her exotic-sounding pen name. "Ouida" was actually her childish pronunciation of "Louisa." Her mother was pretty, middle-class Susan Sutton, her father an ugly but fascinating Frenchman who settled in the village briefly enough to marry Susan and spend her dowry. Ramé flitted in and out of his daughter's life, filling her ears with tales of intrigue, high society and romance. Ouida adopted "de la Ramée" as her surname.

At eighteen, Ouida, precocious and ambitious, persuaded her doting mother and elderly grandmother to move to London so she could pursue her ambition of becoming a rich and famous novelist. An acquaintance happened to be the cousin of W. Harrison Ainsworth, author of popular historical novels and editor of *Bentley's Miscellany*. Ainsworth immediately serialized one of Ouida's stories, publishing eighteen over the next three years, launching Ouida as a popular writer.

Her first full-length novel, *Held in Bondage*, was published in three volumes in 1863, earning Ouida £50. The typical plot concerned a cavalryman, a wicked lady bigamist and a melancholy count. A twenty-six, Ouida had the compliment of being ranked with Disraeli, Tennyson, Dickens, Browning and Eliot for salability on the Continent.

The middle-class apparently was enthralled with Ouida's naughty, dramatic pictures of the aristocracy of which she knew nothing, while the upper class was amused by her imaginative flights and "Ouidaisms." Some even thought Ouida might be George Eliot writing under pseudonym. Success going to her head, Ouida became legendary as an intractable snob and guest, snubbing other women.

A dog-lover who frequently wrote about dogs as characters, Ouida became a passionate antivivisectionist. In 1866, Ouida set up a *salon* notorious because only gentlemen, mainly the Brigade of Guards, were invited, and smoking was permitted. Proper Ouida was always chaperoned by her mother.

Her appearance was equally eccentric. Ouida wore her thin hair down. Her gowns, no matter the style of the day, were designed to show off her only beauties, her tiny wrists, hands, and feet. A male poet once described her: "sinister, clever face, hair down, small hands and feet, voice like a carving-knife."

Every year a new novel was released. She was popular in America as well as England and the Continent, with a Pre-Raphaelite following. Freethought and women's journals invariably contained advertisements for her latest book.

Ouida moved to Europe in 1871 and wrote a collection of stories, *A Dog of Flanders*, which won acclaim from Ruskin. She settled in Florence, rented an expensive villa, outspent her income, acquired a menagerie of cosseted dogs that she refused to house-train, and put on lavish entertainment for local aristocrats.

She began writing about the Italian poor, alienating some society contacts. *Pascarel* was about Tuscan peasants. *Two Little Wooden Shoes* inspired Mascagni's opera "Lodoletta." A novel attacking the sufferings of Italian peasants, *A Village Commune*, once more won Ruskin's approbation. *In Maremma* (1882) was considered the best of her peasant novels. Her career had peaked. After she turned forty she and her mother spent much of the next decade moving from hotel to hotel to escape creditors.

Ouida wrote political and nonfiction pieces, most published in the *Fortnightly Review* or *North American Review* on such subjects as "The New Priesthood: A Protest Against Vivisection." Ouida was evicted from her villa in 1894, and retired to Lucca with at least thirty dogs. She helped found the Italian Society of Prevention of Cruelty to Animals, and wrote articles and pamphlets for the British Humanitarian League. *Views and Opinions*, containing her essay expressing her lifelong freethought views, "The Failure of Christianity," was published in 1895. [See selection] The volume is a strange mixture of radical and reactionary, humanitarian and misanthropic. At the turn of the century, *Critical Studies*, more essays, was published to success, going into three editions.

After she died of pneumonia, she was buried at Bagni di Lucca under a bier showing her prone figure with a dog at her feet. The *Daily Mirror* in London erected a drinking fountain for horses and dogs in her memory at her despised hometown of Bury St. Edmunds in 1909. Despite her irreligion, an inscription reads: "Here may God's creatures whom she loved assuage her tender soul as they drink." Forty-seven books had been published, including an unfinished posthumous novel. Ouida is considered an influence on such authors as Edith Wharton and John Galsworthy.

The Failure of Christianity

Excerpted is this chapter from **Views and Opinions** *(1895).*

CHRISTIANITY IS A FORMULA: it is nothing more. The nations in which daily services in its honour are said in thousands and tens of thousands of cathedrals and churches, sell opium to the Chinese, cheat and slay red Indians, slaughter with every brutality the peaceful natives of Tonquin and Anam, carry fire and sword into central Asia, kill Africans like ants on expeditions, and keep a whole populace in the grip of military service from the Spree to the Elbe, from the Zuider Zee to the Tiber, from the Seine to the Neva. Whether the nation be England, America, France, Russia, Italy, or Germany, the fact is the same; with the gospels on its reading-desks and their shibboleth on its lips, every nation practically follows the lusts and passions of its human greeds for possession of territory and increase of treasure. Not one amongst them is better in this matter than another. Krupp guns, shrapnel shells, nitro-glycerine and submarine torpedoes are the practical issues of evangelicism and catholicism all over the civilised world. And the nations are so sublimely unconscious of their own hypocrisy that they have blessings on their warfare pronounced by their ecclesiastics, and implore the Lord of Hosts for his sympathy before sending out armoured cruisers.

This is inevitable, is the reply: in the present state of hostility between all nations, the first one to renounce the arts of war would be swallowed up by the others. So it would be, no doubt; but if this be the chief fruit of Christianity, may not this religion justly be said to have failed conspicuously in impressing itself upon mankind? It has impressed its formulas; not its spirit. It has sewn a phylactery on the hem of humanity's robe: it has never touched the soul of humanity beneath the robe. It has produced the iniquities of the Inquisition, the egotism and celibacy of the monasteries, the fury of religious wars, the ferocity of the Hussite, of the Catholic, of the Puritan, of the Spaniard, of the Irish Orangeman and of the Irish Papist; it has divided families, alienated friends, lighted the torch of civil war, and borne the virgin and the greybeard to the burning pile, broken delicate limbs upon the wheel and wrung the souls and bodies of innocent creatures on the rack: all this it has done, and done in the name of God.

But of mercy, of pity, of forbearance, of true self-sacrifice, what has it ever taught the world?

A while ago there was published an account of the manufacture of the deadliest sort of dynamite on the shores of Arran. Full in the front of the great sea, with all the majesty of a rock-bound and solitary shore around them, these hideous works raise their blaspheming face to Nature and pollute and profane her most solemn glories; and there, on this coast of Arran, numbers of young girls work at the devilish thing in wooden huts, with every moment the ever-present risk of women and huts being blown into millions of atoms if so much as a shred of metal, or even a ray of too warm sunshine, strike on the foul, sickly, infernal compound which their fingers handle. A brief while since two girls were thus blown into the air, and were so instantaneously and utterly annihilated that not a particle of their bodies or of their clothing could be recognised; and all the while the sea-gulls were circling, and the waves leaping, and the clouds sailing, and deep calling to deep, 'Lo! behold the devil and all his works.' And there is no devil there at all except man—man who makes money out of this fell thing which blasts the beauties of Nature, and scars the faces of the hills, and has made possible to civilisation a fashion of wholesale assassination so horrible, so craven, and so treacherous that the boldness of open murder seems almost virtue beside it.

The manufactory of nitro-glycerine on the Arran shore is the emblem of the world which calls itself Christian. No doubt the canny Scots who are enriched by it go to their kirk religiously, are elders of it, very likely, and if they saw a boy trundle a hoop, or a girl use a needle on the Sabbath day, would think they saw a crime, and would summon and chastise the sinners. Pontius Pilate was afraid and ashamed when he had condemned an innocent man; but the modern followers of Christ have neither fear nor shame when they pile up gold on gold in their bankers' cellars through the death which they have manufactured and sold, indifferent though it should strike down a thousand innocent men.

Even of death Christianity has made a terror which was unknown to the gay calmness of the Pagan and the stoical repose of the Indian. Never has death been the cause of such craven timidity as in the Christian world, to which, if Christians believed any part of what they profess, it would be the harbinger of glad tidings, the welcome messenger of a more perfect life. To visionaries like Catherine of Siena, it may have been so at times, but to the masses of men and women professing the Christian faith, death has been and is the King of Terrors, from whose approach they cower in an agony which Petronius Arbiter would have ridiculed, and Socrates and Seneca have scorned. The Greek and the Latin gave dignity to death, and awaited it with philosophy and peace; but the Christian beholds in it innumerable fears like a child's terror of ghosts in darkness, and by the manner of the funeral rites with which he celebrates it contrives to make grotesque even that mute majesty which rests with the dead slave as much as with the dead emperor.

Christianity has been cruel in much to the human race. It has quenched much of the sweet joy and gladness of life; it has caused the natural passions and affections of it to be held as sins; by its teaching that the body should be despised, it has brought on all the unnamable filth which was made a virtue in the monastic orders and which in the Italian, the Spanish, the Russian peoples, and the poor of all nations is a cherished and indestructible habit. In its permission to man to render subject to him all other living creatures of the earth, it continued the cruelty of the barbarian and of the pagan, and endowed these with what appeared a divine authority—an authority which Science, despising Christianity, has yet not been ashamed to borrow and to use.

Let us, also, endeavour to realise the unutterable torments endured by men and maidens in their efforts to subdue the natural desires of their senses and their affections to the unnatural celibacy of the cloister, and we shall see that the tortures inflicted by Christianity have been more cruel than the cruelties of death. Christianity has ever been the enemy of human love; it has forever cursed and expelled and crucified the one passion which sweetens and smiles on human life, which makes the desert blossom as the rose, and which glorifies the common things and common ways of earth. It made of this, the angel of life, a shape of sin and darkness, and bade the woman whose lips were warm with the first kisses of her lover believe herself accursed and ashamed. Even in the unions which it reluctantly permitted, it degraded and dwarfed the passion which it could not entirely exclude, and permitted it coarsely to exist for the mere necessity of procreation. The words of the Christian nuptial service expressly say so. Love, the winged god of the immortals, became, in the Christian creed, a thrice-damned and earth-bound devil, to be exorcised and loathed. This has been the greatest injury that Christianity has ever done to the human race. Love, the one supreme, unceasing source of human felicity, the one sole joy which lifts the whole mortal existence into the empyrean, was by it degraded into the mere mechanical action of reproduction. It cut the wings of Eros. Man, believing that he must no longer love his mistress, woman, believing that she must no longer love her lover, loved themselves, and from the cloisters and from the churches there arose a bitter, joyless, narrow, apprehensive passion which believed itself to be religion, but was in truth only a form of concentrated egotism, the agonised desire to be 'saved,' to ascend into the highest heaven, let who else would wait without its doors or pine in hell. The influence of this is still with the world, and will long be with it; and its echo is still loud in the sibilant voices which hiss at the poet who sings and the poet who glorifies love.

And herein we approach that spurious offspring of Christianity which is called cant.

Other religions have not been without it. The Mosaic law had the Pharisee, who for a presence made long prayers. The Greek and the Latin had those who made oblations to the gods for mere show, and augurs who served the sacred altars with their tongue in their cheek. But from Christianity, alas! has arisen and spread a systematic hypocrisy more general, more complete, more vain, more victorious than any other. The forms of the Christian religion facilitate this. Whether in the Catholic form of it, which cleanses the sinner in the confessional that he may go forth and sin again freely, or in the Protestant form, which, so long as a man listens to sermons and kneels at sacraments, does not disturb him as to the tenor of his private life, the Christian religion says, practically, to all its professors: 'Wear my livery and assemble in my courts; I ask no more of you in return for the moral reputation which I will give to you.'

Its lip-service and its empty rites have made it the easiest of all tasks for the usurer to cloak his cruelties, the miser to hide his avarice, the lawyer to condone his lies, the sinner of all social sins to purchase the social immunity from them by outward deference to churches.

The Christian religion, outwardly and even in intention humble, does, without meaning it, teach man to regard himself as the most important of all created things. Man surveys the starry heavens and hears with his ears of the plurality of worlds; yet his religion bids him believe that his alone out of these innumerable spheres is the object of his master's love and sacrifice. To save his world—whose common multitudes can be no more in the scale of creation than the billions of insects that build up a coral-reef beneath the deep sea—he is told that God himself took human shape, underwent human birth, was fed with human food, and suffered human pains. It is intelligible that, believing this, the most arrogant self-conceit has puffed up the human crowd, and that with the most cruel indifference they have sacrificed to themselves all the countless suffering multitudes which they are taught to call 'the beasts which perish.' It is this selfishness and self-esteem which, fostered in the human race by Christianity, have far outweighed and overborne the humility which its doctrines in part strove to inculcate and the mercy which they advocated.

It is in vain that the human race is bidden to believe that its Creator cares for the lilies of the field and for the birds of the air: it is the human race alone for which its God has suffered and died, so it believes, and this solitary selection, this immense supremacy, make it semi-divine in its own sight. It is the leaven of egotism begotten by the Christian creed which has neutralised the purity and the influence of its teachings. Here and there saintly men and women have been guided by it solely in the ways of holiness and unselfishness; but the great majority of mankind has drawn from it chiefly two lessons—self-concentration and socialism. 'Rock of ages, cleft for *me*,' sighs the Christian; and this 'immense Me' is, as Emerson has said of it, the centre of the universe in the belief of the unconscious egotist.

Christians repeat like a parrot's recitative the phrase that no sparrow falls uncounted by its Creator, and they go to their crops and scatter poison, or load fowling-pieces with small shot to destroy hundreds of sparrows in a morning. If they believed that their God saw the little birds of the air fall, would they dare to do it? Of course they would not; but they do not believe: it only suits them to use their formula, and they are never prevented by it from strewing bird-poison or setting bird-traps.

Behold their priests taking on themselves the vows of poverty, of chastity, and of renunciation, and whether they be the Catholic cardinal, stately, luxurious and arrogant, or whether they be the Protestant bishop, with his liveried servants, his dinner parties, and his church patronage, what can we see more widely removed in unlikeness from all the precepts of the creed which they profess to obey? What fiercer polemics ever rage than those which wrangle about the body of religion? What judge would not be thought a madman who should from the bench counsel the man who has received a blow to bear it in meekness and turn the other cheek? What missionary would be excused for leaving his wife and children chargeable

on parish rates because he pointed to the injunction to leave all that he
had and follow Christ?

What attempt on the part of any community to put the precepts of
Christianity into practical observance would not cause them to be denounced to magistrates as communists, as anarchists, as moonstruck dreamers, as lunatics? There are sects in Russia which endeavour to do so, and
the police hunt them down like wild animals. They are only logically trying to carry out the precepts of the gospels, but they are regarded therefore as dangerous lunatics. They can have no place in the conventional
civilisation of the world. What judge who should tell the two litigants in
any lawsuit concerning property that they were violating every religious
duty in wrangling with each other about filthy lucre would not be deemed
a fool, and worse? The French Republic, in tearing down from its courts
of law and from its class-rooms the emblems of Christianity, has done a
rough, but sincere and consistent, act, if one offensive to a great portion of
the nation; and it may be alleged that this act is more logical than the acts
of those nations who open their tribunals with rites of reverence towards
a creed with which the whole legislature governing these tribunals is in
entire and militant contradiction. . . .

How is it to be accounted for—this impotence of Christianity to affect
the policies, politics, legislation and general life of the nations which think
their salvation lies in the profession of its creed? How is it that a religion
avowedly making peace and long-suffering of injury the corner-stone of
its temple has had as its principal outcome war, both the fanaticism of
religious war and the avarice of civil war; a legislation founded on the *lex
talionis* and inexorable in its adherence to that law; and a commerce which
all the world over is saturated with the base desire to overreach, outwit
and outstrip all competitors?

It is chiefly due to the absolutely 'unworkable' character of its injunctions; and partly due to the Jewish laws entering so largely into the creeds
of modern Christians: also it is due to the fact that even in the purer creeds
of the evangelists there is so much of egotism. 'What shall it profit a man
if he gain the whole world and lose his own soul?' 'His own'—that throughout is to be the chief thought of his existence and its constant end. The
greatest of the Christian martyrs were but egotists when they were not
matoïdes. Their fortitude and constancy were already rewarded, in their
belief, by every sweetness of celestial joys and glories. It may be doubted

whether they even felt the scourge, the torch, the iron, or the rods, so intensely in their exaltation was their nervous system strung up to ecstasy. What could the poor offer of earthly life seem worth to those who believed that by thus losing it they would enter at once and forever into the exquisite consciousness of a surpassing beatitude? An intense, though innocent, selfishness was at the root of all the martyrdoms of the early Christian Church. There was not one amongst them which approached for unselfishness the death of Antinous. And it is surely this egotism which is an integral part of the Christian creed, and which has been at once its strength and its weakness; its strength in giving it dominion over human nature, and its weakness in allying it with baser things. The alloy has made the gold more workable, but has destroyed its purity.

. . . A religion which is founded on the desire of men to attain eternal felicity will be naturally seductive to them, but the keynote of its motive power can never be a lofty one. The jewelled streets of the New Jerusalem are not more luxuriously dreamed of than the houris of the Mohammedan paradise. Each form of celestial recompense is anticipated as reward for devotion to a creed. And as all loyalty, all loveliness, all virtue *pêchent par la base* when they are founded on the expectation of personal gain, so the Christian religion has contained the radical defect of inciting its followers to obedience and faithfulness by a bribe—a grand bribe truly—nothing less than eternal life; such life as the soul of man cannot even conceive; but still a bribe. Therefore Christianity has been powerless to enforce its own ethics on the world in the essence of their spirit, and has been perforce contented with hearing it recite its formulas.

What will be its future? . . . Christianity can only be one of two things— either a nullity, as it is now in all national life, or a dynamic force allied with and ruling through socialism, and destroying all civilisation as it, at present, stands.

Which will it be? There is no prophet to say. But whichever it be, there will be that in its future which, if it remain dominant, will make the cry of the poet the sigh of Humanity:

> 'Thou hast triumphed O pale Gallilean,
> And the world has grown grey with Thy breath!'

Marilla M. Ricker
(The Schlesinger Library, Radcliffe College)

20

Marilla M. Ricker

DISTINGUISHED ATTORNEY, FREETHOUGHT MISSIONARY

March 18, 1840 – November 12, 1920

*Children should be taught that no amount of so-called religion will
compensate for rheumatism; that Christianity has nothing to do with
morality; that vicarious atonement is a fraud and a lie; that to be born well
and strong is the highest birth; that the Bible is no more inspired than The
Philistine; that sin is a transgression of the laws of life; and that the blood of
all the bulls and goats and lambs of ancient times, and the blood of Jesus or
any other man never had nor can have the least effect in making a life what
it would have been had it obeyed the laws of life.*

"What Is Prayer?" **The Four Gospels**, *1911*

MARILLA M. RICKER, a trail-blazing nineteenth-century attorney, abolitionist, pioneer suffragist and humanitarian, devoted her last decades to the promotion of freethought.

Marilla Marks Young was born at her family farm in Durham, New Hampshire, the second of four children. Her mother Hannah Stevens Young was a Free-Will Baptist. Her father Jonathan was a freethinker, an early woman suffragist, and, reportedly, a relation of Mormon Brigham Young.

Her father educated her in politics by taking her to courtrooms and town meetings. At sixteen the tall teenager began teaching to acclaim at her local school, after a year at Colby Academy in New London, New Hampshire.

At age twenty-three she married John Ricker, a fifty-six-year-old farmer who believed in equality. She was widowed five years later and, childless, inherited $50,000. She spent four years visiting and studying in Europe, then settled in Washington, D.C., determined to read law to help the less fortunate. She passed the District of Columbia bar with the highest grade of any who had been admitted in 1882. As if that were not flourish enough, Marilla's first public courtroom appearance was as assistant counsel to Robert G. Ingersoll in the Star Route mail fraud cases.

Her practice gradually expanded from criminal to financial and banking law, and finally labor reform. When President Arthur appointed her as a notary public, she took depositions for destitute prisoners at no charge. In 1884, Marilla became the first female U.S. commissioner and examiner in chancery in the district. The U.S. Supreme Court admitted her to its bar on May 1, 1891.

Known as the "prisoner's friend," Marilla successfully challenged the district's "poor convict's law," which had indefinitely confined poor criminals unable to pay fines. In 1879, she had an executive hearing before the governor and council of New Hampshire to protest cruel treatment of prisoners there, resulting in passage of an act guaranteeing that convicts could send sealed, unmonitored letters to the heads of government.

An active suffrage proponent, Marilla demanded the right to vote in New Durham in 1870 as an "elector" under the Fourteenth Amendment. Her first ballot was invalidated but *The History of Woman Suffrage* records that the following year she had the distinction of being the first U.S. woman to vote using this argument (II: 586). When Belva Lockwood ran for president under the Equal Rights party in 1884, Marilla campaigned for her. In 1890 Marilla secured the right of women to practice law in New Hampshire. She was a member of the National Woman Suffrage Association, the New Hampshire organization, and became a life member of the merged National American Woman Suffrage Association. She was also active as a Republican in traditional politics but her request to be appointed to a diplomatic post by President McKinley, an effort to break a barrier for women, was rejected.

Marilla announced her candidacy for governor of New Hampshire in 1910 on a woman's rights platform. *The Truth Seeker* praised her as "the intellectual equal of any man ever elected to the office of governor of New Hampshire." The Attorney General ruled her ineligible to run.

She began contributing articles to *The Truth Seeker* around the turn of the century, and continued to do so for two decades. Marilla offered to buy the full twelve-volume Dresden edition of the *Works of Ingersoll* for any library in New Hampshire that would accept them. She habitually paid taxes with a protest, in her suffragist days against her disenfranchisement, and later against the exemption of churches. Upon her death, she was fondly remembered for distributing perhaps more copies of *The Truth Seeker* than anyone else. Marilla described herself as a "free-thought missionary . . . doing my 'level best' to drive superstition, alias Christianity" from the minds of humankind. (*I Am Not Afraid Are You?*: 82) She died at age eighty of a stroke.

Marilla Ricker's books included *Four Gospels* (1911), favorably comparing Paine and Ingersoll with John Calvin and Puritan Jonathan Edwards, and two volumes of practical, folksy essays, *I Don't Know Do You?* (1916) and *I Am Not Afraid Are You?* (1917). She quipped about "the Christian who prays and spells it with an *e.*"

𐂷

The following quotes, from her essay "Science Against Creeds," (*I Am Not Afraid Are You?*) illustrate her plain-spoken New England approach to freethought:

"If you must believe in anything, believe in yourselves, in your senses and in your minds. To accept a religious creed is to accept another's mind in place of your own, and generally contrary to your own. When religious belief comes in brains go out."

"Creeds are not guide-boards; they are tombstones. On every creed can be read three words: 'Here lies'—and such lies!"

"[Science] does not promise to take man to Heaven, and leave him in the cemetery as religion does. . . . [Religion] has spent its time and talent blessing nursing bottles and baptizing babies. In the great Marathon race of the forces of humanity, religion is *not* the hero of the day, but the zero. In any exposition of the products of brains, the Sunday-School takes the booby prize."

"Is it any wonder that children lie when they are taught to read the Bible as true? We shall never have a race of men and women who love the truth, and who tell the truth on this earth, until every vestige of a miracle is swept from the pages of our literature."

"Man has asked for the *truth* and the Church has given him *miracles*. He has asked for *knowledge*, and the Church has given him *theology*. He has asked for *facts*, and the Church has given him the *Bible*. This foolishness should stop. The Church has nothing to give man that has not been in cold storage for two thousand years. Anything would become stale in that time."

"The Church is no more supplying the world with its moral and intellectual nourishment than is the man selling whisky, tobacco and opium furnishing pure food for man's consumption."

"A great many things are protected and praised that should be exposed and denounced. One of them is religion. A religious person is a dangerous person. He may not become a thief or a murderer, but he is liable to become a nuisance. He carries with him many foolish and harmful superstitions, and he is possessed with the notion that it is his duty to give these superstitions to others. That is what makes trouble. Nothing is so worthless as superstition. . . ."

Why I Am An Agnostic

*This is excerpted from a chapter in **I Don't Know Do You?** (1916), describing Marilla Ricker's experiences with differing sects, from the Millerites to the Methodists (who, judging from the racket they made, "appear to think their God is deaf"). After listening to a description of hell that "went on for nearly two hours" in her mother's Free-Will Baptist Church, Marilla wrote: "Do you wonder that I, a child of ten years, said to my father, who was a freethinking, infidel, atheist, or whatever else you please to call him: 'I hate my mother's church. I will **not** go there again!' "*

THERE ARE MORE THAN ONE THOUSAND RELIGIONS. They are founded mostly on fraud. All their saviors had virgins for mothers, and gods for fathers.

The churches own more than thirteen billions of property, and they are *all* too dishonest to pay honest taxes. Many of the churches couldn't be run three weeks without the women. They do all the work, for which they get no credit.

The churches claim all the distinguished people, especially after they are dead and hence can not deny their claims. They have many times claimed that Abraham Lincoln was a churchman. The Honorable H. C. Deming, of Connecticut, an old friend of Lincoln, said it is false. Lincoln belonged to no church, and at one time said, "I have never united myself to any church, because I have found difficulty in giving my assent without mental reservation to the long, complicated statements of Christian doctrine, which characterize their articles of belief, and confessions of faith." But still they claim him. Honest, very!

No institution in modern civilization is so tyrannical and so unjust to women as is the Christian church. The history of the Church does not contain a single suggestion for the equality of woman with man, and still the Church claims that woman owes her advancement to the Bible. She owes it much more to the dictionary.

History, both ancient and modern, tells us that the condition of women is most degraded in those countries where Church and State are in closest affiliation (such as, Spain, Italy, Russia and Ireland), and most advanced in nations where the power of ecclesiasticism is markedly on the wane. It has been proved that, whatever progress woman has made in any department of effort, she has accomplished independent of, and in opposition to, the so-called inspired and infallible Word of God; and that the Bible has been of more injury to her than has any other book ever written in the history of the world.

William Root Bliss, in his *Side Glimpses From the Colonial Meeting-house*, tells us many startling truths concerning the Puritans, and reminds me of what Chauncey M. Depew said—that the *first* thing the Puritans did, after they landed at Plymouth, was to fall on their knees, and the *second* thing was to fall on the Aborigines.

The business of trading in slaves was not immoral by the estimate of public opinion in Colonial times. A deacon of the church in Newport esteemed the slave trade, with its rum accessories, as home missionary work. It is said that on the first Sunday after the arrival of his slaves he was accustomed to offer thanks that an overruling Providence had been pleased to bring to this land of freedom another cargo of benighted heathen to enjoy the blessings of a Gospel dispensation.

At a Bridgewater town meeting of the year Sixteen Hundred Seventy-six, a vote was called to see what should be done with the money that was made from selling the Indians.

John Bacon of Barnstable directed in his will that his Indian slave Dinah be sold and the proceeds used "by my executors in buying Bibles." By men who sat in the Colonial meetinghouse, the first fugitive-slave law was formed. This law became a part of the Articles of Confederation between all the New England Colonies.

The affinity between *rum* and the religion of Colonial times was ex-emplified in the license granted John Vyall to keep a house of entertain-ment in Boston. He must keep it near the meetinghouse of the Second Church, where he extended his invitation to thirsty sinners who were go-ing to hear John Mayo or Increase Mather preach.

The importation of slaves began early. The first arrival at Boston was by the ship *Desire*, on February Twenty-sixth, Sixteen Hundred Thirty-seven, bringing negroes, tobacco and cotton from Barbados. She had sailed from Boston eleven months before, carrying Indian captives to the Ber-mudas to be sold as slaves, and thus she became noted as the first New England slave-ship.

In time, slaves were brought to Boston direct from Africa.

Advertisements of just-arrived negroes to be sold may be seen in the Boston *News Letter* of the years Seventeen Hundred Twenty-six and Seventeen Hundred Twenty-seven. The pious Puritans did not hesitate to sell slaves on the auction-block. I find in the Boston *News Letter* of September Nineteenth, Seventeen Hundred Fifteen, a notice of an auction-sale at Newport, Rhode Island, of several Indians, men and boys, and a very likely negro man. They were treated in all respects as merchandise, and were rated with horses and cattle.

Peter Faneuil, to whom Boston is indebted for its Cradle of Liberty, was deep in the business. In an inventory of the property of Parson Williams of Deerfield, in Seventeen Hundred Twenty-nine, his slaves were rated with his horses and cows. "Believe and be baptized" is all that was essential.

❧

Teach children that no amount of so-called religion will compensate for rheumatism; that Christianity has nothing to do with morality; that "vicarious atonement" is a fraud, and a lie; that to be born well and strong is the highest birth; that to be honest and pay one's debts spells peace of mind; that the Bible is no more inspired than the dictionary; that sin is a transgression of the laws of life, and that the blood of all the bulls and goats and lambs of ancient times, and the blood of Christ or any other man, never had, and never can have, the least effect in making a life what it would have been had it obeyed the laws of life. If you have marred your life, you must bear the consequences. If you have made a mistake, be more careful in the future. Let the thought that the past is irretrievable make you more careful in the present and for the future.

And, above all, teach children that prayer is idiotic. There may be one God or twenty. I do not know or care. I am not afraid, and no priest or parson can make me believe that my title to a future life, if there be one, is defective. And the great and good man Thomas Paine, who wrote the *Age of Reason*, and said, "The world is my country, and to do good my religion," is a good enough god for me. And the great Ingersoll, who said, "I belong to the great Church that holds the world within its starlit aisles; that claims the great and good of every race and clime; that finds with joy the grain of gold in every creed and floods with light and love the germs of good in every soul," is in my opinion an excellent god—as good as any that ever lived, from Confucius to Christ. A friend of mine said to me, "Ingersoll should have been a Christian." I replied, "The dog-collar of

Christianity did not belong on his neck: he preached the truth; he preferred that to the Bible. I can not imagine the great Ingersoll preaching from II Kings xiv: 35."

When I was a child I heard very little about Christmas and nothing about Lent and Easter. I was taught to be honest and truthful and to pay one hundred cents on a dollar. In my opinion there is no Bible extant so good as Ingersoll's Complete Works.

Annie Besant

21

Annie Besant

THE QUIXOTIC VICTORIAN

October 1, 1847 – September 20, 1933

"God" is always the equivalent of "I do not know."
"The Gospel of Atheism"

ONE OF THE MORE NOTORIOUS AND CELEBRATED freethought orators in Victorian Great Britain, Annie Besant rose on the freethought scene in 1874, becoming more famous yet by her shocking conversion to theosophy in 1889. As an atheist, she teamed up with famed Charles Bradlaugh, president of the National Secular Society and editor of *The National Reformer*, in iconoclastic writing and speaking campaigns.

Her father William Wood, a skeptic, died of consumption when Annie was five. Annie had a broad but religion-filled education provided by an evangelical gentlewoman. Enthralled by tales of religious martyrs, she tellingly admitted in her second autobiography, written as a Theosophist: "I [was] of the stuff of which fanatics are made." (*An Autobiography:* 24)

A sheltered twenty, she married the unpleasant Rev. Frank Besant (rhymes with "pleasant").

"My dreamy life, into which no knowledge of evil had been allowed to penetrate, in which I had been guarded from all pain, shielded from all anxiety, kept innocent on all questions of sex, was no preparation for married existence, and left me defenseless to a rude awakening." (p. 71)

She was depressed and dissatisfied with her marriage to Besant, who, she quipped, had "very high ideas of a husband's authority and a wife's submission." (p. 81)

After her baby daughter Mabel almost died of whooping cough, Annie revolted against the idea of a deity who could allow such suffering. Meeting a dissenting Anglican minister and liberal Unitarian Moncure Conway, she embarked on a course of reading, and soon after gave up Christianity, calling the struggle keen but short.

At age twenty-five Annie began her career as pamphleteer. Figuratively thumbing her nose at her husband, she signed her first pamphlet, "By the Wife of a Beneficed Clergyman." She and her husband separated. Annie's mother died shortly after, her prophetic last words: "it has been darling Annie's only fault; she has always been too religious." (p. 24)

In 1874, Annie met Charles Bradlaugh, forty, radical, renowned and with an impressive reputation as an attorney for the poor and defenseless. Bradlaugh offered her a nominally paid position on the weekly *National Reformer,* launching a freethought career that would last a decade and a half. Petite, pretty and charismatic, she was praised as an orator. George Bernard Shaw called her "the greatest orator in England, and possibly in Europe."

Annie Besant and Bradlaugh, both unhappily married to others, shared an intimate but platonic relationship, becoming the target of slander and accusations of immorality. Her arduous speaking tours often attracted hecklers; once she was cut on the forehead by a thrown stone.

To challenge the Obscene Publications Act, Annie persuaded Charles that they should reprint *The Fruits of Philosophy*, a book about birth control by physician Charles Knowlton. They were arrested, tried and narrowly avoided jail. Annie shrewdly rewrote the outdated booklet, her version becoming a bestseller and hastening the birth control movement worldwide. But her involvement lost her custody of her eight-year-old daughter.

When London University agreed to admit women in 1878, Annie became a student, receiving the only honors award given in botany in 1881 in Prof. Thomas Huxley's class. She was the first woman on the London School Board and became an advocate of working-class women. Her relationship with Bradlaugh grew strained due to her restless enthusiasms for other men and other causes, especially her Fabianism. Her conversion to theosophy, officially announced in 1889, was a shock and disappointment to Bradlaugh and his daughter Hypatia, and to the freethought world. Bradlaugh gently summed up Annie as "quixotic."

On a trip to England in 1890, Elizabeth Cady Stanton recorded in her diary a visit from Annie Besant. "Mrs. Besant was full, too full, of theosophy, to which she says she became converted last year. I liked her better when she was associated with Bradlaugh in the Free Thought and democratic movement. 'The Fabian Society can do more for the amelioration of humanity than the Theosophical Society,' I ventured to remark. But I saw this pained her, so I let her go on in her enthusiasm for Mme. Blavatsky, 'of whom I am a devoted pupil,' she said." (Stanton and Blatch, *Elizabeth Cady Stanton Revealed* II: 264)

Annie became successor to the mystic, occultist Theosophical Society, following the death of Blavatsky, and died a famous figure at the age of eighty-five in India. There she had been a prime player in political and educational reforms, celebrated, somewhat ambivalently, among Indians for her support of Indian Home Rule.

She never lost her affection or respect for Bradlaugh and her freethought experiences. She regarded atheism as her stepping stone to theosophy, which she maintained was rational:

". . . I rejoice that I played my part in that educating of England which has made impossible for evermore the crude superstitions of the past, and the repetition of the cruelties and injustices under which preceding heretics suffered." (*Autobiography:* 174)

Definitive biographer Arthur H. Nethercot summed up her life as dominated by a fanatical quest for "Truth," but considered her a true reformer. Without her, the admittance of women to English colleges, the acceptance of birth control, the establishment of free public education and meals for London children all would have been delayed. She organized female strikers and offered other significant service as a secular reformer. Had India followed the advice of her party in 1929, it might have obtained dominion status far sooner, and headed off other problems, wrote Nethercot, who praised the "hard bedrock of common sense" even her occultism could not overshadow. Jawaharlal Nehru praised this would-be "Mother of India" on the anniversary of her birthdate in 1956 for her conspicuous role in India's fight for freedom.

❧

Although her hundreds of unreadable theosophy works vastly outnumbered freethought writings, Annie was a prolific, capable expositor and popularizer of atheist views. Freethought works include *The Freethinker's Text-Book, Part II*, a reference book. More interesting are her freethought tracts, such as "The Gospel of Atheism," "Gospels of Christianity and Freethought," "Life, Death and Immortality," "True Basis of Morality," "Why I Do Not Believe in God," "World Without God," and many essays appearing in *My Path to Atheism*.

Besant's "God's Views on Marriage: As Revealed in the Old Testament" had sold 6,000 copies by 1883; this was mischievously "dedicated to the Bishop of Manchester," and is an energetic, feminist summary of marital immorality in the bible. Most tracts sold for one- or twopence. She also edited *Our Corner*, a multifaceted journal touching on her many literary and social interests.

Is Christianity A Success?

This was published as a one-penny pamphlet by Annie Besant and Charles Bradlaugh in 1885.

SOME TIME AGO IT WAS PUBLICLY STATED that the Japanese authorities had sent over some trustworthy agents to report on the condition of Christendom, with a view of instituting Christianity in Japan if it proved satisfactory in the lands in which it prevailed. The report was unfavorable: it was stated that there were more dishonesty, more drunkenness, more poverty, more misery, in Christian countries than were found in Japan, and judging the trees by their fruits, the Japanese religion proved to be the better of the two.

For eighteen hundred years Christianity has been preached; for fifteen hundred years Christianity has wielded supreme power. It came to the world with tremendous claims. Founded by an incarnate God; protected by his abiding presence; inspired by a Divine Spirit; what greater advantages could be possessed by any religion? What has it done? Has it been a success? A survey of the world will be the best answer.

In its earliest days it appealed to the ignorant and the superstitious, finding its readiest disciples among the most childish-minded of the populace. "Not many wise men after the flesh are called" (1 Cor. 1., 26); "Thou hast hid these things from the wise and prudent, and hast revealed them unto babes" (Matt. xi., 25). Spreading among the ignorant, it gathered numerous adherents, until at last, in a strife for empire, the number of the Christians made them politically important, and Constantine embraced their creed to win them to his side in the struggle. The ignorance which was the birthmark of the religion now spread its blighting influence over the whole Roman empire: the schools, built by Roman emperors for the training of the young, fell into the hands of the clergy, and monkish fables and silly traditions of saints were gabbled in the rooms that had resounded to the wisdom of Greece and Rome, to the dialectics of Socrates, to the philosophy of Epicurus, Aristotle and Lucretius. Darker and darker became the ignorance, until in the ninth century not even a priest in England could translate Latin, nor one priest in a thousand in Spain could write an ordinary letter; until at the end of the tenth century scarce a person in Rome knew the elements of letters (see "Europe during the

Middle Ages", Hallam, ed. of 1869, pp. 595, 596). When in that same tenth century a little light of knowledge began to glimmer, the fire was lighted by Mahommedan hands in Moorish Spain, and spread thence slowly, against every effort of the Church to quench it, over Christendom. Never did a religion do more to foster ignorance, more to destroy learning, than has been done by the Church of Christ.

Take again, glancing over history, the fashion in which Christian nations have ever dealt with savage tribes. Charlemagne Christianised the Saxons with fire and sword, breaking them into the obedience of the Church. The Spaniards Christianised the Peruvians in similar fashion, turning the happy flowery land of the Sun into a slave-filled shambles. The English have Christianised Indians and Africans, Maories and Australians, in good old historic manner by murder and fraud and theft. Look where we will at the treatment experienced by the savage at Christian hands, and we find ever the same old story—cruelty that sickens, treachery that disgusts, brutality that appals.

Studying Christianity in the lands in which it has ruled for centuries, the indictment against it but grows longer and heavier. Slavery in Christendom has been the most cruel and hopeless that the world has known. Hear the passionate cry of Charles Dickens, himself a Christian: "Judaism, the Greek and Roman times, Mahommedanism, all recognised the rights of nature in their slaves. Christianity is the only faith whose professors have violated and destroyed those rights" (*Household Words*, vol. xiv., p. 137). Persecution also in Christendom has been more ruthless, more bloody, more refined in cruelty, than in lands subject to any other form of faith.

And look at Christendom now. Not a Christian country in which drunkenness and prostitution do not pollute the streets, the "Reformed Christian" countries bearing away the palm for widespread intoxication. Not a Christian country in which poverty does not gripe great masses of the people, or in which diseases that grow out of bad feeding and bad sanitation do not hold high festival. Between the nations that worship "one Father" and "one Lord Jesus Christ," bitter jealousy, hot suspicion, breaking out from time to time in war, and evidenced always by huge arrays of armed men, bringing the burden of poverty and the curse of prostitution on every land they guard.

More condemnatory still, perhaps, of Christianity is the fact that these great social evils are regarded as necessary and inevitable. Prostitution is accepted and is legislated for; no attempts are made to radically cure poverty, only charity is called in to alleviate it; morality in national policy is openly scoffed at by the Christian press. Those who seek to abolish poverty, to realise the brotherhood of man, to bring about the submission of international disputes to an International Court of Law, are derided as dreamers when they are not denounced as revolutionaries.

Is Christianity a success? The state of Christendom proves it to be the ghastliest failure the world has ever known: prodigal in its promises, superb in its claims, it is a pitiable breakdown in the lands in which it is supreme.

Can we, by looking at the doctrines of Christianity, find any reason for this widespread failure? It seems to me that any impartial judgment of its doctrines would result in expectancy of just such a result as has historically accrued.

In the first place the whole scheme of Christianity was originally based on the expectation of Christ's speedy return. He himself declares: "The Son of man shall come in the glory of his Father, with his angels, and then he shall reward every man according to his works. Verily I say unto you, There be some standing here, which shall not taste of death, till they see the Son of man coming in his kingdom" (Matt. xvi., 27, 28). The words are as explicit as words can be, and can only be got rid of by most irrational twisting of them. Again, after describing the darkening of the sun and moon and the coming of the "Son of man" "with power and great glory," Jesus proceeds: "Verily I say unto you, This generation shall not pass till all these things be fulfilled. Heaven and earth shall pass away, but my words shall not pass away[!]. But of that day and hour knoweth no man, no, not the angels of heaven, but my Father only. . . . Therefore be ye also ready: for in such an hour as ye think not, the Son of man cometh" (Matt. xxiv., 29, 30; 34–36; 44). These precise declarations of Christ were answered by the faith of the early Church. Not to needlessly multiply quotations, I may note 1 Cor. xv., 51, 52: "We shall not all sleep, but we shall all be changed, in a moment, in the twinkling of an eye, at the last trump: for the trumpet shall sound, and the dead shall be raised incorruptible, and we [mark the *we*] shall be changed." Again: "This we say unto you by the word of the Lord, that we which are alive, and remain unto the coming of the Lord, shall not prevent them that are asleep. For the Lord himself shall descend from heaven with a shout, with the voice of the archangel, and with the trump of God: and the dead in Christ shall rise first: then we which are alive and remain, shall be caught up together with them in the clouds, to meet the Lord in the air" (1 Thess. IV., 15–17). Jude declared that those he addressed were living "in the last time," pointing to the mockers among them (Jude, 17–19); and the pledge, "Surely I come quickly" (Rev. XXII., 20) closes the canon of Scripture.

From a religion which looked for the speedy destruction of the world, no moralising of the world could be expected. The "strangers and pilgrims," whose "citizenship was in heaven" had no time to spare for the improvement of the earth they despised. To be "saved" was the one thing needful, and little cared they for the world which was so soon to be "burned up."

Even after the prophecy of Christ had been proved false, the belief in his speedy return still remained, and Hallam tells us that "in the tenth century an opinion prevailed everywhere that the end of the world was approaching. Many charters begin with these words: 'As the world is now drawing to its close' " ("Middle Ages," p. 599). The result of this faith was that fields were left untilled, all the concerns of life were neglected, and famine punished those who were foolish enough to look for the return of a dead man.

On this basis of a speedy return of Jesus was built up an ascetic, impracticable morality, one utterly unfitted for a society intended to endure. The non-resistance of evil taught by Christ, the submission to forceful theft and unlimited borrowing (Matt. v., 39–42), were doctrines which, permanently practiced, would render society impossible. The avoidance of marriage taught by Christ (Matt. XIX., 12), and Paul (1 Cor. VII., 7, 8; 28; 32–34; 37–40), would have in a short time depopulated the Church; a point of great importance if the Church was to endure for centuries, but not of the slightest moment if Christ was to return before the generation then living passed away.

Out of this magnification of celibacy grew one of the most corrupting influences of Christianity. Monasteries and nunneries were everywhere accompanied by the foulest licence of manners, and "unmarried" priests kept "housekeepers" who were admittedly wives in all but legal status. The corruption of the "religious" naturally extended to the "worldly," while the degraded position assigned to women by Christianity led to their still further degradation at the hands of the superior sex. In Christendom the brothel took the place of the harem, and women sacrificed to men's passions did not receive from the Christian even the protection, shelter, food and clothing which were freely given by the Oriental and the Turk. The doctrine of vicarious sacrifice was thoroughly carried out with regard to women, and the degradation and pollution of one class bought for another its safely guarded home.

The doctrine of non-resistance alluded to above, further tended to injure Society, by the aid it gave to tyrants and the discouragement it threw on manly self-assertion against wrong. Taught, as Christians were, that they were bound to render obedience to "the higher powers," on the ground that "the powers that be are ordained of God" (Rom. xiii., 1), they naturally regarded rebellion against a tyrant as treason to their God. In view of the speedy return of Jesus, the meek submission of Christians to earthly tyranny was a matter of small moment; but when this temporary and unimportant submission became the permanent duty of whole nations, the mischievous influence of Christianity on political institutions was very speedily manifested. Tyrants lent all their aid to its propagation, for it rendered their subjects nerveless and submissive. Thus Mosheim tells us of Charlemagne that he fought against the Saxons to "engage them to embrace the Christian religion," hoping that their conversion would "induce them to submit more tamely to the government of the Franks" ("Eccles. History," p. 170).

The sanctification of poverty was another of the curses brought by Christianity. "Blessed be ye poor; for yours is the kingdom of God. Blessed are ye that hunger now: for ye shall be filled . . . But woe unto you that are rich: for ye have received your consolation. Woe unto you that are full! for ye shall hunger" (Luke vi., 20, 21; 24, 25). The people were bribed into quiescence under poverty by promises of reward in a future life, and when beggars grew clamorous the parable of Dives and Lazarus smoothed them back into passivity. Like other Eastern fanatics Jesus denounced the mere possession of wealth as a crime: "A rich man shall hardly enter into the kingdom of heaven. And again I say unto you, It is easier for a camel to go through the eye of a needle, than for a rich man to enter into the kingdom of God" (Matt. xix., 23, 24). This apotheosis of poverty led to the begging friars who swarmed over Europe like locusts, and the Church utilised the teachings of its God to sweep into its own coffers the perilous wealth which might otherwise have damned men's souls.

Thus in the doctrines of Christianity we find the seeds of the worst curses of Christendom, prostitution, tyranny, pauperism. Originally intended to last for a few years, it has endured for centuries. Originally intended for a small Jewish sect, it has become a world-wide creed. The false morality, the false sociology, which would have been comparatively harmless restricted within the narrow circle for which they were intended, have become world-poisoning, spread beyond their original limits of time and race; and the relatively harmless fanaticism of a band of Jewish zealots has become the curse of modern civilisation.

The rougher and more brutal side of Christianity has resulted from the acceptance by the Church of the Jewish Old Testament. Growing out of Judaism as it did; with a Jew for its God; with Jews for its founders; with Jerusalem for metropolis; it is not surprising that the Jewish Scriptures were received as sacred and inspired.

When we read that slavery has been co-existent with Christianity, we remember that it was commanded in the Old Testament and was sanctioned in the New. When we read of the thousands done to death for religious heresy, by the Inquisition in France, Spain, and Italy, by the governments of Germany, Switzerland, England, Scotland, Ireland, the United States; we remember the bloody commands of Jahveh, the massacres of Moses and Joshua, the social ostracism decreed by, and the bloodthirsty rejoicings over vengeance of, "John the Divine." When we sicken over the stories of the Crusades; of the bloody wars waged by Christians; of the shocking revenge taken by English Christians after the Indian Mutiny; of the cruel stamping out of aboriginal populations by Christian settlers; we remember the tale of God's "chosen people," of their ravaging whole regions with sword and fire, of the brutal cry: "The Lord is a man of war; the Lord of hosts is his name." When we read of diseases decimating populations; of physicians punished as magicians; of processions of saints' images and relics to avert the Divine wrath; we remember that both in the Old and New Testaments disease is represented as the scourge of God; that a king was punished because he sought physicians instead of Jahveh; that Christians are to heal the sick by laying on of hands and anointing with oil, not by science and curative drugs. And so we come to recognise that man's ignorance has been perpetuated, man's brutality fostered, man's progress retarded, by the very agency which claimed to elevate, to purify, to moralise him.

General immorality has been still further increased by the Christian doctrine of the vicarious atonement made by Jesus Christ. His outrageous doctrine that the repentant sinner caused more joy in heaven than the "just persons" has been the fruitful mother of crime. The granting of indulgences was a perfectly logical deduction from the teaching of Jesus, and the Pope who pardoned crime to the son of the Church but followed in the steps of Paul, who declared that salvation was by faith without works. The story of the dying thief, to whom Jesus promised immediate Paradise, bore fruit in hundreds of death-bed repentances; criminals, when death was inevitable and when the power to sin had gone, "repented," received absolution, and were sealed for heaven. Even now the most brutal of murderers is "washed in the blood of the lamb" between his sentence and his execution, and poses as a dying saint in the columns of the Christian press. In fact the surest way to heaven is via the gallows, for time is always given to the murderer to make his "peace with God," and he is given no opportunity of starting a new quarrel.

Verily Christianity is condemned by its failure. Its God, its heaven, its hell, all fail as motives to good conduct. The policeman influences the thief more than God does; worldly prosperity is a surer bait than heaven; the gaol is a more efficacious threat than hell. The wrath of God can be escaped by sheltering behind Jesus; whereas the policeman is not so easily thrown off the track. Heaven can be won by a prayer when earth is lost; hell escaped by a prayer when successful fraud has secured worldly comfort. Christianity is the nursing mother of social evil, for it winks at all oppression by the wealthy, and condones every crime in the believer.

The new creed which is arising in the place of Christianity gains a hearing very largely because of the failure of the religion which it is seeking to destroy. Instead of meeting poverty with a benediction, it regards it as a curse to be abolished by better social arrangements. Disease to it is not the scourge of God, but the scourge of dirt and ignorance, to be broken by cleanliness and knowledge. Sin to it is not an object of divine wrath, but a subject for human skill, to be cured by healthy environment.

The new creed proclaims that morality is as binding on man as on woman. That woman was not created for man, to be the slave of his passions, but that each sex has equal rights, equal liberties, equal duties. It declares that prostitution is not a necessity, but a crime; that the prostitute is no viler than the man who consorts with her; that prostitution may be put an end to by the economic independence of women, and by early marriage conjoined with parental prudence.

The new creed enjoins on all the duty of labor. It points out that so long as some are idle, so long must others do more than their fair portion of work; that over-leisure for the few means over-labor for the many. It admits no right of idleness in any; no right of support by others without fair equivalent given in exchange, save for children, sick, and aged. It claims for all equality of education, equality of comfort, equality of opportunity. It recognises neither privilege nor disability. To its all-embracing charity no man, no woman, is "common or unclean."

The new creed declares against all divisions of classes; knows nothing of "masters" and servants," nothing of "upper" and "lower" ranks of society. Without God in heaven, it is without master on earth, and to it the common good is the supreme law.

Susan H. Wixon

22

Susan H. Wixon

"BORN A LIBERAL"

c. late 1840's – August 28, 1912

Freethought has always been the best friend woman had . . .
"Woman—Four Centuries of Progress," 1893

SUSAN H. WIXON, A WOMAN'S RIGHTS ADVOCATE and respected freethought writer, was "born a Liberal," according to freethought biographer Samuel P. Putnam. Susan's broad-minded parents were Bethia Smith Wixon and Captain James Wixon of Dennis, Massachusetts. Her favorite childhood pastime was contemplating the changing vista of Cape Code from the height of the pine trees she loved to climb. Susan had an early contretemps with an Orthodox Sunday school teacher over the scheme of redemption, asserting that anyone who would make a lake of fire and brimstone in which to incinerate his children ought to be the first one burned in it.

Always head of her class as a public school student, Susan began teaching school in her thirteenth year, placing first in the teacher's examination. She attended a seminary for one year, then continued to teach school in Massachusetts and Rhode Island, moving with her family to Fall River, Massachusetts, and attending the Universalist church. Her father reportedly had told her as a child, "Were you a boy I would send you to college"—thereby converting her to woman suffrage.

By adulthood a radical freethinker, Susan successfully argued as a stockholder against corporate funding of sectarian activities. A local newspaper recorded:

"We honor the heroism of the young lady, a stockholder, who had the devotion to principle and the moral courage to attend a meeting of stockholders where she was the only woman present, and, with thrilling eloquence, to advocate the rights of those who were thus attempted to be despoiled of their own, by the combined action of corporate sectarian influence, and whose strong logic, forcible appeal, cutting and convincing arguments, roused a majority to side with right and justice. When Roger Williams, the apostle of religious liberty, fled from Massachusetts to Rhode Island, he declared for 'soul liberty.' Let credit be given to Susan H. Wixon for the same noble sentiment." (Putnam, *Four Hundred Years of Freethought*: 826)

She became the first woman to lecture at Paine Hall in Boston, embracing reform topics such as temperance, labor and education. She successfully appealed to the governor of Massachusetts to appoint women as factory inspectors in 1891.

She represented Massachusetts and spoke at the 1890 convention of the Woman's National Liberal League founded by Matilda Joslyn Gage. She traveled abroad in 1892 to collect statistics on woman's work and wages, a subject she lectured on as well as free trade.

Despite her controversial views, she was a member of the Fall River school board for twenty-one years, beginning in 1873, and president and founder of the Women's Educational and Industrial Society, as well as a member of various reform-minded and charitable movements.

She wrote verse and prose for the freethought press, occasionally reported for local press and was once a staff member of the Boston *Sunday Record*. She was elected to the committee on woman's industrial advancement in the inventor's department of the World's Columbian Exposition. Her poem, "When Womanhood Awakes," was widely cited among woman's advocates of her day. Books include the novel *All in a Lifetime*, *Apples of Gold* (1876, short stories), and *The Story Hour* (1885), advertised as the only illustrated freethought storybook for children in the nineteenth century. She also wrote *Sunday Observance; or, How to Spend Sunday* (1883), and *Summer Days at Onset* (1887). She served for at least a decade in the 1880s and 1890s as editor of the children's department, The Children's Corner, of *The Truth Seeker*.

※

Susan's best-known freethought work was "Woman: Four Centuries of Progress," a lecture delivered at the Freethinkers' International Congress, Chicago, Illinois, October 1893, and reprinted as a thirty-four page pamphlet by the Truth Seeker Company that December, an overview of the history of the harm of Christianity to women from a feminist viewpoint. "Woman was the beast of burden," Susan argued, "born and reared in subjection."

"The cause of the subjugation of woman reaches far back, and is wound around with the rusted chain of ancient theology and a false faith. Under pagan rule woman was treated with honor and regard, and she had many rights and privileges which were lost to her under Christian rule.

"If ever there was an ingeniously woven plot, it is that of the 'Fall of Man,' with Paul of Tarsus for its mouthpiece." [See selection]

Woman: Four Centuries of Progress

This speech was first delivered at the Freethinkers' International Congress in Chicago, Illinois, in October 1893. The Truth Seeker Company issued it in pamphlet form in December 1893. The following are excerpts.

The Canon Law

THE CANON LAW COMPRISES THAT SYSTEM OF LAWS established by the Christian church in the ninth century, and based upon the Bible. These laws are the root and cause of the subjugation and degradation of women in Christian countries.

In 1632 a book was published in England in which it is declared that "the reason why women have no control in Parliament, why they make no laws, consent to none, abrogate none, is because of their original sin"!

This is the whole story in a nutshell. All the abuses, humiliations, cruelties, and indignities heaped upon woman in Christian countries may be traced directly and squarely to this source, and nowhere else—the fable of original sin.

Listen to this from St. Chrysostom, Greek father of the church, commonly known as the golden-mouthed saint. This may be one of his golden utterances. Judge ye: "Woman is a necessary evil, a natural temptation, a desirable calamity, a domestic peril, a deadly fascination, and a painted ill."

Hark ye to what the great authority, Tertullian, a Latin father of the church, said: "Woman, thou shouldst ever be clothed in rags and in mourning, appearing only as a penitent, drowned in tears, and expiating thus the sin of having caused the fall of the human race. Woman, thou art the gate of the devil. It is thou who hast corrupted those whom Satan dare not attack face to face."

You will note that Tertullian regarded woman as worse than the devil.

❦

St. Jerome wrote that "woman is the gate of the devil, the road to iniquity, the sting of the scorpion, in a word, a dangerous species." Jerome was the dirty fellow who lived in one garment till he died, letting his body go unwashed and half-starved, despising and mortifying the same, in order to preserve his soul. At the death of this notable saint, his ragged garment, full of lively tenants, was held up as proof of his right to be known as a saint and blessed martyr. This gave him the undoubted right to thus discourse regarding women.

St. Gregory said that "woman had no comprehension of goodness," and the poet Milton has pictured her in "Paradise Lost" as "the embodiment of sin, half woman and half serpent, chief doorkeeper of the infernal regions." He also wrote of the angels in heaven as being all men. How many of you, gentlemen, would care to purchase tickets to such a heaven as that?

The canon law held that the deposition of a woman was unworthy of credence, although women are not more given to lying than men.

St. Augustine authorized every husband to slap his wife in the face. Upon some such authority as this, undoubtedly, was based the old English law that says a man may beat his wife with a stick, not larger round than his thumb. If larger than that, the beating might incapacitate her for work. The canon law also decreed that woman was so vile, that while the Lord's supper might be allowed her, yet she should not receive it in her naked hands; and the council of Macon in the year 581 solemnly debated with itself whether woman had a soul or not—whether she was a beast or a human being.

St. John Damascene, once Christian governor of Damascus, wrote: "Woman is a daughter of falsehood, a sentinel of hell, the enemy of peace." Another Christian saint said: "Of all wild beasts woman is the most dangerous."

She was regarded as simply a chattel, an unfortunate creature that man felt obliged to provide for, if married to one, while all unmarried women were bound over to slavish toil, by law, from eleven to forty years of age.

It was not till the tenth century that a Christian wife of a Christian husband was allowed to eat at the same table with her husband. The more Christianity prevailed the worse it was for woman. When Christianity wore its highest crown of power, then was the worst period of woman's enslavement.

Lecky, in his history of European morals, writing of this time, says: "Woman was represented as the door of hell—the mother of all ills. She was taught that she should be ashamed of the very thought that she is woman. She should live in continual penance on account of the curses she has brought into the world. She should be ashamed of her dress, for it is the memorial of her fall. She should be especially ashamed of her beauty, for it is the most potent instrument of the demon."

These are some of the degrading sentiments crushing woman to the dust. And they bore the sanction of the then greatest power in the civilized world! How many men could stand up under such an avalanche? I pause for a reply.

These and similar declarations were not treated lightly as in the present, but were held to be gospel truths.

When the witchcraft frenzy broke out in Europe, who but women and female children were the principal victims? It was women who were accounted as having dealings with Satan, and the Bible declares, "Thou shalt not suffer a witch to live." Pope Innocent VIII considered it sufficient authority upon which to issue his famous bull against witchcraft. In Geneva five hundred women were for this cause executed within three months. In Germany it is estimated that one hundred thousand victims to the delusion lost their lives, while the clergy, in mad excitement, preached notable "witch sermons," as they were called, condemnatory of women as witches and vile emissaries of Satan. England sent thirty thousand poor, defenseless creatures to death on the charge of riding through the air on a broomstick! Not only in the old countries did this foolish delusion of witchcraft prevail, but it showed itself in the New World as well, and the first two centuries of the settlement of America bear testimony in the colonial records of frequent arrests, trials, persecutions, and executions of women for practicing witchery. In the United States one hundred and fifty were imprisoned on the charge of witchcraft, nineteen were executed, some upwards of eighty years of age.

These women were believed to be in league with the devil, and were consequently regarded with the utmost horror and suspicion. The persecutions came from the church, and George Combe says, in speaking of this shocking state of affairs, that "religion was employed to fan the flame of cruelty and superstition." John Wesley had said that to destroy the belief in witchcraft was to destroy the Bible—and Wesley was certainly right. The old superstitions have gone, many of them, and where, let me ask, is the Bible to-day?—tottering in weakness, a moldy mass of ignorance and superstition.

But little progress was made, or could be expected under a general belief that woman had the power to change herself at will into a black cat, and in this guise perform all kinds of villainy, cruelty, and depredation, to cause pain and sickness, to blight crops and torture the innocent, to maliciously injure, to destroy and kill.

Satan was thought to be trying to go the Almighty one better, if I may be pardoned the phrase, in getting possession of the saints, and any maimed, unattractive, aged woman was liable to be accused of being a witch. In the present, times are so changed and opinions, that the young and attractive among women are the most bewitching witches.

It seems almost incredible that such men as Sir Matthew Hale in old England, and Cotton Mather in New England should lend themselves to gravely preside over a delusion like witchcraft. Yet such is superstition, and when blinded by religion, no one can calculate its harmful and deleterious effects upon the human mind.

Woman was now regarded with more suspicion than ever, and was continually urged by the fathers of the church to repent of her sins. Her business was to work and pray, and her only recreation a walk in the graveyard to view the place where she might shortly lie.

In such a situation she found herself hedged about and circumscribed, unable, from ignorance, to define her position, and too bewildered to lift herself above it if she knew it.

In England, as is stated by Herbert Spencer, "wives were bought from the fifth to the eleventh century. Women were whipped on slight provocation, and Christian gentlemen arranged pleasure parties to go to Bridewell to see the women whipped." And this public whipping of women was not abolished in England until 1817. In that country the wife calls her husband "master" to this day. In this country wives were bought by the early settlers in Virginia, and the price paid was one hundred and fifty pounds of tobacco. (See Eggleston's Hist.) The first persons publicly whipped in this country were women. They were tied to the tails of carts and whipped on their naked backs through the streets of Boston. Our police courts everywhere are still disgraced by wife-beaters, the frequency of whose appearance before the bar of so-called justice is a disgrace to present civilization.

As a result of the shameful burdens and bondage of woman, the ownership and slavery of the same, the Christian world has been, and is still, a hot-bed of sensuality and vice. When the mother is regarded solely as a house-cleaner, a scrub, drudge, and breeder of children—and I regret to say that too many regard her in this light only even to-day—what can be the outcome but laxity of morals and crime? When Lust is concealed under the title of Love, what can you expect but sin and sensuality? As the offspring of the inferiority and degradation of woman, planted and maintained by theology, behold in every town and city throughout the Christian world wells of immorality, sinks of iniquity, disgraceful to humanity and shocking to the moral sense of communities.

Two standards of morality have been adopted as a result of the teaching of the early theologians, one for woman, and another, quite different, for men.

And there can never be any great moral progress until there is but *one* code of morality, and that for all the universe alike.

The first Synod of the Reformation passed laws sanctioning polygamy. Martin Luther himself favored it, and the Bible gave it sanction.

Out of it has come the prostitution, that goes hand in hand with our boasted civilization, planting itself before every church-door in Christendom, and which the church candidly admits it is powerless to wipe out.

Thus woman was stranded, as it were, on the rocks of superstition, a helpless and almost hopeless wreck, made so by ecclesiastical rulings and decisions, based entirely upon false and ruinous charges. . . .

The whole duty of woman had been assigned her by the early Christian rulers—to make bread, and keep the cradle rocking—to bear children in sorrow and silence, and to bear the burdens not only of the household, but of out-door labors as well. Her path was indeed a weary one, marked by insult, wrong, blood, and tears, from which there seemed to be no appeal.

Theology Never Helpful To Woman

In the face of a history replete with abuse, cruelty, scorn and dogmatic insolence toward woman, the Christian church still has the audacity and impudence to declare that it has been her friend—that it has done everything for her elevation and advancement. It says that what she is to-day she owes to the church. A blacker falsehood was never uttered.

After the crusades the respect and deference first proffered to woman came from the Moors and Saracens of Spain. In America, it was Thomas Paine who first spoke for equal rights for woman. And her first step in progressive lines began with her defiance of, and indifference to, churchly rules.

Within the last hundred years her march has been steadily onward. But it has not come through the channels of the church, or by theological dogma.

Why, theology forbade a mother to kiss her babe on a Sunday morning. It told her when her unbaptized little ones died that an extraordinary use of their skulls was made in repairing old sidewalks in the regions down below, where asphalt pavements and other modern improvements are unknown. This was consolation with a vengeance.

Within the present century, when a young lady, having taken cold at a ball, became ill with pneumonia and died, the clergyman who officiated at her funeral, administered consolation to the bereaved parents in this wise: "I have no doubt," said he, "that she is now dancing amid the pains and tortures of hell-fire!" And then proceeded to declaim against the sin (?) of dancing.

Theology the friend of women! What did this boasted friend do when woman insisted on her right to free speech? I will tell you, friends. It hanged her in the person of Mary Dyer, to a tree on Boston Common till she was deed. It banished Anne Hutchinson to the wilderness for saying that the clergy of Boston preached a covenant of faith instead of works.

What was the consequence when the beautiful Madame Roland declared her sentiments for truth and justice? She was rendered speechless by severing her head from her body.

What was the answer when woman asked for a little more education? Christianity bade her go home, sew on shirt buttons, mend the stockings, and mind her husband.

When did Christianity, that boasts of being so friendly to woman, ever advocate her right to representation? her right to self-ownership? Never. . . .

When, a hundred years ago, Mary Wollstonecraft spoke brave words for the amelioration of the condition of her sex, how was she received? With derision, scorn, and contumely. Frances Wright was driven from a hotel in New York out upon the street, a stranger in a strange land, to find lodging where she might, because of her advanced views. Ernestine L.

Rose and others who followed her have felt, in their own persons, the cruel shafts of ridicule and insult, for endeavoring to lift woman from the quagmires of superstition in which she was placed by an ignorant past. . . .

Freethought, The Benefactor of Woman

There is one force, and but one, that has brought about this condition of things and assisted woman to the place in which she finds herself to-day. Freethought—call it Liberalism, education, or whatever you will—is the one power which has broken the chains of woman and started her on the road to Freedom. . . .

Freethought has broken every barrier to woman's enfranchisement that so far has been broken and will yet beat down the remaining stumbling blocks in her pathway. . . .

Freethought has always been the best friend woman had—the noblest, truest ally and champion. It has ever sought to place her in her own true light before the world—the guide, counselor, and friend of man; queen not only of home and household, but of every domain where her worth and work is required, and equal sharer in life's pursuits, duties, and emoluments—the undwarfed, unfettered, real complement of man. . . .

To destroy mental slavery is the work of the great future, for that is the vulture still preying upon the vitals of our common humanity. This cannot be accomplished without first making woman herself free. Her condition decides that of the race. Elevate her, and you lift the whole human family. Degrade her, and disgrace and shame become the lot of man.

Ella Wheeler Wilcox
Photo by G.V. Buck, Washington, D.C.,
(State Historical Society of Wisconsin, WHi(x3)24847)

23

Ella Wheeler Wilcox

"JUST THE ART OF BEING KIND"

November 5, 1850 – October 30, 1919

THE ENORMOUSLY POPULAR WISCONSIN-BORN POET was not, according to today's critics, a minor poet—but a bad major one. Her fame was launched on notoriety, when a Chicago firm refused to publish a collection of emotional love poems, calling them immoral. As a result, after *Poems of Passion* was published in 1883, it sold 60,000 copies in two years. She enjoyed courting controversy, veiling herself in unorthodoxy.

Ella was well-known for her moral and temperance poems, including her collection, *Drops of Water*; but had a theatrical nature, enjoying fame and life as a socialite. After attending the funeral of Queen Victoria, she wrote "The Queen's Last Ride," launching her fame in Great Britain. A romantic correspondence with James Whitcomb Riley fizzled when the two met in person. She married Robert Marius Wilcox. Following his death in 1906, she once more became bane to clergy by becoming interested in theosophy, convinced she could commune with the dead. Her orthodox and unorthodox poems probably cancel each other out, and she departed life as an irrationalist, though embracing pantheism and "New Thought." But on the strength of her four-line poem, "The World's Need," Ella deserves to be considered an honorary freethinker.

The World's Need

So many Gods, so many creeds,
So many paths that wind and wind,
When just the art of being kind
Is all this sad world needs.

Helen H. Gardener

24

Helen H. Gardener

"INGERSOLL IN SOPRANO"

January 21, 1853 – July 26, 1925

I do not know the needs of a god or of another world. . . . I do know that
women make shirts for seventy cents a dozen in this one.

Men, Women and Gods, *1885*

HELEN HAMILTON GARDENER WAS DUBBED "Ingersoll done in soprano" by the
New York Sun and "The pretty infidel" by the *Chicago Times* after undertaking a
successful freethought lecture series in her mid-thirties on "Men, Women, and
Gods." One of the best-known American women freethinkers of her day, Helen
became a dedicated activist in the woman's rights movement, achieving respectability as a suffragist. In the tradition of Ingersoll, Helen, too, had the ear of a
President. Her appointment to the Civil Service Commission in 1920 made her
the first woman to occupy such a high position in federal government.

Née Alice Chenoweth, she adopted the name Helen Hamilton Gardener as
both her personal and professional name in her thirties. "Alice," the youngest of
six children, was born near Winchester, Virginia. Her father, the Rev. A.G.
Chenoweth, inherited slaves, freed them and moved north before the war when
Helen was less than a year old. Her great grandfather had married Hannah
Cromwell, granddaughter of Oliver Cromwell.

Her father left the Episcopal church to become a circuit rider in the Methodist
church. The family moved first to Washington, D.C., and then to Greencastle,
Indiana, where he preached. During the war, he guided Union troops to the
Shenandoah Valley from his native state of Virginia and died two years later.
Helen's mother remained a lifelong Calvinist.

Helen was graduated in June 1873 from the Cincinnati Normal School. She
taught school until, at twenty-two in 1875, she married Charles Selden Smart, a
forty-year-old Virginian who was a state school commissioner in Ohio. Helen

studied biology at Columbia when the couple moved to New York City about 1880, when Smart entered the insurance business. She lectured at the Brooklyn Institute of Arts and Sciences in sociology, and wrote for newspapers under male pseudonyms.

She met Robert and Eva Ingersoll during this time, who encouraged her to undertake her 1884 lecture series, published the next year by *The Truth Seeker* in book form, *Men, Women and Gods, and Other Lectures.* In his foreword, Col. Robert Ingersoll noted, "No human being can answer her arguments." Helen charged the bible with degrading and belittling women, using the bible as "chief witness."

Helen became friends with Elizabeth Cady Stanton, and was a member of *The Woman's Bible* committee. Stanton chose Helen to deliver her memorial speech. Helen quipped in that memorial address that while most suffragists found the *Woman's Bible* too radical, she found it not radical enough.

Described as slight and delicate, with brown eyes and hair, Helen was praised as a sweet and graceful orator.

A special interest became the study of the brain. Helen sought to prove whether the common scientific assertion of the day was true—that women were inferior because they had smaller brains. The former United States Attorney General had claimed in an article appearing in *Popular Science Monthly* in 1887 that the inferiority of the female brain was measurable, a claim used as a weapon against women's rights.

In their 1893 book *Woman of the Century*, Frances E. Willard and Mary A. Livermore wrote: "Her investigations, in which she was aided by the leading alients and anthropologists of America and Europe, caused her to discover the utter fallacy of the theory upon which this dicta, as to sex difference in brain, is based. Her work in that direction is the first scientific, basic work and the most thorough that has ever been done, and she settled beyond question the error of the assertion that there is any difference known to science, in brains, because of sex." (p. 313)

Helen presented her findings to the Woman's International Congress held in Washington in 1888 in an address, "Sex in Brain," which was excerpted in the *Popular Science Monthly*.

Proof of her stature was the invitation to deliver three separate papers before the Congress of Representative Women held in conjunction with the World's Columbian Exposition in Chicago in 1893.

Determined to reach the general public with her ideas, she turned to storywriting. A collection of her short stories, *A Thoughtless Lass*, was published in 1890. Her first and most popular novel, *Is This Your Son, My Lord?* came out the same year with 25,000 sold in the first five months. While it did not have staying power, it was a passionate denunciation of legalized prostitution and the scandal-ously low age of consent laws of the time, describing the ruin of an innocent girl by "respectable" men. A second volume of short stories, *Pushed By Unseen Hands*, was published in 1892 along with a novel, *Pray You, Sir, Whose Daughter?* Considered her best work, a war novel based on her father's life, *An Unofficial Patriot*, came out in 1894, and was dramatized by playwright James A. Herine in 1899 as "The Reverend Griffith Davenport."

Helen contributed articles to a wide array of publications, from *Popular Science Monthly* to *Free Thought Magazine* and *The Arena*, a reform journal put out in Boston by Benjamin O. Flower. Her first husband Col. C. Selden Smart was business manager and helped to subsidize *The Arena* magazine during the time Helen edited it (about 1894–97). Smart died in 1901.

The following year Helen married Col. Selden Allen Day, a retired army officer, and set off on a six-year world tour, including some lectures and a long stay in Japan. She retired into the Washington, D.C., social scene upon their return, but was soon cajoled back into activism by Anna Howard Shaw and other suffrage leaders. Helen was able to use her social and governmental connections to advantage in lobbying efforts for the suffrage amendment. She helped reorganize a Congressional committee of the National American Woman Suffrage Association after the original committee resigned to join Alice Paul's militant Congressional Union. Helen became a vice-president of the NAWSA in 1917 working as the chief liaison with President Wilson's administration. She met with Wilson more than twenty times in the next two years, influencing his public pro-suffrage statements.

Although Helen believed in no miracles, she was credited by co-workers with making them, as recalled Maud Wood Park, chair of the Congressional Committee: ". . . this may truly be said, that whenever a miracle has appeared to happen in our behalf, if the facts could be told they would nearly always prove that Mrs. Gardener was the worker of wonders . . ." (*History of Woman Suffrage* V: 567).

At age sixty-seven, Helen became the first woman appointed to the United States Civil Service Commission, serving with distinction for five years and looking after the interests of federal employees, particularly women workers.

When Helen died of heart disease at Walter Reed Army General Hospital in 1925, she was described as a "leader in suffrage cause" in full reports in the *New York Times*. She requested a nonreligious funeral; among those paying tribute was Carrie Chapman Catt. Her body was cremated and the ashes interred at Arlington National Cemetery. Per her instructions, her brain was willed to Cornell University—this news and her brain's shipment followed breathlessly by *The New York Times*.

Men, Women and Gods, predating *The Woman's Bible* by a decade, was a slim but meaty 158-page book including a succinct section on the treatment of women in the Old and New Testaments (limited only to portions that would not "soil my lips nor your ears" to hear about). Part II is a strong section on "vicarious atonement." [See selection]

❦

Among her observations:

"This religion and the Bible require of woman everything, and give her nothing. They ask her support and her love, and repay her with contempt and oppression." (*Men, Women and Gods*, p. 9)

". . . there is no book which tells of a more infamous monster than the Old Testament, with its Jehovah of murder and cruelty and revenge, unless it be the New Testament, which arms its God with hell, and extends his outrages throughout all eternity !" (p. 12)

"It is thought strange and particularly shocking by some persons for a woman to question the absolute correctness of the Bible. She is supposed to be able to go through this world with her eyes shut, and her mouth open wide enough to swallow Jonah and the Garden of Eden without making a wry face. . . . Of all human beings a woman should spurn the Bible first." (pp. 1, 24)

"The bible teaches that a father may sell his daughter for a slave [Ex. xxx, 7], that he may sacrifice her purity to a mob [Judges xix, 24; Gen. xix, 8], and that he may murder her, and still be a good father and a holy man. It teaches that a man may have any number of wives; that he may sell them, give them away, or swap them around, and still be a perfect gentleman, a good husband, a righteous man, and one of God's most intimate friends; and that is a pretty good position for a beginning. It teaches almost every infamy under the heavens for woman, and it does not recognize her as a self-directing, free human being. It classes her as property, just as it does a sheep: and it forbids her to think, talk, act, or exist, except under conditions and limits defined by some priest." (p. 14)

"Every injustice that has ever been fastened upon women in a Christian country has been 'authorized by the Bible' and riveted and perpetuated by the pulpit." (p. 14)

Vicarious Atonement

This is from a selection in Men, Women, and Gods, 1885.

Fear

EVERY EARNEST THOUGHT, like every earnest thinker, adds something to the wealth of the world. Blind belief in the thought of another produces only hopeless mediocrity. Individual effort, not mere acceptance, marks the growth of the mind. The most fatal blow to progress is slavery of the intellect. The most sacred right of humanity is the right to think, and next to the right to think is the right to express that thought without fear. . . .

Because I, a woman, have dared to speak publicly against the dictatorship of the Church, the Church, with its usual force and honor, answers argument with personal abuse. One reply it gives. It is this. If a woman did not find comfort and happiness in the Church, she would not cling to it. If it were not good for her, she in her purity and truth would not uphold it in the face of the undeniable fact that the present generation of thinking men have left it utterly.

You will find, however, that in every land, under every form of faith, in each phase of credulity, it is the woman who clings closest and longest to the religion she has been taught; yet no Christian will maintain that this fact establishes the truth of any other belief. ["Exactly the same thing may be said of the women in the harem of an Oriental. They do not complain. . . . They think our women insufferably unfeminine."—*Mill.*]

They will not argue from this that women know more of and have a clearer insight into the divine will! If she knows more about it, if she understands it all better than men, why does she not occupy the pulpit? Why does she not hold the official positions in the Churches? Why has she not received even recognition in our system of religion? Who ever heard of a minister being surprised that God did not reveal any of the forms of belief through a woman? If she knows and does the Will of God so much better than man, why did he not reveal himself to her and place his earthly kingdom in her hands?

That argument won't do! As long as creed and Church held absolute power there was no question but that woman was a curse, that she was an inferior being, an after-thought. No Church but the Roman Catholic has the decency to recognize even the so-called mother of God! The Church has never offered women equality or justice. Its test of excellence is force. The closer a Church or creed clings to its spirit, the more surely does it assume to dictate to and control woman and to degrade her. The more liberal the creed the nearer does it come to offering individual justice and liberty.

The testimony of our own missionaries, as well as that of many others, assures us that it is not the Turk but his wives who hold fastest to their faith. The women of the harem, whom we pity because of the injustice of their religious training, are the last to relinquish their god, the most bitter opponents of the infidel or sceptic in their Church, the most devout and constant believers of the faith, and the most content with its requirements. They are the ones who cling to the form even when the substance has departed—and it is so with us!

Among the "heathen" it is the women who are most shocked and offended by the attacks made upon their superstitions by the missionaries whom we pay to go to them and blaspheme their gods and destroy their idols.

Go where you will, read history as you may, and you will find that it is the men who invented religion, and the women who believed in it. They are the last to give it up. *The physically weak dread change.* Inexperience fears the unknown. Ignorance shuns thought or development. The dependent cannot be brave.

We are all prepared to admit, I think, that, with but few marked exceptions here and there, the women of most countries are physically and mentally undeveloped. They have had fear and dependence, the dread enemies of progress and growth, constantly to retard them. Fear of physical harm, fear of social ostracism, fear of eternal damnation. With rare exceptions a child with a weak body, or any other dependent, will do as he is told; and women have believed to order. They have done so not only in Christianity but in Buddhism, Mohammedanism, Mormonism, and Fetichism—in each and all of them. Each and all of these religions being matter of faith, religion was the one subject in which every Church alike claimed ignorance as a virtue; and the women understood that the men understood it as little as they did. It was a field where credulity and a solemn countenance placed all on an intellectual level—and the altitude of the level was immaterial.

Women have never been expected to understand anything; hence jargon about the "testimony of the spirit," the "three in one" absurdity, the "horns of the altar," or the widow's oil miracle was not more empty or unmeaning to her than a conversation about Bonds and Stocks, Political Economy, or Medical Science. She swallowed her religion just as she did her pills, because the doctor told her to, and said there was something wrong with her head—and usually there was.

Beginning to Think

The past education of woman gave her an outlook which simply embraced a husband or nothing at all, which was often only a choice between two of a kind.

There are a great many women to-day who think that orthodoxy is as great nonsense as I do, but who are afraid to say so. They whisper it to each other. They are afraid of the slander of the Church.

I want to help make it so that they will dare to speak. I want to do what I can to make it so that a mother won't have to evade the questions of her children about the Bible.

Creeds.

I am sometimes asked, "What do you propose to give in place of this comforting faith? It makes people so happy. You take away all this blessing and you give no other in its place. What is your creed?"

It has never seemed to me that a creed was the staff of life. Man cannot live by creeds alone. I should not object, however, to one that should read something like this:

I believe in honesty.

I believe that a Church has no right to teach what it does not know.

I believe that a clean life and a tender heart are worth more to this world than all the faith and all the gods of Time.

I believe that this world needs all our best efforts and earnest endeavors twenty-four hours every day.

I believe that if our labors were needed in another world we should be in another world; so long as we are in this one I believe in making the best and the most of the materials we have on hand.

I believe that fear of a god cripples men's intellects more than any other influence. I believe that Humanity needs and should have all our time, efforts, love, worship and tenderness.

I believe that one world is all we can deal with at a time.

I believe that if there is a future life, the best possible preparation for it is to do the very best we can here and now.

I believe that love for our fellow-men is infinitely nobler, better, and more necessary than love for God.

I believe that men, women, and children need our best thoughts, our tenderest consideration, and our earnest sympathy.

I believe that God can get on just as well without any of these as with them. If he wants anything he can get it without our assistance. It is people with limitations, not gods without limitations, who need and should have our aid.

I believe that it is better to build one happy home here than to invest in a thousand churches which deal with a hereafter.

If a life that embraces this line of action does not fit a man for heaven, and if faith in vicarious atonement will, then such a heaven is not worth going to, and its god would be unworthy to make a good man's acquaintance.

But suppose that faith in a myth is destroyed and another mysticism be not set up in its place, what then? If a mother takes her child away from the fire, which it finds beautiful, and believes to be a nice toy, is it necessary for her to give it a kerosene lamp in its place? She destroys a pleasant delusion—a faith and a delightful hope and confidence—because she knows its danger and recognizes its false foundation. It is surely not necessary that she should give to the child another delusion equally dangerous and false. She gives it something she knows to be safe; something she understands will not burn; something which, though not so bright and attractive to the child at first, gives pleasure without pain, occupation without disaster. Is she cruel or only sensible? If I were to pretend to a knowledge of a divine creed, a superhuman system, I should be guilty of the same dishonesty, the same deception of which I complain in the Church.

I do not know of any divine commands. I do know of most important human ones. I do not know the needs of a god or of another world. I do not know anything about "a land that is fairer than day." I do know that women make shirts for seventy cents a dozen in this one. I do know that the needs of humanity and this world are infinite, unending, constant, and immediate. They will take all our time, our strength, our love, and our thoughts; and our work here will be only then begun.

Why not, if you believe in a God at all, give him credit for placing you where he wanted you? Why not give him credit for giving you brains and sympathies, as well as the courage to use them. Even if Eve did eat that apple, why should we insist upon having the colic?

Self-Control What We Need.

I want to see the time come when mothers won't have to explain to their children that God has changed his mind about goodness and right since he used to incite murder; that eighteen hundred years ago he was a criminal with bloody hands and vile, polluted breath; that less than three hundred years ago his greatest pleasure was derived from witnessing the agony of pure young girls burning alive, whose only crime was beauty of face or honesty of thought. [See Gage, "History of Woman Suffrage," p. 766.]

I want it so that she won't allow her children to hear and believe such a statement as Bishop Fallows made not long ago. He said, in effect, that sins of omission are as heinous as those of commission; that Saul committed two sins in his life, and that one of them was a refusal to commit a coldblooded murder! He spared the life of a conquered enemy! Out of a whole nation he saved one life—and that was a crime, a sin! Bishop Fallows said that God expressly commanded Saul to utterly exterminate that whole nation, and not only the nation but its flocks; and that God took Saul's kingdom from him because he saved the life of one fallen enemy.

That story, I think, is a libel; and I believe that if there is a God he was never such a fiend! And I want it so that no mother will allow her child to hear such an infamous travesty of the character of a Deity who is called good.

I want it so that all the lessons of the week, all the careful training of a wise father or a good mother, will not be antagonized on Sunday by such a statement as the Rev. Mr. Williamson made at a large church convention recently. Speaking of prayer, he said: "We should offer to God, by prayer, our virtue, our purity, and our pious aspirations" (so far I do not object, for if it means anything I fail to grasp it), "for by not doing so we claim self-control, which is displeasing to God!"

I object! The lesson of self-control is precisely what we need. And when we control ourselves and regulate our lives on principles of right and truth, instead of allowing a Church to regulate them through a fear of hell, we shall be a better people, and character will have a chance to grow.

Then this same gentleman added: "We should also give him our vices, our worry, our temper, and our passions, so that he may dispose of them."

Dispose of them yourselves! Don't try to shift your responsibilities on to somebody else. Don't drive your tack into the brain of justice, expecting to save your own soft skull. Don't enervate your strength to do right by accepting the fatal doctrine of vicarious atonement. It weakens every character that it touches.

Vicarious Atonement Not A Christian Invention.

The doctrine of vicarious atonement is found in some form in most religions, and it is the body and soul of ours. The idea is not a Christian invention. It caused the Carthaginians to put to death their handsomest prisoners if a battle were won, the most promising children of their own nobility if it were lost. They were offerings to appease the gods.

In old times there were peoples who believed that if a chief was guilty of a misdemeanor it was just to punish or enslave any one of his tribe. That was their idea of liberty and justice. If a father committed a crime it could be expiated by the murder of his son. That was the doctrine of vicarious atonement in all its pristine glory. So they adopted that style of justice in our religion, and condemned the whole lot of us to the eternal wrath of God on account of that little indiscretion attributed to Eve. It seems a very little thing for anybody to get so mad at us all about, and stay mad so long! It doesn't seem to me that if one of you were to eat every apple I had in my orchard, I should want to murder and eternally damn all the folks that live [in] Asia Minor. Do you think you would?

In the 11th verse of the 12th chapter of the second book of Samuel it is claimed that God said he was going to be revenged for the crimes of some men by a vile punishment of their wives.

Only a short time ago a man tried that same style of justice in one of our Western towns. He claimed that Smith had alienated the affections of his wife, so he went over to Smith's house and *whipped Mrs. Smith!* And do you know that the judge who tried that case (not being a good Bible student) actually sent that good, pious man to the house of correction—that man who not only believed in his Bible, but lived by it! And just as likely as not that judge will be elected again. Truly we have fallen on degenerate times!

Legal minds outgrew the idea of vicarious punishment long ago. Physical liberty came to have a new meaning, and punishment was awarded more nearly where it was due. But the religious mind never outgrows anything. It is born as big as it ever gets. Development is its terror. It abhors change. It forces you to sin by proxy, to be redeemed by proxy; and the only thing it does permit you to receive at first hand is Hell. That is the only one thing you can't delegate to somebody else.

If you commit no sin, you are responsible for the sins of other people—dead people, too, that you can't look after. If you are good and true and noble—even if you are a Christian—you don't get any credit for it. If there is any one thing above another that God detests it is to have a man try to be grand and noble and true, and then get the credit of it. "To Christ belongs all the honor, the praise, and the glory—world without end, Amen."

But when it comes to the punishment, the vicarious notion doesn't seem to work. There is the one point where you are welcome to your own, and no discount allowed to heavy takers. Hell is always at par and no bail permitted. Even ignorance of the requirements is no excuse. If you did not know any better, somebody else did, and you've got to pay for it.

Now if the vicarious principle is not big enough to go clear round, I'll leave my share off at the other end. If the Church wants to take my hell (vicariously) it is welcome to it. I will let it go cheap.

Awhile ago a man stayed some time at a hotel in New York, and when the time came for him to pay his bill he hadn't the money. Well, the proprietor felt sorry for him and said, "I tell you what I'll do about that bill, I'll throw off half." His guest was overwhelmed by this liberality, and with tears of gratitude said, "I cannot permit you to outdo me in generosity; I'll throw off the other half and we'll call it square."

So if the Church desires all the credit, it is also welcome to all the blame. I cannot permit it to outdo me in generosity. But I'd rather be responsible for just my own sins, and then I can regulate them better, and I can take care of my own reward when I get it. I shall not want to deposit it with the clergy. A profit and loss system that is chiefly loss will not pay me.

The doctrines of vicarious atonement and original or inherited sin are the most infamously unjust dogmas that ever clouded the brain of man.

Twin Monsters Inherited From Intellectual Pigmies.

They are twin monsters inherited from intellectual pigmies.

Let me read you a little prayer based upon this idea of right. I heard it offered as a thanksgiving tribute. "Oh, God, we do thank thee that thou didst give thy only son to die for us! *We thank thee that the innocent has suffered for the guilty,* and that through the suffering and death of thy most holy son our sins are blotted out!"

Monstrous! How would that work in a court of justice? What would you think of a person who coolly thanked a judge who had knowingly allowed the wrong man to be hung? What do you think of a code of morals that offers as one of its beautiful provisions the murder of the innocent instead of the punishment of the guilty?

People ask what good I expect to come of an attack on Christianity. They ask me if I think Christianity does any direct harm. Yes! *It makes a man unjust to believe in unjust doctrines.* Any man who honestly believes in the righteousness of a system of vicarious rewards and punishments is ripe for any form of tyranny. And the more honestly he believes in it the less will he be a good man from principle.

I want men and women to be good and true because it is right towards each other, and not because they are afraid of Hell. Honor towards people in this world, not fear of a fiend in the next—that is my doctrine. That is the way to make men and women strong and brave and noble. Stop telling them they can't be good themselves; teach them that they must do right themselves. Make them self-dependent. Teach them to stand alone. Honor towards others, kindness, and love—these are what make a man a good husband, a noble father—king in his household.

Fear never made any man a gentleman. Fear never made any woman a true wife or a good mother. Fear never covered the pitfalls of vice with anything stronger than the gloss of hypocrisy.

When Reason's torch burned low, Faith led her victims by chains of ignorance into the land of hopeless superstition, and built her temple there.

25

Ellen Battelle Dietrick

RICH, RIPE THOUGHT

The day has gone by when a monk can tear a Hypatia from the pursuit of philosophy and throw her to a rabble of insane monastics to be dragged to a violent death. . . . Man has made himself a law unto himself, publishing it in his pretended "heavenly" revelations, dogmas, and statutes. Woman is now constructing a law unto herself, and she is putting it forth, not on a pretendedly supernatural, but on a natural, basis.

"Cardinal Gibbons' Ignorance," **Liberty,** *1895*

ELLEN BATTELLE DIETRICK SERVED ON Elizabeth Cady Stanton's *Woman's Bible* committee and was prominent at some of the national woman's suffrage conventions. She was elected a vice-president of the Kentucky Equal Rights Association in 1888. Moving to Boston by 1890, she became president of the Boston Suffrage League.

Her importance to freethought lies in her two existing essays, "Cardinal Gibbons' Ignorance" (*Liberty*, April 20, 1895), and a short book on the history of women in the early church, published posthumously. [See *Women In The Early Christian Ministry*] In "Cardinal Gibbons' Ignorance," she wrote:

"Cardinal Gibbons might just as well make up his mind that women are slipping out of the clutches of the priest. And, in so doing, they are, for the first time in the history of the world, becoming truly religious, for they are learning what is religion,—the tie that binds; they have discovered that it is nothing but the common tie of our common humanity, the brotherly and sisterly love of a world-wide family."

Something of Ellen's personality and interests can be gleaned from references to her in *The History of Woman Suffrage*. At the National American Woman Suffrage convention of 1893 in Washington, D.C., all of Ellen's resolutions were adopted without dissent, except her last:

"*Resolved,* That we especially protest against this present attempt to force all the people to follow the religious dictates of a part of the people, as establishing a precedent for the entrance of a most dangerous complicity between Church and State, thereby subtly undermining the foundation of liberty, so carefully laid by the wisdom of our fathers."

History of Woman Suffrage (IV: 217) reported: "This precipitated the discussion as to the opening of the World's Fair on Sunday which had been vigorously waged during two preceding conventions without resulting in definite action. It was now continued during three sessions and then, by the majority vote, indefinitely postponed." Putting the NAWSA on record against the closing of the World Fair on Sunday had been Elizabeth Cady Stanton's final request when she had attended her last national convention in 1892. Its reactivation the following year without her presence indicated she had strong, minority support.

Ellen's death, sometime prior to the annual suffrage convention of January 23–28, 1896, was reported by the *History of Woman Suffrage:*

"The loss of Mrs. Ellen Battelle Dietrick came with crushing force, as her services to the association were invaluable. To her most intimate friend, the Rev. Anna Howard Shaw, was assigned the duty of speaking a word in her memory, and in broken sentences she said: 'I never knew such earnest purpose and consecration or such a fund of knowledge in any one as Mrs. Dietrick possessed. She never stopped thinking because she had reached the furthest point to which some one else had thought. She was the best antagonist I ever saw; I never knew any one who could differ so intensely, and yet be so perfectly calm and good-tempered. What she was as a friend no one can tell. . . . It seemed as if she had a premonition that her life would soon end, for she sat at her desk writing hour after hour. I believe it shortened her life. She had just finished a book—Women in the Early Christian Ministry—and she left many other manuscripts. It would be a pity if the rich, ripe thought of this woman should not be preserved. . . .'

"Miss Anthony, who was to close the exercises, was too much affected to speak and motioned that the audience was dismissed, but no one stirred. At length she said: 'There are very few human beings who have the courage to utter to the fullest their honest convictions—Mrs. Dietrick was one of these few. She would follow truth wherever it led, and she would follow no other leader. Like Lucretia Mott, she took 'truth for authority, not authority for truth.' " (IV: 259–60)

Dietrick, who was on the *Woman's Bible* Revising Committee, would not have found that Convention's subsequent action to disavow *The Woman's Bible* as much of a tribute to her views. Part II of *The Woman's Bible*, published in 1898, was dedicated to her memory "in whose death we lost the ablest member of our revising committee."

Anna Shaw's concern that "the rich, ripe thought of this woman" might not be preserved was all too valid.

Women in the Early Christian Ministry
A Reply to Bishop Doane, and Others

This is excerpted from the 1897 book, published posthumously.

To ALL COURAGEOUS WOMEN who desire to put away childish things, this study of the childhood of orthodoxy is affectionately dedicated. . . .

Persistently leavening public opinion, in a grossly superstitious age, with the theological doctrine of popular preachers, that woman is a sex of superior wickedness and inferior mentality, could have but one general result throughout Christendom. Not only did it gradually create within women themselves a passion of self-depreciation, humility and a self-hatred which led thousands of them to slowly and persistently torture themselves until relieved by insanity or death, it planted within the minds of men a jealous hatred and superstitious horror of the natural powers of women, which ultimately culminated in a veritable crusade of ecclesiastics against womankind. That such should be the case, was as simply inevitable as is the misery of one girl and the contemptuous tyranny of one boy in a family whose heads openly and constantly teach a brother that he is superior, by virtue of sex, and has a right to lord it over his sister. As Emerson says of similar teaching, it is the same in the case of millions as it is in the case of two, and the sooner we learn this truth, the more careful will society be to frown down an ecclesiastical or political dogma which we now would abhor as between one brother and one sister.

Ecclesiastical law in Christendom, growing out of the Eve dogma, gradually converted marriage into a system of legalized slavery for all women, mitigated only by the chance that the wife might, by personal charm, win good treatment from the master to whom she was obliged to swear obedience, and by the chance that the master would not abuse the power his laws granted to him. This degradation of the wife, naturally enough, suggested the exclusion of women from that political rule which they had always shared with men since political rule had been instituted among mankind; and the Salic law in France, the elimination of women from the succession to the throne in Russia, and the exclusion of women from participation in political affairs in the so-called democracies of the United States and modern France, are all fruits of the Pandora-Eve dogma. (It must be remembered that government in Pagan Greece and Rome, to the last, was chiefly theocratic, and that women, even after they ceased to mingle in men's common councils, yet enjoyed great political dignity as a sex, by virtue of their office as deliverers of "inspired" oracles, every political event of note being referred to their decision.) Finally, the lowest depth of woman's degradation in Christendom was reached in the public sentiment (guided by ecclesiastics) which condemned thousands of poor creatures to be tortured and publicly burnt alive at the stake for their imaginary league with Christendom's imaginary devil! Roman Catholics and Protestants, Europeans and Americans, alike, were changed from naturally good and kind men into practical likeness to that mythical chief of tortures, the "devil," upon whom their fevered imaginations constantly dwelt, and defenseless women, whom Nature designed to be men's greatest joy and necessary complement, were the victims of that monstrously false conception of pure ignorance. Now, there is no doubt that those woman-torturers were men *naturally* as good, as sincere, as anxious to do right as, undoubtedly, are our Bishop Doanes, Cardinal Gibbons, Rev. Peter J. Eastons, and other woman-subjectors to-day. There is no doubt that they were sane on every point save in regard to that cruel *idée fixe*— that God had qualified them to govern women on account of "Eve's sin." What a comment does the history of the men perverted by that error provide on the awful danger of trying to force society to abjure reason and follow blind credulity! Elevating "belief" into the chief duty of all virtues, and constantly publishing "doubt" as the chief of all sins, they, inevitably, came to treat belief as the only virtue and doubt as the only sin; and the very professional leaders and exemplars of morality, led astray by their false conception of virtue, plunged into every genuine sin and crime and cruelty conceivable to monstrously distorted minds! As early as the fifth century, the absolute powerlessness of belief in Christian dogmas to promote true morality had manifested itself, and an honest Christian wrote, "The very church which should be the body to appease the anger of God, alas! what reigns there but disorders calculated to incense the Most High! It is more common to meet with Christians who are guilty of the greatest abominations, than with those who are wholly exempt from crime. . . . Their prayers are criminal meditations rather than vows of expiation. Scarcely is the service ended before each returns to his old practices. Some go to their wine, others to their impurities, still others to robbery and brigandage, so that we cannot doubt that these things had been occupying them while they were in church. Nor is it the lowest of people who are thus guilty. There is no rank whatever in the Church which does not commit all sorts of crime." (Salvian, of Marseilles, 440 A.D.)

Nor can our Protestants flatter themselves that any better results flowed from their transfer of belief from a Church to a Book. The punishments of Protestant Christendom, though declining in cruelty as reason gains increasing power over belief, have never during three centuries ceased to be inexpressibly more criminal than the crimes they were meant to correct. It is doubtful if untaught savages ever dealt with that natural enemy—a stranger from a rival tribe—as the Christian officials of Scotland dealt with poor Allison Balfour, accused of "league with the devil," in the year 1593, an account of which is preserved in the official report of the Scottish court. "Towards the end of 1593," says Froude, "there was trouble in the family of the Earl of Orkney. His brother laid a plot to murder him, and was said to have sought the help of a 'notorious witch' called Allison Balfour. When Allison Balfour's life was looked into, no evidence could be found connecting her either with the particular offense or with witchcraft in general; but it was enough in these matters to be accused. She swore she was innocent; but her guilt was only held to be aggravated by her perjury. She was tortured again and again. Her legs were put into the caschilaws—an iron frame which was gradually heated until it burned into the flesh—but no confession could be wrung from her. The caschilaws failed utterly, and something else had to be tried. She had a husband, a son and a daughter, a child seven years old. As her own sufferings did not work upon her, she might be touched, perhaps, by the sufferings of those who were dear to her. They were brought into court and placed at her side; and the husband was first placed in the 'long irons'—some accursed instrument, I know not what. Still the devil did not yield. She bore this; and her son was next operated on. The boy's legs were set in 'the boot'—the iron boot you may have heard of. The wedges were driven in, which, when forced home, crushed the very bone and marrow. Fifty-seven mallet stroves were delivered upon the wedges. There was no confession yet. So, last of all, the little daughter was taken. There was a machine called the 'piniwinkies,'—a kind of thumb-screw, which brought blood from under the finger-nails, with a pain successfully terrible. These things were applied to the poor child's hands, and the mother's constancy broke down, and she said she would admit anything they wished. She confessed her witchcraft—so tried, she would have confessed to the seven deadly sins—and then she was burned, recalling her confession, and with her last breath protesting her innocence." Such was the government of men over women, when women were, by the aid of superstition, reduced to subjection most complete. And, though the form of torture is changed, and the material instruments of torture are no longer used in open court, men's torture of women in attempts to govern them have not yet ceased, but simply grow more refined as men grow less militant. . . . But, terrible as was the involuntary torture of women under the influence of the possessed-of-the-devil idea, the voluntary torture which the poor wretches, weighted down with the sinfulness of their sex, inflicted upon themselves, was no less terrible. The hair-cloth garments worn next the delicate skin, which so irritated the system that outraged Nature protested in violent fevers and nervous convulsions, and the scourges whose power of injury was increased by thickly set iron points, were but successive steps toward the life-long burial in dungeons which furnished every element of horror that a diseased imagination could devise. Victor Hugo tells us of one of these coffins for the living which he saw in this century, about twenty miles from Brussels—in the heart of Christian civilization!—at the Abbey of Villars. "In the middle of the meadow which was once the court-yard of the cloister, and on the banks of the Dyle, are four stone cells of the secret dungeons, half underground and half under water. These were *in pace*. Each of these dungeons has a remnant of an iron wicket, a closet, and a barred skylight, which, on the outside, is two feet above the surface of the river, and from the inside is six feet above the ground. Four feet in depth of the river flows along the outer face of the wall; the ground of the cell near by is constantly wet. This saturated soil was the only bed of the *in pace* occupant. In one of these dungeons there remains the stump of an iron collar fixed in the wall; in another may be seen a kind of a square box, formed of four slabs of granite, too short for a human being to lie down in, too low to stand erect. Now, in this was placed a being like ourselves, and then a lid of stone was closed above her head. There it is. You can see it; you can touch it. These 'places of peace'; these dungeons; these iron hinges; these metal collars; this lofty skylight on a level with which the river runs; this box of stone, covered by its lid of granite, like a sepulchre, with this difference, that it shut in the living and not the dead; this soil of mud, this cess-pool; these oozing walls. Oh! what declaimers!"

And well may we echo, Oh! what declaimers of the evil power of ignorance were both the Protestant forcible torture of the poor women believed to be possessed of the devil, and the Roman Catholic voluntary self-torture of the poor women themselves! But what, save an age of insanity, could have been expected when Reason abdicated her throne and drunken Credulity drove Christendom amuck into the realm of Chaos?

The only method of restoring the natural equality of dignity between men and women, lies in the demolishment of that elaborate theological structure which maintains that woman is made for the possession of man in a sense in which man is not made for woman, and that celibacy, *per se*, is a state of superior purity. Nature and common sense (not metaphysical sense) demonstrate that there is no good reason why any man or any woman should take, claim, or wield "lordship" over another. With the coming of a good strong breeze of common sense—such sense as every little girl displays when she asks why the girl should be locked up and the boy allowed to run free in order to protect the girl from the boy—we may reasonably expect that the cobwebs which ignorance wove in the human brain will be swept away, and that the spiders will become an extinct species. . . . And, in spite of a superficial appearance of stability which still hangs about dogmatism, the era of its overthrow is close at hand. True religion, the tie which binds human hearts in love for each other generated by love for a common good, though of slow growth, is yet more flourishing and widespread than at any previous period in the world's history, but "orthodoxy" is tottering towards its final fall. After the invention of printing, it was only a question of time as to when knowledge should be so widely diffused that "authoritative revelations" would become impossible. Now that every two-penny journal of Christendom has taken the Garden of Eden myth as a standing object for ridicule, the corner-stone of the ecclesiasticism built thereupon is, indeed, crumbling, and the subjection of woman to man maintains its tenure by a thread whose brittleness no sagacious person can fail to see. Already the more Christ-like denominations of Christianity—the Unitarians, Universalists, Quakers, etc.—have opened their doors for the women's re-entrance into that equality of ministry from which thirteen centuries of brutal ignorance have excluded them; and the time is undoubtedly approaching when Methodists, Episcopalians, Roman Catholics, and other sects, will either follow that example or else drop out of existence, for the life of each of these sects depends upon the support of women, and an enlightened womanhood will no longer uphold any body which despises one half the human race, and believes that the other half is conceived in sin and inherently evil. . . .

As women, in this era, compose the bulk of adherents to the "revelation" theory, it is they who must deliver the world from the curse of theology-engendered hatred, by setting themselves mutually free from that most pernicious fallacy. They must *think* their own way out of this bondage, for, as Jesus well said, as one thinketh, so is she. It is not enough that a man or woman claims to be "inspired," speaks with uncommon wisdom, points to the multitudes who credulously accept such pretensions, or even to the admitted fact that many of these credulous believers are in many respects very intelligent. There has been no theological doctrine so monstrously absurd, among all the grotesque absurdities conceived by the still imperfectly working human brain, from Tertullian to Joseph Smith, from the All-Friend Jemima to Madame Blavatsky, or Mrs. Eddy, that it could not find a large number, even of the best educated people, to swallow it blindly, *for a time.* Tertullian actually taught that the more absurdly impossible a dogma appeared to the reason, the greater the virtue of the blind faith which professed belief in it! Such teaching places mankind below the level of intelligent brutes. It is no wonder that it led numbers of early Christians to live in caves or to burrow, nearly naked, in the ground, like wild beasts, suffering such self-imposed tortures as only de-humanized man can know. (See Jerome's letter on the Celibate Life.)

The human race is guided by its own ideas, and only by its ideas. If thought were left perfectly free from ban of legislative or ecclesiastical censor, the best thoughts would as naturally prevail over the worst as the best seeds of the forest naturally triumph over the worst seeds. . . . Our race experience should now help us to reject slavery to the mean, cowardly ideas begotten of the myths of Eve and Pandora, and help us to choose voluntary service to the noble idea of trust in our common human nature. The most profoundly vital idea of mankind is that which concerns the right relation of the sexes, and the only revelation concerning this relation is found in a study of Nature and of universal human experience. If there be such a thing as the "Word of God," it must be in the one common book—accessible to all races—the book of Nature. Of this book only may we say, adapting the words of Martin Luther: It is the common heritage of the whole human race, each member of which may make himself or herself competent to understand it.

26

Josephine K. Henry

AWAKENING KENTUCKY WOMANHOOD

February 22, 1846 – 1928

Is not the Church to-day a masculine hierarchy, with a female constituency,
which holds woman in Bible lands in silence and in subjection? No institution
in modern civilization is so tyrannical and so unjust to woman as is the
Christian Church. It demands everything from her and gives her nothing in
return.

Statement, The Woman's Bible, *1898*

JOSEPHINE KIRBY WILLIAMSON, born in Newport, Kentucky, was a noted woman
suffragist and freethinker. Josephine led her state's woman suffrage party, struggling with "supreme prejudice and sublime mediocrity" to awaken Kentucky
womanhood. (Willard, *A Woman of the Century:* 372)

She married Captain William Henry, a Confederate soldier and distinguished
scholar, in 1868. Frederick, their only child, was killed in a railroad accident in
Crete, Illinois. Settling in Versailles, Kentucky, she was known as an accomplished
musician, pianist and vocalist, and also wrote poetry.

Josephine was the first woman in the South to run for State office. As a candidate of the Prohibition party of Kentucky for clerk of the Court of Appeals in
1890, she did not win but received almost five thousand votes in the notoriously
antisuffrage state. She addressed the legislature and constitutional convention, as
well as large audiences throughout the state on the issue of woman suffrage.

Just as an atheist, Ernestine Rose, was the main lobbyist for passage of the
first Married Woman's Property Act in New York in 1848, it was Josephine, a
freethinker, who was credited as the main force behind the adoption of the 1894
Woman's Property Act in Kentucky. Almost half a century after Rose's work,
Kentucky women were the last in the union to be granted such basic rights as
property ownership, guardianship of their children, and the right to make a will.

Josephine organized a petition drive garnering ten thousand signatures on behalf of property rights, and also oversaw passage of a bill eliminating unfair inheritance laws.

More than three hundred of her articles were published on such subjects as "Married Women's Property Rights" and "Kentucky Women and the Constitution," as well as editorials in Versailles' *Clarion* reprinted by newspapers around the country.

Her address at the 1895 National American Woman Suffrage Association, where she was introduced as "the daughter of Kentucky," won her this report from the *Constitution*: "If the spirit of old Patrick Henry could have heard the eloquent plea of his namesake, he would have had no reason to blush for a decadence of the oratory which gave the name to the world." Josephine answered the assertion that "the women of the South do not want the ballot," contending, "Past civilization has not troubled either dumb creatures or women by consulting them in regard to their own affairs."

She concluded: "The most pathetic picture in all history is this great conflict which women are waging for their liberty. Men armed with all the death-dealing weapons devised by human ingenuity, and with the wealth of nations at their backs, have waged wars of extermination to gain freedom; but women with no weapon save argument, and no wealth save the justice of their cause, are carrying on a war of education for their liberty, and no earthly power can keep them from winning the victory." (*History of Woman Suffrage* IV: 244–245)

❧

Josephine was on the Revising Committee of Stanton's *The Woman's Bible;* her contributions are in the form of two ringing statements published in the appendix, one in response to Frances Willard's letter upholding the bible:

"We claim that woman's advancement is due to civilization, and that the Bible has been a bar to her progress," Josephine asserted.

"Has the Church ever demanded that woman be educated beyond the Bible (and that interpreted for her) and the cook book, or given a chance in all the callings of life to earn an honest living? Is not the Church to-day a masculine hierarchy, with a female constituency, which holds woman in Bible lands in silence and in subjection?

"No institution in modern civilization is so tyrannical and so unjust to woman as is the Christian Church. It demands everything from her and gives her nothing in return. The history of the Church does not contain a single suggestion for the equality of woman with man. Yet it is claimed that women owe their advancement to the Bible. It would be quite as true to say that they owe their improved condition to the almanac or to the vernal equinox. Under Bible influence woman has been burned as a witch, sold in the shambles, reduced to a drudge and a pauper, and silenced and subjected before her ecclesiastical and marital law-givers. 'She was the first in the transgression, therefore keep her in subjection.' These words of Paul have filled our whole civilization with a deadly virus, yet how strange it is that the average Christian woman holds the name of Paul above all others, and is oblivious to the fact that he has bought deeper shame, subjection, servitude and sorrow to woman than has any other human being in history. . . .

"The fact is that woman has been elevated in spite of Bible influence. Every effort that woman has made to secure education has been challenged by popes, bishops, priests, moderators, conferences and college presidents, yet against all these protests she has battered down the doors of Christian colleges and is now studying the Bible of Science in conjunction with the Bible of the Christian religion. With increasing knowledge woman is founding her faith on reason and demonstrated truth, instead of taking it second-hand from priest, parson or presbyter.

"Remove from Bible lands the busy brains and hands which have guided the plow and the locomotive, driven the machinery of the mine, the foundry, the factory, the home, the mental and the physical labor which have brought material prosperity, broadened the mind, subdued the brutal instincts, and humanized the race—remove all these and leave but the Bible and its influence, and where, let me ask, would woman be to-day? Where, indeed, would man be? A crouching and cowering slave to the Bible doctrine of the Divine right of kings, living as the brutes of the field, as he did when Bible Christianity was at the zenith of its power. Whenever in Christian lands man has been a slave, woman has been the slave of a slave." (*Woman's Bible:* 203, 205–207)

She elaborated on some of the points in her thirty-page booklet, "Woman and the Bible" published in Versailles, Kentucky in 1905. [See selection]

❧

As was true for many feminist leaders who criticized religion, Josephine was ostracized by orthodox peers. She was declared an "undesirable member" of the Kentucky Equal Rights Association after joining Stanton's revising committee. She followed "Woman and the Bible" with a second controversial work, "Marriage and Divorce" (c. 1907), criticizing the marriage institution, ceremony, and woman's loss of name and identity upon marriage. That book concludes:

". . . if one thought I have expressed will start a rill of thought in the minds of women and men, who love their fellows, and desire justice and happiness for them, and will nerve their hearts to help right these wrongs, my reward will be great indeed." A forgotten figure, she died after a stroke in 1928.

Woman and the Bible

This is excerpted from a booklet published in 1905.

A Lance Broken On Behalf Of Woman.

"All the wisdom of Vedas, and all that has been written in books, is to be found concealed in the heart of a woman."—Vedas.

"When women are honored the divinities are content."—Parsee Bible.

THE OBJECT OF THIS PAMPHLET is to arouse the latent power of thought in the minds of women, that they may read the Bible for themselves, put their own interpretation upon it, have the courage to express their opinions about its teachings, regarding their sex, without any interference, influence, or interpretation from the clergy—Save a few texts that are worn thread bare the Bible is a sealed book to woman kind.

If the Bible says what it means, and means what it says, the woman of ordinary mentality will discover that in the part of the Holy Book which is devoted to her sex, she will find horrors, terrors and obscenities that she had never dreamed of which her clerical teachers had never told her of, and that much of the teaching from the pulpit regarding women is not true.

Women are a very small factor in Holy Writ, as but one-eleventh of the Bible refers to them at all, and in the interest of justice and good morals it is a pity much of that was ever written.

The Bible estimate of woman is summed up in the words of the President of a Presbyterian Theological Seminary in his address to a class of young preacher. He said: "My Bible commands the subjection of women forever;" that man had searched the scriptures and found out what they taught.

The Bible says: "A tree is known by its fruit," yet this tree is carefully pruned, watered, and tended as the "tree of life" whose fruit in the word of Archdeacon Farrar "alone elevates woman, and shrouds as with a halo of sacred innocence the tender years of the child." As the world is swarming with miserable women, who are robbed of their human rights, bearing children against their will, who are filling our reform schools, poor houses, and prisons, the "elevation" for women and the "sacred halo" for children not having arrived yet after being on the way for 2,000 years, has so far proved to be a mere pipe-dream of this cleric.

The Bible records that God created woman by a method different from that employed in bringing into life, any other creature, then cursed her for seeking knowledge, yet the Scriptures say, "My people are destroyed for lack of knowledge: because thou hast rejected knowledge, I will also reject thee" (Hosea 4–6). "Add to your faith virtue; and to virtue knowledge" (2nd Peter 1–5), yet we have the injustice and inconsistency of God cursing Eve, and through her the race for seeking knowledge. Ever since Eve was cursed, the priest with the Bible in his hands has pronounced woman the most unnatural, untrustworthy and dangerous creature of God.

In the tenth commandment Exodus 20–17, she is classed with the ox and the ass; she is "given away" as a sheep at the marriage altar, and cursed in maternity. Psalms 51–5 says, "Behold, I was shapen in iniquity; and in sin did my mother conceive me." Surely there is nothing elevating about that to woman. This declaration puts the brand of infamy upon every woman that ever bore a child.

The wife who places her destiny in the keeping of the father of her children, bestows upon him the wealth of her affection, who goes "down into the valley and shadow of death" to give birth to children, who are to bear the blood and name of her husband to conquests, yet undreamed of, and to generations unborn, is by divine decree made a fountain of iniquity. Would not men and women rather pluck their tongues out by the roots than thus brand the mothers who gave them birth?

The law of God given to Moses in the 12th chapter of Leviticus, clearly pronounces a woman who becomes a mother to be unclean and impure. If she had borne a son she was not allowed to touch any hallowed thing, or enter the sanctuary for three and thirty days, but if she had borne a daughter she was doubly impure, and was unhallowed and barred out of the temple for sixty-six days. This estimate of woman permeates all Jewish and Christian canons. Today to bear a son is considered more honorable and desirable than to bear a daughter, yet our civilization swarms with sons who are worthless, or dissipated, or dishonest, or who wreck the fortunes and happiness of the family while daughters are as a rule, the comfort and mainstay of parents in their declining years.

The Episcopal prayer-book commands the Churching of Women, which service consists of mothers prostrating themselves at the altar, and giving offerings to the Lord to atone for the crime of having borne children.

What worse can be said of a book, or a religion, than that it treats as essentially unclean, the holy office of motherhood?

This insult includes all women, for even the Virgin Mary had to pass through "the days of her purification."

To say the least, this Christian tenet tends to throw suspicion on the "Immaculate Conception."

Place the Bible trinity, "Father, Son and Holy Ghost," beside the Homeric trinity "Father, Mother, and child" and prove that the Bible has elevated woman. The Homeric conception of woman towers like the Norway pine above the noxious growth of the Mosaic ideal.

Compare the women and men of the Bible with the stately figures culled from the temple of Pagan antiquity, Zipporah denouncing Moses as a "bloody husband," Abraham sending Hagar and his child into the desert, and pocketing twice over the gains from his wife's prostitution. Lot and his daughters, Judah and his daughter-in-law, Anan, Tamar, the Levite and his concubine, David and Bathsheba, Solomon in the sewer of sensuality, Jacob, Saul, Rahab, Aholibah, Mary of Bethlehem, Mary Magdala, and a host of other Bible figures. Place these beside the man and woman, Hector and Andromache of the "Iliad," who called upon the immortal gods to bless their child of love. Isis and her son Horus, Devaki and her divine child, Chrishna, the Vedic Virgin Indrance, the mother of the Savior god Indra, Pandora, Protogenia, Plotina, Cornelia and Penelope and a host of the noble and virtuous of Pagan history.

Prove by comparing these with the position of woman in Christendom, that woman owes all that she is to the Bible.

There were grand and noble women and men in the Pagan world, ten centuries before the laws of Moses or Christ were promulgated.

If women will lay aside their religious bigotry, they will discover that our boasted Christian civilization literally puts into practice, the crimes, the Bible records against their sex, and how well it is being done, the press attests, as never in the history of the world were such atrocious crimes committed against maidens, wives, pregnant, insane, and aged women. As the Bible is said to be the guide for American civilization no wonder we have a carnival of blood curdling crimes of every description. The Bible tells of the incest of a father with his own daughter, Genesis 19-32, the 34th chapter of Genesis contains debauchery, female commodity, lying, deceit, murder, theft, hypocrisy and cowardice. If all this is taught in one chapter of the Christian's guide book, is it any wonder that our civilization is overflowing with crime? The murdering of women and the ravishing of little girls is taught in Numbers 31, 17–18, the treacherous rape of maidens Judges 19-23, and filthy stories about concubinage in Judges 19. Perhaps the example of the holy men and women in the Holy Bible accounts for the epidemic of brutality and moral leprosy in Christendom. There is no use having a guide book unless you are guided by it. Bible Christians have no warrant for respecting womanhood, either as maid or mother, and the claim that woman owes all she possesses of personal purity, domestic happiness, and social consideration to the Bible is false and absurd. There is not a single Bible character, either woman or man, that is a perfect model for the women and men of today to copy after. Some of them illustrate noble traits of human character, but even these are so enveloped in brutality, deception and sensuality they are hard to discover.

Let Christian women and men of today be up to such tricks as are recorded of Abraham, Sarah, Jacob, Rebecca, Leah, Noah, Lot and his daughters, David, Solomon and their lady friends, Samson, Delilah, Sisera, Jael, Abimelech, Naomi, Ruth, Esther, Martha, all the Marys and even St. Paul, the premier saint of the Christian calendar, and they would not only be ostracized by society, but many of them would find themselves behind prison bars.

When woman reasons more and believes less, then, and not till then, will her charter to liberty be signed.

The rib doctrine is the tap root of her inferiority and degradation. The hour is here now, when women are calling theologians to the bar of reason, and they will no longer believe the supernatural, miraculous fables of the Bible that put the brand of inferiority upon their sex. . . .

Keep on searching the scriptures, dear sister, that is a Bible command, and if your preacher will not interpret the diabolisms against your sex, be a self-respecting woman and interpret them for yourself, then read the history of Christianity, and you will come face to face with the truth, that Christian women are the slaves of a superstition that degrades them.

Etta Semple (left) with Laura Knox, editors of The Free-thought Ideal, *1899
(Kansas State Historical Society)*

27

Etta Semple

"SCATTERING SEEDS OF KINDNESS"

September 21, 1855 – April 11, 1914

I never yet have seen the person who could withstand the doubt and unbelief that enter his mind when reading the Bible in a spirit of inquiry.

"A Pious Congressman Twice Answered," **Truth Seeker,** *1895*

WHEN SHE WAS BORN MARTHA ETTA DONALDSON into a Baptist family in Quincy, Illinois, no one could have foretold she someday would become the target of an assassin for her freethought views. Etta married a man named Killmer, they had two sons, and she was widowed in 1887. She married Matthew Semple, a barrel maker from Ottawa, Kansas, and they had one son, named for the American reformer Wendell Phillips.

She became Ottawa's town radical, espousing freethought, feminism, championing the working class, protesting racial bigotry, and opposing capital punishment and "blue laws." Her novels included *Society* and *The Strike*, dedicated to all working classes. She helped to found the Kansas Freethought Association to "fight ignorance, superstition and tyranny," and to ensure that constitutional freedoms would be "untrammeled." In 1897 she was elected its president. From her parlor she began publishing the bimonthly *Freethought Ideal*, an eight-page newspaper with a circulation of two thousand.

Her essay "A Pious Congressman Twice Answered," published in *The Truth Seeker* on February 23, 1895, answered attacks against Ingersoll in a sermon by Elijah A. Morse of the Eastern Presbyterian church of Washington, which had been published in *The Washington Post*, January 15, 1895. She wrote:

"My little five-year old boy, Wendell Phillips, puts it in this way: 'Mamma, if there is a God, why doesn't he come down and show himself?—then we would believe.' . . . Not in all the cycles among all the innumerable millions of people who have inhabited this globe, has even one seen God or seen anyone else who had. Nor has anyone seen his handiwork except as they have called Nature such. Then why not study Nature, and cease to worship a myth which ignorance and superstition have placed behind it?"

When a Christian woman said Etta was little better than a whorehouse madam, she replied: "If heaven is composed of such hatred, such abuse, such tyrannical onslaughts, such Christian love, I don't want to go there. Hell is far preferable."

Etta, who supported temperance, amused Ottawans in the summer of 1901 by strolling arm-in-arm with Carry Nation, prompting a local observer to quip: "One believes in no saloons, and one believes in no god." That year her husband's illness and financial problems caused her to fold the *Ideal*, but she remained an active freethinker, named vice-president of the American Secular Union.

She opened an osteopathic hospital for the sick and lame, building a three-story "Natural Cure" sanitarium in 1902 with thirty-one rooms, never turning away anyone. "No tramp ever went away hungry, and no fallen woman has been kicked down by us," she once wrote.

While the *Evening Herald* of Ottawa, Kansas, hailed Etta as a "Good Samaritan" and "one of the greatest benefactors for humanity Ottawa has ever had," she was stalked by an assassin. In an unsolved murder on March 28, 1905, an elderly patient at the hospital, Caroline Hostetter Jobe, was bludgeoned in bed. Authorities believed Etta was the intended victim.

Etta ran for state superintendent of education on the Socialist Labor ticket and for the State Board of Education, losing but making respectable showings.

When Etta died of pneumonia in 1914 at age fifty-nine, court was adjourned and crowds filled the cemetery for a godless oration in the spring sun. The *Ottawa Herald's* banner headline read: "A Philanthropist Will Long Be Remembered Here" and "Good Deeds of A Good Woman Are on the Tongues of Ottawa Today."

She had suggested her own tongue-in-cheek epitaph, should there be money for one: "Here lies a woman that through her peculiar disposition lived a life of turmoil, as did all who knew her."

Mourners sang one of her favorite secular songs, "Scattering Seeds of Kindness," which the local newspaper called "emblematic of Mrs. Semple's life."

The obituary reported:

"She did not believe in the general idea of God or of the existence of a soul. Her idea of the hereafter was that a person's life will have a good or evil influence after death, wholly dependent upon the life lived by the person. Believing in this faith she strove to live a conscientious life, helping the sick, afflicted and distressed. . . .

"She believed that a good life will inspire others to be better and will have influence for the betterment of the world. This was her idea of the soul."

"Liberty of Conscience Is All That We Ask"

This was a typical editorial appearing in Etta Semple's publication, The Free-thought Ideal, c. 1898.

It has been claimed by many that Freethought does away with churches, creeds, Christs and even a God. So it does to a certain extent, but not as feared by Christians. Freethought has never said pull down your churches, burn up your creeds, crucify your savior or reject your god. No one ever knew a Freethinker to try to make laws to control people. All their efforts have been the other way, trying to tear down laws already made which control by "thou shalt" and "thou shalt not." If those who oppose Free-thought did not strive to *force all* to think as they do, accept Christ by faith, believe the bible to be infallible, keep Sunday as a holy day, and work for a future reward, then our fight would be at an end instantly. Liberty of conscience is all we ask—not control of any class, creed or sect.

Every true Freethinker accords to each individual the right to mental freedom. Where this freedom leads is no concern of others so long as it encroaches not upon their rights.

If I deny the existence of a God—if I deny the idea of a gold paved city with pearly walls and jasper gates somewhere out of knowledge and space and prefer to die and trust to the unfaltering laws of nature—if, in plain words I don't want to go to heaven, whose business is it but my own?

Hypatia Bradlaugh Bonner

28

Hypatia Bradlaugh Bonner

ATHEIST EDITOR, EDUCATOR

March 31, 1858 – August 23, 1934

Heresy makes for progress.

Reformer, 1897

Less power to religion, the greater power to knowledge.

"Testament," 1942

HYPATIA BRADLAUGH WAS THE DAUGHTER of the great British atheist leader Charles Bradlaugh, who triumphed after a long battle to be seated in Parliament as an atheist. She was the namesake of Hypatia of Alexandria, a pagan lecturer and intellectual who was torn to pieces by a mob of Christians in 415. This leader in thought was a credit to the first Hypatia, as well as to the memory of her activist father—but without suffering more than the occasional slanders and the modest lifestyle necessitated by placing an unpopular cause ahead of creature comforts.

When Hypatia was ten and her sister Alice twelve, their father, who had struggled out of poverty to practice law, first ran as a candidate for Parliament. Bradlaugh was sinking in debts due to costs of defending his *National Reformer* from prosecution, and his wife's extravagances in her decline into alcoholism. With Bradlaugh's atheist notoriety costing him clientele, he decided to give up his practice and devote himself to the movement. His wife and daughters lived in the country; Bradlaugh rented two rooms for himself in London.

The girls attended a country school, alternating visits on an irregular basis with their father in London. They enrolled in 1872 in a school in Paris after their father, determined that they should learn French, scraped the money together. As the daughter of an infamous atheist and the frequent target of embarrassing attempts to single her out, Hypatia humorously recalled an incident from Paris: "Before we left Madame la Directrice asked what was our religion. Mr. Bradlaugh, inwardly expecting difficulties, answered: 'None, Madame.' Madame's 'Ah! Monsieur, that saves trouble' brought a smile of surprise and amusement to my father's face." (Bonner & Bonner, *Hypatia Bradlaugh Bonner*: 8)

When their mother died in 1877, the girls kept house for their father in London. Hypatia was recruited to take over her father's affairs during his and Annie Besant's prosecution for publishing a book on birth control. Hypatia and Alice witnessed with fright the sentencing of their father to six months' imprisonment, with a fine of £200. Suddenly the judge stayed the proceedings pending an appeal, which quashed the indictment in February 1878. The victory of that reprieve was overshadowed by violence soon after. Hypatia witnessed Bradlaugh's campaign rally in Hyde Park being mobbed. Young medical students bearing sticks advanced in gangs to the podium where her father and the Hon. Auberon Herbert stood, destroying the platform. Although panicked supporters screamed that Bradlaugh had been killed, he emerged unscathed.

In 1877, Hypatia was admitted to the City of London College, but took only one course before the College reversed its ruling to admit women. In 1879 she enrolled in courses sponsored at the Hall of Science by her father's National Secular Society, studying inorganic chemistry and animal physiology. She took an advanced course of practical work at the Science and Art Department's Laboratory in South Kensington, later matriculating at London University, and becoming a teacher at the Hall herself. In 1882, teaching a mathematics course, she met her future husband, Arthur Bonner. That year she assumed long-held duties as volunteer business secretary of the Society. She and Arthur married in 1885, merging their surnames. In 1886, she gave birth to Kenneth Bradlaugh Bonner, who died at six months. After her sister Alice died from typhoid in 1888, the couple moved in with Bradlaugh, and Hypatia again served as her father's secretary. Bradlaugh's grandson Charles was born in 1890.

When Bradlaugh died in January 1891, Hypatia immediately set about writing his biography, a task she had hoped to do at his side. She was forced by constant slanders and rumors of deathbed conversions to continually correct the public record, and even took successful legal action against one malicious and fraudulent biographer. Eventually she wrote a pamphlet, "Did Charles Bradlaugh Die an Atheist?" expressly to counter the absurd rumors. Hypatia regretfully folded her father's weekly journal, *National Reformer*, in 1893, after thirty-three years of publication.

She had begun lecturing in 1881 and spoke throughout her life in numerous provincial cities. An ardent opponent of the death penalty and proponent of penal reform, she worked on the executive council of the Humanitarian League. Her lecture "The Gallows and the Lash" was reprinted in 1897 as a pamphlet. She worked with the Women's Liberal Association and the International Arbitration and Peace Association, later founding the Rationalist Peace Society in 1910.

A Thomas Paine aficionado, she edited a complete edition of his *Rights of Man*, which came out in 1895, and the following year reissued *Age of Reason* through the A. and H. Bradlaugh Bonner publishing house. Their firm also produced a special edition of Bradlaugh's *Collected Speeches.*

She launched a new journal, the *Reformer* (1897–1904), with a broad humanistic agenda, predicated on her belief that "heresy makes for progress." She lectured for the newly-formed Rationalist Press Association, joining its board in 1916. Hypatia listed prosecutions for heresy and blasphemy through the ages in her 1912 book *Penalties Upon Opinion*, reprinted several times. In 1913, her book *The Christian Hell* forced an examination of the savagery of the doctrine of eternal punishment. In 1919, *Christianity and Conduct* was published. [See selection]

In 1920 Hypatia was pleased to attend the first International Freethought Congress held after the war. She euphorically reported that the streets of Prague were full of hundreds of persons wearing the Congress badge and the pansy, a symbol of freethought. Delegates were welcomed by the President of the State, the mayor and other officials. The organizer of that Congress, Dr. Bartosek, was one of the first Prague citizens jailed and condemned by the Nazis.

Hypatia returned to her work against blasphemy laws after J.W. Gott was prosecuted under them in 1921, receiving a heavy sentence in 1922, despite her efforts. Bertrand Russell, then a member of Parliament, was only able to muster seven peers to support his attempt to repeal the blasphemy laws.

As a reward for forty years of public service, Hypatia was appointed Justice of the Peace for London in 1922, and sat at the bench until 1934, working with probation officers and taking a special interest in incarcerated juveniles.

By the time she had lost her voice in 1924, barely able to speak above a whisper after developing paralysis of a vocal cord, Hypatia had delivered more than one hundred and twenty separate addresses in more than two hundred places.

The year 1933 marked the centenary of her father's birth. Hypatia was very touched by the tributes and festivities. In 1934, she was diagnosed with cancer, and had surgery on May 15. Cognizant of the rumors circulated by Christians after her father's death, she took care to write her "testament" for the *Literary Guide*. [See selection]

After her death, Chapman Cohen, president of the National Secular Society, noted that Hypatia Bradlaugh Bonner belonged to "that small army of brave people who made it their duty, without thought of themselves or hope or expectation of reward, to strive for unpopular causes." (*Hypatia Bradlaugh Bonner:* 124)

Her husband Arthur devoted most of the years before he died in 1939 to compiling a biography, *Hypatia Bradlaugh Bonner: The Story of Her Life.* The book was finished by their son Charles and published in 1942.

Christianity & Conduct

Christianity and Conduct; Or, The Influence of Religious Beliefs on Morals
by Hypatia Bradlaugh Bonner was published by Watts & Co. in London in 1919.
Excerpts from several chapters follow.

Slavery

In this chapter, Bradlaugh Bonner pointed out that African slavery "was inaugu-
rated by that pious mariner, John Hawkins, whose slaving vessel, the Jesus, sailed
for West Africa on its first voyage to kidnap negro slaves in October, 1564, under
the blessing of Almighty God."

IT WAS NOT CHRISTIANITY WHICH FREED THE SLAVE: Christianity accepted
slavery; Christian ministers defended it; Christian merchants trafficked in
human flesh and blood, and drew their profits from the unspeakable horrors of the middle passage. Christian slaveholders treated their slaves as
they did the cattle in their fields: they worked them, scourged them, mated
them, parted them, and sold them at will. Abolition came with the decline
in religious belief, and largely through the efforts of those who were denounced as heretics. In America Thomas Paine was the first person to
publicly advocate the emancipation of the slave, and the work was taken
up and carried to success three quarters of a century later by Abraham
Lincoln. Lincoln was certainly not an orthodox Christian; at most he was
a Deist, and it is extremely doubtful whether he was even that. He was an
eager reader and admirer of Thomas Paine and of Volney; he himself
wrote an attack upon Christianity. So general was the Christian opposition to abolition in the United States that even in Boston itself all the
churches and the schools, which were at that time under the control of the
churches, were closed against the anti-slavery advocates. The only hall
open to that most eloquent abolitionist, William Lloyd Garrison—for the
kidnapping of whom Georgia offered a reward of five thousand dollars—
was one belonging to Abner Kneeland, the despised "infidel" who had
been imprisoned for his heresy. During the anti-slavery struggle in America,
so closely were emancipation and unbelief associated in the popular mind
that "abolitionist" and "infidel" were frequently used as synonymous terms.

War

Before August, 1914, it was the correct thing to proclaim Christ as the Prince of Peace and Christianity as the religion of love and the brotherhood of man. We had a Peace Sunday each year when lip-service was paid to Peace from thousands of pulpits. After August, 1914, these same pulpits resounded with praises of the Lord as a man of war (*Exodus*, xv, 3) and declarations that the great European War was a Christian war, sent directly by Almighty God himself. The earlier attitude, disassociating Christianity from war, was both dishonest and, to say the least of it, ungrateful; for Christianity has been nursed, nourished, and spread abroad by war and by what we now call frightfulness.

During the first three centuries, when its adherents were few and humble, with a considerable proportion of women among them, besides a number of slaves and paupers, Christianity was no doubt a religion of peace. It could hardly have been otherwise. But all that changed from the moment Constantine took it under his protection in the year 312.... For the first three centuries Christianity was, no doubt, a religion of peace; for the last sixteen the cross has been both figuratively and actually the handle of the sword.

Liberty

Bonds, whether they be material or mental, tend to deformity. The cramped foot of the Chinese woman may be thought beautiful in China. The cramped mentality of the priest may be thought beautiful at the Vatican in Rome, or at Lambeth Palace in London. To the Rationalist both are equally ugly.

... Militarism enslaves the body; religion enslaves the mind: when the two go together the servitude is complete.

... Both in the etymological meaning of the word and in actual practice religion means bondage. And, unfortunately, it not only binds its own adherents, but nearly every religion seeks to punish here or hereafter, or both, those who refuse their adherence and are unable to accept its particular dogmas and precepts.

... the Jews do not stand alone as victims of Christian ruthlessness. To realize the extent of the relentless enmity of the Church to all who refused submission to her authority we have only to recall the horrible persecutions organized by the Christian Church and carried on systematically for nearly six centuries under the Inquisition, or such savage massacres as that of St. Bartholomew. Human memory is short, otherwise one might have imagined that it would require centuries of unblemished virtue on the part of Christians everywhere, great and small, high and low, to cleanse their shield from the bloodstain of these awful crimes. But official Christians have either no memory or no shame. By some curious mental twist they can ignore their dark record and boast of the reign of love and brotherhood of man inaugurated by Christianity. There are some of us living even at the present day who have learned by bitter experience that their love begins only where their power to strike has become paralysed by the growth of a sane Rationalism. To-day the Christian Church no longer dares to torture or put to death whole communities; but it has not yet ceased to oppress individuals who venture to think for themselves.

Women

It is difficult to exaggerate the adverse influence of the precepts and practices of religion upon the status and happiness of woman. Owing to the fact that upon women devolves the burden of motherhood, with all its accompanying disabilities, they always have been, and always must be, at a natural disadvantage in the struggle of life as compared with men. . . . With certain rare exceptions, women all the world over have been relegated to a position of inferiority in the community, greater or less according to the religion and the social organization of the people; the more religious the people the lower the status of the women. . . .

The rise which has taken place recently in the status of women in certain countries is due almost wholly, if not entirely, to the decline in religious belief. Among our own people, where circumstances have been specially favourable to the growth of the spirit of liberty, the independence of women and the equalization of their rights have come only little by little; every step has been gained in defiance of the Church and the teachings of the Scriptures, and in no way through their aid. When women cease to kiss the rod which has chastised them for the past sixteen centuries, their emancipation will be still further hastened, their characters strengthened, and their activities given full scope, not only in England, but in France, Italy, Spain, and in the other of the Christian countries in the world. The wider education of women should do much to improve their condition; it should make them more respected, and what is of equal importance, it should make them respect themselves more. The more women know, the less they will "believe." And once released from the thraldom of belief, they will be free to prove their own worth. The more heretical women become—*i.e.*, the more they think, criticize, and make up their minds for themselves, instead of humbly asking their husbands, as enjoined by St. Paul—the sooner they will reach a position of dignity and independence.

Conclusion

Christian morality depends finally upon the belief in immortality, with—in most cases—a belief in a future state of rewards and punishments of some kind or another. . . . Necessarily, therefore, the individual believer is much more concerned about the welfare of his own soul in eternity than about the welfare of the bodies of others sojourning here on earth for a short space of time.

The mental outlook of the man without religion is in complete contrast to that of the believing Christian. This life is all he has: it is all his brother has. When death's long sleep comes to end the chapter, the book is closed. There is no sequel, no after-life, good or bad. Hence it becomes the duty of every man to live the best life he can, so that he may leave the world, the only world he will ever know, better than he found it. . . .

Happily for the world, except under stress of fanaticism or bigotry, men in the mass are almost always better than their creed. The desire for the common good, rooted deep in the primitive instinct for self-preservation, is constantly triumphing over the combined forces of self-interest and religious authority. But in future ethics, in rational ethics, the general interest of humanity should be no rival; it must be supreme. For on the broad foundations of human welfare, and on that alone, can men ever hope to build up a truly sane and lofty morality.

"Testament"

Written for future publication in the Literary Guide when she was dying, this was reprinted in **Hypatia Bradlaugh Bonner: The Story of Her Life** *by Arthur Bonner and Charles Bradlaugh Bonner (1942).*

IT IS THE 9TH OF MAY. I am a sick woman—sick in body, but sound in mind. On May 15 I have to undergo a rather serious abdominal operation, which to a person of my age is not without danger. So it has occurred to me, sitting here in my familiar surroundings, at my familiar writing table, that I would jot down a few notes as to my position in regard to religion.

I do not for one moment suppose that my personal opinion matters one way or the other, but I have a too painful experience of the misrepresentations made by a certain class of Christians not to be well aware that they are quite capable of circulating false stories of the 'death-bed' conversion of Charles Bradlaugh's daughter.

Now, in my seventy-eighth year, being of sane mind, I declare without reserve or hesitation that I have no belief, and never have had any belief, in any of the religions which obsess and oppress the minds of millions of more or less unthinking people throughout the world. All, or most, of these religions have their god or gods, and their adherents profess to adore, to worship, their chosen Deity. What a misuse of words—to 'adore,' to 'worship,' or to 'love' stocks, or stones, or figures of wax dressed in gaudy garments, or figments of the imagination in ancient languages!

There is little in any of those religions, nothing at all in any of their gods, to attract reasoning, thinking minds. Here and there we find teaching helpful to good living, but for the most part these consist of precepts which have been taught by other peoples at other times. They are the result of age-long experience, crystallized into the 'sayings of the day.' But too often even helpful teachings are rendered nugatory by others of a positively contradictory character.

Looking back over the history of our own country, what has Christianity done for it and us? What have the Churches, what have the priests, done? It is only as our peoples have emerged from the domination of the Church, and reason has asserted its powers over the minds of men, that we see improvement. A hundred and fifty years ago people were in bonds to the Church; they were ignorant, their poor homes insanitary, they starved helplessly; their condition was one of degradation and servitude. Compare 1800 with 1935! It is complained that the churches are empty to-day. In 1800 if you did not go to church you were taken to the stocks or suffered imprisonment. That comparison lights up the whole difference: less power to religion, the greater power to knowledge.

Away with all these gods and godlings; they are worse than useless. I take my stand by Truth—by tested truth, which includes sincerity and honesty. I do not mean a truth which changes colour from day to day according to the barometer of an emotional mind. The truth I stand by may be enlarged, or in some degree modified, in the course of years by the increase in our knowledge, but in essentials it remains to-day much as it did for me seventy years ago. Honesty, courage, steadfastness, and sympathy: these, I hope, have been the guiding lights of my life. I have made mistakes—as everyone has—some of which I have been very sorry for; but this I can say with confidence, that I have never willfully injured anyone, and that I have always endeavoured to see and understand the other point of view.

And so Good Night.

Charlotte Perkins Gilman, with portrait of her mother
(The Schlesinger Library, Radcliffe College)

29

Charlotte Perkins Gilman

"LIKE LIGHT FROM A DIAMOND"

July 3, 1860 – August 17, 1935

. . . [Let us inquire] what glory there was in an omnipotent being torturing forever a puny little creature who could in no way defend himself? Would it be to the glory of a man to fry ants?

His Religion and Hers, 1923

BORN IN CONNECTICUT SHORTLY AFTER THE PUBLICATION of Darwin's *On the Origin of Species*, Charlotte Anna Perkins spent her life proposing a rational attitude toward women, work and family predicated on her interpretation of evolutionary principles. One of the most celebrated feminists of her time, she was a respected poet, author, editor and theorist admired by H. G. Wells, George Bernard Shaw, Theodore Dreiser, Zona Gale and contemporary suffragists. In 1924 Rebecca West called her "the greatest woman in the world today." When the tenth anniversary of passage of the woman's suffrage amendment was marked in 1930 with a book honoring four women thinkers, Charlotte Perkins Gilman received top billing. Her *Woman and Economics* was compared to John Stuart Mill's *On Liberty*. Her last book, *His Religion and Hers*, provides a stunning denouement of patriarchal religion.

Charlotte's father Frederick Beecher Perkins was the grandson of evangelist Lyman Beecher. Her mother Mary Ann Fitch Westcott virtually was abandoned by Frederick when, after three babies in three years, a doctor warned that another pregnancy would kill her. Charlotte recorded in her autobiography that her mother resolved to save her from similar grief by withholding all expression of affection from her. Charlotte had almost no formal education so she educated herself, embracing daily exercise and eschewing corsets.

Charles Walter Stetson, a dashing young artist, began to court the twenty-one-year-old. Two years later, they married. Charlotte suffered from lifelong bouts of depression, which deepened into paralyzing proportions after giving birth to her only child, Katherine, in 1885. A bedrest "cure" far worse than the disease, ordered by a fashionable physician, was immortalized in Charlotte's 1890 classic feminist horror story, "The Yellow Wallpaper."

Charlotte blossomed after her 1887 separation from Stetson, settling in California and launching an impressive career as lecturer, journalist and author. Although never free of financial worry, she supported herself and helped support a number of relatives. With Charlotte's blessing, Stetson married her lifelong friend Grace Ellery Channing in 1894. Charlotte sent her daughter, then nine, to live with them until Katherine reached her mid-teens. The divorce and Charlotte's arrangements for her daughter received painful national publicity.

But her reputation soared. At age thirty-five she went on a five-year speaking campaign, with the Hull House her first stop, hobnobbing with key social reformers. Lecture topics included: "Woman Suffrage and Man's Sufferings," "How to Get Good and Stay So," and "A New Way to Heaven."

Her first book, *In This Our World*, a collection of poems, was printed in 1893. It went into a second edition in 1895 and was also published in London. One poem, "To the Preacher," jeers: "Preach about yesterday, Preacher!" and concludes: "Preach about the other man, Preacher!/Not about me!" A whimsical poem, titled "The Holy Stove," gently pokes fun at "The Altar of the Home." In 1894 she started work as editor of an alternative journal, eventually founding the *Forerunner* (1909–1916), a thirty-two-page monthly entirely written by her. Her diverse lectures, prolific articles and serializations became the foundation of books.

When she attended her first National American Woman Suffrage Association convention in 1896, it merited this write-up in the *Woman's Journal*:

"Those of us who have for years admired Mrs. Stetson's remarkably bright poems were delighted to meet her, and to find her even more interesting than her writings. She is still a young woman, tall, lithe and graceful, with fine dark eyes, and spirit and originality flashing from her at every turn like light from a diamond. She read several poems to the convention, made an address one evening and preached twice on Sunday; and the delegates followed her around, as iron filings follow a magnet." (*History of Woman Suffrage* IV: 256)

Charlotte was one of eleven women there who spoke against the resolution disassociating the group from Elizabeth Cady Stanton's *Woman's Bible*.

The publication in 1898 of her *Woman and Economics: A Study of the Economic Relation Between Men and Women as a Factor in Social Evolution* made her an international figure. The book went into a ninth printing by 1920 and was translated around the world. Other nonfiction included: *Concerning Children* (1901), *The Home: Its Work and Influence* (1903), *Human Work* (1904), *The Man-Made World; or, Our Androcentric Culture* (1911), *His Religion and Hers: A Study of the Faith of*

Our Fathers and the Work of Our Mothers (1923) and her autobiography *The Living of Charlotte Perkins Gilman* (1935). Her most enduring fiction is the feminist-like utopian novel *Herland* (1915).

She entered what she called a "happily ever after" thirty-five-year marriage with her younger first cousin George Houghton Gilman in 1900. A firm believer in euthanasia, Charlotte took her own life in 1935, using chloroform, when pain from inoperable breast cancer became unbearable.

❦

Although the Beecher clan was known for its piety, and its first famous woman, Catherine Beecher, for her enthusiastic domesticity, Charlotte broke the mold, embracing humanism and repudiating religion. She trenchantly rejected the "family values" of her day, finding the traditional home a prison for women. Women were relegated to the abnormal and degrading position of being the personal servants of adult men. Women's access to work would be the "humanizing of women," the way to growth. She was disgusted with the Hebrew view of work as a "curse." She advocated rational parenting, educational daycare and nurseries, not only to free women but to benefit children.

A poem expressed her rational views:

> Once we thought the earth was flat—
> What of that?
> It was just as globos then
> Under believing men
> As our later folks have found it,
> By success in running round it;
> What we think may guide our acts,
> But it does not alter facts.

Her book *His Religion and Hers*, written when she was sixty-three, like its author, flashes spirit and originality "like light from a diamond." Its supposition: "That a normal feminine influence in recasting our religious assumptions will do more than any other one thing to improve the world. . . ." (p. 7)

She repudiated a "morbid preoccupation with death and 'another world.' " *His Religion and Hers* asked: "What would have been the effect upon religion if it had come to us through the minds of women?" Although predicating her thesis on evolutionary principles, she attacked that "shop-worn shibboleth, 'The struggle for existence, and the survival of the fittest,' " finding the language used to describe evolution as "heavily masculinized." (p. 92) Evolution is growth, Charlotte wrote, and it can be assisted by cultivation, as Luther Burbank demonstrated. Instead of honoring war and competition, society should honor that which advances humanity.

"If we once admit that our life here is for the purpose of race-improvement, then we question any religion which does not improve the race, or the main force of which evaporates, as it were, directing our best efforts toward the sky. . . . Improvement in the human race is not accomplished by extracting any number of souls and placing them in heaven, or elsewhere. It must be established on earth, either through achievement in social service, or through better children." (p. 10)

"We grovel and 'worship' and pray to God to do what we ourselves ought to have done a thousand years ago, and can do now, as soon as we choose." (p. 13)

The book reiterated her abiding faith in work ("Work is human") and her conviction that "woman is the race type of humanity." (pp. 77, 82)

Hypothesizing how death-based religions started, Charlotte observed: "Thinking is fun to a normal mind, like any other natural exercise, and those very ancient ancestors of ours had lively brains, with no ballast. They were so intrigued by thinking on subjects concerning which nobody knew anything, that they hardly cared for the more difficult topics of real life, wherein one's glad imaginings are so brutally interrupted by stubborn facts." (p. 40)

Submission and eternal damnation were roundly rejected: "Why should so much mental activity have stopped there, and not inquired what glory there was in an omnipotent being torturing forever a puny little creature who could in no way defend himself? Would it be to the glory of a man to fry ants?" (p. 160)

She refreshingly rejected the biblical injunction, "having no parallel in nature," to honor parents, calling it a "peculiar inversion of a natural relation." (p. 179)

Always came her theme against women's servitude to men: "One religion after another has accepted and perpetuated man's original mistake in making a private servant of the mother of the race." (p. 217)

Charlotte advanced proverbs to replace religious ones, from the woman's point of view (pp. 170–171):

WHAT HURTS THE MOTHER HURTS THE RACE.

A BABY IS MORE IMPORTANT THAN A CORPSE.

'T IS A WEAK MAN THAT NEEDS A WHOLE WOMAN TO WAIT ON HIM.

SPEND ON THE SCHOOL AND SAVE ON THE PRISON.

MAKE FEWER LAWS AND KEEP MORE.

A RATIONAL AND STRENGTHENING PHILOSOPHY OF LIFE WILL COME TO US

THROUGH THINKING MOTHERHOOD. IT IS TIME.

While she spared some kind words for a nonsupernatural Jesus, she explicitly rejected Christianity and its "scheme of salvation," also castigating many teachings of Buddhism, Hinduism and Islam, especially Buddha's view that existence is evil because it is subject to death and decay. For the individual it may seem an evil, she pondered, but for the race it is "as unnoticeable as is the death, in a living body, of daily millions of its innumerable constituent cells."

Without defining "religion," she promoted one based on "natural laws," a life philosophy that was not to be believed in but applied. Although she appeared to be a loose Deist, making reference to a "God" as a "naturally possessed power," she rejected the unprovable afterlife, faith, obedience, sin, belief, "past-worship," rites, ceremonies and holy books.

"One and all, religions have their original prophets, their sacred books, their traditions of ages gone. One and all require us to accept without question what other people long dead have said or written; to obey without question the commands of those behind us . . . . No matter what the belief, if it had modestly said, 'This is our best thought, go on, think farther!' then we could have smoothly outgrown our early errors and long since have developed a religion such as would have kept pace with an advancing world. But we were made to believe and not allowed to think. We were told to obey, rather than to experiment and investigate." (pp. 188–190)

In Zona Gale's foreword to Charlotte's autobiography, Gale called Charlotte "one of the great women of the two centuries." Charlotte's leitmotif, Gale wrote, was "Life is growth." Zona recalled a remark Charlotte had made following a conference both writers had attended at the University of Wisconsin in Madison:

"Emerging on that campus, the summer school students streaming over its green swell in the slanting late afternoon sunlight, bright colored groups under the trees, the university band playing, she said: 'There's heaven. There it is. What more do we mean? People, free to come together, and in beauty—*for growth.*' "

In her autobiography Charlotte wrote that "the stony-minded orthodox were right in fearing the first movement of new knowledge and free thought. It has gone on, and will go on, irresistibly, until some day we shall have no respect for an alleged 'truth' which cannot stand the full blaze of knowledge, the full force of active thought." (Gilman, *The Living of Charlotte Perkins Gilman:* 322)

His Religion and Hers
The Two Beyonds

The following is from Chapter II of Gilman's 1923 book, **His Religion and Hers.**

MAN'S INTEREST IN SOMETHING BEYOND THE PRESENT is undeniable, and is, in its higher forms, peculiar to himself.

It is true that many of our zoological inferiors provide by a blind instinct for the advantage of the next generation, and that some of them seem intelligently to foresee the deprivations of the coming winter, arranging for food and shelter during its rigors.

But this short-range and purely practical provision is nothing compared with our limitless and spiritual prevision. We do, indeed, like the mud wasp, lay up supplies for our children, and buy coal in April,—if we can afford it,—but belief in these matters merits no martyrdom. The faith we passionately uphold is in what we call life after death, "the great beyond."

That life goes on after death is clear; no one is so fondly egotistical as to assume that life stops just because he is dead. Human life, with all its adventures and misadventures, has been going on for a long time, and shows no signs of stopping. This, however, is not the point of interest. It is not the undeniable "beyond" of our life here, but that of our life somewhere else about which each is excited. The beyond, for the individual, after his death, is the key-note of most of our great religions. Neither the individual nor the religion thinks or cares about the beyond of human life on earth.

The general interest of humanity in the future life seems to rank almost as a race instinct. As such it might be held to indicate, in our social consciousness, a dim prevision of improvement, a sort of psychic recognition of social evolution. It has not been so understood, but is held to prove some other life, knowledge of which will guide our conduct in this one.

The earthly paradise of a Promised Land, flowing with milk and honey, assured to them and their children in this life, was no more compelling a spur to action to the early Hebrews than was the hoped-for Valhalla, flowing with beer and bloodshed, to early Teutonic peoples. No future life offered has been more practically popular than that of the Moslem. When he died, most particularly when he died in battle for his faith, he went directly to a scene of bliss which any man was quite competent to enjoy, an eternity of feasting and dalliance with ladies of imperishable youth and beauty.

While considering the attractions of the various beyonds as set forth in one religion after another, recognition is due to what is absolutely the most prodigious prize ever offered the human soul, the dazzling future of the good Mormon.

The God worshipped by Jew, Christian, and Moslem, Mormons esteem to be the especial deity of this earth and its people, who are literally his children through Adam; the universe full of countless inhabitable earths, and to each earth its god. To these illimitable worlds will come in time their deities, recruited from the ranks of Latter-day Saints. The perfected Mormon soul, in the fullness of time, becomes God; not resolved into an Infinite Being, as believes the humbler Buddhist, but a quite separate divinity, all by himself. There is a delicious Americanism in this idea. Not only may any little boy be President, but he may be God.

A rather conspicuous point to be noted in all these joy-promising futures is their naïve masculinity. Never a feminine paradise among them. Happy Hunting-Grounds—no happy Nursing-Grounds. No seductively mustached he houris, eternally gallant and devoted, beckon to pious lady Moslems. It is the man Mormon who soars to divinity; the women, in indefinite numbers, may also soar if properly married to him, but their position is distinctly subordinate, as here.

The Christian heaven is as appealing to women as any; but if that decoratively imaged city of golden streets and pearly gates, with its later envisaged choirs of angels with harp and crown, does please them more, it seems on the other hand less attractive to men. No man can rush to death in battle as much stimulated by the hope of a harp as of a houri.

With us the beyond which has had the most force is not heaven but hell. Any study of old sermons shows this in overwhelming proportion. We were told that heaven was our home, to be sure, and in truth it was shown most desirably contrasted with the alternative, but little eloquence was spent in depicting its allurements compared with the fervid orations on the terrors of hell.

Times change; habits change; even human nature, usually advanced as the type of immutability, changes, and with these have changed our precise ideas about the still-desired beyond. On what, as a matter of fact do these ideas depend? On three sources—revelation, imagination, and information, all of which vary. Every religion has its revelations, and even within a religion revelations do not always agree.

If there are any who question this, still holding that every word of our Scripture is true, and none contradictory of another, let them be referred to Ecclesiastes III, 19 and 20, on this very topic:

> For that which befalleth the sons of men befalleth beasts; even one thing befalleth them: as the one dieth, so dieth the other; yea, they have all one breath; so that a man hath no preeminence above a beast; for all is vanity.

The Preacher was in a gloomy mood and felt as he spoke, but few of us believe that what he felt was true.

Imagination has had a greater share in our general beliefs about the beyond than we are commonly aware. Dante and Milton are responsible for most of our views on the subject. The fluent sermonizer and pious hymn-maker have added their contributions. Many of our popular beliefs find their only base in these imaginings.

Then comes information, at present the most accepted source. During all the ages, under the heaviest pressure of revealed religion and in spite of the best efforts of imagination, we have always been intrigued by the idea of direct communication with some one who had been there. So many went,—all of us, in fact, as time passed,—it did seem as if they might get word to us. Never has this feeling been stronger than now. Revelation does not bind as it did, imagination is too easy; we want the facts from eye-witnesses.

So the modern world, with its popular education, its scientific training, its laboratory methods and what not, is now eagerly receiving reports from those "on the other side."

Even here we do not find agreement. It seems virtually impossible to gather any clear and convincing impression as to what awaits us in this beyond, the personal life after death.

How about the other beyond, the human life after our death, here, which we all know does go on, such as it is? There are marked points of difference between this beyond and the spiritual. For one thing, it is finite, a little period, variously estimated among the hundreds or thousands of millions of years; we are more attracted by the idea of eternity. An odd preference, this, because in this life we soon weary of anything that lasts too long, but so it is.

Neither does the earthly beyond have the unchangeable character of the eternal one, but it has altered continuously from its beginning, each age modifying the future for the next. It is usually believed that by careful conduct we may affect our position in the future life, but we may not change its conditions. Whereas the future conditions of all who follow us on earth it is within our power to change, for better or for worse.

In those portions of the earth's surface which have been completely deforested by previous occupants, the future life of all later ones has been made more difficult. We in America, rapidly and recklessly deforesting our rich country, are making the future life of our own descendants poorer and harder.

Those who have contributed to mankind the accumulated discoveries and inventions, the accruing knowledge and skill, the lasting works of use and beauty, have improved the future life of each following generation. For the most part it has been done unwittingly, for advantage in the present life rather than a desire to improve the future, but the benefit remains.

Our personal interest in a future life on earth has been shown mainly in the wish to be remembered, by the most meager gravestone or the pyramid of Cheops. By means of hospital beds, memorial windows, or other name-labeled endowments and bequests we seek to linger in the minds of our fellows, and sometimes we are "immortalized" by poet or sculptor. Undying fame is a dear ambition, though seldom realized.

> "They have ceased, but their glory shall never cease,
> Nor their light be quenched in the light of peace,
> For the rush of their charge is resounding still
> That saved the army at Chancellorsville."

The desire to insure some persistence of the individual life in an earthly beyond, involves no interest in the life of other people. It is a fairly common sentiment, but by no means so compelling as concern for the unearthly one; the wish to live in the minds of our fellows bears no comparison to the wish to live, eternally, somewhere else. . . .

If religion had concerned itself with our earthly future, it would have had a strong influence. Such pictures as it has given us of a vague millennium have been, if anything, less convincing than the Utopias. We can more easily believe in people's behaving well toward one another—as, indeed, many of them do now—than in contiguous naps of lions and lambs. The most frequent assumption of religion regarding our earthly future (I speak here of the Christian religion) is that we shall go from bad to worse and end in total destruction—except of course in the case of those who have handled this life with an eye single to their personal interest in another one, or, in a still narrower view, of a mere handful arbitrarily "elected." This is clearly a misnomer; it should have been "selected"; there was, surely, no vote taken upon members of either the upper or the lower house!

Yet if we lack revelation and information on this really important beyond, we have one base the other lacks—facts to build on. This practical future of ours has been in the building for a long time, quite long enough to show clearly what behavior it is which makes the lives of those who follow it better or worse. . . .

The trouble is that those heavily modifying forces, religion, law, custom, and public opinion, have never concerned themselves with this handmade future of ours; the real, solid, unavoidable future which comes rolling down the ages toward us,—sure to come but ours to mold as we prefer,—hell, heaven, or the confused mixture we call human life and are so discouraged about.

There is inspiration in thinking that the earthly future is for children to be born into, while the other is for our own elderly souls, of which some of us are already tired and some frankly ashamed. The unconscious happiness of children, their swift development, their easy acceptance of all lovely surroundings, make it a pleasure to provide for them. Surely fathers, not to speak of mothers, should be more concerned about what will happen to their living children in the world we are making, than about what may happen to themselves after they are dead!

Our behavior as it affects other people has not been taken seriously enough by religion. After all, it is comparatively a small affair what happens to a single soul, no matter how eternally, compared with what is done to the world. Yet we go on, reaping what our ancestors have sown and sowing for our descendants to reap, as unconcernedly as if we really had no responsibility except in securing our own personal advantage. Furthermore, if religion would be clear and strong on the subject, it becomes plain that the very behavior which builds the best future for our descendants in this life, is conducive to our chances of happiness in the next, whereas the special rites and ceremonies which we were told would benefit us are of no possible benefit to our children.

Perhaps the other-life future is more attractive to us because it is more easily attained. One may be helped in. Methods vary according to different faiths, but most of them are elastic. A person may "sin" in some ways and make up for it in others; or, no matter how much a sinner, he may be forgiven at the last minute, and find his future unimpaired by his behavior. Not so here.

The earthly future, bright though it shines as something within our power to make, has its gloomy side. There is no "forgiveness" in the transmission of sins from father to son. The erring father, spiritually forgiven, may live in heaven as happy as a grig, but the innocent child, inheriting the future his father made, lives on earth in misery. We are so long-sighted in our passionate desire for an eternal existence in the other life, so short-sighted in our indifference to the really respectable number of millions of years before us in this one!

If only religion could be brought to take an interest in this earthly future, what a help it would be! Think of the hymns chanting tunefully of the beautiful life just before us, so easily ours to make. Think of the pulpit eloquence, painting in words of penetrating force our splendid, never-ending opportunity to make our future life on earth worthy of the God we believe in. Think of the appeal to the less spiritual of us, to those who never did get enthusiastic about eternity, or care so tenderly about their own souls, yet who could rise to the thought of improving this world for the children they love, and their children after them.

Then too, if this view were taken up by religion, it might affect public opinion, and perhaps, in time, the law. Even governments held to such a standard would be kept more strictly to the path of far-sighted economy and steady provision for the public good.

Privately, one's future in the other life is one's personal affair.

Publicly, our common future in this life is our common affair, a social responsibility. . . .

"A Sin To Doubt"

This is an excerpt from the chapter "Behavior" in Gilman's **His Religion and Hers.**

A MYSTERY IS NOT MERELY A THING YOU DO NOT KNOW; it is a thing you must not know, which it is wrong to think about.

An odd idea, this! But child or savage takes easily to it; it soon became a race habit of mind, and the priesthood seized upon it as a wonderful protection for their imperfect thought.

Some religious theory or doctrine would be developed which was absurd enough to rouse comment and question. That would never do. So there grew up, as naturally as a running vine, the wonderfully interlocking self-protective structure of a great religion,—any of the religions; they are all alike in this claim,—"Here is something more important than anything else: it must be believed; if you do not believe you will be terribly punished."

Since it was apparent that believers in other religions were tolerably prosperous, the punishment was alleged to take place after death—when none could contradict.

One wonders here whether our hideous hell idea was developed to meet the persecutions of early Christianity. Since the torments inflicted upon people in this life were terrible beyond belief, it was necessary to think up something sufficiently worse to strengthen the martyr to endurance. And—wonderful tribute to the power of a concept!—the fear of a hypothetical roasting in hell enabled men to endure very practical roasting in this.

By the power of ideas over conduct each religion maintains its hold; and since the hold is absolutely dependent upon the ideas, it becomes a sin to doubt them. The more patently absurd they may be, the more necessary it is that they be shrouded by mystery, guarded by sanctity.

The enormous influence of religion upon conduct is obvious. Unfortunately, the conduct demanded was seldom of any value in promoting our happiness and progress, but mostly concerned those rites and ceremonies and those sacrifices either in goods or money essential to the maintenance of the established religion. . . .

"To Believe and to Obey"

*This is an excerpt from the chapter "Religion and Conduct" in Gilman's **His Religion and Hers**.*

THE MOST CONSPICUOUS FEATURE OF ANY RELIGION is in its rites and ceremonies. We might fill a book with endless lists of such detailed practices, from solemn sacrifice and grand processional to ridiculous minutiæ of costume and diet.

See what religion has done with prayer, for instance.

Prayer, the direct reaching out of the personal consciousness toward the divine force, is obscured, in one religion after another, with all manner of petty directions. We are instructed to pray at certain hours, as if God was to be reached only by appointment; in certain postures, as if the soul could move freely only when the body was on its knees; facing in a given direction, taking off the shoes, holding the hands thus and so, and using various set forms of speech. In the Christian churches God is still addressed in "King James's English." "O Thou!" we say, when we should consider it undignified and foolish to begin, "O You!" and "Thou knowest," rather than the tedious colloquialism, "You know!"

Praying with a string of beads is a widely known method in more than one religion, somewhat as the abacus is used in counting; and in Tibet we find not only beads but the ever-working prayer-mill and the practical but, to our minds, undignified, prayer-spit-ball.

Jesus, used to close contact with the divine spirit, gave clear directions to his followers not to make long prayers in public like the Pharisees, but for each man to go into his closet and pray alone. Yet in our highly elaborated Christian religion a regular ceremony in church, and in other meetings, is precisely that forbidden by Jesus—the making of long prayers in public.

Selected days and seasons for special religious ceremonies, some wholly arbitrary, some mere survivals of ancient customs, are another instance. We have a particularly amusing case in point in our patching together of Sunday and the fourth commandment.

The Sabbath day, to be kept holy, was distinctly described as the seventh day of the week, following upon six days of our labor as it did upon six days of God's labor in making the earth. This day was so kept and is still kept without break by the Hebrews, to whom the direction belongs. Jesus, it will be recalled, paid small attention to it. The Christian church in its mistaken attempt to connect the two religions, adopted the commandments, but selected another day to keep holy. That it should choose the first day of the week instead of the seventh, and use this day in commemoration of the resurrection of Jesus, is as reasonable as any other choice, but that it should advance a commandment applying to another day, commemorating another event to buttress its selection, is not so reasonable. Nothing but minds whose reasoning processes had been paralyzed for ages could build religious ceremonies and civil laws about a certain day, and quote as authority directions clearly applying to another one. . . .

But we have not yet reached the most general, far-reaching, and disastrous of these effects. Whatever were the doctrines held, the one universal requirement of all religions was belief. Whatever the laws laid down, always the universal requirement was obedience. To believe and to obey—these were the chief demands of religion upon the human mind. Moreover, this belief and this obedience were always given to the Past.

A religion is the strongest cultural influence affecting humanity. One and all, religions have their original prophets, their sacred books, their traditions of ages gone. One and all require us to accept without question what other people long dead have said or written; to obey without question the commands of those behind us. . . .

"Death Based Religion"

*This is an excerpt from the chapter "Results Of His Religion" from Gilman's **His Religion and Hers**.*

THE PECULIARITY OF ALL DEATH-BASED RELIGIONS is that their subject-matter is entirely outside of facts. Men could think and think, talk and argue, advance, deny, assert, and controvert, and write innumerable books, without being hampered at any time by any fact. The nearest they came to such foundation was in seeking to establish some facts as to the lives of their various religious teachers, or the identity of their sacred books; and even here there is far more of myth and legend than any certainty.

Thus we have almost from the beginning the assertion of authority which it was impossible to disprove, a sin to doubt, an indiscretion even to consider. Then, with this arbitrary basis, the minds of men soared happily in unbridled conjecture, and built up colossal systems of thought, racial "complexes" or states of mind, which were imposed upon the world. Each ancient religion has its form of established church, its priesthood or clergy, its temples and system of ceremonies; and each, as a social phenomenon, stands in history as a social complex, "a state of mind," a system of ceremonies, rather than as an agent of improvement. . . .

In economics we see the enormous evils still visible from the institution of slavery and its resultant false views of labor. In the sex relation itself the evil wrought is evident to any student; as is the further mischief of degrading the character of women and retarding normal race-improvement. But under and over and beyond all these is the wholesale crippling of the human mind, by insisting on unreasoning belief in early misconceptions and forbidding the use of reason in the most important field of our conscious life—the development and application of higher forms of religion.

It cannot be too strongly asserted that the insistence on blind, unreasoning faith is due mainly to the maintenance of a subject-matter upon which there was no knowledge, namely the "other world"; and that this basis was assumed because of early man's preoccupation with death. It is, unfortunately, quite possible to believe a thing which is contradicted by facts, especially if the facts are not generally known; but if the whole position on which we rested our religions had been visibly opposed by what we did know, even the unthinking masses would, in time have noticed it.

For instance, if we were told that a bad man could never grow rich, it would overtax our most willing faith to believe it. But when we are told that it is difficult, well-nigh impossible for a rich man to get into heaven, we can believe that easily, especially if we are poor men; there is no evidence against it.

The soaring, imaginative minds of men, constructing lofty, shimmering piles of abstract thought, and taking as their postulate a revelation from God, gave us religions which could not possibly be maintained without belief and obedience: all early religions demand these. In proportion as they are given, the religions endure, and we find them most permanent and changeless among peoples who make the least effort to square their beliefs with the laws of life.

It is not mere ignorance which holds down a religion. The wisdom of each age was largely developed by the priests. But this wisdom was never applied to their basic doctrines; these were immovable. It was not lack of capacity for thought which maintained absurdities and contradictions. The Hindu mind is perhaps more highly developed in concentrated, abstract thought than that of any other race, but the Hindu's limitless range of meditation and deduction all starts from certain assumed premises, unprovable premises, "irrelevant, incompetent, and immaterial" premises, and we see that tremendous mental exercise resulting in a race of a few sublimely intellectual and useless devotees and preachers, with millions of pathetically ignorant and unprogressive believers. . . .

The original basing of religion upon extra-mundane assumption, and the ensuant erection of immense complicated systems of theology and intricate rules for wholly irrelevant conduct, have had a widely injurious effect in their influence upon education.

In normal mental action, consistency, connection between ideas, is required. The major distinction of our human mind is in the ability to see connections, to put two and two together. As reasoning beings we are revolted by an illogical absurdity. But if the oldest, strongest, most universal cultural influence for all mankind is based on unprovable assumptions, involves gross inconsistencies, yet is enforced by all authority, then we deliberately cultivate in the race an artificial capacity for unreasonableness.

Our unreasonableness has been carried on still farther through systems of education. At first the social function of education was wholly in the hands of the priesthood. The teacher as such appeared later, and his work was largely the teaching of religion, as is still seen where little Moslems are taught the Koran, little Hindus taught from their sacred books, little Hebrews from theirs; and in our own public schools we still sought to impart something of our religion until our Hebrew and Romanist citizens objected.

The direct teaching of religion is small part of the effect in question. More serious is the acquired ability to dissociate ideas instead of connecting them. To this influence is traceable our adoption of an arbitrary division of studies, the mind of the scholar jerked from one subject to another at the stroke of the clock, without the faintest connection in thought. By such means we train learned men, profoundly informed in certain lines, totally uninformed in others, and never even feeling the need of any connection between what they know and the life and progress of mankind.

Because for so long the Christian church carried on its services and preserved its sacred books in Latin, with Greek and Hebrew behind that, there is still an "odor of sanctity" about these ancient tongues and because, further in the Renaissance, so many ancient though secular books in Greek and Latin were brought to life, for many years education continued to place most of its emphasis upon knowledge of dead languages.

That educated men, men more learned than others, should often at the same time be less reasonable, argues some strange peculiarity in our methods of mental training. This peculiarity is directly inherited from religion. "Learning" for long consisted solely in reading what was written and trying to remember it. As a matter of fact, students never *learned* anything, but confined themselves strictly to what was known before. We are but now beginning to *learn*, by investigation, by experiment, by the honest effort of free and active minds to add to human knowledge, instead of everlastingly repeating old theories.

Even if all the bases of religion had been correct, the enforcement of blind faith, the prohibition of intelligent inquiry would have had an injurious effect upon the mind. A sincere devotion to truth has quite different results. Truth is an ever-opening vista, a thing to be always followed and never caught.

Voltairine de Cleyre
(University of Michigan Library)

30

Voltairine de Cleyre

WOMAN VERSUS ORTHODOXY

March 10, 1866 – June 30, 1912

The question of souls is old—we demand our bodies, now. We are tired of promises, God is deaf, and his church is our worst enemy.

"Sex Slavery," *1890*

I can see no reason, absolutely none, why women have clung to the doom of the gods. I cannot understand why they have not rebelled.

"The Case of Woman Vs. Orthodoxy," *1896*

NAMED VOLTAIRINE DE CLAIRE IN LESLIE, Michigan, this dainty baby girl was born to French immigrant Hector De Claire and Harriet Billings, of Rochester, New York. An admirer of Voltaire, De Claire coined a new, most fitting name for his third daughter. Voltairine's family was poor and deprived, her stern father an itinerant tailor, her mother taking in sewing.

At four, bright "Voltai," indignant that the school in St. Johns would not admit her, taught herself to read. She set up a desk with a board in the branches of a maple tree where she would think, write and draw. Her first poem, written at about age six, expressing her lifelong love of privacy, was called "My Wish." Composed in the tree, it appropriately began: "I wish I was a little bird/To live up in a tree."

Her father left the family, settling in Port Huron, sending money when he could. In 1879, Voltai became miserably homesick when sent to live with her father, and even more so when, in 1880, he enrolled her in the Convent of Our Lady of Lake Huron at Sarnia, Ontario. After one runaway attempt, Voltai settled down to become head of her class.

Not unnaturally, she became preoccupied with religious questions: "I suffered hell a thousand times while I was wondering where it was located . . ." she once wrote. In the essay "The Making of an Anarchist," she recalled: "How I pity myself now, when I remember it, poor lonesome little soul, battling solitary in the murk of religious superstition, unable to believe and yet in hourly fear of damnation, hot, savage, and eternal, if I do not instantly confess and profess!" (Berkman, *Selected Works of Voltairine de Cleyre:* 289, 155–56)

She wrote in an autobiographical sketch: "In the heart of Catholicism, the child of fourteen became a freethinker, and frequent and bitter were the acts of rebellion and punishment engendered by the gradual growth of the notion of individual right as opposed to the right of inflexible rule. It was only after re-peated insubordination and subsequent, partial submission, that she was finally allowed to go before the examiners and awarded the gold medal of the institu-tion." (Wess Papers, cited by Avrich, *An American Anarchist: The Life of Voltairine de Cleyre:* 36)

"I struggled my way out at last, and was a freethinker when I left the institu-tion, three years later, though I had never seen a book or heard a word to help me in my loneliness," wrote Voltairine. "It had been like the Valley of the Shadow of Death, and there are white scars on my soul yet, where Ignorance and Supersti-tion burnt me with their hellfire in those stifling days. Am I blasphemous? It is their word, not mine. Beside that battle of my young days all others have been easy, for whatever was without, within my own Will was supreme. It has owed no allegiance, and never shall; it has moved steadily in one direction, the knowledge and the assertion of its own liberty, with all the responsibility falling thereon." (*Selected Works:* 156)

At seventeen, Voltairine began offering private lessons in music, French, and "fancy penmanship." At nineteen, she declared herself a freethinker, marking the moment with a poem, "The Burial of My Past Self," pledging: "And now, Hu-manity, I turn to you/I consecrate my service to the world!"

In 1886, she moved to Grand Rapids, Michigan, became editor of *The Pro-gressive Age*, adopted the penname "Fanny Fern," and changed the spelling of her name to "de Cleyre."

She began lecturing before freethought groups in Michigan in 1887, touring Chicago, Ohio and Pennsylvania for the American Secular Union, and writing for freethought papers. Tall, slim, with arresting features, blue eyes and soft, curly brown hair, she made an impression in her version of a Greek toga, two plaits of hair flowing down her back. She considered herself a lecturer, not an orator, reading her speeches, but Emma Goldman remembered "her pale face lit up with the inner fire of her ideal," praising her speeches as "richly studded with original thought." (Goldman, *Voltairine de Cleyre:* 9, 32, cited by Avrich: 42)

In "Secular Education" (*The Truth Seeker,* December 3, 1887), Voltairine wrote that parents should teach children "that it is better to study how to live rather than how to die; that it is better to have a religion of deeds rather than a religion of creeds; that it is better to work for humanity than for God."

"Secularism owes this duty to itself—that it instruct its children in their earliest infancy to think—think for themselves. . . . Earliest impressions are most enduring, and earliest superstitions are hardest to be rid of.

"Do not deceive yourselves. If you do not educate your children, the church will do it for you, and with an object. . . .

"I know of what I speak. I spent four years in a convent, and I have seen the watchwords of their machinations. I have seen bright intellects, intellects which might have been brilliant stars in the galaxies of genius, loaded down with chains, made abject, prostrate nonentities. I have seen frank, generous dispositions made morose, sullen, and deceitful, and I have seen rose-leaf cheeks turn to a sickly pallour, and glad eyes lose their brightness, and elastic youth lose its vitality and go down to an early grave murdered—murdered by the church."

"The Freethinker's Plea," written in 1887, is her most famous freethought poem. Others include "The Gods and the People" (1897) and "The Cry of the Unfit" (1893), in which she wrote of: "We children, who've hung the Christmas stocking/And found it empty two thousand years."

The execution of four innocent anarchists in 1887 for the Haymarket bombing was the turning point in her life. She dedicated herself to anarchism, calling piecemeal reforms "folly," freethought taking second billing to anarchism. Her essay, "Economic Tendency of Freethought" (*Liberty*, February 15, 1890) was a typical effort to convert freethinkers to anarchism. Anarchy of thought overthrew ecclesiastical tyranny, she argued. "Only by deposing priests, only by rooting out their authority, did it become logical to attack the tyranny of kings." Carrying freethought to its logical conclusion meant overthrowing the authority of the state, she wrote, chiding freethinkers for "digging, mole-like, through the substratum of dead issues," wasting "energies gathering the ashes of fires burnt out two centuries ago," lancing "shafts at that which is already bleeding at the arteries," and ranging "battalions of brains against a crippled ghost. . . .

"They would realize that, unless the freethought movement has a practical utility in rendering the life of man more bearable, unless it contains a principle which, worked out, will free him from the all-oppressive tyrant, it is just as complete and empty a mockery as the Christian miracle or Pagan myth. Eminently is this the age of utility; and the freethinker who goes to the Hovel of Poverty with metaphysical speculations as to the continuity of life, the transformation of matter, etc.; who should say, 'My dear friend, your Christian brother is mistaken; you are not doomed to an eternal hell; your condition here is your misfortune and can't be helped, but when you are dead, there's an end of it,' is of as little use in the world as the most irrational religionist."

At twenty-one, Voltairine was seduced, then abandoned by a former preacher from Scotland lecturing on socialism. Her natural melancholic bent became more pronounced. A powerful poem written after the episode, "Betrayed," is addressed to a prison chaplain in the voice of a desperate young woman jailed for infanticide after she and her starving baby were scorned, and abandoned by a preacher.

> I don't know, but sometimes I used to think that she, who was told
>> there was no room
> In the inn at Bethlehem, might look down with softened eyes thro'
>> the starless gloom.
> Christ wasn't a woman—he couldn't know the pain and endurance
>> of it; but *she,*
> The mother who bore him, she might know, and Mary in Heaven
>> might pity me.
> Still that was useless: it didn't bring a single mouthful for me to
>> eat,
> Nor work to get it, nor sheltering from the dreary wind and the
>> howling street.
> Heavenly pity won't pass as coin, and earthly shame brings a
>> higher pay.

The poem concludes: "There is no avenging God on high!—we live, we struggle, and—we *rot.*"

Voltairine moved to Philadelphia in 1889 and remained there until 1910. She lived and worked among anarchist Jewish immigrants, teaching English and math for a small fee as her primary income, learning Yiddish, translating foreign anarchist classics. Her lifestyle ranged from near-starvation to genteel poverty; occasional bursts of prosperity were shared with her mother or others, including numerous stray cats and animals.

She met freethinker James B. Elliott, a Thomas Paine aficionado like herself, and on June 12, 1890, gave birth to their baby boy, Harry. It was not parenthood by choice. Voltairine left Harry with Elliott and his mother to raise. After his birth she lectured for nearly a year in Kansas for the Woman's National Liberal Union. A relationship with anarchist Dyer Lum ended with his suicide in 1893. Ill-fated in love, Voltairine next put an undeserving lover through medical school.

When Emma Goldman was arrested in 1893 at a rally in Philadelphia after saying starving people denied jobs had the right to take bread, Goldman was impressed when "this brilliant American girl" took her place on the podium.

Voltairine delivered "In Defense of Emma Goldman and the Right of Expropriation" while Emma was in prison, pointing out that Paine advised that "men should not petition for rights but take them." The two eventually had a rift only repaired years later; Goldman wrote Voltairine's biography in 1932.

Eschewing respectability and bourgeois tendencies, Voltairine was a purist with a punishing lifestyle, tutoring, arranging meetings, writing for anarchist newspapers for no fee, lecturing on anarchism and freethought, and commemorating the Haymarket martyrs: "men who bowed at no shrine, acknowledged no God, believed in no hereafter, and yet went as roundly and triumphantly to the gallows as ever Christian martyr did of old." (*The Rebel*, November 20, 1895, cited by Avrich: 97)

She founded the Ladies' Liberal League in Philadelphia in the early 1890s as a forum for freethought and "non-acquiescence to injustice." Her lectures included "Those Who Marry Do Ill," "Sex Slavery," and other feminist themes. Eloquent "Sex Slavery" was a speech delivered after Moses Harman was sentenced to five years in prison under the Comstock Act for publishing medical details of a case of marital rape. [See selection] Addressing men, Voltairine wrote: "The earth is a prison, the marriage-bed is a cell, women are the prisoners, and you are the keepers!"

"And that is the vilest of all tyranny where man compels the woman he says he loves, to endure the agony of bearing children that she does not want, and for whom, as is the rule rather than the exception, they cannot properly provide. It is worse than any other human oppression; it is fairly *God*-like! To the sexual tyrant there is no parallel upon earth; one must go to the skies to find a fiend who thrusts life upon his children only to starve and curse and outcast and damn them! And only through the marriage law is such tyranny possible." (*Selected Works*: 344, 345)

She advocated adopting a day to recognize Mary Wollstonecraft as freethinkers had done for Paine. "The spirit of marriage makes for slavery," she lectured in Scotland in 1897, counseling "every woman contemplating sexual union of any kind, never to live together with the man you love, in the sense of renting a house or rooms, and becoming his housekeeper." ("The Woman Question," *The Herald of Revolt*, September, 1913, cited by Avrich: 160)

Foreshadowing Virginia Woolf, she wrote her mother: "Every individual should have a room or rooms *for himself exclusively*, never subject to the intrusive familiarities of our present 'family life.' A 'closet' where each could 'pray in secret,' without some persons who love him assuming the right to walk in and do as they please." (January 13, 1894, cited by Avich: 161)

When a would-be anarchist shot President McKinley in 1901, Senator Joseph R. Hawley offered a thousand dollars for the chance to shoot an anarchist.

Voltairine, in an open letter to Hawley published in *Free Society*, offered herself, signing her name and address. Her pacifist views evolved into a philosophy which embraced "direct action," blaming the state and privileged classes for inciting retaliatory violence.

On December 19, 1902, Voltairine was stepping onto a streetcar when Herman Helcher, a deranged former pupil, shot her with a pistol at close range above the heart, firing two more bullets into her back. The bullets were considered unremovable and her wounds fatal. However, she was released after two weeks in the hospital, returning to the lecture circuit by mid-March 1903. From her hospital bed she dictated a public statement detailing her assailant's homeless, pathetic condition, saying it would be "an outrage against civilization if he were sent to jail for an act which was the product of a diseased brain." She raised defense funds, and delivered an eloquent denunciation of punishment and imprisonment for its own sake. Her speech "Crime and Punishment," preaching self-government, held Christianity accountable for a "new class of imbruted men." [See selection]

In early 1904, Voltairine fell ill with a sinus infection, a lifelong proclivity, that spread to the middle ear and head, leading to hospitalizations, then daily convulsions. She partially recovered by the spring of 1906, but was left with a never-ceasing pounding in her ears.

She was among a number of prominent persons, including Eugene V. Debs, Clarence Darrow, and Jack London, to speak at a free speech mass meeting in 1909: "There is but one way that free speech can ever be secured, and that is by persistent speaking . . . *Speak, speak, speak*, and remember that whenever any one's liberty to speak is denied, your liberty is denied also, and your place is there where the attack is." ("On Liberty," *Mother Earth*, July 1909, cited by Avrich: 204)

Voltairine repudiated her early individualism, and rejected the "Dominant Idea" of the age—the acquisition of material possessions, wealth and power. She had a horror of communism, instead advocating "mutualism," her heart swelling at the pitiful toil of the poor. She did not believe any system of economy so far proposed was "entirely compatible with freedom." She wrote in *Mother Earth:* "I am an Anarchist, simply, without economic labels attached."

In her last few years, Voltairine began to doubt the worth of anarchism, confessing in a letter to Alexander Berkman: "I cannot preach Anarchism now, because I do not believe it with any great force or strength." (February 17, 1910, cited by Avrich: 215)

She moved to Chicago in 1910, only stirred to her original fervor by the revolution in Mexico in 1911. In April, 1912, she fell ill with sinus problems, diagnosed as an inflammation of the middle ear which penetrated the brain. Two operations were performed. She suffered for nine weeks, unable to speak, finally dying on June 20, 1912.

She was buried in the Waldheim Cemetery next to the graves of the Haymarket anarchists, as two thousand people watched. Berkman, editor of *Mother Earth*, edited the posthumous *Selected Works of Voltairine de Cleyre*.

In a eulogy appearing in *The Agitator* on July 15, 1912, Jay Fox wrote:

"Nature has the habit of now and then producing a type of human being far in advance of the times; an ideal for us to emulate; a being devoid of sham, un-compromising, and to whom the truth is sacred; a being whose selfishness is so large that it takes in the human race and treats self only as one of the great mass; a being keen to sense all forms of wrong, and powerful in denunciation of it; one who can reach in the future and draw it nearer. Such a being was Voltairine de Cleyre."

Sex Slavery

*"Sex Slavery" was a speech delivered after freethinker/feminist Moses Harman was sentenced to five years of hard labor in prison for publishing medical details about a particularly heinous case of marital rape in Lucifer, The Light-Bearer in 1890. This speech was reprinted in **The Selected Works of Voltairine de Cleyre** (1914), edited by Alexander Berkman. Much of the content of "Sex Slavery" sounds contemporary; the passage dealing with religion is excerpted here.*

. . . Let woman ask herself, "Why am I the slave of Man? Why is my brain said not to be the equal of his brain? Why is my work not paid equally with his? Why must my body be controlled by my husband? Why may he take my labor in the household, giving me in exchange what he deems fit? Why may he take my children from me? Will them away while yet unborn?" Let every woman ask.

There are two reasons why, and these ultimately reducible to a single principle—the authoritarian, supreme-power, *God*-idea, and its two instruments, the Church—that is, the priests—and the State—that is, the legislators.

From the birth of the Church, out of the womb of Fear and the Fatherhood of Ignorance, it has taught the inferiority of woman. In one form or another through the various mythical legends of the various mythical creeds, runs the undercurrent of the belief in the fall of man through the persuasion of woman, her subjective condition as punishment, her natural vileness, total depravity, etc.; and from the days of Adam until now the Christian Church, with which we have specially to deal, has made *woman* the excuse, the scapegoat for the evil deeds of *man*. So thoroughly has this idea permeated Society that numbers of those who have utterly repudiated the Church, are nevertheless soaked in this stupefying narcotic to true morality. So pickled is the male creation with the vinegar of Authoritarianism, that even those who have gone further and repudiated the State still cling to the god, Society as it is, still hug the old theological idea that they are to be "heads of the family"—to that wonderful formula of "simple proportion" that "Man is the head of the Woman even as Christ is the head of the Church." No longer than a week since an Anarchist (?) said to me, "I will be boss in my own house"—a "Communist-Anarchist," if you please, who doesn't believe in "*my* house." About a year ago a noted libertarian speaker said, in my presence, that his sister, who possessed a fine voice and had joined a concert troupe, should "stay at home with her children; that is *her place.*" The old Church idea! This man was a Socialist, and since an Anarchist; yet his highest idea for woman was serfhood to husband and children, in the present mockery called "home." Stay at home, ye malcontents! Be patient, obedient, submissive! Darn our socks, mend our shirts, wash our dishes, get our meals, wait on us and *mind the children!* Your fine voices are not to delight the public nor yourselves; your inventive genius is not to work, your fine art taste is not to be cultivated, your business faculties are not to be developed; you made the great mistake of being born with them, suffer for your folly! You are *women!* therefore housekeepers, servants, waiters, and child's nurses!

At Macon, in the sixth century, says August Bebel, the fathers of the Church met and proposed the decision of the question, "Has woman a soul?" Having ascertained that the permission to own a nonentity wasn't going to injure any of their parsnips, a small majority vote decided the momentous question in our favor. Now, holy fathers, it was a tolerably good scheme on your part to offer the reward of your pitiable "salvation or damnation" (odds in favor of the latter) as a bait for the hook of earthly submission; it wasn't a bad sop in those days of Faith and Ignorance. But fortunately fourteen hundred years have made it stale. You, tyrant radicals (?), have no heaven to offer,—you have no delightful chimeras in the form of "merit cards"; you have (save the mark) the respect, the good offices, the smiles—of a slave-holder! This in return for our chains! Thanks!

The question of souls is old—we demand our bodies, now. We are tired of promises, God is deaf, and his church is our worst enemy. Against it we bring the charge of being the moral (or immoral) force which lies behind the tyranny of the State. And the State has divided the loaves and fishes with the Church, the magistrates, like the priests take marriage fees; the two fetters of Authority have gone into partnership in the business of granting patent-rights to parents for the privilege of reproducing themselves, and the State cries as the Church cried of old, and cries now: "See how we protect women!" The State has done more. It has often been said to me, by women with decent masters, who had no idea of the outrages practiced on their less fortunate sisters, "Why don't the wives leave?"

Why don't you run, when your feet are chained together? Why don't you cry out when a gag is on your lips? Why don't you raise your hands above your head when they are pinned fast to your sides? Why don't you spend thousands of dollars when you haven't a cent in your pocket? Why don't you go to the seashore or the mountains, you fools scorching with city heat? If there is one thing more than another in this whole accursed tissue of false society, which makes me angry, it is the asinine stupidity which with the true phlegm of impenetrable dullness says, "Why don't the women leave!" Will you tell me where they will go and what they shall do? When the State, the legislators, has given to itself, the politicians, the utter and absolute control of the opportunity to live; when, through this precious monopoly, already the market of labor is so overstocked that workmen and workwomen are cutting each others' throats for the dear privilege of serving their lords; when girls are shipped from Boston to the south and north, shipped in carloads, like cattle, to fill the dives of New Orleans or the lumber-camp hells of my own state (Michigan), when seeing and hearing these things reported every day, the proper prudes exclaim, "Why don't the women leave," they simply beggar the language of contempt.

When America passed the fugitive slave law compelling men to catch their fellows more brutally than runaway dogs, Canada, aristocratic, unrepublican Canada, still stretched her arms to those who might reach her. But there is no refuge upon earth for the enslaved sex. Right where we are, there we must dig our trenches, and win or die. . . .

These two things, the mind domination of the Church, and the body domination of the State are the causes of Sex Slavery. . . .

Now for the remedy. It is in one word, the only word that ever brought equity anywhere—LIBERTY! Centuries upon centuries of liberty is the only thing that will cause the disintegration and decay of these pestiferous ideas. Liberty was all that calmed the bloodwaves of religious persecution! You cannot cure serfhood by any other substitution. . . .

The Case of Woman Versus Orthodoxy

This lecture, apparently originally given at Eastertime, was reprinted on the front page of the Boston Investigator (September 19, 1896), billed as "An Original Lecture."

"I WILL GREATLY MULTIPLY THY SORROW and thy conception; in sorrow shalt thou bring forth children, and thy desire shall be unto thy husband, and he shall rule over thee." Thus descended the anathema from the voice which thundered upon Sinai; and thus has the curse gone echoing from away back there in the misty darkness before the morning of history rose upon men. Sorrow, sorrow, sorrow—and oh! how many million voices wail, wail endlessly. "Sorrow is my portion and pain is my burden; for so it was decreed of the Lord God, the Lord God who ruleth and whose creature am I. But oh, the burden is heavy, very heavy. I have been patient; I have borne it long; I have not complained; I have not rebelled; if I have wept, it has been at night and alone; if I have stumbled, I have gone on the faster. When I have lain down in the desert and closed my eyes and known no more, I have rebuked myself. I have remembered my mother, and been patient and waited, waited. But the waiting is very long."

This is the cry of the woman heard in the night of the long ages; ghost-forms flitting through the abyss, ghost-hands wrung in the ancient darkness come close and are laid upon the living, and the mournful cadence is reintoned from the dead by the quick, and the mournful, hopeless superstition which bound the hearts and the souls of our foremothers, lengthens out its weary chain and binds us, too. Why it should be so, why it has done so for so long, is one of the mysteries which a sage of the future may solve, but not I. I can see no reason, absolutely none, why women have clung to the doom of the gods. I cannot understand why they have not rebelled. I cannot imagine what they ever hoped to gain by it, that they should have watered their footsteps with tears, and borne their position with such abnegation. It is true that we are often offered explanations, and much force may be in them, but these explanations may serve only to account for the position. They do not account for woman's centurian acceptance of, and resignation to, it. Women are, we know, creatures of their environments, the same as are men; and they react on their environment in proportion to their capacities.

We know that women are not now, and, with some few tribal exceptions, probably never were, as strong as men are physically. But why in common sense sorrow should therefore be their lot, and their husbands should rule over them, and why they should uncomplainingly accept this regime, is one of the, to me, incomprehensible phenomena of human history. Men, enslaved, have, to speak expressively, "kicked"—kicked vigorously, even when the kicking brought to them heavier chains; but we have never, till very recently, had anything like a revolt of women. They have bowed, and knelt and kissed the hand which smote them. Why? Notwithstanding all of its pretensions to be the uplifter and the glorifier of women, there never has been, there never will be, anything for them in orthodoxy but slavery. And whether that slavery be of the sordid, gloomy, leaden, work-a-day sort or of the gilded toy-shop variety, whether it be the hard toil and the burden of workwomen or the canary-bird style of the upper classes, who neither toil nor spin, the undertone and the overtone are still the same: "Be in subjection; for such is the Lord's will." In order to maintain this ideal of the relation of master and of subject between men and women, a different method of education, a different code of morals and a different sphere of exertion were mapped out for women, because of their sex, without reference to individual qualifications. As a horse is designed to draw wheels because it is a horse, so have women been allotted certain tasks, mostly menial, because they are women. The majority of men actually hold to that analogy, and without in the least believing themselves tyrannical or meddlesome, conceived themselves to be justified in making a tremendous row if the horse attempted to get over the traces.

That splendid old veteran of Freethought, George Jacob Holyoake, in a recent article, one of a series now running in the Open Court, has pertinently observed that the declaration that thought is by its very essence free is an error, because as long as speech, which is the necessary tool of thought, is not free, the intellect is as much hampered in its effort to think as a shoemaker without tools is in attempting to make a pair of shoes. By this same method, viz., the denial of the means of altering it, was the position of woman maintained, by subordinating her physical development to what was called delicacy, which *ought* to have been called by its proper name, *weakness*, by inculcating a scheme of morals which made obedience the first virtue, suppression of the will in deference to her husband (or father, or brother, or, failing these, her nearest male relative) the first deduction therefrom, by a plan of education which omitted all of those branches of knowledge which require the application of reason and of judgment, by all of these deprivals of the tools of thinking the sphere was circumscribed and guarded well. And by the penalties inflicted for the breaking through of these prescriptions, whether said penalties were legal or purely social and voluntary, the little spirit which was left in woman by these limitations was almost hopelessly broken. It is apparent, therefore, that if in all these ages of submission women have hopelessly accepted that destiny, if they have never tried to break these forbidding barriers, they will not do so now, with all of their added centuries of inheritance, unless the relentless iron of circumstances drives them across. (Later, it will be my endeavor to show that this iron is already pressing down.)

It may not be flattering to have this conviction thrust upon us; but it may be less disagreeable if I explain what I mean. In former times, when people trod upon the toes of gods every time they turned about, moral ideals and social ideals were looked upon as things in themselves descended from on high, the gift of the gods, Divine patterns laid down without reference to climate, to race, to social development, or to other material things, matters of the soul without relation to bodily requirements. But now that gods speaking the tongues of men have vanished like vapors at sunrise, it is necessary, since it is evident that morality of some sort exists everywhere out of very different sorts of different conditions, to find some explanation of these psychic phenomena correlated with the explanation of physical phenomena. For souls are no longer perceived as monarchs of bodids laying down all manner of laws for the bringing into subjection of the physical members, but rather soul, or mind, or whatever name may be given to the psychological aspect of the bundle called an ego, is one with the body, subject to growth, to expansion and to decay, adapting itself seasonally to time and to circumstances, modified always by material conditions, intimately connected with the stomach, indissolubly related to the weather, to the crops, and to all other baldly commonplace things. In contemplating this revised version of the soul one will, according to the bent of one's nature, regard this view as a descent from spiritual heights, rendering things coarse and gross, or, on the other hand, he will see all things clothed in the glory of superb equality, he will not say: "I am sunken to the indignity of a cabbage," but "this common plant is my brother and the brother of things greater than I, serving equally well his part; there is no *more* or *less*, *smaller* or *greater*; Life is common to us all."

Now, therefore, upon this basis, the basis of the perpetual relation between physical foundations and ethical superstructure, it is seen that if this be an acting principle now, so it has ever been, and will be as long as mind and matter constitute reality. Hence the ethics said to have been delivered by Jehovah upon Sinai was truly the expression of social ideas compatible with the existing physical conditions. Not less so the ethics of bees, of ants, or birds, and of the Fiji Islanders; and not less so the ethics of to-day, which, despite the preservations of the outward shell of the decalogue, are indeed vastly changed.

The conclusion to be drawn from the foregoing in regard to the status of woman is this:—Material conditions determine the social relations of men and women; and if material conditions are such as to make these relations impossible of maintenance, they will be compelled to assume others. This is the explanation of the expression, "driven across the barriers." What no amount of unseasonable preaching can accomplish material necessity will force even in the face of sermons to the contrary. Not that I undervalue the service of the advance guard, the preaching of new thought. On the contrary, the first and best praise is due to the "voice crying in the wilderness." And I say that such a voice is the first faint vibration of the world-soul in response to the unease of world-body created by the shifting of conditions,—whether it so proclaims or not, whether it cries wisely or not. I say that those who call for the breaking of the barriers will always precede the general action of the masses; but I add that were it not for the compulsion of material necessity the preaching would be barren. What I wish to express in order to illustrate my point clearly is, first, that the orthodox view of the ethics of woman's relations and her social usefulness was a view compatible with a tribal organization, narrow geographical limits, the reign of muscular force, the necessity of rapid reproduction; second, that those conditions have given place to others demanding an utterly different human translation.

Before the invention of the means of transportation, when, according to the story, it took forty years for the Israelites to explore a tract some three hundred miles in length (though one may perhaps venture to credit them with better time than they credit themselves with), when, at any rate, a high mountain was a serious obstacle and a good-sized river a natural boundary for tribal wanderings, people were necessarily very ignorant of the outside world. Within the limits valuable pasture and farm lands were debatable grounds, debatable by different tribes, in terms of hue and cry, of slungshot and arrows, and other such arguments. War was a constant condition, the chief occupation of man. Now we who are evolutionists know that those tribes and species survived in the world which obeyed the fundamental necessity of adaptation; and it is easy to see that with a rapid rate of mortality and a non-correspondent rate of increase a tribe must have rapidly gone to the wall. Any nation which might have put its mothers up in battle would have been weeded out simply because the part played by the mother in reproduction requires so much longer a period than that played by the father. To produce warriors—that was the chief purpose of a woman's existence! Nothing in herself, she became everything when regarded as the race preserver. Therein lay her great usefulness; and in reading the sometimes nauseating accounts of the behavior of women in ancient times in Judah, the phase of human development in its entirety should be borne in mind. The mothers of Isaac and of Ishmael, Tamar, the daughter-in-law of Judah, the daughters of Lot, should never be viewed from the standpoint of nineteenth century morals, but from that of the tribal organization and the tribal necessities, which forced upon them the standard of "Multiply and replenish the earth" as the highest possible conception of conduct.

Yet, singular to observe, co-existent with this very ideal and with the very polygamous practices of the patriarchs, are found records of the most horrible punishments inflicted upon women for the breaking of the seventh commandment. As may be seen in the story of Tamar and Judah, the punishment to be inflicted upon her was burning alive, though nothing is said of Judah's. The Talmud has many accounts of tests by "the bitter water" for women, while men were subjected to nothing more than a fine. (Bitter water was simply poisoned water; the innocent were supposed not to be injured, the guilty to fall dead in the marketplace, exposed to the public gaze.) Nevertheless, such was the stringent necessity for rapid reproductions that women defied danger and instinctively continued to fulfill that race-purpose, though the law of Moses, already codifying the conditions of peace (not as yet existent), recognized war and its accompaniments as transient, and giving place to a stricter moral behavior.

As I said before, I do not perceive for the life of me what the women saw in all of this for them; I don't see why they should have been interested in the tribal welfare at all, or in the dreary business of bearing sons for other women's sons to slay. But since the war-environment was the one under which they were born and reared, since no other purpose for them had ever been thought of, by either the dead or the living, it is not surprising that they did not see matters at all as I do. Nowadays, that the majority of English and of French speaking peoples at least see that the requisite ethics is the *limitation of population* within the means of subsistence, these direct descendants of the Judaic ideal are subject rather to a jest among the enlightened of their own race. Thus Zangwill, in the "Children of the Ghetto," puts this speech in the mouth of one of the Jewish grandmothers: "How is Fanny?" inquired the visitor. "Ah, poor Pesach! He has never done well in business! But blessed be He. I am soon to have my seventh grand-child." How fearfully potent is the force of heredity may thus be seen, since to this day these women walk through your streets, wan, faded, humped, distorted, hideous women—women all bone and jaw and flabby flesh, grotesque shadows from the past, creatures once trim and beautiful, but whose beauty went long ago to fulfill the order of the Lord of Sinai.

The primal division of labor is thus seen to have been one of sex. The business of men was to fight, of women to produce fighters. To men were the arts of war; to women were those of peace. Later in the time of Solomon, when material conditions among the Jews had already altered, we see the effect of the continuance of this division beyond the epoch which created it. Already nomadism has been abandoned; and the settled mode of life has been begun. The conditions of war, though still often maintaining, bore no comparison to former prevalence; and the aforeward warrior was hence frequently idle. Was it thus with woman? Oh, no,

> Men may come and men may go,
> But she goes on forever

With her work.

Listen to this delectable account in Solomon, said to be the opinion of King Lemuel concerning a truly blessed woman; behold how her duties have gone on increasing. 'Tis the thirty-first chapter of Proverbs; and let no one with an appreciation of the humorous miss it. It begins rather inconsequently with something about wine-drinking, and runs into the question at issue in the tenth verse; just why, no one is able to understand. It bears no relation to what has preceded it. Here it is:

"Who can find a virtuous woman? for her price is far above rubies." (You'll be convinced of that before you've done;—diamonds either.)

"The heart of her husband doth safely trust in her, so that he shall have no need of spoil." (They don't generally need much of that if Lemuel means the sort of "spoil" which most modern husbands get.)

"She will do him good and not evil all the days of her life." (That's in general; what follows is specific.)

"She seeketh flax and wool and worketh willingly with her hands." (So much for clothes; victuals now.)

"She is like the merchants' ships; she bringeth food from afar." (Goes where she can get it cheap, of course.)

"She riseth also while it is night, and giveth meat to her household, and a portion to her maidens." (Careful that they should not overeat and get sluggish. It is well to keep the girls tolerably hungry if you want them up before daylight.)

"She considereth a field and buyeth it; with the fruit of her hands she planteth a vineyard." (Trades, too, see?)

"She girdeth her loins with strength and strengtheneth her arms." (Nowadays she'd do that with a bicycle instead of a plow.)

"She perceiveth that her merchandise is good; her candle goeth not out by night." (That means that she works all night, too; for she wouldn't burn candles for nothing, being economical.)

"She layeth her hands to the spindle, and her hands hold the distaff." (The woman is all hands!)

"She stretcheth out her hands to the poor; yea, she reacheth forth her hands to the needy." (Hands again!)

"She is not afraid of the snow for her household, for all her household are clothed in scarlet." (How Mephistophelian the whole household must have seemed.)

"She maketh herself coverings of tapestry; her clothing is silk and purple." (The woman must have had forty days in a month and thirteen months in a year.)

"Her husband is known in the gates when he sitteth among the elders of the land." (I thought that he'd be up somewhere about the gates! I thought that he wouldn't be having much to do but sit with the elders! I thought that he'd not be stopping about the house much!)

"She maketh fine linen and selleth it, and delivereth girdles unto the merchant." (I should think that she might send him around delivering.)

"Strength and honor are her clothing, and she shall rejoice in time to come." (There is certainly not much chance for her to rejoice in the time which has already come.)

"She openeth her mouth with wisdom, and in her tongue is the law of kindness." (Verily, I should have expected her to be shrewish.)

"She looketh well to the ways of her household, and eateth not the bread of idleness." (This paragraph was unnecessary; we had reached that conclusion before.)

"Her children arise up and call her blessed; her husband also, and he praiseth her." (Well, in all conscience, 'tis as little as he could do; and he ought to do it well, since there is a deal of fine rhetoric usually going about among the elders and around the gates; and he has plenty of leisure to "get onto it.")

"Many daughters have done virtuously; but thou excellest them all." ("Sure.")

"Favor is deceitful and beauty is vain; but a woman that feareth the Lord, she shall be praised." (That is to console her for getting ugly with all of that work.)

"*Give her of the fruit of her hands;* and let her own works praise her in the gates." Oh, thou who has bought and planted and reaped and sold, spun and woven and girdled and clothed, risen and travelled and gathered and given, borne all, done all, ordered all, saved all, we will "*give* thee of the fruit of thy hands," and prate about it up at the gates! Verily, verily, the woman is far above rubies.

But alas for Lemuel and for Solomon, conditions then were also mutable. And perhaps a friend of mine who has expressed herself upon this passage, is right in her judgment that, as men never exalt a thing until it is beginning to wane and to vanish away, therefore it must have been that this sort of woman was on the decrease before Solomon began to repeat Lemuel. It does not lie within the scope of my lecture to trace the economic development which multiplied the diversion of labor, creating classes having separate and conflicting political interests, which will continue to clash until the process has either, by being pushed to its extremity, destroyed itself and reaccomplished independent production, or until some more correct political solution be found than any at present existing. What I wish to observe is merely that up to the dawn of the Revolutionary period this manifold splitting of humanity's occupations did not affect the primal division of the complementary labors of the sexes. Within the limits set by the original division, however, classes did arise. Among women these classes were principally two; the overworked drudges of the poor, and the pampered daughters of wealth. It is not possible to say whose condition was the most lamentable. For to both was still maintained by preacher, by teacher, by lawyer and by doctor the old decree: "Thy husband shall rule over thee." Of the latter class there were but few previous to the Revolution. The rugged condition of pioneer life in the New World afforded small opportunity for the growth of a purely parasite class; that has arisen since. But in the Old World the women of the landed aristocracy, as likewise those of the developing mercantile class, constituted, though not a majority, yet a good percentage of the whole sex. So large a portion, in fact, that a whole stock of literature, which might have been labelled, "The Gospel of Jesus specially adapted to the use of society women," arose and flourished; preachers busied themselves with it; doctors wrote scores of verses on the preservation of beauty and the delicacy of the lazy; rhetoricians frilled and furbelowed the human toy by way of exercising their art; lawyers rendered learned opinions upon "lovely woman"—they all took their turn and they all did her a bad turn. The entire science of life, as laid down in this literature for women, was to make husband-traps of themselves. Their home training and their educational facilities were in line therewith. Nothing solid, nothing to develop or even to awaken the logical faculties, everything to develop the petty and the frivolous. The art of dressing, the tricks of assumed modesty, the degradation of intellect by continually curbing and straining it in to fit the patterns of God and of his servants—such was the feminine code.

About this time there arose the inevitable protest which conditions were bound to force. It was all very well for the dumb drudges and the well-fed toys; but society has ever between its extremes a middle product which fits in nowhere. This is recruited from both sides, but, at that time mostly from the upper classes being squeezed down into the ranks of the non-possessors. There were women, daughters of the formerly well-to-do, incapable of the very laborious life of the lowly, unable to reascend to their former superior position; upon these were forced the necessity of self-support. Most of them regarded it as a hard and bitter lot, and something to be ashamed of. Even literature, now considered a very fine source of support for women, was then a thing for a woman to keep still about if she engaged in it. The proper thing to do was to lay hold of an honorary sort of husband, support one's self and him, and pretend that he did it. So disgraceful was social usefulness in woman! Such was the premium on worthlessness!

Now, out of this class one who did not do the proper thing, one who protested against the whole scheme arose,—the woman whose name many now delight to honor as the author of the "Vindication of the Rights of Woman,"—Mary Wollstonecraft. One of her biographers, Mrs. Pennel, states that she was the first woman in England who openly followed litera- ture as a means of livelihood. (It is worthy of note that Mr. Johnson, her employer, was one of the Freethinkers of the time, Paine's printer, as well as Mary Wollstonecraft's.)

Nowadays the idea conveyed by the expression, "Women's Rights" is the idea of casting a ballot. Then it meant the right to be treated as serious beings having some faint claim to comprehension. The orthodox code never had, never has, admitted, and never will admit, anything of the kind until it is forced to do so. It is not surprising, therefore, to know that this woman was not orthodox. She found out that if ever a woman expected to have rights she must first pitch the teachings of the priests overboard. And not only priests, but their coadjutors, men of the scientific "cloth" indeed, who see that priestcraft is all wrong for them, but all right for women— men who hunt scientific justifications for keeping up the orthodox stan- dard.

For a long time the seed sown by the author of the "Rights of Woman" lay on seemingly barren ground; and the great prophet of the coming woman was, as usual, maligned, travestied, hissed and hooted, save by the select few. The reason for this is now apparent. Conditions had not so far developed as to create a *class* of women having none to depend upon ex- cept themselves; there were only sporadic specimens here and there, thence the old traditions fortified by the ancient possibilities remained firm. But now that the irresistible tide of economic development is driving women out of the corner wherein they lay drifted for so many thousand years, the case is different. And I, for one, bless the hour when a stinging lash drove women forth into the industrial arena. I know that it is the habit of our labor reformers to bewail the fact that men can no longer "support their wives and their daughters;" it is held up as the chief iniquity of the capital- ist that he has broken up the poor man's family life; the "queen," poor tinsel queen, has been taken from her realm, the home, into the factory. But while I credit the capitalist with no better motive than that of buying in the cheapest market, I bless him from the crown of his head to the sole of his foot for this unintentioned good. This iron-shod heel has crushed the shell of "woman's sphere;" and the wings will grow—never fear, they will grow. No one will accuse me of loving the horrors of modern society, no one will suppose that I want them to continue for one moment after the hour when it is possible to be rid of them. I know all of the evils result-ant to woman from the factory system; I would not prolong them. But I am glad that by these very horrors, these gigantic machines which give to me the nightmare with their jaws and teeth, these monstrous buildings, bare and many-windowed, stretching skyward, brick, hard and loveless, which daily swallow and spew out again thousands upon thousands of frail lives, each day a little frailer, weaker, more exhausted, these unhealthy, man-eating traps which I cannot see blotting the ground and the sky with-out itching to tear down, by these very horrors women have learned to be socially useful and economically independent—as much so as men are. The basis of independence and of individuality is bread. As long as wives take bread from husbands because they are not capable of getting it in any other way, so long will the decree obtain: "Thy desire shall be to thy hus-band, and he shall rule over thee," so long will all talk about political "rights" be empty vagaries, hopeless crying against the wind.

There are those who contend that once the strain and the stress of commercialism are over, women will resume their ancient position, "natu-ral," they call it, of child nurses and home-keepers, being ruled and pro-tected. I say, NO: the broken chain will never be re-forged. No more "spheres," no more stops or lets or hindrances. I do not say that women will not be nurses and home-keepers at all; but I *do* say that they will not be such because they have to, because any priest so reads the ancient law—because any social prejudice checks them and forces them into it rather than allowing full, free development of natural bent. I say that the factory is laughing at the church; and the modern woman, who grasps her own self-hood, is laughing at the priest. I say that the greater half of the case of Orthodoxy *vs.* Woman is won—by woman; through pain, and misery, and sweat of brow and ache of hand, as all things worth winning are won. I don't mean that nothing remains to be done; there is as much in pursuing a victory as in winning it in the first place. But the citadel is taken—the right of self-maintenance—and all else must follow.

From the aforetime sterile ground the seeds are springing green. This is the season to pluck life from the tombs, the time of transfiguration when every scar upon the earth changes to glory, when before the eyes of man appears that miracle, of which all traditions of resurrection and of ascension are but faint, dim images, figures passing over the glass of the human mind, the projection of man's effort to identify himself with the All of Nature. This miracle, this blooming of the mold, this shooting of green peas where all was brown and barren, this resurrection of the sunken snow in tree-crowns, these workings, these responses to the knocking of the sunlight, these comings forth from burial, these rendings of shrouds, these ascensions from the graves, these flutterings, these swift, winged shadows passing, these tremolos high up in the atmosphere,—is it possible to feel all of this miracle and not to dream? Is it possible not to hope? The very fact that every religion has some kind of symbolic festival about the returning time of the seen [sic], proves that man, too, felt the upspringing in his breast—whether he rightly translates it or not, 'tis sure that he felt it, like all organic things. And whether it be the festival of a risen Christ, or of the passage of Judah from the bondage of Egypt, or the old Pagan worship of light, 'tis ever the same—the celebration of the breaking of bonds. We, too, may allow ourselves the poetic dream. Abroad in the April sunlight we behold in every freedom-going spark the risen dead—the flame which burned in the souls of Hypatia, Mary Wollstonecraft, Frances Wright, Ernestine L. Rose, Harriet Martineau, Lucretia Mott, that grand old negress, Sojourner Truth, our own brave old Lucy N. Colman, and all of the beloved unknown whose lives ingrafted on the race what *their* tongues spoke. We, too, proclaim the Resurrection.

Crime and Punishment

This speech was delivered after Voltairine de Cleyre recovered from being shot at close range by a mentally ill man in 1902. It was reprinted in **The Selected Works of Voltairine de Cleyre** *(1914), edited by Alexander Berkman.*

THE CONSERVATIVE HOLDS THAT . . . crime is a thing-in-itself, with no other cause than the viciousness of man; that punishment was decreed from Mt. Sinai, or whatever holy mountain happens to be believed in in his country, that society is best served by strictness and severity of judgment and punishment. And he wishes only to make his indifferent brothers keepers of other men's consciences along these lines. He would have all men be hunters of men, that crime may be tracked down and struck down.

The radical says: All false, all false and wrong. Crime has not been decided from all time: crime, like everything else, has had its evolution according to place, time, and circumstance. "The demons of our sires become the saints that we adore,"—and the saints, the saints and the heroes of our fathers, are criminals according to our codes. Abraham, David, Solomon,—could any respectable member of society admit that he had done the things they did? Crime is not a thing-in-itself, not a plant without roots, not a something proceeding from nothing; and the only true way to deal with it is to seek its causes as earnestly, as painstakingly, as the astronomer seeks the causes of the perturbations in the orbit of the planet he is observing, sure that there must be one, or many, somewhere. And Punishment, too, must be studied. The holy mountain theory is a failure. And it is a failure not because men do not hunt down and strike enough, but because they hunt down and strike at all; because in the chase of those who do ill, they do ill themselves; they brutalize their own characters, and so much the more so because they are convinced that this time the brutal act is done in accord with conscience. The murderous deed of the criminal was *against* conscience, the torture or the murder of the criminal by the official is *with* conscience. Thus the conscience is diseased and perverted, and a new class of imbruted men created. We have punished and punished for untold thousands of years, and we have not gotten rid of crime, we have not diminished it. Let us consider then. . . .

I am no disciple of that school whose doctrine is summed up in the teaching that Man's Will is nothing, his Material Surroundings all. I do not accept that popular socialism which would make saints out of sinners only by filling their stomachs. I am no apologist for characterlessness, and no petitioner for universal moral weakness. I believe in the individual. I believe that the purpose of life (in so far as we can give it a purpose, and it has none save what we give it) is the assertion and the development of strong, self-centered personality. It is therefore that no religion which offers vicarious atonement for the misdoer, and no philosophy which rests on the cornerstone of irresponsibility, makes any appeal to me. I believe that immeasurable mischief has been wrought by the ceaseless repetition for the last two thousand years of the formula: 'Not through any merit of mine shall I enter heaven, but through the sacrifice of Christ.' . . .

Let this be put as strongly as it can now, that nothing I shall say hereafter may be interpreted as a gospel of shifting and shirking.

But the difference between us, the Anarchists, who preach self-government and none else, and Moralists who in times past and present have asked for individual responsibility, is this, that while they have always framed creeds and codes for the purpose of *holding others to account*, we draw the line upon ourselves. Set the standard as high as you will; live to it as near as you can; and if you fail, try yourself, judge yourself, condemn yourself, if you choose. Teach and persuade your neighbor if you can; consider and compare his conduct if you please; speak your mind if you desire; but if he fails to reach your standard or his own, try him not, judge him not, condemn him not. He lies beyond your sphere; you cannot know the temptation nor the inward battle nor the weight of the circumstances upon him. You do not know how long he fought before he failed. Therefore you cannot be just. Let him alone.

This is the ethical concept at which we have arrived, not by revelation from any superior power, not through the reading of any inspired book, not by special illumination of our inner consciousness; but by the study of the results of social experiment in the past as presented in the works of historians, psychologists, criminologists, sociologists, and legalists.

Very likely so many "ists" sound a little oppressive, and there may be those to whom they may even have a savor of pedantry. It sounds much simpler and less ostentatious to say 'Thus saith the Lord,' or 'The Good Book says.' But in the meat and marrow these last are the real presumptions, these easy-going claims of familiarity with the will and intent of Omnipotence. It may sound more pedantic to you to say, 'I have studied the accumulated wisdom of man, and drawn certain deductions therefrom,' than to say 'I had a talk with God this morning and he said thus and so'; but to me the first statement in infinitely more modest. Moreover there is some chance of its being true, while the other is highly imaginative fiction. . . .

Emma Goldman
(State Historical Society of Wisconsin, WHi(X3)24378)

31

Emma Goldman

THE "RED" ATHEIST

June 27, 1869 – May 14, 1940

Have not all theists painted their Deity as the god of love and goodness? Yet after thousands of years of such preachments the gods remain deaf to the agony of the human race. Confucius cares not for the poverty, squalor and misery of the people of China. Buddha remains undisturbed in his philosophical indifference to the famine and starvation of the outraged Hindoos; Jahve continues deaf to the bitter cry of Israel; while Jesus refuses to rise from the dead against his Christians who are butchering each other.

"**The Philosophy of Atheism,**" 1916

"SINCE MY EARLIEST RECOLLECTION of my youth in Russia I have rebelled against orthodoxy in every form," wrote the anarchist Emma Goldman in her 1934 article "Was My Life Worth Living?"

Her father's cruelty toward her as an unwanted daughter set her in revolt. Once, he threw her French grammar into the fire, shouting, "Girls do not have to learn much! All a Jewish daughter needs to know is how to prepare *gefüllte* fish, cut noodles fine, and give the man plenty of children." (Goldman, *Living My Life:* 12)

As a seventeen-year-old emigré from Russia's Jewish ghettos, she settled in Rochester, New York, with her beloved sister Helena, taking a factory job paying $2.50 a week. After an early marriage failed, she set off to fulfill her dream of political activism in New York City, galvanized by the 1887 Haymarket bombing and execution of Chicago anarchists. Sustaining herself by sewing, factory work, and later nursing, Goldman discovered her "ecstatic song" of oratory.

The "free love" label brandished without factual basis against so many feminists and freethinkers was embraced by Goldman, who, unable to have children, vowed to give and withdraw her love freely without aid of law or rabbi. "Free love? As if love is anything but free!" she wrote in her essay "Marriage and Love" published in *Anarchism and Other Essays* (1911). She asked: "how can such an all-compelling force [love] be synonymous with that poor little State- and Church-begotten weed, marriage?"

She and Alexander "Sasha" Berkman dedicated themselves to "a supreme act." Berkman spent fourteen years in prison for wounding Henry Clay Frick, chair of Carnegie Steel Corporation, a company which had killed striking workers and injured hundreds after calling in armed Pinkertons. Goldman later repudiated her youthful conviction that the ends justify the means.

In 1893 she was arrested and found guilty of inciting a riot for saying at a mass rally at Union Square: "If they do not give you work, demand bread. If they deny you both, take bread. It is your sacred right!" She was sentenced to Blackwell's Island for a year.

"I was called before the head matron, a tall woman with a stolid face. She began taking my pedigree. 'What religion?' was the first question. 'None, I am an atheist.' 'Atheism is prohibited here. You will have to go to church.' I replied that I would do nothing of the kind. I did not believe in anything the Church stood for and, not being a hypocrite, I would not attend." (*Living My Life:* 133)

Becoming a famed lecturer she received a singular invitation in 1898, to speak from a Detroit pulpit, her sermon announced by such lurid headlines as "Congregational church to be turned into hotbed of anarchy and free love." Hostile questions followed her tactful speech, and Goldman was provoked into scandalizing the congregation by saying: "I do not believe in God, because I believe in man. Whatever his mistakes, man has for thousands of years past been working to undo the botched job your God has made." She was greeted with cries of "Blasphemy! Heretic! Sinner!"

She added: "There are . . . some potentates I would kill by any and all means at my disposal. They are Ignorance, Superstition, and Bigotry—the most sinister and tyrannical rulers on earth." Even Robert Ingersoll, she noted, "joined the chorus," telling the press: "I think that all the anarchists are insane, Emma Goldman among the rest." (pp. 205–207) The next generation of agnostic intellectuals felt differently. John Dewey called Goldman "a romantically idealistic person with a highly attractive personality." Bertrand Russell, in the 1920s, found "both her and Berkman very interesting, and, although I have never been an Anarchist, I had much sympathy with them." (Drinnon, *Rebel In Paradise:* viii)

Goldman became *persona non grata* in 1901 when a self-professed anarchist assassinated President William McKinley, saying he had once attended one of her lectures. With no evidence against her, she was released, but the backlash was so severe she had to go underground. In 1906, she launched *Mother Earth*, her journal of art, politics and ideas, also starting Mother Earth Publishing Association.

In demand for lectures, she spoke more than one hundred times in thirty-seven cities to 25,000 paying listeners during a 1910 tour. Among her causes was "family limitation," a special interest to her as a midwife and nurse. Contemporary Margaret Anderson, editor of *The Little Review*, wrote: "In 1916 Emma Goldman was sent to prison for advocating that 'women need not always keep their mouths shut and their wombs open.' " (Shulman, *Red Emma Speaks:* 105)

She and Berkman were arrested and charged with conspiracy to obstruct the draft in 1917 for setting up No-Conscription Leagues. She served two years in prison, where the warden said women worshipped her as an idol. Pacifist prisoner Kate O'Hare called Emma Goldman ten thousand times more helpful than all the priests, preachers and religious organizations because Emma fed, fought for, nursed, and cheered the women prisoners.

At the age of fifty, she, Berkman and two hundred and forty-seven other "Reds" were deported to the Soviet Union through the efforts of J. Edgar Hoover. "I consider it an honor to be the first political agitator to be deported from the United States," she said during an official farewell.

Goldman left Russia thoroughly disillusioned with Bolshevism. In 1925 she became a British citizen. In 1931 she wrote her autobiography. She died in Canada at seventy of a stroke. Her body was returned to America and buried next to Voltairine De Cleyre's grave in Chicago's Waldheim Cemetery where a monument stands to the Haymarket martyrs.

❦

Goldman was an outspoken atheist rebelling against the "burden of dead ideas."

In addition to her 1913 essay "The Failure of Christianity" [see selection], Emma wrote "The Philosophy of Atheism" in February 1916. Goldman described atheism as "the concept of an actual, real world with its liberating, expanding and beautifying possibilities, as against an unreal world, which, with its spirits, oracles, and mean contentment has kept humanity in helpless degradation. . . . Man has been punished long and heavily for having created its gods; nothing but pain and persecution have been man's lot since gods began."

She asked: "where are the gods to make an end to all these horrors, these wrongs, this inhumanity to man? No, not the gods, but *man* must rise in his mighty wrath. He, deceived by all the deities, betrayed by their emissaries, he, himself, must undertake to usher in justice upon the earth. . . ."

The Failure of Christianity

This first appeared in Mother Earth, April 1913.

THE COUNTERFEITERS AND POISONERS OF IDEAS, in their attempt to obscure the line between truth and falsehood, find a valuable ally in the conservatism of language.

Conceptions and words that have long ago lost their original meaning continue through centuries to dominate mankind. Especially is this true if these conceptions have become a common-place, if they have been instilled in our beings from our infancy as great and irrefutable verities. The average mind is easily content with inherited and acquired things, or with the dicta of parents and teachers, because it is much easier to imitate than to create.

Our age has given birth to two intellectual giants, who have undertaken to transvalue the dead social and moral values of the past, especially those contained in Christianity. Friedrich Nietzsche and Max Stirner have hurled blow upon blow against the portals of Christianity, because they saw in it a pernicious slave morality, the denial of life, the destroyer of all the elements that make for strength and character. True, Nietzsche has opposed the slave-morality idea inherent in Christianity in behalf of a master morality for the privileged few. But I venture to suggest that his master idea had nothing to do with the vulgarity of station, caste, or wealth. Rather did it mean the masterful in human possibilities, the masterful in man that would help him to overcome old traditions and worn-out values, so that he may learn to become the creator of new and beautiful things.

Both Nietzsche and Stirner saw in Christianity the leveler of the human race, the breaker of man's will to dare and to do. They saw in every movement built on Christian morality and ethics attempts not at the emancipation from slavery, but for the perpetuation thereof. Hence they opposed these movements with might and main.

Whether I do or do not entirely agree with these iconoclasts, I believe, with them, that Christianity is most admirably adapted to the training of slaves, to the perpetuation of a slave society; in short, to the very conditions confronting us to-day. Indeed, never could society have degenerated to its present appalling stage, if not for the assistance of Christianity. The rulers of the earth have realized long ago what potent poison inheres in the Christian religion. That is the reason they foster it; that is why they leave nothing undone to instill it into the blood of the people. They know only too well that the subtleness of the Christian teachings is a more powerful protection against rebellion and discontent than the club or the gun.

No doubt I will be told that, though religion is a poison and institutionalized Christianity the greatest enemy of progress and freedom, there is some good in Christianity "itself." What about the teachings of Christ and early Christianity, I may be asked; do they not stand for the spirit of humanity, for right and justice?

It is precisely this oft-repeated contention that induced me to choose this subject, to enable me to demonstrate that the abuses of Christianity, like the abuses of government, are conditioned in the thing itself, and are not to be charged to the representatives of the creed. Christ and his teachings are the embodiment of submission, of inertia, of the denial of life; hence responsible for the things done in their name.

I am not interested in the theological Christ. Brilliant minds like Bauer, Strauss, Renan, Thomas Paine, and others refuted that myth long ago. I am even ready to admit that the theological Christ is not half so dangerous as the ethical and social Christ. In proportion as science takes the place of blind faith, theology loses its hold. But the ethical and poetical Christ-myth has so thoroughly saturated our lives that even some of the most advanced minds find it difficult to emancipate themselves from its yoke. They have rid themselves of the letter, but have retained the spirit; yet it is the spirit which is back of all the crimes and horrors committed by orthodox Christianity. The Fathers of the Church can well afford to preach the gospel of Christ. It contains nothing dangerous to the regime of authority and wealth; it stands for self-denial and self-abnegation, for penance and regret, and is absolutely inert in the face of every [in]dignity, every outrage imposed upon mankind.

Here I must revert to the counterfeiters of ideas and words. So many otherwise earnest haters of slavery and injustice confuse, in a most distressing manner, the teachings of Christ with the great struggles for social and economic emancipation. The two are irrevocably and forever opposed to each other. The one necessitates courage, daring, defiance, and strength. The other preaches the gospel of non-resistance, of slavish acquiescence in the will of others; it is the complete disregard of character and self-reliance, and therefore destructive of liberty and well-being.

Whoever sincerely aims at a radical change in society, whoever strives to free humanity from the scourge of dependence and misery, must turn his back on Christianity, on the old as well as the present form of the same.

Everywhere and always, since its very inception, Christianity has turned the earth into a vale of tears; always it has made of life a weak, diseased thing, always it has instilled fear in man, turning him into a dual being, whose life energies are spent in the struggle between body and soul. In decrying the body as something evil, the flesh as the tempter to everything that is sinful, man has mutilated his being in the vain attempt to keep his soul pure, while his body rotted away from the injuries and tortures inflicted upon it.

The Christian religion and morality extols the glory of the Hereafter, and therefore remains indifferent to the horrors of the earth. Indeed, the idea of self-denial and of all that makes for pain and sorrow is its test of human worth, its passport to the entry into heaven.

The poor are to own heaven, and the rich will go to hell. That may account for the desperate efforts of the rich to make hay while the sun shines, to get as much out of the earth as they can: to wallow in wealth and superfluity, to tighten their iron hold on the blessed slaves, to rob them of their birthright, to degrade and outrage them every minute of the day. Who can blame the rich if they revenge themselves on the poor, for now is their time, and the merciful Christian God alone knows how ably and completely the rich are doing it.

And the poor? They cling to the promise of the Christian heaven, as the home for old age, the sanitarium for crippled bodies and weak minds. They endure and submit, they suffer and wait, until every bit of self-respect has been knocked out of them, until their bodies become emaciated and withered, and their spirit broken from the wait, the weary endless wait for the Christian heaven.

Christ made his appearance as the leader of the people, the redeemer of the Jews from Roman dominion; but the moment he began his work, he proved that he had no interest in the earth, in the pressing immediate needs of the poor and the disinherited of his time. What he preached was a sentimental mysticism, obscure and confused ideas lacking originality and vigor.

When the Jews, according to the gospels, withdrew from Jesus, when they turned him over to the cross, they may have been bitterly disappointed in him who promised them so much and gave them so little. He promised joy and bliss in another world, while the people were starving, suffering, and enduring before his very eyes.

It may also be that the sympathy of the Romans, especially of Pilate, was given Christ because they regarded him as perfectly harmless to their power and sway. The philosopher Pilate may have considered Christ's "eternal truths" as pretty anæmic and lifeless, compared with the array of strength and force they attempted to combat. The Romans, strong and unflinching as they were, must have laughed in their sleeves over the man who talked repentance and patience, instead of calling to arms against the despoilers and oppressors of his people.

The public career of Christ begins with the edict, "Repent, for the Kingdom of Heaven is at hand."

Why repent, why regret, in the face of something that was supposed to bring deliverance? Had not the people suffered and endured enough; had they not earned their right to deliverance by their suffering? Take the Sermon on the Mount, for instance. What is it but a eulogy on submission to fate, to the inevitability of things?

"Blessed are the poor in spirit, for theirs is the Kingdom of Heaven."

Heaven must be an awfully dull place if the poor in spirit live there. How can anything creative, anything vital, useful and beautiful come from the poor in spirit? The idea conveyed in the Sermon on the Mount is the greatest indictment against the teachings of Christ, because it sees in the poverty of mind and body a virtue, and because it seeks to maintain this virtue by reward and punishment. Every intelligent being realizes that our worst curse is the poverty of the spirit; that it is productive of all evil and misery, of all the injustice and crimes in the world. Every one knows that nothing good ever came or can come of the poor in spirit; surely never liberty, justice, or equality.

"Blessed are the meek, for they shall inherit the earth."

What a preposterous notion! What incentive to slavery, inactivity, and parasitism! Besides, it is not true that the meek can inherit anything. Just because humanity has been meek, the earth has been stolen from it.

Meekness has been the whip, which capitalism and governments have used to force man into dependency, into his slave position. The most faithful servants of the State, of wealth, of special privilege, could not preach a more convenient gospel than did Christ, the "redeemer" of the people.

"Blessed are they that hunger and thirst for righteousness, for they shall be filled."

But did not Christ exclude the possibility of righteousness when he said, "The poor ye have always with you"? But, then, Christ was great on dicta, no matter if they were utterly opposed to each other. This is nowhere demonstrated so strikingly as in his command, "Render to Caesar the things that are Caesar's, and to God the things that are God's."

The interpreters claim that Christ had to make these concessions to the powers of his time. If that be true, this single compromise was sufficient to prove, down to this very day, a most ruthless weapon in the hands of the oppressor, a fearful lash and relentless tax-gatherer, to the impoverishment, the enslavement, and degradation of the very people for whom Christ is supposed to have died. And when we are assured that "Blessed are they that hunger and thirst for righteousness, for they shall be filled," are we told the how? How? Christ never takes the trouble to explain that. Righteousness does not come from the stars, nor because Christ willed it so. Righteousness grows out of liberty, of social and economic opportunity and equality. But how can the meek, the poor in spirit, ever establish such a state of affairs?

"Blessed are ye when men shall revile you and persecute you, and say all manner of evil against you falsely, for my sake. Rejoice, and be exceeding glad: for great is your reward in heaven."

The reward in heaven is the perpetual bait, a bait that has caught man in an iron net, a strait-jacket which does not let him expand or grow. All pioneers of truth have been, and still are, reviled; they have been, and still are, persecuted. But did they ask humanity to pay the price? Did they seek to bribe mankind to accept their ideas? They knew too well that he who accepts a truth because of the bribe, will soon barter it away to a higher bidder.

Good and bad, punishment and reward, sin and penance, heaven and hell, as the moving spirit of the Christ-gospel have been the stumbling-block in the world's work. It contains everything in the way of orders and commands, but entirely lacks the very things we need most.

The worker who knows the cause of his misery, who understands the make-up of our iniquitous social and industrial system can do more for himself and his kind than Christ and the followers of Christ have ever done for humanity; certainly more than meek patience, ignorance, and submission have done.

How much more ennobling, how much more beneficial is the extreme individualism of Stirner and Nietzsche than the sick-room atmosphere of the Christian faith. If they repudiate altruism as an evil, it is because of the example contained in Christianity, which set a premium on parasitism and inertia, gave birth to all manner of social disorders that are to be cured with the preachment of love and sympathy.

Proud and self-reliant characters prefer hatred to such sickening artificial love. Not because of any reward does a free spirit take his stand for a great truth, nor has such a one ever been deterred because of fear of punishment.

"Think not that I come to destroy the law or the prophets. I am not come to destroy, but to fulfill."

Precisely. Christ was a reformer, ever ready to patch up, to fulfill, to carry on the old order of things; never to destroy and rebuild. That may account for the fellow-feeling all reformers have for him.

Indeed, the whole history of the State, Capitalism, and the Church proves that they have perpetuated themselves because of the idea "I come not to destroy the law." This is the key to authority and oppression. Naturally so, for did not Christ praise poverty as a virtue; did he not propagate non-resistance to evil? Why should not poverty and evil continue to rule the world?

Much as I am opposed to every religion, much as I think them an imposition upon, and crime against, reason and progress, I yet feel that no other religion has done so much harm or has helped so much in the enslavement of man as the religion of Christ.

Witness Christ before his accusers. What lack of dignity, what lack of faith in himself and in his own ideas! So weak and helpless was this "Saviour of Men" that he must needs the whole human family to pay for him, unto all eternity, because he "hath died for them." Redemption through the Cross is worse than damnation, because of the terrible burden it imposes upon humanity, because of the effect it has on the human soul, fettering and paralyzing it with the weight of the burden exacted through the death of Christ.

Thousands of martyrs have perished, yet few, if any, of them have proved so helpless as the great Christian God. Thousands have gone to their death with greater fortitude, with more courage, with deeper faith in their ideas than the Nazarene. Nor did they expect eternal gratitude from their fellow-men because of what they endured for them.

Compared with Socrates and Bruno, with the great martyrs of Russia, with the Chicago Anarchists, Francisco Ferrer, and unnumbered others, Christ cuts a poor figure indeed. Compared with the delicate, frail Spiridonova who underwent the most terrible tortures, the most horrible indignities, without losing faith in herself or her cause, Jesus is a veritable nonentity. They stood their ground and faced their executioners with un-flinching determination, and though they, too, died for the people, they asked nothing in return for their great sacrifice.

Verily, we need redemption from the slavery, the deadening weakness, and humiliating dependency of Christian morality.

The teachings of Christ and of his followers have failed because they lacked the vitality to lift the burdens from the shoulders of the race; they have failed because the very essence of that doctrine is contrary to the spirit of life, exposed to the manifestations of nature, to the strength and beauty of passion.

Never can Christianity, under whatever mask it may appear—be it New Liberalism, Spiritualism, Christian Science, New Thought, or a thousand and one other forms of hysteria and neurasthenia—bring us relief from the terrible pressure of conditions, the weight of poverty, the horrors of our iniquitous system. Christianity is the conspiracy of ignorance against reason, of darkness against light, of submission and slavery against independence and freedom; of the denial of strength and beauty, against the affirmation of the joy and glory of life.

Zona Gale
(State Historical Society of Wisconsin, WHi(X3)27348)

32

Zona Gale

PULITZER-PRIZE WINNER

August 26, 1874 – December 27, 1939

I remember well my mother telling me, at five: "Some little girls and boys think that Santa Claus comes down the chimney Christmas eve and brings the toys." And that I said decisively and rudely: "You can't make me believe any such stuff as that."

Zona Gale's Unfinished Autobiography

WISCONSIN AUTHOR ZONA GALE WON A PULITZER PRIZE for her play "Miss Lulu Bett" in 1921.

Zona's biographer August Derleth felt her life's theme was a belief that "Life is something more than that which we believe it to be." This conviction, wrote Derleth, was "not a religious concept at all, in the sense in which she used it, but an attempt to define that ageless groping of mankind for the experience, the emotion that lies just beyond the rim of living, just beyond some remote door that seems always just within reach and is almost always out of reach." (Derleth, *Still Small Voice:* 3)

Following a long siege of diphtheria, Zona, who had been a plump four-year-old, emerged with delicate health and a lifelong fragility, turning to imaginative play since hardier varieties were off limits. Her parents were respectable Presbyterian churchgoers. Her mother was ultra-religious, but had delayed joining a church until she was twenty due to her reluctance to quit dancing. Although immersed in religion through most of Zona's life, she came to believe: "It was the life of Christ that mattered, not His death." Zona's father stopped attending church, entertaining a very private nonconformity.

Zona the child was a scoffer. In her incomplete autobiography, she recalled:

"I remember well my mother telling me, at five: 'Some little girls and boys think that Santa Claus comes down the chimney Christmas eve and brings the toys.' And that I said decisively and rudely: 'You can't make me believe any such stuff as that.' So I never had the pleasure of a moment's credence of the Santa Claus myth. On the other hand I always had, and have yet, a sneaking belief in fairies." (p. 280)

In *When I Was a Little Girl*, Zona wrote about a conversation she had with friends on the subject of bedtime.

"Who *made* bed-time?" I inquired irritably.

"S–h–h!" said Delia. "God did."

"I don't believe it," I announced flatly.

"Well," said Delia, "anyway, he makes us sleep."

This I also challenged. "Then why am I sleepier when I go to church evenings than when I play Hide-and-go-seek in the Brice's barn evenings?" I submitted.

This was getting into theology, and Delia used the ancient method.

"We aren't supposed to know all those things," she said with superiority, and the council broke up. (Gale, *When I Was a Little Girl*: 7–8)

A chance encounter when she was eleven with a dashing college boy named Will Breese, who offered her a toboggan ride, was not forgotten. At fourteen Zona told her friends she was going to marry him someday. She did, in midlife, in 1928. "That life-long glamour has never failed me." (p. 14)

She received her degree in literature from the University of Wisconsin in 1895, then worked for the *Evening Wisconsin* and the *Milwaukee Journal*. She obtained her Master of Literature degree in 1899 (later honored with a Doctor of Literature degree in 1929). Zona made an effect on people. Novelist Edna Ferber, recalling their first meeting, said Zona was a "fragile and lovely creature whose skirts rustled silkenly as she moved." (p. 1) After writing constantly over a ten-year period, often late into the night, mostly of castles and romance, Zona had sold only one fictional story. Moving to New York in 1901, she became a reporter for the *Evening World*, then a free-lance writer.

Her first book was *Romance Island* (1906). A collection of her published stories, *The Loves of Pelleas and Etarre*, appeared in 1907. She then launched her successful sentimental stories, "Friendship Village," about small-town life, first appearing in such periodicals as the *Atlantic* and *Woman's Home Companion*, later published in four volumes from 1908 to 1919.

She moved back to Wisconsin in 1911, spending several months a year in New York. She not only supported herself—however legendary her modest, vegetarian, birdlike meals were—but sent money to her parents, eventually buying them a new home.

She and her father both became staunch supporters of Progressive Senator Robert La Follette, Zona writing for his magazine. A pacifist, she was radicalized by World War I, continuing her peace efforts through the year of her death, when she appeared with Eleanor Roosevelt on a National Peace Program in Green Bay, Wisconsin. She became friends with Jane Addams [see Additional Biographical Sketches], whom she had first met as a student reporter, and Charlotte Perkins Gilman. She served as vice-president of the Wisconsin Woman Suffrage Association and the Wisconsin Peace Society. Reflecting her burgeoning social consciousness were her books, the antiwar *Heart's Kindred* (1915), and *A Daughter of the Morning* (1917), about working women. She shifted from sentimentalism to realism. The critical response to her liberalism by her community contributed to her important tragedy, *Birth* (1918).

Miss Lulu Bett (1920), an ironic, feminist look at small-town life, became a best-seller. Zona's dramatization of the novel for a production of the book brought her the 1921 Pulitzer Prize for drama. She continued writing, served a six-year term on the Wisconsin Board of Regents, established a series of lectureships, served on the Wisconsin Free Library Commission, campaigned for La Follette's Progressive party, and remained active in causes. Derleth wrote that Zona went through a mystical phase, but that her view on religion coincided with her father's: "The spirit of man is God; that is the only God there is."

Two decades before her death from pneumonia, Zona had penned her own lighthearted epitaph for *Vanity Fair:*

> The only snobbish deed within her store
> And one which no one's envy need arouse,
> Was moving in this present type of house
> Where neighbors cannot enter the back door.

Why

From the chapter "Why" in Zona Gale's autobiographical novel of childhood, **When I Was A Little Girl** *(1913). Zona's character has lost two "naughty" playmates to the punishment of being confined to their rooms in the course of one evening, and is discussing the nature of "wickedness" with her remaining play-mates:*

As WE WENT, Mary Elizabeth was asking:

"Is telling a lie and not feeding your canary as wicked as each other?"

It seemed incredible, and we said so.

"Well, you get shut up just as hard for both of 'em," Mary Elizabeth reminded us.

"Then I don't believe any of 'em's wicked," said I, flatly. On which we came back to the garden and met Grandmother Beers, with a great bunch of sweet-peas in her hand, coming to the house.

"Wicked?" she said, in her way of soft surprise. "I didn't know you knew such a word."

"It's a word you learn at Sunday school," I explained importantly.

"Come over here and tell me about it," she invited, and led the way toward the Eating Apple tree. And she sat down in the swing! Of course whatever difference of condition exists between your grandmother and yourself vanishes when she sits down casually in your swing.

My Grandmother Beers was a little woman, whose years, in England, in "New York state," and in her adopted Middle West, had brought her only peace within, though much had beset her from without. She loved Four-o'clocks, and royal purple. When she said "royal purple," it was as if the words were queens. She was among the few who sympathized with my longing to own a blue or red or green jar from a drug store window. . . .

What child of us—of Us Who Were—will ever forget the joy of having an older one enter into our games? I used to sit in church and tell off the grown folk by this possibility in them—"She'd play with you—she wouldn't—she would—he would—they wouldn't"—an ancient declension of the human race, perfectly recognized by children, but never given its proper due. . . . I shall never forget the out-door romps with my Father, when he stooped, with his hands on his knees, and then ran *at* me; or when he held me while I walked the picket fence; or set me in the Eating Apple tree; nor can I forget the delight of the playhouse that he built for me, *with a shelf around*. . . . And always I shall remember, too, how my Mother would play "Lost." We used to curl on the sofa, taking with us some small store of fruit and cookies, wrap up in blankets and shawls, put up an umbrella—possibly two of them—and there we were, lost in the deep woods. We had been crossing the forest—night had overtaken us—we had climbed in a thick-leaved tree—it was raining—the woods were infested by bears and wolves—we had a little food, possibly enough to stave off starvation till daylight. Then came by the beasts of the forest, wonderful, human beasts, who passed at the foot of our tree, and with whom we talked long and friendly—and differently for each one—and ended by sharing with them our food. We scraped acquaintance with birds in neighbouring nests, the stars were only across a street of sky, the Dark did its part by hiding us. Sometimes, yet, when I see a fat, idle sofa in, say, an hotel corridor, I cannot help thinking as I pass: "What a wonderful place to play Lost." I daresay that some day I shall put up my umbrella and sit down and play it.

Well—Grandmother Beers was one who knew how to play with us, and I was always half expecting her to propose a new game. But that day, as she sat in the swing, her eyes were not twinkling at the corners.

"What does it mean?" she asked us. "What does 'wicked' mean?"

"It's what you aren't to be," I took the brunt of the reply, because I was the relative of the questioner.

"Why not?" asked Grandmother.

Why not? Oh, we all knew that. We responded instantly, and out came the results of the training of all the families.

"Because your mother and father say you can't," said Betty Rodman.

"Because it makes your mother feel bad," said Calista.

"Because God don't want us to," said I.

"Delia says," Betty added, "it's because, if you are, when you grow up people won't think anything of you."

Grandmother Beers held her sweet-peas to her face.

"If," she said after a moment, "you wanted to do something wicked more than you ever wanted to do anything in the world—as much as you'd want a drink to-morrow if you hadn't had one to-day—and if nobody ever knew—would any of those reasons keep you from doing it?"

We consulted one another's look, and shifted. We knew how thirsty that would be. Already we were thirsty, in thinking about it.

"If I were in your places," Grandmother said, "I'm not sure those reasons would keep me. I rather think they wouldn't,—always."

We stared at her. It was true that they didn't always keep us. Were not two of us "in our rooms" even now?

Grandmother leaned forward—I know how the shadows of the apple leaves fell on her black lace cap and how the pink sweet-peas were reflected in her delicate face.

"Suppose," she said, "that instead of any of those reasons, somebody gave you this reason: That the earth is a great flower—a flower that has never *really* blossomed yet. And that when it blossoms, life is going to be more beautiful than we have ever dreamed, or than fairy stories have ever pretended. And suppose our doing one way, and not another, makes the flower come a little nearer to blossoming. But our doing the other way puts back the time when it can blossom. *Then* which would you want to do?"

Oh, make it grow, make it grow, we all cried—and I felt a secret relief: Grandmother was playing a game with us, after all.

"And suppose that everything made a difference to it," she went on, "every little thing—from telling a lie, on down to going to get a drink for somebody and drinking first yourself out in the kitchen. Suppose that everything made a difference, from hurting somebody on purpose, down to making up the bed and pulling the bed-spread tight so that the wrinkles in the blanket won't show. . . ."

At this we looked at one another in some consternation. How did Grandmother know. . . .

"Until after a while," she said, "you should find out that everything—loving, going to school, playing, working, bathing, sleeping, were all just to make this flower grow. Wouldn't it be fun to help?"

Yes. Oh, yes, we were all agreed about that. It would be great fun to help.

"Well, then suppose," said Grandmother, "that as you helped, you found out something else: That in each of you, say, where your heart is, or where your breath is, there was a flower trying to blossom too! And that only as you helped the earth flower to blossom could your flower blossom. And that your doing one way would make your flower droop its head and grow dark and shrivel up. But your doing the other way would make it grow, and turn beautiful colours—so that bye and bye every one of your

— 398 —

bodies would be just a sheath for this flower. Which way *then* would you rather do?"

Oh, make it grow, make it grow, we said again.

And Mary Elizabeth added longingly:—

"Wouldn't it be fun if it was true?"

"It is true," said Grandmother Beers.

She sat there, softly smiling over her pink sweet-peas. We looked at her silently. Then I remembered that her face had always seemed to me to be somehow *light within*. Maybe it was her flower showing through! . . .

Margaret Sanger
Passport photo, circa 1916
(Sophia Smith Collection, Smith College)

33

Margaret Sanger

"WOMAN OF THE CENTURY"

September 14, 1879 – September 6, 1966

I wanted each woman to be a rebellious Vashti, not an Esther.

An Autobiography, *1938*

WHEN ANNE PURCELL HIGGINS DIED at age forty-eight of tuberculosis after bearing eleven children, that fact not only changed the course of her daughter Margaret's life, but ultimately changed world history.

Margaret Higgins Sanger began the crusade, in 1914, to provide effective, accessible, inexpensive, safe birth control and maternal health care to women. She became a fugitive, was jailed eight times, was censored and shunned, but she prevailed. Margaret brought the lawsuit overturning the repressive Comstock laws. She was responsible for the distribution of diaphragms in the United States, the development of effective contraceptive jelly, the education of physicians in birth control techniques, the proliferation of birth control clinics in the United States, the founding of Planned Parenthood, and ultimately, the creation of the birth control pill. Doing more to free women than any other single individual, Margaret Sanger, appropriately, was named "Woman of the Century" in 1966.

Margaret's childhood, spent in the largely Roman Catholic community of Corning, New York, was dominated by her father, a freethinking Irishman who was better at stirring up controversy than providing for his family. Her first introduction to the power of the Catholic Church to lock the doors against social change was witnessed as a young child when the local priest locked out agnostic Robert Ingersoll, whom her father had invited to speak. [See "From Which I Spring"]

After three years in Claverack, a private, coeducational school in the Catskills, Margaret returned home in 1896 to nurse her dying mother, apparently becoming infected herself with tuberculosis. Margaret attended a nursing school in

White Plains, New York. She nursed arduous obstetrics cases, while running fevers and being operated upon twice for "tubercular glands."

After marrying an artistic architect named William Sanger, she had three children, Stuart (1903), Grant (1908) and beloved daughter Peggy (1910). She spent most of her first pregnancy at a sanitarium and nearly died after her son was born. After a long convalescence, she settled into tranquil life as a homemaker in wealthy Westchester County, New York.

The family moved back to New York City in 1912, then abuzz with radicals, reformers and socialism. Rubbing shoulders with such iconoclasts as Emma Goldman and Bill Haywood at the radical salons of Mabel Dodge, Margaret soon was drawn into reform, serving as supervisor of a campaign to relocate the children of striking textile workers in Lawrence, Massachusetts. Police violence resulted in a Congressional investigation. The testimony of the slight, quiet, red-haired nurse with a Madonna-like serenity captured headlines.

When the International Workers of the World ("Wobblies") erected a huge banner at Madison Square Garden proclaiming "No God, No Master" in a demonstration planned by John Reed, the slogan obviously caught Margaret's eye.

Returning to obstetrical nursing of the poor, she was repeatedly begged for "the secret" that would let desperate women avoid serial pregnancies. She began writing a weekly Sunday column, "What Every Mother Should Know," for *The Call*, the paper of the Socialist Party, later published in pamphlet form. A second series, "What Every Girl Should Know," an introduction to sex for adolescents, was censored because she referred to "syphilis" and "gonorrhea" by name.

The turning point, she wrote poignantly in her autobiography, came in July, 1912, when she was called to nurse Sadie Sachs, a twenty-eight-year-old mother of three who had nearly died from a self-induced abortion. Margaret overheard the woman timidly ask the doctor how she could avoid another unwanted pregnancy: "Tell Jake to sleep on the roof" was his now-notorious reply. Three months later Margaret was called back to the flat, and helplessly watched the comatose Mrs. Sachs die. That evening she resolved to find out how to help women control fertility. She decided that "the basis of Feminism might be the right to be a mother regardless of church or state. . . ." (*An Autobiography:* 109)

She journeyed to the Library of Congress, medical libraries and then, with her husband, to Paris in search of answers. In 1914, she began publishing a monthly newspaper, *The Woman Rebel*, to challenge the 1873 Comstock Act, instigated by Anthony Comstock, a religious fanatic and special agent for the Postmaster General. The Act defined "prevention of conception" as "obscene, lewd, lascivious, filthy and indecent." Comstock bragged about convicting 3,760 individuals of violating the Act and driving fifteen persons to suicide.

The Woman Rebel debuted in March 1914; its motto was "No Gods—No Masters." Although "gentle" is a recurring adjective used by colleagues to describe Margaret, she wanted *The Woman Rebel* to be "as red and flaming as possible." (Sanger, *My Fight for Birth Control:* 80) In the first issue, Margaret counseled women "To look the whole world in the face with a go-to-hell look in the eyes; to have an ideal; to speak and to act in defiance of convention." During this heady time, she and friends brainstormed for a needed name for the contraceptive movement, and the term "birth control" was born.

That August she was indicted on nine counts of violating the Comstock law and faced forty-five years in prison. Winning a delay, she wrote "Family Limitation," containing everything she had learned about birth control, describing condoms, tampons, suppositories and douches. She had 100,000 printed and ready to be released. In October 1914, with one day's notice, *The People v. Margaret Sanger* was called. Her hastily hired labor attorney was denied a month's delay and advised her to plead guilty. Margaret, agonizing over leaving her children, fled the country that night through Canada, bound for England as "Bertha Watson," leaving directions that "Family Limitation" be released. It would sell ten million copies and be translated into thirteen languages.

She studied the history of contraception at the British Museum, reading Malthus on overpopulation, becoming familiar with the early birth control advocates, many of them freethinkers such as John Stuart Mill, Robert Dale Owen and Annie Besant. Margaret began her long friendship with Havelock Ellis, the British sexologist. She also interned at a family planning clinic in the Netherlands, fitting seventy-five women with diaphragms.

She returned to the states after her estranged husband was entrapped. William Sanger was personally arrested by Comstock for giving a copy of "Family Limitation" to an undercover officer and was jailed one month. Comstock died of complications of a cold caught during William's trial. Mary Ware Dennett of the National Birth Control League, which Margaret had organized, turned down, Margaret's request for support with her pending prosecution. In November 1915, daughter Peggy died of pneumonia. During this grim time, attorneys advised Margaret to plead guilty. Taking a lesson from Annie Besant, she vowed to defend herself. H. G. Wells and other famous British authors wrote President Wilson on Margaret's behalf. By early 1916 with a new trial pending, feminists gravitated to her support. Margaret made a passionate debut speech at a Night-Before-Trial dinner in her honor, describing herself as a nurse working in the slums who saw a fire and was shouting for help. Her trial made front pages, even during the Battle of Verdun. Charges were dropped, but the law was unchanged.

She launched a lecture tour in April 1916, sparking regional birth control leagues wherever she spoke, Catholics protesting her at every city, sometimes successful in halting her lectures or getting her arrested. Realizing that women needed clinics, not speeches, she resolved to open one in an immigrant neighborhood. No doctor could be found to help, but on October 16, 1916, she, her sister Ethel Byrne and supporter Fania Mindell opened their Brooklyn clinic. One patient told her how the priest advised her to have lots of children. "I had fifteen. Six are living. I'm thirty-seven years old now. Look at me! I might be fifty!"

Wrote Margaret: "That evening I made a mental calculation of fifteen baptismal fees, nine baby funerals, masses and candles for the repose of nine baby souls, the physical agonies of the mother and the emotional torment of both parents, and I asked myself, 'Is this the price of Christianity?' " (*Autobiography:* 219)

Ten days later the clinic was raided. Police harassed patients and confiscated four hundred and sixty case records. Ethel, tried first, was convicted and sentenced to a month on Blackwell's Island where she started a food and water strike, was brutally forced fed, and nearly died. Her plight raised national consciousness of the birth control cause. Margaret and supporters obtained a gubernatorial pardon and rescued Ethel, who convalesced a year to recover from ten days in prison. Margaret served a thirty-day sentence at the Raymond Street jail, befriending prisoners and lecturing in corridors about sex hygiene. She lost fifteen pounds (from bad food, not from fasting), and emerged with reactivated tuberculosis.

In 1917 the New York State Supreme Court upheld her conviction, but ruled that contraceptive advice could be given for cure and prevention of disease.

During a three-month rest cure in California with her ten-year-old son Grant, Margaret wrote *Woman and the New Race*, which appeared in 1920 and sold a quarter-million copies. She quietly championed women's right to erotic fulfillment and unflinchingly named the enemy of women's emancipation:

"If Christianity turned the clock of general progress back a thousand years, it turned back the clock two thousand years for woman. Its greatest outrage upon her was to forbid her to control the function of motherhood under any circumstances, thus limiting her life's work to bringing forth and rearing children. Coincident with this, the churchmen deprived her of her place in and before the courts, in the schools, in literature, art and society. They shut from her heart and her mind the knowledge of her love life and her reproductive functions. They chained her to the position into which they had thrust her, so that it is only after centuries of effort that she is even beginning to regain what was wrested from her." (p. 175)

Margaret next launched the American Birth Control League, and planned the first National Birth Control Conference. She became a cause célèbre when her lecture "Birth Control—Is It Moral?" at Town Hall in New York City was cancelled at the orders of Catholic Archbishop Patrick J. Hayes, and she was arrested when she tried to speak.

Along with Albert Einstein, Bertrand Russell and H. G. Wells, she was invited to take part in lectures by four leaders in Western thought in Japan, but the country denied her a visa in 1922. Finally permitted to enter Japan, she gave thirteen lectures and an estimated five hundred interviews.

That year, she recruited a woman physician to run a birth control clinic in New York. Margaret, believed to have had among the highest volume of mail received by a private citizen, was flooded with requests from women around the country for help. Those letters formed the basis of her book *Motherhood in Bondage* (1928). She didn't just publicize their needs. She financed a gynecologist, Dr. James F. Cooper, to lecture for two years to audiences of physicians. Cooper gave more than seven hundred speeches teaching techniques and signed up 20,000 physicians who agreed to take referrals of patients needing birth control.

By 1923 Dr. Hannah Stone donated her services to run the Brooklyn clinic. Cooper and Stone, at Margaret's behest, designed an inexpensive contraceptive jelly to use with diaphragms, based on lactic acid and glycerine. Margaret provided her clinic with five hundred to one thousand diaphragms a week, illegally bootlegged, biographer Emily Taft Douglas discovered, through the Canadian factory of Margaret's second husband, oil tycoon Noah Slee. Slee loaned money to two birth control advocates who started a U.S. factory to manufacture diaphragms.

Margaret raised $25,000 to organize the Sixth International Conference on birth control, attended by eight hundred delegates from eighteen nations, resulting in worldwide education and major press. Dr. Stone's statistics, finding the diaphragm ninety-eight percent effective when used with jelly, were the pinnacle of the conference.

Catholic officials continued to try to censor Margaret. After five years of operation, her clinic, the Clinical Research Bureau, was raided in 1929 at the demand of Archbishop Hayes. Slee purchased a mansion to house the clinic, which served eighteen hundred women a month. Margaret continued planning other international conferences, determined to ignite physicians and researchers into helping women.

By 1931, when she wrote *My Fight for Birth Control*, there were fifty birth control clinics in the United States and another fifty in Europe. Interested in an improved Japanese diaphragm, Margaret had samples ordered. They were destroyed by Customs under the Comstock law. She went to court. Turning her attention to Congress, Margaret unsuccessfully campaigned for a "doctors' bill," getting support from the General Federation of Women's Clubs. At a Congressional hearing dominated by religionists, she was forced to close "my eyes to this monotonous, repetitious chant of medieval dogmas." Her response, in part, was to testify: "Jesus Christ was said to be an only child." (*Autobiography:* 421, 422)

In 1934, Federal District Judge Grover Moscowitz of New York ruled in *United*

States v. One Package that the Comstockian Revenue Act did not apply to contraceptives. The Circuit Court of Appeals agreed and the government did not appeal, making the victory final in January 1937. Margaret's case thus ended the sixty-three year reign of Comstock. By June 1937, the American Medical Association endorsed birth control. There were more than three hundred birth control centers but Margaret wanted ten times that number by the year's end.

Although she had been forced out of her original birth control league, in 1939 a merger took place and Margaret became honorary president of the group that later became Planned Parenthood. She toured India, facing Catholic opposition even there, but got forty-five medical societies to launch birth control programs.

After World War II, she revived the worldwide birth control movement. General MacArthur personally barred her from visiting Japan, at the demand of Catholic groups, but she finally made the trip back at age seventy-three in 1952. She planned a successful world conference in India that year, sponsored by Eleanor Roosevelt and Albert Einstein, among others. That conference resulted in the organizing of the International Planned Parenthood Federation, which elected her president. Her travel and activism was accomplished in spite of many hospitalizations and illnesses.

Seeking a better form of birth control, Margaret, in the 1950s, through the financial sponsorship of Mrs. Stanley McCormick, set up Gregory Pincus, an expert in mammalian biology, to study steroid hormones. No federal funding was available due to fear of the Catholic Church. McCormick and Sanger also sponsored laboratory studies by Dr. M. C. Chang while Dr. John Rock, "Father of the Pill," tried out steroids on volunteers. The "pill," tested more than any drug in history, was released in 1960.

Her other books include: *Pivot of Civilization* (1922), *Married Happiness* (1926), and *An Autobiography* (1938). She also edited and published two journals, *Birth Control Review* (1917–1940) and *Human Fertility* (1940–1948).

Margaret Sanger died at nearly eighty-seven in a Tucson nursing home, living long enough to savor the June 1965 decision of the United States Supreme Court, *Griswold v. Connecticut*, invoking the constitutional "right of privacy" striking down a law declaring contraceptives to be criminal.

In the memorable words of H. G. Wells:

"Alexander the Great changed a few boundaries and killed a few men. Both he and Napoleon were forced into fame by circumstances outside of themselves and by currents of the time, but Margaret Sanger made currents and circumstances. When the history of our civilization is written, it will be a biological history and Margaret Sanger will be its heroine." (Douglas, *Margaret Sanger: Pioneer of the Future*: 142–143)

From Which I Spring

This is excerpted from chapter I of **Margaret Sanger: An Autobiography** *(1938).*

IN THE PREDOMINANTLY ROMAN CATHOLIC COMMUNITY of Corning, set crosses in the cemeteries were the rule for the poor and, before they went out of style, angels in various poses for the rich. I used to watch father at work. The rough, penciled sketch indicated little; even less did the first unshaped block of stone. He played with the hard, unyielding marble as though it were clay, making a tiny chip for a mouth, which grew rounder and rounder. A face then emerged, a shoulder, a sweep of drapery, praying hands, until finally the whole stood complete with wings and halo.

Although Catholics were father's best patrons, by nature and upbringing he deplored their dogma. He joined the Knights of Labor, who were agitating against the influx of unskilled immigrants from Catholic countries, and this did not endear him to his clientele. Still less did his espousal of Colonel Robert G. Ingersoll, a man after his own heart, whose works he had eagerly studied and used as texts. Once when the challenger was sounding a ringing defiance in near-by towns, father extended an invitation to speak in Corning and enlighten it. He collected subscriptions to pay for the only hall in town, owned by Father Coghlan. A notice was inserted in the paper that the meeting would be held the following Sunday, but chiefly the news spread by word of mouth. "Better come. Tell all your friends."

Sunday afternoon arrived, and father escorted "Colonel Bob" from the hotel to the hall, I trotting by his side. We pushed through the waiting crowd, but shut doors stared silently and reprovingly—word had also reached Father Coghlan.

Some were there to hear and learn, others to denounce. Antipathies between the two suddenly exploded in action. Tomatoes, apples, and cabbage stumps began to fly. This was my first experience of rage directed against those holding views which were contrary to accepted ones. It was my first, but by no means my last. I was to encounter it many times, and always with the same bewilderment and disdain. My father apparently felt only the disdain. Resolutely he announced the meeting would take place in the woods near our home an hour later, then led Ingersoll and the "flock" through the streets. I trudged along again, my small hand clasped in his, my head held just as high.

Who cared for the dreary, dark, little hall! In the woodland was room for all. Those who had come for discussion sat spell-bound on the ground in a ring around the standing orator. For them the booing had been incidental and was ignored. I cannot remember a word of what Colonel Ingersoll said, but the scene remains. It was late in the afternoon, and the tall pines shot up against the fiery radiance of the setting sun, which lit the sky with the brilliance peculiar to the afterglows of the Chemung Valley.

Florid, gray-haired Father Coghlan, probably tall in his prime, came to call on mother. He was a kindly old gentleman, not really intolerant. Shutting the hall had been a matter of principle; he could not have an atheist within those sacred walls. But he was willing to talk about it afterwards. In fact, he rather enjoyed arguing with rebels. He was full of persuasion which he used on mother, begging her to exercise her influence with father to make him refrain from his evil ways. She had been reared in the faith, although since her marriage to a freethinker which had so distressed her parents, she had never attended church to my knowledge. The priest was troubled to see her soul damned when she might have been a good Catholic, and implored her to send her children to church and to the parochial school, to stand firm against the intrusion of godlessness. Mother must have suffered from the conflict.

None of us realized how the Ingersoll episode was to affect our well-being. Thereafter we were known as children of the devil. On our way to school names were shouted, tongues stuck out, grimaces made; the juvenile stamp of disapproval had been set upon us. But we had been so steeped in "heretic" notions that we were not particularly bothered by this and could not see ahead into the dark future when a hard childhood was to be made harder. No more marble angels were to be carved for local Catholic cemeteries, and, while father's income was diminishing, the family was increasing.

Occasionally big commissions were offered him in adjacent towns where his reputation was still high, and he was then away for days at a time, coming back with a thousand or fifteen hundred dollars in his pocket; we all had new clothes, and the house was full of plenty. Food was bought for the winter—turnips, apples, flour, potatoes. But then again a year might pass before he had another one, and meanwhile we had sunk deeply into debt.

Towards orthodox religion father's own attitude remained one of tolerance. He looked upon the New Testament as the noble story of a human being which, because of ignorance and the lack of printing presses, had become exaggerated. He maintained that religions served their purpose; some people depended on them all their lives for discipline—to keep them straight, to make them honest. Others did not need to be so held in line. But subjection to any church was a reflection on strength and character. You should be able to get from yourself what you had to go to church for.

When we asked which Sunday School we should attend, he suggested, "Try them all, but be chained to none." For a year or two I made the rounds, especially at Christmas and Easter, when you received oranges and little bags of candy. It was always cold at the Catholic church and the wooden benches were very bare and hard; some seats were upholstered in soft, red cloth but these were for the rich, who rented the pews and put dollars into the plate at collection. I never liked to see the figure of Jesus on the cross; we could not help Him because He had been crucified long ago. I much preferred the Virgin Mary; she was beautiful, smiling—the way I should like to look when I had a baby.

Saying my prayers for mother's benefit was spasmodic. Ethel, the sister nearest my own age, was more given than I to religious phases and I could get her in bed faster if I said them with her. One evening when we had finished this dutiful ritual I climbed on father's chair to kiss him good night. He asked quizzically, "What was that you were saying about bread?"

"Why, that was in the Lord's Prayer, 'Give us this day our daily bread.' "

"Who were you talking to?"

"To God."

"Is God a baker?"

I was shocked. Nevertheless, I rallied to the attack and replied as best I could, doubtless influenced by conversations I had heard. "No, of course not. It means the rain, the sunshine, and all the things to make the wheat, which makes the bread."

"Well, well," he replied, "so that's the idea. Then why don't you say so? Always say what you mean, my daughter; it is much better."

Thereafter I began to question what I had previously taken for granted and to reason for myself. It was not pleasant, but father had taught me to think. He gave none of us much peace. When we put on stout shoes he said, "Very nice. Very comfortable. Do you know who made them?"

"Why, yes, the shoemaker."

We then had to listen to graphic descriptions of factory conditions in the shoe industry, so that we might learn something of the misery and poverty the workers suffered in order to keep our feet warm and dry.

Father never talked about religion without bringing in the ballot box. In fact, he took up Socialism because he believed it Christian philosophy put into practice, and to me its ideals still come nearest to carrying out what Christianity was supposed to do. Unceasingly he tried to inculcate in us the idea that our duty lay not in considering what might happen to us after death, but in doing something here and now to make the lives of other human beings more decent. "You have no right to material comforts without giving back to society the benefit of your honest experience," was one of his maxims, and his parting words to each of his sons and daughters who had grown old enough to fend for themselves were, "Leave the world better because you, my child, have dwelt in it."

This was something to live up to.

Marian Noel Sherman, M.D. (inset)
and photographed as a child
(British Columbia Archives and Records Service)

34

Marian Noel Sherman, M.D.

MISSIONARY DOCTOR TO ATHEIST WITH A MISSION

1892 – 1975

A believer is not a thinker and a thinker is not a believer.
Interview, Daily Colonist, c. *1969*

BORN IN ENGLAND, MARIAN NOEL BOSTOCK, the oldest of eight children, emigrated with her parents to Victoria, British Columbia, Canada. Her mother was quietly freethinking, well-read and committed to the education of women. Her father, more orthodox, was first elected as a Liberal to Parliament in 1896. She finished her schooling in England, studying at the London School of Medicine, and became a fellow of the Royal College of Surgeons specializing in gynecology. She worked as a medical missionary from 1922–1934 in India.

The doctor married banker Victor Sherman in 1928. In 1936 they moved back to Victoria. Marian, busy with domestic concerns and church work, did not reexamine her faith until 1946. She attributed her sudden realization that there is no god to events such as the suffering she had witnessed in India, and the two world wars. Following her atheistic epiphany, Marian became a cofounder of the Victoria Humanist Fellowship.

"The concepts of personal immortality and a personal deity are irrational. That which cannot be made clear in words (e.g., God) cannot exist," she told *The Star* (Victoria), March 17, 1955.

Her suggestion at age seventy-one to start an atheist information center was reported in the *New York Times* on October 6, 1963. She debated a United Church chaplain from the University of British Columbia in 1965, calling God a "divisive concept" and observing, "Every child is born an atheist, and would not have a belief in God if it were not taught by parents."

"How people hate the word atheist. They think there is something evil about it. It only means a person who doesn't believe in a supernatural being over us."

Marian was named 1975 Humanist of the Year in Canada.

What Makes An Atheist Tick?
by Sylvia Fraser

This article originally appeared in Toronto's The Star Weekly, September 11, 1965.

NOW IT'S POSSIBLE FOR THEM TO BECOME CITIZENS. But how about the prejudices they encounter every day? Here is the frank story of Dr. Marian Sherman, a militant Victoria, B.C., non-believer.

❧

Last September, New Democratic M.P. William Howe brought to the attention of Parliament the strange plight of Ernest and Cornelia Bergsma of Caledonia, Ont. A Dutch immigrant couple with nine years' residence in Canada, they had been denied citizenship by Haldimand County Judge W.L. Leach because they could not state positively that they believed in God.

The result of this parliamentary revelation was immediate—and explosive. Reporters converged on the hard-working, plain-living Bergsmas and, overnight, they became front-page news—along with the broader question of atheism itself.

More surprising than the fact of this controversy was the lopsided shape it soon began to take: Editorials roundly denounced the rejection of the Bergsmas' citizenship application as flagrant discrimination; most church leaders praised the Dutch couple's honesty, and affirmed their right to become Canadians; an overwhelming percentage of the mail the Bergsmas received was openly sympathetic.

This liberal attitude—perhaps unthinkable even a few years ago—was reflected in the government's decision to finance an appeal of the Bergsma case to a judge of the High Court of Justice for Ontario. When this appeal was dismissed, the case was taken to the Court of Appeals for Ontario. There, on July 22, three judges unanimously decided that "lack of religious belief alone is not a ground upon which a Citizenship Court should decide against application for citizenship." The Bergsmas had won their fight. They were welcome to become Canadians.

From this swift, sure chain of events, it would seem that atheism, once considered an undercover evil somewhat akin to witchcraft, is now at least officially tolerable in our society. . . . But what does atheism ("There is no God"), or even agnosticism ("I don't know if there is a God"), mean in terms of practical, day-to-day living? . . . Is an atheist less moral than a Christian? Is he a sour-faced cynic—or does he have positive beliefs of his own? Does he encounter prejudice in daily life? And what makes a person an atheist in the first place?

As an insight into the position of an atheist, at a time when many Canadians are curious and concerned, The Star Weekly presents the unusual story of one militant non-believer.

❦

Seventy-three year old Dr. Marian Sherman of Victoria is an atheist. A former medical missionary to India, she astounded friends and family one day in 1946 by dramatically changing from a soft-spoken Anglican into an outspoken non-believer—apparently overnight.

She explains: "I was looking out the window of my home in Victoria, watching the waves wash the rocks and praying quietly to myself, when suddenly the thought struck me that there really was no personal God. That the word 'God' merely meant human love. I went to see the Anglican bishop for instruction, and he cautioned me: 'Don't give up your church connection and don't talk about your new ideas to the ladies of the Woman's Auxiliary or they'll surely throw you out.' And that's exactly what happened. When I told the women, they started asking: 'How can she be president of the W.A. if she doesn't believe in the Virgin birth?' When they demanded my resignation, I suggested we discuss the matter, but the parson's wife drew herself up haughtily and exclaimed: 'I *never* discuss religion!' And so they kicked me out."

Dr. Sherman's embarrassing wrong-way conversion also got her into trouble with her socially prominent family. "They started whispering with my husband about psychiatrists and long rest cures," says Dr. Sherman, whose father, Hewitt Bostock, was speaker of the Canadian Senate from 1923 till his death in 1930. "They had such *fixed* ideas. I couldn't make them see the joy I felt at finally freeing my mind from the fetters of faith and dogma."

Undaunted by stiff-backed, stiff-lipped opposition, the redoubtable Dr. Sherman prepared a pamphlet in which she expounded on her theory

"God is human love." Then she travelled from home to home in her comfortable, conservative neighborhood dropping copies into mailboxes.

"Oh, there was such an outcry over that," she says. "The vicar of St. George the Martyr came to see me to tell me that since I was an atheist I wasn't to come to church any more. I replied: 'You can't forbid me the church. My husband and I worked as hard as anyone else to get it built.' However, I only went a couple of times after that. At first I had thought, in my innocence, that I could help re-vitalize the church from within, but everyone was too fearful and too rigid."

Since those first hectic, heretic times, Dr. Sherman, who was widowed four years ago, has indefatigably devoted herself to spreading her own gospel: disbelief in a supernatural God, love of all people and a devotion to progress through the social sciences. She writes letters to newspapers and occasionally is a guest on local radio programs. She publicly and privately challenges clergymen on all phases of their belief. She works for half a dozen welfare organizations—slyly smuggling in her scientific-atheistic views under the bland guise of "mental health." And she worries about the influence of evangelists, such as Billy Graham, with their "unhealthy," emotion-charged brand of religion, on the minds of the young, in the same way that other parents worry about the influence of the Rolling Stones or Beatlemania.

All this unorthodox activity soon made Dr. Sherman No. 1 atheist in the west.

"I rather wickedly came to consider myself 'the hammer of the clergy,' " she says. "One reason why I have remained aggressive and what many people think is too outspoken through the years is that I don't have to fear public opinion: I am financially secure and I have no job to lose. Of course, I've lost some friends, but that's to be expected—it's all part of life and growth. The main problem with being a freethinker is that people try to hush you up so you won't 'hurt' the Christians. All I want to do is to wake them up—to get them thinking and discussing. Every area of life should be open to scientific scrutiny. There should be no such thing as 'unthinkable' thoughts!"

Some of the "unthinkable thoughts" which Dr. Sherman has been in the habit of publicly expressing are:

On the Bible: "It is a remarkable collection of writings—but no more remarkable than many other collections. If it were used as a textbook on psychology instead of as the Great Authority, I think it would be very fine indeed. Take that poor child Samuel, now: When you condition someone the way he was conditioned, he can't help but see visions."

On God: "There is no evidence at all for the existence of a supernatural Supreme Being. Some people say they know God exists because they feel him in their hearts. Again that is just childhood conditioning. Others are fond of saying that there had to be someone, or something to act as a First Cause, but even a child can see through that argument. If you tell a child 'God made the world' he will usually ask 'Then who made God?' If we reply, as the catechism states, 'No one made God. He always was,' then why couldn't we just say that about the world in the first place?... No, man is the measure of all things. It's only fear of death and egotism that makes us invent a God who will give us everlasting life. Religious people often accuse atheists of being arrogant and of placing ourselves in the position of God, but really it is the theist who has all the vanity. He can't stand to think that he will ever cease to exist. As Freud said, Christianity is the most egotistical of the religions. It is based on the premise 'Jesus saves *me.*'"

On Jesus Christ: "If he lived—and I'm not sure he did—I don't think it matters much. The story of his divinity is just a wonderful, dramatic tale. You can see how it got started—all the Jewish mothers were steeped in the Scriptures, and every one of them thought she could be the mother of the Saviour."

On Christian ethics: "The core of Jesus' teachings is 'Love one another' and I accept that wholeheartedly. However, such teachings were not original to Jesus."

On death: "It is the end of the organism. All we can hope is that we have found some sort of happiness in this life and that we have left the world as a little better place."

On the clergy: "They are so pathetically pleased with any small move that indicates their churches are coming a little closer together, but they are just whistling in the dark to keep their spirits up. I listen to them on the radio every once in a while to see how they are coming along—the way you check a cake to see how it's baking. They're progressing—but, alas, so slowly."

On the church: "Religions inhibit growth. They divide people into little groups with fixed ideas that are sacred, and so can't be changed.

However, we are entering an era of co-operation and science, and I think that religions will evolve out of existence."

Already, widespread changes in traditional patterns of belief are causing major upheaval, and thoughtful reassessment, within the Christian churches themselves.

In a just-published national survey, conducted by the board of evangelism and social service of the United Church of Canada, it was found that: Of a representative sample of 1,955 regular church-goers, occasional church-goers and infrequent church-goers from 209 congregations, sixteen per cent did not believe in a personal god; nineteen per cent did not accept the divinity of Christ; thirty-five per cent did not accept the Virgin birth of Christ; forty-four per cent did not accept the idea of personal existence after death; and sixty per cent rejected the Biblical account of miracles.

Perhaps even more startling: Rev. E.M. Howse, moderator of the United Church of Canada, recently stated that he himself did not personally believe in the physical resurrection of Jesus Christ.

Apparently there is a large segment of the Canadian population—including church members themselves—who now hold views almost as "blasphemous" as the ones which earned Dr. Sherman her cloven hooves. Most of these people do not stir up conflict because most do not issue disturbing challenges or wave banners. Dr. Sherman does: Like a zealous Christian, she unabashedly attempts to gain converts for atheism—and many proselytizers from the other side are shocked and offended.

"The most vitriolic letter I ever received came from a parson," she says. "He insisted, among other things, that the fires of hell were waiting to consume me."

On another occasion, when she spoke in a newspaper interview about setting up an Atheist Information Centre in Victoria, she received nation-wide press coverage—and a spate of angry mail. "One woman rang me up on the phone, shouted 'You are Satanic!' and then slammed down the receiver."

Other believers find it more comfortable simply to dismiss Dr. Sherman as a crazy crackpot: But she is not. At seventy-three, she is articulate, well-educated and well-read. She is up-to-date on world and local affairs, retains a sharply analytic mind and is keenly interested in other people's ideas. She also possesses more energy than the average person of twenty-three, and devotes herself to community and welfare work—for the senior citizens and the victims of multiple sclerosis; as a member of the Canadian Mental Health Association, the Women's Institute, the Local Council of Women and the NDP.

She is not a Communist: "Some people brand all atheists as Communists," says Dr. Sherman. "In my opinion, communism has the same fault that religions have: too many fixed ideas."

Nor is she a cynic. She is a warm and outgoing woman—a happy optimist who believes that, for the majority of people, the world has never been better. In fact, she looks like someone's sweet gray-haired grandmother—which she is, though she certainly doesn't sound like one.

"My two granddaughters are being brought up as unbaptized, happy little heathens," she says contentedly. "The important thing with children is to get them to see that the world is a wonderful place, full of marvels, but not miracles of the supernatural variety. Fortunately, both my stepdaughter and her husband are freethinkers—though I never could bring my husband around. He attended the Anglican church till his death."

In philosophic terms, Dr. Sherman call herself a humanist.

"Humanism seeks the fullest development of the human being," she explains. "Humanists acknowledge no Supreme Being and we approach all life from the point of view of science and reason. Ours is not a coldly clinical view, for we believe that if human beings will but practise love of one another and use their wonderful faculty of speech, we can make a better world, happy for all. But there must be no dogma."

Though Dr. Sherman describes conversion to the atheistic-humanistic position as the result of an instantaneous flash of insight, in reality the evolution of her philosophy took years of reading and thinking.

It also took her over three continents and from the polar position of Christian missionary to that of atheistic spokesman.

Dr. Sherman was born in 1892 in Epsom, England, the daughter of Hewitt Bostock, a wealthy Englishman. When she was just eighteen months, her parents emigrated to Victoria, and later to a ranch near Kamloops, where she was raised—as a proper Anglican—with seven brothers and sisters. At age fifteen, she was sent to school in England.

"Many of my English relatives were very churchy," she says. "People quoted the Bible more frequently in those days, and I remember I was particularly puzzled by the text: 'All sins can be forgiven but the sin against the Holy Ghost.' Now, what on earth is the sin against the Holy Ghost? That sticks in my mind because at church service I used to notice an old parson who kept banging his head against the wall. Once I asked my aunt why he did that, and she replied: 'He thinks he has committed the sin against the Holy Ghost.' "

This formal religious training was partly offset by a liberal education under teacher Julia Huxley, the niece of essayist Matthew Arnold and the mother of author Aldous Huxley. "She was a freethinker, though she was careful not to teach too many ideas that would upset. I was very fond of her and she planted seeds which germinated later."

In 1911, when she was 19, Marian Bostock studied at the London School of Medicine and, upon graduation, she was one of a very few women to become a Fellow of the Royal College of Surgeons in England. Then, in 1922, she decided to go to India as an interdenominational medical missionary.

From 1922 to 1927, Dr. Bostock worked with another woman doctor in a women's and children's hospital near Patna, where she had an opportunity to observe first-hand the unnecessary misery caused by custom and fixed religious beliefs.

"Pregnant women, at the time of childbirth, were considered taboo and so they were put in dirty old cowsheds and looked after by old women with no idea of cleanliness," she says. "The rest of the time their Hindu and Moslem husbands kept them in *purdah*, which meant they were smothered in veils and shut up in their homes. If they were ill and there was no woman doctor, they were left to die, because no man other than their husbands could see them—oh, sometimes one was allowed to stick her tongue out through a piece of cloth for the doctor, but a lot of good that did."

The caste system in particular caused much hardship. "For every patient we admitted into the hospital, we had to admit a relative to cook for her because she would lose caste if someone lower on the social scale touched her food. She would lose caste if she died in a bed, so when a patient became very ill the relatives would take her home to die on the floor, and she would lose her one chance of recovery."

Off-duty the doctors lived with two nursing sisters and a full-time evangelist in a primitive six-room bungalow with no plumbing. "Visitors often said to me: 'How wonderful to be able to help these people,' but I began to feel that what India needed far more than medical help was education. There was very little schooling on any level. In fact, when a Hindu set up as a teacher or lawyer it was quite common for him to proudly post a sign saying 'Failed B. A.' since it was so prestigious to have come even *that* close to a degree.

"What the Indians certainly didn't need was more religion—Christianity or any other," continued Dr. Sherman. "They were already trapped in a web of custom and religious belief that was completely divorced from reality. I took part in various Christian prayer meetings, but I knew it was foolish to try to convert the Indians. A Hindu woman couldn't possibly become a Christian and remain with her husband. Christianity could only confuse her further. For example, I remember our evangelist telling one little patient that God answers prayer. 'I know that,' she replied solemnly. 'I prayed to him to make my husband die so that I could join the mission, and my husband *did* die.' "

The extreme suffering of the Indian women made Dr. Bostock begin to doubt the existence of an all-powerful, all-loving God. "If there is a God of love, how could He let the women of India endure so much? What sins were they punished for?. . .The English had passed a law forbidding the burning of widows on their husbands' funeral pyres, but even in my day there were one or two cases of women throwing themselves into the flames. The lot of Indian widows was so miserable they probably thought they'd be better off dead."

While in India, Dr. Bostock married Victor Sherman, an English bank manager, and in 1936 they moved to Victoria. For ten years Dr. Sherman kept busy with church work, extensive reading, running her home and bringing up her young stepdaughter. Then, in 1946, she abruptly "went to the devil."

"In looking back, I often wonder why it took me so long to become an atheist," says Dr. Sherman. "Probably one reason was that I had the best and kindest of parents and when you admire your father and mother it's more difficult to think of them as having been wrong. It's much easier to reject parental teachings if you feel rebellious."

In 1956 Dr. Sherman banded together with a dozen other freethinkers to form the Victoria Humanist Fellowship, which later became an affiliated chapter of the American Humanist Association. Since then, the group, now numbering twenty-five, has met regularly to discuss social, scientific, religious and welfare problems.

"There are also humanist groups in Montreal, Saskatoon, Winnipeg, and Toronto; in Britain and in other European countries, particularly Holland," says Dr. Sherman.

Outstanding humanists include Brock Chisholm, director-general of the World Health Organization from 1948 to '53; philosopher Lord Bertrand Russell; biologist Sir Julian Huxley; and Margaret Sanger, founder of the Planned Parenthood Association.

Last September the Victoria Humanist Fellowship launched a sixteen-page magazine which ranges over such topics as capital punishment, evolution and birth control. In the eight years since the group's founding, it has also involved itself in a few offbeat controversies that unmistakably show Dr. Sherman's guiding hand.

One of these took place in February when the B.C. Department of Health attempted to combat the growing incidence of venereal diseases in the province by putting up posters in public washrooms showing a slinky redhead and reading "four out of five pickups have V.D."

"That made my blood boil. It wasn't fair to blame the spread of V.D. completely on the women," indignantly exclaimed Dr. Sherman, who has a broad streak of the suffragette in her.

With backing of the other humanists, she wrote to Minister of Health Eric Martin requesting the removal of the signs. "The few that were left were taken down," she says. "But by then most had been snapped up by souvenir-hunters. Apparently you can still buy them at premium prices."

Today Dr. Sherman feels that one of the main stumbling blocks to social acceptance for the atheist is still the old concept that religion is necessary to morality.

"Because I'm not a moral degenerate people keep saying to me 'You *can't* be an atheist.' When I insist I am, they reply 'You're not. I don't believe you.' It's most annoying."

However, Dr. Sherman feels there are clear indications that the position of the atheist is improving both in Canada and in the world. One national example is the success of the Bergsma case. Another is a just-published United Church of Canada survey in which ninety per cent of the clergy supported freedom of speech "even for Communists, French-Canadian separatists and atheists."

The Vatican has also taken a more charitable view of the atheist: Before Easter it was announced that Pope Paul had revised the title of the Good Friday "Prayer for the Conversion of the Infidels" to "Prayer for the Conversion of Non-Believers."

Even Dr. Sherman, long an outcast of traditional religion, is beginning to feel the warm winds of change. "Some months ago I received a nice letter from the St. George's Women's Auxiliary inviting me to their sixtieth reunion," she says wryly. "The women even ended up having their pictures taken with me for the newspapers . . . Times *are* better than ever."

Dora Russell

35

Dora Russell

THE HERETICAL "GIRTON GIRL"

1894 – May 31, 1986

It is no mere accident that Christianity is a good fighting religion.
The Right To Be Happy, 1927

DORA BLACK RUSSELL IS BEST-KNOWN for her marriage to Bertrand Russell, but was a British activist and writer in her own right. The couple, who had two children, John and Kate, opened a progressive school for children, Telegraph House, in West Sussex in the 1920s.

Dora was part of a happy family which let her be a tomboy and enrolled her in a competitive girls' high school. She became one of the elegant "Girton girls" and a freethinker, joining the Heretics' Society and attending many lectures in Cambridge.

"I can recall the very moment when, at my prayers, it occurred to me that the extreme of Christian renunciation amounted to the virtual annihilation of oneself." (Russell, *Tamarisk Tree*: 38) She rejected Pascal's wager as unworthy and Paley's evidences as absurd.

In her autobiography Dora wrote: "At Girton I still wore boned corsets with back lacings which, still proud of small waists, we would pull in tightly. . . . Looking back I have wondered how women ever managed to free themselves from their corsets, frills and furbelows and the iron straight-jacket imposed on them by religion, morality and social sanctions. One might wonder also at the emancipation of men's minds from dogma and the abstruse and obscurantist flights of traditional idealistic philosophy which took place during the first quarter of the twentieth century." (pp. 40–41)

During her first meeting with Russell in 1916, the student Dora expressed a desire to be a mother and a wife someday, which appealed to Russell, fatherless and in his forties. Eventually Dora gave up a fellowship from Girton to be with

Bertie; Dora agreed to accompany Russell to China where he had accepted an invitation to teach for a year at the National University of Peking. They got married when Dora was pregnant.

Dora noted: "I became ever more hostile to religious teaching, seeing it as the negation of life; what is more, it was the basis of our whole economic and political structure. Like Voltaire I cried: *Ecrasez l'infame!*" (p. 176)

Dora was an advocate of birth control, attending several world conferences meeting on "the sex question," and petitioning the government for reform. In 1924, Dora and a colleague coined a saying: "It is four times as dangerous to bear a child as to work in a mine, and mining is men's most dangerous trade." A return visit to the Soviet Union, where abortion had been legalized, piqued her interest in abortion rights. She was instrumental in screening a Russian medical film about abortion in Great Britain in 1929.

Her first book, *Hypatia*, dedicated to her daughter Kate and published in 1925, responded to an antiwoman book called *Lysistrata*. In the preface, Dora wrote:

"Hypatia was a University lecturer denounced by Church dignitaries and torn to pieces by Christians. Such will probably be the fate of this book: therefore it bears her name. What I have written here I believe, and shall not retract or change for similar episcopal denunciations."

The 81-page book, written in an exuberant style of dated romanticism, dealt with the "sex war" and feminist issues, advocating liberated clothing and exercise for young women, their right to sexual pleasure and birth control, and a rational attitude toward pregnancy and motherhood, with criticism of Christianity implicit throughout. A review in the *Sunday Express* called it a "book that should be banned." Consequently, it sold six hundred copies in a week, and was later translated in many countries.

Her next book, *The Right To Be Happy* (1927), was "my manifesto against that religion of the machine age . . . I had more and more come to believe that the dualism of mind and matter was at the root of what was false and dangerous in Western philosophy and religion." In it she wrote: "It is no mere accident that Christianity is a good fighting religion. . . ." (pp. 193, 265)

In 1928 she was invited to the United States for a lecture tour. "Chiefly my audiences were interested in advanced views on sex and marriage, but at that date there was much less freedom in speaking about sex in the States than at home in England," Dora wrote. "I remarked that in England you might say what you liked on these topics so long as you *did* nothing, whereas in America you might *do* as you wished provided you did not speak of it." (*Tamarisk Tree:* 203)

An advertised lecture on the protection of women at the University of Wisconsin resulted in a ban on speaking on sex questions by President Glenn Frank. Her rather academic lecture, defying the ban, must have seemed anticlimactic, she thought.

Dora was the practical administrator of the Telegraph Hill school, which she kept going for several years after she and Bertie divorced, messily, in 1935. Their "open marriage," then not-uncommon among leftist couples, led to the disintegration of their relationship after Bertie "transferred his affections" to another woman, and after Dora gave birth to two additional children fathered by a lover.

❦

While overshadowed by her famous former husband, Dora retained a lifelong interest in progressive questions. She recorded that H. G. Wells once sent her an admiring postcard: "Bertie thinks, I write, but you DO." (*Tamarisk Tree:* 189)

She participated in the Independent Labour Party, and was treated as a subversive when she represented the Womens' International Democratic Federation at the United Nations in 1954. In 1958 she led a Women's Caravan of Peace to European countries.

Besides her autobiographical series, she also wrote *In Defense of Children* (1932) [see selection] and co-wrote with Russell *Prospects of Industrial Civilization*. In her last book *The Religion of the Machine Age*, first started in 1922 but finished sixty years later, Dora expressed her views on the origin of religion, and its harm:

"When the male of the species, enamoured of his stargazing, set up a God outside this planet as arbiter of all events upon it, and repudiated nature, together with sex, for a promised dream of a future life, he turned his back on that creative life and inspiration that lay within himself and his partnership with woman. In very truth he sold his birthright for a mess of pottage." (p. 236)

She retained her deep feminist commitment and continued to speak before groups such as the Rationalist Press Association, giving one of her best talks on a "Challenge to Humanism" in 1982 before that body: "It is time for humanity to reach maturity and at long last assume responsibility—as far as it in us lies—for creating a tolerable existence for everything that lives on our planet." (Spender, *Dora Russell Reader:* 233) Dora received a posthumous "Distinguished Service Award" from the American Humanist Association.

"Religious Training"

This is excerpted from the chapter "Religious Trainers" from Dora Russell's book **In Defense of Children** *(1932).*

PROBABLY MANY PEOPLE WHO, as children, were fed with religious ideas can remember as I can the haunting god figures of their fantasy. To these one made expiatory sacrifices, calling upon the gods of the sea to come up and devour sand-castles on which patient hours of work had been expended, in the avowed service of the god who was to eat them. Sometimes the gods were given the names of clergymen, or of male father substitutes, known and admired. Such fantasies were always tinged with the fear of wrath and a sense of sin and helpless submission. In spite of kind parents and a happy life the vision of God as all-pervasive, sheltering love fails to penetrate. I doubt if there is any way to teach belief in God to a young child without making him afraid. Fear is always waiting round the corner for him, anyway. The warm familiar bed and sunlit nursery are greater reassurance than adding yet another to the prowling power shadows. How terrifying are the stories of this queer God read aloud in church every Sunday or absorbed in Sunday school and Bible-reading! God is being taught in just this way, as I write, to the majority of children in Christendom.

Let us go back to the analysis of Christian psychology. Is not its central fallacy that it glorifies the flowers and leaves, while despising the roots? Each of us a unique individual before God, we were told to love and understand each neighbour as a unique individual. But biological preoccupations, loyalties and rivalries were too strong to permit that sudden spring forward. We issued from these preoccupations and, at each attempt to escape, they surge back upon us like a sea, God the Father riding the waves. It is quite true that at the bottom of each of us lies a hard core of self-preserving egoism. Family feelings, such as they are, are the only instinctive means we have of dissolving this selfishness. When the Christian idealist bade us turn from the family to a wider generosity, we hastily severed our family roots from which alone our generous impulses sprang. Then, facing our lonely selves, we found out just how selfish we are. Prisoners of our self-regarding dreams and desires, we were unable to project our sympathy deep into our neighbors. So we turned on ourselves, preaching and scolding, as so often the disappointed idealist turns on the society he wants to reform. Thus were we convicted of sin, and saw no escape from our heritage of iniquity. Soon we drew our neighbour into the circle of condemnation. We did indeed regard him as ourselves, and as a very wicked person at that. One step more, and we had forgotten ourselves in our righteous zeal to punish him.

Something like this seems to me a consequence of the Christian approach to psychology.

Does not this analysis offer some explanation of how Christian morality, as it became a social force, has twisted love and distorted human rights? An individual truly conscious of the sin of selfishness must be humble; he could have no "rights," nor admit that his neighbour had them. "In the course of justice none of us should see salvation, we do pray for mercy—" but "that same prayer" does *not*, in practice, "teach us all to render the deeds of mercy." [Portia's court speech in *The Merchant of Venice*.] On the contrary, it makes us think of Christian charity or love as something condescending and magnanimous. We may extend it to fellow sinners, as grace or pardon, but not as their right. And the more conscious we become of the gulf between our natural fleshly selfishness, and the ideal of all embracing generosity the more do we separate the weak flesh from the soaring spirit. That goes on until we live in two worlds, the one of dreams and the other of sinful earthly life into which we are born, to which we are bound and from which we can only escape by death into the kingdom of heaven.

This Christian paradox is amazing. It is through the body that we immolate ourselves in love for one another, through the body that we bring forth children, toil to feed them, die to make room for them. . . . Yet we have turned on the body, beating it, starving it, despising it, hating and fearing its beauty, denying to it its pleasures. So doing, we have retarded for generations the coming of the blessed kingdom we professed to desire. We have demanded fruits and flowers without roots or soil. For everything that we are capable of proceeds from the body—our love, our imagination, our intellect, our power to acquire knowledge, our strength and health to put knowledge to use. The technique of our repressive morality has failed utterly. To find another and a more hopeful one, we must not only revise but tear up root and branch our fundamental assumptions.

See how vitally our philosophy has affected the rearing of children. They were the weakest in our midst, with the greatest claim to our mercy and understanding. But we have felt them to be partners in our human sin and suffering. They had to be born haphazard and endure, like ourselves, at God's will. So that for a long while we did not extend to them even the amount of concern we gave to the cattle in the stall or the sheep upon the moor. We did not stop to think, as we did perforce about the food plants on which we depended, what might be the needs of their tender bodies and minds, or how they might differ from us in capacity to understand the rules by which we lived. They had immortal souls but they, like us, were born in sin. So we beat them until they acted according to our morality and consented to learn what we wished in the way we wished to teach it. If they seemed stupid, we took it as another sign of their stubbornness and unregeneration. It did not occur to us until very recent times that they might be ill or defective or terror-struck. . . . Our social care of human beings is still, in the main, remedial patchwork because we have in our bones the old religious notion that life is a suffering of punishment for sin.

Our knowledge of medical science, of how to prevent or assist birth or mitigate pain, our study of human anatomy and psychology, our inventions for making economic life more comfortable and secure, have been impeded for centuries by the same kind of religious prejudices. It was wrong to try and escape pain, wrong to seek comfort, wrong to study our sinful and mortal bodies. Divine knowledge in sacred books should occupy the human intelligence; contemplation of the divine attributes of God or the kingdom to come should fill the human imagination.

We are often reminded that the first hospitals, orphanages and schools were founded under religious auspices. This is true enough, but it does not alter the fact that the bias, and presently the very existence, of these was a barrier to scientific progress. Thought struggled free finally only in the seventeenth century. Scientific thought has had two hundred years; religious systems all the past before that. Comparison between what the two methods have done for humanity needs no emphasis.

The new approach is a complete reversal of the old. It starts at the bottom instead of the top; it builds a morality slowly, instead of framing arbitrary laws; it analyses details and pieces them together, instead of imposing a synthesis of general principles. It works in the concrete instead of the abstract. It assumes a right not to suffer, to control destiny instead of enduring it. Instead of comforting with dreams it tries to make dreams come true. To help the human being, his body is studied, his heredity examined, his mother's pregnancy cared for, his birth well attended. When he is in the world,—which is the matter we are concerned with here—his egoism is accepted as the prime basis of his life instead of being scolded as sin. His nature is seen as something whose germ he derives first from his heredity and then slowly builds about him like a silkworm its cocoon, out of all the experiences that befall him. He is not mind and body, but one stuff, woven into a pattern. He has no mind or soul until he has built one up out of his sensuous experience. At no point can you jerk him violently onward without risk of tearing his warp and woof. You cannot make him love, or make him "good" or make him learn, any more than you can actually force him to grow. You can help him to do these things and you can twist him so that he hates or closes himself to learning, just as you can, by clumsy feeding or care, make him have crooked legs. How he grows and assimilates, how best to teach him at all stages, must be the objects of patient and sympathetic research, like watching the growth of crystals, the genetics of plants or the processes of chemistry. For this task no human being with the religious bias is fitted. Yet these are the kind of people to whom child care is traditionally committed. Morally speaking, good, unselfish, devoted people, upheld by strong principles and beliefs. Psychologically speaking, clumsy brutes, like bulls in a china shop or gardeners whose heavy boots go down inadvertently on the seedlings. Their methods are raw and uncivilised. This is good, that bad; this is punished, that rewarded; this may be said, that must be repressed. Children are beaten and despised; young minds and growing bodies are ridden with a steam-roller and a harrow.

No person who continues to hold traditional morals and religion can get free of the guilt idea in dealing with children. Nurses are frequently good and devoted; they are trained to be so, whether they are sick nurses or specialised for child care. But their conventional moral bias is profound. Once I tried to find a school matron with good training who believed, positively, in not teaching religion to children. One historic English paper refused my advertisement. When I interviewed applicants, they all said that they had supposed I meant undenominational religion, but they could not entertain the thought of no religion at all. One by one they faded out of the door. One of the most up-to-date bureaus in London for supplying trained nurses would not help me because I refused to conceal any of the facts of sex from children under my care. . . . You may say that if children are not punished they will not be good; if they are not rewarded, they will not work; if they know everything about sex, they will be nasty and immoral; if they can say and do what they please, they will be rough and bullying. Or that a child cannot have anything worthwhile to express until he has learnt some of the wisdom and beauty of the ages. Dear adult, he is potentially more virtuous than you, more industrious, less bored, less vindictive, clearer in his bodily impulses and curiosities, more ready than you to speak kindly when he feels so, just as he is more prompt to express his resentment. He is more ready than you for give and take and, when he really feels, more deeply compassionate. Give him the right to the core of his egoism, to pride in his body and his achievements. It is through these, and through contact and conflict with the same things in others that he learns to love, to tolerate and to admire. Not by the dark road of self-doubt and humiliation.

And has he nothing to express? Of course not, if you have frightened him with taboos on subjects, manners and words. If you have not, the flood of his knowledge and of his emotions, the beauty of his language, the grace of his movement and gesture, will overwhelm you, if you watch carefully. Free and healthy children are never bored and empty. The world is their oyster. I have seen children take off their mental, moral and physical clothes, seen how their backs can straighten, limbs ripen and turn brown, eyes brighten. I have seen them make and remake morals by direct experience, seen them turn in happiness and pride to tasks they would never have voluntarily undertaken in sorrow and humiliation.

To see such things has made me more than ever a rebel against what religion has done.

Meridel Le Sueur
(Photograph by Paul Gaylor)

36

Meridel Le Sueur

LUMINOUS WITH AGE

February 1900 – November 14, 1996

Women especially would like to believe that her [my mother's] talents were God-given. But it was not so. Her anger, her strength, her determination, even her brilliance and her oratory were things she developed, often alone, and struggled and fought for, as much as Frederick Douglass had to struggle even to read. In Texas her husband divorced her on the grounds of dangerous thoughts gleaned from reading books!

Crusaders, 1955

Freethinker Meridel Le Sueur

by Annie Laurie Gaylor

This article originally appeared as "She is Luminous with Age" in the Feminist Connection, Madison, Wisconsin, October 1982.

WHEN MIDWEST AUTHOR MERIDEL LE SUEUR wrote "Annunciation," an evocative story about a woman's feelings about her pregnancy, one of the male editors to whom she submitted the piece said to her:

"You write about such strange things—a childbirth!?!"

When Meridel pointed out it was not a strange subject to half the human race, the editor told her to try writing more like Ernest Hemingway.

If she spoke anything like she does today, her response must have rung out clear, crisp and quick:

"Fishing, fighting, and fucking," Meridel told her editor, "are not my major interests!"

"Annunciation," one of the first short stories examining the emotions of pregnancy, was published privately in 1927, then included in an anthology of best short stories of the year.

Today readers can find it and many of Meridel Le Sueur's stories and reportage in an anthology published in 1982 by Feminist Press, appropriately entitled *Ripening*. Appropriate because, as she writes in one of her recent poems, she is "luminous with age."

Meridel's age is etched artistically in a plenitude of soft wrinkles and wonderfully wrinkled dimples, her face framed by silky white hair. But it is her eyes that draw an observer—they are a rich brown and stand out boldly in her pale face, hinting at her Indian ancestry.

But no one must forget to remark on her nose, once called "too Semitic" by a Hollywood producer. His contract requiring that she have it broken and reset disgusted her and tolled the death knell of a career in the new moving pictures she hadn't been particularly interested in to begin with.

Feminist writer Patricia Hampl once said of Meridel: "Bedecked with Indian turquoise bracelets and rings, a string of large ominous teeth around her neck, a bright multicolored serape covering her body—this walking heap of archetypal images is not your idea of somebody's grandmother. A grandmother, no; a wise and maybe occasionally avenging ancient goddess, yes."

The description may be apt (Meridel is still sporting a magnificent piece of Indian artistry around her neck) but its conclusions are wrong. Meridel is very much a mother, grandmother, and even great-grandmother (of twenty—"all socialists" no less). She is quick to admit, "you don't have to do anything but live long enough" to achieve such a status, but her pleasure in her descendants is clear.

Meridel Le Sueur made a visit to Madison in mid-September at the request of Madison admirers, and during an interview with the *Feminist Connection*, she was warm, responsive, downright jolly. Afterwards, she leaned forward expectantly for a goodbye kiss she knew was her due. Meridel Le Sueur definitely is more than "an ancient goddess."

True, a small band of listeners paid her homage during the interview, listening eagerly, and the evening before, one hundred and fifty came to pay their respects. After the interview, U.S. Rep. Bob Kastenmeier paid a surprise courtesy call.

But if homage is being given, it is in recognition of the ritual performed by her pen moving over countless sheets of paper for almost seven decades. Meridel's listeners also realize, as they know when confronted with any "ancient," that they are looking at a precious piece of history with all its secrets.

It is not often we hear our grandmothers speak of hobnobbing with the likes of Emma Goldman, being blacklisted during the McCarthy era, and of marching on countless picket lines.

Grandmotherhood came passively if pleasantly enough to Meridel, but motherhood was something she chose as deliberately as she chose her political and creative work. She explains that in the twenties, in her strata, people took seriously H. L. Mencken's admonition against producing more "cannon-fodder." Meridel had to justify, in a time of depression, her choice.

She remembers the precise moment she made that choice.

She and many others were arrested and jailed protesting the Sacco and Vanzetti execution, and were kept imprisoned until it was all over. That evening, Meridel resolved to have a child. She thought, "The only thing to do was replace their lives."

She had two daughters, Rachel and Deborah, who figure highly in her writings of the thirties and who, Meridel says, now mother her.

At eighty-two years, she walks slowly and is of an age to need some mothering. She is feisty yet, with work to accomplish before what she has called the time when she "drops from the peach tree."

For example, she has accumulated four boxes of research on Robert Emmett, the last Irishman hanged by the English.

Then there are four novels she plans to finish "before the Great Reaper mows me down."

Excerpts of some of her most recent work—she writes eight hours a day "no matter what"—are included in *Ripening*. For the first time, Meridel says "I am writing what I want to write. I don't know if anyone is going to read it," she adds with the pragmatism of someone whose work was virtually banned for years. "I don't even think about it. I just love it. It's a wonderful gift to have a passion like that."

It is Meridel's opinion that there is not only a greater creative life for women after menopause, but that "You may have greater creative life after seventy."

When she turned seventy, she relates whimsically, a doctor, commenting on her age, advised, "Just take these tranquilizers." He proceeded to regale her with a numbing description of decay.

She assured him that she "expected to do my best work" in the next decade, a prophecy she feels she has fulfilled.

Wryly, she says as an afterthought, "In three years, that doctor was dead."

Her four new novels are essentially written, but she is revising them. She calls it "getting in my crop before the frost."

Life began for Meridel in Iowa in February 1900. Eventually, her family moved to Texas. When she was about nine, her mother Marian Wharton "kidnapped" Meridel and her siblings from their preacher-father and from Texas.

Oklahoma, a brand new state, was then very radical—for the first two years women could even vote—and her father's extradition attempts failed.

Not without a fight, however. When Meridel was about eleven, she had to go to court to choose which parent she wished to stay with.

"The judge told me my mother could never make a living." He also told her that her mother was a "whore"! "I didn't know what that was," so Meridel didn't mind. Besides, "I knew we would never starve."

Marian Wharton soon became a lecturer on the famous Chautauqua circuit. Her topic: "Love and Bread;" the theme, that it is foolish to talk of love if you have no bread.

"Women used to come after the lecture and *beg* for contraception or abortion information," Meridel recalls. The penalty, she said, could be life imprisonment for such treacherous talk.

Her mother was arrested for giving what advice she could to a woman with fourteen children. "The only thing that saved her is the woman refused to identify her," Meridel explained. She was released in about a year, and in the meantime Meridel's mother and other community women helped take care of her children.

Meridel let this information digest for a moment, then added, "We've come pretty far!"

Her mother was a feminist, who, after leaving her husband, "became very different kinds of radicals, testing it out." She married Arthur Le Sueur, a socialist lawyer, and became involved in populist movements both in Fort Scott, Kansas, and later in St. Paul, Minnesota.

Meridel's grandmother had likewise been an activist, who obtained a divorce and supported her children at a time when divorce was nearly taboo. She divorced her husband because he was "drinking up the farm."

Her grandmother as a single parent not only succeeded in sending both her daughters to college, but was active in the Women's Christian Temperance Union. She traveled all over Oklahoma in a buggy holding a shotgun for the WCTU, "fearless and indefatigable."

Meridel hastens to explain that the temperance movement was radical in concept, similar to the movement today to help battered women.

Meridel's grandmother was also a Puritan, even denying the Indian heritage of her Iroquois mother.

"I could never find out her name," Meridel says. "The family never accepted her." The marriage license simply lists Meridel's great-grand-mother as "Squaw."

With Meridel's rich and varied background, influenced by active and aware women, it should not be so surprising that by age eleven, Meridel was already a socialist, and already conscious of a void in literature, a fail-ure to describe the lives of women and the real people she knew. She be-gan to write.

By age fifteen, Meridel quit high school, briefly studied dance in Chi-cago, and began studying acting in New York at the American Academy of Dramatic Art.

"My *mother* wanted to be an actress so she sent *me* to the American Academy to fulfill her interest," Meridel noted drily. For Meridel herself was "timid and shy."

While studying and working in New York, she originally went to live at the Anarchist's House—her mother was trying out anarchism at the time.

Emma Goldman lived there too. Describe Emma Goldman? Her in-terest to Meridel was as "the first sexually 'free' woman" she met. "The women and feminists of that period never dealt with sex. They were Puri-tans."

Meridel at fifteen had an introduction to one interpretation of "free love" herself, when attending a salon held by Mabel Dodge, a rich patron of radicals. ("Emma was good at getting rich women to give money.")

At Meridel's first salon, "Theodore Dreiser spent the entire evening—I was fifteen years old!—chasing me around the library."

Meridel had read Dreiser's banned book, *Sister Carrie*. "He kept say-ing, don't you know who I am? and I said, yes, I thought you were the greatest author in the country but I didn't know you were a satyr!"

To this day Meridel cannot imagine why Dreiser would imagine himself a Don Juan: "He had a face that looked like someone just threw him together."

As fifteen year old Meridel fled her literary satyr, she recalls, Edna St. Vincent Millay happened on the scene. Meridel thought she was saved, but Millay left, finally returning later to rescue the besieged girl.

Millay then criticized Meridel for resisting. "Your children could know you'd slept with Theodore Dreiser," she told the unimpressed Meridel, who replied, "But I don't even know him!" After a long lecture, Millay then "did a terrible thing." She publicly related the story to salon-goers, calling Meridel "the corn virgin from Kansas."

Meridel left the commune when she offended Emma Goldman because she went to dinner with a soldier from the midwest going overseas. Radicals had already been arrested for protesting World War I.

Meridel never regretted the dinner; it was to be his last in America. He was killed in the war.

Meanwhile Meridel continued working on stage; "I didn't have any other skills." One job included being in the chorus of "Leave It To Jane," where she had to step on an electric grill that made her hair stand on end.

At twenty-one she went to Hollywood, which, she said, has been built upon "the bodies of beautiful midwestern girls, including myself."

Meridel described the morning lineup. "They'd look at you, pull up your skirt to look at your legs like a mare, look at your teeth." Not surprisingly, she said, huge prostitution rings existed within the system.

Meridel found work as a stunt-woman. "Many were killed doing stunts, and I was almost killed jumping off a burning ship." Meridel also worked as a stand-in for Pearl White in "The Perils of Pauline."

The final straw came when she was presented with a contract which required her to have surgery performed on her nose. She remembers being told, "No American heroine could have a Semite nose like mine."

This "insult to my feminist integrity" prompted her to check out of Hollywood and into California theater.

The twenties were hard years for Meridel and many of her friends. Many radicals were harassed in the political crackdown following the war of the world.

Through it all Meridel wrote. She also supported herself, just as her mother and grandmother had done before her.

Meridel's work was first published in 1927. "I never thought of being a writer. I thought more of being an interpreter, or recorder."

In addition to her published work, Meridel has one hundred and forty notebooks stored in her basement in St. Paul.

"Tillie Olsen ('Tell Me a Riddle') came down to my basement last year and burst into tears" at the sight of them, Meridel noted. She tried to persuade Meridel to Xerox them as a precaution, but Meridel only wonders where she would store the copies.

Several state historical societies have contacted Meridel about obtaining her journals and papers, but Meridel can only think: "Then they would belong to the state. I've been fighting the state all my life!"

She wonders whether her papers would be safe, should another era of repressions swoop down on America. And she has a right to wonder and worry, because her books were virtually banned for about twelve years. "They even had to sell my children's books like contraband."

That was not the extent of it. FBI agents tailed Meridel. When she worked as a teacher, students were followed and warned away.

Restaurant owners who hired her as a waitress were contacted, and fired her. "For two years we had two men sitting outside our door. That must have cost a fortune." Her phone was tapped.

"People couldn't speak to you. I stopped going to the theater because I felt sorry for the people who couldn't speak to me.

"They made you an invisible person."

Eventually Meridel and her mother, then seventy-five, opened a rooming house. The FBI made it impossible to find renters after her mother died. Finally, the FBI planted two dope sellers.

What did she do then? "I got a job as a chauffeur for a woman with one leg. Best job I had. She didn't mind the FBI. I could write then." However, the desperation of the times had severely interrupted her writing.

Looking back at that period, Meridel muses, "It's really hard to describe how you can fill a city with terror. When you look at it chronologically, it's terrifying to see how close you are to fascism."

The repression of her work was successful until six women from Boston in the early 1970s contacted her about republishing some of her writings from the 1930s. They printed it in an anthology, *Song For My Time*.

In 1973, West End Press published *The Girl*, a book that had been in

Meridel's basement since the 1930s, which became a bestseller in anti-Establishment circles.

Meridel has enjoyed being "rediscovered" by the feminist press, particularly because of her chance to work with women editors.

Her male editors typically had "such a superior attitude—even in punctuation." Whereas, she contrasts, "The Feminist Press wouldn't even change a comma without asking." The format of *Ripening*, with its biography, commentary and scrapbook photos, "would never have been conceived in male printing," she notes.

Trashing the women writers has resulted in the neglect of twenty midwest women writers—"some as good as Sandburg or Lewis"—now out of print, Meridel says unhappily.

She cites as an example her friend and Wisconsin author Zona Gale, who won a Pulitzer Prize in 1921 ("for a feminist story"), yet is virtually forgotten and unread today.

Meridel "repudiates categories of male literature." She politely answered all questions about times and dates, but mildly remarked, "Linear thinking is patriarchal."

Meridel is acutely aware of politics (she reads the *Wall Street Journal* to "find out what those rascals are doing") and current literature ("some of the best poetry is being written by three American Indian women"). She is also optimistic.

"The whole temper of the world is in a much higher consciousness than I've even seen it—there's a global consciousness. I think we're on the verge of a new humanity if we don't blow it up!"

Her advice to the women's movement is to avoid male prototypes: "It has to be a collective vision. The time is over entirely for private vision, or private greed. We're entering a new era of the same fate for all."

Perhaps Meridel Le Sueur's wisest and most comforting words to women of the world are found in a line of a poem of solidarity she composed for the North Vietnamese Women's Union:

"It was the bumble bee and the butterfly who survived, not the dinosaur."

37

Margaret Knight

BBC'S "UNHOLY MENACE"

November 23, 1903 – 1983

Ethical teaching is weakened if it is tied up with dogmas that will not bear examination.

Morals Without Religion, 1955

BORN IN HERTFORDSHIRE, ENGLAND, Margaret Horsey attended Girton, Cambridge, receiving her Bachelor's degree in 1926 and her Master's in 1948.

"I had been uneasy about religion throughout my adolescence, but I had not had the moral courage to throw off my beliefs until my third year at Cambridge," Margaret wrote in the preface to *Morals Without Religion*. After reading philosophers such as Bertrand Russell: "A fresh, cleansing wind swept through the stuffy room that contained the relics of my religious beliefs. I let them go with a profound sense of relief, and ever since I have lived happily without them."

From 1926–1936, Margaret worked as editor of the journal published by the National Institute of Industrial Psychology, and also as their librarian and information officer. She married Arthur Knight, a professor of psychology, in 1936, and moved to Aberdeen, Scotland, lecturing in psychology at the University of Aberdeen from 1936–1970.

She wrote several textbooks with her husband, including *Modern Introduction to Psychology*, first published in 1948, which went into a seventh edition in 1966, and *William James: A Selection from His Writings*, 1950.

Margaret became a celebrity across Great Britain when she achieved the freethought *coup* of giving a series of freethought lectures on the BBC radio.

"I was convinced that, besides millions of frank unbelievers, there are today large numbers of half-believers to whom religion is a source of intellectual and moral discomfort. . . . Today, the position of the doubter is in some respects more difficult than it was in my youth," pointing to the stereotype of "atheistic communism."

"It is difficult, none the less, for the ordinary man to cast off orthodox beliefs, for he is seldom allowed to hear the other side. . . . Whereas the Christian view is pressed on him day in and day out."

In 1953, several years after the Corporation had announced that it affirmed the need to broadcast differing beliefs, even unbelief, Margaret submitted a draft script. It got into the hands of a Catholic in a key position, and "was rather forcibly rejected," she recalled. She did not give up, and in July 1954, was invited to Broadcasting House to discuss her proposal, which centered on criticism of the idea that moral education for children must be in the context of religious instruction. The BBC suggested that since she was a psychologist, she could broaden her approach to include "positive advice to nonChristian parents on the moral training of children."

Her goal was "to show the intellectual weakness of the case for theism, but my chief aim was to combat the view that there can be no true morality without supernatural sanctions. So I argued at length that the social, or altruistic, impulses are the real source of morality, and that an ethic based on these impulses has far more claim on our allegiance than an ethic based on obedience to the commands of a God who created tapeworms and cancer-cells."

She gave her first talk on January 5, 1955 to uneventful press, but soon the fireworks began. The *Daily Express* wrote an accurate account of her lecture, headlined: "Woman Psychologist Makes Remarkable Radio Attack on Religion for Children." A *Daily Telegraph* columnist demanded that God and the BBC forbid a second broadcast. The *Sunday Graphic* ran a snapshot of Margaret next to a headline with two-inch letters, "The Unholy Mrs. Knight." It began, "Don't let this woman fool you. She looks—doesn't she—just like the typical housewife; cool, comfortable, harmless. But Mrs. Margaret Knight is a menace. A dangerous woman. Make no mistake about that."

After her second broadcast, the uproar continued, although she simply issued solid, humanistic advice to parents, such as "to provide a firm, secure background of affection so that it never occurs to the child to doubt that he is loved and wanted." Parents can help curb aggressive tendencies, without setting impossibly high standards of unselfishness. The problematic act, not the child, should be condemned, she said. Despite hyperbole and condemning headlines, the accurate news reports conveyed her message to an even larger audience. Following her final broadcast, she returned home to Aberdeen to find five hundred letters awaiting her.

Her BBC lectures appeared in her 1955 book, *Morals Without Religion*. She compiled a *Humanist Anthology* in 1961 which was revised in 1995 by James Herrick.

Morals Without Religion

This is from the first chapter of the book **Morals Without Religion** *(1955).*

THESE TALKS ARE ADDRESSED to the ordinary man and woman, whose attitude towards religion is that they do not quite know what they believe. They were married in church; they have had the children baptised; and they still on rare occasions go to church, though mainly for social reasons; but they do not pretend to believe the creeds they repeat there. Their general feeling is that it does not much matter what views a man holds on the higher management of the universe, so long as he has the right views on how to behave to his neighbour. And they are not at all troubled about religion, except for one thing: what shall they teach the children?

For where intellectual doubts are concerned, this ordinary parent's feeling is: 'Who am I to judge? I find these doctrines hard to believe, but many very able men believe them—men who have studied the subject much more fully than I have.' Furthermore, parents are repeatedly told that Christianity is the only alternative to communism, and that there can be no sound character-training that is not based on religion. When juvenile delinquency increased after the war, they heard on all sides that this was the inevitable result of the decay of religious belief and the lack of sound religious training in the home; and in 1944 a new Education Act was passed, by which daily prayers and religious instruction were made compulsory in the state schools. So, on the whole, our ordinary parent thinks it is best to take no risks. When the children are older they can decide for themselves; meanwhile, better bring them up in the orthodox way—talk to them about God; teach them to say their prayers; take them to church occasionally; and try to stave off awkward questions.

I want here to make three suggestions: first, that the doubts the ordinary man feels about religion are justified, and need not be stifled or concealed; second, that there is no ground for the view that Christianity is the only alternative to communism, or that there can be no sound character-training that is not based on religion; and, third, I want to make some practical suggestions to the parents who are not believers, on what they should tell the children about God, and what sort of moral training they should give them.

The first thing I want to do is to define 'religion,' for it is a term that is used in a great many senses. Sometimes when people say they 'believe in religion' they turn out to mean little more than that they believe in a moral standard, or that they believe there are more important things in life than money and worldly success. I need scarcely say that I have no quarrel with religion in either of these senses. But this is not really a correct use of the term. The *Oxford Dictionary* defines 'religion' as 'Recognition on the part of man of some higher unseen power as having control of his destiny, and as being entitled to obedience, reverence and worship.' That is the sense in which I shall use the term religion in these talks; and by 'Christianity' I mean over and above that, the beliefs essential to the Christian religion—that is, at least, that this 'unseen power' is omnipotent, and wholly good; that Christ was divine; that he rose from the dead; and that human beings survive bodily death. That is a bare minimum of Christian belief: there is far more than that in the official creeds of the Churches.

I am not out to destroy the Christian convictions of people in whom they are deeply implanted and to whom they mean a great deal. And I am sure that nothing I say here will have the slightest effect on believers of this type. But what I do want to argue is that, in a climate of thought that is increasingly unfavourable to these beliefs, it is a mistake to try to impose them on children, and to make them the basis of moral training. The moral education of children is much too important a matter to be built on such foundations.

In any religious argument, one is sooner or later reminded that 'science isn't everything' and that 'logic isn't everything.' That is perfectly true; there are many human activities—art, music, poetry, for example—to which science and logic are more or less irrelevant. But religion is not in this category, for religion, unlike art and music and poetry, is a system of belief. And a system of belief that is to be acceptable must satisfy the ordinary criteria of reason: the beliefs must be consistent with each other and not obviously in conflict with fact. Orthodox Christian beliefs, I suggest, do not satisfy these criteria.

I will just take one point which I think is crucial. Orthodox Christian theology is completely inconsistent with the facts of evil. This was not so obvious in the old days when people believed in the Devil. To regard the universe as a battlefield between God and the Devil, with the odds on God, so to speak, at least did not do violence to the facts. But now most

Christians have ceased to believe in the Devil; and the orthodox view is (as indeed it always was, but the Devil got slipped in somehow) that the universe is controlled by a single, all-powerful and wholly benevolent Power, and that everything that happens, happens by his will. And that raises insuperable intellectual difficulties. For why should this all-powerful and wholly benevolent Being have created so much evil? It is no answer to say that evil is just a means to good. In the first place, there is no reason to believe this is always true; and in the second place, even if it were true it would not be an answer; for a Being who was really all-powerful would not need to use evil means to attain his ends. It is no answer to say that God is not responsible for the evil—that evil is due to man, who has misused his freewill and defied God's edicts. Because it is not true that all the evil in the universe is due to man. Man is not responsible for leprosy and gangrene and cancer, to take a few obvious examples.

Some Christians, when they are faced with these facts, try hard to convince themselves that illness and pain and misery are not really evils; they are desirable states, blessings in disguise, if we could only see it. But, if that is really so, why do we try to cure illness, and think it wrong to inflict pain? Why did Christ heal the sick? But in any case we can leave human suffering out of the argument, because animal suffering sets a still greater problem. Why should an omnipotent and benevolent Power have made animals prey on one another for food? Why implant in the cat the instinct, not merely to kill mice, but to torture them before it kills them? There is no possible answer to the dilemma that so troubled St. Augustine: Either God cannot prevent evil, or he will not. If he cannot, he is not all-powerful; if he will not, he is not all-good.

This difficulty arises for all religions which hold that there is an omnipotent and benevolent power in control of the universe. The specifically Christian doctrines raise still further difficulties, on which I need not enlarge. I do not suggest that these doctrines have been disproved—most of them are not susceptible of disproof. But it is undeniable that in the present scientific climate of thought, belief in these doctrines is becoming more and more difficult to maintain. Just as, to take what I should regard as a parallel case, it is now almost impossible for anyone to believe in witches, though I do not imagine any scientist has ever disproved their existence.

Actually, there is not much attempt today to defend Christian dogma by reasoning. The fashionable attitude among orthodox believers is a defiant anti-intellectualism. The popular Christian apologists are men like Kierkegaard—who made the famous pronouncement 'Christianity demands the crucifixion of the intellect,' as though this were a great point in Christianity's favour. It is surely pessimistic to suggest that doctrines which even their own adherents describe in such terms provide the natural basis for morals and the only alternative to communism? The position is more hopeful than that.

However, as regards the moral training of children, I realise that a case can be made, and is sometimes made, even by unbelievers. . . . People say: 'Of course I realise that these beliefs are not literally true. But then children are not literal-minded, they think naturally in terms of symbol and legend. So why not make use of this tendency in character-training? It is no use giving the child cold-blooded lessons in ethics—moral teaching has got to have colour and warmth and interest. So why not give them that by the means that lie ready to hand—the myths of religion, and the moving and beautiful ceremonies of the Church? The child will cease to believe in the myths as he grows older, but that won't matter—they will have served their purpose.'

I agree that moral training cannot be coldly rational. There must be colour and warmth and interest. One of the best ways to give that is to give the child plenty of models that he can admire and imitate. Tell him plenty of stirring stories about courageous, heroic, disinterested actions—stories that will move and excite him, and make him think that that is the sort of person he would like to be. This may be far more effective, even at the time, than tying up the idea of goodness with the Church, and religion: and there is not the same risk that, later on, if the child leaves the Church and casts off the religion, he may cast off the morals as well.

But let us consider the young child first. If he is brought up in the orthodox way, he will accept what he is told happily enough to begin with. But if he is normally intelligent, he is almost bound to get the impression that there is something odd about religious statements. If he is taken to church, for example, he hears that death is the gateway to eternal life and should be welcomed rather than shunned; yet outside he sees death regarded as the greatest of all evils and everything possible done to postpone it. In church he hears precepts like 'Resist not evil,' and 'Take no thought for the morrow'; but he soon realises that these are not really meant to be practiced outside. If he asks questions, he gets embarrassed, evasive answers: 'Well, dear, you're not quite old enough to understand yet, but some of these things are true in a deeper sense'; and so on. The child soon gets the idea that there are two kinds of truth—the ordinary kind, and another, rather confusing and slightly embarrassing kind, into which it is best not to inquire too closely.

All this is bad intellectual training. It tends to produce a certain intellectual timidity—a distrust of reason—a feeling that it is perhaps rather bad taste to pursue an argument to its logical conclusion, or to refuse to accept a belief on inadequate evidence. And that is not a desirable attitude in the citizens of a free democracy. However, it is the moral rather than the intellectual dangers that I am concerned with here; and they arise when the trustful child becomes a critical adolescent. He may then cast off all his religious beliefs; and, if his moral training has been closely tied up with religion, it is more than possible that the moral beliefs will go too. He may well decide that it was all just old wives' tales; and now he does not know where he is. At this stage he could be most vulnerable to communist propaganda, if a communist were to get hold of him and say: 'Well, you've finished with fairy-tales—now you're ready to listen to some grown-up talk.' Far from being a protection against communism, tying up morals with religion could help to drive people into its arms.

On the subject of communism, it is a mistake, I suggest, to think of Christianity and communism as the two great rival forces in the world today. The fundamental opposition is between dogma and the scientific outlook. On the one side, Christianity and communism, the two great rival dogmatic systems; on the other, Scientific Humanism, which is opposed to both. To try to combat communism by reviving Christianity is a hopeless task. It is like—what shall I say?—like trying to combat the belief in flying saucers by reviving the belief in witches riding on broomsticks. I do not want to press that analogy too closely—but what I mean is, it is trying to drive out a new myth by reviving an old one, instead of going forward to something sounder than myth. Scientific Humanism—that is the constructive answer. By calling it scientific I do not mean that it is crudely materialist, or that it thinks nothing is important but what happens in laboratories: far from it. But scientific in that it does not regard it as a virtue to believe without evidence; scientific in that it deals with hypotheses, not dogmas—hypotheses that are constantly tested and revised in the light of new facts, rather than with alleged immutable truths that it is heresy to question. And humanist because it is concerned with human beings and with this life, rather than with supernatural beings and another world; because it believes that the primary good lies in human happiness and development—men and women realising to the full their capacities for affection, for happiness, and for intellectual and aesthetic experience—and regards these things as more important than any ideology or abstraction, whether it is the Church, or the state, or the five-year plan, or the life hereafter. . . .

Christianity: The Debit Account

This was first published by the National Secular Society, London (1975).

IN 1955 I GAVE TWO BROADCAST TALKS on Morals without Religion, in which I suggested that Scientific Humanism was the natural successor to Christianity. The broadcasts caused some excitement: and many Christians protested, with varying degrees of vehemence, that it was a pity I did not know more about the religion I had so irresponsibly attacked.

I thought there might be something in this. Up to the time of the broadcasts, I had been interested in philosophical theism rather than in historical Christianity, about which I knew no more than the average layman who has had a nominally Christian education. So I decided to fill this gap in my knowledge. In the last few years I have studied the Bible diligently, and now, I suspect, know a good deal more about it than the average vicar; and I have also read many books about the origins and history of the Church. This reading has altered my view profoundly.

At the time of the broadcasts, I held two assumptions that were common among the more highbrow type of sceptic. These were: (i) that Jesus, though he was deluded in believing himself to be the long-awaited Jewish Messiah, was, nevertheless, a great moral teacher, and a man of outstanding moral excellence, and (ii) that though Christianity is now rapidly being outgrown, it was a great force for good in its day. In the light of wider knowledge, both assumptions now seem to me to be false. I now incline to the view that the conversion of Europe to Christianity was one of the greatest disasters of history.

"Gentle Jesus"

To deal first with the personality of Jesus. If one reads the Gospels with a fresh mind, one gets a picture of the founder of Christianity that is quite startlingly different from the traditional "gentle Jesus." The conception of Jesus as meek and gentle may derive in part from his refusal to plead his cause before Pilate. But Jesus may well, by this time, have identified himself with the "suffering servant" of Isaiah 53 ("He is brought as a lamb to the slaughter, and as a sheep before her shearers is dumb, so he openeth not his mouth")—and have been consciously fulfilling the role for which he believed he was prophetically destined. In his preaching, he continually extolled lovingkindness and meekness, but, as so often happens, his practice fell short of his precepts. He was, it is true, gentle and affectionate towards his disciples and towards those who took him at his own valuation: and he was tolerant towards self-confessed sinners. But he was a fanatic; and, like most fanatics, he could not tolerate disagreement or criticism. Towards the Pharisees and others who were sceptical of his messianic pretensions, he was often savagely vindictive. Any hint of criticism, any demand that he should produce evidence for his claims, was liable to provoke a torrent of wrath and denunciation. Most of Chapter 23 of St. Matthew's Gospel, for example, is not, as we are encouraged to regard it, a lofty and dignified rebuke: it is what on any other lips would be described as a stream of invective. "Woe unto you scribes and Pharisees, hypocrites! for ye are like unto whited sepulchres, which, indeed, appear beautiful outward, but are within full of dead men's bones, and of all uncleanness . . . Ye serpents, ye generation of vipers, how can ye escape the damnation of hell?" This can hardly be called loving one's enemies.

Jesus, in fact, was typical of a certain kind of fanatical young idealist: at one moment holding forth, with tears in his eyes, about the need for universal love; at the next, furiously denouncing the morons, crooks and bigots who do not see eye to eye with him. It is very natural and very human behaviour. But it is not superhuman. Many of the great men of history (for example, Socrates) have met criticism with more dignity and restraint.

Historical Christianity

Clerics frequently refer to "the Christian message" of love and human brotherhood. But there is nothing exclusively Christian about this message; it is basic to modern Humanism, as it was to the pre-Christian Humanism of China, Greece and Rome. In the sixth century B.C. Confucius propounded the Golden Rule, and Lao-Tzu enjoined his followers to "requite injuries with good deeds." And later the Stoics, among others, emphatically proclaimed the brotherhood of man regardless of race or nation. There is no ground whatever for the claim, so often made by religious apologists, that these ideals are specifically Christian and originated with Jesus.

What *were* specifically Christian were some less enlightened teachings, which have done untold harm. Christians claim that organised Christianity has been a great force for good, but this view can be maintained on one assumption only: that everything good in the Christian era is a result of Christianity, and that everything bad happened in spite of it. But, as a matter of historical fact many of the worst features of life in the ages of faith (and later) have stemmed directly from the teaching of the Church. Outstanding among these features are the doctrine of hell, intolerance and persecution, anti-intellectualism, asceticism, otherworldliness, and the condonation of slavery.

The hideous doctrine of eternal torment after death has probably caused more terror and misery, more cruelty and more violation of natural human sympathy, than any religious belief in the history of mankind. Yet this doctrine was unambiguously taught by Jesus. "The Son of Man shall send forth his angels, and they shall gather out of his kingdom all things that offend, and them which do iniquity; and shall cast them into a furnace of fire: there shall be wailing and gnashing of teeth" (Matt. Ch. 13). "Then shall he say also unto them on the left hand, Depart from me, ye cursed, into everlasting fire ... And these shall go away into everlasting punishment" (Matt. Ch. 25). "He that shall blaspheme against the Holy Ghost hath never forgiveness, but is in danger of eternal damnation" (Mark, Ch. 3).

The Roman Catholic Church still teaches the doctrine of eternal punishment, but the current tendency among Protestants is to say that Jesus's pronouncements on this subject were "symbolic." But no one has yet answered the question why, if Jesus did not intend his statements about hell to be taken literally, he made them in a form that ensured that they *would* be taken literally. Why, in other words, did he deliberately mislead his hearers? If he was God, he must surely have been able to foresee what disastrous results would follow.

Intolerance and Persecution

No other religion has such a bloodstained record as Christianity. During the ages of faith the Church argued, not illogically, that any degree of cruelty towards sinners and heretics was justified, if there was a chance that it could save them, or others, from the eternal torments of hell. Thus, in the name of the religion of love, hundreds of thousands of people were not merely killed but atrociously tortured in ways that make the gas chambers of Belsen seem humane.

Europe, also, was frequently devastated by religious wars, which destroyed a far higher proportion of the population than the global wars of the twentieth century. The Thirty Year's War, for example, reduced the population of Germany by a third.

Anti-intellectualism

Jesus exhorted his followers to "become as little children," and the Church throughout history has extolled credulity, and feared and distrusted the free intelligence. During the Dark Ages the Church was in control of education, and for centuries scarcely anyone who was not a potential priest learned to read or write. One of the most persistent fallacies about the Christian Church is that it kept learning alive during the Dark and Middle Ages. What the Church did was to keep learning alive in the monasteries, while preventing the spread of knowledge outside them. To quote W. H. Lecky, "The period of Catholic ascendancy was on the whole one of the most deplorable in the history of the human mind . . . The spirit that shrinks from enquiry as sinful and deems a state of doubt a state of guilt, is the most enduring disease that can afflict the mind of man. Not till the education of Europe passed from the monasteries to the universities, not till Mohammedan science, and classical free thought, and industrial independence broke the sceptre of the Church, did the intellectual revival of Europe begin" *(History of European Morals,* Ch. IV). Even as late as the beginning of the nineteenth century, however, nine-tenths of Christian Europe was illiterate.

Asceticism and Otherworldliness

Jesus was a celibate, who appeared to regard sexual love as displeasing to God. "The children of this world marry, and are given in marriage: but they which shall be accounted worthy to obtain that world, and the resurrection from the dead, neither marry nor are given in marriage" (Luke, Ch. 20). "There be eunuchs, which have made themselves eunuchs for the kingdom of heaven's sake" (Matt., Ch. 19). This tendency was even stronger in Paul. "It is good for a man not to touch a woman . . . But if they cannot contain, let them marry: for it is better to marry than to burn" (I Cor., Ch. 7). This attitude accounts in part for the strong neurotic and masochistic strain in Christianity.

Jesus believed that the Last Judgment was at hand: "Verily I say unto you, Ye shall not have gone over the cities of Israel till the Son of Man be come" (Matt. Ch. 10). "There be some standing here that shall not taste of death, till they see the Son of man coming in his kingdom" (Matt., Ch. 16). "This generation shall not pass till all these things be fulfilled" (Matt., Ch. 24). "The kingdom of God is at hand" (Mark, Ch. 1).

Jesus's moral teaching was therefore directed mainly towards getting believers into heaven: he showed little concern for the affairs of this world. Later, the Church ceased to believe that the end of the world was imminent, but it still held that this life was no more than a momentary prelude to eternity, and of little importance except as a preparation for the life to come. Thus throughout most of its history the Church has been indifferent to social progress and social reform. It has encouraged its members to regard suffering and misery as part of the inscrutable decrees of Providence; to be patient under wrong and oppression; to accept evil instead of resisting it: all in the certainty that things would be put right in the next world. To a privileged minority this attitude has obvious advantages, in that it helps to keep the unprivileged majority resigned to their lot, but it has retarded human progress for centuries. The emancipation of slaves and of women, and factory reform in the nineteenth century are three progressive struggles which the laity waged themselves with little or no support from the clergy.

Slavery

There is no justification for the common claim that Christianity was responsible for the abolition of slavery. The Negro slave trade—a far more infamous practice than slavery in the ancient world—was initiated, carried on and defended by Christian men in Christian countries. To quote H. A. L. Fisher, "It is a terrible commentary on Christian civilisation that the longest period of slave-raiding known to history was initiated by the action of Spain and Portugal, France, Holland and Britain, after the Christian faith had for more than a thousand years been the established religion of Europe" *(History of Europe*, Chap. 23).

The abolitionist movement took its impetus . . . from the secular humanitarianism of the Enlightenment. Many of the leading abolitionists were unbelievers—Condorcet . . . in France, Abraham Lincoln in America, Fox and Pitt in Great Britain. Christians like William Wilberforce who actively opposed the slave trade were far from typical: with the honourable exception of the Quakers, the attitude of most of the Churches towards abolition was in America actively hostile, and in Britain (to use Wilberforce's own words) "shamefully lukewarm." The Churches, of course, had no difficulty in citing scriptural authority for their attitude. The Old Testament sanctions slavery (cf. Leviticus 25, 44–46): the New Testament contains no condemnation of it: and St. Paul told slaves to obey their masters (Colossians, 3, 22). (The Greek word for slave, *doulos*, is wrongly translated in the New Testament as "servant.")

The Establishment

The indictment against Christianity is formidable: and when Christians today grow indignant about obscurantism, intolerance and ideological persecution in Communist countries, they would do well to remember that the Church in the ages of faith had a far worse record. This is not to deny that the Church has also done some good; so, too, has Communism. But the crucial fact, surely is that, as Voltaire remarked, men who believe absurdities will commit atrocities. One of the best ways to improve men's behaviour is to enlighten their minds: and today, against the strong opposition of the Church and the Establishment, Scientific Humanism is attempting to do just that.

PRICE 25c

Queen Silver's Magazine

Vol. I, No. 3   Inglewood, California   Second Quarter 1924

—International News Reel Photo

QUEEN SILVER

With Sallie and Billie, famous Chimpanzees owned by Mr. J. S. Edwards

| Evolution---From Monkey to Bryan | PAGE THREE |

From a 1924 cover of Queen Silver's Magazine

38

Queen Silver

"GIRL PHILOSOPHER"

Born December 13, 1910

The greatest contribution nonbelievers have made to the world has been the Constitution of the United States. Consider how very heretical to a religious world was the idea of a Constitution predicated on "We, the People."

"Humanity's Gain From Unbelief"

WHILE FREETHOUGHT HAS HAD ITS SHARE of geniuses young and old, Queen Silver has a unique place in freethought history as a child atheist lecturer. Queen was born to Grace Verne Silver in Portland, Oregon, where her mother was stranded during a tour for the Socialist Party. At ten-days-old, Queen took the first of countless railway journeys with her mother. With two suitcases (one for literature), her baby, and later a baby carriage, Grace continued her lecturing career.

Upon the advent of World War I, they settled in the Los Angeles area, her mother establishing "The Socialist Bookstore" for a time. Starting in 1917, mother, daughter and later a stepfather became extras in motion pictures to supplement a sparse income.

Queen exemplified her mother's conviction that "The precocious child is the normal child." In an article appearing in the September 1922 *National Brain Power Monthly* written by Henry H. Roser, Grace Silver described "the Home Teaching Methods that Have Made Queen Silver the Marvel of the School World."

Her mother believed: "In the eyes of modern educators, individuality is a great sin, to be ruthlessly suppressed. The child is refused the right to reason for itself, and, if bold enough to do so, its thought processes are promptly crushed by the steam roller of the 'system.' The educators of our schools worship a holy trinity of their own, namely, *Average, Authority,* and *Standardized Methods.*"

There was nothing average about her child Queen, pictured in the press of her childhood as a waif-like pixie cuddling kittens ("Not too wise to love a kitten," read one cutline), arranging her beribboned, bobbed hair, and as a delicate little girl, standing on a lecture platform surrounded by admiring adults.

Grace Silver was twenty-one at the time of Queen's birth. Whenever she wanted to read a book, she read it aloud to her infant daughter. Queen as a baby accompanied her mother to all her lectures.

"Queen was three years of age before she made an effort to pronounce a single word. I never tried to induce her to talk, and that first word ever pronounced developed into a speech, delivered when some friends lifted her to the platform, while I stood out of sight in the wings, and some one told her to 'make a speech' like mother. She talked over five minutes, repeating verbatim the peroration of a speech I had been giving on one-night stands all winter."

Shortly after that, someone threw a lighted cigarette out of an open window in San Francisco, where it landed in Queen's left eye, nearly destroying the optic nerve, requiring a six-month recuperation in a dark room, and another year of light avoidance. Her mother continued her education by reading to her. When Queen's eye had recovered sufficiently by age six, she learned to read. According to her mother, "Before she was seven years of age she had read every nonfiction book in the juvenile department of the Los Angeles Public Library that was worth reading."

Her mother prided herself on never reading a myth, fairy story or work of fiction to her daughter: "Fact was as interesting to her as fable is to most children."

By seven and a half she was reading Darwin and Haeckel. At age eight and a half Queen delivered a series of six lectures in Los Angeles, including the topics: "Darwin's Theory of Evolution," "From Star Dust to Man," "Human Nature in the Animal World," "Human Nature in the Plant World," "Mexico" and "Peru." Her mother illustrated them with stereopticon views while Queen delivered them extemporaneously from her own notes. The *Los Angeles Record* carried an article about the series in its December 24, 1919 issue, although today Queen calls its inaccuracies "a perfect example of how a newspaper can blow up facts to make a good story." At ten a Los Angeles newspaper published her feature article on the theory of relativity.

At age eleven, Queen publicly challenged William Jennings Bryan to a debate on evolution. Bryan declined. *The Daily News* in Inglewood carried a front-page article on June 29, 1925, headlined: "Inglewood Girl Wonder May Go To Chattanooga, Aid Evolutionists" featuring a photo of Queen Silver holding a chimpanzee:

"Inglewood's famous girl philosopher, writer and talker, Queen Silver who has written a lecture entitled 'Evolution, from Monkey to Bryan,' may take part in the famous Dayton trial of Dr. Scopes who is alleged to have preached the theory of evolution in a public school." A pro-evolution paper started a subscription fund to pay the cost of sending Queen Silver to Dayton. Although Queen did not make it to the trial, at least one thousand pamphlets of her lecture were distributed.

Queen did not attend school, "except to lecture." Starting when she was twelve, from the years 1923–1934, Queen published *Queen Silver's Magazine*, a sixteen-page periodical with a national subscription. Almost no copies are available today.

In the *National Brain Power Monthly*, Grace Silver summarized her daughter's achievements:

"Queen is studying all the time, writing, speaking, and, like most every one in Los Angeles, has worked in motion pictures. She has earned her own clothes, bought a typewriter for her own use, besides over a hundred books, and has paid her board from her earnings since the age of seven. Not the least important part of her education has been the fact that she has been taught to be self-reliant, to be responsible to herself, financially and otherwise, to find her way about a large city alone, on foot or on the street cars, to go to a restaurant for meals, to the stores to make purchases, etc. At present, she has her own room, furnished for housekeeping, buys her supplies and cooks her own meals. . . . We do not look upon her as a prodigy. She has simply been educated along lines for which heredity, environment, and ability have fitted her."

Queen took seasonal office work during the Depression. In 1936 she held her first permanent job as a junior typist clerk, earning $70 a month. Queen later went to school at night, graduating from the Los Angeles City College in the 1960s with an associate degree in arts.

Queen stayed in state civil service, spending her last sixteen years, before retirement in 1972, as a court reporter, taking shorthand at two hundred and forty words per minute for civil hearings.

She helped to found a Los Angeles group which later became Atheists United, serving on the Board for several years, most recently as recording secretary, and has been a member of many freethought and humanist organizations.

Humanity's Gain From Unbelief

This is adapted from a speech given to a California freethought group by Queen Silver when she was in her eighties. The speech, whose title is borrowed from the nineteenth-century British freethinker Charles Bradlaugh, updates his thesis.

UNBELIEF IS THE SOURCE OF THE PROGRESS that the human race has maintained. The spirit of religion, which teaches "revelation"—that answers are given on high—has tried to squelch curiosity and stop us from seeking answers.

During the Scopes trial in Tennessee, fundamentalist William Jennings Bryan was questioned by famed agnostic attorney Clarence Darrow about biblical scriptures, becoming rattled and confused. Bryan finally admitted, "Well, I believe it because it's in the Bible, the Bible says it and that's it." Darrow asked him, "Well, were you never curious? Didn't you ever think about it?" And Bryan replied, "I never think about things that I don't think about." Darrow next asked, "Did you ever think about things that you do think about?" Darrow ringingly concluded: "I tremble for fear about the state of learning in this country if everyone shared your boundless curiosity."

Bryan had read "The Book," he believed "The Book," he had swallowed "The Book." If that type of mindset always had been victorious, we would still be living in a world in which the Earth had four corners, was flat, was orbited by the Sun, and where Heaven was about three miles straight up. We would never have discovered our boundless universe.

The greatest contribution nonbelievers have made to the world has been the Constitution of the United States. Consider how very heretical to a religious world was the idea of a Constitution predicated on "We, the People," with no reference to God at all!

We have freethinkers to thank for the first steps in being able to limit our families. The battle for abolition in this country was led by freethinkers and free inquirers, because religion taught that slavery was ordained by God. Women can thank freethinkers and nonbelievers for the rights we have now and the attempts to gain the rights which we don't yet have. If the freethinkers had had their way, women's advancement would have been effected long ago.

If you have ever eaten a nice luscious baked potato, you can thank another unbeliever, Luther Burbank, whose work to develop what later became the Idaho russet potato, saved the potato crops in the United States and other parts of the world. When Burbank was growing up, his mother frequently said to him: "Luther, I wish you would make this world a better place to live in than it was before you lived." She lived to be ninety-seven, so she had the satisfaction of seeing how well he heeded her wish. Burbank developed new strains of potatoes that better withstood pests, and put the potato back on the table. The United States Department of Agriculture, in 1906, estimated that Burbank's work with the potato was worth at least $17 million dollars a year to the United States economy. We can thank another unbeliever, Charles Darwin, who wrote *Variation of Animals and Plants Under Domestication*, in which Burbank found the information that enabled him to save the potato. Burbank had asked that his funeral eulogy be given by Judge Benjamin Lindsey of Denver, Colorado. Another nonbeliever, Judge Lindsey was the founder of the first juvenile court in the United States and wrote the still timely *The Revolt of Modern Youth*, proposing certain solutions to mitigate many of the juvenile problems we face today.

Unbelief was prominent in disease control. A thoroughly religious person in the orthodox tradition believes disease is caused by God, who is punishing someone for a sin. This mentality still is reflected today over AIDS, and used to be the prevailing attitude about disease in general. But skeptics unwilling to accept the traditional wisdom of the time realized, "This is not a curse from God, this is something we can cure."

Unfortunately, in the process of discovering how the facts of nature contradicted the dogmas of theology, some people were burnt, some people were imprisoned, some people simply became too scared to continue research or speak out. We now benefit from the fact that there were people who dared to investigate, dared to be curious.

We walk in the footprints of freethinkers and reformers who did not expect immortality, whose only immortality is that they are in the loving memory of the people who came after them. The best memorial is to ensure that the work that they did continues. We must not allow the religious fanatics of our period to take away from us the contributions to humanity brought to us by hundreds of years of toil and strife against superstition.

A historic moment for Vashti McCollum

39

Vashti Cromwell McCollum

CHAMPION OF THE FIRST AMENDMENT

Born November 6, 1912

Between being praised and persecuted, condoned and condemned, I might
understandably have become bewildered, particularly at the brand of ethics
sometimes displayed by the staunch defenders of Christianity. But of one thing
I am sure: I am sure that I fought not only for what I earnestly believed to be
right, but for the truest kind of religious freedom intended by the First
Amendment, the complete separation of church and state.

One Woman's Fight, 1951

A REVERED NAME IN THE HISTORY of constitutional law, Vashti Cromwell McCollum
won a landmark challenge of religion in public schools at the U.S. Supreme Court,
"after three years of headlines, headaches, and hatred." Significantly, *McCollum
v. Board of Education* (1948) was the first Supreme Court decision to declare a
state's religious law unconstitutional according to the First Amendment, as applied through the "due process" clause of the Fourteenth Amendment.

Born Vashti Cromwell in Lyons, New York, the daughter of Arthur G. and
Ruth Cromwell, she was named by her mother for the biblical character who was
"the first exponent of woman's rights."

She studied at Cornell, then transferred to the University of Illinois and was
on the verge of graduating in 1934 when she married John Paschal ("Pappy")
McCollum, who became associate professor of vegetable crops in the Horticul-
tural Department. She had three children—James Terry, Dannel, and Errol—
before completing her degree in political science and law in 1944. The couple's
idyllic life as a faculty family in Champaign, Illinois, changed radically when their
oldest boy, Jim, entered the fourth grade, and was pressured to participate in
religious classroom instruction, a phenomenon sweeping the nation's public school
system in the 1940s. After a number of unpleasant experiences for her son Jim,

and after her objections were ignored, Vashti filed suit to stop the unconstitutional religious instruction. Branded as "that awful McCollum woman," she and her family were treated like outcasts. She lost at both the trial and appeals court levels. On March 8, 1948, the U.S. Supreme Court, in a decision delivered by Justice Hugo Black, vindicated Vashti and the constitution in an eight-to-one decision against religious instruction in public schools. While a student was overheard saying Vashti should be lynched, an atheist supporter wrote her parents: "No Catholic can adore the Virgin Mary more than I adore Vashti McCollum."

Her book *One Woman's Fight*, first published by Doubleday and Co., in 1951, is a testament to the personal toll exacted when the wall of separation is violated at the expense of citizens—especially school children. [See selection] As Vashti told her superintendent, "instead of fostering equality, religious instruction in the schools fosters discrimination because it makes children conscious of differences that before they didn't know existed. The moment children are separated for religious instruction there is new emphasis placed on the distinctions of Jewish or Gentile, or churched and unchurched. The public schools are our greatest hope for teaching and driving home the lessons of democracy; there, children of all creeds, races, and colors meet on common ground, and work and play together.

"There should be no Jews, no Catholics, no Protestants in public schools."

Vashti served two terms as President of the American Humanist Association, also receiving its "distinguished service" award. She earned her Master's degree in mass communications from the University of Illinois as a returning student. Beginning in the late 1950's, she became a world traveler, often going "surface." She has been around the world four times, having visited close to one hundred and fifty countries and all seven continents—including Antarctica in a 1991 adventure. She has won awards for her photography, producing forty-five slide shows culled from her travels. The octogenarian, still busy with travel and photography, was inducted into the National Women's Hall of Fame in 1996. Her son Jim is now a retired attorney, Errol is a retired businessman, and Dannel, in a fitting conclusion to the long struggle, is mayor of Champaign, Illinois.

An honorary officer of the Freedom From Religion Foundation, which recently reprinted *One Woman's Fight*, Vashti is featured in the Foundation's film, "Champions of the First Amendment" (1988). In an on-screen interview, she noted: "I just hope the decision in the *McCollum* case, which in the past has been the precedent, will prevail, because if we have prayer in the public school, whose prayer?"

Vashti added: "I have had a very happy life, and a very fruitful life. I don't feel the need for any organized, supernatural religion, and never have."

Christian Halloween

*This is excerpted from Chapter 11 of Vashti McCollum's book, **One Woman's Fight**, originally published in 1951, about her landmark lawsuit against religious instruction in the public schools. This chapter records some of the community harassment that took place while her lawsuit was pending. The supportive minister referred to was Unitarian.*

The phone calls were bad enough, and so were some of the letters, but the biggest attack on us came in person the Halloween night after the trial.

Halloween is the season for pranks in this vicinity, as it is everywhere, I guess. The pranksters are around every night for nearly a week before they climax their activities on Halloween. Nightly we were serenaded by the teen-age crowd singing, "Onward, Christian Soldiers," which seemed to be the theme song of the hecklers.

"ATHIST" was scribbled on the windows of the family Chevy and on the windows of the house, its misspelling indicating either that an "atheist" was too recent a being in Champaign to be known or else that the schools could have spent some of that religious-instruction time in spelling drill.

The night before Halloween the callers became bolder and after the usual serenade came up and banged on the front door. Pappy and I had just stepped out to mail some letters, leaving the heavy oak door ajar. Banging against it, several of the invaders were surprised to find themselves inside the house. Jim, awakened by the commotion, ran downstairs, sized up the situation, and passed out the "treats" so they would go away.

The next day was a bad one right from the beginning. I'd been fighting a cold and sore throat and was miserably sick. Danny had been in the hospital recovering from an appendectomy, and we went over to bring him home in the afternoon. That evening Pappy went to a lecture—ironically enough, Ely Culbertson on "World Peace"—and Jim and Errol went Halloweening around the neighborhood. Danny and I, the two sick ones, were kept busy handing out treats to the small fry who kept our doorbell ringing continuously.

Errol came in early and went to bed, and shortly afterward Jim came in also. While I was upstairs, making Danny comfortable for the night, a large group of serenaders came around. When they rang the bell I started down the stairs to get more treats ready, as our supply by the front door was exhausted. Jim was struggling out of his costume before answering the bell. Promptness is imperative in answering the bell, as the youngsters are usually impatient to start in on the tricks. Realizing this, I grabbed the rest of our wartime hoard of candy and dashed for the door.

As I opened it I was met by a shower of everything the victory gardens had to offer that year. Rotten tomatoes smashed against the walls, splattered in my hair and over my clothes. Huge cabbage plants, roots, mud, and all, came careening through the open door and into the living room.

Weakened by fever and exhausted by the activities of the evening, this was the last straw for me. I called the police and they arrived shortly. All they did was pick up a cabbage or two as they walked out and suggested that perhaps they'd better drive around the block a couple of times. Naturally it was too dark for them to see or identify anyone. All the time the hoodlums were concealed in the shrubbery in front, so when I went out to shake the throw-rug free of debris, I was greeted by, "So you don't like it? You had to call the police, you atheist," and much more. There were teenagers' voices among them, but they were liberally fortified by adults.

All was quiet for nearly half an hour, and then they returned again, singing, "Onward, Christian Soldiers." There was no doubt it was the same crowd, so I didn't answer the bell. Whereupon they determined to push in the door, probably thinking it would give as easily as it had the night before. Disappointed in their first attempt, they would start out at the street and with a running start ram against the heavy oak door with such violence that our whole house, a stone one, seemed to shake.

All three of the boys were awakened and frightened by this mob violence. I didn't dare open the door but waited out the storm, and eventually they left after piling trash and leaves two feet high on our front doorstep. Our pet kitten disappeared, too, that night. Poor pagan pussycat, even she had to pay for belonging to a family of nonconformists!

The local papers always carry a story on the previous night's Halloween activities. While the *Courier*, accurate as usual, reported the attack under the head "McCollum Home Target," the *News-Gazette* reported call after call from the police records but not the call made by me.

The item in the *Courier* didn't go unnoticed. An august professor at the university read it and called my husband to "apologize for the community." He then called three or four ministers of the largest churches in

Champaign and explained what had happened and strongly urged that they deliver a sermon on the assault, expressing as vehement an opposition to such tactics as they had previously to me and my suit. Unfortunately, the ministers were unable to do this, as their services had all been planned in advance. As far as I know, no mention of it was made by any of the clergy to their flocks.

One minister, however, saw to it that his congregation heard of the goings on of this fine group, the products of that highly moral religious education, who had apparently profited so richly from those precepts, "Love thy neighbor as thyself" and "Do unto others as you would have them do unto you." That minister, of course, was Phil Schug, and he reported it all—the barrage of "fruit of doubtful value," the plight of the police who "found high-school youngsters hard to find in the dark."

His heading of it was especially appropriate.

He called it simply, " 'Christian' Halloween."

Ruth Hurmence Green
(Photograph by Paul Gaylor)

40

Ruth Hurmence Green

THE BORN AGAIN SKEPTIC

January 12, 1915 – July 7, 1981

There was a time when religion ruled the world.
It is known as the Dark Ages.

RUTH HURMENCE GREEN FIRST READ THE BIBLE cover to cover when convalescing from cancer in her early sixties.

"My agnostic brother told me it was a waste of time . . . but I plodded through it, to my increasing incredulity and horror. I was a half-hearted Methodist who had always disliked religion, but, like ninety-seven percent of Christian laity, I had been taught that the bible was a good book and Jesus was a wonderful man. I think the shock I suffered was worse than the trauma caused by my illness. The superstitious ignorance, the atrocious inhuman cruelty, the obvious derivation from mythology, and above all the depravity of bible personalities—they all left me stunned." (Ruth Green to Anne Gaylor, September 1978)

After two years of studying the bible, Ruth wrote *The Born Again Skeptic's Guide to the Bible*, which was first published by the Freedom From Religion Foundation in 1979.

"There wasn't a page of the bible that didn't offend me in some way," Ruth discovered. "I had always been told the bible was a book about love, but I couldn't find enough love in it to fill a salt shaker. God is not love in the bible; God is vengeance. There is no other book between whose covers life is so cheap."

In the preface, Ruth wrote: "I'm fond of saying that reading the Bible turned me into an atheist." But the seeds were planted in childhood, at her astonishment that bible legends were considered true, rather than as an "extension of Grimm's and Andersen's Fairy Tales." She quipped that the bible is "a Grim Fairy Tale."

"When I was young, Easter was a time of horror for me . . . and I still cannot bear the sight of a crucifix," Ruth continued. She coined the memorable phrase, "the Christian torture symbol," to describe the cross.

"... I am now convinced that children should not be subjected to the fright-fulness of the Christian religion. . . . If the concept of a father who plots to have his own son put to death is presented to children as beautiful and as worthy of society's admiration, what types of human behavior can be presented to them as *reprehensible?*" (*Born Again Skeptic's Guide to the Bible:* vii, viii)

Ruth vowed "never to be seen in public with an unconcealed bible." (Green, *Book of Ruth:* 59)

Ruth grew up in a conventional Methodist family in Sumner, a small Iowa town, described in two autobiographical essays, "The Way We Were" (1979), and a more reflective piece completed the month before she died. Ruth wrote of growing up in a "wide circle of love." Her favorite childhood pastime was snug-gling into a featherbed with her favorite snack, salted "pie plant," while reveling in her favorite "sadistic" book, *Elsie Dinsmore*.

Even with the knowledge that she was dying of incurable throat cancer, Ruth wrote:

"Part of me wants to be ten again, sauntering barefoot down the alley behind our house, curling my insteps around the sharp rocks, wincing at the hot Iowa earth, sucking in my breath trying for the hundredth time to whistle a tune, think-ing how grown-up I was becoming and how everything was right with the world. But another part of me knows that I wouldn't want to go back, and I ponder the strangeness of the certainty that I would reject any offer to make me that child again, with all the growing up and living to do over. . . .

"How many of us would say in honesty, 'Let me live my life over again; let me have the same experiences once more'? Does this reluctance tell us that existence is not as appealing as it is perceived to be, that we see it, approaching its close, as, if not an ordeal, a sort of unpredictable gauntlet that we are forced to run by the bittersweet circumstance of being? Is life a boon, then, or a condition which few would choose, in full understanding of what it entails? Perhaps, after all, life as a gift is a myth, and we are destined to be so bewildered at our unsolicited and seemingly purposeless coming-about that we create gods to bestow prestige upon us." (*The Book of Ruth:* 74)

A tomboy and a free spirit, Ruth was a conscientious student. When her fam-ily moved to Lubbock, Texas, she attended Texas Tech as a journalism major, receiving her degree in 1935. She married Truman Green, an engineer, and gave birth to a daughter and two sons. In 1950, the family moved to Jefferson City, Missouri.

Ruth underwent a radical mastectomy in 1960 shortly after her only sister died of breast cancer. Several years later she was treated for skin cancer, then was diagnosed with throat cancer in 1975. She did not wait "for help from the super-natural": "There *are* atheists in foxholes, and they fare very well." (*Born Again*

Skeptic: viii) She had thirty-seven radiation treatments.

When she realized the throat cancer had returned by 1981, Ruth kept the diagnosis to herself, carrying on normally as long as she could. The morning of July 7, 1981, she took her own life by swallowing painkillers. In her last letter to friend Anne Gaylor, president of the Freedom From Religion Foundation, written on July 4, 1981, Ruth wrote: "Freedom From must grow and prosper . . . freedom depends upon freethinkers."

Her life and death touched the lives of many, including members of the media such as novelist Jacquelyn Mitchard, then a columnist with *The Capital Times* who once had interviewed Ruth. After reading of Ruth's death, she wrote in an August 1981 column:

"I can't really say Ruth was a friend of mine. We'd rambled through a funny, enlightening couple of hours over coffee once and I'd written a story about her book, *A Born Again Skeptic's Guide to the Bible.*

"I liked the book. It was like Ruth: salt-plain, sprinkled with anger and wisdom, prickly with humor. Ruth had gone to church almost all her life. She didn't see any reason not to, though she'd never had a particular yen for religion. Ruth was a Missourian, you see. You had to show her.

"Once she saw a reason not to, and trusted it, she stopped. Her relatives roared—Granny? An atheist? But that didn't faze Ruth. Like the good Christian she wasn't, she went on loving them while they shook their heads over her. She studied the Bible, and what she saw as its contradictions, and came to believe that goodness and mercy and tolerance were not 'Christian' values. They were the values of good people.

"*She was a good person.*

"That was all I knew of her. A couple of letters traded. A few hours' talk. So I was surprised that what I felt when I read of her death was not just regret. It was sorrow. . . . She took her own life because she believed profoundly it was hers to take."

Ruth unknowingly echoed the conviction of Elizabeth Cady Stanton when she expressed that her "dearest wish" was to alert women to the sexism in religion "before they get to be sixty-six, like me."

A series of useful and pithy columns, essays, letters and speeches was published posthumously in 1982 as *The Book of Ruth.* She wrote:

"Let us use our energy and our initiative to solve our problems without relying on prayers and wishful thinking. When we have faith in ourselves, we will find we do not have to have faith in gods."

What I Found When I "Searched the Scriptures"

*This lecture was given by Ruth Hurmence Green at the Unitarian Church, Columbia, Missouri, November 16, 1980, and is reprinted from **The Book of Ruth** (1982).*

THIS MORNING I'M GOING TO TELL YOU what I found when I joined that small group of masochists who regularly decide to muddle through the entire Bible, even if it kills them.

My text is taken from the 5th chapter of John, the 39th verse, wherein Jesus instructs someone who probably can't even read, to "search the scriptures."

Today when the Fundamentalists are once more insisting that the fundamentals of fundamentalism are fundamental to our being No. 1 on the Lord's totem pole, it's very brave of you to invite the "resident atheist" of mid-Missouri to share her thoughts with you. Did you know that this SIXTY-FIVE year-old grandmother has become a threat? When I appear infrequently on talk shows, it is not unusual for listeners to be warned to turn off their sets, if they are thin-skinned. I assume that all of you have examined your epidermis and found it to be of sufficient density to permit you to listen to me. And as for those other listeners, as far as I know, none of them ever turns off the set. They pounce upon me, via the telephone, and accuse me of excerpting and of taking out of context. I always agree to stop, just as soon as the preachers do.

Some Christians accuse me of misappropriating the title of born again. They say you have to have a "religious experience" to be re-born. But I *have* had a religious experience. It began when I was a child reared in a small Iowa town by parents who were less than devout Methodists but who required their children to attend church and Sunday School and Epworth League regularly, and it ended when my reading of the entire Bible for myself started a train of thought. This led to my conviction that the natural is so awesome that we need not go beyond it and that there is no evidence in nature for gods with or without bodies, parts, or passions. A purposeless, non-discriminatory/amoral universe exists, and I am part of it and subject to its apparent laws. How all this came about I don't as yet know, and neither does anyone else, and I'm inclined to assign the same ignorance to the Bible writers. Today evolution of human intelligence has advanced us to the stage where most of us are too smart to invent new gods but are reluctant to give up the old ones.

❦

My text is taken from the words of Jesus to the Samaritan woman at the well, one of the rare times when Jesus addressed anyone who was not a pure Jew. Most of the time he adhered to the law whereby Jews did not associate with Gentiles except perhaps to do business with them. If a Jew married a Gentile, unless the Jew was Moses or Solomon of course, the Lord would reward anyone who thrust them through their bellies, or so my scripture search revealed. Almost the whole Bible is anti-Gentile. The most glowing prophecies, which Jesus said he came to fulfill, described the annihilation of the Gentiles on the Day of the Lord. "The lion is come up from his thicket and the destroyer of the Gentiles is on his way."

Today when I hear the Christian clergy encourage the laity to search the scriptures, I fear one of the Lord's many lying spirits has found a home. Secretly proselytizers must pray the Bible will continue to gather dust on the shelf so that *they* can continue to conspire with the media to expunge passages like: "O princes of the house of Israel, who pluck off their skin from off them and their flesh from off their bones, who also eat the flesh of my people and flay their skin from off them, and they break their bones and chop them in pieces, as for the pot and as flesh within the cauldron." God is speaking, and here is his description of the day of the Lord: "Everyone that is found shall be thrust thru, and everyone that is joined unto them shall fall by the sword. Their children also shall be dashed to pieces before their eyes; their houses shall be spoiled, and their wives ravished." The Lord could certainly use some help in promoting his big events.

There wasn't one page of this book that didn't offend me in some way. In fact, after a session of searching the scriptures, I always wanted to take a bath with Grandma's lye soap. And when I encountered the Bible's disdain for women, I very often almost pitched the good book across the room. I vowed never to be seen in public with an unconcealed Bible in my hands. Thomas Paine, the true savior of the world, denounced the Bible for me: "I sincerely detest it as I detest everything that is cruel."

But it wasn't only the cruelty and the unimaginable atrocities. If there is *obscenity*, you'll find it in this book. If there is *pornography*, you'll find it in the scriptures, and you won't even have to search. I don't advise opening the Bible aimlessly and reading aloud the first passage that meets the eye. You might violate a censorship law. Strict censorship would mean that the Bible would have to be sold from under the counter.

You can know just how much religion meant to me as a child when I tell you how I used to amuse myself in church by making rubbings from the covers of the song books, but I was a staunch little participant when it came time for hymn singing. Today I shudder at the awful content of some of those hymns, based as they were on the Christian precept that "without shedding of blood is no remission." "Let the water and the blood from thy wounded side which flowed be of sin the double cure, save from wrath and make me pure." Now I wonder why any god would have to die to save sinners from his own wrath. I was "washed in the blood of the lamb." There was a "fountain filled with blood," and I sang loud and clear about it. I had a good idea of how I rated with God every time I sang, along with the rest of the poor wretches in the congregation, "Would he devote that sacred head to such a worm as I?" We were all crawling on our bellies at the feet of a capricious fiend who might, as the *patriarchs* were in the habit of doing, put his feet upon the necks of his enemies at any time. And we were concurring with the pagans that sacred blood could purify, pagans who let the blood of sacred bulls pour over them.

I looked forward to "Communion Sundays." To me grape juice was grape juice was grape juice, and a wafer was a wafer was a wafer. We Methodists practiced the pagan cannibalism of eating the flesh and drinking the blood of a god, but we were nicer about it than the Catholics. Besides, on Communion Sundays the sermons were shorter and sometimes we got to the Doxology more quickly, that testimonial to the Platonic Trinity, which for several hundred years confounded the Church Fathers and divided the Roman Empire into at least eighteen quarreling sects, none of whom knew what they were fighting about, and which schisms contributed to the decline and fall of this greatest of states. Rome had thrived for one thousand years with pagan gods at the helm and expired after only one hundred and fifty years under the Christian banner.

But what *did* I find when I finally searched the scriptures? In two words: Disillusionment and Release. The "blessed assurance" finally came over me that the Bible and its gods were the products of folk tales and invention all mixed up with a dash of history and seasoned with vast quantities of superstition, and at last I was able to "let a little sun shine in" to dispel the pollution of fear and guilt that befogs the mind of every indoctrinated person. I became the born again skeptic who rejected all gods.

I never thought of myself as a juvenile sinner, at least not a bad one, but I was one, according to the Bible. Paul says avoid foolish questions, and I had some. I never put them to anyone, so perhaps that lets me off the hook. It's hard to tell. One tiny sin even thought about can damn you forever, but I'm not sure at what age children can be excused from the flames, or is it the boiling waves? Jesus didn't seem to know whether hell was a furnace or a lake of fire, and there's very little talk of it in the Old Testament at all, and even less of Satan, who is very polite and nobody seems to be trying to chain him up again after his expulsion from the battlegrounds of heaven, where even the angels weren't happy. But Jesus turned down his generous offer of all the kingdoms of the world, and even after letting old Lucifer set him on a steeple and after camping out in the wilderness with him, Jesus never does reprove Satan for that scene in the Garden. After all these shenanigans, the Bible tells me that *Jesus* died to cause the death of *Satan*, but the Lord works in mischievous ways his blunders to perform and Satan still walks about winning most of our souls. I ask you, who is ahead in the mystic struggle between good and evil?

Apparently Satan is indestructible, even by an omnipotent god. He is always there to create that "superfluity of naughtiness" which James deplores but which comes as such a relief on the heels of Paul's righteousness, whenever we dare to "put our affections on things on the earth" and forget for a few refreshing minutes about being Paul's living sacrifices to God.

In all frankness, I'm very proud of the child that I was, because, you see, even then I thought the Bible was a book of fairy tales. I realize now it was the only way I could accept the hideous stories of the Flood, Abraham and Isaac, Jephthah's daughter, Samson pulling down the temple, the execution of the Hebrew babies by Pharaoh, the midnight slaughter of the Egyptians, and last but most repulsive to me on the biblical horror scale: the crucifixion, which has given us a heritage of and a landscape made ugly by that Christian torture symbol, the Cross. I'm sure they won't be satisfied until the bleeding victim is hanging on every one. I am not convinced that execution scenes inspire and uplift us.

Today Christian parents can purchase recordings, advertised as very realistic, of the infant death scenes in Egypt and the Holy Land as recreated by the industry, and they can buy Bibles in comic book form with every ghastly tale completely illustrated. And these people have the nerve to condemn TV violence. And, by the way, in time for Christmas buying, there is offered a replica of The Last Moment, a Jesus head in its final stages of agony. Christianity has a special propensity for making a silk purse of a sow's ear. It is this unique talent that has enabled the Church to peddle the Bible as the Good Book, this book in which human life is the cheapest commodity and human sacrifice the most valued abomination.

When I was growing up, we read Grimm's and Andersen's Fairy Tales avidly, and surely many of the stories told of cruel deeds, but these deeds were *condemned*, not approved, and besides we knew it was all make believe. I remember the very day it finally registered with me that the Bible stories were supposed to be true and there actually was a Holy Land and a real human god who did miraculous things. I was stunned, and from that illuminating day on for much of my life, I always felt a distaste for religion. My distaste joined hands with my doubts.

It took me three hundred pages to tell in my book what I found when I finally searched the scriptures, and it's very hard to condense all that. Let me begin by saying that I *didn't* find the Wonderful Words of Life, another one of the melodious descriptions of the biblical message I learned in the church. I expected to find a semblance of love, but what I found were vengeance and threats and curses. The word curse and its various forms appear two hundred and five times in the Bible, and a curse isn't always called a curse. The last word in the Old Testament is curse, and I was so happy in the book of The Revelation to read that "there shall be no more curse." I felt that would truly be heavenly. I was so tired of curses like "The blood of your lives shall I require." This bloodthirsty god made sure that his appetite would be satiated by cursing humanity with the Bible and the Cross. The Bible, itself the ultimate curse, is an in-depth profile of the divine spleen.

Human beings start out under a curse and are forced to suffer from it all through their lives as punishment for original sin, but under divine justice they have still not made atonement but are now required to kill their redeemer, as if one sin will be wiped out by the commission of another. This second sin does not anger the Lord, however. He is happy if, now that his wicked children have tortured him to death, they will feast upon his body and call him a Savior. These reprobates he now considers attractive enough to spend eternity with him, as a reward for turning him into a human sacrifice to himself.

I kept waiting and waiting for human beings to do something admirable in the Bible. I read way through to Omega, and don't waste your time, folks. You're a stinker all the way through. But don't worry about it, because the Lord loves stinkers. It is the happy, successful people who use their minds to accomplish something that he hates.

I had always heard the words "free will" bandied about, but I never could see how God's will could prevail if human beings could do anything they wanted to do. And do you know I was right? I found out that God is the Malevolent Manipulator, the potter who fashions the clay to "honor or dishonor," as Paul and Isaiah agree. I was horrified to read how he hardened Pharaoh's heart, and then I read in the New Testament that as many as were ordained to eternal life believed. And there was more about strong delusion, and there was Jesus saying the way was deliberately obscured even from righteous people who want to know it and that his stories, which I call the terrible parables because they're usually about tormentors and slaves, could be understood by only the disciples. Honestly, now, have you ever known of a bigger bunch of clods than the disciples? After all, Luke tells us that they "understood none of these things." A friend of mine says Jesus was the Rodney Dangerfield of the Holy Land. He just couldn't get any respect from his family, his neighbors, John the Baptist, the disciples, or the Jews, not even from a fig tree, and I wondered if he was the first omnipotent god to come to earth and not be recognized.

But then I began to admire the disciples. You see, they were wonderful skeptics. They demanded evidence right up to the time tongues of fire landed on their heads, an event which reinforced my belief that any god who wanted to be a savior could reveal itself equally to all. I think a tongue of fire on the head would persuade me. How about you?

But I still didn't know what kind of monster was this god, until I saw that Jesus *deliberately* hid his light under a bushel. "Tell no one" was often his command.

Why, I asked myself, is the human race denied evidence about Christianity? Why is it a virtue to accept *any* religion without it, when it would seem the one area to require it, if the punishment for error is unforgivable? Even Abraham asked for evidence, and the Lord obliged him with a magic trick. The Old Testament Jews repeatedly exacted signs and wonders, and God even had to make a sun dial shadow go backward. Why is it a *sin* for people to demand evidence about Christianity? Truth is not stashed in the F file under Faith, and no virtue should be attached to belief in what *is* stashed there.

🦋

Christians tell me that they have a higher destiny than the lower animals, because Homo sapiens can reason. But the Bible tells me that this gift of reason, which they call god-given, may be the match that lights the fires of hell for all who dare to use it, since whatever is not of faith is sin.

Next I came across all the predestination stuff and how the names of the saved are already written in the book of life from the foundation of the world. No preacher ever told me about that, and I certainly see why. And I began to wonder a little (actually a lot) about the Master Plan of the Great Designer, who does everything on impulse and whose every bungled procedure leads to the Cross. I was desperately trying to assign some purpose to the Almighty Architect. But in spite of all the How-Great-Thou-Art's, the devil kept popping up with these nagging questions. After losing out with Job, he'd been racking up victories all over the world and had moved on to me. I could see no motivation for the creation, Adam was an afterthought *gardener*, Eve had to be fashioned as his helpmate when the lower animals didn't fit the bill, and childbirth was declared a curse. Now there's a plan!

And the question that nagged me the most about the New Testament master plan is one which Christians ignore today but which bothered Paul. Since Jesus suddenly appeared with the gift of eternal life, what was the fate of all who lived before he came? Paul's notoriously big heart bleeds, but he concludes that the pre-Jesus Jews are denied eternal life. At the same time he doesn't assign them to hell, so we are left to assume that all human beings who existed for four million years before Christianity are mouldering forever in their graves.

The plan was for Jesus to come to earth two thousand years ago with a pocketful of miracles and souls for the people who were then alive. After his return to heaven from Earth (it is about twelve septillion miles from Earth to the edge of our galaxy with four hundred billion suns to dodge) he is going to build those mansions, come back before his generation dies out, finally put an end to the world which has been such a rotten disap-

— 478 —

pointment, and deposit *most* of these souls in hell. No wonder heaven is only 12,000 furlongs wide, long, and high.

So much for the justice we are supposed to find in this book where we are told to look for behavior guidelines. Guidelines which go on to teach that it is ethical for the innocent to suffer for the guilty, and that morality is served when we let a blameless person pay for our misdeeds, as if expiation could ever be achieved in such a way. And how can the Bible teach responsibility when everything is preordained and predestined? Fay Wray in the hands of King Kong had more control over her fate than human beings at the mercy of the Bible deity.

And guess what further entrapment I discovered on his part?

Paul, that lyncher who never became less cruel and struck people blind as he set the example for elitist Christians in their dealings with non-believers, saying "From such withdraw thyselves" and "let every unbeliever be accursed," tells us that everyone was declared a sinner intentionally by the Lord so that Jesus could come with the gift of grace. Did humankind fall, then? Or were they pushed because Eve wanted to eat of the tree of knowledge?

Paul goes on to reveal (after all, he is the only one to whom the mystery has been exposed) that God *next* formulated the *Mosaic* Law in order to *increase* sin (disobedience to the law) so that *more* grace might be *needed*.

I simply could not absorb what I was being told. I decided that if, by god, we mean rascal, then the god of the Bible was the greatest god who had ever lived in the minds of human beings. And I took a second look at him as a Santa Claus. His gift of grace was given to all who believed, but only those ordained to eternal life *believed*. And the Jews were deliberately given the "Spirit of Slumber" so that they could not see or know the truth. By this time I was completely bewildered. The Lord who established Judaism had now come up with a plan to damn all Judaists to hell!

And what about this eternal life business? Didn't God make Adam and Eve leave the garden because he feared they would eat the fruit of another tree and live forever? My head was spinning. And didn't this Lord say, "Beside me there is no Savior?" And don't the Jews believe in one-third of the Trinity, and doesn't any third equal the whole? And don't the gates of the New Jerusalem have inscribed over them the names of the 12 tribes of Israel? And aren't the ones closest to the Lamb during eternity going to be 144,000 male Jewish virgins? Help, theologians! Tell me how you turned the Chosen People into the Damned People!

I'm only kidding. The Bible told me how they did it. The Jews didn't recognize their Messiah, that's how. They didn't know he was supposed to be the Lord in human form. Now, really. It was obvious to me by this time that the Jews had created the Lord, instead of the other way around, as I had been taught. I was familiar with some mythology, and now I began to deprogram myself, and I saw that the Lord was just as fabulous as Zeus and Horus, and Jesus only one of many crucified saviors. I saw that gods come in very handy. They may explain the Unknown, and they might help you if you treat them right. And if you want to be important, how better than to make up a supreme being who names you his Chosen People and despises everyone else? If you want to control your people, how better than to put a thousand rules into a god's mouth and have him annihilate anyone who disobeys them? If you want to take other people's land, how better to justify it than to have your god tell you to do it and leave no one breathing? If you want to be sexist and racist, how better to condone it than by having a sexist, racist god not only approve it but order it? If you are typical of the times and inclined to be cruel, how better to burn, hang, drown, smite, mutilate, and torture than to have your god command you to do it and set the example himself? If you want to kill your neighbor, your friend, and members of your family, and thrust your children through when you're not beating them black and blue, what better way to get permission than from a god who is an amoral fiend himself? Poor God! We can't always choose our biographers.

❦

To me the Bible seemed a book written by nobody knows whom in a barbaric age, solely about the Jews and their superstitions. Sometimes I wonder why the Jews don't renounce it as defamatory and that goes for both Testaments. A similar record of most ancient cultures would read much the same. But let me go back to the Messiah, who was supposed to save the Jews from the Gentiles and reestablish the Jewish kingdom.

It is absolutely ludicrous for Christianity to be telling the Jews that their Messiah has come and turned out to be their Lord in person. Most of the time the Jews had no problem recognizing the Lord in the Old Testament, even when he wrestled with them and disguised himself as a pillar of cloud or smoke. This god didn't do anything but hover over the

Jews for 4,000 years, and I'm supposed to believe they don't know him as Jesus? After all, the Bible made it clear to me that Jesus did not fulfill some of the important prophesies, such as the one that Elijah must first appear and anoint the Messiah. When confronted with this, Jesus said that John the Baptist was Elijah, but John said he was not. In fact, Jesus was never anointed, and for the Jews he was anything but a deliverer.

Personally, I felt that the angel Gabriel should be belled, not only to protect unwary women from him and his Holy Ghost partner in crime, but to warn everyone that this angel of the Lord is very careless of the truth. Not only did Jesus not save the Jews from their sins, but he never occupied David's throne or ruled over the House of Jacob for one hour.

Even many people who reject Christianity have been reluctant to criticize Jesus the person, and I fully expected to find the Sweet Jesus we hear about today on every side. And of course I used to warble about being in the garden with Jesus and "he walks with me and he talks with me."

Well, I was hard pressed to find any place in the gospels where Jesus walked with anyone or talked with anyone without castigating them and calling them names. "Blind guides! Fools! Whited Sepulchres! Faithless and perverse generation! Woman (for his mother)!" Jesus was sweet only when you agreed with him, and even then you had better pay attention. His usual discourse included one of his terrible parables, after which he abruptly departed.

Oh, how Jesus was served up to me in church! I heard only the nice things most of the time, and some of the questionable behavior and teachings once more became the silk purse, but the Jesus of the gospels was a stranger to me, and again, I see why. Recently the pope has accused people of tampering with the simplicity of the words of Jesus. He should be eternally grateful for the tampering that's been so carefully accomplished. Should the *gospel* Jesus ever be resurrected, the astonishment I felt would be widespread.

The other day I went into the store where I usually buy paint. I was greeted at the door by a sign: If you OPEN your heart, Jesus will come in. They gave me a paint stirrer on which was their lettered conviction: Jesus is Lord. I wanted to ask them if they'd ever heard of the Crusades and the Inquisition and the Dark Ages, all of which could be laid at the door of Sweet Jesus? I wondered if they knew that his words had often led to some of the most reprehensible crimes against humanity and some of the most immoral personal behavior ever documented. And you can rest assured I was never told that he was an exorcist who talked to devils, that he believed certain maladies were caused by possession, that he healed with spit; that he knew nothing of the Universe and believed the earth to be flat, that he cursed a fig tree for not bearing out of season, that he had to be persuaded to heal a Gentile child because he said his message was only for the lost tribes of Israel, that he refused to wash his hands, that he damned three cities for not welcoming him, that he was rude to his mother and lied to his brothers and taught family abandonment, that he cast devils into 2,000 pigs who ran into a lake and were drowned, that he defended slavery and told how to beat servants, that he told people to hate their lives, to mutilate their bodies, to drink poison, handle snakes, and jabber nonsense, that he said he came with a sword to cause hatred and division. I was told only the same old tired parables, never the brutal ones. I wasn't told that he was superstitious and believed in the evil eye, and I was not aware that he loved to describe the sufferings of the damned and seemed always to be plotting to trap as many of them as he could. Sure, I knew all about the adulteress he defended, but it was never pointed out that he let the adulterer go or that he told a story about ten virgins awaiting one bridegroom and said woe to pregnant women and those who are suckling babies at the end of the world. Jesus is Lord and everything that supported that statement is what I was told.

Can you imagine how many sermons I listened to without realizing that Jesus convinced his followers that he was coming right back before his generation died out and that they were so sure of this that they made such statements as: "Now once in the end of the world hath he appeared." This was supposed to mean that the end of the world at that time would make it unnecessary for Christ to come again and again to forgive the sins of succeeding generations. As a child I was terrified about the End of the World. I didn't know the moon had to turn to blood first. Or that there would be swords and kings and horses. When I finally faced up to the fact that I could not admire in a deity what I condemned in human beings, I knew that I could not denounce Torquemada and Hitler and worship their Bible counterpart who knew that his salvation plan would be damnation for most people of the world. Didn't he say that many are called but few are chosen and that strait is the gate and narrow is the way and few there be that find it? Not only is he comfortable with this situation but so seem to be those who worship this divine sadist. We all know that Christians are the only happy people. The Christian business of making themselves happy is a twenty billion dollar one.

But it wasn't only the gods of the Bible that I found not to my taste. I searched the scriptures in vain for someone to serve as a role model for human beings who wished to lead exemplary lives. Let's see now. There was Abraham, a pimp for his wife, and a blackmailer who would have been charged with abandonment and child abuse in today's society. Lot was next, a drunkard guilty of incest with his two virgin daughters, one of nineteen cases of incest in the Bible (not counting the children of Adam and Eve). Then there was Noah, another drunkard, who curses his grandson for his son's behavior. I waded through the other family scandals till I got to David, and we all know about him, except I hadn't been told that he hated the lame and the blind, tortured captives, and hamstringed horses. Samson was another animal torturer; he tied three hundred foxes together two by two and set their tails on fire. Solomon was so wise he had a thousand wives and concubines. And Gideon! I wonder if the Gideons ever read about how he slaughtered and tortured thousands with the Lord's help. As far as getting acquainted with your hero or heroine goes, women who belong to Esther societies in their churches would be scandalized if they actually became familiar with this hard-hearted Hannah of the Persian court. And I certainly hoped my parents hadn't named me after Ruth, when I read about her sordid seduction scene with her kinsman. I finally happened upon one reputable person in the Old Testament. He was distinguished by his coat of many colors and his honorable and forgiving nature. Joseph, of course. He was one of the gems I sometimes speak of that can be found by wading through the muck of most of the Bible.

But my greatest revulsion towards those who were next to God's own heart has to be reserved for Peter. If I were the pope, I would not smile when I was addressed: "Thou art Peter." I was already familiar with Peter's cowardly behavior and Jesus's sometime contempt for him, but little did I know how low he could sink when it came to revenue and profit. I have pity for him if he was crucified either right side up or upside down, but he never did have to answer for frightening two converts to death for withholding some money from the communist Christian church and throwing their bodies into the ground with nary a last rite or extreme unction. Speaking of murder, Moses was guilty, and Paul was an accessory. The Bible does not allow any murderer to enter the kingdom of heaven, but St. Peter even has the keys.

I don't know how the courts can make criminals swear upon the Bible, when this book is a chronicle of every kind of crime committed by the Lord and his favorites. If I were a defense lawyer, I would say, Look, Judge, my client only did what so and so does in the Bible.

❦

You know, as we get older, we are sometimes afflicted with palsy, an uncontrollable shaking of the head. Age hasn't yet given me this malady, but I read the Bible, and I've been shaking my head ever since. Even my husband is a victim. Sometimes, upon hearing the traditional propaganda about the Good Book, we can be seen shaking our heads at each other. As long as this forbidding tome is left to the clergy, they will make of it what they will. That is why I call it a behavior grab bag. It is possible to pull out justification for imposing your will on others, simply by calling your will God's will. I can even use the Bible to forbid you to jog, practice law, take a census, or sleep on a downy pillow.

History and current events prove my point. The divine tyrant of the Old Testament still has his feet on the necks of Judaists, Christians, and Moslems, and they refuse to shake him off. They have prostrated themselves before the imagination and superstitions of the long ago and choose to be enslaved to the morality of an age of ignorance and savagery. People have made an idol of the Bible. And they call all this freedom. Pardon me while I shake my head.

I didn't know whether to laugh or cry when I encountered the taboos and make believe of the Bible. By spending a few minutes with the Lord, I experienced medievalism again, with its myths and bugaboos of our fearful, groping ancestors . . . virgin births, angry gods, human and animal sacrifices, purification by fire and blood, angels, devils, spirits, souls, ghosts, crucified redeemers, heavens and hells, signs and wonders, resurrections. Incidentally, I found nine specific resurrections of the dead in the Bible, several ascensions, miracle workers by the number. I found that Jesus wasn't unique in any way that would make him divine, and as for the prophets, do guesses about the future make you messengers of a god? And anyone can have a revelation or be inspired at any opportune time.

I shudder when I hear people demand that we go back to the Bible. I have just one suggestion for them, that they read the Mosaic Law of the Old Testament and remember that Jesus said he came to uphold that law by every jot and tittle. Then let them read Paul and see how his theology nullifies our Bill of Rights, opposes science, forbids pleasure, discourages any accomplishment and personal pride, recommends that mouths must be stopped and books burned, that women submit to their husbands totally, and that men not even touch women.

While I was finally searching the scriptures, I had to keep pinching myself to be sure I existed. The Bible's language is so sexist that most of the time one is not conscious of the female sex, *and* most of the time that's probably just as well, since from Eve on, women are the culprits and the disposable property of the male population. The double standard waves over every page. Sex is sinful. Eunuchs and celibacy are praised as signs of holiness and purity. Several million monks and nuns testify to this recommendation.

I did become convinced that Eve should replace Mary as the heroine of Christianity. The Bible tells me that Eve was responsible for the fall of man. No fall—no need for a redeemer—no Christianity. Mother Eve, you gave birth to the new faith. In sin did you conceive it.

I am pleased as punch no longer to believe in a god who declares reason a sin, who will not choose many noble and great and wise things but has chosen the base things of the world, the foolish things, the weak things and the things which are not. A god who can choose his companions in eternity and prefers Jerry Falwell and Tammy Bakker over Albert Einstein and Marie Curie. I am no longer a fool for Christ's sake. And I have no more desire to be a sheep than to be a fool.

Skepticism is the way to knowledge, and that is why I am proud to be a skeptic.

Catherine Fahringer
(Photo by Robert McLeroy, San Antonio Express-News Magazine)

41

Catherine Fahringer

LONE STAR ACTIVIST

Born September 18, 1922

We would be 1,500 years ahead if it hadn't been for the church dragging science back by its coattails and burning our best minds at the stake.

Portrait of an Atheist

by Craig Phelon

This article originally appeared in the San Antonio Express-News Magazine as "Catherine Fahringer: Speaking Out For Separation Of Church And State, Speaking Up For Equality For The Non-Religious" on Sunday, March 24, 1991.

WHEN MAYOR LILA COCKRELL GATHERED CITY LEADERS for a February prayer breakfast in the Convention Center, another much smaller group led by Catherine Fahringer broke bread at a local restaurant to protest the event.

Relatively few San Antonians were aware of the protest dinner, which commemorated the birthday of Revolutionary War patriot and religion critic Thomas Paine.

If the media had given the protest wide coverage, which it didn't, many residents might be outraged at the protest, or bewildered.

They might ask, "What's wrong with the mayor's having a prayer breakfast?"

Well, Fahringer says, there's plenty wrong.

The organization she founded and directs, Freethought Forum, issued a press release that expresses "dismay and outrage" that the mayor should use her elected office and city funds and facilities to organize a religious exercise.

"San Antonio is particularly lax about observing the wall of separation of church and state," the release reads. "Mayor Cockrell's affiliation with Trinity Baptist Church in organizing a prayer breakfast is not only repugnant because of its unconstitutionality, but it is also embarrassing to have a mayor think that prayer will solve the problems she was elected to address."

Cockrell says she established the mayor's prayer breakfast during her previous term in the early 1980s. It was patterned after the National Prayer Breakfast in Washington, D.C.

She resumed the practice after the first year of her current term "at the specific request of two citizens who came to my office."

The suggestion involved including spiritual guidance along with other approaches to deal with a number of problems, she says.

"It was an ecumenical service. No one was excluded and a very modest fee ($5) was charged to cover the actual expenses," she says. "The idea was to try to have it a break-even event."

Wouldn't it have been more productive and cost-effective, Fahringer wonders, if the mayor had spent the same amount of time and money on a gathering of free-thinking intellectuals for a brainstorming session on solving the city's problems—instead of on a religious rite?

Opinions like that one make Fahringer unpopular. She represents a minority viewpoint that often is ignored.

In fact, she believes her organization represents the "voice of reason," that is not only ignored, but actively suppressed.

While religious messages seem to be everywhere on television and radio, Fahringer has been trying for four years to get a sixty-second pro-atheist commercial aired on local TV stations.

All the stations she approached have refused to run it.

The commercial was made by the Freedom From Religion Foundation in Madison, Wisconsin. It featured Dan Barker, a musician and former fundamentalist preacher.

It opens with a few bars of "Onward Christian Soldiers," fades to a testimonial by Barker, and closes with the final bars of "Let Freedom Ring."

The text reads:

Hello, I'm Dan Barker.

I'm a former minister, a former evangelist. For many years I preached the Gospel of Jesus, the Bible, miracles and faith.

Now I'm an atheist.

I'm an atheist because in my search for truth I discovered that religious beliefs do not withstand the test of evidence and reason.

As a freethinker I now see the dangers of fundamentalism, and I've become a member of a freethought group which is working to keep state and church separate. Won't you join in this critically important effort? Write to me.

KSAT, KMOL, KENS, and KRRT turned down the spot. Station managers gave reasons including: "not in line with community standards" and "disparaging" content.

"I don't know what they're afraid of," Fahringer says. "Maybe that the stations will be bombed or something."

More recently, she tried to get KENS to run an series of short spots that have Dan Barker quoting Thomas Jefferson, George Washington, James Madison, Benjamin Franklin, and Thomas Paine on the church/state issue.

The station returned her tape without explanation.

Fahringer sees this as an indication of how far religion has come in suppressing freedom of expression: Quotes from America's founding fathers are considered too controversial to air on television.

"The fact that the founders of this country would not be allowed to purchase air time for their ringing messages of truth, reason, justice, equality and freedom is beyond belief," a news release from Fahringer's organization reads.

"Freedom of religion apparently means: If you've got one, you're free. But, by God, if you don't have one, you have no rights anywhere along the line," says Fahringer.

Despite constitutional guarantees of free speech, the non-religious frequently suffer discrimination, she says.

❦

She mentions an ongoing dispute in Indiana, where the state government allowed Gideon bibles to be placed in state-park hotel rooms, but barred an atheist group from leaving pamphlets there.

The usual excuse that criticizing religion might offend someone reflects the genius of religious mind-control techniques, Fahringer says. The best way to keep followers from hearing the voice of reason is to brand sacrilegious anyone who questions church teaching.

"I figure that faith is pretty shaky if it can't stand criticism," she says.

However, religious people seem to have no qualms about telling non-believers they're going to roast in hell if they don't mend their ways, Fahringer says.

"I don't understand why we have to be worried so about their feelings when they ride roughshod over ours.

"I think it's really offensive when I get corralled in some prayer situation. I thought it was a secular event and I went and suddenly someone decides to lead a public prayer."

Christians assume it's okay to impose their beliefs on others at all sorts of public events, such as business luncheons, PTA meetings and football games, she says. But what would happen if an atheist stood up and asked for equal time to reflect on the importance of human reason?

Fahringer is the city's most high-profile atheist. She's frequently called the Madalyn Murray O'Hair of San Antonio—a comparison Fahringer doesn't like.

"Madalyn is the only known atheist," she says. "There *are* other atheists out there. They are beautiful people. Madalyn's not, unfortunately."

O'Hair has a reputation for being hot-tempered and arrogant.

"That was the first organization I joined," says Fahringer. "It was the first one I knew about, and I lasted about a year. And I found out that Madalyn Murray O'Hair is to atheism what Jim and Tammy Bakker were to Christianity."

O'Hair runs a large, high-profile, and highly financed organization, Fahringer explains, adding she's not saying O'Hair is involved in fraud.

Fahringer says she joined the Austin-based American Atheists because she agrees with O'Hair's philosophies. However, she says she was turned off by that organization's emphasis on fund-raising.

Now she's affiliated with the Wisconsin-based Freedom From Religion Foundation. Last year, Fahringer appeared with two other foundation members on TV's Sally Jessy Raphael Show.

Fahringer remembers the show with mixed feelings. It was supposed to have been a debate between three atheists who were once religious and three religious people who were once atheists.

Before the show, both sides were encouraged to interrupt their opponents. "We were told, 'We don't want this to be an intellectual discussion,' " she says.

The audience was overwhelmingly hostile to Fahringer's side.

Locally, she is a frequent contributor to newspaper editorial pages—although she says her file of rejected letters is much thicker than the one of those that were printed.

She formed the Freethought Forum as a local chapter of the Freedom From Religion Foundation with co-director Jeff Levan.

Though her opinions are unappealing to many religious people, Fahringer is personally charming. She is a petite, sunny-faced Alamo Heights homemaker who just happens to believe it's her calling to defend the principle of separation of church and state.

She has several other interests and supports other causes, such as the American Civil Liberties Union—though she scolds the ACLU for not being more active in church/state issues.

"I read constantly," she says. And she used to love to scour garage sales for antiques, though she was more apt to come away with a stuffed animal.

When she couldn't find something else she wanted, "I would buy one of those as a consolation." She has several stuffed animals and she periodically gives some away to various charities or children. She calls it "thinning her herd."

She laces her comments with humor and sarcasm.

In her frequent letter exchanges with public officials, religious leaders or the media, that sarcasm can cut to the quick.

She wrote to Bob Rogers, news director at KENS, congratulating him for announcing in response to an anti-war broadcast that even unpopular causes deserved to be heard.

That must mean the station was ready to air the atheist ad, she wrote. "Oh, at long last I am going to have my faith in freedom and justice restored! Oh, thank you, Mr. Rogers!"

The station still refused her commercial.

Mike Simpson, general sales manager at KENS, says he wants to reserve comment on the proposed freethought commercial until he has investigated the situation further. Simpson is responsible for accepting or rejecting ads for broadcast.

The Freethought Forum and Secular Humanist Association of San Antonio combined have about one hundred members. That's obviously small compared to the number of San Antonians who attend churches and synagogues. However, Fahringer says if the organization included all those

San Antonians who don't have any particular religious faith, the membership would be substantial.

Freethinkers aren't joiners, she says.

"A freethinker just doesn't want to be boxed in. They just aren't great for belonging and they're not great on action, either."

❦

Fahringer and others who are activists in the name of secular humanism feel they're playing an important role in preserving the American way of life by fending off religion's attempts to control society.

They argue that if the principle of separation of church and state had not been inserted into the U.S. Constitution, America would be a Christian version of Iran or Iraq.

That is, we would have a society in which all behavior is strictly controlled by religious doctrine, minority religions or philosophies are persecuted as heresy, and freedoms of speech and intellectual pursuits are curtailed.

Evidence of increasing attempts by religion, especially fundamentalist Christians, to control the rest of society can be seen regularly in newspaper headlines, she says.

The Religious Right is the major force behind the anti-abortion movement, she says, as well as attempts to curtail National Endowment for the Arts funding for artists who may criticize religion or explore sexual themes.

Religion affects the way our culture views life in many subtle ways, she says. Religions typically involve some sort of suppression of sexuality, which has led to many psychological problems—as natural feelings often conflict with religious teachings.

Religious teachings have been used to justify slavery, suppress women and promote violence and child abuse, she says.

"I lay practically every ill of our society at the foot of the Bible," she says.

"We would be 1,500 years ahead if it hadn't been for the church dragging science back by its coattails and burning our best minds at the stake."

Fahringer answers to any number of different titles for her point of view—atheist, agnostic, secular humanist, etc.—but the title is less important than the fact that she simply doesn't subscribe to a particular religious dogma.

"I've always had a problem with titles or names or categories," she says. "I like the word *freethinker* the best."

Fahringer has a mountain of paperwork supporting freethinking.

The information arrives at the *Magazine* in an avalanche of letters, brochures and documents. There's even a cassette titled "My Thoughts Are Free," containing freethinker songs.

"I bet I've gained ten pounds today licking stamps," she says. "I just read where they have a tenth of a calorie."

※

Judging from the materials, secular humanism covers a wide spectrum of personal opinions. It includes a large number of people who are simply indifferent to religion, as well as those who believe all organized religions, including Christianity, are based on nothing more than myths.

Secular humanists take the position that nobody really knows for sure what's out there, Fahringer says.

While there are many religions in the world, there is no universally accepted concrete historical or scientific proof that any one of them is correct, she says.

"Nobody knows anything, really. The big question is still out there."

Adopting a belief system and wishing it were true with all your heart doesn't make it true no matter how many people believe it with you, says Fahringer.

What's more, forcing the mind to adopt a rigid belief system may interfere with an individual's power to reason, she adds.

Religions create intellectual limits, Fahringer says. "They (believers) just have a cutoff point beyond which they cannot go, they cannot think."

Some secular humanists may feel, or think they feel, the presence of some external force, says Fahringer. But if there were such a force existing in nature, why worship it? That's like worshipping gravity—or fire.

"I've felt it, too—a sort of belongingness to nature," she says.

"We (atheists) have our thrilling moments. But we don't get them on our knees in some stuffy old building."

Critics of secular humanism frequently view this philosophy as simply another religion that happens to substitute mankind for a god figure. They say the various issues concerning separation of church and state involve substituting secular-humanist values for religious values.

Fahringer disputes this assertion. Secular humanists don't worship anything or require a belief in anything.

In fact, it is the neutral secular "umbrella" provided by the First Amendment that allows the practice of various religions in our multicultural society, she says.

She believes that both freethinking and freedom of religion are endangered when government representatives stray from secular neutrality. When presidents, mayors and schools call upon citizens to pray, they are promoting religion.

It may seem harmless, but the underlying message is: Your government thinks you ought to believe in a deity—and preferably a Christian one, because that's what the rest of us believe.

That's not far from establishing a state religion, she says.

Some of the key issues Fahringer's group and other freethought organizations work with involve fending off what they see as threats to freedom of thought:

The movement to revive organized school prayer—"That's another thing that's so misunderstood," she says.

"Everybody thinks prayer was taken out. It was only *organized* prayer. Anybody who wants to pray at any time is free to do so."

Individual students may pray whenever they want, she says. But a principal, teacher or coach leading students in prayer or telling them it's time to pray or suggesting they ought to pray amounts to state-promoted religion.

When a high-school football coach gathers his players for a moment of prayer before a game, he probably feels he's promoting good moral character in his boys, she says. But he is violating the Constitution, according to current law.

The praying principal or coach is also violating the students' constitutional rights by using his position of authority to impose his religion on a captive audience, she says. The additional message given is that it's okay to ignore the law if you don't agree with it.

From a secular-humanist point of view, the praying coach (or other school authority) sets a bad example in two ways: He violates the Constitution; he tells the students they ought to believe in a myth instead of logic and reason.

"This area is primed and ready and trembling on the brink for some good lawsuit to come along," Fahringer says.

Prison Ministries—"It's hard to understand how religion got such a hammerlock on patriotism and goodness," Fahringer says.

"These people go to prison and they find Jesus and right away they're going to let them out on parole. I'm really sorry about that, but I don't think that's a reason to let them out to rape or do whatever they did again.

"They're a captive audience in prison, too. They have these ministries that go around, and it looks good on your record (if you go along with them). A prisoner might go along with them because he's afraid if he doesn't, it will look bad to the parole board."

Courtroom Oaths—O'Hair's organization already has taken the issue of courtroom oaths to the U.S. Supreme Court—and lost.

However, the standard oath that requires jurors and witnesses to say, "so help me God," still rankles atheists. So does the traditional swearing-in ceremony for judges and other public officials.

Fahringer sees a sad irony when judges swear to defend the Constitution as they violate the principle of separation of church and state with their hands on Bibles, pledging oaths to God.

"If that isn't oxymoronic, I'll eat my hat," she says. "He trashes the Constitution as he swears to uphold it. He ought to be impeached right then and there."

Tax-supported Preaching—Fahringer says many religious-based charities get money from federal and state governments to manage various programs. But the recipients of this tax-supported aid must often sit through sermons and prayers to get the help they need. . . .

Fahringer disputes a common assumption that religious people are more moral than the non-religious.

In her view, the non-religious are more moral because they take responsibility for their actions rather than depend on someone to tell them what's right.

"Our standards are such that people who embrace all those idiotic things like talking snakes are saved and pure and those who don't believe in them, like me, are rotten," she says.

🌾

These and similar issues seem nit-picking to many, but Fahringer echoes the sentiments of other activists—whether their special concerns are racial discrimination, women's liberation or gun control: Most freedoms are not suddenly eliminated, but gradually eroded with seemingly harmless policies.

"Every time something happens and nobody makes a fuss, it goes on and sets a precedent," she says. "Two of the worst things that happened for freethinkers were the inserting of 'under God' in the Pledge of Allegiance and 'In God we trust' on our money."

That happened in the mid-1950s. Now they are brought out as justification for further violations of the separation of church and state, she says.

Fahringer says her evolution as a freethinker activist took several years and was not based on any faith-shattering incident.

"They always say, 'Oh, you must have had a terrible experience. It turned you against something.' You can't turn against something that isn't there."

She was born in Utah to a military family and lived in various cities before her family came to San Antonio when she was twelve.

She was raised an Episcopalian and remained one—at least in name—until adulthood. She began to question her religion when she became a mother.

She was living in England with her husband, who was in the military and stationed there.

Family members said it was her duty to provide religious teaching.

"I was busy coping with how to keep warm. It was plenty cold there," she says, adding it was also difficult to get to a Sunday school.

"So I went out and got 'The Golden Book of Bible Stories.' I thought, 'Let me refresh my memory as to what the bible stories are about.'

"I started reading these stories. And—these are for kids—I didn't like what I was reading. I said to my husband, 'I can't teach this stuff to my kids.' I said, 'I'm nicer than God.'

"I mean, it was, 'get out there and punish somebody if they don't do that or they don't do this.' Mean! So that was the end of Sunday school."

However, Fahringer didn't become an activist until 1987, after she attended a Freedom From Religion convention in St. Louis.

"It seemed so terribly dull when I got back to San Antonio," she says. "No one was doing anything here (in defense of separation of church and state).

"So I figured, why not me?"

Fahringer says she realizes her opinions upset a lot of people, but she says it's not unusual for freethinkers to be in the minority.

She adds that most of civilization's progress has been due to freethinkers who took a stand against the majority point of view.

She mentions a long list of freethinkers who made major contributions to humankind.

It includes Italian astronomer and physicist Galileo, who was imprisoned by the Inquisition; Thomas Alva Edison; Albert Einstein; Thomas Jefferson; James Madison; Mark Twain; Robert Burns; Bertrand Russell; horticulturist Luther Burbank; American Red Cross founder Clara Barton; women's suffrage leader Elizabeth Cady Stanton; economist John Stuart Mill; and many others.

"Sometimes I feel like Alice looking into the looking glass and everything is not the way it ought to be. It's all backwards," Fahringer says.

Of course, the debate will continue over who represents the reality and who represents the mirror's distorted image until mankind's big question is finally answered to everyone's satisfaction.

Meanwhile, Fahringer wants to make sure the great debate includes a few words from freethinkers.

Barbara Smoker

42

Barbara Smoker

PRESIDENT OF NATIONAL SECULAR SOCIETY

Born June 2, 1923

People who believe in a divine creator, trying to live their lives in obedience to his supposed wishes and in expectation of a supposed eternal reward, are victims of the greatest confidence trick of all time.

"So You Believe in God!" 1974

BARBARA SMOKER, WHO WAS A CRADLE CATHOLIC, has been President of the National Secular Society (NSS), the most militant of the organizations in the British secular humanist movement, since 1971.

As a girl, Barbara was torn between the ambitions of becoming a nun or becoming a writer—in either case, for the greater glory of God. For peace of mind and intellectual integrity, she was finally forced to renounce the Catholic faith (and with it all religious faith) at the age of twenty-six in 1949, and immediately found her way into the secular humanist movement.

One of her presidential duties is that of officiating at secular humanist funerals, which have been a feature of the NSS from the time of Charles Bradlaugh and Annie Besant. She has now conducted more than four hundred funerals, and has passed on her expertise to an increasing number of officiants in the humanist movement. During the past few years she has also officiated at humanist wedding ceremonies, as well as analogous ceremonies on behalf of the Gay and Lesbian Humanist Association, of which she is a founding member and Vice-President.

On the lighter side, she published for some years a range of "anti-Xmas" greeting cards, known as Heretic Cards. Over the years she has been active in various other social campaigns, including nuclear disarmament, prison reform, alphabet reform, homelessness, and voluntary euthanasia.

In 1980 she was elected to the executive committee of the Voluntary Euthanasia Society (then called Exit), and was its chairwoman from 1981 to 1985. In that connection, she compiled and edited *Voluntary Euthanasia: Experts Debate the Right to Die*, published by Peter Owen (February 1986).

Her writings include a book of satirical verse, *Good God!—a string of verses to tie up the deity;* a cassette script, *Atheism on a Soap-box;* and a school textbook on *Humanism,* first published as part of the Ward Lock Educational Company's "Living Religions" series in 1973. One of the NSS' most popular leaflets is Barbara's "So You Believe in God!" written in 1974. [See selection]

Becoming actively involved in the campaign to prevent a statutory ban on embryo research, she wrote an illustrated polemical pamphlet, *Eggs Are Not People,* which was distributed by the NSS to all members of Parliament in 1985. That year she recorded a script "Why I Am An Atheist" for the BBC. [See selection]

"Religionists—taking the absolutist line that all human life is sacred and in God's hands—generally see no reason to look into the biological facts, but simply assert 'Life begins at conception.' However, this is not so: life is a continuum," she wrote.

A letter she had written on the dangers inherent in segregating the children of immigrant families in their own denominational schools was counter-signed by twenty-two distinguished persons and published in full in *The Guardian* and elsewhere in July 1986.

When Muslims held a London demonstration on May 27, 1989, against Salman Rushdie, Barbara stood (together with Nicolas and Christine Walter) near Hyde Park, holding aloft a homemade banner reading "Free Speech," and was physically attacked by a surge of demonstrators. She was saved from serious injury by a large plainclothes police officer.

Her various interests have led to innumerable speaking engagements and radio and television broadcasts for more than four decades.

Her writings have been featured regularly in the NSS publication, *The Freethinker.*

In "Mother Teresa—Sacred Cow," Barbara Smoker wrote:

"In the West, among people of all religions and none, Mother Teresa has become a sacred cow; . . . it would require a knowledge of modern psychology and of Christian theology to understand the deep masochistic motivation of a woman who, as a lifelong 'bride of Christ,' sacrifices herself to a lost cause while eschewing the one chance of making any progress with it; and all for the passionate love and adoration of an all-powerful, invisible, aloof being, who apparently, chooses to create this colossal mess faster than she can mop it up, while 'calling' her to dedicate her life to this Sisyphean task. . . . Mother Teresa sees daily the appalling suffering caused by overpopulation, yet she refuses to accept the need for population control or the humane preferability of birth control over death control." (*The Freethinker,* February 1980)

Barbara Smoker

Why I Am An Atheist

This was Barbara Smoker's script for the BBC World Service recorded in June 1985. It was broadcast four times in 1985 and four times the following year.

WHY AM I AN ATHEIST? The short answer is that I cannot accept any of the alternatives. I simply don't find them believable.

Oh, yes—I once had an orthodox creed. I was brought up in a devout Roman Catholic family, and had an old-style convent education—and throughout my childhood and adolescence I was a steadfast believer. That was in the days (before the Second Vatican Council) when the Catholic Church was still Catholic and the pope was infallible—so I was given absolute certitude about God and the universe and my place in it. But in the end—and it took me a very long while—I grew up.

Whenever I mention my Catholic childhood, people tend to assume that the reason I have rejected religion so completely is that an extreme version of it was drummed into me as a child—but it wasn't like that at all. No one needed to drum religion into me: I lapped it up like a thirsty puppy. And by the time the good nuns got hold of me, at the age of four, I was hooked on the supernatural.

At home I was regarded as the pious one of the family—which is saying a great deal—and the nuns at my first convent school seem to have cast me in the role of a future saint. Whenever there was any school entertainment, I was given some religious poem to recite, and once, when they put on a little play in which Jesus appeared, I was given that role, without any competition—though, admittedly, my auburn curls may have contributed to the choice.

There was a large sentimental painting on our classroom wall of a guardian angel hovering protectively over a child on the edge of a precipice—and I accepted it quite literally. I never got on a bus or a train without quickly reminding my guardian angel to keep an eye out for danger.

At home, as in most large families, we were always playing competitive games among ourselves—and Rule Number One, which became standard for any competitive family game, was "No praying." This was at the insistence of the others, who thought that praying would give me an unfair advantage.

On one occasion, when our family, together with a number of aunts, uncles, and cousins, were spending Sunday afternoon at Grandma's, our uncle priest offered a shilling to the best behaved child at the tea-table. When, after a tea-time of unusual restraint, the children were told they could leave the table, I was the only one who remained to say my grace—and that, of course, won me the shilling. The others protested that they too had remembered to say their grace after meals—but quietly, with a less ostentatious sign of the cross. This, however, was apparently not believed. To this day, half a century later, some of my cousins still hold this shilling against me—maintaining that I cunningly planned the whole thing: but it is really not so. I would simply never have thought of eating even a biscuit without saying a grace both before and after.

My gullibility embraced not only the supernatural and miraculous, but also the magical. Amazing though it may seem in these days of advanced childhood knowledge, I was actually ten years old by the time I realised that Christmas presents were not really left by an old red-coated gentleman coming down the chimney. When I upbraided my mother for having told me such lies, she protested that Santa Claus did, in a sense, exist—as the spirit of generosity and giving. But it was too late to give me a metaphorical explanation. I had accepted it literally for too long.

Empathising with younger children on whom the same confidence trick was being imposed, I embarked on a crusade around the neighbourhood, telling all the kids that there was no Santa Claus. This reached the ears of the father of a neighbouring family, who reproved me for spoiling it for the little ones. Spoiling it! I could not understand what he meant. To my mind, they were being made fools of, and I was only saving them from this indignity.

I now see this as the beginning of both my loss of faith and of my persistent missionary zeal in proclaiming scientific truth—but it was many years before Jesus was to go the way of Santa Claus.

At my secondary school—also a convent—the other pupils laughingly referred to me as "the saint," but I was fortunate in that somehow my piety did not make me unpopular. Eventually, however, even the nuns told me to spend less time in church and the convent chapel, and more time in study.

By the time I was fourteen, I had no wish to be anything but a nun—not in a teaching order, but in the Carmelite (enclosed) order. I was already saving up half my pocket-money towards my dowry—and I would gladly have entered at fifteen, as St. Therese did. But my mother said I must wait until the age of nineteen, and then see if I felt the same. She said the same to one of my sisters who, similar to me in temperament, is nine years younger than I—but whereas the second world war started when I was sixteen, and I then left school and went out first into the world of work and then into the Women's Royal Naval Service, my sister, in the post-war years, remained at school until the age of nineteen, and then went straight from one convent as a pupil into another as a novice, with no time between to change her mind. She is still a nun.

In my last year at school I was awarded the religious knowledge medal by the diocesan inspector because, when he unexpectedly departed from the set catechism questions and asked for a proof of Christ's divinity, I was the only student ready with an answer. To me it was obvious that God would not otherwise have given Jesus the power to perform miracles, since this would mislead people as to his divine claims. It did not occur to me at the time that it was an unproved assumption that the gospel stories were true. And no one pointed this out.

On other occasions, I would ask the nuns quite probing theological questions—but, of course, my teenage naivety was no match for their comparatively sophisticated replies, and so, though generally of a questioning turn of mind, I accepted the Catholic creed *in toto*. Indeed, in those days of papal authority it had to be all or nothing; and I remember how amazed I was to hear of a Catholic who had given up practising and yet had remained a believer in Christianity. For me, there was never any possibility of a halfway house between the Catholic Church and atheism.

At the same time, I must already have begun to fear a loss of faith, for I remember praying daily that this would never happen to me. It took ten more years to complete the process.

At the age of nineteen, when, at my naval training camp, I found that there was no provision for Catholics to hear Mass on January the 1st (the feast of the Circumcision) or January the 6th (the Epiphany), which were then holidays of obligation, I successfully requested special 6 a.m. "liberty boats" for that purpose. How my fellow Catholics must have hated me for forcing them to go out on dark, wet mornings, instead of having another two hours in bed!

A year later I was in Ceylon (now Sri Lanka), where I served king and country for the next eighteen months. There I not only mixed with non-Catholic Christians, with some of whom I used to discuss moral theology, but I also visited Hindu temples and Buddhist shrines, and so widened my perspective on religion. Consequently, by the time I returned home after the war, I was no longer sure I wanted to be a nun, though I was still a staunch believer. However, my theological doubts now began to build up, and became more and more insistent.

In confession, I was told that I was suffering from intellectual pride. Who was I to pit my puny intellect against the teaching of Holy Mother Church? I saw the force of this argument—especially as there were important Catholic writers I admired, such as G. K. Chesterton, who, though obviously far more intelligent and learned than I, apparently had no difficulty in accepting doctrines that seemed to me to be irrational and at odds with the world around us. Now, of course, I realise that many people of undoubted mental ability manage to cling to their supernatural beliefs by keeping them, as it were, in different mental compartments from everyday knowledge, not subjecting them to the same sort of scientific scrutiny or rigorous evidence that they would demand for anything else.

As for the accusation of intellectual pride, surely the boot is on the other foot. Atheists don't claim to know *anything* with certainty—it's the believers who know it all.

At school, we were taught that there is no such thing as an atheist—and to some extent I think the nuns were right in this, because they took the word "atheist" to mean someone who categorically denies the existence of any kind of god. Obviously, it must depend on the definition of the word "god," which can mean anything from the very human and immoral Old Testament god, Jehovah, to some sort of abstract god, such as Bernard Shaw's Life Force, or even something as indisputable as the whole of existence. The only objection one can make to that last god-concept is to the confusing use of the word "god" as a synonym for everything.

However, the one function that most gods seem to have in common is to give human existence some ultimate purpose—and, while it is not possible to disprove an ultimate purpose, there does not seem to be any evidence for it. This is not to say, of course, that there is no purpose in life at all: we all make our own purposes as we go through life. And life does not lose its value simply because it is not going to last for ever.

For most believers, however, the important thing is that death is not the end, either for themselves or for their relationship with close friends who have died. Most of us would find it comforting to believe that—but the fact that a belief is comforting does not make it true. And I suppose I just happen to be the sort of person who cannot derive comfort from a belief that has no evidence to support it.

In fact, all the evidence is *against* a personal survival of death: it just doesn't make sense. How could anything that survived the death of the body still be the same person? Just think, what makes you *you?* Isn't it the historical continuity of your body, from conception throughout life, and the genes you were born with, and the things that have happened to you, and your likes and dislikes, and funny little ways, and the memories in your brain? All these things depend on a living body. And how would you recognize a friend in another life without his body—without his face or his voice or anything you knew him by in life? Even the doctrine of the resurrection of the body, on the last day, means having to wait until the end of time before recognising one another. And which body are we supposed to get then? The body we had at birth, or as a teenager, or a fifty-year-old, or a ninety-year-old? If you are going to rise again as a child, so as to be recognised by your grandmother, you'll hardly be recognisable by your grandchildren.

As for the idea that the universe was deliberately created, it fails to explain existence—for one is still left with the question "Who made God?" It is less complicated to suppose that particles of matter and waves of energy have always existed than to suppose they were made out of nothing by a being who had always existed. Besides, if I did accept the idea of deliberate creation, all the suffering there is in life—for so many people, and also for animals—would make it impossible for me to worship the creator. I would have to heap curses on him—or her, or it. But there is just one thing to be said for this creator-god, and that is his evident non-existence. If there were a creator, he could not possibly be both good and almighty—he could either be sadistic and almighty, or good and incompetent, but he could not possibly be both good and almighty.

In the late 1940s, remembering from school theology lessons that, according to Thomas Aquinas, it was possible to come to faith through reason, I decided to try giving my faith a boost through reason stimulated by a course of reading. So I read book after book—mainly books written by Catholic apologists, but also some by moral philosophers, including non-believers. And the more I read, the less I could believe.

Finally, one Saturday morning in November 1949, actually standing by the philosophy shelves of my local public library, I suddenly said to myself, with a tremendous flood of relief, "I am no longer a Catholic." And that, for me, meant I was no longer a Christian or a theist of any kind.

After so much mental turmoil, I did not imagine I had really come to the end of it: I expected to go on having doubts—doubts now about my disbelief. But in fact this never happened. I have never found any reason to suppose that my decision that morning thirty-six years ago was a mistake.

That is not to say that I have not sometimes hankered after my old childhood beliefs—but it is no more possible for me to go back to believing in a god and a heaven than it is to go back to the belief that an old red-coated gentleman climbs down chimneys with presents on Christmas Eve.

So You Believe In God!

Written about 1974, this article has been distributed as a leaflet by the National Secular Society.

PEOPLE WHO BELIEVE IN A DIVINE CREATOR, trying to live their lives in obedience to his supposed wishes and in expectation of a supposed eternal reward, are victims of the greatest confidence trick of all time.

A children's hospital will provide you with ample evidence against the existence of a being that is both all-powerful and all-loving. And even if some specious explanation is contrived for the sufferings of humanity—such as its giving us opportunities for merit, or its being caused by the "sin" of Adam or that of ourselves or our parents—what about the suffering of animals, during the many millions of years before humankind came on the scene?

Since all life and its evolution are based on the principle of the weakest going to the wall, the creator, if the universe really were deliberately created, would be a monster of unimaginable cruelty—enjoying the sight of one animal devouring another, condoning the wastage of a myriad doomed species, and taking sadistic pleasure in the miseries of humankind. If our promised heaven means spending eternity in the company of such a monster, let alone in lickspittle adoration of him or it, what self-respecting human being would want "salvation"?

If the alleged creator really were all-powerful, then he certainly could not be a god of love. If he really were a god of love, then he must be so incompetent that it would surely have been better had he left creation uncreated.

What is the I.Q. of "divine intelligence"? Since it apparently scores no better than random chance, and has learned nothing at all from billions of years of trial and error, "divine intelligence" would be put to shame by the powers of adaptability exhibited by the least of its supposed creatures.

To say that God is good is meaningless unless his alleged goodness is to be judged by some independent criterion—that is, by human values. Therefore, when god-believers argue that human values must come from God they are chasing their own tails.

Most god believers also postulate God as an explanation for existence itself. But if existence needs to be explained, the god-theory fails to explain it, for it leaves us with the necessity of explaining why and how God exists. The assertion that God has existed from all eternity, uncaused, is no advance on the hypothesis that matter (or energy) has existed in varying forms—from all eternity, uncaused.

Now just consider the vastness of the universe in relation to ourselves. Would an overlord of the universe be likely to take a special interest in the doings of individual members of a particular animal species, recently evolved on a small satellite of an inconspicuous star, among the billions of stars of a certain galaxy, itself one of billions of galaxies?

Is ours the only planet anywhere inhabited by a species comparable in intelligence with us? If so, and if the creator's main concern is therefore assumed to be with us, why should he create such a vast universe to house so few of us? Besides, with such a huge choice of territory available, why did he not choose a less hostile environment for us?

If the more likely supposition is made that there are other colonies of intelligent sentient beings scattered about the universe, then god-believers must assume either that God has an equal concern for all—presumably, for instance in Christian terms, sacrificing his son more than once—or else, with supreme arrogance, that earth is his chosen planet and humankind his chosen species.

Even more arrogant, and selfish in the extreme, is the assumption, within the context of our own planet at this particular moment in time, that I and mine (especially in the more affluent areas of the planet) are

God's chosen few. Although this is rarely admitted, it is clearly implied in every prayer of thanksgiving. To say grace, knowing that people on this globe are starving, indicates a highly selfish acquiescence in the arrogantly supposed favouritism of the almighty. A really decent god-believer, far from giving thanks for the food and good health and fortune enjoyed by himself and his family and close friends, would surely curse God for his neglect of the hungry, the sick and the tormented, throughout the world.

To imagine that God wants prayers and hymns of praise is to make him out a sort of oriental potentate; while praying for favours is an attempt to get him to change his allegedly all-wise mind.

To say that "God moves in mysterious ways" is to put up a smokescreen of mystery behind which fantasy may survive in spite of all the facts.

Anne Nicol Gaylor
(Photograph by Bill Fritz)

43

Anne Nicol Gaylor

FOUNDER, FREEDOM FROM RELIGION FOUNDATION

Born November 25, 1926

There are no gods, no devils, no angels, no heaven or hell. There is only our natural world. Religion is but myth and superstition that hardens hearts and enslaves minds.

Wording for a monument to counter religious displays, 1995

FEMINIST, FREETHINKER AND ABORTION RIGHTS ACTIVIST Anne Nicol Gaylor was born at her family's farm on Thanksgiving night, 1926. A second-generation free-thinker, she was the youngest child and only daughter of Jason Theodore Nicol and Lucie Sowle Nicol. Her father, a graduate of the Agricultural Course at the University of Wisconsin, farmed and managed a cooperative grain and feed store in nearby Tomah, Wisconsin, a Monroe County community of 5,000 about fifty miles from the Mississippi River. Her mother, who had graduated from Milwaukee State Teachers College, had been an elementary school teacher in and around Tomah for several years before her marriage.

Scottish in nationality, her father's ancestors had come to the United States in the mid-1800s. An aunt used to chuckle, telling Anne that her great-grandfather had come through the wonderfully fertile soil of southern Wisconsin "to find some sand and hills like he was used to" in Monroe County. Her mother's family traces its beginnings in America to the Mayflower. George Soule (Sowle), a carpenter's apprentice, was one of the hardy few surviving the difficult first winter at Plymouth Colony.

Anne's mother died unexpectedly in 1928 when Anne was not yet two years old, and her brothers were four, seven and eight. A practical nurse/housekeeper had come to care for the children for two weeks while their mother was hospitalized for surgery, but instead stayed ten years, caring for the children and farm home throughout the Great Depression. Of Irish background, her songs and recitations were a nostalgic part of Anne's childhood, as were the farm's many pet animals—a bevy of cats, two appealing dogs and a very special pet lamb, Judy Plum, named for a character in a Lucy Maud Montgomery novel. As a little girl she played in the creek that ran through the farm, wading out to a tiny, cowslip-covered island, the beginning of a lifelong fascination for islands, which later became her favorite travel destination.

She started first grade at a one-room country school at age four and soon read almost everything there. She recalled how gratifying it was to have her own card at the Carnegie library in town with its shelves of books waiting to be read.

A graduate of Tomah High School, she received a Bachelor of Arts degree from the University of Wisconsin in Madison with an English major in 1949, financing her education through room and board and summer jobs. Following graduation she married Paul Joseph Gaylor in 1949 in Springfield, Missouri, and they returned to live in Wisconsin where their four children were born: Andrew Joseph, twins Ian Stuart and Annie Laurie, and Jamie Lachlan.

An entrepreneur, Anne started the first temporary office help service in Madison in 1958 and, with a partner, the city's first private employment agency in 1959. After the sale of her successful small businesses in 1966 she and her husband owned a suburban weekly newspaper for three years. As editor, she transformed the *Middleton Times Tribune* into a lively, award-winning piece of community journalism—too lively for the tastes of some in the staid religious community when she ran the first editorial in the state calling for the legalizing of abortion in 1968.

She became a pioneering abortion rights advocate, establishing a referral service three years prior to *Roe v. Wade*. Since 1972 she has administered, as a volunteer, the Women's Medical Fund charity, which has helped more than seven thousand needy Wisconsin women pay for abortions. She was active in several women's rights groups, serving as vice-president central of the National Abortion Rights Action League from 1972–1978.

"There were many groups working for women's rights," she realized, "but none of them dealt with the root cause of women's oppression—religion."

In the mid-seventies, with her daughter Annie Laurie and an elderly friend, John Sontarck of Milwaukee, she started the Freedom From Religion Foundation, "a dining-room table cause group" until 1978, when it was organized as a national association with Anne as president, a post she still holds. The Foundation's focus has been the separation of church and state and the education of the public about nontheism.

Under Anne's direction, the group launched the only existing freethought newspaper in North America, *Freethought Today*, in 1984, produced two documentary films, "A Second Look at Religion" and "Champions of the First Amendment," brought a variety of lawsuits around the country to protect the First Amendment, published books, held annual national conventions, popularized the nineteenth-century term "freethinker," and handled a multitude of protests against religious incursion in government and public schools.

In 1983, when Congress passed a law designating it as the "Year of the Bible," Anne was chief plaintiff in an attempt, unsuccessful but widely reported, to enjoin President Ronald Reagan from signing the proclamation. In 1995 the Foundation succeeded in overturning a Wisconsin statute that designated worship on Good Friday and established it as a state holiday. Continuing her feminist work Anne successfully sued a Wisconsin Attorney General, Donald Hanaway, in 1989, when he illegally placed the State of Wisconsin on a friend-of-the-court brief before the U.S. Supreme Court seeking to overturn *Roe v. Wade.*

Anne was the guest on numerous radio and television talkshows in the 1970s and 1980s—local, regional and national. She appeared on most of the early programs in Wisconsin on the subject of abortion rights, then still a near-taboo topic. In Philadelphia she was choked on the set of a television program by a member of the audience who was going to "drive the devil out of her." She tangled with Catholic talkshow host Phil Donahue in Chicago when he refused to show her book on abortion because of its positive title—*Abortion Is A Blessing.* As they were about to go on the air, Donahue told Anne that her book was "tasteless" and "would create shock waves across America." However, toward the end of the show in response to a call about the power of religion in the media, Anne said, "Let me tell you about the power of religion. I am probably the first person ever to appear on the Donahue show whose book could not be shown because of religious prejudice. Because I dared to write a book with a positive title about abortion, my book may not be shown. Yet I have referred thousands of women for abortion. They have been as young as twelve and as old as fifty-two. Many of them have had nine and ten children. Many have been ill. I *know* that abortion is a blessing. It is a blessing for women and a blessing for society." A sheepish Donahue displayed the book; America survived the "shock wave."

Anne's awards include: Zero Population Growth Recognition Award, 1983; Humanist Heroine Award, American Humanist Association, Feminist Caucus, 1985; Commitment to Women Award, Women's Political Caucus (Wisconsin), 1989; Feminist of the Year Award, National Organization for Women (Wisconsin), 1994; Citation by the Wisconsin State Senate (1994).

Her two published books are *Abortion Is A Blessing* (1976) and *Lead Us Not Into Penn Station* (1983), a collection of essays. [See selections].

Anne's best-known aphorisms: "Nothing fails like prayer."

"There can be no religious freedom without the freedom to dissent."

"It is possible to speculate endlessly about the nonexistent."

What's Wrong With The Ten Commandments?

*These essays were included in the book **Lead Us Not Into Penn Station** (1983).*

CRITICS OF THE BIBLE OCCASIONALLY CAN SCORE a point or two in discussion with the religious community by noting the many teachings in both the Old and New Testaments that encourage the bible believer to hate and to kill, biblical lessons that history proves Christians have taken most seriously. Nonetheless the bible defendant is apt to offer as an indisputable parting shot, "But don't forget the ten commandments. They are the basic bible teaching. Study the ten commandments."

Do study the ten commandments! They epitomize the childishness, the vindictiveness, the sexism, the inflexibility and the inadequacies of the bible as a book of morals.

Actually, only six of the ten commandments deal with an individual's moral conduct, which comes as a surprise to most Christians. Essentially, the first four commandments say:

1. Thou shalt have no other gods before me.

2. Thou shalt not make thee any graven images or bow down to them, and if you do I'll get you and your kids and their descendants.

3. Thou shalt not take the name of the Lord in vain.

4. Keep the Sabbath holy.

The exact terminology is found in chapter five of Deuteronomy. Two other versions of the "ten commandments" can be found in the Old Testament. One version, in Exodus 20, differs slightly from the Deuteronomy version, while a third, in Exodus 34, is wildly different, containing commandments about sacrifices and offerings and ending with the teaching: "Thou shalt not seethe a kid in its mother's milk." This is the only version referred to in scriptures as the "ten commandments."

In essence, the first four commandments all scream that "the Lord thy god" has an uneasy vanity, and like most dictators, must resort to threats, rather than intellectual persuasion, to promote a point of view. If there were an omnipotent god, can you imagine him or her being concerned if some poor little insignificant creature puttered around and made a graven image? Do you think that any god, possessing the modicum of good will you could expect to find in any neighbor, would want to punish children even "unto the third and fourth generation" because their fathers could not believe? How can anyone not perceive the pettiness, bluster, bombast and psychotic insecurity behind the first four commandments? We are supposed to respect this!

"Honor thy father and thy mother" is the fifth commandment, and it is, of course, an extension of the authoritarian rationale behind the first four. Honor cannot be bestowed automatically by an honest intellect. Intellectually honest people can honor only those who, in their opinion, warrant their honor. The biologic fact of fatherhood and motherhood does not in and of itself warrant honor. Until very recently parenthood was not a matter of choice. It still is a mandatory, not optional, happening for many of the world's people. Why should any child be commanded to honor, without further basis, parents who became parents by accident—who didn't even plan to have a child? All of us know children who have been abused, beaten or neglected by their parents. What is the basis for honor there? How does the daughter honor a father who sexually molests her? "Honor only those who merit your honor" would be a more appropriate teaching, and if that includes your parents, great! "Honor your children" would have been a compassionate commandment.

Commandments six through nine—thou shalt not kill, commit adultery, steal or bear false witness—obviously have merit, but even they need extensive revision. To kill in self-defense is regrettable, but it is certainly morally defensible, eminently sensible conduct. So is the administration of a shot or medication that will end life for the terminally ill patient who wishes to die.

Adultery, the subject of the seventh commandment, again raises the question of an absolute ban. For the most part fidelity in marriage is a sound rule, making for happiness, but some marriages may outlast affection. Some couples may agree to live by different rules. Until relatively recent times Christian marriages were not dissolvable except by death, so the ban of divorce coupled with the ban of adultery obviously created great distress. Adultery, it must be remembered, involves an act between consenting adults. How much more relevant and valuable it would be to have, for instance, a commandment that forbids the violent crimes of rape and incest.

"Thou shalt not steal" raises questions regarding the usefulness of a blanket condemnation, and may put squatter's rights ahead of public and private welfare. Should people who are cold or ill steal to ameliorate their situations? Should the child who is hungry steal? Surely this command-ment cries for some amending clauses. One is reminded of the comment of Napoleon, who really had religion figured out: "How can you have order in a state without religion? For, when one man is dying of hunger near another who is ill of surfeit, he cannot resign himself to this differ-ence unless there is an authority which declares, 'God wills it thus.' Reli-gion is excellent stuff for keeping people quiet."

In general, to bear false witness is construed to mean "don't lie," and that is a valuable moral precept, except again it is stated in absolute terms. Lies have saved lives, they have preserved relationships, and every day they save hurt feelings. The truth is not always a reasonable or kind solu-tion. Interestingly, in biblical times the dictum not to bear false witness against a neighbor was a tribal commandment and meant to apply only to persons within the tribe—it was quite all right to bear false witness against "strangers."

Finally, the tenth commandment, which riles the feminist blood, says: "Neither shalt thou desire thy neighbor's wife, neither shalt thou covet thy neighbor's house, his field, or his manservant, or his maidservant, his ox, or his ass, or anything that is thy neighbor's." In addition to rating a wife with an ox and an ass, the bible loftily overlooks the woman who might desire her neighbor's husband. Covetousness somehow does not seem like such a crime. If you can't have a comfortable house or a produc-tive farm, what is the great harm in wishing you did? Covetousness may be nonproductive and unpretty, but to make a big, bad deal out of it is ridiculous. Bible apologists sometimes will excuse the triviality of the tenth commandment on the basis that to covet, in a more superstitious age, meant "to cast an evil eye." Someone who coveted "his neighbor's house" was purportedly casting an evil eye on that property with a view toward its destruction. Whether one accepts the apologist's definition of covet or the more popular meaning, the tenth commandment lacks real impor-tance.

Little in Christianity is original. Most of it is borrowed, just as the celebration of Christmas was borrowed from Roman and earlier pagan times. When the "Lord" supposedly wrote his commandments on two tablets of stone and delivered them to Moses (Deut. 5:22), he was only aping earlier gods: Bacchus, Zoroaster and Minos.

Reflect for a moment that almost anyone reading this essay could write a kinder, wiser, more reasonable set of commandments than those that Christians insist we honor. Try it!

❦

In the United States in the past few decades, tombstone-like monuments engraved with the ten commandments have been scattered across the country. Some are placed, appropriately enough, on private property, but most appear in public parks, on public courthouse lawns, or even on statehouse grounds. Most are the property of the government entity displaying them. Challenges in the courts have failed to dislodge them. Counter displays have been refused. Judges, immersed in religion since infancy, have failed to see a problem, yet they need to read no further than the first commandment to see the unconstitutionality of such governmental display. "Thou shalt have no other gods before me" makes a mockery of constitutionally guaranteed freedom of religion. In the United States citizens are free to have one god, many gods, any god they choose or no god at all. Their government should not be telling them which god to honor.

A Critique of the Scriptural Jesus

Originally published with the title: "Was Jesus A Horse Thief?"

THE ONE-ROOM COUNTRY SCHOOL I ATTENDED when I was a little girl was not at all fussy about what age you were when you started, so I got to start first grade when I was four. Consequently, I learned to read at an early age, I loved to read, and I read everything I could put my hands on.

Since country schools in the 1930s were very poor, there were not all that many books available. Our school library, unlike school libraries today, was not a room, or even an alcove. It was a piece of furniture—an old oak bookcase whose glass doors had been broken out years before. It held only about ninety books for the children in our eight grades, and, of course, it did not take too long for a hungry, growing reader to go through them. Soon, I was reading the adult books at home, including some memorably bad turn-of-the-century novels. Occasionally, in desperation, I even read my father's agricultural journals. But one book available to me that I could never read because it repelled me so was the bible. I tried it, I dipped in here and there. But it did not seem to make much sense, and far from impressing me or comforting me, it frightened and dismayed me.

At the time I decided that the bible, unlike those turn-of-the-century novels, really was supposed to be an adult book, and that I might appreciate it more when I was older. About that time I got a card at the Andrew Carnegie library in town, and my problems of what to read were ended. There I found shelves and shelves of books, and I could choose what pleased me. (Thank you, Andrew Carnegie.)

Except to check an occasional verse or biblical allusion, I did not read the bible again until I was a college student, and certain palatable parts of both the Old and New Testaments were required reading for a literature course. I decided then that it made more sense than when it had frightened me as a child, but I was still unconvinced of its merit. I thought some of the prose quite stately and some of the poetic images very lovely, but the content and teachings still troubled me. Unlike so many books that drew me back, I definitely did not want to return to the bible. Again, I decided the problem was my own immaturity, that in a few years I might understand what all of the excitement was about. After all, at age nineteen you are inclined to accept professorial judgment without question. If they and all those clergypersons thought it great literature and immortal truth, the fault was probably mine.

Busy with children, career, causes, and always with a good supply of delightful books on my night table, I had no occasion to read the bible again until I found myself disagreeing with an acquaintance about the respect due Jesus. There was a ferocious flap in the 1960s brought on by the Beatles' rather innocuous remark that they were now "more popular than Jesus." Widely circulated, the famous quotation caused a huge uproar in this country, with hundreds of boycotts of Beatles music by disc jockeys, passionate denunciations from pulpits, and a rash of bonfires of Beatles records and sheet music, especially in the south. My friend, a churchy type, argued that he did not like to see anyone's religion belittled, adding that whatever one thought of the divinity of Jesus, surely he was a wise and admirable man.

Somehow I didn't remember Jesus that way! And so, it was back to the bible. And this is what I found.

1. *Jesus believed in "demons."* Jesus believed that "demons" caused ill-

ness, both mental and physical illness. The New Testament swims in this. Jesus spoke not a word about germs, bacteria, viruses, contagion and the importance of sanitation. He did not know about these things; he believed "demons" to be responsible for sickness.

2. *Jesus unnecessarily killed animals*, e.g., pigs. For the most part a pig is a very gentle and intelligent animal, and clean, given the chance. (Most pigs are penned in small spaces where they have no chance to be clean.) A pig can be a delightful pet, affectionate, and as companionable as a dog. Yet Jesus, who had the power to still the seas and calm the winds, chose to drive "demons" from people into pigs. In one report (Mark 5:13) 2,000 pigs whom the "unclean spirits" had entered "ran violently down a steep place into the sea." One can only wonder at Jesus' irrationality. With his supernatural powers, why not drive the "demons" directly into the sea, and spare 2,000 pigs?

3. *Jesus told the people he spoke to that the world would end in their lifetime.* Obviously, this was a rather serious error, and must have caused a great deal of unnecessary fear and apprehension.

4. *Jesus believed in and promoted the idea of everlasting punishment*, even for offenses such as calling someone a fool (Matthew 5:22). Most wise and kind persons do not believe in hell; they do not accept the idea of a creator who punishes the objects of his creation.

5. *Jesus had an uneasy vanity.* He frequently became quite vindictive if people did not believe in him. A wise person would understand that there was cause for questioning.

6. *Jesus destroyed a fig tree out of peevishness.* With a disciple, he came upon a fig tree that had no fruit, for the very good reason that it was not the season for figs. Finding no figs, Jesus caused the tree to shrivel and die, thereby assuring no future figs for hungry persons.

7. *Jesus was a horse thief.*

And it came to pass, when he was come nigh to Bethphage and Bethany, at the mount called the mount of Olives, he sent two of his disciples,

Saying, Go ye into the village over against you; in the which at your entering ye shall find a colt tied, whereon yet never man sat; loose him, and bring him hither.

And if any man ask you, Why do ye loose him? thus shall ye say unto him, Because the Lord hath need of him. (Luke 19:29–31)

These verses cannot help but give a thoughtful person pause. Why was it that someone with the magical powers of Jesus would choose to put his disciples at risk to steal a horse for him; here was someone with the supernatural ability to feed a multitude with a bit of bread and fish, yet he could not manage to slip that horse's rope and get it to trot past him. Horses were very valuable in those days, even young horses "not yet rid by man." Stealing horses was a very dangerous pastime. The horse belonged to someone; it was tied.

His unwitting disciples, who could not have been unmindful of Jesus' preaching a day or two earlier that it was wrong to steal (Luke 18:20) did as they were told and survived a challenge.

So, in scripture, Jesus was a horse thief. In a sense, he was worse than a horse thief, because he made others do his stealing for him.

Someone once called Jesus "a mediocre preacher who had mistaken ideas about practically everything." The most cursory reading of the New Testament will confirm that evaluation. Far from being omniscient, as would be anyone's expectation for a reputed "god," Jesus actually was superstitious and most ignorant of science. He thought the sun could stand still and the moon had a light of its own. He was an exorcist, preoccupied with demons. He liked to call people names—fools, serpents, dogs, hypocrites, vipers are a few of the epithets he uses regularly. He encouraged his followers to mutilate their bodies, to drink poison and to handle snakes, and some of them still follow those lethal teachings today. He based his ministry on a sense of guilt and the fear of physical punishment. His style was to mix threats and curses with promises, and he cursed not only individuals but whole cities. Most philosophers who make claims present arguments to support them, but the biblical Jesus backs his claims only by threats of eternal damnation. His "cures," sometimes effected with holy spit and followed by admonishments to "tell no one," must perplex even modern day Christians. Why would not a "god" with the power to cure not want to cure as many persons as possible?

On close scrutiny, far from being a great moral teacher—a description that even some nonbelievers apply to Jesus—this deity of the New Testament emerges as an unadmirable, unconvincing myth.

The Religious Battered Woman

AT LONG LAST, THE CAUSE OF THE BATTERED WOMAN has become "fashionable." There has been a spate of articles, a book or two and a movie, with actress Sally Struthers getting convincingly roughed up. Even the male-dominated wire services in the United States are recognizing that, yes, there is a problem, and, really, men shouldn't be treating women that way. Battered women finally are getting "P.R."

But there are still those who, just as they did for rape, blame the woman, who is the victim, for her predicament. "Why does she stay?" they ask.

Why does she stay? Why does the woman, whose husband uses her as a private punching bag, stick around? The answers are so clear one wonders why the question is ever asked. She stays because she has nowhere else to go. She stays because she is economically and emotionally dependent. She stays because she may have small children or because her children may not want the family broken up. She stays because she is ashamed to tell anyone that her husband beats her. She stays because she fears the unknown; she has learned to cope, after a fashion, with being beaten, but she fears she might not be able to cope with whatever lies beyond her home. What she has, bad as it is, might be better than what would happen to her if she left. She stays because she has been told repeatedly by her husband that she is no good, no one would want her, she could never make it on her own. Her self-esteem is nil. She is isolated. Her husband's behavior has cut her off from friends and family, and she is beaten, in every respect.

"But," says the doubter, "She must really like to be beaten." That myth persists. Surely a grown woman must have something wrong with her to stay in her situation, the skeptic says. She must be a masochist. She must enjoy abuse. Somehow, this woman herself is to blame.

The myth dies hard. It is a simple truth, but one impossible for many to understand, that nobody likes to be beaten. Men don't like to be beaten, children don't like to be beaten, women don't like to be beaten. That is the fact of the matter. Just as a child may continue to love a parent who beats him or her, so a woman may continue to love her batterer. It is a form of childish dependency. And even if there no longer is affection, only fear, the woman stays because she is trapped. And there is always tomorrow. She can still hope that tomorrow will be better.

The religious woman will have even more difficulty extricating herself from a battery situation.

According to Mandy Stellman, a Milwaukee attorney and feminist who deals daily with battered women: "A religious woman refuses to believe that her marriage is not forever, and therefore convinces herself that her husband is a loving spouse. She will deny that he ever abused her or beat her; she believes God will punish her if she complains. So she will never tell anyone that her husband has, in fact, battered her or sexually abused her. Finally, she is so traumatized by fear of her husband, and by the humiliation, that she lies to herself and denies the facts of the abuse."

Battered women have traits and circumstances in common, and these make up the "battered woman syndrome." The battered woman is someone who denies the abuse, at first to others, eventually to herself. She is someone who "bruises easily." Every battered woman in the country will tell you that she "bruises easily." Always, she feels guilty. Somehow, she thinks, she must be at fault. She believes she must be doing something wrong, or this wouldn't be happening. Often, the battered woman is someone who "had to get married," and the battery usually started before the marriage. Interestingly, the battered woman is almost always someone who is much smarter than her husband. This fact is all but ignored in the literature on the subject; apparently that frail, male ego must be protected at all costs. Frequently she is someone who was victimized as a child, either by battering or sexual abuse. She is accustomed to being a victim. She enters the relationship with her batterer with an already low self-image. Although he will beat her drunk or sober, almost invariably the husband of a battered woman has a drinking problem.

Often, the battered woman is religious, a threefold problem. First, most religions teach that marriages, if not actually made in heaven, should last, and divorce, even if allowed, is a disgrace. Secondly, the religious battered woman has read the bible and knows very well its opinion of women. There are in excess of two hundred bible verses that specifically belittle and demean women. Her low opinion of herself is buttressed by her religion. Third, she has been praying when she should have been acting. Surely, she thinks, god will help her if she prays hard enough and long enough. Not only does her god not help her, her clergyman, if she dares confide in him, will probably urge her to "work harder at her marriage." Because she is religious, she has developed no inner strength that is meaningful or useful to her in times of crisis. She has relied on prayer to the extent that she has lost the power to act, to cope, to initiate, to solve problems, to reason.

If anyone helps her, it will be other women, feminists who have established counseling centers, legal services and shelter homes. Shelter homes are a temporary answer at best, and one wonders at a society that tolerates them as a real solution. The abused woman must uproot herself, bundle up her children, live in inadequate, cramped housing when she is the victim! Why doesn't society uproot the male? He is the problem. He is the one guilty of battery. Why isn't he hustled away? It is reminiscent of those curfews for women in some foreign countries because women are being attacked on the streets. Why aren't there curfews for men? . . .

What are the answers? Clearly, men who batter must be worked with as well as the victims who are battered. Certain men's need to inflict pain must be analyzed; these men must be rehabilitated. There are so many of them, it would be impossible just to lock them up.

And the battered women? Their immediate needs must be met. They must be helped to remove themselves from their dangerous situations, to start new lives, if possible. They must recognize self-worth; they must know that their partners' expressed opinion of them is not the opinion of others, the opinion of society.

Finally, we must change the way we look at women, the way we "bring up" girls. Young women must know that they are *not* inferior human beings, that it is not their duty to please men. This business of romantic love—that there is only one true love, and if you blow that, forget it—must be dispelled. Women must know that it is not necessary to live in fear, that the men who beat them or abuse them can be arrested and imprisoned, that battery is a crime, that women are not possessions.

The religious battered woman must come to see reality—that religion has been part of her problem, and that true mental and emotional health can come about only when she can reject her religious dependency sufficiently to recognize a fact: that the degradation of women is a cornerstone of religion.

Meg Bowman

44

Meg Bowman

ATHEIST, FEMINIST, EDUCATOR

Born June 28, 1929

Why burn? The answer is simple. Read the Bible—the Koran—the theologians and philosophers of the world.

Why We Burn: Sexism Exorcised, 1988

MARGARET ("MEG") MARIE GUNNERUD WAS BORN IN RUGBY, North Dakota, a town of 3,000, to Hazel and Al Gunnerud, pillars of the Methodist church. Meg's maternal grandmother, Anna Elise Thoreson Whiting ("Grandma Liz") was married to Ben Whiting, who played professional baseball at the turn of the century. Ben's salary, under $10 a month, plus Liz's sale of butter and eggs, kept the family solvent. Grandma Liz later ran a dairy farm near Fargo, not only doing the housework, gardening and canning, but milking the cows, stacking hay, shocking and threshing, also boarding teachers, serving as midwife, and raising three children. Meg's paternal grandmother Hanna Olsen Gunnerud saved money to buy passage from Norway to the United States by working as housekeeper and "baby-tender," marrying a widower with two children in Minnesota. They homesteaded in North Dakota, where Grandma Gunnerud gave birth to eleven children, teaching herself to read and write English.

Meg's mother held local/district/state/regional/national/international positions in the Methodist church, "thus allowing her to travel," observed Meg. "A woman traveling without her husband was 'suspect' but as long as she was attending church conferences, no one in this little town could say anything negative!" Meg's father eventually owned a chain of hardware and furniture stores and lumber yards in North Dakota.

"Because we both loved to read, I had one close friend (JoAnn Grier—now deceased) in this little town in North Dakota and we both became atheists," Meg wrote.

She left North Dakota during high school to attend a girls' boarding school in Illinois. She attended college in Arizona, where she became active with the Progressive Party in 1948. She married Richard Samuel Turner, had three sons, and divorced. She earned her Bachelor of Arts degree from Colorado College, Colorado, 1954, then a Master's from Arizona State University in 1961. When she married again, she moved to northern California where she taught innovative classes in sociology on the junior college and university level. Meg earned a Ph.D in 1985.

She organized and was executive director of Fremont Human Rights Committee, a California civil rights group which supported Mississippi Freedom Schools in the 1960s. She persuaded the city of Fremont and the county of Alameda to establish an active Human Relations Commission, and to sponsor United Nation's Day programs, human rights essay contests and other activities. Meg participated regularly in area civil rights and peace marches. She became president of Fremont Unitarian Fellowship in the 1960s and has been active in her area chapter of National Organization for Women and the San Jose Unitarian Church. She is active in the Unitarian-Universalist Women & Religion Task Force and Older Women's League. She is also co-chair of the Feminist Caucus of the American Humanist Association.

Since 1986, Meg has collected monies to sponsor impoverished young women through school in western Kenya and Romania. One recipient is now a nurse in Kenya, another is in an accounting program and other young women are college-bound.

Her second husband, Alden Humphreys Bowman, is deceased. Meg has five grandchildren, and is "almost" retired from San Jose State University.

A popular speaker at Unitarian, humanist and freethought gatherings, Meg has written and published eight books through her Hot Flash Press, including *Goddesses, Witches & the Paradigm Shift, Memorial Services for Women, Dramatic Readings on Feminist Issues, Women's History: Dramatic Readings, Readings for Older Women*, with Diane Haywood, and *Feminist Classics: Women's Words That Changed the World*. Most of her participative readings, predicated on the thesis that learning should be fun and history should come alive, dramatize the lives and views of women freethinkers and pioneers. She has written presentations on Hypatia, Anne Hutchinson, the Seneca Falls convention, Susan B. Anthony, and Emma Goldman, among others. Her essay, "Misogyny: Men Don't Really Hate Women, Or Do They?" was published in *Z Magazine* and is featured in a college text, *Human Sexuality*, published by Dushkin Publishing Co., 1995.

An intrepid world traveler, Meg has organized many international tours with a feminist and freethought emphasis.

Why We Burn: Sexism Exorcised

This is adapted from a chapter in **Dramatic Readings on Feminist Issues** *(1988) by Meg Bowman. When performed, each sexist religious quote is burned after being read aloud.*

IN 1971 THE WOMEN'S GROUP of St. Clement's Episcopal Church, New York City, rewrote the liturgy from the Book of Common Prayer, read sexist statements from the Bible, brought them to the altar, set them on fire and presented them as a burnt offering.

In 1972, at the Democratic National Convention, women repeated the ritual in the streets of Miami Beach. Our coast-to-coast "burnings" in 1975 were a prelude to feminist fireworks set off in 1976, our Bicentennial, to "Remember the ladies," as Abigail Adams asked John to do in 1776.—John forgot.

From Berkeley to Boston, Maine to Miami, we have burned. Omaha women drew the biggest audiences as they ignited the streets of Nebraska. And, yes, radical feminism has even "played in Peoria"—pyromaniacally.

Why burn? The answer is simple. Read the Bible—the Koran—the theologians and philosophers of the world. Look in your hymnals and then ask, "What better way to raise the religious consciousness of obtuse, callous, sexist societies?"

Our foremothers, Susan B. Anthony, Elizabeth Cady Stanton, Matilda Joslyn Gage, Sojourner Truth and Alice Paul knew that the major force *against* women's rights came from the male clergy.

Elizabeth Cady Stanton said, "The Bible and the church have been the greatest stumbling blocks in the way of women's emancipation." She got together with other women and they put together the "Woman's Bible"—noting all passages that relate to women.

Betty Friedan told the world (including the Pope personally) "the church is the enemy."

Dr. Rosemary Ruether, one of the first two women to become a lecturer at Harvard Divinity School, said that since the time of the earliest Christian fathers, women have been viewed as ". . . flesh, a sort of headless body"—"the symbol of sin"—for the spiritually superior male to control and use, "either as the means of procreation or the remedy for their sexual desires."

Both the early fathers and the medieval theologians agreed "that for any spiritual companionship another male is always more suitable."

"Not too surprising," Ruether went on—"the most concerted foes of the women's movement in the nineteenth century and down to our own times have been the Christian clergy, and it has been the Biblical, especially the Pauline, texts which have been used continually as the bludgeon to beat women back into their traditional place."

That same year—1973—Dr. Mary Daly, professor of theology at Boston College, spoke before the Nobel Conference: "Compare the high status of women under the Celts with that of women under Christianity . . . a patriarchal religion which functions to maintain patriarchy. Male Deity, the incarnation of God, in a male Christ, feminization of evil, sexist scriptures, disregard of women's experience are means by which this is achieved. A sexist society spawns a sexist religion, which, in turn, produces a sexist society."

In her book *The Church and The Second Sex*, Dr. Mary Daly notes that ". . . a woman's asking for equality in the church would be comparable to a black person's demanding equality in the Ku Klux Klan."

Women will never have equal rights—will never be liberated—until either the major religions are abolished or women assume leadership and drastically change them.

You say we are too radical? Read your history. Read your bibles. Read the words of the church fathers and the philosophers. It's all there.

It is time to exorcise the sexism out of religion!

❧

One of the worst sexists was the revered sage *Confucius*. This respected religious leader said, "One hundred women are not worth a single testicle." This respected authority on how to live wrote in the *Confucian Marriage Manual* (551–479 B.C.E.): The five worst infirmities that affect the female are indocility, discontent, slander, jealousy and silliness . . . Such is the stupidity of women's character, that it is incumbent upon her, in every particular, to distrust herself and to *obey her husband.*

The *Hindu Code of Manu*, dated about 250 B.C.E., regulates social customs and lists detailed precepts for daily life, such as: "In childhood a woman must be subject to her father; in youth to her husband; when her husband is dead, to her sons. A woman must *never* be free of subjugation."

Also from this most impressive law book: "If a wife has no children after eight years of marriage, she shall be banished; if all of her children are dead, she can be dismissed after ten years; and, if she produces only girls she shall be repudiated after eleven years."

Tertullian, the founder of Western theology, said in A.D. 22: "Woman is a temple built over a sewer, the gateway to the devil. Woman, you are the devil's doorway. You should *always* go in mourning and in rags." He also wrote: "Do you know that each of your women is an Eve? The sentence of God—on this sex of yours—lives in this age; the guilt must necessarily live, too. You are the gate of Hell, you are the temptress of the forbidden tree; you are the first deserter of the divine law."

And the church father *St. Clement of Alexandria* wrote in 96: "Let us set our womenfold on the road to goodness by teaching them . . . to display . . . submissiveness, to observe silence. Every woman should be overwhelmed with shame at the thought that she *is* a woman."

St. John Chrysostom (345?–407), Patriarch of Constantinople: "Among all savage beasts none is found so harmful as woman."

St. Ambrose, author and composer of hymns, bishop of Milan (340?–397): "Adam was led to sin by Eve and Eve by Adam. It is just and right that woman accept as lord and master him whom she led to sin." (I say, "Eve Was Framed!")

The "moral majority" has been around a long time. Listen to this early Christian church father *St. Augustine* (354–430): "Any woman who acts in such a way that she cannot give birth to as many children as she is capable of, makes herself guilty of that many murders . . ."

Council of Macon: In the year 584, in Lyons, France, forty-three Catholic bishops and twenty men representing other bishops, held a most serious debate: "Are Women Human?" After many lengthy arguments, a vote was taken. The results were thirty-two yes, thirty-one no. Women were declared human by *one vote!*

The *Koran*, the catechism, the holy book of Islam, (Circa 650): Men are superior to women.

Daily prayer of the *Orthodox Jewish Male* (still in use today): "Blessed art thou, O Lord our God and King of the Universe, that thou didst *not* create me a woman."

The Old Testament book of Deuteronomy (22:20–21) notes that if a woman be found not to be a virgin, ". . . then they shall bring the damsel to the door of her father's house and the men of the city shall stone her with stones that she die."

Exodus 20:17 and 22:16–17 declares as law that if a man seduces a virgin who is not betrothed (thus damaging the father's property)—he (the rapist) shall marry her. (Can you imagine having to marry your rapist?!) If the father doesn't wish this, the rapist shall pay money equivalent to the marriage/bride price for virgins.

Job 25:4: "How can he be clean that is born of woman?"

Leviticus 12:1–2, 5: And the Lord spake unto Moses saying: speak unto the children of Israel, saying: if a woman be delivered, " . . . and bear a *man*-child then she shall be unclean for seven days . . . . But if she bear a *maid*-child, then she shall be unclean for two weeks . . ."

In 1847, a British obstetrician, Dr. Simpson, used chloroform as an anesthetic in delivering a baby. A scandal followed, and the holy men of the Church of England prohibited the use of anesthetic in childbirth, citing Genesis 3:16: "God said to woman Eve, I will greatly multiply thy sorrow and thy pain in childbearing. In *pain* thou shalt bring forth children . . . and thy desire shall be to thy husband and he shall *rule over thee.*"

Ecclesiastes 7:26–28: "I find a woman more bitter than death; she is a snare, her heart a net, her arms are chains. No wickedness comes anywhere near the wickedness of a woman. May a sinner's lot be hers."

New Testament: I Corinthians 11:7–9: Man is the image of God . . . whereas woman reflects the glory of man. For man did not originally spring from woman, but woman was made out of man; and man was not created for woman's sake, but woman for the sake of man.

I Timothy 2:9–12, 15: I desire that "women should adorn themselves modestly and sensibly . . . *not* with braided hair or gold or pearls or costly attire . . . Let a woman learn in silence with all submissiveness. I permit no woman to teach or have authority over men; she is to keep silent. Yet women will be saved through bearing children, if she continues in faith and love and holiness, *with modesty.*"

I Corinthians 14:33–36: It is shameful for a woman to speak in church. Wives should regard their husbands as they regard the Lord. Women are not permitted to speak, but should be subordinate. If there is anything they desire to know, let them ask their husbands at home.

The Coptic text of the *Gospel of Thomas* (these are the Gnostic texts discovered in 1945) translates: (114) Simon Peter said to them, "Let Mary leave us, for women are not worthy of life." Jesus said, "I myself shall lead her in order to make her male, so that she too may become a living spirit resembling you males. For every woman who will make herself male will enter the Kingdom of heaven."

Moving into the Middle Ages, *St. Thomas Aquinas*, the well-known 13th-century Italian theologian, said: "Woman is defective and accidental . . . and misbegotten . . . a male gone awry . . . the result of some weakness in the (father's) generative power."

The renowned Protestant clergyman, *Martin Luther* (1483–1546), said: "God created Adam lord of all living creatures, but Eve spoiled it all." And: "Women should remain at home, *sit still*, keep house and bear and bring up children." Again: "If a woman grows weary and, at last, dies from childbearing, it matters not. Let her die from bearing; she is there to do it." [*Die Ethnik Martin Luthers*, Althaus, p. 100; or, this may have been said by Philip Melancthon, an associate of Luther.]

John Knox, sixteenth-century founder of Scottish Presbyterianism, declared: Woman in her greatest perfection was made to serve and obey man, *not* rule and command him.

Samuel Butler (1612–1680), the English poet, wrote: "The souls of women are so small that some believe they've none at all."

French philosopher *Jean Jacques Rousseau* (1712–1778): The whole education of women ought to be relative to men. To please them, to be useful to them . . . to make life sweet and agreeable to them.

Swiss Protestant theologian *Karl Barth* (1886–1968) said: "Woman is ontologically subordinate to man."

Pope Pius XII said in 1941 (He reigned 1939–1958): "The pains that, since original sin, a mother has to suffer to give birth to her child only draw tighter the bonds that bind them; she loves it the more, the more pain it has cost her."

Dr. C. W. Shedd, Presbyterian minister in Houston, Texas, wrote this advice in *Letters on How to Treat a Woman* (1968): "It seems to me that nearly every woman I know wants a man who knows how to love with authority. . . . Our family airedale will come clear across the yard for one pat on the head. The average wife is like that. She will come across town, across the house, across the room, across to your point of view, and across almost anything to give you her love *if* you offer her yours with some honest approval."

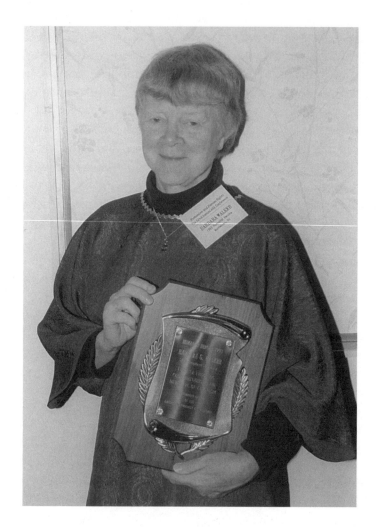

Barbara G. Walker

45

Barbara G. Walker

THE SKEPTICAL FEMINIST

Born July 2, 1930

The real reason for the persistence of the witchcraft idea was that Christian authorities couldn't let it die, without admitting that God's word was wrong, and God's servants had committed millions of legal murders and tortured millions of helpless people without cause.

The Woman's Encyclopedia of Myths and Secrets, *1983*

BARBARA G. WALKER REJECTED RELIGION as a child:

"To be locked into a religious mold is slavery to the mind."

Born in Philadelphia, she first read the King James Bible as a young teenager: "It sounded cruel. A God who would not forgive the world until his son had been tortured to death—that did not strike me as the kind of father I would want to relate to."

At twelve, she found her first love, astronomy, studying stars through her telescope every night. Then came her "horse phase," interrupted by a major in journalism at the University of Pennsylvania. She married research chemist Gordon Walker, moved to Washington, D.C., and worked at the *Washington Star.* After they relocated to Morristown, New Jersey, she taught the Martha Graham dance technique.

She became a knitting expert, writing ten volumes on the craft, including the classics, *Treasury of Knitting Patterns* and *A Second Treasury of Knitting Patterns. Vogue Knitting* once declared that "knitting without them is like writing without a dictionary."

Her feminist interest was heightened in the mid-seventies when she worked on a local hotline, receiving calls from battered women and pregnant teenagers. She soon delved into the "new feminist wave," reading authors such as Mary Daly and Merlin Stone.

She wrote the monumental feminist-freethought encyclopedia *The Woman's Encyclopedia of Myths and Secrets* in 1983, its goal to trace the "transition from female-oriented to male-oriented religions in western civilization." She is the well-known author of many feminist books published by Harper & Row, including *The Crone: Woman of Age, Wisdom, and Power; The I Ching of the Goddess; The Skeptical Feminist: Discovering the Virgin, Mother, and Crone;* and *Women's Rituals: A Sourcebook.*

An atheist, she finds "the archetypical Goddess image" to be of psychological importance to women. Branching off from feminist research, she has examined crystals and minerals, and the symbolism of tarot, calling fortune-telling "just a parlor trick." She is one of the few scholars to offer a critical analysis debunking New Age assertions about crystals.

"Crystals . . . [are] inert, inorganic substances. And for people to claim they're going to cure cancer with crystals is, I think, highly irresponsible. It's a scam aimed at getting more money."

Barbara is "an incessant reader," admitting "I never take a bath without a book," even propping them on the stove when she cooks. "It's astonishing how much time one has for creative activities when the idiot box is eliminated from one's life," she has said of television.

In an interview with *Book Resources*, Barbara pointed out: "what is moral is simply what does not hurt others. Kindness . . . sums up everything."

❧

In the introduction to *The Woman's Encyclopedia of Myths and Secrets*, Barbara wrote that "God is a human projection of the image of man."

"Modern Christians take it for granted that they must revere the figures of a Father and a Son, never perceiving divinity in corresponding Mother and Daughter figures, as the ancients did."

"As a salvation cult, early Christianity based its scheme of redemption on the premise of female wickedness."

"The Christian hell was the most sadistic fantasy ever to masquerade as fact."

The Skeptical Feminist

*This was delivered as a speech at the annual conference of the American Human-
ist Association in Philadelphia, Pennsylvania, in May 1993, following the presentation of the "Humanist Heroine" award by the AHA Feminist Caucus to
Barbara G. Walker. It is reprinted here for the first time.*

I TURNED TOWARD SKEPTICISM at a very early age in my childhood when a
beloved dog died, and a few weeks later our minister dropped in to visit
my mother. I seized the opportunity to ask him what it would be like when
I met my dog again in heaven. He told me that I would not meet my dog
in heaven because dogs don't have souls and don't go to heaven.

At this I was heartbroken, crushed. I tried to negotiate. He said I would
meet all my loved ones in heaven, and I was perfectly willing to trade a
couple of aunts and uncles for my dog, but he was adamant and I couldn't
move him. Eventually, although I was a rather quiet child, I threw a tan-
trum and I stamped my foot and I said, "I don't want anything to do with
your rotten old God and nasty old heaven." I ran into my bedroom weeping, and my mother was mortified. It was a terrible occasion, but this was
actually the first time that I began to doubt and to think that maybe what
I had been told about God, that he was kind, was not so true.

A little later I entered Sunday school and the first thing I saw when I
entered Sunday school was a life-sized crucifixion scene with a lot of agony
and twisted muscles and it was horrible. I was told that God had decreed
that this had to be done to his dearly beloved son. And I thought perhaps
that must have been why Jesus ran away from heaven, because if I had a
father that wanted to do that to me, I certainly would run away.

And then we children were taught that not only was this poor man
tortured on the cross but we had to become cannibals and eat him. And
his flesh and blood were magically transposed into bread and wine, but
nevertheless we were assured it was flesh and blood. I began to think in
my childish way that the God who decreed all this was some kind of a
lunatic.

When I got into my early teens, I set myself to study a very subversive
book that gave God a very nasty character. This book was called the Bible,
and from the Bible I learned that God did not like people very much. He
created them and he called them his children, but he frequently repented

of this and destroyed whole populations at a time. He set one tribe against another. He fomented ruthless wars with casualties in the hundreds of thousands. And the same God who said, "Thou shalt not kill," on the very next page recommended the killing of men, women and children, of the little ones of every city. This was very difficult for me to understand. He forbade any show of mercy. He reveled in the murders of, I quote first Samuel: "Man and woman, infant and suckling, ox and sheep, camel and ass." I think it was the mention of the animals that really got to me. Neither was he very kind to his chosen people. Periodically, he wiped out sizable numbers of them for relatively trivial offenses. He threatened them with the most colorful set of curses imaginable. This is one of my favorite passages: "pestilence, corruption, fever, inflammation, extreme burning, blasting, mildew, hemorrhoids, the botch, the scab, the itch, madness, blindness, slavery, plague and barren lands." It sort of seemed like overkill.

God particularly disliked women. He hit women where they live by making their motherhood a curse, and giving men permission to lord it over them. We all know that passage from Genesis 3. And I realized that when I grew up I would be one of this accursed sex. And I began to look upon God with extreme distrust. It made me very uneasy to learn, for example, that God commanded that any girl found not to be a virgin on her wedding night must be stoned to death by the men of her village, (this is in Deuteronomy 22), however, no such punishment was meted out to the promiscuous bridegroom. And I wondered: if unmarried women remained virginal on pain of death and if married women were also off limits, who's left for the promiscuous young men to be promiscuous with? It is some failure of communication here.

But eventually, I came to realize that there is a strong element of woman hatred in every form of patriarchal religion but also, a form of hatred of human beings in general. Faith in God necessarily implies a lack of faith in humanity. The profoundly cynical premise of all religionists is that people are not capable of behaving decently toward one another unless they are lured with promises of pie in the sky and simultaneously terrorized by threats of extreme nastiness in the eternal afterlife in hell.

Now this process begins in childhood, and is known as "putting the fear of God into children," which is usually a euphemism for harsh punishment. Every psychologist knows that childhood fears eventually become adult cruelties and/or dysfunctions. Being forced into unnecessary fear is not really the best route to mental health and confidence in adulthood. On the contrary, the very fears and guilts imposed by religious training are responsible for some of history's most brutal wars, crusades, pogroms, and persecutions, including five centuries of almost unimaginable terrorism under Europe's Inquisition and the unthinkably sadistic legal murder of nearly nine million women. History doesn't say much very good about God. Nowadays the more modern religionists are trying to get around their legacy of millennia of violence, and sexism, and obfuscation, and just plain lying, by viewing God as more symbolic than literal and by tacitly admitting that he is a human creation rather than creator. Men get together in pretentious councils to decide what God is, what God thinks, what God wants the rest of us to do for him, and the one thing he never fails to want is more money.

P. T. Barnum once made God his partner in the amusement industry by saying that any entertainer "is in a business established by the Author of our nature; if he worthily fulfills his mission and amuses without corrupting, he need not feel that he has lived in vain." This was the same man who said, "There's a sucker born every minute." Now, we know how he defined amusement, but we also have to wonder how he would define corruption. Strictly speaking, it might be considered corrupt to diddle the public as often and as successfully as Barnum did in order to amass large sums of money for himself, which seemed to be his mission in life, worthily fulfilled. To fool people and make them pay for it might be viewed as a nutshell description of corruption, even if the suckers are entertained in the process. Reasoning of this sort has provided self-justification for all kinds of charlatans, flimflammers and fakers throughout history, allowing them to feel good about themselves as they busily relieve the sheep of their fleeces. They know that the mark isn't being amused, he is earnestly believing, not because he thinks it's fun, but because he thinks it's real.

Our society is becoming increasingly sheeplike, in its attitudes toward our present-day Barnums, various spellbinders, preachers, gurus, psychics, channelers, spiritualists, fortune tellers, and miracle-mongers, who swarm on the fringes of our collective consciousness, and get rich by entertaining the credulous. No matter how many times it is demonstrated that psychics' predictions don't come true, telepathy doesn't work, crystals don't cure diseases, transcendental meditators don't levitate, dead people don't talk, and many other assorted absurdities are debunked over and over, yet large

numbers of people are obsessed by an indomitable will to believe the un-
believable. Why is this?

It is very curious that so many human beings are more willing to believe what doesn't make sense, than to believe what does. Perhaps it's only
another one of the insanities of our culture. From earliest childhood, many
of us are given to understand that fantasies are fun and exciting, whereas
facts are dull. Stories are more interesting than real life. Many adults seem
to accept it as axiomatic that children are entertained by fantasy and bored
by fact, even though children do incessantly ask questions about the real
world. Why is the sky blue? Why don't fish drown? Why does water freeze?
What makes a car run? How does a telephone work? How do germs make
one sick? Too often their factual curiosity goes unsatisfied by ignorant
parents who don't know the answers and won't take the trouble to find
out. Questions concerning nature may be answered by a vague allusion to
God. Questions concerning technology may simply be passed over.

Barnum was right, in another sense, when he referred to God as the
original founder of the flimflam business. Credulity as a character trait is
encouraged in every child who grows up with religious training, which
invariably insists on the virtue of blind faith and the sinfulness of doubting
and questioning. Children who accept indoctrination into the faith of their
fathers, must suppress any rudimentary critical sense they may have to
believe in the miracles and magic promulgated by religion, or to choose
religion's unscientific and usually untenable notions of cosmic origins ahead
of the more plausible scientific views.

When skepticism is regarded as a vice, skeptics are forced into a minority position and forced to live in a world whose majority opinions they
find very distasteful. Yet no one politely refrains from offending the skeptic's
philosophical position in the same way that people usually refrain from
offending the views of a believer. Churches as well as psychics entertain
the credulous with fakery, in so far as any religious ritual is supposed to be
doing something real, outside of the human psyche (bread and wine actually becoming flesh and blood, or prayer becoming a mechanistic cause of
events).

Religion's war against fringe beliefs is not a contest of rational and
irrational. It is a contest between different fantasy systems, one having
more political and financial clout then the others, and therefore, able to
advertise itself into respectability. Because religious training means cre-

dulity training, churches should not be surprised to find that so many of their congregations accept astrology as readily as theology, or a channeled Atlantean priest as readily as a biblical prophet.

If a deity is to exist in the collective mind, as a symbol of life, love or nature as they are perceived by human beings, then it seems to me that the mother Goddess makes a far better symbol than the male God with his unsavory past. Mother nature or mother earth is the anthropomorphic or gynomorphic personification of what really makes life possible on this planet. This is the only living planet that we know or ever are likely to know. We have also come to understand the crucial influence of mothering behavior in the development of personalities, animal or human, and the necessity for men to practice their own versions of this kind of behavior, in order to become decent people. If humanity continues to need a parent figure, then in my opinion, it is far better seen as an immanent Mother rather than a transcendent Father. That's why I'm a feminist. I also think that we must make clearer distinctions between the supernatural and the symbolic, so that we understand our own spirituality in a realistic way that cannot be threatened or destroyed by education.

Feminists may be anti-God, but they are not anti-men. The feminist message is that patriarchy hurts men, too. Our world is violent for the very reason that it's full of men who have been wounded by oppressive father figures, both real and imaginary. This can be changed by bringing us all down to earth in the practice of enlightened humanism, that recognizes our physiological needs, and takes sensible precautions for the preservation of our mother earth and our own species. It is my profound hope that the near future will see this come about.

Sherry Matulis

46

Sherry Matulis

ABORTION RIGHTS ADVOCATE

Born July 9, 1931

If every criminal and inhumane act ever committed were traced to its root cause, that root would be buried deep in religion.

"Paradise Lost, Paradise Found," *1981*

"I WAS BORN AN ATHEIST (aren't we all?) in the small town of Nevada, Iowa," writes Sherry Scott Matulis. She moved to Peoria, Illinois in 1942, and married John Matulis in 1948. "Reared in Iowa farm country, I learned to prod with a pitchfork," she quipped in a column about religion, "Maybe One of These Centuries, They'll Grow Up."

"You couldn't go out to play hopscotch or kick-the-can without tripping over a church or two. (Or a tavern. The churches had a reciprocal arrangement, I think . . .)

"But tripping over all those churches wasn't the real problem. The real problem was all that time spent inside them—skipping over the facts of reality. Listening to all that 'Hellfire & Brimstone' hype," she said in "Speaking of Religious Experiences," a speech delivered on October 24, 1981, at the annual convention of the Freedom From Religion Foundation, Louisville, Kentucky.

A poet and writer, Sherry became a national spokeswoman for abortion rights in the 1980s. Her experience seeking an illegal abortion was first published as "Never Again" in the *Feminist Connection* in June 1981, later reprinted in the *Progressive* magazine as "Abortion 1954." Sherry spoke about her experiences before a United States Senate Judiciary Subcommittee, chaired by Orrin Hatch, in 1981. She has testified before state legislatures and in 1990 spoke at the United States Senate committee hearings on the Freedom of Choice Act.

She served both as a state and a national representative for the "Silent No More" campaign sponsored by the National Abortion Rights Action League in

1985. As an advocate for reproductive freedom, she has appeared on numerous radio and television programs, including the "Oprah Winfrey" and "Sally Jessy Raphael" talkshows, and has spoken for choice on college campuses. Sherry is featured in "Personal Decisions," a film produced by Planned Parenthood (1985).

Her column, "The Refractory Relic," appeared in the *Feminist Connection*, Madison, Wisconsin, from 1981–1984. Her essays on feminism, politics, peace and freethought examined the new Religious Right and trenchantly rejected "stuporstition." In her column "Paradise Lost, Paradox Found," Sherry wrote:

". . . for centuries ignorance has existed. And has been *religiously* protected. It has gone forth and been fruitful and multiplied like mad, unquestioning and un-questioned. It has had fear on its right flank and avarice on its left—formidable foes, both, of reason. It has, in the name and under the protective guise of reli-gion, twisted and trampled and tortured those very billions of souls it has pro-fessed to 'save.' It has been and it yet is solely responsible for every act of inhu-manity ever committed. It exists. It is. But that is no reason for it to continue."

Sherry's articles, stories and poetry have been published in such periodicals as *Redbook, Isaac Asimov's Science Fiction magazine, Questar, Analog, Freethought Today, The Rationalist* and *The Arizona Journal.* She has completed two "fiercely femi-nist, uncompromisingly irreligious books, one fiction, one poetry, yet to be pub-lished."

Recognition includes the Illinois Pro-Choice Alliance "Sylvia" ("You've Got Guts, Sweetie") Award for Valor in 1986; the National Organization for Women's (Reproductive Rights) Award for Education in 1987; the Feminist Caucus of the American Humanist Association's "Humanist Heroine" Award in 1991; and the Peoria Planned Parenthood's "Betty Osborne" Award (recognizing courage, ex-cellence and leadership in family planning) in 1995.

At age 20, Sherry was surprised to find herself in the first "Miss Universe" contest after she was selected from photographs surreptitiously submitted by her husband. She has written entertainingly about that experience. She has long ad-mired feminist freethinkers Voltairine de Cleyre and Ellen Battelle Dietrick. She became the "village atheist," and has run small businesses and managed income property for many years.

"Rumor has it that I'm the love child of a clandestine affair between Elizabeth Cady Stanton and Jules Verne, but don't you believe it for a moment. Actually, I'm a libertarian feminist who has devoted the first fifty years of her life primarily to the children of her body, five in number, and who is intent on devoting at least the next fifty to the children of her mind, which at last count number somewhere in the gazillions."

How I Earned My Feminist Credentials

This speech was delivered at the fiftieth annual convention of the American Humanist Association in Chicago in May 1991. Sherry received the AHA Feminist Caucus "Humanist Heroine" award for her articulate and courageous activism on behalf of women's rights.

IF IT'S TRUE THAT THERE'S NOTHING AS POWERFUL as an idea whose time has come, I think it's equally true that there's nothing as pervasively harmful as a malefic religious notion whose time won't go. I've spent a good part of my life dealing with such notions, trying to counter them—all the myriad misogynous notions of Fundamentalist religion. But the specific of such notions that's taken most of my attention, the one that has dealt so heinously with the lives of millions of women over the years, is that extremely peculiar notion which persists in the error that the uniting of sperm and ova—oftentimes the *accidental* uniting of sperm and ova—constitutes the Holiest of Holies; a thing so universally meritorious that it should be revered above all else. Including the existent life of every female on the planet.

That this notion is restful to the patriarchal brain, I have no doubt. That it has been highly instrumental in perpetuating a slave mentality/slave morality, with all the *attendant* misery and woe, I wouldn't question for a minute. But: that it corresponds with reality—as any objective truth, or for that matter, any valid notion *must*—is clearly, patently false.

In making this statement before, I've been asked more than once by certain of those in the Right To Lie movement, "Well! Who are you to judge?" And the answer to that has always been the same: I am a person upon whom this notion has been tried and found wanting. I am, in fact, a person who was quite nearly rendered a non-person by this nutso notion. And since the effects of anything can usually best be judged by those who have borne them, I think my "credentials" to judge, in this instance, are probably better than average. Certainly they are better than those of the Pope; and also better than those of the Right To Lie males who invariably question them. I'll recount for you the events that gave birth to those "credentials" and let you decide for yourselves.

Back in 1954, while I was on my way home from work late one night, I was assaulted and very viciously, sadistically raped. I didn't see the person who attacked me—he had come up from behind as I was taking a shortcut across a dark schoolyard close to where we lived; and the first I knew of his presence was when he clapped a big hand over my mouth. My first instinct was to try to bite that hand; and when I did, he brought the other one up full force under my chin and knocked me down and out.

When I came to, I was flat on my back on this blacktopped schoolyard. The back of my head was sticky with blood. My clothes were scattered all around me. And when I tried to sit up, I felt this searing, knifelike pain in my mid-section. Looking down, I saw that there was no knife there, but there had been. It took me probably a full minute to realize that what I was seeing, this odd ugly mass perched atop my abdomen, was part of my intestine. I can joke about it now; I often do, saying that I invented the first "living girdle" long before Playtex came up with theirs. But at the time it was no laughing matter. I literally had to hold myself together with my hands to get the rest of the short distance home.

And fortunately it was a short distance, otherwise I'm sure I wouldn't have survived. However, about a month later, I found myself almost wishing I hadn't.

Contrary to what the purveyors of mystical notions seem to think happens in cases such as this, I discovered that my ovaries hadn't magically shut down; and I had been impregnated by the rape. The feeling that came over me at that time is one I've never really been able to describe. It was part fear, panic, revulsion and, mostly, an overwhelming sense of helplessness—of not knowing where to turn for help because at that time there wasn't any help.

I did go to see two doctors, neither of whom could offer anything more than some totally unacceptable advice; namely, that I carry to term and then put the infant up for adoption. As I told a Senate subcommittee in Washington, D.C., last year, this "advice" didn't take into consideration that I already had two children, that I would later go on to have three more, and that it might be just a little difficult to explain to the world and all why we had put the third kid out to pasture. Nor did it take into account that I considered what had been forcibly and violently implanted within my body to be almost, not quite but almost, as repulsive as the prevailing notion that I was nothing more than an incubator or a brood mare put here to service the whims of others.

Please don't misunderstand: I have nothing against the practice of adoption when it's accomplished freely all 'round. But I have everything against it when it's accomplished in the manner suggested to me. I was a person in my own right then, just as I am now. I agreed no more with the idea of forced pregnancy then, than I do now. And because of this, because of my disagreement with the misogynous mentality of the time, and because I could find no doctor to afford me the medical procedure I needed, I proceeded to try every "home remedy" I'd ever heard of. Up to and including throwing myself down a flight of stairs *and* pounding on my barely healed abdomen with a meat mallet. All of which left me very black and blue, and about one month more pregnant than I'd been when I started.

Up until this time, I had never even considered seeing a back-alley abortionist. I knew that they existed. I'd heard that there was one in our area. A lot of people—including the police, many of whom were taking pay-offs—knew about his "practice." And in fact it was a policeman who gave me the phone number where I could get in touch with him. But after having heard how he "buried his mistakes in the river," things like that, I wasn't any too anxious to give him a call.

However, what it finally came down to, when nothing else worked and there was no place else to turn, was that I had to call that number. Which I think rather pointedly puts the lie to the No-Choice Fantasy that by making abortion illegal again they are somehow going to make it disappear. I had no illusions about what I was letting myself in for. I didn't realize how humiliating or painful it would be; but I did realize that a trip to see the butcher might be the last trip I'd ever make. And still, I consider that preferable to the alternative. It was, for me, the lesser of a lose-lose situation.

So, I made the call. And I was told to meet with his "assistant" at a certain restaurant the following day. And to be sure to bring any evidence I had of a savings or checking account. And naive young thing that I was, I did just that. I took my little savings passbook along and showed this woman that, by scrimping and scraping and doing without for years, I had managed to set aside $987; money that we were hoping to use as a down payment on a home.

She scrutinized the bankbook, asked me a couple of irrelevant questions and said that she'd get back to me. And she did, later that same evening, telling me where to come, what time to be there, to come alone and be sure to bring the "fee" in cash. I was about two and a half months into the pregnancy and, in 1954, when one dollar would have been the equivalent of at least three or four today, they had set that "fee" at $1,000. Which I had to hand them before I ever got through the door; and which bought me two aspirin and the most painful and degrading experience of my life.

I suppose this is why, today, when I hear some notion-peddling No-Choice busybody refer to a clean, well staffed, well equipped clinic as an "abortion mill," I frequently get the urge to temporarily forget that I'm a non-violent person. Actually, I am non-violent; I don't believe that violence has ever resolved anything. And if I were ever going to strike out at anyone, I certainly would have done it by now. So taking up the pushing, shoving, hitting, bombing tactics of the Anti-Choice movement is out of the question for me. I fight with my mouth and my pen. But . . .

If a little blue fairy were to suddenly come on the scene and grant me a request, I think I might ask for a time machine—so I could take these holier-than-thous back thirty-seven years and have them walk alongside me as I trudged up those three flights of dark, smelly stairs and walked down that pitchy corridor—my hands shaking and my heart in my throat—and knocked at that door at the end of it, not knowing *what* was on the other side, or whether I'd ever walk back down those stairs again.

Better yet, if the little blue fairy were in a really accommodating mood, I think perhaps I'd like to have them take that walk: in my place. I'd like to see how they'd fare if *they* were put in the position of being young and raped and pregnant and scared witless that *they* were going to die and leave two little children motherless. I'd like to see if their smug pseudo-morality would hold up if they had to experience, first-hand, what a *real* "abortion mill" was all about:

The incredible, indescribable filth and stench. The cobwebs hanging from the ceiling and the blood-spattered floor. The two aspirin "anesthetic." The slop bucket at the end of the old enameled kitchen table. The drunken old butcher coming at *them*, a whiskey glass in one hand, a sharp instrument in the other; saying to *them*, "You can take your pants down now, but you shoulda'—ha, ha—left 'em on before." Putting his fist in *their* face and saying, "This is gonna' hurt and you'd better keep your mouth shut, or I'll shut it for you!" Whacking away at *their* insides for fifteen eyeball-popping minutes. And then, insult added to injury, offering them $20 of their $1,000 back for "a quick blow job."

This is how I earned my "credentials." This, and the hemorrhaging and the peritonitis and the hospitalization and the blood transfusions that followed is what I had to endure to terminate an unbearable pregnancy; to rid myself of that microscopic "holy alliance" caused by a psychotic rapist's religious hatred of women. And if it makes you shudder, or if you think that my experience was at all unique or the worst possible scenario, I assure you it was not. I survived. I could speak to you for days on end of those who didn't.

Women young, old, black, white—known to the medical books only by their initials and their perforated or Lysol-damaged wombs and their resultant infections and suffering and eventual deaths. Women really too young to be called women, undergoing hysterectomies at sixteen. Women with bottles of household disinfectants, sometimes even Lye; no need for a hysterectomy, nothing left to perform one on. Women with bent heads and unbent coat hangers, screaming in the night, *dead* at 16, 18, 20, 22. Women for whom the phrase "Right To Life" was totally without meaning or substance; who were murdered, as surely as putting a gun to their heads, by the same sort of blue-nosed and hypocritical element in our society that once again rears its ugly unfeeling head to Laud What Might Be and Condemn What Is.

And all for a notion. A malefic, erroneous religious notion whose time won't go . . . until we make it go by insisting that subjective superstition make way for objective truth.

The truth, ladies and gentlemen, that thing which does correspond with reality, is that the Anti-Choice concern is not for that tiny little couplet of sperm and ova; not for the zygote, nor the blastocyst, nor the embryo, nor even the fetus. The concern is for the status quo of the Patriarchy.

The truth is that the issue is not abortion at all; it never has been. As much as eighty percent of *all pregnancies* end in spontaneous abortion. And a rose is a rose is a rose. But you will never hear an Anti-Choice person raise their voice against spontaneous abortion. You will never see them picket or march on Washington or take any other action to try to stop, or even to lessen, this spontaneous "holocaust." And you will certainly never hear them decry their God with his Big Abortion Mill In The Sky for this heavy-handed destruction of "innocent life"; the "mass Murder" of up to eighty percent of all those fertilized eggs they refer to as "unborn children." You won't even find them willing to *discuss* spontaneous abortion. Because to discuss it, to really discuss it, is to put the lie to all their mystical twaddle.

The single notable distinguishing factor between induced and sponta-neous abortion rests, quite simply, with who makes the decision. This is the issue. Whether we will have the non-entities of either a "God" or a State—the Witch Doctor or the Bully Boy, or any of their self-appointed spokespeople—making that decision for the individual or the individual making that decision for herself.

And if we're to abide by the illogic of the No-Choicers—that is, if we're to go along with this noxious notion of letting an indiscriminate nature or an irrational god rule our lives, if we're never to attempt to thwart what they call "the will of God" in the effort to make our lives and the lives of others better, brighter, healthier, more meaningful, then *do* let us remember: never to get out of the way of a tidal wave or a bolt of lightning; never to run from a tornado or an earthquake or a volcanic eruption; never to try to find a cure for cancer or the zillion and one other diseases and infirmities that are, obviously, the "will" of this "God." And, oh, do especially let us remember these things if our name is Jimmy Swaggart or Oral Roberts or Jerry Falwell or Pat Robertson or Henry Hyde or Orrin Hatch or Jesse Helms, et cetera, ad infinitum, ad nauseam.

Hypocrisy is still the language of the land; but fortunately some of us have never learned to speak it. In aspiring to health and well-being, we all overcome conditions of nature, and we overcome them every day of our lives. We build shelters and install indoor plumbing and purchase refrig-erators and sit in air-conditioned living rooms and munch microwaved popcorn and watch TV and condemn purposeful abortion as: "unnatu-ral."

We shampoo and style and perm our hair and bathe and deodorize and perfume our bodies and put clothes upon our backs and shoes upon our feet. And should we spot a tornado coming, we employ those feet to run like hell. We *do* get out of the way of tornados. And we also fend off or attempt to thwart countless other "natural" or "God-willed" things—things that we determine will either lessen the quality of our lives or, maybe, end them altogether.

We do these things, we take these actions, we make these decisions because we are rational human beings, unwilling to have the terms of our lives dictated by an indiscriminate nature or an irrational god. The same god who opposed anesthesia not so long ago because, according to his interpreters, people are *supposed* to suffer. And the more they suffer here, the better their chances of getting into "Heaven;" where, in accord with its description and potential habitants, I suppose they can suffer for eternity.

I've heard more times than I care to recall, from these self-proclaimed "authorities" on what is "natural" and what is not, that induced abortion is both "unnatural" and "unacceptable." In fact, it is neither. The nature of a thing is the nature of a thing. And the nature of human beings, if we wish to remain human beings, is to use our heads for something other than a hat rack.

Brought to the bottom line, whenever *anyone* shampoos his hair or buys a refrigerator or drives a car instead of using his feet or *uses* his feet to get out of the way of a tornado and then talks about making purposeful abortion illegal because it is "unnatural" or against "God's will," no matter how fancily he dresses it, no matter what pro-natalist platitudes he employs, what he is really talking about is: the continued subordination of women.

Thirty-seven years ago, that subordination so dear to the patriarchal heart came within a hairsbreadth of ending my life. And my heart, in the thirty-seven years since, has wanted to break each time I ponder how many lives it *did* end. And how many more it maimed. I will never cease wondering, the question will never leave my mind: how many women lay hemorrhaging, as I did, *afraid* to seek help, as I was, but without the saving grace of a husband who insisted on getting that help? How many women bled to death for a lousy superstitious notion?!

It's especially ironic, sadly ironic, to speak of the inhumane treatment of all these victims of this nefarious notion at a time when we're supposed to be celebrating the two-hundredth anniversary of the most powerful idea in human history—the Bill of Rights; the idea that each of us possesses, *intrinsically*, the right to exist with dignity and self-direction; the right to live our lives rationally and without undue interference from others—especially those "others" who would impose their superstition as a Law.

That idea *is* the Law of the Land. It has been the Law of the Land for two hundred years. And it was made the Law of the Land by people who realized that, unless we wish to march under a false banner, homo sapiens *must* have the right to biological sovereignty. This right is ours by virtue of our existence. It does not come from any "God," any King, *any* man, any source outside the individual; and therefore it cannot be negated by any source outside the individual.

I think a perfectly lovely way to celebrate the two hundredth anniversary of this most powerful idea in human history would be to illuminate it! Make it really shine! Dredge Mr. Madison's ninth amendment out of the mothballs, stick a lot of candles on it, and remind everyone far and near that one of those "rights retained by the people" is the right to reproductive freedom.

And if we want to put some frosting on that two-hundredth anniversary cake, maybe we could "ice" it with the little Italian lady's admonition when she was asked about the Pope's stand on birth control and abortion. She said it all so beautifully and so concisely: "He no play a' da game, he no make a' da rules!"

Temporary Sins, Eternal Punishment

by Sherry Matulis

As elfin brat honoring the wondrous curiosity
Mom Nature so generously accorded,
I nibbled lots of forbidden fruit.
Never took any big bites, but, oh, those nibbles:

"Now don't you kids go near that Holy Roller tent,"
my Methodist ma would warn, as she handed us
the shiny silver dime for the tarnished silver screen.
And whoosh! off to see the Revival Meetin' I'd go;
it was a much better show—none of those Tinseltown
kings and queens could push a potato down
a fifty foot aisle with their nose
while shaking and quaking and speaking
pseudo-orgasmic other-worldly (Plutonian?) prose.

"Young ladies don't chew gum!" my boilermaker-drinking
Presbyterian pa would growl. And quick as his
steely god-fearing fist could knock the Juicy Fruit
from my mouth, I'd be dazedly out the door
looking for some more, as expected.
Maybe Spearmint this time—
its odor wasn't quite so easily detected.

"I don't know what we're going to do with her, Miz Scott!"
my Sunday School teacher would gasp, as she rolled
her eyes in the direction opposite that which she *knew*
I was headed. She was thirty; I but seven
and determined to explain why Jonah,
for goodness-gracious-sakes-alive-in-Heaven,
could not possibly have lazed
in any fish's gut for three hours,
let alone!?three days?!

This disregard for parent/teacher dictates
was minor of this minor's better 'sins.'
I often scorned, disdained and *queried* 'Him.'

Coming home from midweek evening services,
small chin jutting defiantly
at that diamond-studded velvet those poor ancients
erroneously, in their ignorance, deemed a canopy
and we moderns *know* as Heaven,
"Where are you?" I would mumble.
"And why don't you do something?"

"Where are you when my father gets drunk
and parks the black Ford *we* can't sit in
square in front of our Grapes of Wrath house
to make out with his latest painted lady and then,
done, spent, storms through the door
to knock my mother to the floor?
And why don't you *do* something?"

"Where are you when tornadoes come
freight-training through the cornfields
and slap sizzling electric wires
around the eight year old neck
of my very best friend?
And *why* don't you do something?"

"Where are you when dirty old men
of the cloth hump hump hump
defenseless five year olds, admonishing
Eternal Hellfire if they tell, leaving
them bloody and teeth-chattering constrained;
and then walk away from the crime,
skin and bones and reputation intact?
And why don't *you* do something?"

"Where are you when mean people
shoot little puppies because they bark?
When only brothers don khaki and leave home
and return in big ugly boxes?
When good hearts give out too soon,
while bad ones just keep thumping away?
When sisters lie forever cold in pools
of jelling blood because they wanted
to be sisters, not mothers?
And why don't you do *something?*"

"Where are you? Are you busy
pimping for preachers?
Designing a fish without stomach acids?
Planning a bigger, better Flood?
Stoking the Forever Fire?

Build a huge one; you deserve it.
My 'sins' are small and temporary.
For yours, I'd recommend
Eternal Punishment."

Religion's Child

by Sherry Matulis

Aware of light and yet condemned to grope
Through dark regression's cave, told she must find
Life's purpose in that blackness, without hope,
Denied the luminescence of her mind
Until, at last, she finds the darkness kind,
Religion's child—a babe once bright and fair,
Curls up, tucks in her tail, and says her prayer.

Kay Nolte Smith

ON A

WALK

47

Kay Nolte Smith

ATHEIST, ACTRESS, AUTHOR

July 4, 1932 – September 25, 1993

The tragedy is that every brain cell devoted to belief in the supernatural is a brain cell one cannot use to make life richer or easier or happier.

"Truth or the Consequences," *1983*

KAY NOLTE SMITH WAS AN ACTOR, teacher, atheist and award-winning novelist.

Born in Eveleth, Minnesota, she spent her teenage years in small-town Baraboo, Wisconsin, an experience that gave her a yearning for big cities. She received her B.A. from the University of Minnesota in 1952 and her Master's degree in Theater and Speech from the University of Utah in 1955. Thanks to the ubiquitous strong-arm of the Mormon Church, she had difficulty obtaining coffee, tea or carbonated beverages while studying there.

She married Prof. Philip Smith in 1958, who later became chair of the Visual and Performing Arts Department at Brookdale College in New Jersey. She and her husband went into professional theater together, running a summer theater in Michigan, performing at dinner theaters, and co-producing Ayn Rand's "Penthouse Legend" (known as "Night of January 16"). Kay even ventured into television commercials. After performing off Broadway for ten years, she joined several faculties as a teacher, and turned her energies to writing.

Her first novel *Watcher* (1980) won the Edgar Allen Poe award, followed by *Mindspell* (1983), *Country of the Heart* (1988), and *Tale of the Wind* (1991). *Catching Fire* is a suspense story set in the theater.

To write *Mindspell*, Kay delved into the witchhunts, asserting that records of this heinous time should be "mandatory reading in every Sunday school. This is what made me an atheist. Consider how deeply witch craze was rooted in religion. The papal sanction was not abolished for six centuries. How can anyone belong to a church that treated it members this way?"

Truth or the Consequences

This is the text of a speech delivered at the 1983 Freedom From Religion Foundation convention in Peoria, Illinois, originally appearing in the January 1984 Freethought Today.

IN 1589 THE TEN-YEAR-OLD DAUGHTER of a squire of Warboys in England began to have fits. She blamed them on the influence of a respectable, elderly neighbor named Alice Samuel. Soon the girl's four sisters also began to have fits. A local doctor hinted at the possibility of witchcraft, and though the parents were at first inclined to dismiss the whole thing, they reluctantly agreed to confront Mrs. Samuel with the girls. With this, the fits became more dramatic. At last, to placate the family, Mrs. Samuel ceremonially ordered the girls to stop. They did so, which was taken as proof that she was indeed a witch. The local parson nagged her into confessing, and although she retracted her statement the next day, she was held in custody to await the Assizes, along with her husband and her daughter, whom the girls had also implicated by that time. The girls' fits went on, and they began claiming that the Samuels had magically murdered a locally prominent woman. The jury found all three suspects guilty. Old Mrs. Samuels confessed to intercourse with the Devil and she and her husband and daughter were hanged.

Over two hundred and fifty years later—in 1848—the family of John Fox, in upstate New York, began to hear peculiar raps and thumps in the house they had recently moved into. The sounds became more distinct and alarming. One night the Fox daughters began to establish that the sounds were made by a phantom, whom they could question and receive answers from by means of knocks. The neighbors were invited in to witness, and a communication system was set up: The phantom rapped for Yes, and was silent for No. Soon an alphabet system was devised, and the Fox girls learned that the phantom was the ghost of a peddler who had been murdered on the premises. Mrs. Fox and her two daughters became celebrities, and when one of them went to nearby Rochester to visit another married sister, rappings began immediately in that house as well. Soon all the Fox women turned professional. Within three years after those original raps and thumps, they had led to the existence of more than a hundred mediums in New York City alone, and the rapping experiments were being reproduced in a dozen countries. By the 1870s, an estimated one and a half million followers professed to believe in the spirit world, and attended seances.

These two events—the accusation and killing of a witch during the height of the witch-craze, and the beginning of modern spiritualism—took place centuries and countries apart. In my mind, they were first united simply because I came across both of them while doing research for a book, which became *Mindspell.* But I soon saw that the witch-craze and the spiritualist craze are united in deeper, fundamental ways: they are both part of humankind's endless attempt to search for truth by irrational means.

They show us the consequences of that kind of search. They let us contemplate it in forms that are different, yet distressingly similar. For in spite of the fact that the witch-craze took place centuries ago—from the fourteenth to the mid-eighteenth centuries—whereas the spiritualist craze is in its modern phase, considering the two of them together shows us that the more things change, the more they stay the same.

I'd like to talk about three ways in which those two phenomena are the same. First, both dispense with proof and evidence. Second, both are rooted in, and derive their strength from, religion. Third—as a consequence of the first two—both destroy those who come under their influence.

And both, incidentally, have a meaning in our own lives, yours and mine. . . .

Over two thousand years ago Aristotle formulated the axioms of logic, which are the foundation of so much of Western civilization—certainly of our science, and therefore of all the material improvements over the centuries, and of course of all Western jurisprudence. Try to imagine a judicial system in which A is non-A, in which no independent validation of charges is required, in which guilt, not innocence, is presumed—and you have Franz Kafka. Or, you have the trials of the witch-craze, which lasted for over three centuries.

But, as a kind of twisted tribute to whatever is Aristotelian in human nature, the witch trials, in their search for truth, had to claim to be gathering evidence and facts and demanding proof. In doing so, they violated every requirement of logic, law, and reason.

Here, for example, is a summary of the methods used by the Inquisition (as provided by Roger Hart in his book, *Witchcraft*). As you listen, put yourself in the place of the accused—let's say someone charged with being in league with Satan and causing the deaths of a neighbor's wife and infant son:

1. The accused is presumed guilty until she has proved her innocence.

2. Suspicion, gossip, or denunciation is sufficient indication of guilt to haul one before the Inquisition.

3. Witnesses are not identified. Often their accusations are not made known to the defendant. For example, in some localities, a wooden chest was kept in the church so that anyone could throw in a paper containing the name of a witch and the time and place of the crime. But the chest was kept locked, so that the accuser need not be known, except to the inquisitors who regularly opened the chest.

4. Witnesses disallowed in other offenses are encouraged in cases of heretics: for example, convicted perjurers, those without civil rights, young children, and excommunicates. Furthermore, if hostile witnesses should retract their evidence, they will be prosecuted for perjury, but their testimony will be allowed to stand.

5. No witnesses are allowed to testify for the accused, nor is the accused person's reputation as a good citizen or Christian taken into account.

6. The accused is permitted no counsel, since the lawyer would thereby be guilty of defending heresy. (In the seventeenth century, however, this privilege was allowed.)

7. The judges are encouraged to trip the accused into confessing.

For example, the Inquisitorial courts prepared set lists of questions, designed to prove a victim's guilt. All were leading questions, like these:

Why did you become a witch?

Whom did you choose to be your incubus?

What was the oath you were forced to swear?

What demons and what other humans took part in the sabbath?

Who are the children on whom you have cast a spell?

8. Torture is the accepted means of confirming guilt. The practices can range from "swimming" a witch, throwing her into a river bound hand and foot (if she floats, she is guilty), to pricking her naked body with long brass pins (if any spot fails to bleed, she is guilty), to making her walk without stopping for several days and nights, to things that make all of those seem painless and innocent.

9. Having confessed under torture, the accused has to repeat her con-

fession in sight of the torture chamber but "freely and spontaneously, without the pressure of force or fear." In other words, she is finally taken from the torture chamber and told to repeat the confession—or she will be sent back. If she does repeat it, she is considered to have admitted guilt without torture, and the court record will so state.

10. Every accused has to give or invent names of accomplices or those whom he or she suspected of heresy.

11, and last. Generally no appeal will be allowed.

Some voices were raised in protest against these methods. Some witchseekers and judges did try to exercise reason and compassion. Usually they didn't get very far.

Consider the case of Dietrich Flade of Germany, a secular judge who was in charge of prosecuting witches. He tried to be restrained, and demanded careful presentation of evidence. This moderation enraged two of his colleagues, a bishop and a governor, who plotted against him: they got a boy to accuse him of planning to poison the archbishop, and got an old woman who was about to be executed to say that Flade, like her, was a witch. More accusations followed, including the charge that he had persuaded other witches to eat a child's heart. Flade was arrested and tortured. In terrible pain he confessed to such things as intercourse with the Devil, and named his accomplices.

One of the sadder consequences of the witch-craze is that many of the accused came to believe in their own guilt. In the historical record there are tales of those who thought they did have Satanic powers, and could fly through the air, attend Sabbath, copulate with Satan, et cetera. There are of course psychological explanations for these aberrations, but imagine a judiciary system that encourages defendants in their illness, and tries to "prove" to them that their delusions are real—so it may put them to death.

When a judicial system abandons reason, it cannot find truth. And the consequences are horrible.

In spiritualism, by contrast, no one suffers—physically. Everything, in fact, is gentle and soothing—the voices, the atmosphere, and the messages that are brought from the dead. But the suspension of logic, proof, and of all rationality, is just as great.

Like the witchcraft trials, spiritualism pretends to be offering proof—in this case, not proof of Satanic commerce but proof that there is an afterlife. In fact, spiritualism claims to be not only a religion and a philosophy, but also a science. Its proof consists of manifestations from the world of the dead: that is, the voices, forms, and other communications of the spirits. (Incidentally, there are two terms in use: spiritism, which is the belief that one can communicate with the dead; and spiritualism, which is that belief made explicitly religious.)

Before I went to a spiritualist camp, I had done a good deal of research and was aware of what phenomena to expect, as well as how most of them were actually achieved. (For the explanations, I was greatly indebted to a wonderful out-of-print book called *The Psychic Mafia* by a former spiritualist medium who had a change of heart, retired, reformed and wrote a book revealing how he had accomplished all his tricks.)

I was prepared for the spiritualist camp, but I wasn't prepared for the cheapness of the tricks—excuse me, the spirit manifestations—and, above all, for the pathetic gullibility of the clients.

For example, when I told them I was a believer but a novice, they sent me first to a woman who was to give me a "clairvoyant reading." She spoke in such glittering generalities and boring banalities that I gave her a hand: I hinted that I wanted to talk to my dead sister, with whom I'd fought before she died. The woman—Virginia was her name—then began to tell me that my sister was well and happy on the other side and (guess what?) had forgiven me. (No one in the spiritualist psychic world ever tells a client anything unpleasant. It's not good for business.) In a dazzling display of clairvoyant technique, Virginia went on to say that my sister had died of something "around the area of the heart or the stomach." That was safe enough—how many people die of something in the fingers or legs? The only real problem with Virginia's reading was the fact that my sister is alive and well and living in New York City.

Yet I met people at the spiritualist camp who swore by Virginia and were astounded by the accuracy of her messages.

Later, along with a group of regular sitters, I was admitted to a trumpet seance. In this form of spiritualist "proof" the medium goes into a trance and, in darkness, her spirit guide brings various spirits who speak through the trumpet (which is actually a long aluminum cone). My medium, who had a strong Southern accent, produced a complete blackout in the room (darkness was the one thing they were really good at) and then, various spirit voices began to talk through the trumpet. A mother, a brother, an aunt, an old friend—they all came with messages for the sitters. There was only one problem: they all had the same Southern accent as the medium.

It was all so transparent despite the blackout, that I expected the sitters to burst out laughing. Instead, whenever the spirit voices weren't speaking, there was a reverent silence. And when it was over, the sitters were ecstatic in their praises of "the spirits" and the medium who had produced them.

If I hadn't been there, I would not have believed anyone could be taken in by tricks so obvious and shoddy. I had expected more sophistication—after all, I had worked in the professional theater and was aware of many ways in which impressive illusions were created onstage. But what I learned from that camp was that the crudest tricks, which wouldn't fool a five year old for very long, can convince someone who wants to be convinced—and who has abandoned, or never knew, what is meant by evidence and proof. . . .

What permits things like witchcraft and spiritualism to come into existence—and stay in existence? There are many factors: sociological, economic, and of course psychological. But one that deserves a lion's share of the blame is religion.

As long as people believe in a God of some kind, there is no logical reason to reject any other form of supernaturalism. As long as they accept God, why shouldn't they accept Satan and his creatures—namely, witches? As long as they accept God and the concept of an afterlife, why shouldn't they accept the notion that their loved ones can speak to them after they're dead?

Religion is omnipresent in spiritualism. On the walls of the camp I visited were two pictures: a famous Indian spirit guide and Jesus Christ. The camp held straight religious services, and the seances began with prayers and hymns. The mediums call themselves Reverends.

As the author of *The Psychic Mafia* explained, "It's very easy to set up a church and obtain the legal right to call yourself 'Reverend.' A lawyer was needed who, for three hundred dollars, drew up the articles of incorporation. . . . [under those articles], approved by the Florida secretary of state, we could give ourselves virtually any power, authority, or title we wanted. I, who had never taken a theological course, proceeded to conduct weddings and funerals, ordain others to the spiritualist clergy. . . . run a religious school, and certify other congregations that might wish to affiliate with us. . . . In the eyes of the law I had as much ecclesiastical status as the Archbishop of Canterbury or the Pope—and it was all a racket!"

But are the Reverends themselves religious?

"The Bible," he says, "is exhibited in most spiritualist churches but in their hearts mediums scorn it—and openly too, when they're with their own kind. The jokes about Jesus' virgin birth were many and varied but had one thing in common: their scabrous quality."

Of course there are psychics practicing today who are not spiritualists, and there are believers in the psychic world who don't practice any religion. But would there be such heightened interest and belief in all things "psychic" if religion didn't hold such an honored place in our world? If Uncle Sam can become involved in the "Year of the Bible," if his money declares, "In God We Trust," then why shouldn't his citizens try to commune with the dead?

One of the puzzles about widespread belief in the supernatural has been: How can it exist in periods of rationality and scientific advancement? For example, the witch-craze, as well as a general belief in magic, coexisted with the Renaissance; on the one hand were Leonardo, Galileo, Michelangelo, and on the other, the Inquisition. The same thing happened in the nineteenth and twentieth centuries: spiritualism, spiritism, and belief in psychic phenomena co-exist with the Industrial Revolution and with computers, laser beams, and space flight.

So, how is it that periods of rationality and scientific advancement can also be periods of widespread belief in the supernatural? In my view, a large part of the answer—one of the main bridges that lets irrationality co-exist with reason—has been and is religion.

In other words, it's not an accident that a time when I am able to write a novel with the amazing technology of the word processor is also a time when the publishing world clearly prefers occult novels to books like *Mindspell* and when I find, at the college where I occasionally teach writing, that a large percentage of my students are born-again Christians.

Our world, even at its most rational, has never fully rejected the concept of the supernatural, which has been kept alive by the church. And the church is kept alive because it has a stranglehold on the idea of Good and Evil. Human beings need a code of good and evil to live by, and whatever else the church has had to abandon over the centuries, it has convinced most of the world that morality belongs to religion. Witness the historical split between science and ethics, recognized by most thinkers, which amounts to the idea that reason is for use in the practical world of science and commerce, but when it comes to moral issues—to the most personally important kind of truth—then one looks to faith. Or at least, one turns away from reason. The most powerful kingdom on earth—the kingdom of morality—still belongs to God. As long as religion maintains its virtual monopoly on morality, it will be a significant force. And as long as it is, there will be a significant degree of belief in other manifestations of the supernatural. And as long as we have religion, two things will keep taking place in the name of God: fraud and destruction. There is of course no more overwhelming example of destruction in God's name than the witchcraft craze. If I may speak personally: this is what made me an atheist. When I was an adolescent and read about the Inquisition, the church lost forever whatever small territory it had staked out in my mind.

Consider how deeply the witch-craze was rooted in religion: Philosophically, the belief in possession by devils had always been part of Christian doctrine. Witness the madman in the New Testament whose "devil" is cast out by Christ. But religion was also the practical and political basis for the witchcraft craze. For example: Torture as a means to discover heresy was sanctioned by a papal bull in 1257, and that sanction was not abolished for almost six centuries. In 1484 a Dominican inquisitor in Germany persuaded the Pope to issue a bull confirming full Papal support for the work of the Inquisition against witches. Two years later that same Dominican and a colleague, with the Pope's approval, published a book called *Malleus Maleficarum*—"The Hammer Against the Witches"—which became one of the most influential of all early printed books, and the Bible for witchhunters.

In 1532 the Carolina Code was issued in Germany and adopted by the three hundred-odd states of the Holy Roman Empire. It was a code that imposed torture and death for witchcraft.

In the sixteenth century, the Protestant Reformation failed to reform one thing: it did not reject the belief in witchcraft. Luther, in fact, argued that all witches should be burned as heretics for having made a pact with the devil, even if there was no evidence that they had done anyone any overt harm. Perhaps the greatest obscenity of all is that the instruments of torture were usually blessed beforehand by the churchmen who used them, or ordered their use.

During the more than three centuries that the witch-craze lasted, the power of the church and the state were united. Can there be a more powerful argument for their separation?

Where the witch-craze was ugly and terrifying, the spiritualist-psychic craze is merely pathetic and foolish. But both of them, in different ways, have the same consequence: they destroy those who come under their influence.

Their least offensive consequence is the destruction of property. You are probably aware that the goal of spiritualists and psychics is, simply, to fleece their victims. Stories abound of gullible, usually elderly people who give all their savings to some Reverend or spiritualist church. What is not so well known is that many mediums are very well off indeed; ten years ago one of them reported taking in over a thousand dollars a day at a spiritualist camp, where the total take was said to have been over a million dollars a year in the days before inflation.

Venality, it may surprise you to learn, was also a strong motivation in the witchcraft trials. The property of the condemned witch was always confiscated, and records indicate that the witchfinders were on the lookout for well-to-do persons, so the coffers might be filled more quickly. In fact, one authority on the witch persecutions, Russell Hope Robbins, charges that the chief motive behind them was the desire to appropriate the property of the condemned.

But loss of property pales by comparison with another consequence: the loss of life. No one knows for certain how many lives were taken in the witch-craze. At least several hundred thousand, and there are a few scholars who estimate that the figure is in the millions. But even worse than the fact of death was the manner of death. The Nazi gas chambers were kind and swift, compared to the terrible and protracted suffering that every victim of the witch-craze endured.

Here is a verbatim report of the first day's torture of a woman accused of witchcraft in Germany in 1629. It is a list of ten points:

1. The hangman bound her hands, cut her hair, and placed her on the ladder. He threw alcohol over her head and set fire to it so as to burn her hair to the roots.

2. He placed strips of sulphur under her arms and about her head and set fire to them.

3. He tied her hands to her back and pulled her up to the ceiling.

4. He left her hanging there from three to four hours, while the torturer went to breakfast.

5. On his return, he threw alcohol over her back and set fire to it.

6. He attached very heavy weights on her body and drew her up again to the ceiling. After that he put her back on the ladder and placed a very rough plank full of sharp points against her body. Having thus arranged her, he jerked her up again to the ceiling

7. Then he squeezed her thumbs and big toes in the vise, and he. . . .

I'm sorry. I can't finish. It's hard even to read it. Imagine having to live through it . . . hours, days, even weeks of it.

Could there be anything worse than being put to an agonizing death in order to appease a God you probably had loved? Yes, there could be.

You may have noticed that most of the time when I've been referring to victims of the witch-craze, I've said "she." That is no accident. Overall, at least twice as many women as men were accused. Whenever someone uses the word "witch," is there any doubt which sex is being referred to? Here is the *Malleus Maleficarum*, the Bible of witchhunters, explaining how women became the greatest victims of the witch-craze:

"What else is woman but a foe to friendship, an inescapable punishment, a necessary evil, a natural temptation, a desirable calamity, a domestic danger, a delectable detriment, an evil of nature, painted in fair colours. . . . The word woman is used to mean lust of the flesh. . . . [Women] are more credulous; and since the chief aim of the devil is to corrupt faith, therefore he rather attacks them [than men]. . . . Women are intellectually like children. . . . [Woman] is more carnal than a man, as is clear from her many carnal abominations. . . . She is a liar by nature. . . . Let us also consider her gait, posture, and habit, in which is vanity of vanities."

On and on it goes, inflaming the witchhunters. And if women had hoped to find any relief from the Reformation, Martin Luther dispelled that hope. His writings, as one critic puts it, "writhe with fear of women."

Why? Why such virulent misogyny?

There were some practical reasons. For one, in the sixteenth century, a higher proportion of women lived alone than before: widows, unmarried persons, elderly women with perhaps some physical affliction or deformity. Women had survived the plagues in greater numbers than men, who could suspect them of causing that result. And then, women were the usual attendants at childbirth: If anything went wrong with the delivery or the child, and it often did in that time of high infant mortality, the husband could blame the midwife. Women were safe to accuse, because of their lower social position and their inability to defend themselves.

For a deeper explanation of the misogyny behind the witch-craze, consider the view of women that the church had promulgated for centuries: woman was either a virgin or a whore. If she wasn't a saint then she was a carnal hag.

For many women, the ultimate horror of being accused as a witch must have been the realization, however dimly grasped, that she was being destroyed because of the sexual cravings of her accusers and torturers. It's a well established fact of human psychology that a person—or a culture—which represses its sexuality will experience great sexual cravings. And the greater the repression, the more depraved the desires will be. A prudish, Victorian culture has the darkest underside. And a man who has foresworn all sexual contact is going to be tormented by his desires for it. Clearly for some men the witch-craze was a golden opportunity to lust after woman the whore and carnal hag while punishing her for being the object of his fantasies and transgressions.

Consider one Franz Buirmann, whom the Prince Archbishop of Cologne appointed to be a witchseeker in the 1630s. When Buirmann made advances to a woman who refused them, he had her arrested and placed under torture immediately. The torturer's assistant shaved all the hairs off her body and head. While he did so, he was allowed to rape her. Franz Buirmann looked on, and stuffed a dirty rag in her mouth to stifle her cries. She was placed in a hut filled with dry straw and burned alive.

The witch-craze destroyed the property and lives of its victims. It also destroyed something possessed by everyone who was part of it, even the accusers: It destroyed their minds. Before a witchseeker could do violence to his victims, he had to do violence to his own mind. He and all the accusers had to believe in witchcraft; they had to elevate the word of God above every fiber of decency and compassion in their own souls. Probably some of the accusers and witchseekers—perhaps even most of them—had been basically decent people until they joined the witch-hunt. But by giving God's word precedence over their own minds, they destroyed their own humanity, and became torturers and killers. They abandoned their minds, and cast a bloodspell over the Western world. This, to me, is the most tragic consequence of the witch-craze—not the most horrible, but the most tragic: the surrender by thousands and thousands of people, for centuries, of their own minds. That surrender is equally, though less horribly, a consequence of the spiritualist psychic craze.

Listen again to the reformed medium I've been quoting elsewhere: "One of the most alarming things about the mediumistic racket is how completely some people put their lives into the hands of ill-educated, emotionally unbalanced individuals who claim a hot line to heaven. As a medium I was routinely asked about business decisions, marital problems, whether to have an abortion, how to improve sexual performance, and similar intimate and important subjects. That people who ask such questions of a medium are risking their mental, moral, and monetary health is a shocking but quite accurate description of the matter."

It would be some comfort to think he's talking only about people who are as ill-educated as the mediums they consult. But then there are reports like a New York magazine article of a few years ago, which states that the likes of Marion Javits, Cristina Ford, and Virginia Graham were consulting a psychic. So were some Wall Street brokers. They wanted to know the futures of various stocks and bonds, so the psychic gave them something called "pendulum readings." And how many people do we all know who believe that their astrological signs have something to do with their actions and destinies? The tragedy is that every brain cell devoted to belief in the supernatural is a brain cell one cannot use to make life richer or easier or happier.

The witch-craze and spiritualism have a meaning in our lives today, even though one has been over for two hundred years and most of us in this room may never directly confront the other. They affect our lives because of what they have taken from our lives. Who knows what the consequences might have been, what inventions might have been created, what pain relieved, what pleasure brought into existence, if all the mental energy expended throughout history on God, Satan, witches, spirits, et cetera—and some of it was expended by talented and brilliant people—who knows how much better our lives could be if all that power had been spent on seeking truth, and seeking to live, by rational means.

If I may be permitted to quote the heroine of my novel: "Superstition and the supernatural cannot change the world, or alleviate its suffering. Only the power of the mind can do that."

Sonia Johnson
(Photograph by Joan E. Biren, 1983)

48

Sonia Johnson

HOUSEWIFE TO HERETIC

Born February 1936

Women must rise up and be the saviors of the world.

From Housewife to Heretic, 1983

SONIA JOHNSON BECAME A "WOMAN WARRIOR" after being excommunicated from the Church of Jesus Christ of Latter-day Saints in 1979, for her public support of the proposed Equal Rights Amendment to the United States Constitution.

Her treatment at the hands of the Mormon hierarchy catapulted her "from housewife to heretic," turning her into a national celebrity and one of the most ardent supporters of the ERA. Sonia was arrested in November 1980, in Bellevue, Washington, for chaining herself to the gates of a Mormon temple. Her activism culminated in a life-threatening thirty-seven day fast with six other women in the statehouse in Springfield, Illinois, when that state's nonratification became pivotal in 1982. Her hunger strike during the last days of the ERA countdown symbolized how "women hunger for justice." Sonia was named the first "Humanist Heroine" by the Feminist Caucus of the American Humanist Association in 1982.

Sonia ran on a feminist ticket for President of the United States in 1984 as the candidate of the Citizens Party. Her campaign was distinguished as the first third-party presidential candidacy to qualify for primary matching funds. Her campaign helped to pressure the Democrats to offer a woman as a vice-presidential candidate; Geraldine Ferraro made history when she joined the Democratic ticket of Walter Mondale running against Ronald Reagan.

Sonia grew up a fifth generation Mormon in Malad, Idaho. A conscientious intellectual achiever, Sonia took the Mormon church at its professed word, and believed she never wanted to be anything other than "a Mommy." She graduated from Utah State University and was married a year later to Richard Johnson. Sonia pursued her M.A. and Ed.D from Rutgers through many moves, pregnancies and bureaucratic obstacles. She taught English at American and foreign universities, working part-time as a teacher, and accompanied Richard on overseas jobs. After living oversees for some time the family bought a house in the unratified state of Virginia in 1976, and "the rest is history."

She wrote, eloquently, of her experiences in *From Housewife to Heretic* (1981), exposing the role of the Mormon Church in defeating the ERA:

"According to a 1979 Associated Press story the Mormon church brings in nearly four million dollars a day, and a *Fortune* magazine editor told us that the church is one of the twenty wealthiest corporations in this country. With such financial backing and such a ready-made, obedient constituency, it poses by far the greatest threat to equal rights for women in this country of any New Right group. It is the archenemy of the Equal Rights Amendment. It is the archenemy, therefore, of women. If all other opponents of women marched off into the ocean like lemmings and drowned—and let us linger a moment over the pleasant fantasy—the Mormon church could and would defeat the ERA single-handedly."

In becoming a non-Mormon, she wrote:

"A reporter for the *Atlanta Constitution* recently asked me if, now that I was no longer theologically Mormon, I had acquired any non-Mormon habits (alluding, I'm sure, to smoking and drinking). 'Yes,' I replied, 'in fact I have. I have acquired the habit of free thought.' "

In speeches and interviews around the country, she has pointed out: "Nobody's ever fought a revolution for women." She called her excommunication "the best thing that ever happened to me."

"A feminist is a revolutionary, by definition. I like to remind people what radical means—'at the root of things.' It shouldn't be considered a pejorative. There isn't a great name out of history you can pick who wasn't 'radical.' "

Sonia's other books include: *Going Out of Our Minds: The Metaphysics of Liberation* (1987), *Wildfire: Igniting the She/Volution* (1989), and *The Ship That Sailed Into The Living Room: Sex and Intimacy Reconsidered* (1991).

"I have to admit that one of my favorite fantasies," Sonia has said, "is that next Sunday not one single woman, in any country of the world, will go to church. If women simply stop giving our time and energy to the institutions that oppress, they would have to cease to do so." She advocates "faith not in god (or goddess), but in ourselves, in our own voices, in our own judgment, our own abilities."

From Housewife to Heretic

*This speech was delivered at the 1982 convention of the Freedom From Religion
Foundation, in Madison, Wisconsin.*

SHORTLY AFTER I WAS EXCOMMUNICATED from the Mormon church I was in
Boise, Idaho, speaking, and a young TV cameraman came up to me with a
puzzled look on his face and said, "But you're just a mom!" He was really
disappointed because I was the first heretic he'd ever seen, and somehow
he'd hoped for more. I remember thinking, "You know, Sonia, you've come
a long way from housewife to heretic in a very short time."

My husband and I have lived out of this country a lot during our married life, and we've lived in countries where there isn't exactly a booming
women's movement. We've lived in Samoa, Korea, Malaysia and a couple
of countries in Africa. Though I knew there was something called the
women's movement going on in this country, I didn't really know what it
was all about. I didn't feel any antipathy, but then on the other hand it was
quite clear I didn't need it because I was living a perfectly wonderful life. I
was very happy and doing exactly what I wanted to do. So whatever it was
you were up to here, it was simply irrelevant.

In 1976, we moved back to this country, to Virginia, which was then,
as it seems destined to remain, alas, a very unratified state. And I began to
hear immediately about something called the ERA. I heard about it in
church, and what I heard was all bad. I was distressed by that, not because
I even knew what those letters stood for, because I didn't, but because I
was hearing about it over the pulpit. This had not been my experience in
the Mormon church. I found it upsetting and distressing that political
stuff was happening in our most sacred church meetings. It appeared that
in order to be a good Mormon you had to be right-wing in your politics.

When we moved to that part of Virginia, which is close to Washington, D.C., I realized that we had some old friends who lived in that area, a
couple that we had gone to graduate school with at the University of Minnesota about fifteen years before. We'd all been very good Mormons and
very close friends. We'd been newly married; we had our first babies in the
same hospital. So I called them up. And when I hung up the phone I turned
to my husband and said, "Something has happened to Hazel. She sounds
just shocking!" Well, I had just spoken to my first feminist. Maybe you

remember when it happened to you. It really is just shocking. I remember hanging up the phone another time and turning to my husband and saying, "I hope I never sound like Hazel." Which just goes to show because now, of course, I out-Hazel Hazel.

She said I should find out what the women's movement was all about, that it was for happy women too, women like me. (That came as a real surprise.) But she said I should do it gently because the women's movement was a little bit dangerous and slightly painful. You can see, can't you, that Hazel is the mistress of understatement. She had me read a little book to dip my big toe in the icy waters of feminism, a book called *I'm Running Away From Home, But I'm Not Allowed To Cross The Street*.

I asked Hazel, "What is this ERA that we're hearing about in church all the time?" She told me in twenty-four words what the Equal Rights Amendment was all about: "Equality of rights under the law shall not be denied or abridged by the United States or by any state on account of sex."

To my dismay, I couldn't find anything wrong with that. In fact, I liked it. I liked it a lot. And I say "to my dismay" because I'd never been opposed to my church in any serious way about anything, and I didn't want to start. Things were heating up in Richmond about the ERA, which meant things were heating up in the pulpit, which meant pretty soon I was in a state of really serious spiritual conflict on this matter. Therefore, I was very relieved when one night in church it was announced that the next Sunday night we'd have a special meeting, where one of the leaders of the church would come and explain to us in detail why the church opposed the Equal Rights Amendment. I was very impressed by the credentials of this speaker. He was not only a leader of the church, which in those days impressed me very much, but he had been—and this will impress you—the project director for the manned exploration to the moon. I was still so naïve, I thought that meant something. I ran right home. I called up Hazel and said, "You people have got to come out to my ward next Sunday night." ("Ward" is what we call Mormon congregations, which I now think is very appropriate.) I said, "Finally we're going to hear something intelligent on the other side of this issue!" (That was before I knew that there wasn't anything intelligent on the other side of the issue.)

The next Sunday night when the project director got up to speak there were, right there at his feet in the front row, seven or eight of us pro-ERA

Mormons in a room full of thirty or forty of the other sort. He began by telling us that he hadn't prepared anything to say to us that night, and on his way over to the church he got kind of nervous about it. I poked my husband, and I said, "Well, I should think so!" And in his mounting agitation the closer he got to the church, he suddenly remembered, thank goodness, somebody had told him that there was an article about the ERA in the latest *Pageant* magazine. You remember *Pageant?* That deservedly defunct, little B-grade *Reader's Digest* (if that's possible). Miracle of miracles, what should appear on the horizon but a Seven-Eleven store, so he had run in there and bought the *Pageant* magazine. While we were having our opening psalm and prayer he had read that article, and now he was ready to talk to us about the Equal Rights Amendment to the Constitution.

I began to feel a kind of fury rise up inside me from inside someplace deep down, a kind of fury that I had never felt in all my life about anything. I grew up in a culture like yours, only more so, that teaches that any anger is evil, especially for women. I don't think I've been seriously angry since I was a baby, and I was really alarmed by myself. I was so angry I was trembling, and I hardly knew who I was. I didn't know if I had control of this person or not—it was a whole new person. I remember as I was looking at that man, I was thinking to myself of that place in the bible where it says, "Which of you if your child asked for bread, would give her a stone?" (Or something like that.) I remember thinking that *Pageant* magazine is a pretty large stone. And I also thought, as I was looking at him, that he was probably representative of the men of my church, the leaders of my church, men and leaders of other churches, and probably most men, in the way they felt about women's issues. That women's issues are so trivial, so peripheral, so ultimately unimportant that you don't even need to read anything about them. You don't even need to think about them before you come to speak to a group about them. Then he went on to make his second mistake with me. He read the Equal Rights Amendment. I told you that Hazel had told me what it said, and I bet you I'd even read it myself by that time. I was pro-ERA, in a mild sort of way, but when he read it that night, it took hold of my heart and it hasn't let go for one single second, waking or sleeping, since.

After he converted me, heart and soul, to the Equal Rights Amendment he went on to read a letter from the first presidency of the Mormon church explaining its opposition. As he was reading that letter I had an experience that I'd been teaching my students about at universities on this continent and several others for about fifteen years, an experience that I'd never personally had and I'd never known anyone else to have either, so I was beginning to think that people only had this experience in books, primarily James Joyce novels. But I can testify, I'm a living testament, that in fact people really do have Epiphanies in real life because I really had one. When I say epiphany some of you are perhaps inclined, perhaps not, to think of something supernatural. (You know, "God made me have it.") Although the experience I'm about to tell you about is without doubt the most profound spiritual experience of my life, I don't think there was anything supernatural about it at all. I think it has a perfectly rational explanation that I can probably help you understand best by giving an analogy.

All day long and all night long, as long as we're alive, as long as we are sensate beings, we are being bombarded by stimuli from our environment. Millions of little pieces of data are coming at us all the time. Obviously if we take each one of those pieces of data through our conscious minds and think about it, we'd go bonkers on the spot. It would be overwhelming. So we're very selective about what we choose out of all that information to take through our conscious process. We only select those few that we need to keep on looking sane and reasonable to our friends, and the rest of it we file away somewhere. Experts tell us that none of it is ever lost, it's all still there, which means, of course, that each one of us has miles and miles of underground corridors someplace just chock-full of filing cabinets and chock-full of files. Somewhere in all that labyrinth of filing cabinets and all that material, women have a special file. It's titled in big red Magic Marker: "What it means to be female in a male world." As soon as we're born female and someone says, "It's a . . . *girl*," we put our first piece of data in that file. For some women, way out here on this end of the continuum, that file is always open.

Those are the pieces of data they take out of all that barrage of information to think about: "What it means to be female." They're feminists from birth, which must be a very painful way to live; I don't know how they live to grow up, to tell you the truth. But in fact we know that there are some of those hearty souls even now stalking the earth, thank goodness. Then you go along until you get to the middle of the continuum (you know the normal curve)—and here's where there are more women than any other place. These are the women who know they have that file.

They know that there's something peculiar and negative about being female. They can get into that file if they need to. That information sits on the peripheries of their minds. They know it's there, but on the whole they'd just as soon not deal with it today, thank you. Then you go along the continuum until you get clear out here on the other end (and it's no accident that this is my right hand). Way out here are the women who don't have the least idea that they have such a file and they don't want to know. They spend a lot of their time and energy keeping themselves from finding it out. I know about those women, I know about them intimately, because I was one of them.

But that night, as I sat at the feet of the project director, I was forty-two years old and my file was just bulging. It was so full! (Mormon women's files are very full.) You have to remember that my file had just sustained an extraordinarily large piece of data, which was *Pageant* magazine, and it was probably even beginning to tremble a little and the seams beginning to give. This was the way it was when he began to read that letter. As he read that letter a couple of little tiny pieces of data came fluttering down into that file. That was all it took. The thing just burst open and all that information came flooding into my conscious mind. The miraculous thing about an epiphany is that when all that information becomes available to the consciousness it's perfectly organized! I knew exactly what the women's movement was all about, I knew it in my bones. I had always really known it somewhere. I knew where women really were in this culture despite all the rhetoric to the contrary. I knew where we really were and where women had been in all the cultures in the world since written history, at least. And I thought I was going to die of the pain of it. Hazel says that I was shaking my head back and forth and saying in a very loud voice (and this is bizarre in a Mormon meeting): "Oh no! Oh No!" to the alarm and consternation of everybody else in the room. But I was oblivious to them; I didn't care because I remember what I was thinking. And what I was thinking was how was I going to live through the rest of that meeting? It was truly an existential crisis. I thought I might die before I got out.

When I tell you what those two little pieces of data were that had come fluttering down into my file and finally broke it open, it's going to be a terrible anticlimax. You're going to say, "Oh, for heaven's sake! Those are such little things. I've always known that." That's true, they are little things and you probably always have known them. But you have to remember the state of the file. It couldn't take any more data no matter how little. It had come to the end. The really positive and exciting thing is that every single woman out there on that end of the continuum has a *very* full file. The first little piece of data was in the first line or in the first few sentences of that letter, where the leaders of the church said how much the men of the church have always loved us. I'd been listening to that rhetoric for forty-two years and I had never realized how condescending that is! But that night I realized the women of the church would never write the men of the church a letter telling them how much we loved them. Women simply don't know how to *matronize* like that. We're the ones who are patronized, we don't do it ourselves. Then he went on to read how Mormon women have always been held in an exalted position. You obviously know what that means.

To explain to you what I knew it meant is best described by a banner that I saw a year later at the ERA Extension march in Washington. The night of the project director was April 1977. In July of 1978 we marched 100,000 strong down Constitution Avenue in Washington, D.C., on the hottest day in the history of the world, to get the time limit extended to get women into the Constitution. In that march there was a magnificent banner carried by a whole battalion of women from Kansas. It filled up all of Constitution Avenue. It was all white except right in the middle had been painted this big deep hole. Down at the bottom of the hole had been painted two little pedestals, and on those two pedestals were two itty-bitty women. And way up there on ground level were painted these big, heavy boots of the men walking around in the real world, doing the important stuff. Down there at the bottom of the hole one little woman is turned to the other and she's saying, "I'm getting tired of this exalted position!" As Hazel says, "Sonia, what you learned that night is that pedestals are the pits!"

❦

A few months later I was reading Mary Daly's book—I should say I was suffering through her book, *Gynecology*—when I came, to my great delight, upon a definition of the pedestals-are-the-pits syndrome. Mary Daly is one of those theoreticians and philosophers in the women's movement who's doing an absolutely essential service for women, and that is that she is naming women's experience. What she names as the pedestals-are-the-pits syndrome is patriarchal reversal. As the rhetoric in a patriarchal institution or culture rises, it becomes more lofty and lush and purple—"Women are co-partners with God" (therefore we don't rate any protection under the law), and "Women are more spiritual than men" (ditto) and "Women are even more equal than men!" then, "Women have never had it so good," "The women's movement is totally successful." "We've accomplished everything, we've got all the laws we need, my gosh, why don't we just go home and bake a cake or something?" The lid of oppression is going down at the same rate the rhetoric is going up. This rhetoric is an attempt to distract us from what's really happening, to manipulate our perceptions. This is the voice of authority. This is the male voice that has spoken to us from God for nearly 4,000 years. And we have listened to that voice and ignored, denied our own experience, our own feelings, denied what we saw with our very own eyes because we wanted to please God. We really believed that those men had inside lines to deity.

The rhetoric about women has never been better. Why, you would think that we were the queens of the universe (if you believe that stuff). And what is really happening, while all this rhetoric is going on about how magnificent things are for women, is that there goes fifty years of work for women being washed out as if the tide were coming in and washing away the sand castle. Every single so-called safety net under women is going. That's why, of course, we must get the Equal Rights Amendment ratified.

I live near Washington, D.C., and I hear a lot of this nonsense. It spews out of the mouth of the administration—how wonderful things are for women these days. If things are so terrific for women, why is it that a woman with a graduate degree from a university makes, on the average, what a man makes who dropped out of high school at the eighth grade? And why is it, if things are so terrific for women, that of the eighty-eight million people living in official poverty in this country, eighty-four million are women and their children? If this trend continues, and there's no reason why this trend won't continue without the ERA and with the people in office we now have, by the year 2000, according to the National Counsel on Economic Opportunity, the entire poverty population of this country will be women and their children. Why is it, if things are "so terrific" for women, that they are so awful and getting worse by the day?

When I went out of that room that night I understood this phenomenon by which we had been kept oppressed, and which had kept us ignorant of our oppression. I knew that when we hear the establishment, or the people in power, praise us and say how wonderful things are for us, we know that exactly the opposite is the case. Patriarchal reversal is the most useful concept I have ever learned. It explains practically everything that happens to women. When I went out of that room that night, I was such a mass of mixed emotions it's funny I didn't atomize on the doorstep, that you couldn't see me glowing in the dark for miles around. First of all I felt betrayed, because, of course, I had been betrayed. All women have been betrayed by that voice, are daily betrayed by that voice. The voice of power always lies to women. Always, always, always. I felt like such a fool that I hadn't seen that before. I mean, gosh, I had a doctorate. I taught in universities. I thought I was a shrewd cookie. I thought it was hard to pull one over on me. Hard? Why it had been, as my children persist in saying, "a piece of cake." I felt such a fool that I was profoundly humiliated. Right on the tail of humiliation always travels anger. I was so angry that there isn't a word in the man's dictionary for it. Rage is a pale, little word. Fury is sickly. Really, we have got to get our own word. Men have never felt anything like that, just wanting to blow into millions of little pieces when we suddenly understand how we have been systematically duped for millennia.

All under, around and shot through those emotions was the feeling of the most immense sorrow, such sadness for the lives that women have had to live as far back as we have any knowledge of it, such sadness for my grandmother's life, for my mother's life. I can't forgive my mother's life. Sadness for my own life, for your lives.

On the way home in the car I turned to my husband and said something that I had resisted saying for a very long time, and now, seems to me to be the most beautiful word in the whole world: "I am a feminist. In fact, I'm a radical feminist!" I knew what radical meant. Radical means right at the roots of things. I knew that right at the roots of my soul I'd been changed that night, and I would never be the same. When we got home it was quite clear I wasn't going to sleep that night. After I got my family to bed, I went across the breezeway to the big room over the garage and shut and locked the door and let God have it. I told him (because in those days that's who I thought God was) what I thought of a supreme being who had made women so rich and so full, so talented and intelligent, so eager for experience and so able to profit from it, and who had put us in this little box and clamped the lid on it and said, "Now stay there, honey." I told him that that was the angriest, most vicious and ultimately the most evil thing that had ever been done, that if I could get hold of him, I'd kill him.

That is not the way I usually spoke to God. I grew up in a very devout and Orthodox Mormon family where God was much revered and loved. My mother is one of those women who takes that injunction in the scriptures seriously, the one that says pray always. My mother prays all the time. There are always several lines open between mother and heaven. You know that if you want to say something to momma, you're going to have to interrupt her. Back as far as I can remember, I wanted to be exactly like my mother. Since it was clear that her outstanding characteristic was this relationship with deity, it was quite clear I was going to have to have it too, if I was going to be like her. So from an early age I was a very prayerful person, very loving and respectful to God.

I had also read the scriptures. I knew the people who weren't respectful to God got zapped. The bible is full of people who got zapped because they weren't properly respectful. You do have to respect that kind of power, and I always had, but you know, all of a sudden I didn't care if I did get zapped. I figured I had *been* zapped! I figure all women had been zapped; in fact I thought it might be a relief to be zapped because what was I going to do with the contents of that file? The pain was indescribable, as close to unendurable as anything I have ever felt in my life. How could I survive the next fifteen minutes, to say nothing of waking up every morning for the next forty years and looking full in the face what has been done to women? I thought what a relief it would be if out of the ceiling should come this bolt of something and take care of me. I could just leave this immense, gargantuan problem up to all the rest of you. In fact, you can plainly see that that didn't happen.

After a couple of hours of screaming at the top of my lungs (I really hadn't done that since I was a baby either, I hadn't even hollered at the kids a lot), I found myself sitting on the floor exhausted, dripping with perspiration, my vocal cords in shreds, and feeling absolutely wonderful. I had this momentary fantasy that all those beings particularly interested in my life—you know, a guardian angel and all those amorphous sorts just wandering around up there (we don't know what they're doing, but it's good)—had gotten together in this impromptu celebration and were saying, "Oh Sonia, gee, this is wonderful! This really is so terrific that you finally figured this out. Do you know that we thought you never would?

For forty-two years we've been giving you every conceivable clue, but no, never mind, tonight is not the night to vent our frustration. Tonight's the celebration and all we really want to say to you is congratulations and welcome home. Now go do something for women."

Well, the first thing I had to do is something for Sonia because we all have to have our own personal revolutions before we can be of any use in the larger revolution, and, believe me, this *is* a revolution. And mine had to be a religious one, because that's the kind of person I was. I had to come to grips with God and I wish I had read something besides *I'm Running Away From Home, But I'm Not Allowed To Cross The Street*. If I had I would have known that out there in this country, and many other countries, there are thousands of women facing these same questions and feelings, and I would not have had to reinvent the wheel, in my own bedroom, on my own knees, in my own words. One of the very first conclusions I reached was one of the first conclusions everybody else out there was reaching— that men have given us God in their own image to keep control of us. So obviously, it's quite clear what we need to do, isn't it? We need to get some good powerful female representation in the courts, we need to desegregate that Old Boys Club, we need to ratify the ERA!

The second thing I figured out was that every single person born on planet earth in the last 3,500 years since the patriarchal revolution, whether they're conscious of it or not, whether they're religious or not, has believed that God and men are in this Old Boys Club, with God as president. Now because they're all guys, they have a special feeling for one another. They speak the same language, they have a lot of business dealings and they are in the same locker rooms and God just has to take one look at them to see that they're infinitely superior to the rest of us because they look like him, therefore he trusts them a lot. He wants them to be the prime ministers, kings and monarchs of the world. He wants them to be the popes, prophets and the priests. He wants them to own all the corporations, businesses and universities. He wants them to own all the property, make all the money and boss everybody around and make all the decisions. Needless to say, he wants them to be the bosses of all the women and children. And there are the rest of us out there, with our faces pressed up against the glass, trying to see what's going on in there.

Pretty soon one of those men comes out of that meeting. Oh, we're so grateful we're going to hear something about what's been going on. We say, "What's God saying in there?" And he leans up against the pulpit and he says, "God told me to tell you that he wants you to be my helpmeet." Pretty soon another man comes out and leans against the pulpit and says, "God told me to tell you that he wants you to be sweet and gentle. To have a soft voice and make sure that I always feel just terrific, and that my business flourishes and that I'm healthy, warm and well-fed. He wants you to think about me all the time. Just concentrate all your efforts on me. He wants you to always do everything that I say and obey me in everything and not make any rift, and not give me any grief. That's what *He* really wants. That is what God told me to tell you." So we've known for a very long time that in order to propitiate God, who is the President of the club, we're going to have to please his cronies—the men. That, in a thimble, is patriarchy. That's the system under which women have tried to survive for nearly 4,000 years. Mary Daly sums it up in one very wise, very wonderful and true sentence: "As long as God is male, male is God."

I had a little easier time than some getting some good female representation on high, because Mormons believe in a mother in heaven. I have to admit they don't say anything at all about her. Nevertheless, there she is. One day when the men were off to some meeting they had left the clubhouse door open and she sneaked in and wrote a hymn. The last verse says (it's a quaint little nineteenth century poem): "In the heavens are parents single? No, the thought makes reason stare. Truth is reason, truth eternal tells me I have a mother there." Mother, the subversive word in the last line, was a very wily woman as we have had to learn to be. She named that hymn, "Oh My Father." When the men came back they discovered this wonderful hymn just full of this father stuff. They took it instantly to their bosoms. I don't think they read clear down to the bottom where that little word was lurking. So that's the way "mother in heaven" slipped into tradition and then into doctrine. There she sits, a lovely time bomb under the Mormon church just waiting to go off.

The Mormon church is preparing a wonderful drama, but I only hope you enjoy it half as much as I'm going to. I remember the first night I prayed to "Mother in heaven," feeling very wicked and subversive, as one does when one knows they are doing something deliberately wrong. I wasn't very deeply into that prayer before it was quite clear to me why men have loved praying to a male deity all these years. I felt so powerful, so strong, even invincible. I thought, with her on my side, how can I not be victorious? I remember thinking how wonderful it was to pray to a deity who had had not just a lifetime of, but millions of years of menstrual cycle! I had no sooner thought that, then I suddenly understood the most diabolical and most successful patriarchal reversal of them all. Of all that had been perpetrated upon us, this has got to be the king. Men took that menstrual cycle, that which, in the human animal, is the most closely aligned to divinity—it makes people, it's godly, holy and divine (if that's what godly is), the most sacred thing (and I don't want to romanticize motherhood, but try to think of anything more powerful than what women do in their bodies), the most powerful attribute—and turned it upside down. They made it the most degrading, most filthy, most loathsome and revolting and disgusting of all human functions.

The man came out of the Old Boys Club and leaned against the pulpit. He said, "God told me to tell you that your menstrual cycle is really gross. How do you expect us to feel comfortable with you sitting on our boards when you might be doing . . . *it*? When at any moment you could just bleed all over everything." We said to ourselves, "Oh my word, that is truly awful, isn't it? We can't even get a grip on ourselves. We can't even stop doing this truly disgusting thing." And we believed them. We believed that this really made us just a little above the animals, surely subhuman. We shouldn't be kings and ministers. We shouldn't own corporations or universities because we just don't have any self-control. In that way, they stole our power from us. I hope every women out there laughs herself into hysterics every time she hears the term "Penis Envy." That is so ridiculous. Because truly the primeval envy is womb envy—all women know that, and any man who's thoughtful at all knows what the true envy is, and how men took from us the tremendous power that that is.

When I got up off my knees that night I wasn't the same woman I had been when I had knelt down, thank goodness. And although that's not where I am theologically now, or religiously, it was one of the phases through which I had to go. What I'm telling is history. That's where I was when we marched in July 1978 for the ERA extension. In that march, although the pedestals-are-the-pits banner is a wonderful banner, ours was the best. It said, "Mormons for ERA." As the *New York Times* wrote around the time I was being excommunicated, "Mormons for ERA, isn't that a little like Astronauts for a Flat Earth?" Nobody who ever saw that banner forgot it, as we had reason to discover. A few weeks after that march the extension bill passed the House of Representatives of the 95th Congress and went over to the Senate for hearings to be put on the calendar. Senator Biden, who was then Chairman of the Senate Subcommittee on Constitutional Rights, decided to hold another hearing. He'd asked his staff to get together a religious panel. One of the women in his office remembered the "Astronauts for a Flat Earth" banner and thought it might be interesting to have this bizarre little group on that panel. So she tried to find us. At that time there were four of us—Hazel and her three friends. Hazel was entirely impossible to find. She and the others had become such important women in their professions that they're just not ever there. But I was a full-time homemaker and we're easy to find. I was in the kitchen one afternoon when the phone rang. This woman from Senator Biden's office said she'd like one of us Mormons for ERA to be on this religious panel; it was 4:30 in the afternoon and she had to have the name by 5 p.m. I said to her, "You have found the only Mormon for ERA that I know where she is. So I'll have to do it."

I prepared a five-minute statement to read and so did three other people from other religious groups. We all read our five-minute statements, and then the subcommittee responded, Senator Biden first. Then it was the turn of the ultra-conservative Utah Senator Orrin Hatch. Orrin began at one end of the table with two women and did such a good job of questioning them, I was proud of him. (You see, we *can* matronize, can't we? Not that we ought, but with Orrin, I think we're obliged.) Then he got to me and I had one of those little moments of insight that you have at least dozens of times a day after your feminist awakening, and they're all hideous. He put on his churchman's voice for me. I said to myself, "For heaven's sake, Sonia, do you mean to say that the men in your church have been speaking to you like that for forty-two years and you never even heard it?" He began by looking down his nose and saying (I don't do this part very well, because I haven't been trained from birth to condescend as Orrin has), "Mrs. Johnson, you must admit that nearly one hundred percent of Mormon women oppose the Equal Rights Amendment." And I said, "Oh, my goodness!" (That's in the Congressional Record, by the way. How not to go down in history.) "I don't have to admit any such thing, it simply isn't true." Well, I didn't know it wasn't true, but I wasn't going to tell him that. When you've just spoken in your churchman's voice, which is the voice of authority, of God, you don't expect to be answered back like that.

Especially not by a woman. Orrin was much annoyed and we began to have what I thought was a delightfully brisk little interchange. I was enjoying it a lot. It became evident early on that Orrin was not enjoying it nearly as much as I was. In fact, it wasn't very long into all of this before he lost his composure altogether, and became completely unglued. It was simply wonderful! I do wish all of you had been there to see it. It was impossible to tell at the outset of this little statement that he was going to lose his cool, make history and hate himself. He began by saying (you'll love this, it's a very Orrinish statement), "It's implied by your testimony that you're more intelligent than other Mormon women, and if they were all as intelligent as you they'd all support the Equal Rights Amendment." Then he banged on the table in front of him and shouted at the top of his lungs: "Now that's an insult to my wife!" The whole audience inhaled as one. Everybody woke up, including the Associated Press and the United Press International reporters who had been dozing through this boring religious stuff. They came rushing up and thrust the microphones under our noses and flipped on their tape recorders and the next day people all across the country were reading about how the "Mormon Senator and Mormon woman sparred." The one I like best was: "Mormon family feud on Senate floor." (Those media people, really!)

Among those who read these newspaper accounts were Mormons who supported the Equal Rights Amendment, and they had thought until then that they were the only ones in the whole church who did, and now there were two of us. They had to find me. When I tell you within the next three months over five hundred Mormons did find me and what they had to do in order to do that, I think that you'll understand that when the Mormon church said, "We're not having any trouble with women in our church, all is well in Zion," that perhaps they were not being totally candid. What those people had to do to find me was call every single Johnson in the Northern Virginia telephone directory. Six pages, back and front until they got to the letter "R." My name was Richard in those days. Typically what would happen is that late at night I'd get this phone call, and on the other end would be this exhausted little voice, sounding more like a tape recording or a robot, saying, "I'm looking for the Mormon woman who testified before the Senate Subcommittee," and I'd say, "This is she," and they'd start to cry, men and women, so it shows you what a trauma it had been to call all those Johnsons.

One day, four founding mothers, Mormons for ERA, were standing over this broad land and we recognized that without ever dreaming of such a thing, without even being organized locally (we were just a little guerilla group—we struck here, struck there) we had become, overnight, a national organization and so of course we declared ourselves a national organization. We've always been deeply grateful to Orrin Hatch for making us one. Mormons for ERA think it's the best thing he ever did and I personally think it's the only good thing the man ever did.

That was August 1978. The church had only made me a feminist. I was still so apolitical that if they got me in the voting booth, and I knew both names of the two major candidates for president of the United States, I figured that I was on top of it politically. In the fall of that year, the church, having made me a feminist, decided to go one step further and make me a political activist overnight. I began organizing all through the church states and wards of Zion against the ERA, organizing political action committees. I finally went to the leaders of the church in my area and said to them that the problem was not just that they were doing it, but they were doing it covertly, not telling anybody who they were, going in massive numbers to legislatures and lobbying. Nobody knew where these people were coming from; they thought they were just private citizens, just coming out of their own private consciences. Well, there's nothing private, consciously, about those folks at all. If the president of the Mormon church changed his mind about the Equal Rights Amendment tonight, the whole Mormon church would be pro-ERA by morning.

I said, "Look, if you're going to go into politics up to your ears, be above board, be open about this. Come out and say who you are. Say we're the Mormon church, we're fighting the Equal Rights Amendment, we've got a Political Action Committee." It is not fair for the proponents of the Equal Rights Amendment and the unratified states not to know that they have this powerful secret enemy. It's like having termites in the beams of your house. One day the house falls in in Virginia, Georgia, Florida, Oklahoma, Illinois. Everybody wants to know what's happening and I say to them, "You've got Mormons." But the Church insisted that they didn't have to tell, they weren't doing anything wrong, that they were going to go on like that. I said, as I was going out the door, words that I can now look back on as though they were famous last words: "If *you* don't tell what the church is doing, I will."

I remember the day I called up the *Washington Post* with a very trembly voice saying something assertive like, "I'm sure you're not the least bit interested in knowing what the Mormon church is doing against the Equal Rights Amendment." Were they interested! So were all the local newspapers, the Virginia newspapers.

Pretty soon the whole story was out, and I began to figure prominently in those stories. It was about eighteen months later that they excommunicated me, and for a good reason. As you can plainly see, I was cruelly disloyal to the patriarchy. It was the best thing that ever happened to me. I must say I thank them daily. At the time it was all happening to me, the reporters from everywhere asked me, "Why does the church oppose the Equal Rights Amendment?" You see, it was before the term "Moral Majority" had been spawned. We weren't really aware of the "new right" yet. We were just on the brink of all this discovery. Reporters have a nose for things that are about to happen. The reason my case got so much publicity is because they sensed that it wasn't just a story about this little woman from Virginia. The case was symbolic of something happening. I shared the front page of the *New York Times* with the Ayatollah and Hans Kung. That should have told us all something, shouldn't it? I was kind of a harbinger of this whole religious repressive political stuff that was about to happen. But we weren't quite on to it yet. We didn't have it nailed down, and they were asking me why do Mormons oppose this?

I told them I understood the patriarchy. Even then I knew the patriarchy means the "rule of the fathers." It means if you're born male, you're born into a ruling caste. If you're born female, you're one of the ones left over to be rulees. Nobody ever said to us when we were little girls, "Now you just be good, competent, smart, nice and kind, and one of these days you'll be a man." No man can ever be bad enough to suddenly wake up and find himself a woman. It's absolutely a caste system that's immovable. There is an enormous stake in keeping it just that way because rulers have terrific privilege. There's no reason to be a ruler—it's a lot of work—unless you get some privilege from it. Heaven knows the men have enormous privilege. They codify that privilege into the law. They make the laws, they interpret the laws and they enforce the laws. They do all those things so we'll stay here (below) and they stay there (above).

That, of course, was the reason we needed the Equal Rights Amendment and the reason the New Right came out and fought it tooth and nail. They'd have killed to defeat the ERA because they know what it means is the collapse of the only social organization we have ever known on this world in written history, which is patriarchy. That's what the Equal Rights Amendment is, the most revolutionary statement in the history of the world. It signals an end to that social system which oppresses women and destroys men's characters. I didn't get a grip on the whole thing until I went to Copenhagen to the World Conference on Women in the summer of 1980 and heard the Secretary General of the United Nations address a press conference. He told all of us who had assembled that, according to United Nations surveys and studies, women do two-thirds of the world's work and make one-tenth of the world's money and own one-hundredth of the world's property. Those are not the statistics of oppression; those are the statistics of slavery.

I know there is hope because I remember what Frederick Douglass said once—that the limits of the oppressor are set by how much the oppressed will bear. We have come to the place where we are not willing to bear any more, so perhaps it truly is the end of patriarchy.

Once, I was speaking to an enormous group of people at Northwestern University. Right in the front row was a man who I wasn't sure was going to live through my speech. I thought he might have an aneurysm or a stroke or something. He was squirming and periodically burying his face in his hands. He was moaning out loud and turning from side to side, going red in the face. Finally, when I opened up the discussion for questions at the end he just leaped up and threw his arm in the air. He said, "You know, you don't seem to me to be, well . . . balanced! Would you say that you're obsessed by the Equal Rights Amendment?" I said, "Well, if you mean by obsessed that I'd give my life to see it ratified, yes, I suppose you could say I am obsessed."

When I said that I saw, as it crossed the faces in the audience, looks of the most acute embarrassment. I could just hear them saying to themselves, "Oh, that really is immoderate. That is too extreme. I knew she was going to say something kooky before this was over." I could hear some women say, "We're going to lose our credibility," and other women say, "It's going to hurt the movement." It really made me angry, because of course, that's baseline sexism and I told them so. I reminded them that in every country in the world where we celebrate some man's birthday we do so because he was a man willing to give his life, and probably did give his life for the human and civil rights of his fellow men. When Patrick Henry said, "Give me liberty or give me death!" nobody said, "Oh, that is so immoderate!" because everybody knows that men's rights are worth that kind of sacrifice, but women's? Huh, don't be ridiculous. We know that if those patriots that went to the tyrants and said, "Let my people go!" had looked out the window and had seen that their people were all women, they would have said, "Oh, well, never mind," and would have gone home to supper, because nobody has ever fought a revolution for women. Nobody's ever made any serious and sustained sacrifices for women because everybody knows that women aren't worth it.

You remember when that man came out of the Old Boys Club meeting and leaned up against the pulpit and said, "God told me to tell you . . . that he wants you to sacrifice! He wants you to sacrifice your time, talents and energy for me, the kids, the PTA, the church, the community and the nation. He wants you to sacrifice, sacrifice, sacrifice! But he wants me to make sure to make one thing very clear to you, and don't you ever forget it. Nobody is ever going to sacrifice for you." So we've always known that if God didn't think we were worth sacrificing for, heaven knows, who are we to contradict God?

Once after I finished speaking, a woman came up to me lickety-split in a state of extreme agitation. She took me by both arms and shook me hard and said, "Sonia, don't you dare die for me and don't you let anybody else do it, either! I'd feel so guilty. Now, after we get the economy on its feet, and there's no more energy crisis, and the nuclear threat is under control, and there's no more famine or wars or rumors thereof, when the ozone layer has thickened up a lot and the whales are safe, and the fields are okay, after all the really important things have been taken care of, after the sun burns right out of the sky, then maybe I won't feel guilty. We'll start talking about my dignity and my human rights."

One of the reasons we feel that way is that the message to us from men has been clear for a very long time. It has been that if you make any demands on me, I won't love you any more. We needed that love because we didn't even exist without that. We didn't even have an identity, we just sort of homed into view when we became Mrs. Him. Until then we were told we were invisible, we didn't count, we didn't figure into any scheme of anything so we needed it for our own identity. Also, we had all these little children we sure could use some help with. So we said, "Oh, don't you worry, honey. I won't rock the boat at all. I'll compromise, I'll temporize, I'll make peace. I'll make myself the very doormat of the world if you'll just love me." Then we began to make a hideous discovery. Men don't love doormats and neither do we. Nobody loves a doormat.

There was another message that came to us from men that was even more vicious than the first, although more subtle. It was one of the strongest taboos governing women in this world. By taboo I mean it is not conscious. We're not aware of it but it governs our every move. Women are always afraid because the message to us from men in power is, in insidious and subtle ways: "If you get out of your place, we won't allow you to live." We know that that's no idle threat. We know that in times past we haven't been allowed to live when we've been perceived as getting out of our place. We know that between the thirteenth and sixteenth century millions of us—not the thousands of us that male historians want us to believe—but millions of us, were burned at the stake as witches, burned alive because we were perceived by the churchmen of Europe and England, the Catholics and Protestants, as getting out of our place. Burned alive after having perpetrated upon our bodies the most violent and ugly and vicious sexual crimes that you can even begin to imagine (I couldn't even imagine them until I read them) by the churchmen of England and Europe. We know that that's no idle threat. We know that the women who are afraid to find out what I've been telling you tonight are not afraid because they are not courageous women, or because they're stupid, but because it's perfectly reasonable to be afraid. It would be foolish not to be afraid.

We've come to a new time in history when there are now millions of women upon the earth who are no longer willing to live in that kind of fear, who refuse to live in it and to pass on this fear to our daughters. Who insist on standing upright on the face of this planet and saying, "This is my home, too! This is my world. I don't have to ask permission to travel here. I will give my life to make this home to women." That's the women's movement and why I say we're a revolution. We've come to a time in history when we have got to love ourselves as women and value ourselves and that is extremely hard because for 4,000 years we've been told that we weren't worth anything and we believed it. We must never listen to this voice, not ever. We've got to start listening to our own hearts. We're just beginning to learn how. We have got to learn to love and value ourselves and other women, to make the same kinds of sacrifices and take the same kinds of risks for our human rights, dignity and safety that men have always known had to be taken and made, and they've always been willing to take and make for themselves. There's a recipe in how to succeed in this, a recipe for justice. We just have to look out there and see how did men do it? How has it been done in former times? We'll begin to see the ingredients that have to go into a struggle for justice. We'll see that anytime that a civil rights movement has succeeded, that justice is never bestowed. That's what men know and women don't. We keep believing that voice that says, "Don't worry, honey, we'll give it all to you one of these days." It's always a lie. Justice is never bestowed. The powerful never give the powerless power, not ever. Justice is always wrested out of the hands of those in power by the most incredible risk and courage and daring and love and longing that human beings are capable of. There is no other way. There never has been and there never will be.

One time Susan B. Anthony was speaking to a little group of women at a women's college somewhere. She was getting very annoyed because she'd been fighting for women's rights nonstop for sixty years and she couldn't get these young women to even think seriously about women's rights for sixty minutes. Finally, she said, in great annoyance, "Why aren't you all protesting? What have I got to do? When I'm dead and under the sod or I'm cremated and my ashes are floating about in the air, have I got to come back and stir you up? Why aren't you all on fire?"

I invoke those great women who went before us, those great women of whom we are just mere shadows. Why, we don't even begin to measure up to our foremothers. Do you know that Susan B. Anthony would never have been elected President of the National Organization for Women? I try to take that as some comfort because people call me radical. Do you know what she said? She went around this country saying, "Overthrow this government! Burn that bloody contract of the fathers—the constitution!" Because she knew women weren't in it. Imagine! Look at us, we're afraid to say "Boo!" We're afraid to say we want lesbian and gay rights, we think that's really big of us. Isn't that amazing? I invoke our foremothers because we need that kind of spirit. Really, what do we have to lose? Women have nothing to lose. Nothing! And everything to gain. Patriarchy would all be over the minute we realize that it is all a lie.

Susan, Elizabeth, Sojourner, Matilda, Lucretia, Alice . . . you great American women whose liberty-loving ashes float over our heads in this land, come back to us now and stir us up! Help us to burn as you burned. Help us to be all on fire.

Barbara Ehrenreich
(Photograph by Paul Gaylor)

49

Barbara Ehrenreich

ATHEIST COLUMNIST

Born August 26, 1941

What better maxim, for a race of migrants, than "Think for yourself"?
"Cultural Baggage," **New York Times Magazine**, *April 5, 1992*

THE ESSAYS OF AMERICAN WRITER, atheist, socialist and feminist Barbara Ehrenreich are regularly featured in the mass-circulation news weekly *Time*. She has written widely for such periodicals as *The Nation, Ms., Mother Jones, Esquire, Vogue, New Republic* and *New York Times Magazine*.

Born in Butte, Montana, she graduated from Reed College in 1963 and earned her Ph.D. at Rockefeller University in 1968. She was employed as a staff member of the Health Policy Advisory Center, New York City, was an assistant professor of health sciences, 1971–1974, and began writing for publication in 1974. Awards include the Ford Foundation award for Humanistic Perspectives on Contemporary Issues, 1981, and a Guggenheim fellowship in 1987.

Witches, Midwives, and Nurses: A History of Women Healers (Feminist Press, 1972), written with Deirdre English, was a widely acclaimed exposé of male domination of female health care, followed by two other collaborations with English, *Complaints and Disorders: The Sexual Politics of Sickness* (Feminist Press, 1973) and *For Her Own Good: One Hundred Fifty Years of the Experts' Advice to Women* (Doubleday, 1978).

Other books include: *The Hearts of Men: American Dreams and the Flight from Commitment* (Doubleday, 1983), *Fear of Falling: The Inner Life of the Middle Class* (Pantheon Books, 1989) and *The Worst Years of Our Lives: Irreverent Notes from a Decade of Greed* (Pantheon Books, 1990).

In examining her family heritage, Barbara wrote in "Cultural Baggage" (*New York Times Magazine*, April 5, 1992) that "we are the kind of people . . . who do *not* believe, who do not carry on traditions, who do not do things just because someone has done them before. . . . In my parents' general view, new things were better than old, and the very fact that some ritual had been performed in the past was a good reason for abandoning it now. Because what was the past, as our forebears knew it? Nothing but poverty, superstition and grief. 'Think for yourself,' Dad used to say. 'Always ask why.' "

She added: "The more tradition-minded, the newly enthusiastic celebrants of Purim and Kwanzaa and Solstice, may see little point to survival if the survivors carry no cultural freight—religion, for example, or ethnic tradition. To which I would say that skepticism, curiosity and wide-eyed ecumenical tolerance are also worthy elements of the human tradition. . . .

"A few weeks ago, I cleared my throat and asked the children, now mostly grown and fearsomely smart, whether they felt any stirrings of ethnic or religious identity, etc., which might have been, ahem, insufficiently nourished at home. 'None,' they said, adding firmly, 'and the world would be a better place if nobody else did, either.' My chest swelled with pride, as would my mother's, to know that the race of 'none' marches on."

Barbara penned a freethought classic, "U.S. Patriots: Without God On Their Side," for *Mother Jones* magazine in 1981. [See selection]

Barbara Ehrenreich

U.S. Patriots: Without God on Their Side

This originally appeared in Mother Jones magazine, February/March 1981.

ONLY FIFTEEN YEARS AGO, the best publicity God could get was an obituary. "Is God Dead?" asked an April 1966 cover story in *Time*, and a surprising number of theological experts answered yes, adducing as evidence of his demise the Holocaust, the tragedy of Hiroshima and the ruins of our own inner cities. Reports of his death—or, to put it in less biomedical language, of his abandonment of the human scene—turned out, as we know now, to have been premature. The last couple of years have brought us a trinity of born-again Christian presidential candidates, the new Bob Dylan, the Islamic revival, a mass resurgence of American fundamentalism and the militant medievalism of Pope John Paul II. While predictions of this sort are always risky, God may turn out to be one of the most important public figures of the '80s.

I am an atheist, by family tradition as well as by personal conviction, and I am frankly alarmed. When God was dead, so, in a way, was atheism. At least there did not seem to be any pressing need to debate the divine inspiration of the Scriptures with the fundamentalists, or the existence of a superhuman essence with the Christian radicals. But now, with seventy-six percent of the population favoring that prayer be allowed in public schools, with at least four states requiring that Genesis get equal time with Darwin and with five of the nine Supreme Court justices apparently willing to give organized religion jurisdiction over the uterus, it may be time to dust off Voltaire and reread Tom Paine. In fact, with some of our leading evangelists now preaching that humanism (which presumably includes Unitarianism, Universalism, Ethical Culture and other benign ways of getting through Sunday morning) is "basically Satan's philosophy and program," it may be time to prepare for a second Inquisition. If we're going to burn—not merely the out-of-the-closet atheists but even the lukewarm agnostics, lapsed atheists and all the unchurched believers in some vague sort of transcendent Goodness—we might as well know what for.

The threat we now face is as much political as it is in any spiritual sense "religious." In twentieth-century America, Christian revivalism has usually marched hand in sweaty palm with jingoism, and has passed itself off as the quintessential expression of Americanism. Atheism, obversely, gets tagged as un-American, communistic and even traitorous.

The groundwork for this peculiar mixture of religion and politics (branded "theopolitics" by the irrepressible atheist Madalyn Murray O'Hair) was laid during the Cold War of the '50s—a period when the Christian Right, as we now call it, actually held state power, and anti-Semitism as well as antiatheism were institutionalized features of American society. "Recognition of the Supreme Being is the first, the most basic expression of Americanism," then President Dwight Eisenhower told the nation in 1955. "Without God, there could be no American form of government, nor any American way of life." Senator Joseph McCarthy was, as usual, more explicit, declaring that "the fate of the world rests with the clash between the atheism of Moscow and the Christian spirit throughout other parts of the world."

In 1954, Congress undertook to strengthen our position *vis-à-vis* the Soviets by inserting the phrase "under God" into the pledge of allegiance. Eisenhower's pastor, who had worried that the old God-free pledge "could just as easily be repeated by little Muscovites pledging allegiance to the hammer and sickle," prompted the change, and the American Legion vigorously promoted the idea. Two years later, "In God We Trust" was adopted as the national motto, without any debate or a single dissenting vote in either the House or the Senate. A 1954 survey showed that sixty percent of Americans would not permit a book written by an atheist to remain in a public library, if they could prevent it, and that eighty-four percent believed that atheists should not be allowed to teach in colleges or universities. As a worried writer for *The New Republic* explained (after establishing his own credentials as an Episcopalian and an anti-Communist), Americans no longer distinguished between atheists and Communists anyway.

The ideological amalgam of atheism and communism established both as external forces opposed to human feeling, individual liberty, family life and, of course, nuclear preparedness. It almost seems as if American military power had become so awesome as to require some sort of supernatural sanction. "Kill a Commie for Christ" became a popular slogan just at the time when it had become technologically possible to kill *all* Commies, for *any* reason. Today, when it is possible to kill the same Commies forty times over (a concept which undoubtedly has more meaning to the born-again), there is all the more temptation to link militarism with evocations of the Gentle Redeemer. This—as much as any genuine religious revival—

is what we are up against in today's Christian Right: a theopolitical big-otry which will make no distinctions, in the Armageddon we are so abun-dantly prepared for, between atheism, un-Americanism and the Enemy outside.

I grew up in the '50s as an atheist, which may, I realize now, have been a little like growing up as a red-diaper baby. I knew my family was differ-ent and I learned the hard way to be discreet about the difference. In the fourth grade, however, I was "exposed" by the practice of release time for religious education. Release time meant that on Wednesdays, right after lunch, all the other children lined up to be bused to their respective houses of worship, leaving me visibly rooted to my seat to await the three o'clock dismissal bell. In the inevitable playground confrontations that followed, I was accused of—to my shock—not atheism but communism. I knew, as did every reader of *Life* magazine and the *Weekly Reader*, that communism was something foreign and evil. But atheism seemed to me to be as Ameri-can as my family—blue-eyed, Scotch-Irish Montanans—most of whom were Roosevelt Democrats and none of whom, to my knowledge, had ever been the dupe of a foreign ideology. I resented, with my own variety of nativist bigotry, being told by nine-year-old third-generation Polish Ameri-cans to "go back to Russia."

So far as I knew, atheism was an idiosyncrasy of my own family, origi-nating in certain proud and colorful personalities. For example, there was Mamie O'Laughlin Howes. The story goes that when her father lay dy-ing, she sent to the next town for a priest. The message came back that the priest would come only if $25 was sent in advance. This being western Montana in the late 1880s, which was as wild as the West ever got, he may have been justified in avoiding house calls. But not in the price, which was probably more cash than Mamie—with three small children and an errati-cally employed husband—had ever had at one time. It was on account of this sum that the church lost the soul of Mamie O'Laughlin Howes. When she herself lay dying of pneumonia a few years later, it is said that a priest did appear, though she had not sent for him. Because she was too weak to hold the crucifix, he placed it on her chest and proceeded to administer the last rites. But Mamie pulled herself together at the last moment, flung the crucifix across the room and died.

This was my great-grandmother. Her husband, John Howes, had left the company of the faithful in his own way, some years earlier. John Howes is a figure of folkloric proportions in my memory, well-known in Butte as a miner, a fighter and an uncompromising individualist. Nevertheless, the story of his defection from the church is not without its embarrassing side. When he was growing up in Ontario, he once got the idea of peeing in the holy water that was to be used for Easter communion—presumably as a way of enhancing his private enjoyment of the proceedings. He couldn't resist letting a few friends in on the prank, though, and when the story eventually got to the priest, he was informally excommunicated. The full weight of this hit a few years later, when John became engaged to a local woman. The priest refused to marry them and forbade the young woman to marry John anywhere. Rejected, John and his brother set off on the long trek to Butte, but not without (according to one version of the story) dragging the priest out and slugging him.

It was stories like these that explained why we, apparently unlike anyone else in America, did not "believe in God." What I did not know, and could not have found out so easily at the time, was that my family was not at all as different as we seemed in the '50s. America has a rich and venerable tradition of atheism, or, ecumenically speaking, "free thought": anticlericalism, agnosticism, deism, scientific atheism, existential atheism, high-brow atheism, barroom skepticism and all-purpose grassroots irreverence. The republic was founded by men who considered themselves freethinkers, and if atheism came to have a foreign cast, it may be because of the important contributions of later-arriving immigrant German, Italian and Jewish atheists. (Those who persist in condemning atheism as a European ideology should consider the origins of our major religions. With a few exceptions, such as Mormonism, Christian Science and the Jehovah's Witnesses, America's religions are "foreign imports.") Our atheists and freethinkers have been as politically diverse as Andrew Carnegie and Emma Goldman, H. L. Mencken and Eugene Debs.

But by and large, as the McCarthyites perhaps correctly discerned, the American free thought tradition has been a politically radical one. Among the leaders of the American Revolution, for example, practicing Christians were almost a rare as Tories. Men like Thomas Jefferson, Benjamin Franklin, James Madison and, in all likelihood, George Washington, were deists, holding that God had departed shortly after getting the universe started, pausing just long enough to lay down the laws of nature. If the infidel views of the Founding Fathers are not familiar to every schoolchild today, it is not because these men were particularly coy about them. Ethan Allen, the captor of Fort Ticonderoga, authored the first anti-Christian book published in America, entitled *Reason: The Only Oracle of Man.* Jefferson, who liked to needle Christian dinner guests with attacks on the character of Jesus, was baited as an atheist in the presidential campaigns of 1796 and 1800.

There was good reason, then, for the Presbyterian General Assembly of 1798 to lament the young nation's "abounding infidelity, which in many cases tends to atheism itself." The educated eagerly read essays by Rousseau and the philosophical letters of Voltaire. At Princeton in 1782, there were only two students who identified themselves as Christians; at Dartmouth in 1799, only one. The less-educated among the population circulated Tom Paine's strongly worded pamphlets. (His *Age of Reason* is said to have converted thousands to infidelity.)

On the frontiers, the early settlers of the West devoted the Sabbath to what one American historian described as "riot and drunkenness." No one, therefore, thought it strange that the Constitutional Convention in Philadelphia proceeded without religious invocations, or that the Constitution itself makes only one reference to the deity—in the date, "Seventeenth Day of September in the Year of our Lord one thousand seven hundred and Eighty-seven."

Christianity made a rapid rebound in the early nineteenth century, abetted in part by middle-class anxieties over the "excesses" of Jeffersonian democracy. Piety was restored in the Ivy League schools, and atheists of the comfortable classes discreetly regrouped as Unitarians. Truly radical freethought became the almost exclusive property of the lower classes—the "discontented, underprivileged workingmen who agitated in favor of political and social equality"—and, having been squeezed out of the mainstream of respectability, it became a radical social movement again. Between 1825 and 1850, twenty atheist periodicals appeared, dedicated to "the destruction of Christianity and 'superstition' " and the advancement of the working class. Free thought, or "infidel," societies sprang up in the industrial cities of the Northeast, drawing hundreds for solemn commemorations of Tom Paine's birthday, half-ribald lectures on "The Inconsistencies, Contradictions and Absurdities of the Bible" and serious presentations of scientific subjects.

Of all the atheist speakers and organizers of the early nineteenth century, none surpassed, in eloquence or in notoriety, Frances Wright—not only a freethinker but a feminist, abolitionist, Socialist and sexual heretic. So great were the crowds that turned out for her speeches that men and women fainted in the crush, and once, in Louisville, Kentucky, the packed gallery almost collapsed. With a sweeping ecumenicism, she denounced "heavenly kings," "heavenly queens," "apotheosized monarchs," and all "saints, angels, devils, ghosts, apparitions, and sorceries" that had "darkened what every mind blessed with intelligence *knows* to be the light of truth." She exhorted her listeners to "turn your churches into halls of science and devote your leisure day to the study of your own bodies, the analysis of your own minds and the examination of the fair world which extends around you!"

Like Wright, few free thought agitators confined themselves to the issue of religion. Among the causes embraced by the Ohio free thought newspaper the *Regenerator,* for example, were vegetarianism, the water cure, peace, sex education, socialism and spelling reform. Abner Kneeland's *Boston Investigator* advocated public education, abolition, women's rights and herbal medicine. The *Investigator* went on, in the 1840s, to become one of the leading labor papers in the country, though even with this broader focus the editors never let an opportunity go by to cast aspersions on the integrity and morality of the clergy.

If there was one cause which had a logical and consistent affinity with free thought, it was feminism. Nineteenth-century Protestantism waxed unctuous on the subject of women's piety, domesticity and dependence; and anti-feminist polemics were invariably larded with scriptural evidence. Elizabeth Cady Stanton became depressed by the number of women she encountered in her travels who still believed they were doing penance for Eve's transgression. As she went through the Scriptures in preparation for her *Woman's Bible,* Stanton was shocked by the frank misogyny of the original. Genesis, for example, read to her like "gross records of primitive races," and the stories of Lot's daughters (who got their father drunk and then seduced him) and of Tamar (who dressed as a whore to seduce her father-in-law) she found unworthy of comment. As for contemporary Christianity, she wrote: "So long as ministers stand up and tell us that Christ is the head of the church, so is man the head of the woman, how are we to break the chains which have held women down through the ages?"

But the tradition of multi-issue radical irreverence, embodied in women like Frances Wright and Elizabeth Cady Stanton, declined near the turn of the century. For their part, labor and Socialist organizations now had to reckon with a working class swelled by immigrants (Irish, Italian, eastern and southern European) who faced intense anti-Catholic bigotry from the native-born Protestants. The Socialist party took the official position that it was "not concerned with matters of religious belief . . . Anybody who wants to cooperate . . . with us is welcome."

It was not only the need for unity that dictated the religious indifference of turn-of-the-century social movements. Thanks to our freethinking Founding Fathers, church and state were more firmly separated in the United States than in any European nation. Reformers did not have to overthrow an established church in order to expand suffrage or advance the cause of labor—any more than atheists, in good conscience, had to overthrow the state. Furthermore, fundamentalist Protestantism, America's "old-time" religion, had sustained a crushing blow from Darwinism in the late nineteenth century. Liberal theologians beat a hasty retreat from the literal "Word" and appropriated evolution as an even more impressive divine feat than the six-day Creation. The vast popularity of atheist orator "Colonel Bob" Ingersoll in the 1880s and '90s—he made more than $150,000 a year as a speaker—reflected both a softening of religion and the deradicalization of atheism. A few well-known ministers of the time, like Lyman Beecher, openly admired Ingersoll (though others held prayer meetings to petition God for his immediate conversion). Politically, he was entirely respectable: a leading Republican, a corporate lawyer, a close friend of President Garfield's and an announced foe of anarchism and free love.

The gap between free thought and political radicalism widened in the twentieth century. In the '20s and early '30s, Marxists made occasional sallies against the "opium of people," but by the late '30s, the Communist party had pretty much shelved the religion issue. "We felt that the important thing was unity on this earth," says former party leader Dorothy Healey, "and we would find out afterward who was right [about religion]."

The dissociation of atheism and radicalism was probably never so sharp as in our most recent period of social upheaval, the 1960s, and this may explain why radicals were so unprepared for the revival of the Christian Right in the late '70s.

At the beginning of the '60s, a few lone atheist radicals—Lenny Bruce,

Paul Krassner, Madalyn Murray—took their stand against the Christian-conservative consensus. But the "Movement," when it came along, was far from being atheistic or even, as the Left of the '30s had been, accommodationist toward religion. In its tone and often in its approach, the movement *was* religious. As Paul Breines, a veteran of the '60s, put it, religion "provided the symbolic structure of the New Left." The songs sounded like, and sometimes were, made-over hymns. Actions were a way of "bearing witness," rather than dryly carrying out strategy. The utopian vision, initially, was not socialism but the "beloved" or "blessed community." The most visible leaders included men like the Reverend Martin Luther King, Jr., Malcolm X (a Black Muslim) and Fathers Daniel and Philip Berrigan. What '60s historian Sara Evans has called the "biblical cadences" of the early civil rights movement continued to echo throughout the decade. A friend who joined the antiwar movement as a campus activist in 1970, an ex-Catholic, recalls, "It was like coming back to Jesus, what his life meant, making my life like his. I didn't believe in God, but I thought of Jesus a lot."

But for me and other young atheists, the latent religiosity of the movement did not evoke a childhood faith. It was both confusing and, in a strange way, tempting. "My response as an atheist," said Breines, the son of Jewish atheists, "was partly to be attracted by the religious aspects of the movement, but without wanting to believe in God . . . The issue was confused, or maybe repressed. Basically, I guess I thought it just didn't matter." Breines suggested there might also have been a more practical, if not exactly conscious reason why the issue was "repressed" for so long: "The religious aspect of the movement made us less separate from the rest of society. It gave a legitimacy to the politics."

Considering the tenacity of the 1960s-style Christian anticommunism, there may be a good deal of truth to this. It was as late as 1964 that Madalyn Murray was labeled by the national media "the most hated woman in America" for her efforts to ban prayer in schools. She was driven out of her home in Baltimore by neighbors who killed her pets, beat up her sons repeatedly, smashed her windows and scrawled the word *Communist* across her fence. Part of the genius of the political movement of the '60s was the way it dissolved the theopolitical advantage of the Christian Right. You could redbait Martin Luther King (and that did happen), but you could not atheist-bait him. You could call the movement misguided, but hardly immoral. "Christianized," we were protected from the full stigma of our radicalism, and those of us who came from Jewish, atheist and/or really Communist backgrounds may have felt this more than anyone else. It made sense to keep religion a nonissue: if some people felt driven by a superhuman force, rather than by human need or conscience, at least they were going our way.

But today we can no longer afford to dodge the issue—if only because those Americans who are most noisily religious are no longer going our way, nor are they going in any remotely progressive direction. Yet it is they who seem to have the moral initiative now, the emotional fervor and even, sometimes, the sense of community, that once belonged to leftist and feminist movements. While the Left speaks in rational (and increasingly academic) tones about corporate power, oil prices, structural unemployment and so forth, the Right mobilizes around the sanctity of the family, the fetus or the neighborhood school. And as the Right advances, the Left has tended to retreat to ever more arid ground, hoping perhaps that leftist politics which are sufficiently "secular"—which confine themselves to issues of the political economy—can coexist with the most reactionary aberrations in other spheres of life.

But a radical movement which does not have a moral vision of society—both a utopian dream and a day-to-day ethos—cannot succeed. And is probably not worth building. I believe that a moral vision for a born-again radical movement will have to encompass the insights and strivings of all kinds of people—feminists, labor activists, environmentalists, pacifists and, yes, religious activists. Only this time around I would argue that the grounds for a political morality, an activist morality, should not be religious in any sense.

We know what religion is at its worst: an ideology that serves to justify patriarchy and all entrenched authority. But even at its best, it is only a fleshless abstraction of our human concerns, a metaphor for human solidarity rather than solidarity itself. Madalyn Murray (now O'Hair) put it well when I asked her how she felt, as an atheist and a radical, about working side by side with religiously motivated activists. "I'm perfectly willing to work with them or anyone," she said, with uncharacteristic mellowness. "They are caring people. The tragedy to me is they have to think that it's religion that's motivating them. They don't feel that *people* are a good enough reason."

An atheist morality starts with people—you, me and the largest pos-sible "us"—as concrete, physical beings. But it also *stops* with people. There is just us, or, I should say, us and the other living species we share the earth and perhaps the universe with. There is no transcendent Other—whether imagined with a human face or as an unknowable essence—that will inter-vene to set things right or carry on if we extinguish ourselves. This is not a statement of fact, derived from knowledge, but a statement about hu-man responsibility. If we, as living beings, are the only genuine reason to act, we are also the only actors on the scene. Whatever happens—utopia or barbarism—is up to us.

The need to divest ourselves of all invisible Others, eternal spirits, after-lives and other comforting delusions becomes all the greater as we inch toward nuclear destruction. The spokespeople of today's Christian Right, such as Jerry Falwell of Moral Majority, do not flinch at the idea of nuclear confrontation, either because (in the spirit of the Old Testament) they believe Americans are the "chosen people" who can "win" or because (in the spirit of the New Testament) they don't believe this earthly life is worth that much—certainly not worth losing face to the Communists. There are plenty of good Christians who can refute Jerry Falwell and com-pany on their own ground, fighting Scripture, resurrecting the Sermon on the Mount and so forth, and I am glad they are around to do so. But the atheist response is more direct: There is nothing but this earthly life; and, for much the same reason, there are no chosen people, for there is no Other to do the choosing. We are all one human family, and this is all we have.

All this lies well within the tradition of American atheism and would meet with little objection from Thomas Jefferson or Frances Wright or even Robert Ingersoll. But there is one way in which we have to amend, or perhaps transcend, that tradition. A new radical political morality must become more than just old-fashioned atheist humanism, warmed over. Strangely, I agree with the right-wing evangelists on this; there is a certain "sinful arrogance" to humanism. We are not so good, as a species, as to be human*ists* with a chauvinistic inflection. None of us has a claim to a "mo-rality"—left or right, atheist or theist—which exudes self-righteousness and absolutism. It was not always "someone else"—some other sex or race or nation of people—who committed genocide or environmental destruc-tion or the massive theft that we know as "the economy," or who stood by while these things happened.

This century alone should have taught us that human goodness is not something given, as God once was. It is always a project, a project we can undertake only with patience and, it seems to me, a vast sense of irony. If, to use the religious metaphor, God is the goodness in us and our fullest potential as a species, then it follows to me as an atheist that the only truly human project is the creation of God.

Katha Pollitt

50

Katha Pollitt

COLUMNIST, THE NATION

Born October 14, 1949

For me, religion is serious business—a farrago of authoritarian nonsense, misogyny and humble pie, the eternal enemy of human happiness and freedom.

"*Subject To Debate,*" **The Nation,** *December 26, 1994*

KATHA POLLITT, ASSOCIATE EDITOR of *The Nation,* is an atheist, essayist and poet whose work regularly appears in the *New Yorker* and *The New Republic.* Her weekly column for *The Nation* is called "Subject to Debate." [See selection]

Katha received her Bachelor of Arts degree from Harvard University and her Master of Fine Arts degree from Columbia University. Her book of poems, *Antarctic Traveler,* won the National Book Critics Circle Award.

Reasonable Creatures (1994), her most recent book, a collection of essays, has a title taken from Mary Wollstonecraft. Wollstonecraft wrote: "I wish to see women neither heroines nor brutes, but reasonable creatures."

Katha writes in the introduction: "For me, to be a feminist is to answer the question 'Are women human?' with a yes. . . . It's about women having intrinsic value as persons rather than contingent value as a means to an end for others: fetuses, children, 'the family,' men."

In the book's chapter, "Why I Hate Family Values," Katha writes: "Family values and the cult of the nuclear family is, at bottom, just another way to bash women, especially poor women."

Feminist Gloria Steinem has written: "Katha Pollitt's essays are fine, fierce, well-informed and mind-changing. Anyone would be proud to have her good head and good heart on their side."

Katha not only publicly identifies herself as an atheist, but unabashedly has defended atheism on national television. She was named 1995 Freethought Heroine by the Freedom From Religion Foundation. In her acceptance speech delivered on September 29, 1995, in Denver, Colorado, Katha observed:

"Although Christianity and organized religion generally have a lot to answer for historically, I don't think opposition to gun control can be blamed on the Bible. What we are dealing with here is a grab bag of new-right causes and pet peeves that has been given a quick spiritual make-over in order to appeal to the mobilized millions of the Christian Coalition. . . .

"Why do we have this marriage of fundamentalist religion and right-wing politics? From the political side it seems obvious enough. You can't, even today, come right out and say, 'Our basic program is to take away worker's rights, deprive citizens of access to the courts, close down hospitals that serve the poor, starve the public school system and put poor women and children out on the street.' Even Newt Gingrich can't say that. Still less can you say, 'The reason why we want to do all those things is to effect a massive transfer of wealth from the lower end of the income scale to the top, with not too many stops in between.' Even Phil Gramm can't say that. Pat Buchanan certainly can't say that. What you can talk about is responsibility, family, work, faith, values. If you're Phil Gramm, you can throw in the imminent second coming of Christ, as he recently did.

"You can make people feel that the world feels uncertain because the National Endowment for the Arts funds dirty pictures and that the solution to the so-called breakdown of the family is to put men back in charge. In short you can foment a culture war and if you're lucky everyone will be so busy fighting it, they won't even notice that they've become steadily poorer, with fewer rights, fewer public amenities and public services, breathing more polluted air and drinking toxic water. . . .

"The question is, will the rest of America get fed up with fundamentalists before the fundamentalists and the Republican party get fed up with each other? And how much damage will they do before that happy day arrives?"

Subject to Debate

Originally appeared in The Nation, December 26, 1994.

For reasons I have never understood, my left-wing, cosmopolitan parents—he the agnostic Episcopalian, she the atheistic Jew—sent me to a private nondenominational Protestant school for girls. Prayer in the schools? For nine years I had chapel *every day*: three hymns, the doxology, the Lord's Prayer, a Bible reading (or was it two Bible readings?) and, on Fridays, a sacred-music solo from Mr. Crandall, the organist. Never mind that one-third of the student body was Jewish and another third Roman or Eastern-rite Catholic. You don't have to say the prayers, our teachers used to tell us, but you should bow your head as a mark of respect. Not praying was easy, not bowing somewhat less so. It was not singing that was the real challenge. I loved choral singing, which is surely one of life's great pleasures, but since I didn't believe in God, to take part was to participate in falsehood. Truth or beauty? Principled isolation or join the fun? Reign in Hell or serve in heaven? These questions obsessed me for years and, indeed, still do.

What was the effect on me of all this compulsory religion? Well, I don't remember a single word of the doxology, but I do have by heart the words to dozens of hymns that no one sings anymore because the lyrics are too imbued with cultural arrogance or sectarian crankiness. Once I was trapped alone in an elevator and, believe me, I was glad I knew all the verses of "From Greenland's Icy Mountain" and "The Church's One Foundation." Then, too, without all that force-fed Christianity I probably wouldn't have even the modest sense of Jewish identity I possess today. There's nothing like being excluded to make one embrace one's otherness.

Mostly, though, chapel made me loathe religion. I know nonbelievers who find in the occasional church service or high holy day something pleasant and nostalgic. I know believers, too, who don't trouble themselves over the outmoded or bloodthirsty bits of their faith; they just take what they want and leave the rest. Not me. For me, religion is serious business—a farrago of authoritarian nonsense, misogyny and humble pie, the eternal enemy of human happiness and freedom. My family may have made me a nonbeliever, but it took chapel to make me an atheist.

That's why I'm in favor of prayer in the schools. Now that Newt Gingrich has called for swift passage of a school-prayer amendment, just about every liberal columnist in America has pointed out that the separation of church and state is a great boon for religion and has helped make ours easily the most observant country in the West. Quite right. The state-backed religions of Western Europe are pallid affairs compared with our robust industry of Virgin-spotters, tongues-speakers and mitzvah-mobilers. Where is the English Jimmy Swaggart, the French billboard in whose depicted bowl of spaghetti thousands claim to discern the face of Christ? You could say that state support waters down the Living Word, or you could say that when the state underwrites religion the buried links between these two forms of social control stand too clearly revealed for modern, let alone postmodern, people to accept. Or you could say that wherever the state gives it permission, religion invariably overplays its hand and starts acting like it's the seventeenth century. Look at Poland, where it took the Catholic church only a few years of temporal power to squander the moral capital it had garnered during the Communist era as the self-proclaimed defender of human rights and personal liberty. Look at Israel, where civil marriage does not even exist. Look at Iran.

In our country the constitutional separation of church and state has obscured the nonetheless real connection between the two as fellow enforcers of conformity, mystification and hierarchy. Prayer in the school will make it plain to see. It's never too early for the young to take the measure of the forces arrayed against those who would think for themselves. Right now religion has the romantic aura of the forbidden—Christ is cool. We need to bring it into the schools, which kids already hate, and associate it firmly with boredom, regulation, condescension, makework and de facto segregation, with business math and *Cliffs Notes* and metal detectors.

Prayer in the schools will rid us of the bland no-offense ecumenism that is so infuriating to us anticlericals: Oh, so *now* you say Jews didn't kill Christ—a little on the late side, isn't it? I see a big boom in theological casuistry, denominational infighting, schisms and scandals of all kinds. Anti-Semitism will thrive, as it tends to when Christian soldiers start marching as to war, which will be a good lesson for Midge Decter and the other neocon Jews who have been cozying up to the religious right.

Many editorial hands have been wrung on behalf of minority-religion children who will be singled out and humiliated by school prayer, which cannot possibly be formulated so vaguely as not to violate someone's conscience. This too can be a valuable lesson in alienation. And there's a way out: I heard a Christian Action Network fellow, Tom Kilgannon, suggest on the radio that local standards should apply, so that if a neighborhood had, say, a lot of "Islams," the Islams should get to write the prayer. Who knows? We may yet see graduations blessed by anything from the sacrifice of a chicken to a Latin mass.

After a few years it will become clear that prayer in schools does nothing to lower crime or teen pregnancy, much less raise S.A.T. scores. The religious kids will still be devout, but the others—the ones from nonobservant homes, who supposedly need to be forced into piety—will have been moved from apathy to open disgust. And they will be entirely justified. Nothing reveals the bankruptcy of the new conservatism more than its promotion of school prayer. The message to youth is clear: We have nothing for you here, start thinking about the hereafter.

Taslima Nasrin, author of The Game in Reverse
(Photograph by Ulla Montan)

51

Taslima Nasrin

BENGALI "BLASPHEMER"

Born 1962

*I said that Shariat law should be revised. I want a modern, civilized law,
where women are given equal rights. I want no religious law that
discriminates, none, period—no Hindu law, no Christian law, no Islamic
law. Why should a man be entitled to have four wives? Why should a son get
two-thirds of his parents' property when a daughter can inherit only a third?
Should I be killed for saying this? . . .*

The New Yorker, *September 12, 1994*

LIVING PROOF OF THE THREAT POSED TO WOMEN'S LIBERTY by fundamentalist religion is Bengali author and physician Taslima Nasrin, the target of a series of
fatwas, or religious sanctions, condemning her to death in 1994 for blasphemy.

A price was put on her head by her country's "holy men" after she wrote a
novel, *Shame (Lajja),* about the plight of Hindus under Moslem order. Following
pressure by the militant Moslems, the government brought criminal charges
against her for defaming the Moslem faith. Thousands in Bangladesh demonstrated regularly, sometimes daily, to demand her death.

After a terrifying two months in hiding, and fearing the fate of Hypatia, Taslima
fled her native Bangladesh, seeking refuge in Sweden. She remains in hiding
from the Moslem world.

Born in Mymensing, she is the daughter of Dr. Rojab Ali, government physician and practitioner of the Sufi tradition of Islam. Her mother was devoutly
religious. When Taslima was nine, a Sufi holy man who had issued *fatwas* against
village women, confining them to their homes, told Dr. Ali he would burn in hell
along with his family. Taslima became an atheist by the time she was eleven or
twelve. She was kept cloistered from the time of puberty, escorted to school by
her family, access to her small town forbidden her.

Her family encouraged her to become a physician. By 1990 she was working as an anesthesiologist in the gynecological department of a hospital. She began writing poems and articles, her column syndicated in 1990. Atrocities against women drew her attention, including the execution in 1993 of a twenty-one-year-old woman at the behest of a local mullah. Declaring the young woman's second marriage a violation of Islamic law, the mullah gathered the villagers together. First burying her waist deep in a pit, they stoned her with more than one hundred stones. Attacks escalated against women and the schools serving them. In 1992, mobs descended on bookstores carrying Taslima's writings. She was attacked at a book fair.

The first *fatwa* was issued against her in early 1993, right after her novella *Shame* was first published. Sixty thousand copies were sold in five months, but then the book was banned and her passport seized. Bounties were soon offered. That fall, the United States, France and Sweden, as well as amnesty and feminist groups, protested Bangladesh's lack of action against the illegal *fatwas*. Taslima's passport was returned, but fanatics demonstrated in the streets over remarks she made to the Indian press, saying, she later clarified, that "the Koran, the Vedas, the Bible and all such religious texts [are] out of place and out of time."

She told the *New Yorker* on September 12, 1994:

"If the progressive forces in our country don't unite, if they don't stand up to the fundamentalists, then there's no question the fundamentalists will have won."

"Why shouldn't I write about what I've seen? I'm a doctor, remember. Do you know what it's like to see a woman crying out in the delivery room when she gives birth to a girl, terrified that her husband will divorce her? To see the ruptured vaginas of women who've been raped? The six- and seven-year-olds who have been violated by their fathers, brothers, and uncles—by *their own families?* No, I will not keep quiet. I will continue to speak out about these women's wretched lives."

In June 1994, Bangladesh charged Taslima with defaming religion, and she went into hiding the next day. Following negotiations, she was granted bail by a high court and boarded a plane for Sweden.

Taslima has written nine volumes of poetry, a volume of collected essays and the novel *Shame*. *The Game In Reverse,* her first volume of poetry to appear in English translation, was released in 1996, featuring more than forty poems which address subjects such as domestic violence, sexual abuse and the indignities endured by women under Moslem society. Her writing challenges Islamic taboos about women and female sexuality.

"Religion is the great oppressor, and should be abolished," Taslima has often stated.

She was awarded the 1994 Sakharov Prize for Freedom of Thought in 1994.

Taslima Nasrin

On Islamic Fundamentalism

This article is adapted from Taslima Nasrin's April 28, 1996 speech at Harvard University, sponsored by the Humanist Chaplaincy.

"Gradually men will come to realize that a world whose institutions are based upon hatred and injustice is not one most likely to produce happiness. . . . We need a morality based upon love of life, upon pleasure in growth and positive achievement, not upon repression and prohibition."

Bertrand Russell

WE ARE AT THE THRESHOLD of the twenty-first century. The last decade of the twentieth century reminds me of the opening lines of Charles Dickens' *A Tale of Two Cities:*

It was the best of times, it was the worst of times, it was the age of wisdom, it was the age of foolishness, it was the epoch of belief, it was the epoch of incredulity, it was the season of Light, it was the season of Darkness, it was the spring of hope, it was the winter of despair. . . .

How true his remarks are even today! Science and technology have made miracles. Arts and literature have reached new heights. At the close of the twentieth century, human creativity has opened up incredible new possibilities. At the same time, however, we find that large areas of this globe are ruled by bigotry, hatred, and fanaticism in the name of race, religion, and political creed. When we look around, it seems as if a new dark age is descending upon us.

After World War II, people were confronted by a war of political creeds which became known as the Cold War. The whole world was divided into rival camps that competed with each other not only on the ideological level but also in acquiring terrifying weapons of mass destruction. That fear no longer exists. We hear that the Cold War has ended. We even hear that history has reached its end. But has it? Emphatically not.

Instead, humankind is facing an uncertain future; the probability of new kinds of rivalry and conflict looms large—in particular, the conflict between two different ideas: secularism and fundamentalism. I do not agree with those who think that the conflict is simply between two religions—namely, Christianity and Islam. After all, there are fundamentalists in every religious community. Likewise, I do not agree with those people who think that the crusades of the Middle Ages are going to be repeated soon. Nor do I think that this is a conflict between East and West. To me, this conflict is basically between irrational blind faith and the modern rational, logical mind. To me, this is a conflict between modernity and anti-modernism. While some people want to go forward, others are trying to go back. It is a conflict between the future and the past, between innovation and tradition, between those who value freedom and those who do not.

At one point in time, Islam was a powerful force for change, expanding throughout the world and winning the hearts of the multitude. Historians tell us that Islamic civilization was the richest and most advanced culture in the world during the early Middle Ages, particularly in the mid-eighth through the mid-eleventh centuries, and perhaps reached its peak during the ninth century. In comparison, the culture of Europe crept far behind. But gradually this glory faded, and Islamic civilization stagnated and ultimately declined. There were many causes for this: invasion by the Turkoman nomads in the eleventh century, the Crusades in the twelfth century, European exploration in the sixteenth century, as well as a failing economy and social immobility. By the nineteenth century, European imperialism had succeeded in subjugating vast empires—Turkey, Persia, and India—and Islam was pushed into the backyard of modern history.

When the colonial powers finally left the occupied countries of Asia and Africa, some Western scholars thought that these nations had left behind a lasting legacy of secular democratic ideas and institutions in the newly independent states. Most of these newly independent nations proclaimed themselves secular states, including some of the Muslim majority countries. But within fifty years, we find secularism is either giving way to or being threatened by fundamentalism. With the breakup of the Soviet Union and the fall of secular eastern European states, we find a resurgence of different kinds of nationalism where religion is considered vital to national identity. The question arises out of these new developments: was secularism a matter of cardinal faith with the new leaders of Asian and African countries, or was it imposed on them from above by their former colonial masters? This question is not irrelevant. I offer this quote from an observer who, in turn, is quoting from various sources. He makes these observations about the newly independent countries where Muslims constitute the majority:

"Jinnah [of Pakistan], whose country's reason for being was its religion, was quoted as saying after he came to power that 'Pakistan is not going to be a theocratic state ruled by priests with a divine mission.' Sukarno's policy [in Indonesia] was 'to tolerate Islam as a religion to curb it as a political force.' Nasser [in Egypt] restricted polygamy, suppressed religious courts, and instituted votes for women; however his aim was not 'to knock down Islam but to transform it,' 'to *neutralize* Islam in internal politics, while *utilising* it in foreign politics.' Bourguiba [of Tunisia], 'the most iconoclastic of all the contemporary Muslim rulers, while instituting modernist reforms . . . allowed the Ulema a certain visibility and status as religious leaders.' In short, these Muslim rulers, like the Buddhist rulers of Sri Lanka and Burma, sought to use religion as a unifying ideology while adapting it for the purposes of modernization."

Naturally, when the challenge came from religious fundamentalists, the second and third generation of nationalist leaders found it very difficult to hold the fort. The basic argument of the fundamentalists is this: the idea of secularism is Western in origin. The imperialistic West sold its idea of secularism to the nationalist leaders of the newly independent states so that the West could dominate the indigenous culture and religion by proxy. After the breakup of the Soviet Union and the failure of the West to solve all the problems of humankind—because the West is basically areligious and devoid of morality—there was a renewed challenge to the Western value system. A belief grew among the majority people of western Asia and sub-Saharan Africa that Islam should go back to its roots to find an alternative to Western life, culture, values, and institutions. A social scientist has tried to explain this stand by citing some instances of failure on the part of secular democracies:

"In many parts of the world the secular state has not lived up to its own promise of political freedom, economic prosperity, and social justice. Some of the most poignant cases of disenchantment with secularism are to be found among educated members of the middle class who were raised with the high expectations propagated by secular nationalist political leaders. Some of them have now been propelled toward religious nationalism after trying to live as secular nationalists and then feeling betrayed or, at least, unfulfilled. Many of them also feel that the Western societies have betrayed themselves: the government scandals, persistent social inequities, and devastating economic difficulties of the United States and the former Soviet Union in the 1980s and early 1990s made both democracy and socialism less appealing as role models. . . . The global mass media in their exaggerated way have brought to religious leaders in non-Western nations the message that there is a deep malaise in the United States caused by the social failures of unwed mothers, divorce, racism, and drug addiction."

There are, of course, many other reasons for the resurgence of religious fundamentalism in Asia and Africa, but I find it difficult to accept fundamentalism as an alternative to secular ideas. My reasons are: first, the insistence of fundamentalists on divine justification for human laws; second, the insistence of fundamentalists upon the superior authority of faith, as opposed to reason; third, the insistence of fundamentalists that the individual does not count, that the individual is immaterial. Group loyalty over individual rights and personal achievements is a peculiar feature of fundamentalism. Fundamentalists believe in a particular way of life; they want to put everybody in their particular straitjacket and dictate what an individual should eat, what an individual should wear, how an individual should live everyday life—everything would be determined by the fundamentalist authority. Fundamentalists do not believe in individualism, liberty of personal choice, or plurality of thought. Moreover, as they are believers in a particular faith, they believe in propagating only their own ideas (as autocrats generally do). They do not encourage or entertain free debate, they deny others the right to express their own views freely, and they cannot tolerate anything which they perceive as going against their faith. They do not believe in an open society and, though they proclaim themselves a moral force, their language is hatred and violence. As true believers, they are out to "save the souls" of the people of their country by force of arms if necessary.

True, the imperialist West did not establish and rule over its colonies by peaceful means. It did not colonize the new world with idealism, enlightenment, and democratic values. So when the fundamentalists argue that they are paying back their old adversaries in the same coin, they may find some sympathetic listeners even in the West. But, as I said earlier, the fight is not between the former colonial powers and newly independent nations; the war is between two ideas of our time: secularism and fundamentalism. So the doctrine of "life for life, eye for eye, tooth for tooth . . . burning for burning, wound for wound" is totally irrelevant here. The fundamentalists want to replace democracy with theocracy and to impose old theocratic laws instead of modern secular laws on the members of their own society, not on other distant powerful states which they consider their enemies.

Though it has a global dimension, Islamic fundamentalism is also a local phenomenon. In reality, there is no such thing as an "Islamic front" embracing all the states of the world that have a Muslim majority. It has been proved time and again that pan-Islam is just an aspiration. There is no end of fighting between different Muslim states. The war between Iraq and Iran and the Iraqi invasion of Kuwait are examples of the animosity between states run by Muslims. The civil war in Afghanistan is also a reminder of this. In fact, even if we assume that the first loyalty of a Muslim is to his or her religion, that person is first and foremost a member of a nation state.

All the various Islamic groups are actually artificially constituted by the rulers of different countries to buttress their own position. Often these groups are initiated by despotic rulers who use Islam to perpetuate their despotic rule. For example, my country, Bangladesh, was once a part of Pakistan. Pakistan regarded it simply as a colony and exploited its people just like a colonial power would, even though most of the population consisted of fellow Muslims. It tried to impose its own language and culture on our people. When the war of liberation began, Pakistani soldiers brutally murdered the freedom fighters. Like an occupation army, they burnt village after village, raped women, and committed all sorts of crimes against our people. The liberation war of Bangladesh proved that religious unity among Muslims was a myth. It was Bengali culture which unified the Muslims and Hindus of the land and gave them their real identity. Naturally, for me, the question is: what is to be done about the rise of fundamentalism in my country? The global problem can be discussed later.

As I said, in my country the basis of nationalism was Bengali culture. No doubt religion plays an important role in the lives of Bengalees—whether Hindu, Muslim, Buddhist, or Christian. But it was Bengali language and culture that shaped our nationalism. So the founding fathers declared Bangladesh a secular, democratic country. But successive military generals who usurped power gave up secularism and declared the country an Islamic state in order to make themselves popular among the ignorant masses. When, after more than a decade, democracy was finally restored, the elected leaders did not restore secularism as the guiding spirit of the constitution. They, too, feel that, because religion is important to the ignorant, illiterate masses, it is a useful tool for control.

Even the opposition is hesitant to disturb the fundamentalists for fear of losing political support. In short, when almost all the political parties make political hay out of religious sentiments, there is no reason why that situation would not be favorable for the fundamentalists. Bangladesh is not (yet) governed by Mollahs, however; political power is still not in the hands of any religious fundamentalist party. When the Mollahs issue a *fatwah* from time to time, it has no constitutional legitimacy or legal sanction. But seldom is any action taken against them. Doesn't this indicate a compromise with fundamentalism?

How to correct this situation, I do not know. I do not think the government or the other democratic parties are really worried about this development. Some day they may have to pay a high price for today's small gains. In the meantime, common people will have to suffer because of the activities of the fundamentalists. If only there was faster economic growth, less unemployment, better access to education, I think the situation would be different. Until such miracles happen, democrats will have to bear the brunt of fundamentalism in my country. Women will have to suffer not only discrimination but also ignominy and violence, and human rights will remain just a dream for many.

Looking at the world situation, I feel the situation is not as bleak. We hear about the globalization of the economy. Modern technology has made for a globalization of culture, too. In a sense, it seems that the world today is like a close-knit family. Economic activity and cultural give and take has brought nations closer in the past. But to make the global media market into a useful tool for fighting fundamentalism, the advanced nations should be very careful about certain aspects of their drive for a global market. If just greed and profit-making become the guiding forces in this drive, with no consideration for ethics and moral values, fundamentalists will name this globalization as exploitation. Market leaders could be compared to colonial powers of the past.

Similarly, if culture means just Western culture, it will also provoke anger in poorer countries. Personally, I believe in plurality of culture, and I have nothing against Western culture as such. But in the past, feelings of cultural superiority among the Western rulers were a constant irritant to the people of non-Western countries. When fundamentalism looms large, the West should be very careful in handling the culture of Asian, African, and Latin American peoples. There is no such thing as a "superior" or "inferior" culture, there are only various cultural patterns which make up this beautiful, multicolored mosaic.

"The power of reason is thought small in these days, but I remain an unrepentant rationalist," wrote Bertrand Russell. I began this article by quoting him, and so I would like to conclude by quoting him again:

"Reason may be a small force, but it is constant and works always in one direction, while the forces of unreason destroy one another in futile strife. Therefore every orgy of unreason in the end strengthens the friends of reason, and shows afresh that they are the only true friends of humanity."

Mathilde Franziska Anneke
Inset, about twenty-five
(State Historical Society of Wisconsin,
WHi(X3)31173, WHi(X3)36475)

ADDITIONAL BIOGRAPHICAL SKETCHES

These are a sampling of the 83 biographical profiles of women included in Joseph McCabe's **A Biographical Dictionary of Modern Rationalists,** *published by Watts & Co. in London in 1920. Additional sketches by Annie Laurie Gaylor are initialed.*

ADDAMS, Jane, *B.* Sept. 6, 1860, the eighth child of a prosperous family in Cedarville, Illinois, Jane became motherless at three. Her father, Quaker by conviction but not affiliation, served eight terms in the Illinois Senate. At seventeen, Jane went to Rockford Seminary, preparing to attend the Woman's Medical College in Philadelphia. Her health broke down after her father's death. After European travel, she and classmate Ellen Gate Starr opened a settlement home in Chicago in 1889, which expanded services for poor working class to include a girls' home, nursery, labor museum, boy's club, theater. Jane also documented sociological conditions. She worked with reformers and radicals of every stripe, and wrote articles on everything from suffrage to prostitution. Jane was elected national chair of the Woman's Peace Party, which she co-founded, in 1915, which ultimately became the Women's International League for Peace and Freedom. She was a recipient of the Nobel Peace Prize in 1931. In *Twenty Years at Hull-House*, she records the secular nature of her enterprise (pp. 448–450): "A wise man has told us that 'men are once for all so made that they prefer a rational world to believe in and live in,' . . ."

In "A Challenge to the Contemporary Church," an address before the Conservation Congress of the Men and Religion Forward Movement, Addams said the "Supreme religious test of our social order is the hideous commerce of prostitution." Although crediting Jesus, and calling the typical treatment of harlots "irreligious," Addams denounced the church fathers very firmly: "The very word woman in the writings of the church fathers stood for the basest temptations. . . . As women were lowered in the moral scale because of their identification with her at the very bottom of the pit, so they cannot rise themselves save as they succeed in lifting her with whose sins they are weighted." *D.* May 21, 1935—*ALG*

ANNEKE, Mathilde Franziska Giesler, *B.* April 3, 1817, a freethought editor, educator and woman's rights advocate. First of twelve children in a prosperous family in Westphalia, Mathilde was raised a devout Catholic. An unhappy marriage at nineteen to a French wine merchant, during which she battled for custody of her daughter Fanny and had the marriage annulled, turned her more fervently to her faith. She married Prussian artillery officer Fritz Anneke in 1847, published a censored revolutionary journal when he was imprisoned, and became a radical freethinker, meeting Karl Marx and Michael Bakunin. Anneke fought in the German revolutions of 1848 and 1849, then he and Mathilde fled to America with other German "Forty-Eighters." They settled briefly in Milwaukee, where she published the monthly *Deutsche Frauenzeitung*, described as a radical, freethinker's journal dedicated to women's complete emancipation, earning the jibes of the German-language press. She continued the publication for two and a half years when the couple moved to New Jersey, also editing *Newarkerzeitung*. Mathilde attended and spoke at her first woman's rights convention, with Ernestine Rose translating, during the infamous "mob convention" of 1853. (*History of Woman Suffrage* I: 571–573) After three of her six children died of smallpox in 1858, she went abroad when her husband worked as a foreign correspondent, remaining with their children in Switzerland when Fritz returned to America to fight in the Civil War. Mathilde settled in Milwaukee in 1865 without her husband, protesting alcohol, clericalism and nativism, co-founding a Wisconsin suffrage group in 1869. In 1865 she co-founded the Milwaukee Tochter Institut, a highly-regarded German-language girls school, continuing to lecture and write, selling insurance for extra income.

At the 1869 national Equal Rights Association convention in New York, Mathilde spoke: "That which you can no longer suppress in woman—that which is free above all things—that which is pre-eminently important to mankind, and must have free play in every mind, is the natural thirst for scientific knowledge—that fountain of all peacefully progressing amelioration in human history. This longing, this effort of reason seeking knowledge of itself, of ideas, conclusions, and all higher things, has, as far as historical remembrance goes back, never been so violently suppressed in any human being as in woman. But, so far from its having been extinguished in her, it has, under the influences of this enlightened century, become a gigantic flame which shines most brightly under the protection of the star-spangled banner. There does not exist a man-made doctrine, fabricated expressly for us, and which we must learn by heart, that shall henceforth be our law. Nor shall the authority of old traditions be a standard for us—be this authority called Veda, Talmud, Koran, or Bible. No. Reason, which we recognize as our highest and only law-giver, commands us to be free." (*History of Woman Suffrage* III: 393–394) D. Nov. 25, 1884 —ALG

BODICHON, Barbara Leigh Smith, foundress of Girton College. *B.* Apr. 8, 1827. Linked through her father with Cobden and other distinguished politicians, Mme. Bodichon was equally intimate with advanced writers like George Eliot, D. G. Rossetti, and G. J. Holyoake. Several of her pamphlets were published by Holyoake, with whom she agreed. She is the model of George Eliot's Romola. In her early years she had founded *The Englishwoman's Journal* (which had been suggested by Holyoake), and throughout her life she was zealous for the education and emancipation of her sex. "She may justly be regarded as the foundress of Girton College" (*Dict. Nat. Biog.*), of which she devised the plan, and for which she supplied large funds (over £11,000). *D.* June 11, 1891.

BONHEUR, Marie Rosalie ("Rosa"), French painter. *B.* Oct. 22, 1822. She received her artistic education from her father, a Saint-Simonian, and at Paris. Her first picture, an animal picture, was exhibited in 1841, and she won gold medals in 1845 and 1848. In 1853 she painted her famous "Horse Fair" and earned a world-wide repute. She wore the cross of the Legion of Honour. T. Stanton's *Reminiscences of Rosa Bonheur* (1910) contains an interesting discussion of her views on religion (pp. 78–82). Her friend Louis Passy describes her as Agnostic, and she was at the most a Pantheist and non-Christian. She consented to a religious funeral in order to be buried near a friend, and said: "Though I make this concession as to my body, my philosophical belief remains unaltered." *D.* May 25, 1899.

CAPE, Emily Palmer, American writer. *B.* Oct. 6, 1865. *Ed.* Columbia College, Barnard College, and Wisconsin University. Mrs. Cape (*née* Palmer) studied sociology under Prof. Lester Ward, of whom she became an intimate friend and a highly valued assistant. She was the first woman student at Columbia College (now University). She has written several books (*Oriental Aphorisms*, 1906, *Fairy Surprises for Little Folks*, 1908, etc.), but her chief work was to collaborate with Lester Ward in compiling and publishing his *Glimpses of the Cosmos* (12 vols., 1913). Like Professor Ward, she is an Agnostic and an ardent humanitarian. She has founded a School of Sociology in New York which has an important educational influence. Mrs. Cape is also a gifted painter.

CAROLINE, Queen of England. *B.* Mar. 1, 1683, daughter of the Margrave of Brandenburg-Ansbach. It was proposed to marry her to an Austrian Archduke, and a Jesuit was sent to instruct her in the Catholic faith, but, coached by Leibnitz, she routed the Jesuit. She married the Prince of Hanover, in 1705, and reached England as Princess of Wales in 1714. She continued to correspond with Leibnitz and to study philosophy, and her house at Richmond was more or less a Deistic centre. She ascended the throne in 1727, and on several occasions during the King's absence, when she acted as Regent, an Act of Parliament was passed excusing her from taking the oath. She refused to receive the sacrament on her death-bed, though pressed to do so by the Archbishop of Canterbury (see the memoirs of Lord Hervey, her intimate friend, ii, 528). Horace Walpole (*Reminiscences*, p. 66) says that she was "at least not orthodox," and Chesterfield (*Characters*, p. 1406) accurately describes her as "a Deist, believing in a future state." The Earl of Bristol (*Letter-Books of John Hervey*, iii, p. 196) represents her heterodoxy as widely known. *D.* Nov. 20, 1737.

CATHERINE II, Empress of Russia. *B.* May 2, 1729. Sophia Augusta Friederika, as she was originally named, was a daughter of the Prince of Anhalt-Serbst. She was selected in her fourteenth year to be the wife of Peter, heir to the Russian throne, and was sent to Moscow to be educated. Her name was changed to Catherine at her reception into the Russian Church, and she was married in 1745. The irregularities of her later years were in part a natural reaction upon this early union with a drunken and entirely contemptible prince, and in part a defiant disregard of the mingled piety and licence of the Russia of the time. Catherine and her friends deposed her husband in 1762, and he was strangled in prison. There is no evidence connecting Catherine with the crime (see J. McCabe's *Romance of the Romanoffs*). As Empress, Catherine endeavoured to enforce the enlightened humanitarian views of the great French Rationalists, with whom she was in complete sympathy. Her reforms, in regard to education, justice, sanitation, industry, etc., were of great value. In her later years the French Revolution soured her love of France and drove her into a profession of conservatism. *D.* Nov. 10, 1796.

CHAPPELLSMITH, Margaret Reynolds. Born Margaret Reynolds, daughter of a master mechanic in Great Britain, she began to question from an early age why the working poor suffered, talking to her father's customers and workmen. Her early discourses at first brought smiles, but as she grew older she was encouraged to deliver a series of lectures. For a number of years she lectured in England to Liberal and Freethinking societies. Moncure D. Conway called her the first female lecturer of the British Communists established by Robert Owen in the village of Broughton (Harmony Hall), which eventually failed.

Her diverse lectures included "The Education of Women," "My Reasons why I, having been a Calvinist, have Become an Infidel," "The Character of the Priesthood as Given by Themselves," and five lectures on the Protestant Reformation. She and her husband commenced bookselling. She intended to publish a series, " The Historic Value of the Gospels. " The Chappellsmiths settled in the United States in New Harmony, Indiana, set up by Owen's son.—*ALG*

CHÂTELET, Gabrielle Émilie, Marquise du, French writer. *B.* Dec. 17, 1706, daughter of the Baron de Breteuil. She learned Latin, English, and Italian at an early age, and in her sixteenth year translated Vergil. In 1738 the Marquise nearly won the Academy's prize for a dissertation on the nature of heat. She was a woman of remarkable ability and accomplishments. Her chief Deistic work, *Doutes sur les religions révélées* (published posthumously in 1792), is dedicated to Voltaire, with whom she lived for thirteen years. *D.* Sep. 10, 1749.

COLBY, Clara, *B.* Aug. 5, 1846. Born in England, Clara Bewick moved with her parents to a farm near Windsor, Wisconsin, in 1849, where public schools were scarce and public libraries unknown. Clara read early, liked to memorize and recite, and churned butter by keeping time to fearful hymns threatening "the fires of hell," she later recalled in a lecture. At nineteen, she moved to Madison to live with her grandmother, enrolling at the University of Wisconsin. Clara was instrumental in opening admission of the UW to women. She graduated in 1869 as valedictorian, in the first class of women graduated. She taught history and Latin at the UW, married Leonard Wright Colby, and moved to Beatrice, Nebraska. She became well-known for woman's suffrage, managing the 1882 campaign in her state, serving as president for sixteen years of the Woman's Suffrage

Clara Bewick Colby
(State Historical Society of Wisconsin, WHi(X3)36907)

Association there. She organized a free public library in 1873, also founding the *Woman's Tribune* in 1883. Legendary for her energy and hard work, she adopted two children, including a Sioux Indian baby girl, "Lost Bird," found by Clara's husband in the arms of her slaughtered mother after Wounded Knee.

Clara published the *Woman's Tribune* for twenty-five years, an organ of the National Woman Suffrage Association when Elizabeth Cady Stanton was president. At the International Council of Women in Washington, D.C., in 1888, Clara published *daily* right through the woman's suffrage convention the following week, reproducing all speeches. At the union of the two women's suffrage organizations, Susan B. Anthony adopted the competing *Woman's Journal*, edited by Henry Blackwell, as the suffrage organ, a bitter blow to Clara, who continued publishing for twenty years at great effort and personal sacrifice. She even set type, was editor, compositor and sometimes ran the press. She lived in D.C. until 1904, chairing teas and evening lectures. She moved to Portland, Oregon, to aid the suffrage campaign there, and stopped publishing in 1909.

She the first woman designated as a war correspondent during the Spanish War. Clara lectured in nearly every state, and in England, Ireland, and Scotland, helping English suffragists in 1909–1912. She was appointed delegate by the Governor of Oregon to the Great International Suffrage Alliance at Budapest, and the Peace Congress at Hague. After nursing others with grippe in 1916, she fell sick, dying of pneumonia in Palo Alto.

Clara had belonged to the Congregational church, but introduced and defended resolutions denouncing patriarchal religious dogma, notably at the 1885 woman suffrage convention. She featured Stanton's critiques of religion on the front pages of her paper, and lectured herself on women and the bible. Olympia Brown, who wrote a memorial of her, classified Clara's views as "New Thought." She believed, "God and I are one and I am the one." D. Sept. 7, 1916.—*ALG*

CRADDOCK, Ida. Ida Craddock committed suicide rather than serve a second prison sentence under Comstock. According to George Macdonald, "Mrs. Craddock's coeducational hobby was the purification of the marriage relation, which, being something of a mystic, she regarded as a communion with God." She was sentenced to three months at the Work House on Blackwell's Island on March 17, 1902, where inmates called her a "ministering angel." After her release, she continued her writings, and Comstock arrested her on October 10. After bail, she cut the veins of her wrists and turned on the gas in her room, leaving a letter: "I maintain my right to die as I have lived, a free woman, not cowed into silence by any other human being." Wrote Macdonald: "Personally Mrs. Craddock was a surprisingly lovely woman. She and Comstock were the Beauty and the Beast." (*Fifty Years of Freethought*: 217–219)

Craddock was published in *The Truth Seeker*, such as her article, "The Coming Convention of Liberal Women" (February 1, 1890). "For some time past our orthodox brethren and sisters—especially the sisters—not satisfied with their legitimate churchly works of mercy and peace, and the right (inherent in every human being) to moral suasion, have assumed an aggressive position, and are seeking to cram their religious opinions by main force down the throats of those who differ with them. . . .

"It is high time that women outside of orthodoxy awakened to the sense of their powers, as have already their sisters within the pale of the church. It is high time that they realized the mission to which they are called in this nineteenth century, and which they alone can accomplish—the carrying of the human race not alone upward, as their orthodox sisters are seeking to do, but forward to the broader sweep and clear outlook of Liberalism." She was at one time corresponding secretary of the American Secular Union. *D.* Oct. 16, 1902.—*ALG*

DERAISMES, Maria, French writer. *B.* Aug. 15, 1835. *Ed.* Paris. She started her literary career in 1861 with a collection of dramatic sketches. In 1866 she began to take an active part in feminist controversy, and is regarded as one of the founders of the movement in France. She opened the first French Women's Congress (1878), and was President of the Society for the Improvement of the Condition of Women. Mlle. Deraismes was an active Rationalist. She was the first woman Freemason of France (Pesq Lodge of Freethinkers), and president of various Freethought societies. She presided, with V. Schoelcher, at the Anti-Clerical Congress at Paris in 1881. *D.* Feb. 6, 1894.

FREEMAN, Mattie. Called a "bright, brave little moral heroine" by the secretary of the American Secular Union, Mrs. M.A. Freeman was considered a "sparkling" orator on the freethought circuit in the 1880s and 1890s, and held offices in the American Secular Union. She was the daughter of a freethinker, and related to John Quincy Adams on her mother's side of the family. Active with the Chicago Secular Union, she published the *Chicago Liberal* in 1891.—*ALG*

GEOFFRIN, Marie Thérèse, French writer. *B.* June 2, 1699. Daughter of a chamberlain of the Dauphin, she was married to Geoffrin at the age of fourteen, and his death some years later left her rich and independent. Witty and cultivated, she made her home the chief centre for the brilliant Parisian Rationalists of the time; and the *Dictionnaire Encyclopédique* is largely due to her liberality. D'Alembert and Morellet wrote high praise of her (*Éloges de Mme. Geoffrin*, 1812), and published her *Letters* and an essay *Sur la conversation*, which she had written. *D.* Oct. 6, 1777.

GREENAWAY, Kate, painter. *B.* Mar. 17, 1846. *Ed.* Heatherley's Art School, South Kensington, and Slade School. Her first picture was exhibited, in the Dudley Gallery, in 1868; and she exhibited regularly for many years in the Academy and elsewhere. From the illustration of magazines she passed, as her repute grew, especially for her depictment of child life, to issuing books of her own which had a very wide circulation. Ruskin speaks warmly of the delicacy of her art and humour in *Praeterita* and *Fors Clavigera*. In their biography of her (*Kate Greenaway*, 1905) M. H. Spielmann and G. L. Layard quote many letters in which she avows her advanced scepticism. She professes to be religious, but "it is in my own way" (p.

189). She is quite Agnostic about a future life, and considers it "strange beyond anything I can think to be able to believe in *any* of the known religions" (p. 190). She is not even clearly a Theist. *D.* Nov. 6, 1901.

HALL, Sharlot, *B.* October 27,1870. Born in frontier Kansas to an educated mother and a backwards father, she was named Sharlot, an Indian name, by her uncle. Bright and talented, at eleven she moved with her family near Prescott, Arizona, then Dewey. She worked for room and board for a half year to escape the ranch and attend Prescott High School, receiving her first payment for an accepted story that year. When her mother became ill, she had to return to the hard domestic and outdoor work of a ranch. She took up photography and explored ancient Indian cliff dwellings with her brother. Sharlot, seeing the lot of her mother and most women, vowed never to marry, once remarking: "The egotism of the average man is so great that he thinks he is a glorious sight—even with a wad of tobacco in his cheek and the spit drooling off his chin."

Her family attended lectures by freethinker Samuel Putnam in Prescott in 1895. Sharlot joined Putnam on the platform at his final speech, speaking about Thomas Paine. Although Sharlot was twenty-four and Putnam was fifty-six, she fell in love. Putnam's death on December 11, 1896, which made headlines and was treated like a scandal, was a great shock to her. The fully dressed bodies of Putnam and a young woman lecturer, Mary L. Collins, were found on the floor of a hotel room, asphyxiated by a gas leakage. Sharlot sent poetry to *The Truth Seeker* to commemorate him. Widely published in newspapers, she was launched as the protégée of Charles F. Lummis, editor of *Land of Sunshine* in Los Angeles, meeting Charlotte Perkins Gilman and others. Two volumes of her poetry were published. She began taking oral histories of Arizona pioneers, and in 1909 her friend, territorial governor Judge Richard Sloan, appointed her territorial historian, giving her an office in Phoenix. She traveled through Arizona collecting history, supported by the Federation of Women's Clubs. After statehood, the first governor dismissed her in 1912, and soon after, her mother died. Sharlot became reclusive, caring for her father until he died in 1925. At fifty-seven, in 1927, she was given a life lease on the Governor's Mansion to restore it as a museum of early Arizona history by the city of Prescott. She died of heart trouble on April 9, 1943. The mansion and a Sharlot Hall Museum remain. Below is her freethought ditty:

With a Box of Apples

Suppose a modern Eve would come
And tempt you with an apple,
Say just about the size of these?
Would you temptation grapple
And manfully declare: "I won't?"
Or, would you say: "Well, I
Think since you've picked them

Sharlot Hall, c. 1918
(Sharlot Hall Museum Library/Archives)

They'd be best in dumplings or in pie.
And, let us ask the serpent in
To share with us at dinner.
A de'il with taste for fruit like that
Can't be a hopeless sinner."—*ALG*

HARMAN, Lillian. *B.* December, 1870. Freethinker Lillian Harman was the daughter of Kansas freethinker Moses Harman, who was imprisoned under the Comstock Act as publisher of *Lucifer, The Light-Bearer* in the 1880s and 1890s. At a baby-faced sixteen, Lillian entered an "autonomistic marriage" on September 19, 1886 (without benefit of church or state), with Harman's senior editor Edwin C. Walker. Authorities arrested the couple the next day. Lillian was sentenced to forty-five days in jail and Walker to seventy-five, but they were jailed far longer for refusing to pay court costs. The Supreme Court of Kansas, on March 6, 1887, upheld the conviction and they finally paid costs, but legal harassment continued.

From her prison cell, Lillian wrote a letter to a rebuking Christian woman on November 4, 1886: "Is there, in your opinion, no incentive to right-doing aside from the hope that you will sometime obtain a position in the heavenly choir, and with wings growing out of your shoulders, and a crown on your head, stand by the throne of the man-god and twang your harp through all the countless ages; while at the same time you know that many of your friends and relations—perhaps your father and mother or husband and children—are roasting below you in hell? Don't you think that you would get rather tired?"

She defensively opposed feminist efforts to raise the age of consent for women. Her daughter, Virna Winifred Walker, was born in 1893, absentee Walker agreeing to support her. Lillian was elected honorary president of Legitimation League in England, and retired from the cause in 1910, quietly marrying American printer George O'Brien.—*ALG*

HUBBARD, Alice, American writer. *B.* June 7, 1861. *Ed.* State Normal School, Buffalo, and Emerson College of Oratory, Boston. Miss Moore, as she was originally, married Elbert Hubbard, and was general superintendent of his Roycroft Shop, manager of the Roycroft Inn, and principal of the Roycroft School for Boys. Among her books is *An American Bible* (1911), in which she says of her husband: "Content to live in one world at a time, he has the genuine faith which does not peep into the Unknown, but lives to the full to-day, assured that the power which cares for us here will not desert us there" (p. 34). She went down on the *Lusitania* May 7, 1915.

KEY, Ellen Karolina Sofia, Swedish writer. *B.* Dec. 11, 1849. *Ed.* privately. Miss Key is a daughter of the Countess S. Posse, but her father lost his fortune and she became a teacher. She taught in a school at Stockholm from 1880 to 1900, and lectured at the Workers' Institute from 1883 to 1903. Her numerous works on social questions have won for her a remarkable influence in Scandinavia and a high reputation in other lands. Of her thirty volumes seven have been translated into English between 1909 and 1914. She is a Monist, and writes for the organ of Prof. Haeckel's League. L. Nyström's *Ellen Key* (1913) gives a good account of her work and career.

KREKEL, Mattie, *B.* April 13, 1840 in Goshen, Indiana to liberal parents, she expressed thanks to them both for not twisting her life to ecclesiastical influences or enslaving her mind. At fifteen, she began lecturing on the Liberal platform, making her first address in Rockford, Illinois. She married T.W. Parry in 1862 and gave birth to four sons and two daughters. Her second husband was Judge Arnold Krekel of the United States District Court, western district of Missouri, who came to the United States from Prussia, served in the Civil War, and was appointed a federal judge by Lincoln. An agnostic, he died in 1888. In an article appearing in *The Truth Seeker* on February 15, 1890, Mattie P. Krekel wrote: "Freethought means, first of all, mental self-assertion." —*ALG*

LAW, Harriet, lecturer. *B.* 1832. Mrs. Law, a London lady, used to attend the Secular Hall for the purpose of refuting the speakers. Mr. Law, whom she married, shared her work, and both were converted to Secularism. For thirty years she was the only woman Secularist lecturer in England, and she had to endure much insult and even assault. In 1878 she edited the *Secular Chronicle*. D. 1897.

LELAND, Lilian, *B.* October 16, 1857. The daughter of freethinkers, she traveled sixty thousand miles alone around the world at the age of twenty-five for nearly two years, starting with a voyage around Cape Horn. Her mother, Mary A. Leland, was one of the first women to study medicine in the United States, and lectured on anatomy as early as 1852. Her father, Theron C. Leland, was a popular lecturer in the Liberal League. She was brought up to play chess and read widely, conceiving her plan to travel after reading "Merchant of Venice." She wrote a book about her travels, and married the son of Stephen Pearl Andrews, abolitionist and freethinker. —*ALG*

LINTON, Eliza Lynn, novelist. *B.* Feb. 10, 1822. In 1845 she left her home in Keswick for London, and opened a literary career. Her early historical novels were not very successful, and she acted as Paris correspondent of London newspapers (1851–54). In 1858 Miss Lynn married W. J. Linton, but their characters were so ill assorted that they soon separated, retaining a marked affection for each other throughout life. The differences are indicated in her *Autobiography of Christopher Kirkland* (1885). Mrs. Linton's high reputation as a novelist began in 1872 with her *True History of Joshua Davidson*, a Rationalist novel; as is also her *Under Which Lord?* (1879). G. S. Layard, her biographer, amply tells of her Agnosticism (*Mrs. Lynn Linton: Her Life, Letters, and Opinions*, 1901, pp. 66, 155–56, etc.). He includes a statement by Mr. Benn, who knew her well, that she "professed Agnosticism with complete sincerity" (p. 202). In her earlier years she had believed in a Providence, but this she entirely abandoned, and she was severe against Christianity. In the year before her death she wrote a fine Agnostic letter to a clergyman: "I see no light behind that terrible curtain. I do not think one religion better than another, and I think the Christian religion has brought far more misery, crime, and suffering, far more tyranny and evil, than any other" (p. 367). She was a frequent contributor to the *Agnostic Annual*. D. July 14, 1898.

MCQUEEN, Butterfly, actress. *B.* 1911. Butterfly McQueen, best known for her role as "Prissy" in the 1939 MGM movie "Gone With the Wind," was nearly a lifelong atheist. Born in Tampa, she gained her unusual name after dancing in a butterfly ballet as a child in a production of "A Midsummer Night's Dream." She auditioned for the part of the simpleminded slave Prissy at age twenty-six, and was initially rejected as too old, too plump and too dignified. "It was not a pleasant part to play—I didn't want to be that little slave. But I did my best, my very best." Her best was very good, indeed, with Butterfly stealing every scene she was in. She was offered a succession of "maid" roles in such movies as "Duel in the Sun," "Mildred Pierce" and "Cabin in the Sky." She played a WAC sergeant in "Since You Went Away." She quit movie-acting in 1947 to avoid further typecasting. She returned to the maid role on the TV show "Beulah" in 1950–1953, appeared occasionally on Broadway, and supported herself in a succession of jobs as a real-life maid, a companion to an elderly white lady, a taxi dispatcher, a saleslady at Macy's, and a seamstress at Sak's. She returned to films in 1974, playing Clarice in "Amazing Grace" and Ma Kennywick in "Mosquito Coast" in 1986, also appearing in a PBS version of "The Adventures of Huckleberry Finn" that year. A continual student who attended five universities and even read *Gone With the Wind* in Spanish, Butterfly received a bachelor's degree in political science in 1974 at the age of sixty-four from New York City College. An offstage role she enjoyed was that of Santa Claus at children's hospitals. She reported that children were delighted with a black female Santa with a high voice. She "adopted" a public elementary school in Harlem, patrolling the playground. She was a health food advocate, and played and sang from an impressive repertoire of classical music, jazz, and show tunes. She died tragically of wounds suffered in a kerosene-heater accident at her winter home in Augusta, Georgia, on December 22, 1995.

A Life Member of the Freedom From Religion Foundation, she was honored with a "Freethought Heroine" award by that group in Atlanta in 1989. She told reporter Gayle White of *The Atlanta Journal and Constitution* (October 8, 1989): "As my ancestors are free from slavery, I am free from the slavery of religion."

"If we had put the energy on earth and on people that we put on mythology and on Jesus Christ, we wouldn't have any hunger or homelessness." Christianity and studying the bible have "sapped our minds so we don't know anything else."—*ALG*

NIGHTINGALE, Florence, O.M., reformer. *B.* May 12, 1820. *Ed.* in her father's house. As her parents were rich, Miss Nightingale had an excellent education; but she chafed at the limitations of the sphere marked out for women in her time, and in 1844 she began to take an interest in hospital work. She visited the hospitals of France, Germany, and Ireland, and in 1853 she was appointed Superintendent of a Hospital for Invalid Gentlewomen at London. In the following year the Crimean War offered her a great opportunity, and, settling at Scutari, she worked for two years with such devotion, skill, and power of organization that the sufferings of the wounded were incalculably reduced. At the close of the war the nation subscribed £50,000 for a Nightingale School for Nurses. Her health was seriously affected, but she carried on her beneficent work for a further fifty years. She was frequently consulted by the Government. Miss Nightingale was the first woman to receive the Order of Merit; and she had also the freedom of the City of London, the German Cross of Merit, the French gold medal for helping the wounded, and other honours. Sir Edward Cook shows in his *Life of Florence Nightingale* (2 vols, 1913) that, while she was a fervent Theist, she was entirely outside Christianity. He says less than the truth when he observes that "she had little interest in rites and ceremonies as such, and she interpreted the doctrines of Christianity in her own way" (ii, 243). Her own words, in a letter of 1896 which he quotes (ii, 392), are: "The Church is now more like the Scribes and Pharisees than like Christ. . . . What are now called the 'essential doctrines' of the Christian religion he [Christ] does not even mention." In 1873 she wrote two articles on religion in *Fraser's Magazine* (May and July) in which she is not less outspoken. Curiously enough, the Unitarians have included a pamphlet on her (*Florence Nightingale as a Religious Thinker*, 1914) in their "Penny Library," in which the author, W. G. Tarrant, quotes her saying: "I am so glad that my God is not the God of the High Church or of the Low; that he is not a Romanist or an Anglican—or a Unitarian" (p. 12). *D.* Aug. 13, 1910.

PARSONS, Lucy, *B.* March, 1853. Lucy E. Parsons fled Ku Klux Klan-riddled Texas with Albert Parsons for Chicago around 1873, describing herself as Indian and Spanish, although she appeared also to be African-American and a former slave. She was a leader in the working class movement until the end of her life. In 1877, Albert was scapegoated after a strike rally and arrested for the first of many times by Chicago officials. Lucy began writing for the *Socialist*, and opened a dress shop to support the family. She gave birth to a son, Albert, in 1879 and to a daughter, Lulu Eda, on 1881, whom some official designated as "nigger" on the birth certificate. Anarchist "propaganda by the deed" appealed to Lucy, witnessing ugly violence directed at workers, blacks and the homeless. She became known for fiery, incendiary speeches urging bloody revolution. After the "Haymarket Police Riot," Albert was hunted for the bombing, although innocent, and was one of four to hang in 1887, singing his favorite song "Annie Laurie" shortly before his execution.

Lucy Parsons
(University of Michigan Library)

Lucy became a Chicago fixture, handing out leaflets, working for free speech and setting up book stands. She was arrested and jailed many times on speaking tours. On January 23,1889, Lucy spoke to a Knights of Labor meeting on the "Religion of Humanity," saying, "Socialism is the 100-cents-on-dollar religion. . . . We have heard enough about a paradise behind the moon. We want something now. We are tired of hearing about the golden streets of the hereafter. What we want is good paved and drained streets in this world."

Her seven-year-old daughter died in 1889. Lucy published the periodicals, *Freedom* and *Liberator.* By the turn of the century, her political views turned toward trade union advocacy. She had her son Albert, 18, committed for insanity. He died of tuberculosis in 1919 at the asylum. Once arrested for leading a Hunger Demonstration in 1915, Lucy was bailed out by Jane Addams. She worked actively for labor rights until her late eighties, when, nearly blind, she died in a house fire. It was rumored, when her extensive library disappeared, that the FBI had confiscated it, afraid of Lucy Parsons even after death. D. March 7, 1942. *Source: Lucy Parsons: American Revolutionary, by Carolyn Ashbaugh, Charles H. Kerr Publishing Co, 1976—ALG*

RAND, Ayn. *B.* February 2, 1905. Born Alice Rosenbaum in St. Petersburg in a nonobservant Jewish family, she witnessed with initial enthusiasm the revolution of 1916 from her parents' apartment balcony. Enthusiasm was replaced by horror when Bolshevik troops overtook the country, turning a bloodless coup into one of the bloodier revolutions. Her father lost his chemist shop and the family was thrown into deprivation, a nightmare which would shape her future and end for Alice only when she obtained a visa to "visit" relatives in Chicago in 1921. Intense, intellectual, antisocial, and driven, even as a child, Alice spent her spare moments writing fiction. Her themes were Good and Evil; she early developed her penchant for idealistic "heroes," who later surfaced in the form of Howard Roark in her bestselling novels *The Fountainhead* and John Galt in *Atlas Shrugged.* Biographer Barbara Branden in *The Passion of Ayn Rand* records that a diary entry made when Alice was a teenager reads: "Today, I decided to be an atheist." She later told Branden: "I had decided that the concept of God is degrading to men." She also observed that "no proof of the existence of God exists; the concept is an untenable invention." But Rand preferred to battle the underlying rejection of reason.

In the United States, she renamed herself Ayn (rhymes with "mine") after a Finnish woman; the "Rand" was inspired by her Remington-Rand typewriter. She landed in Hollywood, where she caught the eye of Cecil B. DeMille and was offered a job as an extra. She worked for studios intermittently for two decades, including screenwriting. She married Frank O'Connor, a young actor who resembled Gary Cooper, in 1929, at "a 'proper' nonreligious ceremony in a judge's chambers," she wrote. Her first novel *We the Living* fell flat upon its publication in 1936. *The Fountainhead* (1943) secured her place in literature, and was followed by *Atlas Shrugged* (1957). Her novels promote her philosophy, Objectivism.

The famous speech broadcast by character John Galt in *Atlas Shrugged*, gives her views in a 54-page nutshell. Reason, her character John Galt advised humanity, "is your means of survival." "Sweep aside those hatred-eaten mystics, who pose as friends of humanity and preach that the highest virtue man can practice is to hold his own life as of no value."

Galt's soliloquy debunks the idea that faith is "the alleged short-cut to knowledge," calling it "only a short-circuit destroying the mind." Original sin "demands, as his first proof of virtue, that he accept his own depravity without proof." In a critique of prayer, Galt says "feelings are impotent to alter the course of a single speck of dust in space or the nature of any action. . . "

A controversial and enigmatic figure, Rand remains influential and stimulating. Her freethought views are found in "Faith and Force: The Destroyers of the Modern World," a lecture delivered at Yale University on February 17, 1960; at Brooklyn College on April 4, 1960; and at Columbia University on May 5, 1960. D. March 6, 1982—*ALG*

ROALFE, Mathilda, reformer. *B.* 1813. Miss Roalfe was active with Holyoake and Paterson in the London Anti-Persecution Union of the early forties. Hearing in 1843 that an Edinburgh bookseller had been prosecuted for selling Rationalist literature, she went north, opened a shop, and published a defiant circular calling attention to the fact. She was prosecuted, and was imprisoned for two months in 1844; but she resumed her sale of books like those of Paine when she was set at liberty. She afterwards married a Mr. Sanderson, and settled in Scotland. *D.* Nov. 29, 1880.

ROLAND DE LA PLATIÈRE, Marie Jeanne, French patriot. *B.* Mar. 17, 1754. Marie Jeanne Philipon, as she was named before marriage, was a very precocious child. She could read at the age of four, and as she grew up, she devoured books. The works of Bossuet had the effect of disturbing her faith, and she went on to read the works of the great Rationalists of the time, and abandoned Catholicism. As virtuous as she was beautiful and accomplished, she took the Stoic morality for her inspiration. In 1780 she married Roland, a Rationalist like herself, and they worked and studied in close co-operation. She accepted the sober principles of the Revolution, and before long "Mme. Roland" was one of the most familiar names at Paris. She helped to found *Le Républicain*. But their moderation made many enemies, and at the fall of the Girondins her husband had to fly. Mme. Roland was thrust into a prostitutes' jail, and there for five months she helped her unfortunate fellow prisoners and wrote her *Memoirs*. Still a Deist, at the most, she tried to end her life, but the extremists succeeded in bringing her to the guillotine. There was a statue of Liberty near the scaffold, and she uttered the famous words; "O Liberté, que de crimes on commet en ton nom!" Carlyle, who found little good in the Revolution, is dithyrambic in his praise of this wonderful woman (*French Revolution*, III, bk. v, ch. ii), though he has to admit that her "clear perennial womanhood" was nourished only on "Logics, *Encyclopédies*, and the Gospel according to Jean-Jacques." *D.* Nov. 8, 1793.

SAND, George, French novelist, poet, and dramatist. *B.* July 2, 1804. Aurore Dupin, as she was originally named, spent her early years in the country, and was educated by private tutors. She then spent three years (1817–20) with the Augustinian nuns at Paris; but her real education began after her return to the country. She studied Aristotle, Bacon, Locke, Condillac, etc., and lost the pious faith of her earlier years. In 1822 she married Baron Dudevant, but he was totally unworthy, and she soon left him and applied herself to letters. Her first novel (*Rose et Blanche*, 1831) was unsuccessful. The second (*Indiana*, 1832) opened her brilliant career. She had adopted the pen-name of George Sand. In 1833 she went with A. De Musset to Venice, and three years later she secured a judicial separation—divorce being impossible in France—from her husband. *Consuelo* (a novel in eight volumes) was published in 1842. She hailed the Revolution of 1848 with enthusiasm, for she was an advanced democrat, and founded the weekly *La Cause du Peuple*. Her autobiography (*Histoire de ma vie*) runs to twenty volumes (1854–55). George Sand's Rationalist views changed a good deal at different periods, but she never returned anywhere near the Church. She was at one time under the influence of Lamennais, at another time a follower of the mystic Leroux. As Professor Caro says in his *George Sand* (1887), which gives the best account of her opinions, she uses the word God "prodigally" in all her writings, but "it is an avatar of which the meaning is often an enigma." She wavered between Theism and Pantheism, and was even at the last uncertain about a future life. During most of her life she was aggressively anti-clerical, though in her later years she abandoned this attitude. "She remained outside the Church, but thundered not," says Caro (p. 190). From an artist of George Sand's temperament one would not expect a severe and consistent philosophy of religion, but her views were seriously based on philosophical reading, and she was at least consistently non-Christian to the end. *D.* June 7, 1876.

SARRAGA DE FERRERO, Belén, Spanish educationist. Señora Sarraga edited the *Conciencia Libre*, a Rationalist and feminist organ, at Malaga for many years. She is a very eloquent speaker, and had a great influence in emancipating the women of Spain. She was a conspicuous and enthusiastic attendant at the International Freethought Congresses at Rome and Paris (in 1904 and 1905). She is now head of a Normal School in Argentina, and takes no less interest in the spread of Rationalism among the women of South America.

SCHREINER, Olive, novelist. *B.* 1862 (in Basutoland). Her father, a missionary from London, was at work among the natives of South Africa. She wrote the *Story of an African Farm* before she was twenty, and brought it to England for publication. It appeared, under the pseudonym of "Ralph Iron," in 1883; and none suspected that its drastic Rationalism was written by a woman. It is an autobiographical account of the way in which she reacted on her sombre Calvinistic environment and became an Atheist (see pp. 127, 285, etc.). The story was followed by *Dreams* in 1891, and three years later she married Mr. S. C. Cronwright.

As Mrs. Cronwright-Schreiner she has published *Trooper Peter Halket* (1897), *Woman and Labour* (1911), and other works; but her fame rests chiefly on the work of her youth. Mrs. Cronwright-Schreiner's rejection of all religion is partly based on an intense human idealism. "I have seen her," says Edward Carpenter, "shake her little fist at the Lord in heaven, and curse him down from his throne" (*My Days and Dreams*, p. 229). She has taken a very progressive and humane part in the difficult questions of South African life.

SIMCOX, Edith, writer. *B.* 1844. Miss Simcox contributed a Rationalistic volume, *Natural Law* (1877), to "The English and Foreign Philosophical Library." She traced the natural evolution of man and his ideas. She had, under the pseudonym "H. Lawrenny," previously criticized Theistic arguments in the *Fortnightly Review* (1872). Later she published *Episodes in the Lives of Men, Women, and Lovers* (1882) and *Primitive Civilizations* (2 vols., 1894—a substantial work on anthropology). *D.* 1901.

SMITH, Katie Kehm, *B.* 1868. Born in Warsaw, Illinois, she started teaching at seventeen, after graduating from high school in Ottumwa, Iowa. She was a freethinker by sixteen, and began lecturing soon after to turn people's attention from their "souls" to their bodies, encountering flak as a teacher from religionists. She eventually served as secretary of the Oregon State Secular Union. In 1891 she married the supportive Hon. D. W. Smith of Port Townsend, Washington. A freethought lecturer in Oregon, she organized the First Secular Church in Portland in 1893, attracting a congregation of hundreds, also inaugurating the Portland Secular Sunday-school, which sparked similar activities, including the Silverton Secular circuit. She sent regular reports on these proceedings to *The Truth Seeker*. A typical account, "The Cause in Oregon," ran in the April 20, 1895 issue, noting "It is amusing to note how astonished they are that 'Infidels' can have Sunday-schools. . . One of the pious Christians of Silverton inquired of another what we do there. The answer was, 'Why, they do almost everything; they even stand on their heads!' . . ."

After her untimely death, the secular church and Sunday school were conducted by **Mrs. Nettie A. Olds**. Olds wrote *The Truth Seeker* (January 26, 1895): "Secularism must be built upon the social plain . . . . enlist the young in our ranks, and the Christian churches will be compelled to go out of business for want of converts." The Portland group may have popularized observance of the Winter Solstice, which Olds advocated. Another, later promoter of secular Sunday Schools was **Eliza Mowry Bliven,** First Secretary, Materialist Association, Brooklyn, Connecticut, a freethinker and suffragist who wrote in *The Truth Seeker* (September 9, 1911): "Just as long as the priests and preachers have entire control of all Sunday meetings and of all marriages and funerals, the women must remain ignorant and church-bound slaves of superstition, and start all the children in the same beliefs and follies." *D.* 1895—*ALG*

SOMERVILLE, Mary, writer. *B.* 1780. Daughter of Vice-Admiral Sir W. G. Fairfax, she made a thorough study of mathematics and Latin, and early attracted attention by her ability. In 1804 she married Captain Greig, who died three years later, and she then married Dr. W. Somerville. In 1816 they moved to London, and Mrs. Somerville soon had a brilliant circle of admirers. The leading statesmen and men of science in London sought her society, and she was esteemed one of the most charming and most cultivated women of her time. In 1827 she wrote a work on astronomy for the Society for the Diffusion of Useful Knowledge, and it brought her such repute that the Royal Society ordered a bust of her, by Chantrey, to be placed in its hall. In her *Connection of the Physical Sciences* (1834) she pointed out that the perturbations of Uranus probably implied the existence of an outer planet, and this hint led the Cambridge astronomers to look for it and discover Neptune. In 1848 she published her *Physical Geography*. She was elected an honorary member of the Royal Astronomical Society; and she received the gold medal of the Royal Geographical Society (1869) and the gold medal of the Italian Royal Geographical Society. Somerville Hall and the Mary Somerville Scholarship at Oxford perpetuate her memory. Her daughter wrote a kind of biography of her (*Personal Recollections*, 1873), in which she grudgingly admits that Mrs. Somerville was a Rationalistic Theist (pp. 374–76). She discarded Church doctrines at an early age, refused to admit miracles, and took the side of science in the struggle against *Genesis*. On one occasion she was "publicly censured by name from the pulpit of York Cathedral." *D.* Nov. 29, 1872.

STAËL-HOLSTEIN, the Baroness Anne Louise Germaine de ("Mme. de Staël"), French writer. *B.* Apr. 22, 1766. *Ed.* by mother. Her mother, a Protestant Swiss, brought her up in the strictest orthodoxy, but her father, the famous French Minister of Finance, Necker, was more liberal, and in the circle of his friends she soon outgrew the narrow piety imposed on her. She was very clever, and wrote political essays at the age of fifteen. In 1786 she married the Swedish Ambassador, the Baron de Staël. The marriage was not fortunate, and they separated in 1796; but Mme. de Staël returned to take care of him in his last illness (1798–1802). In 1786 she produced a drama (*Sophie*) which opened for her a period of long and fertile literary activity. She studied and followed Rousseau, though the course of the Revolution chilled her democratic ardour. In 1792 she left Paris for five years. Napoleon again drove her into exile, and she travelled in Germany and Italy, producing her long autobiographical novel *Delphine* (4 vols.) in 1802. In Germany she modified her earlier Voltairean attitude, and took up the study of philosophy, but she never returned to Christianity. Chateaubriand said: "My rage is to see Jesus Christ everywhere: Mme. de Staël's is perfectibility." The American envoy J. Q. Adams, who knew her in Paris, says, in a letter to his mother in Nov., 1812: "She spoke much about the preservation of religion, in which, she gave me to understand, she did not herself believe" (*Proceedings of the American Antiquarian Society*, vol. xxiii, 1913, letter dated Nov. 22, 1812). *D.* July 14, 1817.

TAYLOR, Helen, reformer. *B.* July 27, 1831. *Ed.* privately. In 1851 her mother married J. S. Mill. She died seven years later, and Miss Taylor devoted herself to the care of her stepfather and was greatly esteemed by him. She co-operated with him in writing his *Subjection of Women* (1869). After Mill's death she lived mainly in London, and led a very active and useful life. She edited Buckle's works (1872), and Mill's *Autobiography* (1873) and *Essays on Religion* (1874). In 1876, and again in 1879 and 1882, she was elected to the London School Board. Miss Taylor was conspicuous as a friend of the poor children of London. She worked for the abolition of school-fees and the provision of free food and boots for the children of the poorer workers, and exposed many scandals in industrial schools. At her own expense she provided dinners and boots for a large number of children. She worked also for land nationalization and the enfranchisement of women. In 1885 she offered herself at North Camberwell as a Parliamentary candidate, but her nomination paper was rejected. The later years of her life were spent at Avignon. *D.* Jan. 29, 1907.

UNDERWOOD, Sara A., wrote *Heroines of Freethought*, a 327-page book published by Charles P. Somerby in New York in 1876. This book offers a biography, with special emphasis on freethought views, of eleven women: Madame Roland, Mary Wollstonecraft Godwin, Mary W. Godwin Shelley, George Sand (A. L. Aurore Dudevant), Harriet Martineau, Frances Wright D'Arusmont, Emma Martin, Margaret Reynolds Chapplesmith, Ernestine L. Rose, Frances Power Cobbe and George Eliot (Marian Evans Lewes). Some were Deists. Underwood suffers the fate of many biographers—little is known about *her*. Underwood's Preface to *Heroines of Freethought* reads:

"The word Freethinker in times past has implied a censure of the person so designated, and especially if the one so called chanced to be a woman. But, in spite of this fact, here and there in the history of Freethought has appeared a woman strong enough of heart and brain to understand and accept Liberal truths, and brave enough to avow publicly her faith in the 'belief of the unbelievers.' Among these courageous souls we find the names of some of the most brilliant lights of feminine literature. The Orthodox world could not well afford to reject their valuable contributions to the pleasure and well-being of society, but in accepting them did so with an ungracious protest against the religious conclusions of these daring Thinkers."—*ALG*

WATTS Kate Eunice, wife of Charles Watts (who was born in 1835) was author of the pamphlets "The Education and Position of Woman," and "Reasons for Not Accepting Christianity." She was an amateur actress, speaker and well-known freethinker in Great Britain.—*ALG*

Appendix

Pastoral Letter of the General Association of Massachusetts (Orthodox) to the Churches under their care, 1837

This extract of a letter distributed by the Congregationalists of Massachusetts condemning public speaking by American women originally appeared in the History of Woman Suffrage, Volume I, pp. 81–82. The exclamations in parentheses belong to the editors of History of Woman Suffrage. The editors of this volume received the extract from William Lloyd Garrison, who originally and indignantly published it in his periodical The Liberator. According to Garrison, it was written by Rev. Dr. Nehemiah Adams of Boston.

We invite your attention to the dangers which at present seem to threaten the female character with wide-spread and permanent injury.

The appropriate duties and influence of woman are clearly stated in the New Testament. Those duties and that influence are unobtrusive and private, but the source of mighty power. When the mild, dependent, softening influence of woman upon the sternness of man's opinions is fully exercised, society feels the effects of it in a thousand forms. The power of woman is her dependence, flowing from the consciousness of that weakness which God has given her for her protection, (!) and which keeps her in those departments of life that form the character of individuals, and of the nation. There are social influences which females use in promoting piety and the great objects of Christian benevolence which we can not too highly commend.

We appreciate the unostentatious prayers and efforts of woman in advancing the cause of religion at home and abroad; in Sabbath-schools; in leading religious inquirers to the pastors (!) for instruction; and in all such associated effort as becomes the modesty of her sex; and earnestly hope that she may abound more and more in these labors of piety and love. But when she assumes the place and tone of man as a public reformer, our care and protection of her seem unnecessary; we put ourselves in self-defense (!) against her; she yields the power which God has given her for her protection, and her character becomes unnatural. If the vine, whose strength and beauty is to lean upon the trellis-work, and half conceal its clusters, thinks to assume the independence and the overshadowing nature of the elm, it will not only cease to bear fruit, but fall in shame and dishonor into the dust. We can not, therefore, but regret the mistaken conduct of those who encourage females to bear an obtrusive and ostentatious part in measures of reform, and countenance any of that sex who so far forget themselves as to itinerate in the character of public lecturers and teachers. We especially deplore the intimate acquaintance and promiscuous conversation of females with regard to things which ought not to be named; by which that modesty and delicacy which is the charm of domestic life, and which constitutes the true influence of woman in society, is consumed, and the way opened, as we apprehend, for degeneracy and ruin.

We say these things not to discourage proper influences against sin, but to secure such reformation (!) as we believe is Scriptural, and will be permanent.

Ingersoll's Letter Supporting the Woman's National Liberal League

Marietta M. Bones of Webster, South Dakota, sent America's most influential freethinker, Robert G. Ingersoll, a copy of the resolutions adopted by the National Woman's Liberal League in February 1890. Following a scurrilous attack of its author Matilda Joslyn Gage by a male leader of the American Secular Union, Bones sought damage control in winning Ingersoll's endorsement. The June 7, 1890 Truth Seeker reprinted Ingersoll's reply:

New York, April 25 1890.

Mrs. Marietta M. Bones
Webster, S.D.

My Dear Madam:
Accept my thanks for your letter of the 25th of March, endorsing the resolutions passed by the Woman's National Liberal Union, at Washington, D.C. I agree most heartily with the first resolution—that it is essential to the life of the republic that the purely civil character of the government be maintained. I also agree with the second resolution. I am perfectly satisfied that if they ever succeed in getting God into the Constitution, there will be no room left for the folks. So the fourth resolution meets with my approval. I am hardly sure that I am for all of the fifth. I do want to see power centralized to that extent, in the general government, that it can protect all the citizens of the republic, and protect them in whatever state they may happen to be. The sixth is undoubtedly right. No one should be paid for guessing in the public schools. Teachers should be called teachers, because they teach what they know, and what some other person can learn. The seventh is a self-evident proposition. The eighth is absolutely true. The church has taught to women only the slave virtues. Women have always been crawling on the floor of the sanctuary, eating the dust of the temple, and it gave me the greatest pleasure to know that a few women, at least, had outgrown the priest slavery. I have said a great many times, and I say again, that the parasite of the woman is the priest. So the ninth resolution contains a good, wholesome truth. Every church is the enemy of liberty—always has been and always will be

as long as it is orthodox. Woman has been the slave of the church, and not only the slave of the church but the supporter of the church—the carystides beneath the altar are women. So the tenth resolution is historically true. Nothing can be more absurd than the fall of man through the temptation of woman; nothing more idiotic than the doctrine of the atonement, and anything more absurd or immoral than the idea that an innocent man can suffer for the guilty and in that way make the guilty innocent. The eleventh resolution is all right, and is exactly to the point. Nothing is right or wrong by reason of a declaration. A thing is right or wrong according to its consequences, as these consequences exist in the nature of things. Right and wrong do not depend upon authority. We ascertain them by experience—but they exist independently of all authority—in the nature of things. Your last resolution is good, but I like the word "happiness" better. I seek happiness, come whence it may. I deem nothing so beautiful as happiness. No religion can excel happiness. But the last quotation, from Lucretia Mott, "Truth for authority, not authority for truth," is splendid. All I can say, my dear madam, is that I wish you and your Liberal Union the greatest possible success. We never shall have a great generation of men until there has been a generation of great women. When babes sit in the lap of philosophy there will be hope for the world.

I am, with great respect,

Yours sincerely,

R.G. Ingersoll

Eugenics Defined, 1910

Freethinker Moses Harman, who championed women's right to control their own bodies and was convicted twice for obscenity under the Comstock Act, was editor of Lucifer the Light-Bearer, which then became The American Journal of Eugenics, for thirty years. Since the word "eugenics" has an ominous sound today, it is instructive to read the definition of eugenics appearing in every issue:

The Century Dictionary thus defines Eugenics:

The doctrine of Progress, or Evolution, especially in the human race, through improved conditions in the relations of the sexes.

Its central thought is Natural Selection through Freedom of Motherhood, the Self-ownership of Woman in the Realm of Sex and Reproduction—Intelligent and Responsible Parenthood; Woman First, Man Second.

This much neglected, this tabooed, disgraced, and almost unknown Science was named "Eugenics" by Francis Galton, cousin of, and co-worker with, the great Charles Darwin; and now, both in England and in Continental Europe, is beginning to receive the attention its importance demands.

BIBLIOGRAPHY

* Asterisk in front of listing indicates this was the source of the essay or excerpt reprinted in this anthology.

Introduction

Augur, Helen, *An American Jezebel: The Life of Anne Hutchinson*, Brentano's, 1930

Lerner, Gerda, *The Grimké Sisters from South Carolina: Pioneers for Woman's Rights and Abolition*, Schocken Books, 1967

Flexner, Eleanor, *Century of Struggle: The Woman's Rights Movement in the United States*, 1959, reprinted Atheneum, 1968

Gaylor, Annie Laurie, *Woe to the Women—The Bible Tells Me So*, Freedom From Religion Foundation, 1981, Fourth edition 1988

Grimké, Sarah, (Bartlett, Elizabeth Ann, Ed.), *Letters on the Equality of the Sexes*, Yale University Press, 1988

Stanton, Elizabeth Cady, Anthony, Susan B., Gage, Matilda Joslyn, Eds., *The History of Woman Suffrage, I–III* (1881, Susan B. Anthony, Publisher), reprint, Source Book Press, 1971

Sterling, Dorothy, *Ahead of Her Time: Abby Kelley and the Politics of Antislavery*, W.W. Norton & Co., 1991

Mary Wollstonecraft (Chapter 1)

Flexner, Eleanor, *Mary Wollstonecraft, A Biography*, Coward, McCann & Geoghegan, Inc., 1972

Jones, Louis Worth, "The First Feminist Was A Freethinker," *Freethought Today*, December 1987. (Also pamphlet, "What Mary Wollstonecraft Wrote: 180 Quotations," 1984)

Solomon, Barbara H., and Berggren, Paula S., Eds., *A Mary Wollstonecraft Reader, Edited, with an Introduction and Notes*, New American Library, Times Mirror, 1983

Sunsten, Emily W., *A Different Face: The Life of Mary Wollstonecraft*, Harper & Row, 1975

*Wollstonecraft, Mary; Tomaselli, Sylvana, Ed., *A Vindication of the Rights of Men* and *A Vindication of the Rights of Woman, and Hints*, Cambridge University Press, 1995

Wollstonecraft, *A Vindication of the Rights of Woman*, Introduction by Charles W. Hagelman, Jr., W. W. Norton & Co., 1967

Anne Royall (Chapter 2)

Jackson, George Stuyvesant, *Anne Royall: Uncommon Scold*, Bruce Humphries, Inc., 1937

James, Bessie Rowland, *Anne Royall's U.S.A.*, Rutgers University Press, 1972

James, Edward T., Ed. (with James, Janet Wilson, & Boyer, Paul S.), *Notable American Women: 1607–1950: A Biographical Dictionary, Vol. III*, Belknap Press of Harvard University Press, 1971

Porter, Sarah Harvey, *The Life and Times of Anne Royall*, Torch Press Book Shop, 1909

*Royall, Anne, *The Black Book*, Vols. I–III, published by author, 1828–1829
Royall, Anne, *Letters from Alabama 1817–1822*, 1830, reprinted University of Alabama Press, 1969 (with Lucille Griffith)

Frances Wright (Chapter 3)

Eckhardt, Celia Morris, *Fanny Wright: Rebel in America*, Harvard University Press, 1984
Lane, Margaret, *Frances Wright and the 'Great Experiment,'* Manchester University Press, 1972
Rossi, Alice S., *The Feminist Papers*, Northeastern University Press, 1973 (1988 edition)
Stanton, Elizabeth Cady, Anthony, Susan B., Gage, Matilda Joslyn, *History of Woman Suffrage I, II*, Susan B. Anthony, Publisher, Second Edition 1889
Wright (D'Arusmont), Frances, *Life Letters and Lectures*, Arno Press, 1972 Reprint

Harriet Martineau (Chapter 4)

Martineau, Harriet, *Autobiography*, edited by Maria Weston Chapman, James R. Osgood and Company, Boston, 1877, Vols. I, II
Underwood, Sara A., *Heroines of Freethought*, Charles P. Somerby, 1876

Lydia Maria Child (Chapter 5)

Child, L. Maria, *The Progress of Religious Ideas Through Successive Ages*, Vols., I–III, James Miller, Publisher, 1855
Clifford, Deborah Pickman, *Crusader for Freedom: A Life of Lydia Maria Child*, Beacon Press, 1992
James, Edward T., Ed. (with James, Janet Wilson, & Boyer, Paul S.), *Notable American Women: 1607–1950: A Biographical Dictionary, Vol. I.*, Belknap Press of Harvard University Press, 1971

Ernestine L. Rose (Chapter 6)

Barnard, L. E., "Ernestine L. Rose," a sketch, *History of Woman Suffrage* I: 95–98
D'Hericourt, Jenny P., "Ernestine L. Rose," *The Revolution*, p. 171, date unknown, reprinted from *Agitator*, June 25, 1869
DuBois, Ellen Carol, Ed., *Elizabeth Cady Stanton, Susan B. Anthony: Correspondence, Writings, Speeches*, Schocken Books, 1981
Piercy, Blodwen, "Ernestine Rose," *Humanist in Canada*, Winter 1995/96
Stanton, Elizabeth Cady, Anthony, Susan B., Gage, Matilda Joslyn, Eds., *The History of Woman Suffrage, I–III* (1881, Susan B. Anthony, Publisher), reprint, Source Book Press, 1971
*Rose, Ernestine, "A Defense of Atheism: Being a lecture delivered in Mercantile Hall, Boston, April 10, 1861 [microfilm], 3rd ed., Boston, J.P. Mendum, 1889
Stein, Gordon, "Ernestine L. Rose," *The American Rationalist*, Nov.–Dec. 1993
Suhl, Yuri, *Ernestine L. Rose: Women's Rights Pioneer*, second edition, Biblio Press, 1990 (originally *Ernestine L. Rose and the Battle for Human Rights*, Reynal & Co., 1959). *This excellent biography was not footnoted. Unless another source is indicated for quotes and particulars by and about Rose, the Suhl biography is my source.*

Margaret Fuller (Chapter 7)

*Chevigny, Bell Gale, Ed., *The Woman and the Myth: Margaret Fuller's Life and Writings*, The Feminist Press, 1976

James, Edward T., Ed. (with James, Janet Wilson & Boyer, Paul S.), *Notable American Women: 1607–1950: A Biographical Dictionary, Vol. I.*, Belknap Press of Harvard University Press, 1971

Wade, Mason, Ed., *The Writings of Margaret Fuller*, Augustus M. Kelley, Publishers, 1941, reprinted 1973

Emma Martin (Chapter 8)

Underwood, Sara A., *Heroines of Freethought*, Charles P. Somerby, 1876

Elizabeth Cady Stanton (Chapters 9 and 10)

Anthony, Susan B., & Harper, Ida Husted, *The History of Woman Suffrage IV*, Susan B. Anthony, Publisher, 1902

Buhle, Mary Jo and Paul, Eds., The *Concise History of Woman Suffrage: Selections from the Classic Work of Stanton, Anthony, Gage, and Harper*, University of Illinois Press, 1978

DuBois, Ellen Carol, Ed., *Elizabeth Cady Stanton, Susan B. Anthony: Correspondence, Writings, Speeches*, Schocken Books, 1981

Griffin, Elisabeth, *In Her Own Right: The Life of Elizabeth Cady Stanton*, Oxford University Press, 1984

Harper, Ida Husted, *The History of Woman Suffrage V, VI*, National American Woman Suffrage Association, 1922

*Holland, Patricia G., and Gordon, Ann D., Eds., *Papers of Elizabeth Cady Stanton and Susan B. Anthony*, Wilmington, DE, Scholarly Resources Inc., 1991, microfilm

*Library of Congress, *Papers of Elizabeth Cady Stanton*, microfilm

Lutz, Alma, *Created Equal*, Van Rees Press, 1940

Pellauer, Mary D., *Toward A Tradition of Feminist Theology: The Religious Social Thought of Elizabeth Cady Stanton, Susan B. Anthony, and Anna Howard Shaw*, Carlson Publishing Inc., 1991

Stanton, Elizabeth Cady, *Eighty Years and More: Reminiscences 1815–1897*, 1898, reprint, Schocken Books, 1971

Stanton, Elizabeth Cady, Anthony, Susan B., Gage, Matilda Joslyn, Eds., *The History of Woman Suffrage, I–III* (1881, Susan B. Anthony, Publisher), reprint, Source Book Press, 1971

*Stanton, Elizabeth Cady, Ed., *The Woman's Bible Parts I and II*, 1895, 1898, reprint, Arno Press Inc, 1971

Stanton, Theodore & Blatch, Harriot Stanton, *Elizabeth Cady Stanton As Revealed In Her Letters, Diary and Reminiscences*, Harper & Brothers Publishers, 1922

Waggenspack, Beth M., *The Search for Self-Sovereignty: The Oratory of Elizabeth Cady Stanton*, Greenwood Press, Inc., 1989

Wakefield, Eva Ingersoll, Ed., *The Letters of Robert Ingersoll*, Philosophical Library, 1941

Lucy N. Colman (Chapter 11)

*Colman, Lucy N., "Reminiscences," *The Truth Seeker*, Jan. 29, Feb. 19, March 5, March, 12, April 23, 1887

Putnam, Samuel P., *400 Years of Freethought*, The Truth Seeker Company, 1894

Marian Evans ("George Eliot") (Chapter 12)

*Eliot, George, *Essays of George Eliot*, (edited by Thomas Pinney), Routledge and Kegan Paul, 1963
Pinion, F.B., Ed., *A George Eliot Miscellany*, Macmillan Press, 1982

Susan B. Anthony (Chapter 13)

*Anthony, Susan B., "Miss Anthony on the Religious Press," *The Woman's Tribune*, Saturday, June 17, 1893, Clara Bewick Colby, Ed.
Anthony, Susan B., & Harper, Ida Hustad, *The History of Woman Suffrage IV*, 1902, Susan B. Anthony Publisher
DuBois, Ellen Carol, Ed., *Elizabeth Cady Stanton, Susan B. Anthony: Correspondence, Writings, Speeches*, Schocken Books, 1981
Lutz, Alma, *Created Equal*, Van Rees Press, 1940
Harper, Ida Husted, *The History of Woman Suffrage V, VI*, National American Woman Suffrage Association, 1922
Harper, Ida Husted, *The Life and Work of Susan B. Anthony, Vol. I & II*, 1898, *Vol. III*, 1908, Hollenbeck Press
Holland, Patricia G., and Gordon, Ann D., Eds., *Papers of Elizabeth Cady Stanton and Susan B. Anthony*, Wilmington, DE, Scholarly Resources Inc., 1991, microfilm
Pellauer, Mary D., *Toward A Tradition of Feminist Theology: The Religious Social Thought of Elizabeth Cady Stanton, Susan B. Anthony, and Anna Howard Shaw*, Carlson Publishing Inc., 1991
Sherr, Lynn, *Failure Is Impossible: Susan B. Anthony in Her Own Words*, Times Books, Random House, 1995. *Contains excellent chapter on her nonreligious views.*
Stanton, Elizabeth Cady, *Eighty Years and More: Reminiscences 1815–1897*, 1898, reprint, Schocken Books, 1971
Stanton, Elizabeth Cady, Anthony, Susan B., Gage, Matilda Joslyn, Eds., *The History of Woman Suffrage, I–III* (1881, Susan B. Anthony, Publisher), reprint, Source Book Press, 1971
*Stanton, Elizabeth Cady, Ed., *The Woman's Bible Parts I and II*, 1895, 1898, reprint, Arno Press Inc, 1971

Ella E. Gibson (Chapter 14)

MacDonald, E.M., *Fifty Years of Freethought: Story of the Truth Seeker from 1875*, Vol. I, Truth Seeker Co., 1929, Vol. II, 1931
Putnam, Samuel P., *Four Hundred Years of Freethought*, The Truth Seeker Company, 1894

Matilda Joslyn Gage (Chapter 15)

Craddock, Ida C., "The Coming Convention of Liberal Women, *The Truth Seeker*, Feb. 1, 1890
Ingersoll, Robert G., Letter to Mrs. Marietta M. Bones (April 25, 1890), *The Truth Seeker*, June 7, 1890
*Gage, Matilda Joslyn, *Woman, Church & State*, 1893, reprint with Introduction by Sally Roesch Wagner, Persephone Press, 1993

James, Edward T., Ed. (with James, Janet Wilson & Boyer, Paul S.), *Notable American Women: 1607–1950: A Biographical Dictionary, Vol. I*, Belknap Press of Harvard University Press, 1971

Kirkley, Evelyn Anne, *"The Female Peril": The construction of gender in American Freethought, 1865–1915*, [dissertation], Duke University, 1993

Porter, Lois K., "Matilda Joslyn Gage: Feminist and Secular Humanist," *Free Inquiry*, Winter 1993–1994

Stanton, Elizabeth Cady, Anthony, Susan B., Gage, Matilda Joslyn, Eds., *The History of Woman Suffrage, I–III* (1881, Susan B. Anthony, Publisher), reprint, Source Book Press, 1971

The Truth Seeker, "A New Women's Association," unsigned, Jan. 11, 1890

The Truth Seeker, "Comstock after Big Game," Sept. 1, 1894

White, Mary A., "Woman at the Fore," *The Truth Seeker*, January 25, 1890

Willard, Frances E., & Livermore, Mary A., eds., *A Woman of the Century: Fourteen Hundred-Seventy Biographical Sketches Accompanied by Portraits of Leading American Women In All Walks of Life*, Charles Wells Moulton, 1893.

Lois Waisbrooker (Chapter 16)

Sears, Hal D., *The Sex Radicals: Free Love in High Victorian America*, Regents Press of Kansas, 1977

Waisbrooker, *A Sex Revolution*, Introduction by Pam McAllister, New Society Publishers, 1984

Elmina Drake Slenker (Chapter 17)

Colman, Lucy N., "Mrs. Slenker's Arrest an Outrage," *The Truth Seeker*, May 21, 1887

Edward W. Chamberlain, "The Trial of Mrs. Slenker," *The Truth Seeker*, Nov. 12, 1887

Sears, Hal D., *The Sex Radicals: Free Love in High Victorian America*, The Regents Press of Kansas, 1977

Slenker, Elmina D., "Mrs. Slenker in Her Own Defense," *The Truth Seeker*, May 14, 1887

Slenker, Elmina D., "Mrs. Slenker at Home," *The Truth Seeker*, May 21, 1887

The Truth Seeker, May 14, 1887; "The Trial of Mrs. Slenker" (transcript), Nov. 19, 1887

*Slenker, Elmina D., *Studying the Bible*, J.P. Mendum, Boston, 1870

Lillie Devereux Blake (Chapter 18)

Blake, Katherine Devereux and Wallace, Margaret Louise, *Champion of Women: The Life of Lillie Devereux Blake*, Fleming H. Revell Co., 1943

*Blake, Lillie Devereux, *Woman's Place To-Day*, John W. Lovell Co., 1883

James, Edward T., Ed. (with James, Janet Wilson & Boyer, Paul S.), *Notable American Women: 1607–1950: A Biographical Dictionary, Vol. I*, Belknap Press of Harvard University, 1971

Ouida (Louisa de la Ramée) (Chapter 19)

Bigland, Eileen, *Ouida: The Passionate Victorian*, Jarrolds Publishers, 1950

*Ouida, *Views and Opinions*, Methuen & Co., 1895

Marilla Ricker (Chapter 20)

James, Edward T., Ed. (with James, Janet Wilson & Boyer, Paul S.), *Notable American Women: 1607–1950: A Biographical Dictionary, Vol. III*, Belknap Press of Harvard University Press, 1971
Ricker, Marilla M., *The Four Gospels*, Roycrofters, 1911
*Ricker, Marilla M., *I Am Not Afraid Are You?* Roycrofters, 1917
Ricker, Marilla M., *I Don't Know Do you?* Roycrofters, 1916

Annie Besant (Chapter 21)

Arnstein, Walter L., *Atheism, Sex and Politics Among the Late Victorians*, University of Missouri Press, 1965, 1983 Oxford University Press
Besant, Annie, *An Autobiography*, Theosophical Publishing Society, Third Edition 1910
Besant, Annie, *Autobiographical Sketches*, Freethought Publishing Co., 1885
Besant, Annie, *The Christian Creed Or, What it is Blasphemy to deny*, Freethought Publishing Co., 1883
Besant, Annie, John Saville, Ed., *Selection of Social and Political Pamphlets of Annie Besant*, Augustus M. Kelley Publishers, 1970. *Contains nothing on religion.*
Besant, Annie, *The Teachings of Christianity: A Debate Between Annie Besant and the Rev. G. F. Handel Rowe, of Halifax.*
Manvell, Roger, *The Trial of Annie Besant and Charles Bradlaugh*, Elek Books Ltd., Great Britain, 1976
Nethercot, Arthur H., *The First Five Lives of Annie Besant*, University of Chicago Press, 1960
Nethercot, Arthur H., *The Last Four Lives of Annie Besant*, University of Chicago Press, 1963
Stanton, Theodore & Blatch, Harriot Stanton, *Elizabeth Cady Stanton As Revealed In Her Letters, Diary and Reminiscences*, Harper & Brothers Publishers, 1922

Susan H. Wixon (Chapter 22)

Putnam, Samuel P., *Four Hundred Years of Freethought*, The Truth Seeker Company, 1894
Willard, Frances E., & Livermore, Mary A., eds., *A Woman of the Century: Fourteen Hundred-Seventy Biographical Sketches Accompanied by Portraits of Leading American Women In All Walks of Life*, Charles Wells Moulton, 1893.

Ella Wheeler Wilcox (Chapter 23)

Ballou, Jenny, *Period Piece: Ella Wheeler Wilcox & Her Times*, Houghton Mifflin Co., 1940
James, Edward T., Ed, (with James, Janet Wilson & Boyer, Paul S.), *Notable American Women: 1607–1950: A Biographical Dictionary, Vol. III*, Belknap Press Of Harvard University Press, 1971
* Wilcox, Ella Wheeler, *Poems of Power*, Albert Whitman & Co., 1901
Wilcox, Ella Wheeler, *The Worlds and I*, 1918, Arno Press reprint, 1980

Helen Hamilton Gardener (Chapter 24)

James, Edward T., Ed. (with James, Janet Wilson & Boyer, Paul S.), *Notable American Women: 1607–1950: A Biographical Dictionary, Vol. II*, Belknap Press of Harvard University Press, 1971

*Gardener, Helen, *Woman, Man & the Gods: And other Lectures*, Belford, Clarke & Co., 1885

New York Times, "Leader in Suffrage Cause: Author of Many Works on Social and Ethical Reform and a Student of Craniology," dateline July 26, 1925; "Cremation Report Denied: Was Sent to Cornell. University Authorities Have Not Yet Received the Brain, But Are Expecting It," dateline Aug. 4, 1925; and "Brain of Mrs. Gardner [sic] is studied at Cornell: Dr. Papaz Finds It Equal in Weight to That of Dr. Burt G. Wilder," dateline Sept. 2, 1925

Willard, Frances E., & Livermore, Mary A., eds., *A Woman of the Century: Fourteen Hundred-Seventy Biographical Sketches Accompanied by Portraits of Leading American Women In All Walks of Life*, Charles Wells Moulton, 1893.

Putnam, Samuel P. *Four Hundred Years of Freethought*, The Truth Seeker Company, 1894

Dietrick, Ellen Battelle (Chapter 25)

Anthony, Susan B., & Harper, Ida Hustad, *The History of Woman Suffrage IV*, 1902, Susan B. Anthony, Publisher

*Dietrick, Ellen Battelle, *Women in the Early Christian Church Ministry: A Reply to Bishop Doane, and Others*, Alfred J. Ferris, Philadelphia, 1897

McElroy, Wendy, *Freedom, Feminism, and the State: an overview of individualist feminism*, Cato Institute, 1982. *Contains Dietrick's essay: "Cardinal Gibbons' Ignorance."*

Josephine K. Henry (Chapter 26)

Dew, Aloma Williams, "Josephine W. Henry: She was an early advocate of women's rights in Kentucky," *Courier Journal (Louisville)*, August 20, 1995

*Henry, Josephine K., *Woman and the Bible*, Versailles, Ky., 1905

Putnam, Samuel P., *Four Hundred Years of Freethought*, The Truth Seeker Company, 1894

Stanton, Elizabeth Cady, Ed., *The Woman's Bible Parts I and II*, 1895, 1898, reprint, Arno Press Inc, 1971

Etta Semple (Chapter 27)

James J., "Iconoclast outraged Kansas," *Kansas City Times*, July 10, 1987

*Gaylor, Annie Laurie, "Etta Semple: A Woman Of Mystery," *Freethought Today*, April/May 1985

Lambertson, John Mark, "An Ottawa Pioneer With A Touch of Infamy," *Ottawa Herald*, September 25, 26, 1987

Semple, Etta, "A Pious Congressman Twice Answered," *The Truth Seeker*, Feb. 23, 1895

MacDonald, E.M., *Fifty Years of Freethought: Story of the Truth Seeker from 1875*, Vol. II, Truth Seeker Co., 1931

Whitehead, Fred, & Verle, Muhrer, *Freethought on the American Frontier*, Prometheus Books, 1992

Bonner, Hypatia Bradlaugh (Chapter 28)

*Bonner, Arthur & Bonner, Charles Bradlaugh, *Hypatia Bradlaugh Bonner: The Story of Her Life*, Watts & Co., 1942

Bonner, Hypatia Bradlaugh, *Charles Bradlaugh: His Life and Work*, Vol. I, T. Fisher Unwin, 1894

*Bonner, Hypatia Bradlaugh, *Christianity & Conduct, Or the Influence of Religious Beliefs on Morals*, Watts & Co., 1919

Bonner, Hypatia Bradlaugh, *The Christian Hell: From the First to the Twentieth Century*, Watts & Co., 1913

Bonner, Hypatia Bradlaugh, *Penalties Upon Opinion: Or Some Records of the Laws of Heresy and Blasphemy*, Watts & Co., 1934

Charlotte Perkins Gilman (Chapter 29)

Anthony, Susan B., Harper, Ida Husted, Eds., *History of Woman Suffrage, Vol. IV*, Susan B. Anthony Publisher, 1902

Gilman, Charlotte Perkins, *The Home: Its Work and Influence* (1903), University of Illinois Press, 1972

Gilman, Charlotte Perkins, *The Living of Charlotte Perkins Gilman*, D. Appleton-Century Co., 1935

*Gilman, Charlotte Perkins, *His Religion And Hers: A Study of the Faith of Our Fathers and the Work of our Mothers*, Century Co., 1923

Nies, Judith, *Seven Women: Portraits from the American Radical Tradition*, 1979, reprinted Penguin Books, 1986

Stetson, Charlotte Perkins, *In This Our World*, 1893, reprinted 1899 University Press: Small, Maynard & Co.

Voltairine de Cleyre (Chapter 30)

Avrich, Paul, *An American Anarchist: The Life of Voltairine de Cleyre*, Princeton University Press, 1978

Baase, Sara, "Anarchist without Adjectives," *Truth Seeker*, Vol. 120, No. 5, 1993

*Berkman, Alexander, Ed., *The Selected Works of Voltairine de Cleyre*, Mother Earth Publishing Association, 1914

*De Cleyre, Voltairine, "The Case of Woman vs. Orthodoxy," *The Boston Investigator*, Saturday, Sept. 19, 1896

De Cleyre, Voltairine, "The Economic Tendency of Freethought," *Liberty*, Boston, Mass., Vol. XI, No. 25, Feb. 15, 1890

Goldman, Emma, *Living My Life*, 1931, reprinted in one volume by The New American Library, Inc., 1977

McElroy, Wendy, Ed., *Freedom, Feminism, and the State: an overview of individualist feminism*, Cato Institute, 1982

Sears, Hal D., *The Sex Radicals: Free Love in High Victorian America*, Regents Press of Kansas, 1977

Emma Goldman (Chapter 31)

Goldman, Emma, *Living My Life*, 1931, reprinted in one volume by The New American Library, Inc., 1977

Drinnon, Richard, *Rebel in Paradise: A Biography of Emma Goldman*, University of Chicago Press, 1961

*Shulman, Alix Kates, *Red Emma Speaks: An Emma Goldman Reader*, Schocken Books, 1983

Zona Gale (Chapter 32)

Derleth, August, *Still Small Voice: The Biography of Zona Gale*, D. Appleton-Century Co., 1940
*Gale, Zona, *When I Was a Little Girl*, MacMillan Co., 1915
James, Edward T., Ed. (with James, Janet Wilson & Boyer, Paul S.), *Notable American Women: 1607–1950: A Biographical Dictionary, Vol. II*, Belknap Press of Harvard University Press, 1971

Margaret Sanger (Chapter 33)

Baskin, Alex, ed., *Margaret Sanger, The Woman Rebel, and the Rise of the Birth Control Movement in the United States*, State University of New York at Stony Brook, 1976
Sicherman, Barbara & Green, Carol Hurd, Eds., *Notable American Women: The Modern Period*, Belknap Press of Harvard University Press, 1980 *[Note: This is source used for Sanger's birth and death dates.]*
*Sanger, Margaret, *An Autobiography*, W.W. Norton & Co., 1938
Sanger, Margaret, *My Fight for Birth Control*, Farrar & Rinehart, 1931
Sanger, Margaret, *Woman and the New Race*, Brentano's, 1920
Douglas, Emily Taft, *Margaret Sanger: Pioneer of the Future*, Holt, Rinehart & Winston, 1970

Dr. Marian Sherman (Chapter 34)

Brereton, Lloyd, "Canadian Humanist of the Year: Dr. Marian Sherman," *Humanist in Canada*, August 1975
* Fraser, Sylvia, "What Makes An Atheist Tick?" *Star Weekly (Toronto)*, Sept. 11, 1965
Humanist in Canada, "Marian Sherman," November 1975
Don Gaine, "Dr. Marian Sherman," *Victoria Daily Colonist*, reprinted *Humanist in Canada*, #7, early 1969
New York Times, "Woman Missionary Becomes An Atheist," Oct. 6, 1963
Sherman, Marian, "How I Came To Be A Humanist," *Humanist in Canada #6*, late 1968
Spraggett, Allen, "What I saw in India turned me from God," *Daily Star* (no date)
The Star (Victoria, B.C.), "Religion Is Irrational Says Saanich Doctor," March 17, 1955

Dora Russell (Chapter 35)

* Russell, Dora, *In Defense of Children*, Hamish Hamilton, 1932
Russell, Dora, *The Religion of the Machine Age*, Routledge & Kegan Paul, 1983
Russell, Dora, *The Right To Be Happy*, Harper & Brothers, 1927
Russell, Dora, *The Tamarisk Tree*, Virago, 1977
Spender, Dale, Ed., *The Dora Russell Reader*, Pandora Press, 1983

Meridel Le Sueur (Chapter 36)

Le Sueur, Meridel, *North Star Country*, Duell, Sloan & Pearce, 1945
Le Sueur, Meridel, *Ripening: Selected Works, 1927–1980*, Feminist Press

Margaret Knight (Chapter 37)

*Knight, Margaret, *Morals Without Religion and Other Essays*, Dennis Dobson Ltd., 1955

Knight, Margaret, Ed., Herrick, James, Revised Ed., *Humanist Anthology: From Confucius to Attenborough*, 1961, revised, Prometheus Press, 1995

Queen Silver (Chapter 38)

Beckley, Zoe, "Who Is Queen Silver?" Zoe Beckley's Corner, *New York Telegram*, c. February 1924

Daily News [Inglewood, CA], "Inglewood Girl Wonder May Go Chattanooga, Aid Evolutionists," June 29, 1925

Los Angeles Record, "Eight-Year Old Girl To Lecture On Darwinism," Dec. 24, 1919

Roser, Henry H., "Making Your Child a Genius: Grace Verne Silver Tells the Secret of the Home Teaching Methods that Have Made Queen Silver the Marvel of the School World," *National Brain Power Monthly*, September 1922

Vashti McCollum (Chapter 39)

McCollum, Vashti, *One Woman's Fight*, Freedom From Religion Foundation, Inc., 1993 reprint.

Ruth Hurmence Green (Chapter 40)

*Green, Ruth H., *The Book of Ruth*, Freedom From Religion Foundation, Inc., 1982

Green, Ruth H., *The Born Again Skeptic's Guide to the Bible*, Freedom From Religion Foundation, Inc., 1979

Catherine Fahringer (Chapter 41)

*Phelon, Craig, "Portrait of An Atheist," *San Antonio Express-News Magazine*, Sunday, March 24, 1991

Anne Nicol Gaylor (Chapter 43)

Gaylor, Anne Nicol, *Abortion Is A Blessing*, Psychological Dimensions, 1976

*Gaylor, Anne Nicol, *Lead Us Not Into Penn Station*, FFRF, Inc., 1983

Meg Bowman (Chapter 44)

* Bowman, Meg, *Dramatic Readings on Feminist Issues*, Hot Flash Press, 1988

Bowman, Meg, *Goddesses, Witches and the Paradigm Shift*, Hot Flash Press, 1994

Bowman, Meg, *Women's History: Dramatic Readings*, Hot Flash Press, 1994

Barbara G. Walker (Chapter 45)

Walker, Barbara G., *The Skeptical Feminist: Discovering the Virgin, Mother & Crone*, Harper & Row Publishers, 1987

Walker, Barbara G., *The Woman's Encyclopedia of Myths and Secrets*, Harper & Row, Publishers, 1983

Sherry Matulis (Chapter 46)

Matulis, Sherry, *Does It Take One Bird or Two, or What?* H.H. Waldo, Bookseller, 1985

*Matulis, Sherry, "How I Earned My Feminist Credentials" *Freethought Today*, Jan./Feb. 1992

Kay Nolte Smith (Chapter 47)

Gaylor, Annie Laurie, "Exploring The Legacy Of The Witches Trials ('Baraboo Girl Makes Good:' Actress/Author Kay Nolte Smith)," *Feminist Connection*, Dec. 1983
Smith, Kay Nolte, "Truth or the Consequences," *Freethought Today*, January 1984

Sonia Johnson (Chapter 48)

Gaylor, Annie Laurie, "Sonia Johnson: revolutionary for women," *The Feminist Connection*, Madison, Wis., December 1982
Johnson, Sonia, *From Housewife to Heretic*, Doubleday & Co., Inc., 1981

Barbara Ehrenreich (Chapter 49)

Ehrenreich, Barbara, "Cultural Baggage," *New York Times Magazine*, April 5, 1992
* Ehrenreich, Barbara, "U.S. Patriots: Without God On Their Side," *Mother Jones*, Feb.– March, 1981
Lesniak, James G., Ed., *Contemporary Authors*, Gale Research Inc., 1992 (Vol. 37)

Katha Pollitt (Chapter 50)

Pollitt, Katha, *Reasonable Creatures: Essays on Women and Feminism*, Alfred A. Knopf, 1994
*Pollitt, Katha, "Subject to Debate," *The Nation*, Dec. 26, 1994

Taslima Nasrin (Chapter 51)

Burns, John F., "A Writer Hides. Her Country Winces," *New York Times*, July 31, 1994
* Nasrin, Taslima, "On Islamic Fundamentalism," *The Humanist*, July/August 1986
Weaver, Mary Anne, "A Fugitive from Injustice," *The New Yorker*, Sept. 12, 1994

Additional Biographies

Addams, Jane, *The Second Twenty Years at Hull-House*, MacMillan Co., 1930
Addams, Jane, *Twenty Years at Hull-House*, (1910), MacMillan Co., 1959
Ashbaugh, Carolyn, *Lucy Parsons: American Revolutionary*, Charles H. Kerr Publishing Co., 1976
Branden, Barbara, *The Passion of Ayn Rand*, Anchor Books, Doubleday, 1986
Brown, Olympia, *Democratic Ideals: A Memorial Sketch of Clara B. Colby*, Federal Suffrage Assoc., 1917
Johnson, Emily Cooper, *Jane Addams: A Centennial Reader*, New York, 1960
Larson, Orvin, *American Infidel: Robert G. Ingersoll*, Freedom From Religion Foundation, Inc., Madison, Wisconsin, 1993
Maxwell, Margaret F., *A Passion for Freedom: The Life of Sharlot Hall*, University of Arizona Press, 1982
McCabe, Joseph, *A Biographical Dictionary of Modern Rationalists*, Watts & Co., 1920
Putnam, Samuel P., *Four Hundred Years of Freethought*, The Truth Seeker Company, 1894
Rand, Ayn, *Atlas Shrugged*, 1957, Signet Book, Times Mirror
Sears, Hal D., *The Sex Radicals: Free Love in High Victorian America*, Regents Press of Kansas, 1977
Wright, Nancy Kirkpatrick, Ed., *Sharlot Herself: Selected Writings of Sharlot Hall*, Sharlot Hall Museum, 1992, introduction by Margaret F. Maxwell

General Bibliography

Bacon, Margaret Hope, *Mothers of Feminism: The Story of Quaker Women in America*, Harper & Row, Publishers, 1986

Budd, Susan, *Varieties of Unbelief: Atheists and Agnostics in English Society 1850–1960*, Heinemann, 1977

Bullough, Vern L., *The Subordinate Sex: A History of Attitudes Toward Women*, Penguin Books, 1974

Cole, Margaret, *Marriage: Past and Present*, J.M. Dent & Sons, 1939

Courtney, Janet E., *Freethinkers of the Nineteenth Century*, Chapman & Hall, 1920

Crook, Margaret Brackenburg, *Women and Religion*, Beacon Press, 1964

DeBerg, Betty A., *Ungodly Women: Gender and the First Wave of American Fundamentalism*, Fortress Press, 1990

Gray, Carole, "1993 Women of Freethought Calendar," "1994 Women of Freethought Wall Calendar," Black Cat Enterprises, 1992, 1993

Hageman, Alice L., Ed., *Sexist Religion and Women in the Church: No More Silence*, Association Press, 1974

Ingersoll, Robert G., *The Works of Robert G. Ingersoll, In Twelve Volumes*, Dresden Publishing Co., New York , 1900

Kirkley, Evelyn Anne, *"The Female Peril": The construction of gender in American Freethought, 1865–1915*, [dissertation], Duke University, 1993

Lerner, Gerda, *The Creation of Patriarchy*, Oxford University Press, 1986.

Mill, John Stuart, & Mill, Harriet Taylor, *The Subjection of Women (1869) & Enfranchisement of Women (1851)*, Virago Press Ltd, 1983

Post, Albert, *Popular Freethought in America 1825–1850*, Columbia University Press, 1943

Robertson, J.M., *A History of Freethought in the Nineteenth Century*, Vols. I–II, G.P. Putnam's Sons, 1930

Robertson, J.M., *A Short History of Freethought: Ancient and Modern*, Russell & Russell, 1957

Rossi, Alice S., Ed., *The Feminist Papers: From Adams to de Beauvoir*, 1973, reprinted First Northeastern University Press 1988

Ruether, Rosemary Radford, & Keller, Rosemary Skinner, Eds., *Women & Religion in America Vols. II*, Harper & Row, Publishers, 1983; *Vol. III*, 1986

Saadawi, Nawal El, *The Hidden Face of Eve: Women in the Arab World*, Beacon Press, 1982

Schneir, Miriam, Ed., *Feminism: The Essential Historical Writings*, Vintage Books, 1972

Sears, Hal D., *The Sex Radicals: Free Love in High Victorian America*, The Regents Press of Kansas, 1977

Stein, Gordon, Ed., *An Anthology of Atheism and Rationalism*, Prometheus Books, 1980

Stone, Merlin, *When God Was A Woman*, Harvest/Harcourt Brace Jovanovich Book, 1978

Tribe, David, *100 Years of Freethought*, Elek Books Ltd, 1967

Warren, Sidney, *American Freethought 1860–1914*, Columbia University Press, 1943

Special Acknowledgments

First and most of all, my thanks to the James Hervey Johnson Foundation and Bonnie Lange for the grant to the Freedom From Religion Foundation, Inc., making this book possible.

❦

The late Dr. Gordon Stein, Library Director of the Center for Inquiry Library, Amherst, New York, deserves special acknowledgment for providing materials from his personal collection on Hypatia Bradlaugh Bonner, Ella E. Gibson, Emma Martin, and Marilla Ricker. Gordon sent a photocopy of the introduction of Gibson's *Godly Women of the Bible* which would otherwise have been unavailable to me. (Only one public library in the country lists the rare book and would not loan it.) Likewise, Gordon sent copies of the pamphlets of Emma Martin, which are available only through the University of California at Los Angeles, which also refused my Inter-Library Loan request, and a photocopy of Bonner's rare biography by her son. Gordon also sent copies of two representative essays by Marilla Ricker and offered other helpful advice. Although he must have been very ill when I requested help this summer, he responded immediately. His unexpected death from cancer in August 1996, is a loss to freethought research.

Dr. Sally Roesch Wagner, a women's studies historian and performing artist from North Dakota, supplied encouragement and names of some women to investigate for inclusion, and e-mailed me Matilda Joslyn Gage's speech at the 1890 Woman's National Liberal Union. The rare book containing this speech was not made available after my Inter-Library Loan request, so Sally is my source; her help was instrumental.

Edward Weber, director of the Labadie Collection at the University of Michigan, very helpfully went through some of the papers of Voltairine de Cleyre on my behalf, locating and photocopying de Cleyre's piece, "Woman Vs. Orthodoxy," lost in the pages of *The Boston Investigator*, a nice find. Sharon Presley of Resources for Independent Thinking, California, who is working on a book collecting the writings of Voltairine de Cleyre, pointed me to de Cleyre's essay, "The Economic Tendency of Freethought."

Yvonne and Charles Dobson of Sidney, B.C., went out of their way to search the papers of Dr. Marian Sherman on my behalf, trying to find a leaflet Dr. Sherman had written about her freethought views. The couple graciously helped make arrangements when Dan Barker and I went to the Archives at Victoria in person, helping us go through the boxes. The leaflet did not turn up, but I found many interesting items. Thanks also goes to Blodwen Piercy of *Humanist in Canada* for helping me contact the Dobsons and promptly providing additional material about Dr. Sherman on several occasions, and to Dr. Sherman's stepdaughter Ruth Lindsay for her help and correspondence.

Several Foundation members, in learning I was undertaking this collection, offered names and advice, including: Fred Whitehead, of Kansas, author of *Freethought on the American Frontier*, Foundation officer Catherine Fahringer of Texas; James Sanders, of Arizona, who alerted me to the existence of Sharlot Hall and her museum; Allan Rubin of Florida; Ken Malpas of New Jersey, and Paul M. Kay of New Jersey, who pointed out some of Ayn Rand's freethought writings. (Dave Daniels and Andy Gaylor of Frugal Muse Bookstore in Madison, Wisconsin, located a copy of her speech, "Faith and Force: The Destroyers of the Modern World," 1960.)

Jeff Frankel, an aficionado of Helen H. Gardener, had, several years before his untimely death, sent me copies of the *New York Times'* fascinating coverage of her death. The collection of his books inherited by the Freedom From Religion Foundation included several by women included in the anthology.

Joe Horton from the reference bureau of the Kentucky Archives kindly faxed a recent article about Josephine K. Henry appearing in the *Courier-Journal*.

Foundation member Richard Rickard of Ohio fortuitously donated a recent re-issue of all five volumes of *The History of Woman Suffrage* to the Foundation, which proved an invaluable convenience in completing this project.

Barbara Smoker, President of the National Secular Society, drew my attention to and gave me permission to reprint Margaret Knight's essay, "The Debit Account." For locating elusive information, thanks goes to helpful Keith Wood, general secretary of the Society, and Nicholas Walter, director of the Rationalist Press Association. Margaret Sanger's grandson Alexander was most gracious in according me permission to reprint a chapter from her autobiography. Thanks to Prof. Phillip S. Smith for sending a photograph of Kay Nolte Smith, and to Constance Threinen, an "unabashed atheist" and feminist leader in her own right, for providing a photographic image of her famous great-aunt, Margaret Fuller.

My gratitude to the really exceptional resources at my doorstep in Madison, Wisconsin. The University of Wisconsin Memorial Library was persuaded several decades ago to purchase parts of the Hypatia Bradlaugh Bonner Collection to add to its already good freethought collection. The Freedom From Religion Foundation also had supplied close to $10,000 worth of freethought books to the library in the early 1980s, in a project directed by Dr. Gordon Stein. The State Historical Society of Wisconsin boasts an unusually good collection, not the least of which is the wonderful Papers of Elizabeth Cady Stanton and Susan B. Anthony, edited by Patricia G. Holland and Ann D. Gordon. (Unfortunately I did my major research on Stanton directly from the Library of Congress microfilm before I was aware of this Project and before it was acquired by the Historical Society. When it became available to me I took advantage of the project's transcription of Stanton's nearly illegible "My Creed.") This project is a great service to feminist history.

I can only hope and urge that someday the freethought community will boast its own history of freethought microfilm collection to be made available to libraries nationally, and that, to paraphrase the words of Abigail Adams, "the ladies will be remembered" in it. There is no excuse for history's shabby treatment of women freethinkers!

❧

Special thanks to my mother Anne Gaylor, not only for applying for the grant given to the Foundation from the James Hervey Johnson Foundation which made this book possible, but for helping to edit or proof many of the biographies, for suggesting certain women and certain readings, as well as for being a sounding-board regarding some of the selections. Foundation staff, past and present, who typeset some of the writings appearing here include Denise McLaughlin, Amy Cox and especially Shelly Johnson, who transcribed the speech by Sonia Johnson, and did some last-minute scanning and corrections. Student staff member Amy Schernecker obligingly spent an afternoon at two libraries retrieving some last-minute materials for me.

❧

Finally, most of the major essays included in this book were cheerfully scanned into the computer, a tedious task, by my husband Dan, who also provided a patient ear as I regaled him with tidbits from the fascinating lives and writings I encountered. Dan did yeoman's work, including the exacting layout "grunt work" via computer, corrections *and* the indexing, bringing me peace of mind by also proofreading the final version. Thank you, Dan! (Any mistakes are my responsibility, naturally.) Anne, Dan, Shelly and Amy shouldered many of my usual office duties during the final half year of completing the book. (My daughter Sabrina also showed great forbearance at our family's necessary deferment of the many plans and pleasures of a six-year-old as the book neared completion, and Dan uncomplainingly put up with books, files and papers strewn all over the living room floor in the final countdown!)

INDEX

Boldfaced number indicates the start of a major section on this subject.

ABOUT THE EDITOR

Annie Laurie Gaylor co-founded the Freedom From Religion Foundation, an association of freethinkers working for the separation of church and state, with her mother Anne Gaylor in 1976. She received a journalism degree from the University of Wisconsin–Madison in 1980. She founded, edited and published a monthly feminist advocacy newspaper, *The Feminist Connection* (1980–1984). Since 1985 she has served as editor of the Foundation's newspaper *Freethought Today*. Her book about sexism in the bible, *Woe to the Women: The Bible Tells Me So* (FFRF, Inc., 1981) is in its fourth printing. Annie Laurie wrote the first nonfiction book exposing the scandal of sexual abuse of children by clergy, *Betrayal of Trust: Clergy Abuse of Children* (FFRF, 1988). She co-directs the Feminist Caucus of the American Humanist Association. She lives in Madison, Wisconsin, and is married to Daniel E. Barker. They have one daughter, Sabrina Delata Gaylor, born in 1989.